THE DIRECTORY OF BRAND NAME APPAREL MANUFACTURERS

fashiondex.com

Dear Fashiondex Owner,

Fashiondex is pleased to provide you with the most up-to-date resource guide in the apparel industry today.

Every effort has been made to provide you with the must accurate information possible. If you do find an error please let us know so we can correct it for the next edition.

As always our support staff at 212 647 0051 or info@fashiondex.com is ready to answer your questions and take your suggestions and comments or to help you find a source, so we can make The Fashiondex even more useful to you.

Sincerely,

Customer Service
The Fashiondex

P.S. Please let the manufacturer know that you found them in The Fashiondex.

Legal Stuff

The Fashiondex, Inc.

E-Mail : info@fashiondex.com

Printed in the United States of America

May 2016

Womens - Table of Contents

ACTIVE/ATHLETICWEAR 1

BLOUSES/SHIRTS/TOPS 9

BRIDAL & EVENINGWEAR 15

CASUAL SPORTSWEAR 25

CONTEMPORARY SPORTSWEAR 33

DECORATED/EMBELLISHED APPAREL 49

DESIGNER COLLECTIONS 54

DRESSES/SEPARATES/SUITS 63

ECOLOGICAL & ORGANIC 73

INTIMATE APPAREL & LINGERIE 77

JEANS & DENIMWEAR 85

JUNIOR SPORTSWEAR 91

LEATHER & SUEDE 99

LICENSED APPAREL 101

LIFESTYLE COLLECTIONS 104

MISSY/UPDATED SPORTSWEAR 109

OUTERWEAR/COATS & JACKETS 115

PRIVATE LABEL 125

SLEEPWEAR & LOUNGEWEAR 131

SPECIAL SIZES/LARGE 135

SPECIAL SIZES/MATERNITY 143

SPECIAL SIZES/PETITE 145

SWEATERS & KNITWEAR 149

Womens - Table of Contents

SWIMWEAR & BEACHWEAR 161

TEE SHIRTS & BLANKS 167

UNIFORMS 173

COMPANY INDEX 385

RN INDEX 413

LABEL INDEX 417

WWW & E-Mail INDEX 449

Mens - Table of Contents

ACTIVE/ATHLETICWEAR 162

BIG & TALL 169

CASUAL SPORTSWEAR 172

CONTEMPORARY SPORTSWEAR 177

DESIGNER COLLECTIONS 181

ECOLOGICAL & ORGANIC 183

JEANS & DENIMWEAR 185

LEATHER & SUEDE 189

LICENSED APPAREL 191

OUTERWEAR/COATS & JACKETS 193

PRIVATE LABEL 199

SHIRTS: DRESS & SPORT 203

SLEEPWEAR & UNDERWEAR 207

SPORTSMEN'S APPAREL 211

SUITS & SPORTCOATS 213

SWEATERS 215

SWIMWEAR & BEACHWEAR 217

TEE SHIRTS & BLANKS 219

TROUSERS & SLACKS 225

UNIFORMS 227

WESTERNWEAR 231

COMPANY INDEX	361
RN INDEX	387
LABEL INDEX	391
WWW & E-Mail INDEX	421

ACTIVE/ATHLETICWEAR	233
COORDINATED SPORTSWEAR-BOYS	237
COORDINATED SPORTSWEAR-GIRLS	241
DRESSES	245
ECOLOGICAL & ORGANIC	249
JEANS & DENIMWEAR	251
LICENSED APPAREL	253
NEWBORN/LAYETTE/INFANT	255
OUTERWEAR/COATS & JACKETS	259
PRIVATE LABEL	263
SHIRTS: DRESS & SPORT	267
SLEEPWEAR & UNDERWEAR	269
SUITS/SPECIAL OCCASION	271
SWEATERS	273
SWIMWEAR & BEACHWEAR	275
TEE SHIRTS & BLANKS	277
UNIFORMS	281
COMPANY INDEX	361
RN INDEX	387
LABEL INDEX	391
WWW & E-Mail INDEX	421

BELTS	283
BRIDAL/SPECIAL/INTIMATE	289
CHILDREN	291
EYEWEAR	295
FASHION JEWELRY & WATCHES	297
GIFT ITEMS	305
GLOVES	310
HAIR ORNAMENTS	313
HANDBAGS	317
HATS/CAPS/MILLINERY	325
HOSIERY/SOCKS/LEGWEAR	335
LUGGAGE/BAGS/LEATHER GOODS	341
MEN'S TIES & NECKWEAR	345
SCARVES & SHAWLS	349
UMBRELLAS	357
COMPANY INDEX	361
RN INDEX	387
LABEL INDEX	391
WWW & E-Mail INDEX	421

ADIDAS AMERICA, INC.

5055 North Greeley Avenue
Portland, OR 97217
971 234 2300 Fax : 971 234 2450 888 234 3270

Labels *Adidas*
Products *Activewear and athletic apparel.*
Price Points *Moderate to better.*
Production *U.S.A. and import worldwide.*
Sell To *Department stores, mail order catalogues, mass merchants and sporting good stores.*
Private Label *No*
Web Site *www.adidas.com*
Rev. in mil. *+500*

AERO TECH DESIGNS

2345 Preble Avenue
Pittsburgh, PA 15233 cyclewear@aerotechdesigns.com
412 262 3255 Fax : 412 203 1785 800 783 8326

Labels *Aero Tech Designs*
Products *Top quality bicycle apparel.*
Price Points *Better*
Production *U.S.A.*
Sell To *On-line, mail order catalogs*
Web Site *www.aerotechdesigns.com*
Contact *President: Cathy Schnaubelt Rogers*

B.C.T.C.

3322 South Garfield Avenue
Commerce, CA 90040 edward.hu@bctcapparel.com
323 888 9388

Labels *BCTC*
Products *Women's active sportswear tops & bottoms.*
Price Points *Budget, moderate & better.*
Production *U.S.A. & import*
Showrooms *Los Angeles*
Sell To *Department stores, mass merchants.*
Private Label *Yes*
RN Number *RN69587*
Contact *President and Owner: Even Chew*

BADGER SPORTSWEAR

111 Badger Lane
Statesville, NC 28625 tom@badgersportswear.com
704 871 0990 Fax : 704 871 0521 888-871-0990

Labels *Badger Sport*
Products *Special order custom team uniforms & warm-ups.*
Price Points *Better*
Production *U.S.A.*
Sell To *Sporting good stores.*
Corp. Office
Private Label *Yes*
Web Site *www.badgersportswear.com*

RN Number *RN55346*
Rev. in mil. *11-50*

BALTIERRA SURFBOARDS & BALTI GIRL

788 W 16th Street, Unit B
Costa Mesa, CA 92627 rogerbaltierra@sbcglobal.net
949 645 7873

Labels *Balti Girl*
Products *Women's & girls beach wear shorts, tee's, tank tops, drawstring pants & shorts.*
Price Points *Moderate*
Production *U.S.A.*
Showrooms *Costa Mesa*
Sell To *Specialty stores.*
Private Label *Yes*
RN Number *SREAA24-776411*
Contact *President & Owner: Roger Baltierra*

BARRAZA ASSOCIATES LTD

225 West 35th Street, Suite 1502
New York, NY 10001 barrazany@aol.com
212 564 6583

Labels *Paz*
Products *Yoga & spa wear. Unique fabrications and styles in various 100% Eco organic cottons.*
Price Points *Moderate to better.*
Production *U.S.A. & import.*
Sell To *Department stores, specialty stores, boutiques, mail order catalogues.*
Private Label *Yes*
Web Site *www.barrazastyle.com*
Rev. in mil. *2-10*
Contact *President: Maria Barraza, Sales & Marketing: Rafael Romero*

BODY WRAPPERS

65 West 36th Street, 5th Floor
New York, NY 10018 info@bodywrappers.com
212 279 3492 Fax : 212 564 3426 800 323 0786

Labels *Body Wrappers®, Premiere Collection™, totalSTRETCH™ Tights, Angelo Luzio® Shoes*
Products *Activewear, dance, ballroom, recital apparel & team apparel & accessories.*
Price Points *Moderate*
Production *U.S.A.*
Showrooms *New York, Denver, Toronto plus reps throughout the U.S, Canada, Europe & Japan.*
Sell To *Dance specialty stores, boutiques, Nordstrom's, mail order catalogues, website.*
Corp. Office *107 Trumbull Street, Elizabeth, NJ 07206*
Private Label *Yes*
Web Site *www.bodywrappers.com*
RN Number *RN60206*
Rev. in mil. *11-50*
Contact *Sales: Michael Lee, tel: 908 354 7218 ext. 231*

BROOKS SPORTS, INC.

3400 Stone Way North, Suite 500
Seattle, WA 98103 Stephen.Cheung@brooksrunning.com
800 227 6657 Fax : 425 489 1975

Labels *Brooks®*
Products *High performance running shoes, apparel and accessories.*
Price Points *Moderate*
Sell To *Department stores*
Web Site *www.brooksrunning.com*
Contact *Global Marketing: Heather Snavely, US Marketing: Stephen Cheung*

CALIFORNIA RAIN CO.

1213 E. 14th Street
Los Angeles, CA 90021 info@californiarainla.com
213 623 6061 Fax : 213 627 5703

Products *Form fitting fashion blank knit apparel. Missy & junior shirts, sweatshirts & novelty shirts.*
Price Points *Better*
Production *U.S.A.*
Sell To *Department stores*
Corp. Office *Above*
Private Label *Yes*
Web Site *www.californiarainla.com*
RN Number *75443*
Rev. in mil. *11-50*
Contact *President: Jack Chang*

CHAMPION ATHLETICWEAR, INC.

1000 East Hanes Mill Road
Winston Salem, NC 27105 linda.barabasova@hanesbrands.com
336 519 6500 Fax : 336 519 7909 800 999 2249

Labels *Champion*
Products *Womens sports bras, all types of active & athleticwear.*
Price Points *Moderate*
Production *U.S.A. & import from the Orient.*
Sell To *Department stores, mass merchants, mail order catalogues & sporting goods retailers.*
Private Label *Yes*
Web Site *www.championusa.com*
RN Number *RN26094*
Contact *Licensing: Nancy Gendimenico - 212 576-8481*

COLUMBIA SPORTSWEAR CO., INC.

14375 N.W. Science Park Drive
Portland, OR 97229 sales_info@columbia.com
503 985 4000 Fax : 503 985 5800 800 MA BOYLE

Labels *Columbia Sportswear Co.*
Products *Hunting, fishing, sportswear, footwear, active outerwear & active sportswear.*
Price Points *Moderate*
Production *U.S.A.*
Sell To *Department stores, specialty stores, mass merchants.*
Private Label *No*
Web Site *www.columbia.com*

RN Number *RN69724*
Rev. in mil. *+500*
Contact *Chairman: Gertrude Boyle, CEO: Tim Boyle, VIP Sales: Joseph R. Craig*

DIVINA DANCEWEAR

544 West 9560 South
Sandy, UT 84070 divinadancewearusa@gmail.com
800 360 6008 Fax : 801 571 9974

Labels *Divina Dancewear*
Products *Performance apparel that moves with you. Dancewear line that fits and flatters dancers.*
Price Points *Better*
Production *U.S.A.*
Sell To *Department stores, specialty stores, boutiques*
Web Site *www.divinadancewear.com*
Contact *Owner: Christee Roderick*

DONOUGHE SPORT

721 Donoughe Street
Gallitzin, PA 16641 rmapparel@aol.com
814 886 9272 Fax : 814 886 4228

Labels *Donoughe Sport™*
Products *Designers & manufacturers of quality sports apparel & related products*
Price Points *Moderate*
Production *U.S.A.*
Sell To *Specialty Stores*
Corp. Office *Division of R&M Apparel, Inc.*
Web Site *www.donoughesport.com*

FILA U.S.A. INC.

930 Ridgebrook Road, Suite 200
Sparks, MD 21152 ecommusa@fila.com
410 773 3000 Fax : 410 773 4984 800 845 3452

Labels *Fila*
Products *Active sportswear.*
Price Points *Moderate to better.*
Production *U.S.A., Hong Kong, Thailand, Taiwan & Indonesia.*
Sell To *Department stores, catalogues, mass merchants & sporting goods stores.*
Web Site *www.fila.com*

FRUIT OF THE LOOM

PO Box 90015
Bowling Green, KY 42102 fotlcustserv@fruit.com
855 253 4534 Fax : 888 259 6557

Labels *Fruit of the Loom, Russell Athletic, Vanity Fair, Russell Outdoors*
Products *All types of underwear and activewear.*
Price Points *Moderate*
Production *U.S.A.*
Sell To *On-line, department stores, specialty stores.*
Private Label *Yes*
Web Site *www.fruit.com*

HOLLOWAY SPORTSWEAR, INC.

2633 Campbell Road
Sidney, OH 45365
customercare@hollowayusa.com
937 497 7575 Fax : 937 497 7337 800 852 8798

Labels *Holloway*
Products *Women's sportswear, running suits & wool jackets.*
Price Points *Moderate*
Production *U.S.A. & import*
Sell To *Dept., specialty & sporting goods stores, catalogues, mass merchants & ASI distributors.*
Private Label *Yes*
Web Site *www.hollowayusa.com*
Rev. in mil. *51-100*

K & P WEAVER, LLC

527 Carriage Drive
Orange, CT 06477
kpweaver@aol.com
203 795 9024 Fax : 203 795 4294

Labels *K & P Weaver LLC*
Products *Official licensee of the All-American Girls Professional Baseball League & replica uniforms.*
Production *U.S.A.*
Sell To *Specialty & sport stores, historical institutes, mail order catalogues, gift shops & museum stores*
Private Label *Yes*
Web Site *www.baseballamericaspastime.com*
Rev. in mil. *0-2*
Contact *Owner: Paula Weaver, Production: Kenneth Weaver*

MISTER NOAH

1407 Broadway, Suite 707
New York, NY 10018
noah@mrnoah.com
212 354 1700 Fax : 212 354 1740

Labels *Mister Noah, Feathers*
Products *Fashion activewear knit tops & bottoms in junior and missy sizes.*
Price Points *Moderate*
Production *Import*
Showrooms *New York*
Sell To *Department stores, mass merchants, mail order catalogues & off-price.*
Corp. Office *1824 Byberry Road, Bensalem, Pa. 19020 tel: 215-639-9300*
Private Label *Yes*
Web Site *www.feathersgirl.com*
RN Number *RN50110*
Rev. in mil. *11-50*
Contact *Presidents: Bruce Feinberg/Robert Feinberg*

MOTIONWEAR, LLC

1315 Sunday Drive
Indianapolis, IN 46217
bwilson@motionwear.com
317 780 0609 Fax : 317 780 4188 800 869 0609

Labels *Motionwear, Motionwar Gymnastics, Motionwear Cheer*
Products *Dance, gymnastics & cheerleading apparel for women and girls.*
Price Points *Better*
Production *U.S.A. & import*

Sell To *Specialty stores, boutiques, direct internet*
Web Site *www.motionwear.com*
Contact *President: Bob Wilson*

NIKE, INC.

1 Bowerman Drive
Beaverton, OR 97005
503 671 6453 Fax : 503 671 6300 800-806-6453

Labels *Nike*
Products *Active & athletic sportswear collection & accessories.*
Price Points *Moderate to Better.*
Production *U.S.A, & worlwide importer.*
Showrooms *Showrooms throughout the U.S.*
Sell To *Department stores, specialty stores, catalogues, mass merchants & Nike retail stores.*
Private Label *Yes*
Web Site *www.nike.com*
Rev. in mil. *+500*
Contact *President: Thomas Clark*

ROYAL APPAREL, INC.

65 Commerce Drive
Hauppauge, NY 11788 sales@royalapparel.net
631 213 8299 Fax : 631 922 8438 866-Royal-1-S

Labels *Royal Apparel*
Products *Basic & fashion forward blanks, active/athleticwear in a large selection of colors & knit fabr.*
Price Points *Moderate to better.*
Production *U.S.A.*
Showrooms *New York & Allentown, Pa.*
Sell To *Mass merchants, branded labels, screen printers & department stores.*
Private Label *Yes*
Web Site *www.royalapparel.net*
Contact *President: Morey Mayeri, Owners: Morey Mayeri/Abraham Mayeri*

SPORTHILL, INC.

725 McKinley Street
Eugene, OR 97402 info@sporthill.com
541 345 9623 Fax : 541 343 7261 888 645 3627

Labels *Sporthill*
Products *Women's athletic & activewear, gymwear, skiwear & outdoor active sportswear.*
Price Points *Moderate to better.*
Production *U.S.A. & import*
Sell To *Department & specialty stores, catalogues, mass merchants, national & regional chains.*
Private Label *No*
Web Site *www.sporthill.com*
Rev. in mil. *2-10*
Contact *President: James Hill, Production: Taunya Martin*

STANFIELD'S

1 Logan Street, PO Box 190
Truro, Nova Scotia, Canada B2N 5C2 inquiries@stanfields.com
902 895 5406 Fax : 902 893 8187 855-895-5406

Products *Bike shorts, leggings & bodywear.*
Price Points *Moderate*
Production *Canada*
Showrooms *Sales Office: 40 University Avenue, Toronto, Ontario Canada M5J 1T1 (416) 598-8086.*
Sell To *Department stores, specialty stores, boutiques & mail order catalogues.*
Private Label *No*
Web Site *www.stanfields.com*

SWEENIE MANUFACTURING CORPORATION

60 East 9th Street, Suite 315
New York, NY 10003 diane@sweeniemanufacturing.com
646 825 5027 Fax : 646 825 5027

Labels *Naked Sportswear, SUPmerge, bbs, Hotdrop, Torvu, Sthenos, Daniela Corte*
Products *Women's & junior contemporary activewear, boardshorts, dancewear.*
Price Points *Budget to designer*
Production *U.S.A. & import from China, East Asia, Europe & South/Central America*
Sell To *Department stores, specialty stores, boutiques, mass merchants*
Private Label *Yes*
Web Site *www.sweeniemanufacturing.com*
Rev. in mil. *0-2*
Contact *Design & Production: Diane Walker (cell: 914-471-1069),*
Sales & Marketing: Stacey Demar (cell: 646-772-6113)

WASATCH CO.

3287 Marjan Drive
Atlanta, GA 30340 info@wasatcht.com
404 634 3000 Fax : 404 634 1338 800 544 9096

Labels *Gildan, Fruit of the Loom, Jerzees Bella+Canvas, KiddyKats, Paradis Point, Q-Tees of Cali*
Products *Sweatpants, sweatshirts & tee-shirts.*
Sell To *Embroiders, screen printers, wholesalers and retail stores.*
Private Label *Yes*
Web Site *www.wasatcht.com*
Contact *Abdul Samad*

WHITE SIERRA

305 Soquel Way
Sunnyvale, CA 94085 wholesale@whitesierra.com
408 980 6688 Fax : 408 980 6670 1 800 980 8688

Labels *White Sierra*
Products *Sport outerwear, shorts, tee shirts & fleece legging collection.*
Price Points *Moderate*
Production *U.S.A. & Asia*
Sell To *Department stores, specialty stores, mass merchants & sporting good shops.*
Private Label *Yes*
Web Site *www.whitesierra.com*
RN Number *RN58486*
Rev. in mil. *11-50*

A'NUE LIGNE

3300 NW 41st Street
Miami, FL 33142 admin@anueligne.com
305 436 5828 Fax : 305 436 8134

Labels *A'nue Ligne*
Products *All styles of tank tops & essentials in lycra/spandex.*
Price Points *Bridge*
Production *U.S.A.*
Showrooms *New York/Terry Ventre, Dallas/Mike & Co., Los Angeles/Jamie Prince Showroom, Atlanta/Shepard and Tucker*
Sell To *Department stores, specialty stores & boutiques.*
Private Label *Yes*
Web Site *www.anueligne.com*
Contact *Owner: Lois Varat, Design: Lois Varat*

ATOPAPPAREL CORP

214 West 39th Street, Suite 604A
New York, NY 10018 info@atopapparel.com
212 221 7685 Fax : 212 221 7587

Labels *Emil Rutenberg, People Like Frank*
Products *Ladies dresses & tops in junior, missy and plus sizes.*
Price Points *Below wholesale prices*
Production *Import*
Showrooms *Same as Above*
Sell To *Department stores, specialty stores, boutiques*
Corp. Office *Same as Above*
Private Label *Yes*
Web Site *www.emilrutenberg.com*
Contact *Customer Service: Amy (347-688-8781)*

B & B DESIGNS COLLECTION INC. *(Rep.)

300 S. Anderson Street
Los Angeles, CA 90033 info@amandafashion.com
323 261 0000 Fax : 323 261 0001

Labels *Amanda*
Products *Acetate, poly, rayon & slinky tops.*
Price Points *Moderate & Better*
Production *U.S.A.*
Showrooms *Los Angeles*
Sell To *Department stores, specialty stores & boutiques.*
Private Label *Yes*
Web Site *www.amandafashion.com*
RN Number *RN87230*
Rev. in mil. *2-10*
Contact *President and Owner: Bijan Navabian, Sales: Bahman Navabian*

BLUE PLATE INC.

525 Seventh Avenue, Suite 309
New York, NY 10018 bpshowroom@aol.com
212 382 0069 Fax : 212 997 2413

Labels *Blue Plate*

Products *Junior and missy cotton tops.*
Price Points *Moderate*
Production *India*
Showrooms *New York*
Sell To *Department stores, specialty stores, boutiques and mass merchants.*
Private Label *Yes*
Web Site *www.blueplatefashion.com*
Contact *President & Owner: Shashi Anand, Incharge: Seema Anand*

CLASSIX

39360 3rd Street East, #307
Palmdale, CA 93550
vkhachooni@hotmail.com
661 726 9041 Fax : 661 726 9246 800 934-3290

Labels *Classix*
Products *Women's formalwear shirt collection in sizes 4 to 24.*
Price Points *Better*
Sell To *Department stores, specialty stores, formalwear shops.*
Web Site *www.classixshirts.com*

COLLECTION ARIANNE

1655 De Louvain West
Montreal, Quebec, CA H4N1G6
webmaster@ariannelingerie.com
514 385 9393 Fax : 514 385 9281 888 239 8165

Labels *Arianne*
Products *RTW trendy tops & camisoles for everyday wear.*
Price Points *Better to high end*
Production *Canada*
Showrooms *Montreal*
Sell To *Department & specialty stores, boutiques, mail order catalogues.*
Private Label *No*
Web Site *www.ariannelingerie.com*
Contact *President & Owner: Norman Rossy, Design: Anne Pigeon*

DANA EMILIA PRESENTS *(Rep.)

264 West 40th, Suite 503
New York, NY 10018
fashion@danaemilia.com
212 391 4104 Fax : 212 391 4153

Labels *Christopher Calvin, Redwood Court, Peacock Ways, Swish, Vanite Couture, Banaris*
Products *Detailed shirts & blouses in cotton, silk and natural blends.*
Price Points *Better*
Production *U.S.A. & import.*
Showrooms *New York.*
Sell To *Specialty stores, boutiques, chain stores & mail order catalogues.*
Private Label *Yes*
Web Site *www.danaemiliapresents.com*
Contact *President: Dana Harrison*

DORMAN FASHION INC.

850 S. Broadway, #1003
Los Angeles, CA 90014
213 623 7188 Fax : 213 623 7189 800-872-7455
sales@dormanfashion.com

Labels *Dorman Fashion*
Products *Washed 100% silk, poly, crinkle & linen jacksts, blouses and set pieces.*
Price Points *Moderate*
Production *Import*
Showrooms *A386 in the California Market Center*
Sell To *Boutiques and regional chain stores throughout the US and Canada*
Web Site *www.dormanfashion.com*

ELE.PAVONI NEW YORK LTD *(Rep.)

159 West 53rd Street, Suite 29D
New York, NY 10019
212 397 0108 Fax : 212 397 0366
elepavoni@mac.com

Labels *Gossip, Mela Rosa*
Products *Unique hand-painted pieces.*
Price Points *Bridge to designer*
Production *Italy*
Showrooms *New York*
Sell To *Specialty stores & boutiques.*
Private Label *Yes*
Web Site *www.elepavoni.com*
Rev. in mil. *0-2*
Contact *Sales: Eleonora Pavoni*

FLATIRON WORKSHOP

53-55 West 21st Street, 3rd Floor
New York, NY 10010
212 924 8795
flatironworkshop@gmail.com

Labels *Flatiron Workshop*
Products *Blouses, tops & knits, Sizes XS through XL.*
Price Points *Better*
Production *U.S.A. & import.*
Showrooms *Rep. Jill Bredel at 21 East 10th Street, 10th floor, New York tel: 212-331-1390.*
Sell To *Department stores, specialty stores, boutiques*
Private Label *Yes*
Web Site *www.flatironworkshop.com*
Contact *Designer: Sally Lee*

GOLF APPAREL BRANDS

13621 South Main Street
Los Angeles, CA 90061
310 715 1772 Fax : 310 715 1776 800 678 5246
sales@lamode.com

Labels *La Mode, NatureTech, Clark & Gregory, Sahara*
Products *Ladies golf shirts and fleece tops.*
Price Points *Moderate to better*
Production *Domestic and import from Korea, China, Hong Kong, Malaysia*
Sell To *Specialty stores, off-price and golf shops.*
Private Label *Yes*

Web Site *www.lamode.com*
Contact *President/Owner: Eddie Kahn*

HTT HEADWEAR LTD.

41185 Raintree Court
Murrieta, CA 92562 sales@httapparel.com
951 304 0400 Fax : 951 304 0410 800 846 8468

Labels *Head To Toe*
Products *Woven and knit blouses, tops, tees & polos.*
Price Points *Better*
Production *U.S.A., China & Pakistan*
Showrooms *Murrieta, CA*
Sell To *Manufacturers*
Private Label *Yes*
Web Site *www.httapparel.com*
Contact *President: Howard Seegar, Owner: Howard Seegar, Customer Service: Luke Fafara*

ONLY HEARTS

134 West 37th Street, 9th Floor
New York, NY 10018 customerservice@onlyhearts.com
212 268 0886 Fax : 212 268 0922

Labels *Only Hearts*
Products *Flirty and fashioned tops.*
Price Points *Better to bridge.*
Production *U.S.A.*
Showrooms *New York*
Sell To *Speciallty stores, department stores & mail order catalogues.*
Private Label *Yes*
Web Site *www.onlyhearts.com*
Rev. in mil. *2-10*
Contact *Design: Helena Stuart*

REDWOOD COURT BY SILK BOX

PO Box 3019
Princeton Jct, NJ 08543 info@lotusa.com
609 275 4403 Fax : 609 897 1118

Labels *Redwood Court*
Products *Jackets, shirts, blouses in silk blends for missy and plus sizes.*
Price Points *Better*
Production *Import*
Showrooms *None*
Sell To *Department stores & boutiques.*
Private Label *Yes*
Web Site *www.redwoodcourt.com*
Rev. in mil. *0-2*
Contact *Sales: Shirley Fang 609-275-0350 (shirleymfang@gmail.com)*

SQUASHT BY LES

2556 West Chicago Avenue
Chicago, IL 60622
773 292 4123
les@squashtbyles.com

Labels *Squasht by Les*
Products *Halters, dresses, skirts, blouses & tunics in sustainable, natural, and vintage fabrics.*
Price Points *Better*
Production *U.S.A.*
Sell To *Boutiques*
Web Site *www.squashtbyles.com*
Contact *Designer & Owner: Lesley Timpe*

TASHA POLIZZI

287 Main Street
Great Barrington, MA 01230
413 528 6500 Fax : 413 528 6370
jane@tashapolizzi.com

Labels *Tasha Polizzi*
Products *Contempoary embroidered blouses & shirts.*
Price Points *Bridge*
Production *U.S.A.*
Sell To *Department stores, specialty stores.*
Private Label *No*
Web Site *www.tashapolizzi.com*
Contact *Owner: Tasha Polizzi, Sales: Jane Wright*

ADK FASHIONS *(Rep.)

225 West 35th Street, Suite 300
New York, NY 10001 adk@adkfashions.com
212 714 1177 Fax : 212 947 9063

Labels *Georges Chakra "Edition", Maria Coca, Eshel, Julie Vino, Lalla Bee, Meher & Riddhima*
Products *Cocktail dresses, evening separates, social occasion, evening wear and sportswear.*
Price Points *Bridge, Designer, Couture*
Production *U.S.A., Europe, Australia, Canada*
Showrooms *New York.*
Sell To *Department stores, specialty stores & boutiques.*
Private Label *No*
Web Site *www.adkfashions.com*
Rev. in mil. *2-10*
Contact *President: Ab Korine, Owner: Arthur Drogowski*

AIDAN MATTOX

500 Seventh Avenue, 10th Floor
New York, NY 10018 customerservice@aidanmattox.com
212 764 5870 Fax : 212 764 5845

Labels *Aidan Mattox, Aidan*
Products *Eveningwear collection*
Price Points *Better*
Production *Import from the Orient*
Showrooms *New York, Los Angeles & Dallas*
Sell To *Specialty stores, catalogues & department stores.*
Private Label *Yes*
Web Site *www.aidanmattox.com*
RN Number *RN59782*
Contact *President: Frank Borsas*

BARRAZA ASSOCIATES LTD

225 West 35th Street, Suite 1502
New York, NY 10001 barrazany@aol.com
212 564 6583

Labels *BarrazaStyle*
Products *Custom creations, bridal, black tie, mother of the bride and groom.*
Price Points *Moderate to better.*
Production *U.S.A. & import.*
Sell To *Department stores, specialty stores, boutiques, mail order catalogues.*
Private Label *Yes*
Web Site *www.barrazastyle.com*
Rev. in mil. *2-10*
Contact *President: Maria Barraza, Sales & Marketing: Rafael Romero*

BCBG MAX AZRIA GROUP

1450 Broadway, 17th Floor
New York, NY 10018 judy.scarpulla@bcbg.com
212 382 1880 Fax : 212 764 6912 866 518 2224

Labels *BCBG Max Azria, Herve Leger*
Products *Eveningwear & day collection*
Price Points *Better*

Production *U.S.A.*
Showrooms *New York: 1450 Broadway-212-704-4725, Los Angele: 110E 9th St, A571-323-277-5440, Atlanta: 250 Spring St.#11E112-A/B-404-223-2224, Dallas:Ross Ave.-214-744-2226*
Sell To *Department stores & specialty stores.*
Corp. Office *2761 Fruitland Avenue, Vernon, Ca. 90058 - 323-589-2224*
Private Label *Yes*
Web Site *www.bcbg.com*
Contact *President and Owner: Max Azria, President Licensing & International: Sophie Rietdyk, Sales Executive: Judy Scarpulla 212 704-4736*

BERGER & STEVENS *(Rep.)

260 West 39th Street, 7th Floor
New York, NY 10018 aberger@bergerandstevens.com
212 768 0050 Fax : 212 768 3332

Labels *Marisa Baratelli*
Products *After-five silk, European separates, romantic dressing & mother of the bride.*
Price Points *Bridge to designer.*
Production *U.S.A., Europe & Russia*
Showrooms *New York*
Sell To *Specialty stores & better department stores.*
Private Label *Yes*
Web Site *www.bergerandstevens.com*
Contact *Owner: Alana Berger & Jackie Stevens*

BILL BLASS FASHIONS LLC

236 Fifth Avenue, 8th Floor
New York, NY 10001 allison@billblass.com
212 689 8957 Fax : 212 889 0840

Labels *Bill Blass*
Products *Designer & couture sportswear, suit & evening collections.*
Price Points *Designer*
Production *U.S.A. & Italy*
Showrooms *New York/above*
Sell To *Specialty stores.*
Private Label *No*
Web Site *www.billblass.com*
RN Number *RN59126,RN38344*

CARMEN MARC VALVO

132 West 36th Street, 2nd Floor
New York, NY 10018 customerservice@carmenmarcvalvo.com
212 944 7370 Fax : 212 944 8074 888 4 CARMEN

Labels *Carmen Marc Valvo Couture, Carmen Marc Valvo Collection Black and White Label*
Products *Eveningwear & special occasion dresses*
Price Points *Better to designer*
Production *U.S.A. & Hong Kong*
Showrooms *New York*
Sell To *Department stores, specialty stores*
Corp. Office *Above*
Private Label *No*
Web Site *www.carmenmarcvalvo.com*

Contact *Sales Manager: Marcy Maybaum*

CAROL PERETZ

49 Windsor Avenue, Suite 103
Mineola, NY 11501 info@carolperetz.com
516 248 6300 Fax : 516 248 6622

Labels *Carol Peretz*
Products *Eveningwear & special occasion dressing. High fashion designer gowns.*
Price Points *Better to designer.*
Production *U.S.A.*
Showrooms *New York*
Sell To *Specialty stores and boutiques.*
Private Label *No*
Web Site *www.carolperetz.com*
Contact *President: Carol Peretz*

DAMIANOU

60-01 31st Street, 2nd Floor
Woodside, NY 11377 sales@damianouny.com
718 204 5600 Fax : 718 204 5081

Labels *Damianou*
Products *Special occasion, cocktail & mother-of-the-bride dresses. Also in plus sizes.*
Price Points *Better*
Production *U.S.A.*
Showrooms *New York/530 7th Ave., 11th Fl. NYC 212-869-5959, Atlanta/Sharon Putnam 800-522-76(Mid-Atlantic/Marsha Brody 516-378-3553, Mid West/Joan Prikos 312-467-4274.*
Sell To *Department stores, specialty stores, boutiques, mail order catalogues & bridal shops.*
Private Label *No*
Web Site *www.damianouny.com*
RN Number *RN93780*
Contact *Sales: Paul Damianou, Design: Elenitsa Damianou*

DARIAN GROUP INC.

1410 Broadway, Suite 1600
New York, NY 10018 martin@dariangroupinc.com
212 944 6500

Labels *Chetta B*
Products *Day dresses, knit dresses, evening dresses (short and long), evening separates.*
Price Points *Better*
Production *U.S.A. and import.*
Sell To *Department stores, specialty stores, boutiques and mail order catalogues.*
Private Label *Yes*
Web Site *www.dariangroupinc.com*
RN Number *RN89700*
Contact *President and Owner: Martin Schlossberg*

DEBORA RACHELLE INC.

PO Box 16419
Duluth, MN 55816 info@deborarachelle.com
218 727 8100

Labels *DeBora Rachelle, Jamais Rae*

Products *Prom dresses, red carpet gowns, evening & wedding apparel.*
Price Points *Designer*
Production *U.S.A.*
Sell To *Specialty stores & boutiques.*
Corp. Office *Above*
Web Site *www.deborarachelle.com*
Contact *CEO/Designer: DeBora Rachelle*

DEPECHE MODE

230 West 38th Street, 12th Floor
New York, NY 10018 leer@depecheco.com
212 643 6633 Fax : 212 643 1184

Labels *Depeche Mode, Studio*
Products *Special occasion dresses & suits.*
Price Points *Better to bridge, plus off-price.*
Production *U.S.A. & import*
Showrooms *New York.*
Sell To *Department & specialty stores, boutiques, mass merchants, catalogues, chains & off-price.*
Private Label *Yes*
Web Site *www.depecheco.com*
RN Number *RN61812*
Contact *President: Lee Rosenthal, Sales: Joy Villa (joyv@depecheco.com)*

DESSY CREATIONS & AFTER SIX

8 West 38th Street, 4th floor
New York, NY 10018 alan@dessy.com
646 638 9600 Fax : 646 638 9699 800-444-8304

Labels *Dessy Creations & After Six, Alfred Sung*
Products *Women's eveningwear and bridesmaid's dresses.*
Price Points *Moderate*
Production *U.S.A.*
Sell To *Department stores & speciality stores.*
Private Label *No*
Web Site *www.dessy.com*
RN Number *RN91947*
Contact *President: Alan Dessy, Design: Vivian Dessy-Diamond*

EDWARD CROMARTY ART DESIGN STUDIO *(Rep.)

228 East Route 59, #281
Nanuet, NY 10954 edwardcromarty@gmail.com
914 288 5171

Labels *Edward Cromarty Bridal Design Studio, Edward Cromarty Art Design Studio*
Products *Elegant bridal gowns & eveningwear plus bridal veils, wraps & shawls.*
Price Points *High end, designer, & reasonable designer pricing.*
Production *U.S.A.*
Showrooms *Please call for an appointment*
Sell To *Department stores, boutiques & specialty stores.*
Private Label *Yes*
Web Site *www.edwardcromarty.com*
RN Number *RN101294*
Rev. in mil. *0-2*

Contact *President & Owner: Edward Cromarty*

EMA SAVAHL DESIGN

7151 NW 6th Court
Miami, FL 33150
305 754 6717 Fax : 305 754 6787
sales@emasavahl.com

Labels *Ema Savahl Couture*
Products *Handpainted & embellished eveningwear separates& dresses with Swarovski crystals.*
Price Points *Designer to couture.*
Production *USA*
Showrooms *Miami/FL*
Sell To *Specialty stores & boutiques.*
Private Label *No*
Web Site *www.emasavahl.com*
Rev. in mil. *2-10*
Contact *Owner/Designer: Ema Koja*

JLM COUTURE

525 Seventh Avenue, Suite 1703
New York, NY 10018
800 686 7880 Fax : 212 768 2902
tammy@jlmcinc.com

Labels *Alvina Valenta, Blush by JLM, Jim Hjelm, Lazaro, Tara Keely, Hayley Paige*
Products *Bridal gowns, bridesmaid's gowns & flower girl's dresses*
Price Points *Couture*
Sell To *Specialty stores*
Private Label *No*
Web Site *www.jlmcouture.com*
Contact *President: Joe Murphy*

JUSSARA LEE

60 Bedford Street
New York, NY 10014
212 242 4128 Fax : 212 242 4129
mail@jussaralee.com

Labels *Jussara Lee*
Products *Made-to-order bridal, eveningwear, hand tailored coats, jackets, trousers, skirts, shirts & cas*
Price Points *Designer*
Production *U.S.A.*
Showrooms *New York*
Sell To *Department stores, specialty stores & boutiques.*
Private Label *No*
Web Site *www.jussaralee.com*
RN Number *RN89094*
Rev. in mil. *0-2*
Contact *Design: Jussara Lee*

KELLWOOD COMPANY

600 Kellwood Parkway
Chesterfield, MO 63017
314 576 3100 Fax : 314 576 3325
corp_communications@kellwood.com

Labels *David Meister - manufactured under license from David Meister®*
Products *A collection of cocktail dresses, evening and day dresses. (www.davidmeister.com)*

Price Points *Bridge*
Showrooms *New York/212-515-2600, California/626-934-4122*
Sell To *Department stores, boutiques*
Web Site *www.kellwood.com*

LIANCARLO

1737 NW 79th Avenue
Miami, FL 33126
305 591 7332 Fax : 305 477 9679
info@liancarlo.com

Labels *Liancarlo*
Products *Bridal & eveningwear collection made with the finest French & Italian silks, embroideries &*
Price Points *Couture*
Production *U.S.A.*
Sell To *Department stores, specialty stores, boutiques.*
Web Site *www.liancarlo.com*
Contact *Designer: Carlos Ramirez*

MARC BOUWER

141 Fulton Street, 2nd Floor
New York, NY 10038
212 242 7510 Fax : 212 242 2687
info@marcbouwer.com

Labels *Marc Bouwer*
Products *Couture day into eveingwear.*
Price Points *Couture*
Production *U.S.A.*
Showrooms *New York*
Sell To *Department stores & specialty stores.*
Private Label *No*
Web Site *www.marcbouwer.com*
Contact *President and Design: Marc Bouwer*

ROSE TAFT

488 Seventh Avenue, Suite 3C
New York, NY 10018
212 279 8580 1 800 223 0928
mdm@rosetaft.com

Labels *Rose Taft Couture*
Products *Social occasion, special occasion, eveningwear, cocktail dresses & evening suits.*
Price Points *Bridge, designer & couture.*
Production *U.S.A.*
Showrooms *New York*
Sell To *Department stores, specialty stores & boutiques.*
Corp. Office *Miami, Florida*
Private Label *No*
Web Site *www.melanieharrisny.com*
Contact *Sales: Melanie Harris Silverman, Design: Melanie Harris Silverman*

SARA MIQUE

4800 W Hillsboro Boulevard, Suite B6
Coconut Creek, FL 33073
954 531 6800 Fax : 954 531 6688 800 338 6366
info@saramique.com

Labels *Sara Mique*

Products *Non-traditional bridal, mother-of-the-bride, evening & cocktail dresses.*
Price Points *Bridge*
Production *U.S.A.*
Showrooms *East Coast Rep: Adria Galinkin*
Sell To *Specialty Stores*
Private Label *No*
Web Site *www.saramique.com*
Rev. in mil. *0-2*
Contact *Owner: Joan Lamonica*

SENTIMENTAL INC.

214 West 39th Street, Suite 504A
New York, NY 10018 sam@sentimentalny.com
212 221 0282 Fax : 212 302 2959

Labels *Sentimental NY*
Products *Cutting edge evening, prom & special occasion wear, clubwear.*
Price Points *Budget to moderate*
Production *U.S.A.*
Showrooms *New York*
Sell To *Specialty stores, chain stores*
Private Label *Yes*
Web Site *www.sentimentalny.com*
RN Number *124825*
Rev. in mil. *0-2*
Contact *Owner: Sam Hourani*

SOSSY BAGHDOIAN

10131 Riverside Drive
Toluca Lake, CA 91602 sossy.b@sbcglobal.net
818 766 5008 Fax : 818 766 5008

Labels *Sossy Baghdoian*
Products *Missy size bridal gowns & black-tie & cocktail dresses sizes 4 to 14.*
Price Points *Moderate to designer.*
Production *U.S.A.*
Showrooms *Toluca Lake, California*
Sell To *Specialty stores, boutiques & mail order catalogues.*
Private Label *Yes*
Web Site *www.sossysbridals.com*
Contact *Owner and Designer: Sossy Baghdoian*

SUSAN ELIAS

5640 12th Avenue North
St. Petersburg, FL 33710 eliascouture@gmail.com
727 452 6637

Labels *Susan Elias*
Products *One of a kind wedding dresses specializing in beach wedding dresses.*
Price Points *Designer & couture*
Production *U.S.A.*
Private Label *No*
Web Site *www.eliascouture.com*
Contact *President/Designer: Susan Elias*

TERI JON

241 West 37th Street, 2nd Floor
New York, NY 10018
212 398 0480 Fax : 212 302 2726
sales@terijon.com

Labels *Rickie Freeman for Teri Jon*
Products *Evening dresses & suits.*
Price Points *Bridge to designer*
Production *U.S.A.*
Showrooms *New York/above, Dallas/214-637-6962*
Sell To *Department stores, boutiques & specialty stores.*
Private Label *Yes*
Web Site *www.terijon.com*
Contact *President: Rickie Freeman*

WEDDING TROPICS

8608 Utica Avenue
Rancho Cucamonga, CA 91730
844 921 0466
kevin@weddingtropics.com

Labels *Wedding Tropics*
Products *Unique island beach wedding dresses*
Price Points *Bridge*
Sell To *Department stores, specialty stores, boutiques and mass merchants.*
Corp. Office *Above*
Private Label *Yes*
Web Site *www.weddingtropics*
RN Number *117573*
Rev. in mil. *0-2*
Contact *President/Owner: Kevin Baldwin*

5TH & OCEAN CLOTHING LLC/NEW ERA CAP CO.

590 West 83 Street
Hialeah, FL 33014
305 822 4606 Fax : 305 822 4665
laura.garden@neweracap.com

Labels *Major League Baseball, NHL, NBA, NFL, Collegiate teams*
Products *Ladies & Junior sportswear.*
Price Points *Low to moderate.*
Production *Honduras*
Corp. Office *Above*
Private Label *Yes*
Web Site *www.neweracap.com*
RN Number *94989*
Rev. in mil. *11-50*
Contact *Designer: Laura Garden ext. 220*

7 FOR ALL MANKIND

25 West 39th Street, 13th Floor
New York, NY 10018
646 839 5400 Fax : 646 839 5435 866 427 1114
customerservice@shop.7forallmankind.com

Labels *7 for all mankind*
Products *Full collection of casual sportswear, tops and bottoms.*
Price Points *Better to Bridge*
Showrooms *Above, Los Angeles/CA, Dallas/TX*
Sell To *Department stores, boutiques & specialty stores.*
Corp. Office *4440 East 26th Street, Vernon, Ca 90023 tel: 323-406-5300*
Private Label *No*
Web Site *www.7forallmankind.com*

AREA CODE 212 INC.

43 West 33rd Street, Suite 404
New York, NY 10001
212 465 9072
www.areacode212.net

Labels *Area Code 212*
Products *Brand name closeouts plus our own line of fashion tops and activewear*
Price Points *Moderate*
Sell To *Department stores, specialty stores,*
Web Site *ac@areacode.net*

AUGUST SILK, INC.

499 Seventh Avenue, 5th Floor South
New York, NY 10018
212 643 2400 Fax : 212 244 2155
francineshane@augustsilk.com

Labels *August Silk*
Products *Casual separates in silk/rayon/nylon, rayon/spandex, silk/bamboo, cotton/nylon.*
Price Points *Moderate*
Production *Import.*
Showrooms *New York.*
Sell To *Department stores, specialty stores & boutiques.*
Private Label *Yes*
Contact *Sales: Francine Shane - 212-584-0466*

B. BRONSON

1825 South Hill Street
Los Angeles, CA 90015 sales@bbronson.com
213 747 0501 Fax : 213 747 0704

Products *Large variety of fashion junior and missy apparel.*
Sell To *Department stores, clothing boutiques,*
Web Site *www.bbronson.com*

BLUE HAWAII SALES

801 South King Street, Suite 3707
Honolulu, HI 96813 hiblue@hawaii.rr.com
808 277 0368

Labels *Blue Hawaii*
Products *Casual sportswear & tropical wear collection.*
Price Points *Moderate*
Production *U.S.A.*
Showrooms *Honolulu*
Sell To *Department stores & mass merchants.*
Private Label *Yes*
RN Number *RN85143*
Contact *President and Owner: Joni Albao*

CARTISE INTERNATIONAL

6161 Cypihot Street
Saint Laurent, Quebec, Canada H4S 1R3 customerservice@cartise.ca
514 383 3499 Fax : 514 383 5405 1 888 383 1984

Labels *Cartise*
Products *Ladies tops, sweaters, blouses, jackets, pants, skirts, knits, dresses & coats.*
Price Points *Moderate to better*
Production *Domestic & Import*
Showrooms *Montreal, Toronto*
Sell To *Specialty stores and boutiques.*
Corp. Office *Above*
Web Site *www.cartise.ca*
Contact *President: Gadi Padan, Sales: Sharoni Padan, Design: Amy Wu*

EASTWEST CLOTHING

3481 East 14th Street
Los Angeles, CA 90023 avril@languagelosangeles.com
323 980 1177 Fax : 323 980 0551

Labels *Language Los Angeles*
Products *Casual sportswear, specializing in prints, solids & coordinates.*
Price Points *Moderate to better.*
Production *U.S.A.*
Showrooms *New York: 212-840-6300, Dallas: 214-969-5319, Atlanta: 404-355-1644, Chicago: 312-836-1920.*
Sell To *Department stores, speciality stores, boutiques & mail order catalogues.*
Private Label *Yes*
Web Site *www.languagelosangeles.com*
RN Number *RN94062*
Contact *President: Michael Schreier, Owner: Avril Ozen*

EURO JOY SPORTSWEAR CORP.

108 West 39th Street, Suite 1120
New York, NY 10018 jasoneurojoy@aol.com
212 575 4650 Fax : 212 575 4651

Labels *Euro Joy Sportswear*
Products *Active & casual sportswear & related separates.*
Price Points *Moderate*
Production *Overseas*
Showrooms *New York/above*
Sell To *Department stores, specialty stores & catalogues.*
Private Label *Yes*
RN Number *RN57032*
Rev. in mil. *2-10*
Contact *President: Jason Wu*

GRANITE KNITWEAR/CAL CRU CO., INC.

805 S Salisbury Avenue, PO Box 498
Granite Quarry, NC 28072 calcru@mindspring.com
704 279 5526 X254 Fax : 704 279 8205 800 476 9944

Labels *Cal Cru*
Products *Casual sportswear.*
Price Points *Moderate*
Production *U.S.A.*
Showrooms *Granite Quarry, NC/above*
Sell To *Screen printers, embroiderers, gift & souvenir retailers.*
Corp. Office *Same/above*
Private Label *Yes*
Web Site *www.calcru.com*
RN Number *RN41253*
Rev. in mil. *0-2*
Contact *President: Mike Jones, Marketing: Marsha Hartzoge*

HILO HATTIE

670 Auahi Street, Suite 1-03
Honolulu, HI 96813 sales@hilohattie.com
808 535 6500 Fax : 808 356 1510 1 800 233 8912

Labels *Hilo Hattie*
Products *Hawaiian, casual & resort wear for women.*
Production *Domestic*
Sell To *Retail stores and mass merchants.*
Private Label *Yes*
Web Site *www.hilohattie.com*

LIFE & STYLE FASHIONS INC.

1400 Broadway, Suite 815
New York, NY 10018 sunnykakar@hotmail.com
212 629 7314 Fax : 212 840 7433

Labels *Jessica Taylor*
Products *Casual sportswear, dresses and tops*
Price Points *Moderate*

Production *India & China*
Sell To *Department stores, specialty stores, boutiques, mass merchants & mail order catalogues.*
Private Label *Yes*
RN Number *RN77511*
Contact *President: Ajit Kakar, Sales Manager: Sunny Kakar*

MODODOC/GENEXUS INTERNATIONAL

1214 W. Jon Street
Torrance, CA 90502 sales@mododoc.com
310 532 7300 Fax : 310 532 7311 888 680 8910

Labels *Mododoc*
Products *Casual sportswear & knits*
Price Points *Better.*
Production *Import*
Showrooms *Los Angeles/127 E. 9th St., #601, L.A., CA 90015, 213-236-0983*
Sell To *Specialty stores, boutiques and mail order catalogues.*
Private Label *Yes*
Web Site *www.mododoc.com*
Rev. in mil. *0-2*

MOOSE CREEK

20801 Currier Road
City of Industry, CA 91789 richard@moosecreekinc.com
909 869 5859 Fax : 909 869 5873 800 332 2513

Labels *Moose Creek*
Products *Women's active & casual sportswear.*
Price Points *Moderate*
Showrooms *New York/212-967-0999*
Sell To *Department stores & sportsing goods stores.*
Private Label *Yes*
Web Site *www.moosecreekinc.com*
RN Number *RN53623*
Contact *Sales: Richard Bernstein*

NEW ORLEANS KNITWEAR

2917 Magazine Street, Suite 105
New Orleans, LA 70115 info@neworleansknitwear.com
504 891 4502 Fax : 504 891 3875 800 338 4864

Labels *Joan Vass*
Products *Ladies casual tops, bottoms & dresses.*
Price Points *Bridge to designer.*
Production *U.S.A.*
Showrooms *New York*
Sell To *Department stores & specialty stores.*
Private Label *Yes*
Web Site *www.neworleansknitwear.com*

PERSONAL TOUCH INC.

23 Commercial Waye
Hanson, MA 02341
781 447 0467 Fax : 781 447 5172 1 888 447 0496
info@personaltouchinc.com

Labels *Personal Touch*
Products *Casual sportswear & career wear for missy & large sizes.*
Price Points *Moderate*
Production *U.S.A.*
Showrooms *New York/above*
Sell To *Department stores, speciality stores & mail order catalogues.*
Private Label *Yes*
Web Site *www.apersonaltouchinc.com*
RN Number *RN60666*
Contact *President: Richard May*

VENUS FASHION

11711 Marco Beach Drive
Jacksonville, FL 32224
904 997 4000 Fax : 904 641 0977 888 782 2224
email@venus.com

Labels *Venus Fashion*
Products *Women's & junior pants, skirts, skirts, activewear, jeans, tops and dresses.*
Price Points *Moderate to better.*
Production *U.S.A.*
Showrooms *Jacksonville, FL/above.*
Sell To *Specialty stores & boutiques.*
Private Label *No*
Web Site *www.venus.com*
Contact *President and CEO: Jim Brewster*

WEARABLE INTEGRITY/BARBARA LESSER

1158 26th Street, Suite 873
Santa Monica, CA 90403
310 742 7444 Fax : 310 440 0858
mlesser@barbaralesser.com

Labels *Barbara Lesser*
Products *Ladies sportswear, denim, tops & pants.*
Price Points *Better*
Production *Import*
Showrooms *Los Angeles, Dallas, Atlanta, Chicago, Miami & New York.*
Sell To *Department stores, specialty stores, boutiques & mail order catalogues.*
Private Label *Yes*
Web Site *www.barbaralesser.com*
Rev. in mil. *11-50*
Contact *Sales: Mark Lesser, Design: Barbara Lesser*

WILLIAMSON-DICKIE MFG CO.

509 West Vickery Boulevard
Fort Worth, TX 76104
817 336 7201 Fax : 817 810 4342 866 411 1501
customerservice@dickies.com

Labels *Williamson-Dickie*
Products *Quality & style tops & bottons for workwear & playwear.*
Price Points *Moderate*

Production	*U.S.A.*
Showrooms	*Dallas, New York*
Sell To	*Department stores, specialty stores, uniform outlets.*
Private Label	*Yes*
Web Site	*www.dickies.com*
Rev. in mil.	*+500*
Contact	*President: Philip Williamson*

525 AMERICA

525 Seventh Avenue, 10th Floor
New York, NY 10018 mbock@525america.com
212 921 5688 Fax : 212 921 5069 877-246-8609

Labels *525 Womens*
Products *Contemporary knit sportswear plus silk camisoles for layering.*
Price Points *Better*
Production *U.S.A.*
Showrooms *New York & reps throughout the U.S.*
Sell To *Department stores, specialty stores & mail order catalogues.*
Private Label *Yes*
Web Site *www.525america.com*
Contact *President: Robert Bock, Design: Robert Bock, VP Sales: Marianne Bock*

ALICE AND OLIVIA

450 West 14th Street
New York, NY 10014 info@aliceandolivia.com
646 747 1461 Fax : 212 840 0149

Labels *Alice and Olivia*
Products *Sportswear, knits and pants.*
Sell To *Department stores, specialty stores & boutiques.*
Private Label *No*
Web Site *www.aliceandolivia.com*
Contact *Designer: Stacey Bendet*

AVALIN LIMITED

221 West 37th Street
New York, NY 10018 info@avalinknits.com
212 997 0011 Fax : 212 997 0022

Labels *Avalin*
Products *Knit & related separates.*
Price Points *Better*
Production *U.S.A.*
Sell To *Speciality stores & boutiques.*
Private Label *Yes*
Web Site *www.avalinknits.com*
RN Number *RN89128*
Contact *Owner: Zuzu Aghravi*

AZIBI LTD. *(Rep.)

270 West 39th Street, Suite 1501
New York, NY 10018 goodrep@gmail.com
212 869 6550 Fax : 212 764 4764

Labels *Luna Luz, Azibi*
Products *Contemporary sportswear & separates. Lots of garment-dyed styles.*
Price Points *Better*
Production *U.S.A. and Spain.*
Showrooms *New York, Denver, Florida, Texas, Los Angeles, Atlanta.*
Sell To *Department stores, specialty stores, boutiques and mail order catalogues.*
Private Label *Yes*
Web Site *www.lunaluz.net*

RN Number	*RN96314*
Rev. in mil.	*0-2*
Contact	*Rep: Barbara Feldman - 917-331-7536*

B & B DESIGNS COLLECTION INC. *(Rep.)

300 S. Anderson Street
Los Angeles, CA 90033
323 261 0000 Fax : 323 261 0001
info@amandafashion.com

Labels	*Amanda*
Products	*Acetate, polyester, rayon & slinky two piece dressing sportswear.*
Price Points	*Moderate & Better*
Production	*U.S.A.*
Showrooms	*Los Angeles*
Sell To	*Department stores, specialty stores & boutiques.*
Private Label	*Yes*
Web Site	*www.amandafashion.com*
RN Number	*RN87230*
Rev. in mil.	*2-10*
Contact	*President and Owner: Bijan Navabian, Sales: Bahman Navabian*

BABETTE

867 Isabella Street
Oakland, CA 94607
510 625 8500 Fax : 510 986 1402 800 677 7246
mary@babettesf.com

Labels	*Babette*
Products	*Womens sportswear & related separates.*
Price Points	*Better/Bridge*
Production	*U.S.A.*
Showrooms	*West: Diane Vonderheide, 213.488.9334; diane@thevonderheideshowroom.com* *East: Terry Ventre, 212.967.6192; info@terryventreshowroom.com*
Sell To	*Specialty stores & boutiques.*
Private Label	*No*
Web Site	*www.shopbabette.com*
Rev. in mil.	*2-10*
Contact	*President: Steven Pinsky, Design: Babette Pinsky*

BARAMI/FASHION CONCEPTS/PATRIZIA LUCA

519 8th Avenue, 5th Floor
New York, NY 10018
212 629 6464 Fax : 212 695 1417
baman@barami.com

Labels	*Barami, Patrizia Luca, Fashion Concept*
Products	*Contemporary sportswear collection.*
Price Points	*Better*
Production	*U.S.A. and China*
Showrooms	*New York*
Sell To	*Specialty stores, department stores, boutiques & catalogues.*
Private Label	*Yes*
Web Site	*www.barami.com*
RN Number	*RN94992,RN87729*
Contact	*Sales: Bahman Terani, Bahram Hakakian, Merchandising/Personl Relations: Neda Hakak*

BARRAZA ASSOCIATES LTD

225 West 35th Street, Suite 1502
New York, NY 10001 barrazany@aol.com
212 564 6583

Labels *BarrazaStyle*
Products *Silk Dupioni separates that dress up or dress down.*
Price Points *Moderate to better.*
Production *U.S.A. & import.*
Sell To *Department stores, specialty stores, boutiques, mail order catalogues.*
Private Label *Yes*
Web Site *www.barrazastyle.com*
Rev. in mil. *2-10*
Contact *President: Maria Barraza, Sales & Marketing: Rafael Romero*

BASIX OF AMERICA

2778 NW 31st Avenue
Ft. Lauderdale, FL 33311 info@basixofamerica.com
800 236 8150 Fax : 954 486 6580

Products *Contemporary and fashion sportswear. Lots of dresses, fashion tops & a crochet collection.*
Showrooms *Rep: Jessica Corbett - 954-486-6580 - jessicacorbett@basixofamerica.com*
Sell To *Department stores, specialty stores*
Web Site *www.basixofamerica.com*

BCBG MAX AZRIA GROUP

1450 Broadway, 17th Floor
New York, NY 10018 judy.scarpulla@bcbg.com
212 382 1880 Fax : 212 764 6912 866 518 2224

Labels *BCBG Max Azria*
Products *Contemporary womenswear.*
Price Points *Better*
Production *U.S.A.*
Showrooms *New York: 1450 Broadway-212-704-4725, Los Angele: 110E 9th St, A571-323-277-5440, Atlanta: 250 Spring St.#11E112-A/B-404-223-2224, Dallas:Ross Ave.-214-744-2226*
Sell To *Department stores & specialty stores.*
Corp. Office *2761 Fruitland Avenue, Vernon, Ca. 90058 - 323-589-2224*
Private Label *Yes*
Web Site *www.bcbg.com*
Contact *President and Owner: Max Azria, President Licensing & International: Sophie Rietdyk, Sales Executive: Judy Scarpulla 212 704-4736*

BEL ESPRIT SHOWROOM/SHOWROOM INTERNATIONAL *(Rep.)

P.O. Box 30273
Philadelphia, PA 19103 belesprit@ureach.com
215 963 9394 Fax : 419 793 8064

Labels *Bel Esprit, Showroom International*
Products *Contemporary sportswear & careerwear.*
Price Points *Better to designer.*
Production *U.S.A. & import*
Showrooms *Bel Esprit Showroom - The International Showroom for Ethical Fashion. Showroom Internat. The International Showroom for Independent Fashion. Moda 360: A Complete Fashion Revo.*
Sell To *Department stores & specialty stores.*

Corp. Office *Additional websites: www.showroominternational.com, www.moda360intl.com*
Private Label *No*
Web Site *www.belesprit.net*
Contact *CEO: Debora Pokallus*

BERGER & STEVENS *(Rep.)

260 West 39th Street, 7th Floor
New York, NY 10018
212 768 0050 Fax : 212 768 3332
aberger@bergerandstevens.com

Labels *Vitamin, Eva and Claudi, Blair Stanley, Queen, Max Volmary and Alora Knits.*
Products *European sportswear, knitwear. BGS furs...Fur vests and jackets from Russia*
Price Points *Bridge to designer.*
Production *U.S.A., Europe & Russia*
Showrooms *New York*
Sell To *Specialty stores & better department stores.*
Private Label *Yes*
Web Site *www.bergerandstevens.com*
Contact *Owner: Alana Berger & Jackie Stevens*

BETSEY JOHNSON

52-16 Barnett Avenue
Long Island City, NY 11104
866-222-4243
info@betseyjohnson.com

Labels *Betsey Johnson*
Products *Contemporary sportswear & accessory collections.*
Price Points *Better*
Sell To *Department stores & specialty stores.*
Web Site *www.betseyjohnson.com*
RN Number *RN77751*

C.T.C. INC.

1821B Knickerbocker Road
San Angelo, TX 76904
325 947 2106 Fax : 325 944 7371
turnercarol22@aol.com

Labels *C.T.C.*
Products *Missy updated sportswear & coordinating separates*
Price Points *Moderate to better.*
Production *U.S.A.*
Showrooms *Atlanta/Atlanta Mart*
Sell To *Specialty stores & boutiques*
Private Label *No*
Contact *Owner: Randy Turner, Design: Carol Turner*

CAROL PERETZ

49 Windsor Avenue, Suite 103
Mineola, NY 11501
516 248 6300 Fax : 516 248 6622
info@carolperetz.com

Labels *Twisted by Carol Peretz*
Products *Contemporary sportswear, dresses and separates.*
Price Points *Better to designer.*
Production *U.S.A.*

Showrooms *New York*
Sell To *Specialty stores and boutiques.*
Private Label *No*
Web Site *www.carolperetz.com*
Contact *President: Carol Peretz*

CHRISTOPHER & BANKS CORPORATION

2400 Xenium Lane North
Plymouth, MN 55441 info@christopherandbanks.com
763 551 5000 Fax : 763 551 5198 800 890 9601

Labels *Christopher & Banks*
Products *Tops, blouses, pants & skirts for work and leisure in womens size 4 to 16.*
Price Points *Moderate*
Production *Import*
Sell To *Department stores, specialty stores*
Private Label *Yes*
Web Site *www.christopherandbanks.com*

CPT USA, LLC DBA COCKPIT USA

15 West 39th Street, 12th Floor
New York, NY 10018 jacky@cockpitusa.com
212 575 1616 Fax : 212 575 1636 800 228 4739

Labels *Cockpit USA, Blue Eagle by Cockpit USA, Civilian Pilot Training*
Products *Contemporary Americana themed sportswear, bottoms, denims, wovens, knits & leather.*
Price Points *Better*
Production *U.S.A. & import.*
Showrooms *New York.*
Sell To *Department stores, specialty stores, mail order catalogues, specialty chains & internationally.*
Private Label *Yes on a limited basis.*
Web Site *www.cockpitusa.com*
RN Number *RN114345*
Contact *President: Jeff Clyman, Marketing: Jacky Clyman*

CYNTHIA ROWLEY

376 Bleeker Street
New York, NY 10014 kfiorentino@cynthiarowley.com
212 242 0847 Fax : 212 242 4136

Labels *Cynthia Rowley*
Products *Contemporary designer sportswear & dress collection.*
Price Points *Better to designer*
Production *U.S.A.*
Showrooms *New York/above*
Sell To *Department stores, specialty stores & boutiques.*
Private Label *No*
Web Site *www.cynthiarowley.com*
RN Number *RN75150*
Contact *Design: Cynthia Rowley*

CYNTHIA STEFFE

530 Seventh Avenue, 18th Floor
New York, NY 10018 info@cynthiasteffe.com
212 403 6210

Labels *Cynthia Steffe, CeCe by Cynthia Steffe*
Products *Contemporary sportswear and dresses.*
Price Points *Contemporary to designer*
Production *U.S.A. and import*
Showrooms *New York/above*
Sell To *Department stores and specialty stores.*
Private Label *No*
Web Site *www.cynthiasteffe.com*
RN Number *RN77456*
Contact *Design: Cynthia Steffe*

DANA EMILIA PRESENTS *(Rep.)

264 West 40th, Suite 503
New York, NY 10018 fashion@danaemilia.com
212 391 4104 Fax : 212 391 4153

Labels *Christopher Calvin, Redwood Court, Peacock Ways, Swish, Vanite Couture, Banaris*
Products *All types of women's contemporary sportswear.*
Price Points *Better*
Production *U.S.A. & import.*
Showrooms *New York.*
Sell To *Specialty stores, boutiques, chain stores & mail order catalogues.*
Private Label *Yes*
Web Site *www.danaemiliapresents.com*
Contact *President: Dana Harrison*

DEPECHE MODE

230 West 38th Street, 12th Floor
New York, NY 10018 leer@depecheco.com
212 643 6633 Fax : 212 643 1184

Labels *Depeche Mode, Studio*
Products *Contemporary sportswear.*
Price Points *Better to bridge, plus off-price.*
Production *U.S.A. & import*
Showrooms *New York.*
Sell To *Department & specialty stores, boutiques, mass merchants, catalogues, chains & off-price.*
Private Label *Yes*
Web Site *www.depecheco.com*
RN Number *RN61812*
Contact *President: Lee Rosenthal, Sales: Joy Villa (joyv@depecheco.com)*

DKNY

240 West 40th Street, 11th Floor
New York, NY 10018
212 789 1500 Fax : 212 768 5760 800 231 0884

Labels *DKNY*
Products *Designer contemporary collection*
Price Points *Better*

Showrooms *New York*
Sell To *Department stores & specialty stores*
Web Site *www.donnakaran.com*

DREW PHILIPS CORP.

231 West 39th Street, Suite 410
New York, NY 10018 gigi@drewphilipscorp.com
212 354 0095 Fax : 212 354 0080

Labels *Drew*
Products *Contemporary sportswear, knits, dresses, pants & skirts.*
Price Points *Better*
Production *U.S.A.*
Showrooms *New York*
Sell To *Specialty stores, boutiques & catalogues.*
Private Label *Yes*
Web Site *www.drewclothing.com*
Contact *Design: Drew Philips, Sales: Gigi Hoffman*

DUE PER DUE/209WST

209 West 38th Street, Room 401
New York , NY 10018 amyho@dueperdue.com
212 921 7650 Fax : 212 921 4913

Labels *Due Per Due/209Wst*
Products *Contemporary sportswear.*
Price Points *Better*
Production *China*
Showrooms *CA/213-629-1817, Dallas/214-630-2061, Atlanta/704-906-4371, NE/631-424-5733.*
Sell To *Department stores, specialty stores & mail order catalogues.*
Private Label *Yes*
Web Site *www.dueperdue.com*
Contact *Richard Cocheri*

ELAN INTERNATIONAL

15885 N.W. 13th Avenue
Miami, FL 33169 elan@elan-usa.com
954 962 9166 Fax : 954 962 8676 800 645 7873

Labels *Elan™*
Products *Manufacturer & wholesaler of young contemporary lounge-wear and resort-wear collections.*
Price Points *Better*
Showrooms *Los Angeles: 213-622-1514, New York: 800-645-7873, Dallas: 214-634-2164.*
Sell To *Department stores, specialty stores, boutiques*
Private Label *Yes*
Web Site *www.elan-usa.com*
Rev. in mil. *11-50*

EMIL RUTENBERG

719 S Los Angeles Street, Suite 718
Los Angeles, CA 90014 info@emilrutenberg.com
213 489 4374 Fax : 213 489 4402

Labels *Emil Rutenberg*
Products *Contemporary sportswear, skirts and jackets.*

Price Points *Bridge*
Production *U.S.A.*
Showrooms *New York/ Susan Bonomo 212-302-4702*
.
Sell To *Speciality stores & boutiques.*
Web Site *www.emilrutenberg.com*
Rev. in mil. *2-10*
Contact *Sales/LA: Emil Rutenberg*

FRENCH CONNECTION

512 Seventh Avenue, 25th Floor
New York, NY 10018 frenchconnection@frenchconnection-usa.com
212 221 3157 Fax : 212 302 6839 866-932-3285

Labels *French Connection*
Products *Contemporary sportswear collection, European fabrics.*
Price Points *Better*
Production *Global*
Showrooms *Atlanta, Chicago, Los Angeles & New York.*
Sell To *Department stores, specialty stores, boutiques, mail order catalogues & off-price retailers.*
Corp. Office *184-10 Jamaica Avenue, Hollis, New York 11423*
Private Label *Yes*
Web Site *usa.frenchconnection.com*
RN Number *RN53372*
Rev. in mil. *101-500*
Contact *President: Andrea Hyde*

GAIAM

833 W South Boulder Road, PO Box 3095
Boulder, CO 80307 customerservice@gaiam.com
303 222 3600 Fax : 303 222 3700 877 989 6321

Labels *Gaiam*
Products *Enviromentally responsible contemporary clothing in natural & organic knits.*
Price Points *Moderate to better.*
Production *U.S.A.*
Sell To *Specialty stores, boutiques & mail order catalogues.*
Web Site *www.gaiam.com*
Contact *President: Lynn Powers*

H.M.S. PRODUCTIONS

250 West 39th Street, 18th Floor
New York, NY 10018 nubby@nubby.com
212 719 9190 Fax : 212 730 7581

Labels *Cable & Gauge, Cupio, Spense Dress, Spense Blouse, Spense Knits*
Products *Knit tops, cut and sew tops, blouses*
Price Points *Better*
Production *U.S.A. & import.*
Showrooms *New York.*
Sell To *Department stores, specialty stores & catalogues*
Private Label *Yes*
Web Site *www.cableandgauge.com*
RN Number *RN98108*

Contact *President and Owner: Spenser Alpern, Production: Spenser Alpern, Design: Michelle Antonelli*

HEISEL

P.O. Box 792
New York, NY 10002
212 719 3916
contact@heisel.co

Labels *Heisel*
Products *Contemporary sportswear & accessories in sustainable new tech materials.*
Price Points *Contemporary*
Production *U.S.A.*
Sell To *Specialty stores & boutiques.*
Corp. Office *Above*
Private Label *No*
Web Site *www.heisel.co*
Contact *President: Sylvia Heisel*

J.D. FINE *(Rep.)

179 Mason Circle
Concord, CA 94520
925 521 3300 Fax : 925 521 9090
jamief@jdfine.com

Labels *Tart Collections*
Products *Contemporary fashion sportswear.*
Price Points *Better*
Production *Import & some local production*
Showrooms *New York/Cricket Showroom 901 412 5466, Chicago Agents 312 396 0100, Atlanta/ Tryst Showroom 404 749 5115.*
Sell To *Department stores, specialty stores, boutiques*
Private Label *Yes*
Web Site *www.tartcollections.com*
RN Number *97884*
Rev. in mil. *11-50*
Contact *President: Jamie Finegold, National Sales Manager: Jennifer Kreider (jenniferk@jdfine.com*

JUSSARA LEE

60 Bedford Street
New York, NY 10014
212 242 4128 Fax : 212 242 4129
mail@jussaralee.com

Labels *Jussara Lee*
Products *Young bridge contemporary sportswear.*
Price Points *Designer*
Production *U.S.A.*
Showrooms *New York*
Sell To *Department stores, specialty stores & boutiques.*
Private Label *No*
Web Site *www.jussaralee.com*
RN Number *RN89094*
Rev. in mil. *0-2*
Contact *Design: Jussara Lee*

KELLWOOD COMPANY

600 Kellwood Parkway
Chesterfield, MO 63017 corp_communications@kellwood.com
314 576 3100 Fax : 314 576 3325

Labels *XOXO, Briggs New York, Sag Harbor®,*
Products *Contemporary women's sportswear & dress collection*
Price Points *Better*
Showrooms *New York/212-515-2600, California/626-934-4122*
Sell To *Department stores, boutiques*
Web Site *www.kellwood.com*

NUTHATCH

412 Main Street
Rockland, ME 04841 sales@shopnuthatch.com
207 596 0880

Labels *Nuthatch*
Products *Women's sustainable, modern & classic collection.*
Price Points *Better*
Production *USA*
Sell To *Department stores & specialty stores.*
Web Site *www.shopnuthatch.com*
Contact *Designer: Beth Bowley*

OXFORD GOLF

555 S. Victory Drive
Lyons, GA 30436 info@oxfordgolf.com
866 727 4693 Fax : 212 586 8825

Labels *Oxford Golf*
Products *Golf shirts, pants, shorts, skirts, sweaters and jackets.*
Price Points *Better*
Sell To *Golf pro shops, resorts, specialty stores.*
Private Label *Yes*
Web Site *www.oxfordgolf.com*
Rev. in mil. *2-10*
Contact *Beverly Day (bday@oxfordgolf.com), Vicki Robins (vrobins@oxfordgolf.com), Pam Blount (pblount@oxfordgolf.com).*

PARASUCO JEANS INC.

128 Deslauriers Street
St. Laurent, QC, Canada H4N 1V8 customerservice@parasuco.com
514 334 0888 Fax : 514 334 9833 877 PARASUCO

Labels *Parasuco Denim Legend*
Products *Denim sportswear & jeans.*
Price Points *Better*
Production *Canada*
Sell To *Department stores, specialty stores, boutiques & mail order catalogues.*
Corp. Office *Above*
Private Label *Yes*
Web Site *www.parasuco.com*

PHOOL FASHIONS

241 West 37th Street, Suite 518
New York, NY 10018
212 944 0910 Fax : 212 944 0286
phoolfash@aol.com

Labels *Phool*
Products *Missy, junior & women's updated dresses.*
Price Points *Moderate*
Production *Import*
Showrooms *New York*
Sell To *Specialty stores, boutiques, mail order catalogues & chain stores.*
Private Label *Yes*
Web Site *www.phoolfashionusa.com*
RN Number *RN80911*
Rev. in mil. *2-10*
Contact *Owner/Sales: Reena Paintal*

SCULLY

Scully Corporate Plaza
Oxnard, CA 93003
805 483 6339 Fax : 805 483 6439
brianscully@scullyleather.com

Labels *Scully*
Products *Contemporary apparel for ladies. Western, dresses, blouses, skirts and jackets.*
Showrooms *California*
Web Site *www.scullyleather.com*
Contact *Division Director: Brian Scully*

SENTIMENTAL INC.

214 West 39th Street, Suite 504A
New York, NY 10018
212 221 0282 Fax : 212 302 2959
sam@sentimentalny.com

Labels *Sentimental NY, ON TREND*
Products *Chic & contemporary line of pants, tops and clubwear.*
Price Points *Budget to moderate*
Production *U.S.A.*
Showrooms *New York*
Sell To *Specialty stores, chain stores*
Private Label *Yes*
Web Site *www.sentimentalny.com*
RN Number *124825*
Rev. in mil. *0-2*
Contact *Owner: Sam Hourani*

SHOWROOM SEVEN/ERICKSON BEAMON *(Rep.)

263 Eleventh Avenue
New York, NY 10001
212 643 4810 Fax : 646 763 8940
jean-marc@showroomseven.com

Labels *2nd Day, EKAT, Etienne Marcel, PatBo, Maliparmi*
Products *Updated contemporary sportswear.*
Price Points *Contemporary, designer & couture*
Production *International*
Showrooms *New York, Los Angeles, Paris*

Sell To *Department stores, specialty stores & boutiques. International and domestic.*
Private Label *Yes*
Web Site *www.showroomseven.com*
Rev. in mil. *11-50*

SIMON SHOWROOM *(Rep.)

95 Fifth Avenue, 3rd Floor
New York, NY 10003 info@simonshowroom.com
212 242 1565 Fax : 212 242 6836

Labels *IRO, Tatras, Rivieras, Pepin, Sundry, AMO, Antik Batik, Carisa Rene, Foundrae, Essentiel*
Products *Contemporary sportswear, dresses & ready-to-wear.*
Price Points *Better to contemporary.*
Production *U.S.A., France, Hong Kong.*
Showrooms *Los Angeles 213-593-1394*
Sell To *Department stores, specialty stores & boutiques.*
Private Label *Yes*
Web Site *www.simonshowroom.com*
Rev. in mil. *11-50*
Contact *President/Owner: Fifi Simon*

SOPHIE FINZI LTD DBA PASHOOT

255 West 36th Street, Suite 201
New York, NY 10018 sophiefinziltd@aol.com
212 967 4349 Fax : 212 967 5361

Labels *Pashoot, Sophie*
Products *Better sportswear with a European look. Regular & large sizes.*
Price Points *Better*
Showrooms *Chicago/Julie Kipta 219-762-1442, California/Peggy Finnegan 707-778-1592*
Sell To *Specialty stores & boutiques.*
Private Label *No*
Web Site *www.sophiefinzi.com*
Contact *President and Designer: Sophie Finzi*

SUSAN ELIAS

5640 12th Avenue North
St. Petersburg, FL 33710 eliascouture@gmail.com
727 452 6637

Labels *Susan Elias*
Products *Women's couture/contemporary tops, dresses and pants.*
Price Points *Better to designer*
Production *U.S.A.*
Private Label *No*
Web Site *www.eliascouture.com*
Contact *President/Designer: Susan Elias*

TAILOR VINTAGE

12 South Main Street, Unit 403
Norwalk, CT 06854 info@tailorvintage.com
212 840 1871 Fax : 203 286 1055

Labels *Tailor Vintage*
Products *Better contemporary sportswear, shorts, trousers, shirts & jackets. Preppy Cool.*

Price Points *Better*
Sell To *Department stores, specialty stores & boutiques.*
Private Label *Yes*
Web Site *www.tailorvintage.com*
Contact *Owner & Design: Richard Rosenthal*

TASHA POLIZZI

287 Main Street
Great Barrington, MA 01230 jane@tashapolizzi.com
413 528 6500 Fax : 413 528 6370

Labels *Tasha Polizzi*
Products *Contempoary skirts & sportswear.*
Price Points *Bridge*
Production *U.S.A.*
Sell To *Department stores, specialty stores.*
Private Label *No*
Web Site *www.tashapolizzi.com*
Contact *Owner: Tasha Polizzi, Sales: Jane Wright*

TOPSON DOWNS

3840 Watseka Avenue
Culver City, CA 90232 info@topsondowns.com
310 558 0300 Fax : 310 774 3666

Labels *Love, Fire*
Products *Young contemporary line with a touch of vintage flare in tops, bottoms and dresses.*
Price Points *Better*
Production *Import*
Showrooms *NY Showroom: 530 7th Avenue, Suite 1502, New York, NY 10018 (212) 730 7860.*
LA Showroom 110 East 9th Street Suite A803 Los Angeles, CA 90072 310.558.0300
Sell To *Department stores, specialty stores*
Private Label *Yes*
Web Site *www.topsondowns.com*

TRAMP

1407 Broadway, Suite 1404
New York, NY 10018 tramp@trampny.com
212 398 1428 Fax : 212 921 0984

Labels *Tramp*
Products *Young contemporary sportswear, cutting edge fashions.*
Price Points *Better*
Production *U.S.A. & overseas.*
Showrooms *New York*
Sell To *Department stores, specialty stores, boutiques & off-price retailers.*
Private Label *Yes*
RN Number *RN99610*
Rev. in mil. *2-10*
Contact *President: Prim Tolani, Sales: Jackie*

XOXO

1411 Broadway, 7th Floor
New York, NY 10018 suzanne.desiderio@kellwood.com
212 575 0273 Fax : 212 575 0309

Labels *XOXO*
Products *Contemporary sportswear & dresses.*
Price Points *Moderate to better.*
Production *Import*
Sell To *Specialty stores, department stores*
Corp. Office *Kellwood Company, 600 Kellwood Parkway, Chesterfield, MO. 63017, tel#314-576-3100.*
Private Label *No*
Web Site *www.kellwood.com*
Contact *Sales: Suzanne Desiderio*

YON DESIGN, INC.

6057B NW 31st Avenue
Fort Lauderdale, FL 33309 yondesigninc@me.com
954 973 7771 Fax : 954 302 4974

Labels *YonDesign*
Products *All types of contemporary sportswear, resortwear & travelwear for ladies.*
Price Points *Moderate*
Sell To *Specialty stores and boutiques.*
Corp. Office *Above*
Web Site *www.yondesign.com*
Contact *Designer: Yon O. Chang*

ANDERSEN-BECKER INC.

9010 Maier Road, Unit 100
Laurel, MD 20723 info@leeandersen.com
301 725 5555 Fax : 301 725 0155 800 765 5648

Labels *Lee Andersen*
Products *Wearable art clothing, special occasion & outerwear with graphic images & mixed fibers.*
Price Points *Better.*
Production *U.S.A.*
Showrooms *Chicago/312-527-2530, Los Angeles/213-627-3663, Mid-Atlantic/908-725-1255, Dallas/985-674-5036 & Atlanta/727-392-3880*
Sell To *Specialty stores & boutiques.*
Private Label *Yes*
Web Site *www.leeandersen.com*
Rev. in mil. *0-2*
Contact *President: Lee Andersen, Vice-President: Joan Becker, Design: Lee Andersen*

ANNE NAMBA DESIGNS

324 Kamani Street
Honolulu, HI 96813 anne@annenamba.com
808 589 1135 Fax : 808 589 1792 877-578-0001

Labels *Anne Namba Designs*
Products *Unique kimono & Asian inspired looks.*
Price Points *Designer*
Production *U.S.A.*
Sell To *Department stores, specialty stores, boutiques & mail order catalogues.*
Private Label *No*
Web Site *www.annenamba.com*
Rev. in mil. *0-2*
Contact *President & Designer: Anne Namba*

COLORATURA, INC.

P.O. Box 157
Annville, PA 17003 coloratura9@aol.com
717 867 1144 Fax : 717 867 1152 800 825 8288

Labels *Coloratura*
Products *Decorative patchwork & applique outerwear & more in multi tones, textures & fabrics.*
Price Points *Designer*
Production *U.S.A.*
Showrooms *Denver/Frank Levy & Annville, PA.*
Sell To *Specialty stores, boutiques & mail order catalogues.*
Private Label *No*
Web Site *www.coloratura.com*
Contact *President: Alan J. Resnick*

DANA EMILIA PRESENTS *(Rep.)

264 West 40th, Suite 503
New York, NY 10018 fashion@danaemilia.com
212 391 4104 Fax : 212 391 4153

Labels *Christopher Calvin, Redwood Court, Peacock Ways, Swish, Vanite Couture, Banaris*
Products *Wearable art tops & jackets and separates.*
Price Points *Better*

Production *U.S.A. & import.*
Showrooms *New York.*
Sell To *Specialty stores, boutiques, chain stores & mail order catalogues.*
Private Label *Yes*
Web Site *www.danaemiliapresents.com*
Contact *President: Dana Harrison*

EMA SAVAHL DESIGN

7151 NW 6th Court
Miami, FL 33150 sales@emasavahl.com
305 754 6717 Fax : 305 754 6787

Labels *Ema Savahl Couture*
Products *Handpainted & embellished eveningwear separates& dresses with Swarovski crystals.*
Price Points *Designer to couture.*
Production *USA*
Showrooms *Miami/FL*
Sell To *Specialty stores & boutiques.*
Private Label *No*
Web Site *www.emasavahl.com*
Rev. in mil. *2-10*
Contact *Owner/Designer: Ema Koja*

KIPPYS *(Rep.)

2096 Newton Avenue
San Diego, CA 92113 bob@kippys.com
619 435 6218 Fax : 619 238 0670

Labels *Kippys, Manage á Trois*
Products *Embellished leather, suedes, denims, t-shirts & westernwear.*
Price Points *Better to designer.*
Showrooms *Regional shows in Dallas, Los Angeles, New York, Denver, Chicago, Las Vegas. International: Milan and Paris.*
Sell To *Specialty stores & mail-order catalagues.*
Private Label *Yes*
Web Site *www.kippys.com*
Rev. in mil. *2-10*
Contact *Designers: Bob Kipperman & Tarin Brouillette*

STEEL PONY

7758 South 4th Street, Suite 103
Philadelphia, PA 19147 joanne@steelpony.com
215 467 6065 Fax : 215 271 7709

Labels *Steel Pony*
Products *Hand dyed, hand painted sportswear, yogawear & casual dressing in missy & large sizes.*
Price Points *Better*
Production *U.S.A.*
Sell To *Specialty stores, boutiques*
Private Label *No*
Web Site *www.steelpony.com*
Contact *Owner/Design: Dennis Wolk/Joanne Litz*

WAI-CHING

115 Prefontaine Place South, Suite 605
Seattle, WA 98104
206 229 1111
sales@wai-ching.com

Labels	*Wai-Ching*
Products	*Wearable embellished & hand dyed art clothing. Unique bridal, kimono & Asian inspired lo*
Price Points	*Bridge*
Production	*U.S.A.*
Showrooms	*Above*
Sell To	*Specialty stores & boutiques.*
Corp. Office	*Above*
Web Site	*www.wai-ching.com*
Contact	*Designer: Christine W Ching Leung*

Notes

ABS BY ALLEN SCHWARTZ

1231 Long Beach Avenue
Los Angeles, CA 90021 kfoster@absstyle.com
213 895 4400 Fax : 213 895 4401

Labels *ABS by Allen Schwartz, ABS Collection, Allen B. by Allen Schwartz*
Products *Contemporary collection of day into evening dresses & separates.*
Price Points *Better to designer*
Showrooms *New York/ tel # 212 398 0330, Los Angeles & Atlanta.*
Sell To *Department stores & specialty stores*
Corp. Office *Above*
Private Label *No*
Web Site *www.absstyle.com*
Contact *CFO: Kirk Foster, VP of Sales: Lloyd Singer*

ADK FASHIONS *(Rep.)

225 West 35th Street, Suite 300
New York, NY 10001 adk@adkfashions.com
212 714 1177 Fax : 212 947 9063

Labels *Georges Chakra "Edition", JOTA+GE, Lalla Bee, Maria Coca, Vicedomini*
Products *Sportswear, eveningwear, suits and seperates.*
Price Points *Bridge, Designer, Couture*
Production *U.S.A., Europe, Australia, Canada*
Showrooms *New York.*
Sell To *Department stores, specialty stores & boutiques.*
Private Label *No*
Web Site *www.adkfashions.com*
Rev. in mil. *2-10*
Contact *President: Ab Korine, Owner: Arthur Drogowski*

ADRIANNA PAPELL LLC.

500 Seventh Avenue, 10th Floor
New York, NY 10018 customerservice@adriannapapell.com
212 695 5244 Fax : 212 714 1871

Labels *Adrianna Papell*
Products *Day into evening designer collection.*
Price Points *Better*
Production *Import from the Orient*
Showrooms *New York, Los Angeles, Atlanta, Chicago & Dallas*
Sell To *Specialty stores, catalogues & department stores.*
Private Label *Yes*
Web Site *www.adriannapapell.com*
RN Number *RN59782*
Contact *President: Jaynee Berkman*

AIDAN MATTOX

500 Seventh Avenue, 10th Floor
New York, NY 10018 customerservice@aidanmattox.com
212 764 5870 Fax : 212 764 5845

Labels *Aidan Mattox, Aidan*
Products *Eveningwear collection*
Price Points *Better*

Production *Import from the Orient*
Showrooms *New York, Los Angeles & Dallas*
Sell To *Specialty stores, catalogues & department stores.*
Private Label *Yes*
Web Site *www.aidanmattox.com*
RN Number *RN59782*
Contact *President: Frank Borsas*

ANNA SUI

250 West 39th Street, 15th Floor
New York, NY 10018 contactus@annasui.com
212 768 1004 Fax : 212 840 6737

Labels *Anna Sui*
Products *Designer collection.*
Price Points *Designer*
Production *U.S.A.*
Showrooms *New York/above*
Sell To *Department stores & specialty stores.*
Corp. Office *250 West 39th Street, New York, NY 10018, tel: 212 768 1951, fax: 212 302 6199*
Private Label *No*
Web Site *www.annasui.com*
Contact *Sales: Robert Sui, Design: Anna Sui*

BETSEY JOHNSON

52-16 Barnett Avenue
Long Island City, NY 11104 info@betseyjohnson.com
866-222-4243

Labels *Betsey Johnson*
Products *Women's dresses & eveningwear collection.*
Price Points *Better*
Sell To *Department stores & specialty stores.*
Web Site *www.betseyjohnson.com*
RN Number *RN77751*

BILL BLASS FASHIONS LLC

236 Fifth Avenue, 8th Floor
New York, NY 10001 allison@billblass.com
212 689 8957 Fax : 212 889 0840

Labels *Bill Blass*
Products *Designer collection.*
Price Points *Designer*
Production *U.S.A. & Italy*
Showrooms *New York/above*
Sell To *Specialty stores.*
Private Label *No*
Web Site *www.billblass.com*
RN Number *RN59126,RN38344*

BLUESUITS

200 West 70th Street, Suite 14G
New York, NY 10023 jamak@off7th.com
212 787 0278

Labels *Bluesuits*
Products *Women's designer collection including suits, jackets, pants, skirts & dresses in sizes 0 to 20.*
Price Points *Designer*
Production *U.S.A.*
Sell To *Department stores & boutiques*
Private Label *Yes*
Web Site *www.bluesuitsonline.com*
Contact *Designer: Jamak Khazra*

CAROL PERETZ

49 Windsor Avenue, Suite 103
Mineola, NY 11501 info@carolperetz.com
516 248 6300 Fax : 516 248 6622

Labels *Carol Peretz*
Products *Eveningwear & special occasion dressing. High fashion designer gowns.*
Price Points *Better to designer.*
Production *U.S.A.*
Showrooms *New York*
Sell To *Specialty stores and boutiques.*
Private Label *No*
Web Site *www.carolperetz.com*
Contact *President: Carol Peretz*

CYNTHIA ROWLEY

376 Bleeker Street
New York, NY 10014 kfiorentino@cynthiarowley.com
212 242 0847 Fax : 212 242 4136

Labels *Cynthia Rowley*
Products *Contemporary designer sportswear & dress collection.*
Price Points *Better to designer*
Production *U.S.A.*
Showrooms *New York/above*
Sell To *Department stores, specialty stores & boutiques.*
Private Label *No*
Web Site *www.cynthiarowley.com*
RN Number *RN75150*
Contact *Design: Cynthia Rowley*

CYNTHIA STEFFE

530 Seventh Avenue, 18th Floor
New York, NY 10018 info@cynthiasteffe.com
212 403 6210

Labels *Cynthia Steffe, CeCe by Cynthia Steffe*
Products *Designer sportswear*
Price Points *Designer*
Production *U.S.A. and import*
Showrooms *New York/above*

Sell To *Department stores and specialty stores.*
Private Label *No*
Web Site *www.cynthiasteffe.com*
RN Number *RN77456*
Contact *Design: Cynthia Steffe*

DIANE VON FURSTENBERG STUDIO, L.P.

440 West 14th Street
New York, NY 10014 M.Graniela@dvf.com
212 741 6607 Fax : 212 741 8273 888 472 2383

Labels *Diane by Diane Von Furstenberg*
Products *Day into evening designer collection*
Price Points *Bridge*
Showrooms *New York, Los Angeles, Atlanta, Dallas*
Sell To *Department stores, specialty stores*
Corp. Office *Above*
Web Site *www.dvf.com*
Contact *Sales : Marisa Graniela*

DONNA KARAN COLLECTIONS

550 Seventh Avenue, 15th Floor
New York, NY 10018
212 789 1500 Fax : 212 789 1825 800 231 0884

Labels *Donna Karan*
Products *Day into evening designer collection.*
Price Points *Designer*
Showrooms *New York*
Sell To *Specialty stores*
Corp. Office *Above*
Web Site *www.donnakaran.com*

ELE.PAVONI NEW YORK LTD *(Rep.)

159 West 53rd Street, Suite 29D
New York, NY 10019 elepavoni@mac.com
212 397 0108 Fax : 212 397 0366

Labels *Mela Rosa, Tricot Chic, Eugenio Vazzano*
Products *Women's dresses, ensambles, coats & coordinated chic sportswear.*
Price Points *Bridge to designer*
Production *Italy*
Showrooms *New York*
Sell To *Specialty stores & boutiques.*
Private Label *Yes*
Web Site *www.elepavoni.com*
Rev. in mil. *0-2*
Contact *Sales: Eleonora Pavoni*

ELIE TAHARI LTD.

11 W 42nd Street, 14th Floor
New York, NY 10036 questions@elietahari.com
212 763 2000 Fax : 212 763 2299 800 649 6179

Labels *Elie Tahari*

Products *Well-rounded sportswear, dress, day and evening collections. Missy and petite sizes.*
Price Points *Better to bridge.*
Production *Hong Kong and China*
Sell To *Department stores, specialty stores, boutiques and off-price.*
Web Site *www.elietahari.com*
Contact *President: Elie Tahari*

ESCADA USA

1412 Broadway, 10th Floor
New York, NY 10018 customerservice@escadausa.com
212 852 5300 Fax : 212 869 0109 800 869 8424

Labels *Escada USA*
Products *Full sportswear & separates collection*
Price Points *Bridge & designer.*
Production *Europe*
Showrooms *New York/above*
Sell To *Department stores & specialty stores.*
Private Label *No*
Web Site *www.escada.com*

HUGO BOSS U.S.A., INC.

55 Water Street, 8th Floor
New York, NY 10041 customerservice@hugoboss-store.com
212 940 0600 Fax : 212 940 0619 800-484-6267

Labels *Hugo Boss, Boss Hugo Boss, Boss Black, Boss Green, Boss Orange*
Products *Designer collection.*
Price Points *Better*
Production *U.S.A. & import*
Sell To *Department stores, specialty stores, mail order catalogues & mass merchants.*
Private Label *No*
Web Site *www.hugoboss.com*
Rev. in mil. *+500*

MELANIE HARRIS

488 Seventh Avenue, Suite 3C
New York, NY 10018 melanieharrisdesignspr@gmail.com
646 504 9608 1 800 223 0928

Labels *Melanie Harris*
Products *Social occasion cocktail dresses & suits, long gowns plus non-traditional bridal/reception dress*
Price Points *Bridge, designer & couture.*
Production *U.S.A.*
Showrooms *New York*
Sell To *Department stores, specialty stores & boutiques.*
Private Label *Yes*
Web Site *www.melanieharrisny.com*
Contact *Principal/Design: Melanie Harris*

MICHAEL KORS

11 W 42nd Street, 20th Floor
New York, NY 10036 inquiries@michaelkors.com
212 201 8100 Fax : 646 354 4872 800 908 1157

Labels *Michael Kor's, Michael by Michael Kors*
Products *Designer collection.*
Price Points *Bridge to designer.*
Production *U.S.A. & Italy*
Showrooms *New York/above*
Sell To *Department stores, speciality stores & boutiques.*
Web Site *www.michaelkors.com*
Contact *Chairman: Michael Kors*

NORMA KAMALI

11 West 56th Street
New York, NY 10019 sales@normakamalicollection.com
212 957 9797 Fax : 212 265 9154 800 8 Kamali

Labels *Norma Kamali*
Products *Designer clothing and accessory collection for day, evening, active, swim, beauty & wellness.*
Price Points *Designer, bridge to better*
Production *U.S.A. & import*
Showrooms *New York/above*
Sell To *Direct to clients through website & distributors*
Private Label *No*
Web Site *www.normakamalicollection.com*
RN Number *RN47494*

RALPH LAUREN, INC.

650 Madison Avenue
New York, NY 10022 customerassistance@ralphlauren.com
888 475 7674

Labels *Black Label, RRL, Blue Label, Lauren, RLX*
Products *Complete sportswear collection, plus dresses, shirts, polos, skirts, pants/shorts, sleepwear.*
Price Points *Better to designer.*
Production *U.S.A. & import worldwide*
Showrooms *New York/above*
Sell To *Department stores, specialty stores, catalogues, off price & company owned retail shops.*
Web Site *www.ralphlauren.com*
Rev. in mil. *+500*

RODEL U.S.A. INC.

30 Central Park South, Penthouse
New York, NY 10019 rodelusa@aol.com
212 997 9767 Fax : 212 997 9785 866 4CR COAT

Labels *Cinzia Rocca*
Products *European designer outerwear, dress & suit collection.*
Price Points *Better to designer*
Production *Italy*
Showrooms *New York*
Sell To *Department stores, specialty stores & boutiques.*
Private Label *No*

Web Site *www.cinziarocca.com*

ROSE TAFT

488 Seventh Avenue, Suite 3C
New York, NY 10018
212 279 8580 1 800 223 0928
mdm@rosetaft.com

Labels *Rose Taft Couture*
Products *Collection of day & evening dresses.*
Price Points *Bridge, designer & couture.*
Production *U.S.A.*
Showrooms *New York*
Sell To *Department stores, specialty stores & boutiques.*
Corp. Office *Miami, Florida*
Private Label *No*
Web Site *www.melanieharrisny.com*
Contact *Sales: Melanie Harris Silverman, Design: Melanie Harris Silverman*

SHOWROOM SEVEN/ERICKSON BEAMON *(Rep.)

263 Eleventh Avenue
New York, NY 10001
212 643 4810 Fax : 646 763 8940
jean-marc@showroomseven.com

Labels *Anamaria Couture, Patricia Bonaldi, Pier Antonio Gaspari, Cristina Ruales, EKAT, Malip*
Products *Contemporary sportswear, designer sportswear & eveningwear from Europe & Asia.*
Price Points *Contemporary, designer & couture*
Production *International*
Showrooms *New York, Los Angeles, Paris*
Sell To *Department stores, specialty stores & boutiques. International and domestic.*
Private Label *Yes*
Web Site *www.showroomseven.com*
Rev. in mil. *11-50*

ST. JOHN

17622 Armstrong Avenue
Irvine, CA 92614
949 863 1171 Fax : 949 437 8183 877 908 1171
info@sjk.com

Labels *St. John*
Products *Coordinated day into evening collection of dresses & separates*
Price Points *Better*
Showrooms *New York/665 5th Avenue, 2nd Floor, New York, New York, 10022 tel: 212 755 5252*
Sell To *Specialty stores*
Corp. Office *Above*
Private Label *No*
Web Site *www.sjk.com*
Contact *CEO: Glenn McMahon*

SUSAN ELIAS

5640 12th Avenue North
St. Petersburg, FL 33710
727 452 6637
eliascouture@gmail.com

Labels *Susan Elias*
Products *Women's couture/contemporary tops, dresses and pants. One of a kind wedding dresses.*

Price Points *Designer & couture*
Production *U.S.A.*
Private Label *No*
Web Site *www.eliascouture.com*
Contact *President/Designer: Susan Elias*

TERI JON

241 West 37th Street, 2nd Floor
New York, NY 10018 sales@terijon.com
212 398 0480 Fax : 212 302 2726

Labels *Rickie Freeman for Teri Jon, Teri Jon, Jon*
Products *Evening dress, suit collection & sportswear collection*
Price Points *Bridge to designer*
Production *U.S.A.*
Showrooms *New York/above, Dallas/214-637-6962*
Sell To *Department stores, boutiques & specialty stores.*
Private Label *Yes*
Web Site *www.terijon.com*
Contact *President: Rickie Freeman*

TOM AND LINDA PLATT

55 West 39th Street, 17th Floor
New York, NY 10018 info@tomandlindaplatt.com
212 764 1210 Fax : 212 719 1213

Labels *Tom and Linda Platt, Tom and Linda Platt Custom*
Products *Women's designer day, cocktail, evening dresses and separates.*
Price Points *Designer*
Production *U.S.A.*
Showrooms *New York*
Sell To *Department stores, specialty stores, and private clients.*
Private Label *Yes*
Web Site *www.tomandlindaplatt.com*
Contact *Owners/Designers: Tom and Linda Platt*

ABS BY ALLEN SCHWARTZ

1231 Long Beach Avenue
Los Angeles, CA 90021 kfoster@absstyle.com
213 895 4400 Fax : 213 895 4401

Labels *ABS by Allen Schwartz, ABS Collection, Allen B. by Allen Schwartz*
Products *Contemporary collection of day into evening dresses & separates.*
Price Points *Better to designer*
Production *U.S.A.*
Showrooms *New York/ tel # 212 398 0330, Los Angeles & Atlanta.*
Sell To *Department stores & specialty stores*
Corp. Office *Above*
Private Label *No*
Web Site *www.absstyle.com*
Contact *CFO: Kirk Foster, VP of Sales: Lloyd Singer*

ADVANCE APPARELS INC.

15 West 36th Street
New York, NY 10018 sales@advanceapparelsny.com
212 481 7246

Products *A wide collection of stylish and trendy dresses.Handpainted, tube, embroided and great prints*
Price Points *Moderate*
Sell To *Wholesale orders only. Department stores, outlets, bulk orders.*
Web Site *www.advanceapparelsny.com*

ALICE AND OLIVIA

450 West 14th Street
New York, NY 10014 info@aliceandolivia.com
646 747 1461 Fax : 212 840 0149

Labels *Alice and Olivia*
Products *Casual and formal dresses, separates and work attire.*
Sell To *Department stores, specialty stores & boutiques.*
Private Label *No*
Web Site *www.aliceandolivia.com*
Contact *Designer: Stacey Bendet*

ANN TAYLOR

4079 Executive Parkway
Westerville, OH 43081 clientservices@anntaylor.com
800 342 5266 Fax : 866 232 9266 800 342 5266

Labels *Ann Taylor*
Products *Multi-faceted career, casual & dressy collection.*
Price Points *Better*
Production *Import worldwide*
Sell To *Company owned retail stores only.*
Corp. Office *7 Times Square, New York, NY 10036*
Web Site *www.anntaylor.com*

ANNE NAMBA DESIGNS

324 Kamani Street
Honolulu, HI 96813 anne@annenamba.com
808 589 1135 Fax : 808 589 1792 877-578-0001

Labels *Anne Namba Designs*
Products *Kimonos & Asian inspired dresses & bridal gowns.*
Price Points *Designer*
Production *U.S.A.*
Showrooms *Salt & Pepper Sales/Los Angeles*
Sell To *Department stores, specialty stores, boutiques & mail order catalogues.*
Private Label *No*
Web Site *www.annenamba.com*
Rev. in mil. *2-10*
Contact *President & Designer: Anne Namba*

AZIBI LTD. *(Rep.)

270 West 39th Street, Suite 1501
New York, NY 10018 goodrep@gmail.com
212 869 6550 Fax : 212 764 4764

Labels *Luna Luz, Azibi*
Products *Updated missy dresses and separates. Lots of garment-dyed styles.*
Price Points *Better to bridge.*
Production *U.S.A. and Spain.*
Showrooms *New York, Denver, Florida, Texas, Atlanta and Los Angeles.*
Sell To *Department stores, specialty stores, boutiques and mail order catalogues.*
Private Label *Yes*
Web Site *www.lunaluz.net*
RN Number *RN96314*
Rev. in mil. *0-2*
Contact *Rep: Barbara Feldman - 917-331-7536*

BARAMI/FASHION CONCEPTS/PATRIZIA LUCA

519 8th Avenue, 5th Floor
New York, NY 10018 baman@barami.com
212 629 6464 Fax : 212 695 1417

Labels *Barami, Patrizia Luca, Fashion Concept*
Products *Contemporary suit collection.*
Price Points *Better*
Production *U.S.A. and China*
Showrooms *New York*
Sell To *Specialty stores, department stores, boutiques & catalogues.*
Private Label *Yes*
Web Site *www.barami.com*
RN Number *RN94992,RN87729*
Contact *Sales: Bahman Terani, Bahram Hakakian, Merchandising/Personl Relations: Neda Hakak*

BELASSE COLLECTION LLC

2115 Piedmont Road NE, Suite 102
Atlanta, GA 30324 info@belassecollection.com
404 892 5030

Labels *Belasse*

Products	*All occasion dresses are made of 100% silk and silk/cotton blends.*
Price Points	*Better*
Production	*U.S.A.*
Sell To	*Department stores, specialty stores, boutiques*
Web Site	*www.belassecollection.com*
RN Number	*2408904*
Contact	*Designer: Myriam Belasse*

BIANCA NERO

935 South Wall Street, 3rd Floor
Los Angeles, CA 90015 info@biancanero.com
213 236 9282 Fax : 213 236 9271

Labels	*Bianca Nero*
Products	*Contemporary & evening dresses.*
Price Points	*Better*
Sell To	*Department stores, specialty stores & boutiques.*
Corp. Office	*Above*
Web Site	*www.biancanero.com*
Contact	*Designer: Maria Wojciechowski, Sales: Michelle*

BLUESUITS

200 West 70th Street, Suite 14G
New York, NY 10023 jamak@off7th.com
212 787 0278

Labels	*Bluesuits*
Products	*Women's business suits & professional attire including business jackets, pants, skirts & dresses*
Price Points	*Designer*
Production	*U.S.A.*
Sell To	*Department stores & boutiques*
Private Label	*Yes*
Web Site	*www.bluesuitsonline.com*
Contact	*Designer: Jamak Khazra*

C.T.C. INC.

1821B Knickerbocker Road
San Angelo, TX 76904 turnercarol22@aol.com
325 947 2106 Fax : 325 944 7371

Labels	*C.T.C.*
Products	*Missy updated coordinating jackets & dresses*
Price Points	*Moderate to better.*
Production	*U.S.A.*
Showrooms	*Atlanta/Atlanta Mart*
Sell To	*Specialty stores & boutiques.*
Private Label	*No*
Contact	*Owner: Randy Turner, Design: Carol Turner*

CARTISE INTERNATIONAL

6161 Cypihot Street
Saint Laurent, Quebec, Canada H4S 1R3 customerservice@cartise.ca
514 383 3499 Fax : 514 383 5405 1 888 383 1984

Labels	*Cartise*

Products *Dresses, separates & special occasion.*
Price Points *Moderate to better*
Production *Domestic & Import*
Showrooms *Montreal, Toronto*
Sell To *Specialty stores and boutiques.*
Corp. Office *Above*
Web Site *www.cartise.ca*
Contact *President: Gadi Padan, Sales: Sharoni Padan, Design: Amy Wu*

DARIAN GROUP INC.

1410 Broadway, Suite 1600
New York, NY 10018 martin@dariangroupinc.com
212 944 6500

Labels *Chetta B*
Products *Day dresses, knit dresses, evening dresses (short and long), evening separates.*
Price Points *Better*
Production *U.S.A. and import.*
Sell To *Department stores, specialty stores, boutiques and mail order catalogues.*
Private Label *Yes*
Web Site *www.dariangroupinc.com*
RN Number *RN89700*
Contact *President and Owner: Martin Schlossberg*

DEPECHE MODE

230 West 38th Street, 12th Floor
New York, NY 10018 leer@depecheco.com
212 643 6633 Fax : 212 643 1184

Labels *Depeche Mode, Studio*
Products *Day, lunch & dinner dresses & suits. Contemporary, better & bridge dresses.*
Price Points *Better to bridge, plus off-price.*
Production *U.S.A. & import*
Showrooms *New York.*
Sell To *Department & specialty stores, boutiques, mass merchants, catalogues, chains & off-price.*
Private Label *Yes*
Web Site *www.depecheco.com*
RN Number *RN61812*
Contact *President: Lee Rosenthal, Sales: Joy Villa (joyv@depecheco.com)*

DREW PHILIPS CORP.

231 West 39th Street, Suite 410
New York, NY 10018 gigi@drewphilipscorp.com
212 354 0095 Fax : 212 354 0080

Labels *Drew*
Products *Contemporary sportswear, knits, dresses, pants & skirts.*
Price Points *Better*
Production *U.S.A.*
Showrooms *New York*
Sell To *Specialty stores, boutiques & catalogues.*
Private Label *Yes*
Web Site *www.drewclothing.com*
Contact *Design: Drew Philips, Sales: Gary Rosenblum*

EVANESE, INC.

1444 West 178th Street
Gardena, CA 90248
310 532 7004 Fax : 310 532 7070
info@evanese.net

Labels *Evanese, Inc.*
Products *Special occasion & contemporary dresses & separates in missy and plus sizes.*
Price Points *Moderate to better*
Production *U.S.A.*
Sell To *Department stores, specialty stores, boutiques & mail order catalogues.*
Private Label *Yes*
Web Site *www.evanese.net*
Rev. in mil. *0-2*
Contact *Director: Grace Cordeiro, Sales: Justin Kwon, Production: Miya Kim*

H.M.S. PRODUCTIONS

250 West 39th Street, 18th Floor
New York, NY 10018
212 719 9190 Fax : 212 730 7581
nubby@nubby.com

Labels *SPENSE*
Products *Daytime dresses & updated separates.*
Price Points *Better*
Production *U.S.A. & import.*
Showrooms *New York.*
Sell To *Department stores, specialty stores & catalogues*
Private Label *Yes*
Web Site *www.cableandgauge.com*
RN Number *RN98108*
Contact *President and Owner: Spenser Alpern,*
Production: Spenser Alpern, Design: Michelle Antonelli

J.D. FINE *(Rep.)

179 Mason Circle
Concord, CA 94520
925 521 3300 Fax : 925 521 9090
jamief@jdfine.com

Labels *Tart Collections*
Products *Evening and day dresses*
Price Points *Better*
Production *Import & some local production*
Showrooms *New York/Cricket Showroom 901 412 5466, Chicago Agents 312 396 0100,*
Atlanta/ Tryst Showroom 404 749 5115.
Sell To *Department stores, specialty stores, boutiques*
Private Label *Yes*
Web Site *www.tartcollections.com*
RN Number *97884*
Rev. in mil. *11-50*
Contact *President: Jamie Finegold, National Sales Manager: Jennifer Kreider (jenniferk@jdfine.com*

MARC BOUWER

141 Fulton Street, 2nd Floor
New York, NY 10038 info@marcbouwer.com
212 242 7510 Fax : 212 242 2687

Labels *Marc Bouwer*
Products *Couture day into eveing dresses.*
Price Points *Couture*
Production *U.S.A.*
Showrooms *New York*
Sell To *Department stores & specialty stores.*
Private Label *No*
Web Site *www.marcbouwer.com*
Contact *President and Design: Marc Bouwer*

MISOOK

1680 E Touhy Avenue
Des Plaines, IL 60018 customerservice@misook.com
800 447 3556

Labels *Misook*
Products *Elegant separates for the working woman - dresses, pants, skirts, tops.*
Price Points *Better*
Corp. Office *Division of Wdiamondgroup (www.wdiamondgroup.com)*
Web Site *www.misook.com*

ODETT ENTERPRISES

109 West 37th Street, Street Level
New York, NY 10018 info@odettfashion.com
212 921 9690 Fax : 212 768 4760

Labels *Odett*
Products *Day & evening suits.*
Price Points *Budget to bridge.*
Production *U.S.A. & Italy*
Showrooms *New York*
Sell To *Specialty stores, boutiques.*
Private Label *Yes*
Web Site *www.odettfashion.com*
Contact *President: Amir Darouvar, Sales: Farah Darouvar*

ONLY HEARTS

134 West 37th Street, 9th Floor
New York, NY 10018 customerservice@onlyhearts.com
212 268 0886 Fax : 212 268 0922

Labels *Only Hearts*
Products *Flirty and fashioned dresses.*
Price Points *Better to bridge.*
Production *U.S.A.*
Showrooms *New York*
Sell To *Speciallty stores, department stores & mail order catalogues.*
Private Label *Yes*
Web Site *www.onlyhearts.com*
Rev. in mil. *2-10*

Contact *Design: Helena Stuart*

PHOOL FASHIONS

241 West 37th Street, Suite 518
New York, NY 10018 phoolfash@aol.com
212 944 0910 Fax : 212 944 0286

Labels *Phool*
Products *Missy, junior & women's updated contemporary sportswear.*
Price Points *Moderate*
Production *Import*
Showrooms *New York*
Sell To *Specialty stores, boutiques, mail order catalogues & chain stores.*
Private Label *Yes*
Web Site *www.phoolfashionusa.com*
RN Number *RN80911*
Rev. in mil. *2-10*
Contact *Owner/Sales: Reena Paintal*

REBECCA TAYLOR

307 West 36th Street, 16th Floor
New York, NY 10018 sales@rebeccataylor.com
212 704 0607

Labels *Rebecca Taylor*
Products *Perfect prints, delicate knits, flirty dresses, tailored suits for the modern, contemporary women*
Price Points *Better*
Showrooms *Los Angeles, Canada, UK, Italy, France.*
Web Site *www.rebeccataylor.com*

REDWOOD COURT BY SILK BOX

PO Box 3019
Princeton Jct, NJ 08543 info@lotusa.com
609 275 4403 Fax : 609 897 1118

Labels *Silk Box*
Products *Dresses, separates, slacks & tops. Specialize in silk novelty fabrications.*
Price Points *Better*
Production *Import*
Showrooms *None*
Sell To *Department stores & boutiques.*
Private Label *Yes*
Web Site *www.redwoodcourt.com*
Rev. in mil. *0-2*
Contact *Sales: Shirley Fang 609-275-0350 (shirleymfang@gmail.com)*

ROBBIE BEE

1412 Broadway, 8th Floor
New York, NY 10018 rlong@robbiebee.com
212 944 0255 Fax : 212 719 0009

Labels *Robbie Bee*
Products *Casual & dressy dresses.*
Price Points *Moderate.*
Production *U.S.A., Hong Kong, China.*

Showrooms *New York*
Sell To *Department stores, specialty stores, mail order catalogues & off-price.*
Private Label *Yes*
RN Number *RN98582*
Contact *Owner: Maia Chiat*

SENTIMENTAL INC.

214 West 39th Street, Suite 504A
New York, NY 10018 sam@sentimentalny.com
212 221 0282 Fax : 212 302 2959

Labels *ON TREND*
Products *A complete collection of chic dresses, skirts, pants, tops & clubwear.*
Price Points *Budget to moderate*
Production *U.S.A.*
Showrooms *New York*
Sell To *Specialty stores, chain stores*
Private Label *Yes*
Web Site *www.sentimentalny.com*
RN Number *124825*
Rev. in mil. *0-2*
Contact *Owner: Sam Hourani*

SUSAN ELIAS

5640 12th Avenue North
St. Petersburg, FL 33710 eliascouture@gmail.com
727 452 6637

Labels *Susan Elias*
Products *Women's couture/contemporary tops, dresses and pants.*
Price Points *Better to designer*
Production *U.S.A.*
Private Label *No*
Web Site *www.eliascouture.com*
Contact *President/Designer: Susan Elias*

SWIFT ORIGINALS

1 W Flatiron Crossing, Ste 2156
Broomfield, CO 80021 swiftoriginals@gmail.com
303 442 9013 Fax : 303 499 6045 866-704-4024

Labels *Swift Originals*
Products *Daytime & fancy dresses, skirts, sarongs & jackets made with crinkle rayons & nice motifs.*
Price Points *Moderate*
Production *Import*
Sell To *Specialty stores & boutiques.*
Private Label *Yes*
Web Site *www.facebook.com/swiftoriginals*
Contact *President: Andy McPherson*

TOM AND LINDA PLATT

55 West 39th Street, 17th Floor
New York, NY 10018 info@tomandlindaplatt.com
212 764 1210 Fax : 212 719 1213

Labels *Tom and Linda Platt, Tom and Linda Platt Custom*
Products *Day, cocktail, evening dresses and separates. Custom and made-to-measure clothing.*
Price Points *Designer*
Production *U.S.A.*
Showrooms *New York*
Sell To *Department stores, specialty stores, and private clients.*
Private Label *Yes*
Web Site *www.tomandlindaplatt.com*
Contact *Owners/Designers: Tom and Linda Platt*

VENUS FASHION

11711 Marco Beach Drive
Jacksonville, FL 32224 email@venus.com
904 997 4000 Fax : 904 641 0977 888 782 2224

Labels *Venus Fashion*
Products *Women's & junior dresses.*
Price Points *Moderate to better.*
Production *U.S.A.*
Showrooms *Jacksonville, FL/above.*
Sell To *Specialty stores & boutiques.*
Private Label *No*
Web Site *www.venus.com*
Contact *President and CEO: Jim Brewster*

VIVIANA UCHITEL *(Rep.)

12115 San Vicente Boulevard, Suite 410
Los Angeles , CA 90049 pamcarone@gmail.com
310 472 4955 Fax : 310 472 6054

Labels *Viviana Uchitel*
Products *Dresses & knitwear.*
Price Points *Moderate to better*
Production *Import.*
Showrooms *Los Angeles*
Sell To *Specialty stores & boutiques.*
Web Site *vivianauchitel.com*
Rev. in mil. *0-2*
Contact *Sales: Pamela Carone (cell: 310-994-8483), Design: Vivianna Uchitel*

ZELDA

260 West 39th Street, 5th Floor
New York, NY 10018 info@zelda-intl.com
212 764 0020 Fax : 212 764 2588

Labels *Zelda*
Products *Classic signature suiting line.*
Price Points *Bridge.*
Production *Imported & U.S.A.*
Showrooms *New York, Dallas & Los Angeles, with reps in Atlanta*

Sell To	*Specialty & department stores & boutiques.*
Private Label	*Yes*
Web Site	*www.zeldacollection.com*
Rev. in mil.	*11-50*
Contact	*Sales: Lisa Attea*

ACTIVE EDGE, THE/OLD CITY T-SHIRTS

233 Church Street
Philadelphia, PA 19106 actvej@aol.com
215 925 7860 Fax : 215 925 1597 800 343 1497

Labels *Active Edge*
Products *Organic ladies ring-spun cotton tees.*
Price Points *Moderate*
Production *U.S.A.*
Showrooms *Philadelphia.*
Sell To *Specialty stores & boutiques.*
Private Label *Yes*
Web Site *www.theactiveedge.com*
Contact *President: Evan Sharps*

BARRAZA ASSOCIATES LTD

225 West 35th Street, Suite 1502
New York, NY 10001 barrazany@aol.com
212 564 6583

Labels *Paz*
Products *Yoga & spa wear. Unique fabrications and styles in various organic cottons.*
Price Points *Moderate to better.*
Production *U.S.A. & import.*
Sell To *Department stores, specialty stores, boutiques, mail order catalogues.*
Private Label *Yes*
Web Site *www.barrazastyle.com*
Rev. in mil. *2-10*
Contact *President: Maria Barraza, Sales & Marketing: Rafael Romero*

DOLORES PISCOTTA

8865 Sixteenth Avenue
Brooklyn, NY 11214 piscotta@msn.com
718 232 1167 Fax : 718 232 1167

Labels *Piscotta New York, Dolores Piscotta*
Products *Cashmere sweaters & apparel made from organic fibers such as soybeans & organic milk fibe.*
Price Points *Better to designer*
Production *U.S.A., Italy, China, Nepal*
Showrooms *Brooklyn, New York - By appointment only.*
Additional website: dolorespiscottawholesale.com
Sell To *Department stores, specialty stores, boutiques & catalogues.*
Private Label *Yes*
Web Site *www.dolorespiscotta.com*
RN Number *RN97327*
Contact *Owner and Designer: Dolores Piscotta*

GAIAM

833 W South Boulder Road, PO Box 3095
Boulder, CO 80307 customerservice@gaiam.com
303 222 3600 Fax : 303 222 3700 877 989 6321

Labels *Gaiam*
Products *Enviromentally responsible contemporary clothing & sleepwear in natural & organic knits.*
Price Points *Moderate to better.*

Production *U.S.A.*
Sell To *Specialty stores, boutiques & mail order catalogues.*
Web Site *www.gaiam.com*
Contact *President: Lynn Powers*

GOODWEAR USA

239 Western Avenue, Room 2D
Essex, MA 01929 steve@goodwear.com
978 768 7746 Fax : 800 787 4951 800 338 8895

Labels *Goodwear*
Products *Women's upscale dyeable tee-shirts done in sustainable fabrics: organic cotton & bamboo.*
Price Points *Bridge*
Production *U.S.A.*
Showrooms *Tokyo, Osaka, NYC & Essex*
Sell To *Distributors*
Private Label *Yes*
Web Site *www.goodwear.com*
RN Number *75346*
Contact *President: Martha Liquori, Owner: Stephen & Martha Liquori, Sales: Stephen Liquori*

GREEN DRAGON

10700 Valley View
Cypress, CA 90630 info@greendragonstyle.com
714 892 7354

Labels *Pink Lotus, Green Dragon*
Products *Stylish pants, dresses, skirts and tees in organic, sustainable, and/or recycled fabrics.*
Price Points *Better*
Production *U.S.A.*
Sell To *Department Stores, specialty stores, boutiques.*
Web Site *www.greendragonstyle.com*
Contact *President: Michael Keefer*

HYPERCLASH

926 Baca Street #1
Santa Fe, NM 87505 wholesale@hyperclash.com
505 820 0520

Labels *Hyperclash*
Products *Current styles made from reclaimed, organic, sustainable or fair trade earth friendly materi*
Price Points *Moderate*
Production *U.S.A.*
Web Site *www.hyperclash.com*
Contact *Owner: Paloma Navarrete*

INDIGENOUS

6780 Depot Street, Suite 210
Sebastopol, CA 95472 matt@indigenous.com
707 861 9719 Fax : 707 861 9214

Labels *Indigenous*
Products *Contemporary hand made fashion made with organic fibers by artisans worldwide.*
Price Points *Better*
Sell To *Specialty stores*

Private Label *Yes*
Web Site *www.indigenous.com*
Contact *Wholesale Inquiries: Matt Reynolds*

MEHERA SHAW TEXTILES PVT. LTD.

3307 Trice Atwater Road
Chapel Hill, NC 27516 info@meherashaw.com
919 969 2572 Fax : 919 969 6909

Labels *Mehera Shaw, Sweet Blossom, Lolakimoni*
Products *Contemporary artisan design in natural fibers only. Dresses, tops, jackets, trousers & skirts.*
Price Points *Better*
Production *India*
Sell To *Specialty stores, boutiques*
Private Label *Yes*
Web Site *www.meherashaw.com*
Contact *Designer: Shari Keller*

ROYAL APPAREL, INC.

65 Commerce Drive
Hauppauge, NY 11788 sales@royalapparel.net
631 213 8299 Fax : 631 922 8438 866-Royal-1-S

Labels *Royal Apparel*
Products *100% organic apparel for ladies available in various colors and styles.*
Price Points *Moderate to better.*
Production *U.S.A.*
Showrooms *New York & Allentown, Pa.*
Sell To *Mass merchants, branded labels, screen printers & department stores.*
Private Label *Yes*
Web Site *www.royalapparel.net*
Contact *President: Morey Mayeri, Owners: Morey Mayeri/Abraham Mayeri*

STYLE SOURCE INC.

913 Orange Street
Wilmington, NC 28401 geoff@style-source.com
910 399 2288 Fax : 910 399 2289

Labels *Henry Lehr, Mainland Co., Crazy Shirts Hawaii, Motherwear, Garnet Hill*
Products *Product development & private label specialists of organic & bamboo fabrics in ladies tops &*
Price Points *Moderate to better.*
Production *U.S.A.*
Sell To *Specialty stores, boutiques, mail order catalogues, screenprinters and embroiderers.*
Private Label *Yes*
Web Site *www.style-source.com*
RN Number *RN82034*
Contact *President: Geoffrey Krasnov*

Notes

ADEA

197 Prospect Street
Shrewsbury, MA 01545 info@myadea.com
866 798 2332 Fax : 508 845 1449

Labels *Adea*
Products *Underwear, camisoles, slips & bodysuits.*
Price Points *Moderate*
Sell To *Boutiques*
Web Site *www.myadea.com*
Contact *Designer: Jacqueline Durkee*

ARABESQUE DESIGN/PATRICIA FIELDWALKER

1682 West 75th Avenue
Vancouver, BC, Canada V6P 6G2 inquiries@arabesquedesign.com
604 689 1210 Fax : 604 689 1277

Labels *Patricia Fieldwalker, Adagio, Bergdorf Goodman Collection exclusively by Patricia Fieldwa*
Products *Daywear, sleepwear, resort pure silks, cottons & velvets with exclusive French laces.*
Price Points *Designer*
Production *Company owned factory in Vancouver Canada*
Showrooms *Vancouver & New York*
Sell To *Department stores, boutiques, lingerie web stores*
Private Label *Will consider for luxury items*
Web Site *www.pfieldwalker.com*
Contact *Designer/General Manager: Patricia Fieldwalker*

CALVIN KLEIN, INC.

205 West 39th Street, 12th Floor
New York, NY 10018 calvinkleincustomerservice@pvh.com
212 719 2600 Fax : 212 292 9131 866-513-0513

Labels *CK One*
Products *Women's underwear & nightwear.*
Price Points *Moderate to better*
Showrooms *New York*
Sell To *Department stores & specialty stores.*
Web Site *www.calvinklein.com*
RN Number *RN54718*

CARRIEAMBER INTIMATES

9401 Whitmore Street
El Monte, CA 91731 sales@carrieamber.com
626 371 1980 Fax : 626 288 2670 800 870 8680

Labels *Seven 'til Midnight, Spreegirl, Flex, Rockalicious, Carrie Amber,*
Products *Manufacturer of intimate apparel. Innovative colors, styles, prints and fabrics.*
Sell To *Department stores, specialty stores*
Private Label *Yes*
Web Site *www.carrieamber.com*

CHANTELLE LINGERIE INC.

183 Madison Avenue, Suite 707
New York, NY 10016 lgeerhart@chantelle.com
212 689 4735 Fax : 212 689 4953

Labels *Chantelle, Passionata*
Products *Exquisite French bras, pants & control garments in European fabrics & laces.*
Price Points *Designer*
Production *France*
Showrooms *New York.*
Sell To *Department & specialty stores, only the finest boutiques & mail order catalogues.*
Private Label *No*
Web Site *www.chantelle.com*
Contact *President: Sonja Winther*

CHARLEY MORGAN, INC.

2664 Stingle Avenue
Rosmead, CA 91770 info@charleymorganusa.com
213 747 7048 Fax : 626 607 0102

Labels *Made with Love, Coco , Intimate Moments, Bijou*
Products *Bras, Panties, Thongs, Shapewear, Tights*
Sell To *Department stores, specialty stores*
Private Label *Yes*
Web Site *www.charleymorganusa.com*

CHRISTINE VANCOUVER

821 Powell Street
Vancouver, B. C., Canada V6A 1H7 kim@christinevancouver.com
604 253 0350 Fax : 604 253 0351 888 922 0355

Labels *Christine Vancouver*
Products *Lingerie, loungewear & daywear in luxurious silk, cotton, lace & linen.*
Price Points *Designer*
Production *Canada*
Showrooms *Dallas/Rita Harris, Tel: 214 905 2006, Toronto/Dee Dee Crosland 416-849-7943*
Sell To *Department stores, specialty stores, boutiques & mail order catlogues.*
Private Label *Yes*
Web Site *www.christinevancouver.com*
Rev. in mil. *2-10*
Contact *President: Christine Morton, Sales: Erin Williams, Design: Christine Morton*

COLLECTION ARIANNE

1655 De Louvain West
Montreal, Quebec, CA H4N1G6 webmaster@ariannelingerie.com
514 385 9393 Fax : 514 385 9281 888 239 8165

Labels *Arianne*
Products *Lingerie & loungewear.*
Price Points *Better to high end*
Production *Canada*
Showrooms *Montreal*
Sell To *Department & specialty stores, boutiques, mail order catalogues.*
Private Label *No*
Web Site *www.ariannelingerie.com*

Contact *President & Owner: Norman Rossy, Design: Anne Pigeon*

COMME CI COMME CA LTD.

400 Oser Avenue, Suite 900
Hauppauge, NY 11788 liz@malepower.com
631 300 1035 Fax : 631 300 1039 1 800 447 4720

Labels *Lust*
Products *Sexy lingerie for women. Also in plus sizes.*
Price Points *Moderate*
Production *U.S.A.*
Sell To *Retail stores, lingerie stores & mail order catalogues.*
Private Label *Yes*
Web Site *www.magicsilk.com*
Contact *President: Jeff Baker, Sales: Elizabeth*

COOBIE INTIMATES

10309 Norwalk Boulevard
Santa Fe Springs, CA 90670 coobieintimates1@gmail.com
562 906 5200 Fax : 562 906 2500

Labels *Coobie*
Products *Women's bras and underwear.*
Price Points *Moderate*
Production *Import from China*
Sell To *Wholesale only*
Private Label *Yes*
Web Site *www.coobieintimates.com*

COSABELLA

12186 SW 128th Street
Miami, FL 33186 miami@cosabella.com
305 253 9904 Fax : 305 253 1286 800 451 5393

Labels *Cosabella*
Products *Lingerie, easywear & bodywear in novelty & luxurious fabrics.*
Price Points *Designer*
Production *Italy*
Showrooms *Los Angeles, New York & Miami. New Jersey rep: Steven Tamarof 973-495-6398.*
Sell To *Department stores, specialty stores & boutiques.*
Private Label *No*
Web Site *www.cosabella.com*
RN Number *RN77351*
Contact *President: Valeria Campello, Design: Ugo Campello*

DAYLEEN INTIMATES INC.

540 Nepperhan Avenue
Yonkers, NY 10701 mchernoff@dayleen.com
914 840 2729 Fax : 914 969 5922

Labels *Dominique*
Products *Ladies foundation garments*
Sell To *Department stores, boutiques, specialty stores, on-line*
Web Site *www.dominiqueapparel.com*
Contact *President: Michael Chernoff*

EVEDEN INC.

65 Sprague Street, Hyde Park
Boston, MA 02136 usaorders@wacoaleurope.com
617 361 7559 Fax : 617 361 7527 800 467 1269

Labels *Fantasie of England, Freya, Fauve, Goddess, Elomi*
Products *Designer, everyday & special occasion foundations for the full busted woman.*
Price Points *Better to designer.*
Production *Import*
Sell To *Specialty stores & boutiques.*
Private Label *No*
Web Site *www.eveden.com*
Rev. in mil. *2-10*

FLEUR'T, INC./MONTELLE

9250 Park Avenue, Suite 423
Montreal, Quebec, Canada H2N1Z2 info@fleurtintimates.com
866 278 3739 866 278 3739

Labels *Fleurt*
Products *Feminine lingerie that fits and feels good.*
Price Points *Contempory, bridge*
Production *U.S.A.*
Showrooms *East Coast: 212-727-5535, lesliewackerman@aol.com*
West Coast: 301-509-9099 sarah@sfshowroom.com.
Sell To *Specialty stores, boutiques*
Web Site *www.fleurtintimates.com*

FLORA NIKROOZ/DIVISION OF AGE GROUP

2 Park Avenue, 18th Floor
New York, NY 10016 info@agegroupltd.com
212 213 9500 Fax : 212 481 0455 800 899 4391

Labels *Flora Nikrooz Collection, Flora Nikrooz Gold Label*
Products *Lace & embroidered peignoirs, chiffons, sleepwear, camisoles & tops.*
Price Points *Better to designer*
Production *U.S.A.*
Sell To *Department stores, specialty stores, boutiques, catalogues, off-price.*
Corp. Office *Above*
Private Label *Yes*
Web Site *www.flora-nikrooz.com*
Contact *President: Flora Nikrooz Backer, Sales: Deborah (deborah@agegroupltd.com)*

FORT KNOX LINGERIE

2589 Hope Lane West
Palm Beach Gardens, FL 33410 fortknoxlingerie@comcast.net
561 625 9594 Fax : 561 626 7365

Labels *Cotton Club, Selmark*
Products *Importers of Italian & Spanish designer lingerie. Bras, panties, bodysuits & g-belts.*
Price Points *Desigher to couture.*
Production *Italy, Spain*
Sell To *Department stores, specialty stores & boutiques.*
Private Label *No*

Web Site *www.cottonclub.it, www.selmark.es*
Rev. in mil. *0-2*
Contact *President: Michele Krchov, Marketing: Terry Krchov*

GELMART INDUSTRIES INC.

48 West 38th Street
New York, NY 10016 ezran@gelmart.com
212 743 6900 Fax : 212 725 7248 800 746 0014

Labels *Jenna Leigh, Lady M, Bodynaturals*
Products *Intimate apparel & shapewear.*
Price Points *All price points.*
Production *Philippines Islands*
Sell To *Department stores, specialty stores*
Private Label *Yes*
Web Site *www.gelmart.com*

JOCKEY INTERNATIONAL, INC.

2300 60th Street
Kenosha, WI 53140 andy.vacca@jockey.com
262 658 8111 Fax : 262 658 1812 800 Jockey1

Labels *Jockey Classic, Elance®, Jockey Silks®, Jockey Sport, Naturals, Comfies®*
Products *Underwear, bras & tops, hosiery, thermals & sleepwear.*
Price Points *Moderate to better*
Production *U.S.A. & import worldwide.*
Showrooms *New York/1411 Broadway Suite 1010 (tel:212 840-4900)*
Sell To *Department stores, specialty stores, catalogues, off-price retailers & mass merchants.*
Private Label *Yes*
Web Site *www.jockey.com*
RN Number *RN61683*
Contact *President: Edward Emma*

NATORI CO.

180 Madison Avenue, 18th Floor
New York, NY 10016 custserv@natori.com
212 532 7796 Fax : 212 481 7282

Labels *Natori, Josie*
Products *Full range of intimate apparel, lingerie, sleepwear, loungewear & daywear.*
Price Points *Moderate to designer*
Production *Philippines, Turkey, China, Korea & VIetnam*
Showrooms *New York & Dallas*
Sell To *Specialty stores*
Web Site *www.natori.com*
Contact *CEO: Josie Natori*

ONLY HEARTS

134 West 37th Street, 9th Floor
New York, NY 10018 customerservice@onlyhearts.com
212 268 0886 Fax : 212 268 0922

Labels *Only Hearts*
Products *Lingerie.*
Price Points *Better to bridge.*

Production *U.S.A.*
Showrooms *New York*
Sell To *Speciallty stores, department stores & mail order catalogues.*
Private Label *Yes*
Web Site *www.onlyhearts.com*
Rev. in mil. *2-10*
Contact *Design: Helena Stuart*

PARISA

19401 Business Center Drive
Northridge, CA 91324 sales@parisausa.com
818773 5000 Fax : 818 773 5100 800 800 0555

Labels *Parisa*
Products *Fine lingerie*
Price Points *Better*
Production *U.S.A. and import.*
Sell To *Department and specialty stores.*
Private Label *Yes*
Web Site *www.parisausa.com*
RN Number *RN84980*
Contact *President: Amir Moghadam, Jaymi Washburn: Product Development and Merchandising.*

RAGO FOUNDATIONS LLC

18-15 27th Avenue
Long Island City, NY 11102 justin@ragoshapewear.com
718 728 8436 Fax : 718 728 8465 800 982 1113

Labels *Rago, Shapette, Lacette, Special Attention*
Products *Shapewear garments for todays woman in regular & special sizes*
Price Points *Moderate, better*
Production *U.S.A.*
Showrooms *New York/183 Madison Ave., New York, N.Y. 10001 plus reps in LA, Dallas, Atlanta, France, Germany & Japan.*
Sell To *Department stores, specialty stores, boutiques, mail order catalogues*
Private Label *Yes*
Web Site *www.ragoshapewear.com*
Rev. in mil. *11-50*
Contact *President: Justin Chernoff, Marketing: Steve Chernoff*

STANFIELD'S

1 Logan Street, PO Box 190
Truro, Nova Scotia, Canada B2N 5C2 inquiries@stanfields.com
902 895 5406 Fax : 902 893 8187 855-895-5406

Products *Cotton/lycra intimate apparel, underwear & form fitting bodywear.*
Price Points *Moderate*
Production *Canada*
Showrooms *Sales Office: 40 University Avenue, Toronto, Ontario Canada M5J 1T1 (416) 598-8086.*
Sell To *Department stores, specialty stores, boutiques & mail order catalogues.*
Private Label *No*
Web Site *www.stanfields.com*

THEA HAUTE COUTURE

38 Verandah Place
Brooklyn, NY 11201
718 237 8555 Fax : 718 237 8555
sales@theahautecouture.com

Labels *Thea*
Products *Fine, beautifully crafted, white cotton sleepwear.*
Price Points *Better*
Production *Philippines*
Sell To *Lingerie stores, department stores, specialty stores, boutiques & mail order catalogues.*
Private Label *Yes*
Web Site *www.theahautecouture.com*
Rev. in mil. *101-500*
Contact *Sales: Derma Gerety, Designer: Marie de la Soudiere*

Notes

7 FOR ALL MANKIND

25 West 39th Street, 13th Floor
New York, NY 10018
646 839 5400 Fax : 646 839 5435 866 427 1114
customerservice@shop.7forallmankind.com

Labels *7 for all mankind*
Products *Women's jeans & denimwear.*
Price Points *Better to Bridge*
Showrooms *Above, Los Angeles/CA, Dallas/TX*
Sell To *Department stores, boutiques & specialty stores.*
Corp. Office *4440 East 26th Street, Vernon, Ca 90023 tel: 323-406-5300*
Private Label *No*
Web Site *www.7forallmankind.com*

ADRIANO GOLDSCHMIED

860 South Los Angeles Street, Suite 316
Los Angeles, CA 90014
213 689 4867 Fax : 213 683 0035
david@namasteshowroom.com

Labels *AG Jeans*
Products *Contemporary detailed jeans.*
Price Points *Better*
Production *U.S.A.*
Showrooms *New York/646-279-8690, Dallas/214-634-3304*
Sell To *Department stores, specialty stores*
Corp. Office *2741 Seminole Avenue, South Gate, CA 90280, tel#: 323-357-1111*
Web Site *www.agjeans.com*
Contact *West Coast Sales: David Coury*

BERMO ENTERPRISES INC.

12033 U.S. Highway, PO Box 426
Schoolcraft, MI 49087
269 679 2580 Fax : 269 679 2611
info@bermoenterprises.com

Products *Lots of styles & finishes of denimwear in missy and junior sizes.*
Showrooms *350 W 34th St, Suite B2501, New York, NY 10001 Ph: 212 239 7483*
Sell To *Off-price clothing wholesaler*
Web Site *www.bermoenterprises.com*

BOULEVARD APPAREL

2707 South Alameda Street
Los Angeles, CA 90058
213 614 1800 Fax : 213 614 1815 866-967-5919
sales@blvapparel.com

Products *Denim, jeans, skirts & shorts*
Price Points *Budget to designer*
Production *U.S.A & import*
Sell To *Department stores, specialty stores, boutiques, mass merchants, mail order catalogues.*
Private Label *Yes*
Web Site *www.blvapparel.com*
RN Number *111159*
Rev. in mil. *2-10*
Contact *President & Owner: Eugene Kaplan*

BRAZILROXX INC.

1104 Manor Way
Roanoke, TX 76262 eliana@brazilroxx.com
817 886 6710 Fax : 817 431 4934 1 877 285 7735

Labels *BrazilRoxx Jeans*
Products *Jeans & denimwear.*
Sell To *Specialty stores & boutiques.*
Corp. Office *Above*
Web Site *www.brazilroxx.com*
Contact *President: Eliana Solera*

CALVIN KLEIN, INC.

205 West 39th Street, 12th Floor
New York, NY 10018 calvinkleincustomerservice@pvh.com
212 719 2600 Fax : 212 292 9131 866-513-0513

Labels *CK One*
Products *Jean collection.*
Price Points *Moderate to better*
Showrooms *New York*
Sell To *Department stores & specialty stores.*
Web Site *www.calvinklein.com*
RN Number *RN54718*

DIESEL PLANET

220 West 19th Street
New York, NY 10011 customerservice@shop.diesel.com
212 755 9200 Fax : 212 255 6641 877.344.8342

Labels *Diesel*
Products *Sportswear & outerwear.*
Price Points *Moderate to better*
Showrooms *New York & Los Angeles/Tel: 310 652 2322*
Sell To *Department stores, mass merchants & boutiques.*
Corp. Office *Above*
Web Site *www.diesel.com*
Contact *Owner: Renzo*

FRENCH CONNECTION

512 Seventh Avenue
New York, NY 10018 frenchconnection@frenchconnection-usa.com
212 221 3157 Fax : 212 302 6839 866-932-3285

Labels *French Connection*
Products *Contemporary sportswear & jean wear collection*
Price Points *Better*
Production *Global*
Showrooms *Atlanta, Chicago, Los Angeles & New York.*
Sell To *Department stores, specialty stores, boutiques, catalogues & off-price retailers.*
Corp. Office *184-10 Jamaica Avenue, Hollis, New York 11423*
Private Label *Yes*
Web Site *usa.frenchconnection.com*
RN Number *RN53372*
Contact *President: Andrea Hyde*

HENRY AND BELLE

549 West Randolph Street
Chicago, IL 60661 meganw@henryandbelle.com
312 242 2500 Fax : 312 648 4309 888-753-0538

Labels *Henry & Belle*
Products *Jeans of all types and styles.*
Price Points *Better*
Production *U.S.A., China*
Showrooms *New York/Cricket 901 412 5466, SouthEast/ 5 Seasons Showroom 404 549 7160, Midwest/Scout Showroom 773 697 7462, West/Collective Showroom 415 994 5393.*
Sell To *Department stores, specialty stores, boutiques & mail order catalogues.*
Private Label *No*
Web Site *www.henryandbelle.com*
Contact *President and Owner: Robert Mann*

JOU JOU DESIGNS

1407 Broadway, 5th Floor
New York, NY 10018 racampora@joujou.com
212 997 0230 Fax : 212 302 0308

Labels *Jou Jou*
Products *Specialize in jackets and denim.*
Price Points *Moderate*
Sell To *Department stores*
Corp. Office *Division of BBC Apparel, Inc.*
Private Label *Yes*
Web Site *www.joujou.com*
Contact *Sales: Bob Acampora*

LEVI STRAUSS & CO.

1155 Battery Street
San Francisco, CA 94111 questions@levistrauss.com
415 501 6000 Fax : 415 501 3939

Labels *Levi's®, Dockers®, Signature by Levi Strauss & Co.™, Denizen*
Products *Casual sportswear, jeans & westernwear.*
Price Points *Moderate*
Showrooms *New York/1411 Broadway, 11th Floor, New York 10018, Tel: 212-704-3200 Atlanta, Dallas & Chicago*
Sell To *Department stores*
Web Site *www.levistrauss.com*
RN Number *RN36665, WPL00423*
Contact *CEO: Chip Bergh*

PARASUCO JEANS INC.

128 Deslauriers Street
St. Laurent, QC, Canada H4N 1V8 customerservice@parasuco.com
514 334 0888 Fax : 514 334 9833 877 PARASUCO

Labels *Parasuco Denim Legend*
Products *Denimwear, sportswear & jeans.*
Price Points *Better*
Production *Canada*

Sell To *Department stores, specialty stores, boutiques & mail order catalogues.*
Corp. Office *Above*
Private Label *Yes*
Web Site *www.parasuco.com*

PIMLICO PERFORMANCE APPAREL LTD.

118 West Hastings Street
Vancouver, BC, Canada V6B 1G8 adriana@pimlicoperformance.com
604 323 0441 Fax : 604 323 0449

Labels *Dish*
Products *Contemporary jeans and denimwear with performance attributes.*
Price Points *Moderate to better*
Sell To *Specialty stores & boutiques.*
Private Label *Yes*
Web Site *www.dishandduer.com*

ROCKSTAR

5901 S. Eastern Avenue
Commerce, CA 90040 customerservice@rockstaroriginal.com
323 278 3874 Fax : 323 278 3877

Labels *Rockstar*
Products *Women's jeans and denimwear.*
Showrooms *New York & Los Angeles*
Sell To *Departmnent stores, boutiques & specialty stores.*
Corp. Office *Above*
Private Label *No*
Web Site *www.rockstarsushi.com*

ST. JOHN

17622 Armstrong Avenue
Irvine, CA 92614 info@sjk.com
949 863 1171 Fax : 949 437 8183 877 908 1171

Labels *St. John*
Products *Jeans collection for women sizes 2 to 16.*
Price Points *Designer*
Showrooms *New York/665 5th Avenue, 2nd Floor, New York, New York, 10022 tel: 212 755 5252*
Sell To *Specialty stores*
Corp. Office *Above*
Private Label *No*
Web Site *www.sjk.com*
Contact *CEO: Glenn McMahon*

5TH & OCEAN CLOTHING LLC/NEW ERA CAP CO.

590 West 83 Street
Hialeah, FL 33014 laura.garden@neweracap.com
305 822 4606 Fax : 305 822 4665

Labels *Major League Baseball, NHL, NBA, NFL, Collegiate teams*
Products *Junior sportswear.*
Price Points *Low to moderate.*
Production *Honduras*
Corp. Office *Above*
Private Label *Yes*
Web Site *www.neweracap.com*
RN Number *94989*
Rev. in mil. *11-50*
Contact *Designer: Laura Garden ext. 220*

BEACH RAYS/DIV OF J.Y. RAYS, INC.

2023 Chico Avenue
South El Monte, CA 91733 sales@beachrays.com
626 941 0388 Fax : 626 941 0386

Labels *Surfer, Vast, Wet*
Products *Junior apparel, swimwear, printed t-shirts, shirt & skirts.*
Price Points *Moderate to better*
Production *Offshore*
Sell To *Department stores, specialty stores, theme/water parks*
Corp. Office
Private Label *Yes*
Web Site *www.beachrays.com*
Contact *National Sales Manager: Natalie Wierzba*

BLUE PLATE INC.

525 Seventh Avenue, Suite 309
New York, NY 10018 bpshowroom@aol.com
212 382 0069 Fax : 212 997 2413

Labels *Blue Plate*
Products *Junior cotton tops, prairie skirts and cotton crochet dresses.*
Price Points *Moderate*
Production *India*
Showrooms *New York*
Sell To *Department stores, specialty stores, boutiques and mass merchants.*
Private Label *Yes*
Web Site *www.blueplatefashion.com*
Contact *President & Owner: Shashi Anand, Incharge: Seema Anand*

COTTON EMPORIUM, INC.

40 83 Street
Glendale, NY 11385 cottonemporium@aol.com
718 894 3365 Fax : 718 894 3374

Labels *Cotton Emporium, C & E*
Products *Junior sportswear, sweaters and knitwear.*
Price Points *Moderate*
Production *U.S.A.*

Showrooms *530 7th Avenue, Suite 609, New York, NY 10018 212 391 4427*
Private Label *Yes*
RN Number *RN93290*
Rev. in mil. *11-50*
Contact *President and Owner: Joseph Mosheshvili*

DOLLHOUSE

1407 Broadway, Suite 507
New York, NY 10018
212 997 0230
racampora@joujou.com

Labels *Dollhouse*
Products *Fashion forward looks for juniors. Denim, dresses, leggings, outerwear & shoes.*
Price Points *Moderate*
Production *Import*
Sell To *On-line, department stores, specialty stores, boutiques.*
Web Site *www.dollhouse.com*
Contact *Sales: Bob Acampora ext. 243*

EVY OF CALIFORNIA, INC./DBA JALATE

530 Fashion Avenue, Suite 804
New York, NY 10018
212 594 3670 Fax : 212 971 9131
suzannem@evy.com

Labels *Fleurish*
Products *Young contemporary junior line featuring the latest tops, bottoms & dresses.*
Price Points *Moderate*
Production *U.S.A., Mexico, Dubai, China, Central America, Cambodia, India, Vietnam, Philippines*
Sell To *Department stores, specialty stores, boutiques, mass merchants & mail order catalogues.*
Corp. Office *810A S. Flower St, Los Angeles, Ca. 90017 Tel: 213 763 6100, Fax: 213 748 7475.*
Private Label *Yes*
Web Site *www.evy.com*
RN Number *RN17657, RN106895*
Rev. in mil. *51-100*
Contact *CEO: Kurt Kreiser, Office Manager: Nadine (NY Showroom)*

GUESS, INC.

1444 S. Alameda Street
Los Angeles, CA 90021
213 765 3100 Fax : 213 765 5902 877-44-GUESS
vendors@guess.com

Labels *Guess*
Products *Contemporary sportswear separates & outerwear.*
Price Points *Moderate to better*
Showrooms *New York/119 West 40th St, Suite 420, New York, N.Y. 10018, Tel: 212 730 7200*
Sell To *Department stores & specialty stores.*
Corp. Office *Above*
Web Site *www.guess.com*
Contact *CEO: Paul Marciano*

HYPERCLASH

926 Baca Street #1
Santa Fe, NM 87505
505 820 0520
wholesale@hyperclash.com

Labels *Hyperclash*
Products *Current styles made from reclaimed, organic, sustainable or fair trade earth friendly materi*
Price Points *Moderate*
Production *U.S.A.*
Web Site *www.hyperclash.com*
Contact *Owner: Paloma Navarrete*

JONDEN MANUFACTURING CO., INC.

1410 Broadway, Suite 1103
New York, NY 10018
212 730 1741 Fax : 212 730 1742
tsmith@jonden.com

Labels *Jonden*
Products *Junior knit tops & related separates.*
Price Points *Moderate*
Production *U.S.A.*
Showrooms *New York/above*
Sell To *Department stores, specialty stores, mass merchants, mail order catalogues & off-price.*
Private Label *Yes*
Web Site *www.jonden.com*
RN Number *RN85224*

JOU JOU DESIGNS

1407 Broadway, 5th Floor
New York, NY 10018
212 997 0230 Fax : 212 302 0308
racampora@joujou.com

Labels *Jou Jou*
Products *Specialize in jackets and denim.*
Price Points *Moderate*
Sell To *Department stores*
Corp. Office *Division of BBC Apparel, Inc.*
Private Label *Yes*
Web Site *www.joujou.com*
Contact *Sales: Bob Acampora*

KELLWOOD COMPANY

600 Kellwood Parkway
Chesterfield, MO 63017
314 576 3100 Fax : 314 576 3325
corp_communications@kellwood.com

Labels *My Michelle, Rewind*
Products *Junior fashion-forward dresses and related sportswear.*
Price Points *Better*
Showrooms *New York/212-515-2600, California/626-934-4122*
Sell To *Department stores, boutiques*
Web Site *www.kellwood.com*

MISTER NOAH

1407 Broadway, Suite 707
New York, NY 10018 noah@mrnoah.com
212 354 1700 Fax : 212 354 1740

Labels *Feathers*
Products *Junior denim jeans, junior knit sweaters & knit & woven fashion tops.*
Price Points *Moderate*
Production *Import*
Showrooms *New York*
Sell To *Department stores, mass merchants, mail order catalogues & off-price.*
Corp. Office *1824 Byberry Road, Bensalem, Pa. 19020 tel: 215-639-9300*
Private Label *Yes*
Web Site *www.feathersgirl.com*
RN Number *RN50110*
Rev. in mil. *11-50*
Contact *Presidents: Bruce Feinberg/Robert Feinberg*

ROYAL APPAREL, INC.

65 Commerce Drive
Hauppauge, NY 11788 sales@royalapparel.net
631 213 8299 Fax : 631 922 8438 866-Royal-1-S

Labels *Royal Apparel*
Products *Basic & fashion forward blanks, active/athleticwear in a large selection of colors & knit fabr*
Price Points *Moderate to better.*
Production *U.S.A.*
Showrooms *New York & Allentown, Pa.*
Sell To *Mass merchants, branded labels, screen printers & department stores.*
Private Label *Yes*
Web Site *www.royalapparel.net*
Contact *President: Morey Mayeri, Owners: Morey Mayeri/Abraham Mayeri*

SIMON SHOWROOM *(Rep.)

95 Fifth Avenue, 3rd Floor
New York, NY 10003 info@simonshowroom.com
212 242 1565 Fax : 212 242 6836

Labels *IRO, Tatras, Rivieras, Pepin, Sundry, AMO, Antik Batik, Carisa Rene, Foundrae, Essentiel*
Products *Contemporary jeans, skirts, shorts & chic dresses.*
Price Points *Better to contemporary.*
Production *U.S.A., France, Hong Kong.*
Showrooms *Los Angeles 213-593-1394*
Sell To *Department stores, specialty stores & boutiques.*
Private Label *Yes*
Web Site *www.simonshowroom.com*
Rev. in mil. *11-50*
Contact *President/Owner: Fifi Simon*

SURVIVAL INC.

90 C Washington Drive
Centerport, NY 11721 sanjay@survivalrules.com
631 385 5060 Fax : 631 385 5063

Labels *Survival*

Products *Contemporary junior sportswear, knit tops & sweaters.*
Price Points *Moderate*
Production *Import worldwide*
Sell To *Department stores, specialty stores & boutiques.*
Web Site *www.survivalrules.com*
Contact *Sales: Sanjay*

TOPSON DOWNS

3840 Watseka Avenue
Culver City, CA 90232
310 558 0300 Fax : 310 774 3666
info@topsondowns.com

Labels *Tinseltown*
Products *Junior demin brand with trendy silhouettes from 5 pocket pants to bustiers and dresses.*
Price Points *Better*
Production *Import*
Showrooms *NY Showroom: 530 7th Avenue, Suite 1502, New York, NY 10018 (212) 730 7860.*
Sell To *Department stores, specialty stores*
Private Label *Yes*
Web Site *www.topsondowns.com*

TRENDSET ORIGINALS

1407 Broadway, Room 503
New York, NY 10018
212 736 9520 Fax : 212 997 9284
jj@skiva.com

Labels *Trendset*
Products *European junior sportswear tops & bottoms.*
Price Points *Budget to moderate.*
Production *Import*
Showrooms *New York*
Sell To *Department stores, specialty stores, mass merchants & off-price retailers.*
Private Label *Yes*
RN Number *RN48829*
Rev. in mil. *51-100*

TRIPP NYC

69 Saint Marks Place, Suite 6
New York, NY 10003
212 979 8238 Fax : 212 979 8290
wholesale@trippnyc.com

Labels *Tripp NYC, Daang Goodman*
Products *Contemporary junior sportswear.*
Price Points *Moderate*
Production *U.S.A.*
Showrooms *New York/above*
Sell To *Boutiques, specialty stores*
Private Label *Yes*
Web Site *www.trippnyc.com*
RN Number *RN78061*
Contact *Owner: Ray Goodman*

UNIONBAY/SEATTLE PACIFIC INDUSTRIES

1633 Westlake Avenue North, Suite 300
Seattle, WA 98109
253 872 8822 Fax : 253 395 1345
cathie.underwood@unionbay.com

Labels *Unionbay, Reunion*
Products *Casual sportswear. Shorts, crop pants, jeans and tank tops.*
Price Points *Moderate to better*
Production *Import*
Showrooms *New York/70 West 36th Street, NYC 212-947-1888, plus Los Angeles, Atlanta & Seattle.*
Sell To *Department stores, specialty stores, mail order catalogues, mass merchants & off-price.*
Private Label *Yes*
Web Site *www.unionbay.com*
Rev. in mil. *+500*

ANDREW MARC

512 Seventh Avenue
New York, NY 10018 sales@andrewmarc.com
212 840 1800 Fax : 212 575 4717 888 424 6272

Labels *Andrew Marc, Marc New York*
Products *Shearling, leather, suede, cloth & cashmere/wool outerwear.*
Price Points *Better*
Production *Asia & Europe*
Showrooms *New York/above*
Sell To *Department stores, specialty stores, boutiques & mail order catalogues.*
Private Label *Yes*
Web Site *www.andrewmarc.com*
Rev. in mil. *11-50*

KIPPYS *(Rep.)

2096 Newton Avenue
San Diego, CA 92113 bob@kippys.com
619 435 6218 Fax : 619 238 0670

Labels *Kippys*
Products *Leather & suede jackets, pants & skirts.*
Price Points *Better to designer.*
Showrooms *Regional shows in Dallas, Los Angeles, New York, Denver, Chicago, Las Vegas. International: Milan and Paris.*
Sell To *Specialty stores & mail-order catalogues.*
Private Label *Yes*
Web Site *www.kippys.com*
Rev. in mil. *2-10*
Contact *Designers: Bob Kipperman & Tarin Brouillette*

MONTANACO CLOTHING COMPANY

321 W. Galena Street
Butte, MT 59701 info@montanacoclothing.com
406 723 2332 Fax : 406 723 5267 1-888-265-4128

Labels *Montanaco, Deni, Razer*
Products *Women's leather jackets and vests.*
Price Points *Better*
Production *Domestic*
Corp. Office *Above*
Private Label *No*
Web Site *www.montanacoclothing.com*

SCULLY

Scully Corporate Plaza
Oxnard, CA 93003 brianscully@scullyleather.com
805 483 6339 Fax : 805 483 6439

Labels *Scully*
Products *Leather outerwear, Western apparel and accessories.*
Showrooms *California*
Web Site *www.scullyleather.com*
Contact *Division Director: Brian Scully*

TASHA POLIZZI

287 Main Street
Great Barrington, MA 01230
413 528 6500 Fax : 413 528 6370
jane@tashapolizzi.com

Labels	*Tasha Polizzi*
Products	*Contempoary leather & suede outerwear, jackets & sportswear.*
Price Points	*Bridge*
Production	*U.S.A.*
Sell To	*Department stores, specialty stores.*
Private Label	*No*
Web Site	*www.tashapolizzi.com*
Contact	*Owner: Tasha Polizzi, Sales: Jane Wright*

ASPEN LICENSING INTERNATIONAL, INC.

6615 W. Boynton Beach Boulevard, #349
Boynton Beach, FL 33437
561 509 8888 Fax : 561 740 0637 1 888 642 7736
bob@aspenlicensing.com

Labels *Aspen, Aspen Extreme*
Products *Active & outdoor inspired outerwear, underwear, footwear & accessories.*
Price Points *Moderate*
Production *U.S.A. & Orient.*
Showrooms *Call for licensee's showrooms or if your company would benefit by licensing the Aspen name.*
Sell To *Department stores & mass merchants.*
Web Site *www.aspenbrand.com*
RN Number *RN86959*
Contact *Chairman: Robert Maltz*

CHAMPION ATHLETICWEAR, INC.

1000 East Hanes Mill Road
Winston Salem, NC 27105
336 519 6500 Fax : 336 519 7909 800 999 2249
linda.barabasova@hanesbrands.com

Labels *Champion*
Products *Women's tee shirts, jogging suits, sport uniforms & all types of active & athletic wear.*
Price Points *Moderate*
Production *U.S.A. & import from the Orient.*
Sell To *Department stores, mass merchants, mail order catalogues & sporting goods retailers.*
Private Label *Yes*
Web Site *www.championusa.com*
RN Number *RN26094*
Contact *Licensing: Nancy Gendimenico - 212 576-8481*

GLOBAL BRANDS GROUP

350 Fifth Avenue, 7th Floor
New York, NY 10118
646 839 7000
business@globalbrandsgroup.com

Labels *Calvin Klein, Michael Kors, Coach, Frye*
Products *Womens apparel and leather collection.*
Price Points *Moderate & better*
Production *Import*
Showrooms *New York*
Sell To *Department stores, specialty stores, mid-tier, mass merchants & catalogues.*
Private Label *Yes*
Web Site *www.globalbrandsgroup.com*
RN Number *RN82457*
Rev. in mil. *11-50*

HYBRID APPAREL

10711 Walker Street
Cypress, CA 90630
714 952 3866 Fax : 714 952 3874
mlee@hybridapparel.com

Products *Women's & juniors tees, tunics, thermals, hoodies, dresses & separates.*
Price Points *Moderate*
Showrooms *Los Angeles/ 910 South Los Angeles St, Suite 408, Lost Angeles, Ca 90015, New York/530 7th Avenue, NYC 10018 212-997-4688.*

Sell To *Department stores & mass merchants.*
Web Site *www.hybridapparel.com*
Contact *Wholesale: M. Lee*

ANN TAYLOR

4079 Executive Parkway
Westerville, OH 43081 clientservices@anntaylor.com
800 342 5266 Fax : 866 232 9266 800 342 5266

Labels *Ann Taylor*
Products *Multi-faceted career, casual & dressy collection.*
Price Points *Better*
Production *Import worldwide*
Sell To *Company owned retail stores only.*
Corp. Office *7 Times Square, New York, NY 10036*
Web Site *www.anntaylor.com*

ANNE KLEIN

1411 Broadway
New York, NY 10018 customer_relations@anneklein.com
888 841 2229 888 841 2229

Labels *Anne Klein, AK*
Products *Updated sportswear collection.*
Price Points *Bridge*
Production *Import*
Showrooms *New York & Dallas.*
Sell To *Department stores, specialty stores & mail order catalogues.*
Corp. Office *Division of Jones Apparel Group*
Private Label *No*
Web Site *www.anneklein.com*
RN Number *RN82060*

ARAKS

137 Grand Street, 5th Floor
New York, NY 10013 sales@araks.com
212 982 5652 Fax : 212 966 5596

Labels *Araks*
Products *Luxurious and versatile collection of lifestyle garments.*
Price Points *Designer*
Sell To *Boutiques*
Web Site *www.araks.com*
Contact *Designer and Owner: Araks Yeramyan*

BURBERRY

444 Madison Avenue, 14th Floor
New York, NY 10022 us.customerservice@burberry.com
800 284 8480 Fax : 212 977 5521 877-217-4085

Labels *Burberry*
Products *Modern classic & contemporary full lifestyle collection.*
Price Points *Better to designer*
Production *U.S.A. & import*
Sell To *Department stores & specialty stores.*
Private Label *No*
Web Site *www.burberry.com*

G-III APPAREL GROUP

512 Seventh Avenue, 40th Floor
New York, NY 10018
212 403 0500
info@g-iii.com

Labels *Kensie*
Products *Feminine, edgy women's lifestyle sportswear collection.*
Price Points *Better*
Production *Import*
Showrooms *Same as Above*
Sell To *Department stores, specialty stores, boutiques*
Corp. Office *Same as Above*
Private Label *Yes*
Web Site *www.g-iii.com*
Contact *Designer: Kisha Beaugris (646 825 9297)*

J. CREW

770 Broadway, 11th Floor
New York, NY 10003
212 209 2500 Fax : 434 385 5750
contactus@jcrew.com

Labels *J. Crew*
Products *Casual sportswear and lifestyle collection.*
Price Points *Moderate*
Production *Import worldwide*
Sell To *Company owned stores and catalogue only.*
Web Site *www.jcrew.com*

JBD NEW YORK

241 West 37th Street, Suite 518
New York, NY 10018
212 944 0910 Fax : 212 944 0286
vijay@jbdnewyork.com

Labels *JBD New York*
Products *Fashion forward lifestyle women's collection. Highest quality fabrics and printing processes.*
Price Points *Better*
Production *India*
Showrooms *New York*
Sell To *Specialty stores, boutiques, department stores*
Private Label *Yes*
Web Site *www.jbdnewyork.com*
RN Number *RN80911*
Rev. in mil. *2-10*
Contact *Owner/designer: Vijay Paintal*

JOYOUS AND FREE

2233 Faraday Avenue, Suite H and I
Carlsbad, CA 92008
760 385 6999 Fax : 760 268 1112 800 987 8792
sales@joyousandfree.com

Labels *Joyous and Free, Basil & Maude, Faith*
Products *Contemporary clothing in comfortable fabrics. Fun prints. Dresses, tunics & flow pants.*
Production *Bali*
Showrooms *Atlanta/Carroll Apparel 800 3069949 Dallas/B&B Sales 214 630 4410*
Chicago/Cheney & Cohen 312 316 8588 LA/John Walter & Associates 925 5705320

Sell To *Boutiques*
Web Site *www.joyousandfree.com*

KATE SPADE AND COMPANY

2 Park Avenue
New York, NY 10016
212 739 6550
media_relations@katespade.com

Labels *Kate Spade*
Products *All categories of womens apparel & accessories for all aspects of life.*
Price Points *Moderate to bridge*
Production *U.S.A. & import*
Showrooms *New York/above*
Sell To *Department stores, specialty stores*
Private Label *No*
Web Site *www.katespadeandcompany.com*
Contact *CEO: Craig Leavitt*

MT SHOWROOM *(Rep.)

627 West 27th Street
New York, NY 10001
212 354 5678 Fax : 212 354 8654
info@parajumpers.it

Labels *Parajumpers*
Products *Contempory timeless lifestyle collection including jackets, fleece, polo and t-shirts.*
Price Points *Better*
Sell To *Department stores, specialty stores, boutiques & own website.*
Private Label *No*
Web Site *www.parajumpers.it*
Rev. in mil. *0-2*

NIC + ZOE

323 Speen Street
Natick, MA 01760
508 651 0000 Fax : 508 651 0066 800 822 2939
info@nicandzoe.com

Labels *Nic + Zoe*
Products *Updated collection sportswear in missy and petite.*
Price Points *Better*
Production *U.S.A. and import.*
Showrooms *New York/561 7th Avenue, Suite 1002 New York, NY 212-768-8500 and have road reps throughout the U.S*
Sell To *Department stores, specialty stores, mail order catalogues.*
Private Label *Yes*
Web Site *www.nicandzoe.com*
RN Number *RN59351*
Contact *Sales: Julie Jordan Browne*

PIMLICO PERFORMANCE APPAREL LTD.

118 West Hastings Street
Vancouver, BC, Canada V6B 1G8
604 323 0441 Fax : 604 323 0449
adriana@pimlicoperformance.com

Labels *Dish*
Products *Shirts, dresses, skirts & outerwear*

Price Points *Moderate to better*
Sell To *Specialty stores & boutiques.*
Private Label *Yes*
Web Site *www.dishandduer.com*

PVH CORPORATION

200 Madison Avenue
New York, NY 10016
212 287 8000

contactus@pvh.com

Labels *Calvin Klein, Tommy Hilfiger, Heritage Brands*
Products *Lifestyle apparel collection*
Price Points *Better*
Production *U.S.A. & import worldwide*
Sell To *Department stores, specialty stores, mass merchants & mail order catalogues.*
Corp. Office *1001 Frontier Road, MS#44, Bridgewater, NJ 08807*
Private Label *Yes*
Web Site *www.pvh.com*
Rev. in mil. *+500*

ANNE KLEIN

1411 Broadway
New York, NY 10018 customer_relations@anneklein.com
888 841 2229 888 841 2229

Labels *Anne Klein, AK*
Products *Updated sportswear collection.*
Price Points *Bridge*
Production *Import*
Showrooms *New York & Dallas.*
Sell To *Department stores, specialty stores & mail order catalogues.*
Corp. Office *Division of Jones Apparel Group*
Private Label *No*
Web Site *www.anneklein.com*
RN Number *RN82060*

BLUESUITS

200 West 70th Street, Suite 14G
New York, NY 10023 jamak@off7th.com
212 787 0278

Labels *Bluesuits*
Products *Women's sportswear collection including suits, jackets, pants, skirts & dresses in sizes 0 to 20.*
Price Points *Designer*
Production *U.S.A.*
Sell To *Department stores & boutiques*
Private Label *Yes*
Web Site *www.bluesuitsonline.com*
Contact *Designer: Jamak Khazra*

DAILY WEAR SPORTSWEAR/FOREVER YOUNG

1407 Broadway, Suite 2315
New York, NY 10018 dailywearsports@aol.com
212 278 0038 Fax : 718 438 2545

Labels *Daily Wear, Forever Young*
Products *Sportswear & updated active wear. Missy, junior & large sizes.*
Price Points *Moderate*
Production *U.S.A. & import*
Sell To *Department stores & specialty stores.*
Private Label *No*
RN Number *RN93450*
Contact *Owner and President: Isaac Abed*

DANA EMILIA PRESENTS *(Rep.)

264 West 40th, Suite 503
New York, NY 10018 fashion@danaemilia.com
212 391 4104 Fax : 212 391 4153

Labels *Christopher Calvin, Redwood Court, Peacock Ways, Swish, Vanite Couture, Banaris*
Products *Casual to dressy separates in novelty fabrics. Soft separates with versatility.*
Price Points *Better*
Production *U.S.A. & import.*
Showrooms *New York.*
Sell To *Specialty stores, boutiques, chain stores & mail order catalogues.*

Private Label *Yes*
Web Site *www.danaemiliapresents.com*
Contact *President: Dana Harrison*

EILEEN FISHER INC.

111 Fifth Avenue, 11th Floor
New York, NY 10003 customercare@eileenfisher.com
212 420 5900 Fax : 212 228 0533 866 512 5197

Labels *Eileen Fisher*
Products *Bridge sportswear collection. Missy, large & petite sizes.*
Price Points *Bridge*
Production *U.S.A., China & Italy.*
Showrooms *New York/above, Los Angeles, Dallas & Atlanta.*
Sell To *Department stores, specialty stores & boutiques.*
Corp. Office *Two Bridge St., Irvington, NY 10533. Tel: 914-591-5700, fax: 914-591-8900*
Private Label *No*
Web Site *www.eileenfisher.com*
RN Number *RN78121*
Contact *President & Owner: Eileen Fisher*

ELIE TAHARI LTD.

11 W 42nd Street, 14th Floor
New York, NY 10036 questions@elietahari.com
212 763 2000 Fax : 212 763 2299 800 649 6179

Labels *Elie Tahari*
Products *Well rounded bridge collection. Missy and petite sizes.*
Price Points *Better to bridge.*
Production *Hong Kong and China*
Sell To *Department stores, specialty stores, boutiques and off-price.*
Web Site *www.elietahari.com*
Contact *President: Elie Tahari*

EURO JOY SPORTSWEAR CORP.

108 West 39th Street, Suite 1120
New York, NY 10018 jasoneurojoy@aol.com
212 575 4650 Fax : 212 575 4651

Labels *Euro Joy Sportswear*
Products *Casual career missy sportswear line & related separates.*
Price Points *Upper moderate*
Production *Overseas*
Showrooms *New York/above*
Sell To *Department stores, specialty stores & catalogues.*
Private Label *Yes*
RN Number *RN57032*
Rev. in mil. *2-10*
Contact *President: Jason Wu*

GENE EWING BIS

PCH Fashion District, PO Box 326
Malibu, CA 90265 geneewing@geneewingbis.com
323 839 9647 Fax : 323 839 9647

Labels	*Gene Ewing Bis, Bis Woman*
Products	*Innovative collection of designer sportswear & casual into evening dresses.*
Price Points	*Better*
Showrooms	*Los Angeles*
Sell To	*Specialty stores.*
Corp. Office	*Above*
Web Site	*www.geneewingbis.com*
Contact	*President: Gene Ewing*

JONDEN MANUFACTURING CO., INC.

1410 Broadway, Suite 1103
New York, NY 10018 tsmith@jonden.com
212 730 1741 Fax : 212 730 1742

Labels	*Jonden*
Products	*Missy knit tops & related separates.*
Price Points	*Moderate*
Production	*U.S.A.*
Showrooms	*New York/above*
Sell To	*Department stores, specialty stores, mass merchants, mail order catalogues & off-price.*
Private Label	*Yes*
Web Site	*www.jonden.com*
RN Number	*RN85224*

JONES APPAREL GROUP USA, INC

1411 Broadway, 37th Floor
New York, NY 10018
212 642 3860 Fax : 212 921 9124 888 255 7992

Labels	*Jones New York*
Products	*Sportswear & updated dress collection.*
Price Points	*Better*
Showrooms	*New York*
Sell To	*Department stores & mass merchants*
Corp. Office	*180 Rittenhouse Circle, Bristol, PA 19007 215 785 4000*
Web Site	*www,jny.com*

KATE SPADE AND COMPANY

2 Park Avenue
New York, NY 10016 media_relations@katespade.com
212 739 6550

Labels	*Kate Spade*
Products	*Updated womens apparel & accessories for all aspects of life.*
Price Points	*Moderate to bridge*
Production	*U.S.A. & import*
Showrooms	*New York/above*
Sell To	*Department stores, specialty stores*
Private Label	*No*
Web Site	*www.katespadeandcompany.com*

Contact *CEO: Craig Leavitt*

KEMBALI LTD.

87 Alta Avenue
Yonkers, NY 10705 kembali@optonline.net
914 965 2183 Fax : 914 730 9801

Labels *Kembali*
Products *Updated sportswear collection including dresses and separates.*
Price Points *Moderate, better & bridge.*
Production *Indonesia, Nepal, Vietnam*
Sell To *Specialty stores, boutiques, mail order catalogues.*
Private Label *Yes*
Rev. in mil. *0-2*
Contact *President: Michelle LaFond*

LE MIEUX/TARA INTERNATIONAL, INC.

242 Gemini Avenue
Brea, CA 92821 sweta.lmstudio@gmail.com
562 694 6860 Fax : 562 694 6875 877 962 9525

Labels *Le Mieux*
Products *Casual skirts, tops, dresses, 2-piece sets, pants, tees & denim.*
Price Points *Moderate*
Production *U.S.A. & import*
Showrooms *Los Angeles & Texas.*
Sell To *Department, specialty & off-price stores, boutiques, mass merchants & mail order.*
Private Label *Yes*
Web Site *www.lemieux.com*
Contact *President and Owner: Shekhar Agrawal*

ODETT ENTERPRISES

109 West 37th Street, Street Level
New York, NY 10018 info@odettfashion.com
212 921 9690 Fax : 212 768 4760

Labels *Odett*
Products *Updated sportswear & separates in missy & large sizes.*
Price Points *Budget to bridge.*
Production *U.S.A. & Italy*
Showrooms *New York*
Sell To *Specialty stores, boutiques.*
Private Label *Yes*
Web Site *www.odettfashion.com*
Contact *President: Amir Darouvar, Sales: Farah Darouvar*

SUSAN GREENSTADT & ASSOC. *(Rep.)

215 West 40th Street, 9th Floor
New York, NY 10018 susangreenstadt@aol.com
212 302 0600 Fax : 212 302 0680

Products *Contemporary & better missy sportswear. Wovens, dresses, shirtings & t-shirts.*
Price Points *Better, contemporary & bridge.*
Production *U.S.A. & import.*
Showrooms *New York.*

Sell To *Department stores, better specialty stores, chain stores, mail order catalogues & private label.*
Private Label *Yes*
Contact *President: Susan Greenstadt*

WEARABLE INTEGRITY/BARBARA LESSER

1158 26th Street, Suite 873
Santa Monica, CA 90403 mlesser@barbaralesser.com
310 742 7444 Fax : 310 440 0858

Labels *Barbara Lesser*
Products *Better sportswear & items.*
Price Points *Better*
Production *Import*
Showrooms *Los Angeles, Dallas, Atlanta, Chicago, Miami & New York.*
Sell To *Department stores, specialty stores, boutiques & mail order catalogues.*
Private Label *Yes*
Web Site *www.barbaralesser.com*
Rev. in mil. *11-50*
Contact *Sales: Mark Lesser, Design: Barbara Lesser*

ZELDA

260 West 39th Street, 5th Floor
New York, NY 10018 info@zelda-intl.com
212 764 0020 Fax : 212 764 2588

Labels *Z by Zelda*
Products *Modern bridge collection.*
Price Points *Bridge*
Production *Imported & U.S.A.*
Showrooms *New York, Dallas & Los Angeles, with reps in Atlanta*
Sell To *Specialty & department stores & boutiques.*
Private Label *Yes*
Web Site *www.zeldacollection.com*
Rev. in mil. *11-50*
Contact *Sales: Lisa Attea*

Notes

ADRIENNE LANDAU

519 Eighth Avenue, 21st Floor
New York, NY 10018
212 695 8362 Fax : 212 563 2014
sales@adriennelandau.com

Labels *Adrienne Landau*
Products *Fur trimmed coats & all fur coats.*
Price Points *Designer*
Production *U.S.A. & import*
Showrooms *New York*
Sell To *Department stores & specialty stores.*
Private Label *No*
Web Site *www.adriennelandau.com*
Contact *Owner: Adrienne Landau, , Design: Adrienne Landau*

ALPHA INDUSTRIES, INC.

14200 Park Meadow Drive, Suite 110 South
Chantilly, VA 20151
703 378 1420 Fax : 703 378 4910 866 631 0719
wholesale@alphaindustries.com

Labels *Alpha Industries, Alpha U.S.A.*
Products *Fashion cold weather outerwear & apparel with a feminine touch.*
Price Points *Moderate to better*
Production *U.S.A., Far East & Middle East*
Showrooms *Washington DC, NY, Los Angeles, London, Frankfurt, Paris, Seoul, Tokyo, Florence & Shanghai.*
Sell To *Department stores, specialty stores, boutiques & mail order catalogues.*
Private Label *Yes*
Web Site *www.alphaindustries.com*
RN Number *RN35569*

ANDREW MARC

512 Seventh Avenue
New York, NY 10018
212 840 1800 Fax : 212 575 4717 888 424 6272
sales@andrewmarc.com

Labels *Andrew Marc, Marc New York*
Products *Leather, suede, shearling, cashmere/wool & all types of cloth outerwear. Iconic, timeless trench*
Price Points *Better*
Production *Asia & Europe*
Showrooms *New York/above*
Sell To *Department stores, specialty stores, boutiques & mail order catalogues.*
Private Label *Yes*
Web Site *www.andrewmarc.com*
Rev. in mil. *11-50*

BABETTE

867 Isabella Street
Oakland, CA 94607
510 625 8500 Fax : 510 986 1402 800 677 7246
mary@babettesf.com

Labels *Babette*
Products *Outerwear, coats & raincoats.*
Price Points *Better/Bridge*
Production *U.S.A.*

Showrooms *West: Diane Vonderheide, 213.488.9334; diane@thevonderheideshowroom.com*
East: Terry Ventre, 212.967.6192; info@terryventreshowroom.com
Sell To *Specialty stores & boutiques.*
Private Label *No*
Web Site *www.shopbabette.com*
Rev. in mil. *2-10*
Contact *President: Steven Pinsky, Design: Babette Pinsky*

BARRAZA ASSOCIATES LTD

225 West 35th Street, Suite 1502
New York, NY 10001 barrazany@aol.com
212 564 6583

Labels *BarrazaStyle*
Products *Warm practical coats with feminine detailing.*
Price Points *Moderate to better.*
Production *U.S.A. & import.*
Sell To *Department stores, specialty stores, boutiques, mail order catalogues.*
Private Label *Yes*
Web Site *www.barrazastyle.com*
Rev. in mil. *2-10*
Contact *President: Maria Barraza, Sales & Marketing: Rafael Romero*

BLUE DUCK TRADING CO.

463 Seventh Avenue, Suite 1106
New York, NY 10018 barry@blueduckshearling.com
212 268 3122 Fax : 212 268 3125 800 377 9001

Labels *Blue Duck*
Products *Fine luxury outerwear specializing in Spanish Merino Shearlings & fur lined coats & jackets*
Price Points *Better to bridge.*
Production *U.S.A.*
Showrooms *New York*
Sell To *Department stores, specialty stores, boutiques & mail order catalogues.*
Private Label *Yes*
Web Site *www.blueduckshearling.com*
Contact *Founder and CEO Barry Novick*

BURBERRY

444 Madison Avenue, 14th Floor
New York, NY 10022 us.customerservice@burberry.com
800 284 8480 Fax : 212 977 5521 877-217-4085

Labels *Burberry*
Products *Modern classic, traditional & casual outerwear & rainwear.*
Price Points *Better to designer*
Production *U.S.A. & import*
Sell To *Department stores & specialty stores.*
Private Label *No*
Web Site *www.burberry.com*

CASSIN

922 Riverview Drive
Totowa, NJ 07512
973 826 1190
info@cassincollections.com

Labels *Cassin, sherry cassin new york*
Products *Hi-end & bridge designer furs, outerwear (including faux fur), bridal & evening cover ups.*
Price Points *Moderate to designer*
Production *U.S.A. & import.*
Sell To *Department stores, fine specialty stores*
Web Site *www.cassincollections.com*
Contact *Designer: Sherry Cassin*

CEJON ACCESSORIES INC.

390 Fifth Avenue, Suite 602
New York, NY 10018
212 967 4663 Fax : 212 967 4766
rmummert@cejon.com

Labels *Cejon*
Products *Distributor of ladies scarves, pullovers, ponchos & cold weather sets.*
Price Points *Moderate*
Production *U.S.A. & import*
Sell To *Department stores, specialty stores, mail order catalogues & off-price retailers.*
Private Label *Yes*
Web Site *www.cejon.com*
Contact *President: David Seeherman, Sales: Robin Mummert*

COLORATURA, INC.

P.O. Box 157
Annville, PA 17003
717 867 1144 Fax : 717 867 1152 800 825 8288
coloratura9@aol.com

Labels *Coloratura*
Products *Decorative outerwear. Coats, jackets, capes, scarves & vests in patchwork, applique, etc.*
Price Points *Designer*
Production *U.S.A.*
Showrooms *Denver/Frank Levy & Annville, PA.*
Sell To *Specialty stores, boutiques & mail order catalogues.*
Private Label *No*
Web Site *www.coloratura.com*
Contact *President: Alan J. Resnick*

COLUMBIA SPORTSWEAR CO., INC.

14375 N.W. Science Park Drive
Portland, OR 97229
503 985 4000 Fax : 503 985 5800 800 MA BOYLE
sales_info@columbia.com

Labels *Columbia Sportswear Co.*
Products *Active outerwear, skiing, sportswear, footwear & accessories.*
Price Points *Moderate*
Production *U.S.A. & Overseas*
Sell To *Department stores, specialty stores, mass merchants.*
Private Label *No*
Web Site *www.columbia.com*
RN Number *RN69724*

Rev. in mil. *+500*
Contact *Chairman: Gertrude Boyle, CEO: Tim Boyle, VIP Sales: Joseph R. Craig*

DOLORES PISCOTTA

8865 Sixteenth Avenue
Brooklyn, NY 11214 piscotta@msn.com
718 232 1167 Fax : 718 232 1167

Labels *Piscotta New York, Dolores Piscotta*
Products *100% cashmere cloth coats and jackets for women & dogs.*
Price Points *Better to designer*
Production *U.S.A., Italy, China, Nepal*
Showrooms *Brooklyn, New York - By appointment only*
Additional website: dolorespiscottawholesale.com
Sell To *Department stores, specialty stores, boutiques & catalogues.*
Private Label *Yes*
Web Site *www.dolorespiscotta.com*
RN Number *RN97327*
Contact *Owner and Designer: Dolores Piscotta*

ESSEX MANUFACTURING INC.

350 Fifth Avenue, Suite 2400
New York, NY 10118 bbaum@baum-essex.com
212 239 0080 Fax : 212 714 2958 800 648 6010

Labels *Misty Harbor®, CLC*
Products *Rainwear, specialize in PVC & vinyl slickers, raincoats & nylon packaway jackets.*
Production *Import*
Showrooms *Chicago, Boston, Cleveland, Philadelphia, San Francisco & New York.*
Sell To *Department stores, specialty stores, mass merchants & mail order catalogues.*
Private Label *Yes*
Web Site *www.baum-essex.com*
Contact *Rainwear & Outerwear: Bill Baum, Umbrellas: Lance Lovett - llovett@baum-essex.com*

EURO JOY SPORTSWEAR CORP.

108 West 39th Street, Suite 1120
New York, NY 10018 jasoneurojoy@aol.com
212 575 4650 Fax : 212 575 4651

Labels *Euro Joy Sportswear*
Products *Light-weight jackets & active outerwear.*
Price Points *Moderate*
Production *Overseas*
Showrooms *New York*
Sell To *Upper moderate*
Private Label *Yes*
RN Number *RN57032*
Rev. in mil. *2-10*
Contact *President: Jason Wu*

FORI SHOWROOM *(Rep.)

130 West 25th Street, Suite 10B
New York, NY 10001
646 724 2728
jacopo@jacopofoti.com

Labels *Peserico,Katia Serafini, Argonne, Walter Voulaz, Moorer, Rossopuro*
Products *Upscale apparel, coats & jackets.*
Price Points *Bridge*
Production *Italy*
Showrooms *Collection is presented twice a year: Fall and Spring/Summer & sold through specialized agents with showrooms. The best of Made in Italy products.*
Sell To *Specialty stores*
Private Label *Yes*
Web Site *www.forifashion.com*
Rev. in mil. *0-2*

FREE COUNTRY LTD.

1071 6th Avenue, 9th Floor
New York, NY 10018
212 719 4596 Fax : 212 719 2051
rondac@freecountry.com

Labels *Free Country*
Products *Outerwear*
Price Points *Better*
Production *U.S.A. & import*
Showrooms *New York*
Sell To *Department stores, specialty stores & boutiques.*
Private Label *Yes*
Web Site *www.freecountry.com*
RN Number *RN82608*
Rev. in mil. *11-50*
Contact *Design: Ira Schwartz*

FRENCH CONNECTION

512 Seventh Avenue, 25th Floor
New York, NY 10018
212 221 3157 Fax : 212 302 6839 866-932-3285
frenchconnection@frenchconnection-usa.com

Labels *French Connection*
Products *Contemporary leather jackets, down coats & overcoats, European fabrics.*
Price Points *Better*
Production *Global*
Showrooms *Atlanta, Chicago, Los Angeles & New York.*
Sell To *Department stores, specialty stores, boutiques, mail order catalogues & off-price retailers.*
Corp. Office *184-10 Jamaica Avenue, Hollis, New York 11423*
Private Label *Yes*
Web Site *usa.frenchconnection.com*
RN Number *RN53372*
Rev. in mil. *101-500*
Contact *President: Andrea Hyde*

GOLF APPAREL BRANDS

13621 South Main Street
Los Angeles, CA 90061 sales@lamode.com
310 715 1772 Fax : 310 715 1776 800 678 5246

Labels *La Mode, Clark & Gregory, Sahara,*
Products *Ladies golf rain jackets and rain pants.*
Price Points *Moderate to better*
Production *Domestic and import from Korea, China, Hong Kong, Malaysia*
Sell To *Specialty stores, off-price and golf shops.*
Private Label *Yes*
Web Site *www.lamode.com*
Contact *President/Owner: Eddie Kahn*

HARBOUR INTERNATIONAL LLC

1407 Broadway, Suite 1515
New York, NY 10018 tlewis@harbourintl.net
212 868 9128 Fax : 212 868 9129

Labels *Boston Harbour, Proshield, Habour/One, Emanuel Ungaro*
Products *Outdoor wear in leather and cloth for every occasion*
Price Points *Better*
Production *Import*
Sell To *On-line store*
Private Label *Yes*
Web Site *www.bostonharbour.net*
Contact *CO: Tom Lewis*

J RICHARDS INTERNATIONAL

437 Mamaroneck Avenue
Mamaroneck, NY 10543 richard@jrichardsintl.com
212 819 0444 Fax : 212 819 0587

Labels *J Richards*
Products *Coats, jackets, rainwear in cashmere, lambswool, coated & novelty fabrics. Fur & leather tri*
Price Points *Better, bridge & off-price.*
Production *U.S.A.*
Sell To *Specialty stores, boutiques, department stores.*
Private Label *Yes*
Web Site *www.jrichardsintl.com*
Contact *Designer: Jheri Richards*

JOU JOU DESIGNS

1407 Broadway, 5th Floor
New York, NY 10018 racampora@joujou.com
212 997 0230 Fax : 212 302 0308

Labels *Jou Jou*
Products *Specialize in jackets and denim.*
Price Points *Moderate*
Sell To *Department stores*
Corp. Office *Division of BBC Apparel, Inc.*
Private Label *Yes*
Web Site *www.joujou.com*
Contact *Sales: Bob Acampora*

LINDA RICHARDS

209 West 38th Street, Suite 505
New York, NY 10018
212 382 2257 Fax : 212 382 1793
info@lindarichards.com

Labels *Linda Richards*
Products *Outerwear*
Price Points *Better*
Production *U.S.A.*
Sell To *Department stores, specialty stores & boutiques.*
Corp. Office *Above*
Private Label *Yes*
Web Site *www.lindarichards.com*
RN Number *RN28278*
Contact *Sales: Merrisa Alfano (malfano@lindarichards.com*

MARMOT MOUNTAIN LLC.

5789 State Farm Drive, Suite 100
Rohnert Park, CA 94928
707 544 4590 Fax : 707 544 1344 1-888-357-3262
ghouser@marmot.com

Labels *Marmot*
Products *Women's performance outerwear.*
Price Points *Better*
Sell To *Specialty stores and department stores.*
Private Label *No*
Web Site *www.marmot.com*
Contact *Greg Houser*

MT SHOWROOM *(Rep.)

627 West 27th Street
New York, NY 10001
212 354 5678 Fax : 212 354 8654
info@parajumpers.it

Labels *Parajumpers*
Products *Fashion-focused women's ski apparel collection.*
Price Points *Better*
Sell To *Department stores, specialty stores, boutiques & own website.*
Private Label *No*
Web Site *www.parajumpers.it*
Rev. in mil. *0-2*

ODETT ENTERPRISES

109 West 37th Street, Street Level
New York, NY 10018
212 921 9690 Fax : 212 768 4760
info@odettfashion.com

Labels *Odett*
Products *Furs, fur products, coats & jackets.*
Price Points *Budget to bridge.*
Production *U.S.A. & Italy*
Showrooms *New York*
Sell To *Specialty stores, boutiques.*
Private Label *Yes*

Web Site *www.odettfashion.com*
Contact *President: Amir Darouvar, Sales: Farah Darouvar*

PENDLETON WOOLEN MILLS, INC.

220 Northwest Broadway
Portland, OR 97209 pendletoncatalog@penwool.com
503 226 4801 Fax : 503 535 5599 800 522 9665

Labels *Pendleton*
Products *Sportswear, outerwear, jackets, westernwear & accessories.*
Price Points *Better*
Production *U.S.A. & import*
Sell To *Specialty stores & mail order catalogues.*
Private Label *No*
Web Site *www.pendleton-usa.com*
RN Number *RN29685, WPL04378*
Rev. in mil. *+500*

RODEL U.S.A. INC.

30 Central Park South, Penthouse
New York, NY 10019 rodelusa@aol.com
212 997 9767 Fax : 212 997 9785 866 4CR COAT

Labels *Cinzia Rocca*
Products *Luxury outerwear & suit collection.*
Price Points *Better to designer*
Production *Italy*
Showrooms *New York*
Sell To *Department stores, specialty stores & boutiques.*
Private Label *No*
Web Site *www.cinziarocca.com*

SHEDRAIN CORP.

366 Fifth Avenue, Suite 1001
New York, NY 10001 iraw@shedrain.com
212 685 5555 Fax : 212 447 0888 800 722 7246

Labels *ShedRain, WalkSafe*
Products *Women's fashion & basic rainwear.*
Price Points *Moderate to better.*
Production *U.S.A. & Asia*
Showrooms *New York & Portland, Oregon*
Sell To *Department & specialty stores, boutiques, mass merchants, catalogues & corporate sales.*
Corp. Office *8303 N.E. Killingsworth, Portland, OR 97220, Tel:503-255-2200*
Private Label *Yes*
Web Site *www.shedrain.com*
Contact *President: Jeffrey Blauer*

SHEEPSKIN BY SUSAN BRADFORD

8800 Green Valley Road
Sebastopol, CA 95472 susanbradforddesigns@charter.net
802 371 8236

Labels *Sheepskin*
Products *Original, hand-sewn shealring coats and vests.*

Price Points *Designer*
Production *U.S.A.*
Sell To *Specialty stores and boutiques.*
Private Label *No*
Web Site *www.sheepskin-by-susan.com*
Contact *Owner: Susan Bradford*

TASHA POLIZZI

287 Main Street
Great Barrington, MA 01230 jane@tashapolizzi.com
413 528 6500 Fax : 413 528 6370

Labels *Tasha Polizzi*
Products *Contempoary jackets & blanket coats.*
Price Points *Bridge*
Production *U.S.A.*
Sell To *Department stores, specialty stores.*
Private Label *No*
Web Site *www.tashapolizzi.com*
Contact *Owner: Tasha Polizzi, Sales: Jane Wright*

TRENDSET ORIGINALS

1407 Broadway, Room 503
New York, NY 10018 jj@skiva.com
212 736 9520 Fax : 212 997 9284

Labels *Trendset*
Products *Women's outerwear and jackets.*
Price Points *Budget to moderate.*
Production *Import*
Showrooms *New York*
Sell To *Department stores, specialty stores, mass merchants & off-price retailers.*
Private Label *Yes*
RN Number *RN48829*
Rev. in mil. *51-100*

WHITE SIERRA

305 Soquel Way
Sunnyvale, CA 94085 wholesale@whitesierra.com
408 980 6688 Fax : 408 980 6670 1 800 980 8688

Labels *White Sierra*
Products *Active sports outerwear.*
Price Points *Moderate*
Production *U.S.A. & Asia*
Sell To *Department stores, specialty stores, mass merchants & sporting good shops.*
Private Label *Yes*
Web Site *www.whitesierra.com*
RN Number *RN58486*
Rev. in mil. *11-50*

Notes

ANDARI FASHION, INC.

9626 Telstar Avenue
El Monte, CA 91731 info@andari.com
626 575 2759 Fax : 626 575 3629

Products *Private label sweater manufacturer.*
Price Points *Moderate to designer.*
Production *U.S.A. & import*
Sell To *Department stores, specialty stores, boutiques.*
Private Label *Yes*
Web Site *www.andari.com*
Rev. in mil. *2-10*
Contact *Owner: Lillian Wang*

AUTUMN CASHMERE INC.

231 West 39th Street, Suite#1111
New York, NY 10018 info@autumncashmere.com
888 6 AUTUMN Fax : 212 398 2255 1 888 6 AUTUMN

Labels *Autumn Cashmere*
Products *Fashion & novelty 100% cashmere & cashmere blend sweaters. 2 to 20 gauge knits.*
Price Points *Better to designer.*
Production *China & Hong Kong*
Showrooms *New York/Aci NY, 212-398-2244, CA/Sales: 213-893-6995.*
Sell To *Department & specialty stores, boutiques & mail order catalogues.*
Private Label *Yes*
Web Site *www.autumncashmere.com*
Rev. in mil. *11-50*

BARRAZA ASSOCIATES LTD

225 West 35th Street, Suite 1502
New York, NY 10001 barrazany@aol.com
212 564 6583

Products *Private label sportswear & dresses.*
Price Points *Moderate to better.*
Production *U.S.A. & import.*
Sell To *Department stores, specialty stores, boutiques, mail order catalogues.*
Private Label *Yes*
Web Site *www.barrazastyle.com*
Rev. in mil. *2-10*
Contact *President: Maria Barraza, Sales & Marketing: Rafael Romero*

CALIFORNIA RAIN CO.

1213 E. 14th Street
Los Angeles, CA 90021 info@californiarainla.com
213 623 6061 Fax : 213 627 5703

Products *Form fitting fashion blank knit apparel. Missy & junior shirts, sweatshirts & novelty shirts.*
Price Points *Better*
Production *U.S.A.*
Sell To *Department stores*
Corp. Office *Above*
Private Label *Yes*
Web Site *www.californiarainla.com*

RN Number *75443*
Rev. in mil. *11-50*
Contact *President: Jack Chang*

CARRIEAMBER INTIMATES

9401 Whitmore Street
El Monte, CA 91731 sales@carrieamber.com
626 371 1980 Fax : 626 288 2670 800 870 8680

Labels *Seven 'til Midnight, Spreegirl, Flex, Rockalicious, Carrie Amber,*
Products *Manufacturer of intimate apparel. Innovative colors, styles, prints and fabrics.*
Sell To *Department stores, specialty stores*
Private Label *Yes*
Web Site *www.carrieamber.com*

CHATHAM KNITTING MILLS, INC.

119 S. Main Street, PO Box 152
Chatham, VA 24531 mattharris2006@gmail.com
434 432 4701 Fax : 434 432 3742

Products *Windbreaker jackets, work coats, jumpsuits, elastic waist pants, prison clothing*
Price Points *Off-price*
Production *U.S.A.*
Sell To *Off-price & institutional.*
Private Label *Yes*
RN Number *WPL10668*
Contact *President: Matt Harris*

COTTON HERITAGE

6393 E. Washington Blvd.
Commerce, CA 90040 mickey@cottonheritage.com
323 722 5592 Fax : 323 724 0045

Labels *Cotton Heritage*
Products *Women's blank t-shirts, polo's, fleece, outerwear, active and denim wear & jogging sets.*
Price Points *Competitive*
Production *Import*
Showrooms *City of Commerce, CA., Clifton, New Jersey 973-249-5081, Miami, FL. 305-623-1947.*
Sell To *Screenprinters, Embroiders, Resort & Promotional & licensed companies, retailers & discount*
Private Label *Yes*
Web Site *www.cottonheritage.com*
RN Number *75813*
Contact *Vice President: Mickey Sachdeva*

GRUVEN INTERNATIONAL INC.

19 Newgale Gate
Ontario, Canada M1X 5B6 sales@gruven.com
416 292 7331 Fax : 416 754 8675

Products *Activewear, sportswear & outerwear in knit & woven styles.*
Price Points *Moderate to better.*
Production *Canada & Shanghai, China*
Showrooms *Toronto*
Sell To *Specialty stores & boutiques.*
Private Label *Yes*

Web Site *www.gruven.com*

IN STYLE USA, INC. *(Rep.)

307 West 36th Street, 2nd Floor
New York, NY 10018 pauline.lock@instyleusa.net
212 631 0278 Fax : 212 631 0279

Products *Athleticwear, sportswear, dresses, jeans, uniforms and more.*
Price Points *Better to designer.*
Production *U.S.A. & China*
Showrooms *Above*
Sell To *Department stores, specialty stores & boutiques.*
Corp. Office *Above*
Private Label *Yes*
Web Site *www.instyleusa.net*
Rev. in mil. *2-10*
Contact *President: James Mallon*

IN.STYLE EXCHANGE™

1844 W. Division Street, Suite 201
Arlington, TX 76012 info@instyleexchange.com
817 886 9222 Fax : 928 447 3168

Products *Ready-to-wear trendy designs for private label orders.*
Price Points *Competitive to moderate*
Production *U.S.A.*
Sell To *Department stores, specialty stores, boutiques, screenprinters, embroiderers.*
Corp. Office *Arlington, Texas*
Private Label *Yes*
Web Site *www.instyleexchange.com*
Contact *Sales: Jenny Siede*

JULIE HUTTON INC.

140 East 28th Street, Suite 5K
New York, NY 10016 julie@juliehuttoninc.com
212 532 5126

Labels *Emerson Fry, jj threads, Sassy Cyclist, Lorraine Claire, Ashton Bradley, The Essence, House*
Products *Design & sourcing for private & personal label sportswear*
Price Points *Better*
Production *Factories in New York City, China and Turkey*
Showrooms *New York*
Sell To *Specialty stores*
Private Label *Yes*
Web Site *www.juliehuttoninc.com*
RN Number *134008432*
Rev. in mil. *2-10*
Contact *Owner: Julie Hutton*

LEAWOOD APPAREL LLC.

PO Box 55
Flourtown, PA 19031 leawoodapparel@hotmail.com
215 233 1973

Products *Women's private label sweaters and knitwear.*

Price Points *Moderate to better.*
Production *Domestic & Caribbean Basin*
Corp. Office *8900 Carlisle Road, Wyndmoor, PA 19038-7412.*
Private Label *Yes*
Web Site *www.leawoodapparel.vpweb.com*
Contact
President/Owner: Allan Flickstein

MIAMI STYLE INC.

7480 NW 52nd Street
Miami, FL 33166
customercare@miamistyle.com
305 805 1168 Fax : 305 805 0075

Labels *Miami Style*
Products *Manufacturer of active/athletic wear, tee shirts, junior sportswear, swimwear & beachwear.*
Price Points *Moderate*
Production *Bangladesh and China*
Sell To *Department stores, specialty stores, boutiques, mass merchants*
Private Label *Yes*
Web Site *www.miamistylebsd.com*
Contact *Owner: Amnon Bensimon, General Manager: Sofia Rincon*

MISTER NOAH

1407 Broadway, Suite 707
New York, NY 10018
noah@mrnoah.com
212 354 1700 Fax : 212 354 1740

Products *Fashion activewear, sportswear, knit bottoms & sweaters. Also plus sizes.*
Price Points *Moderate*
Production *Import*
Showrooms *New York*
Sell To *Department stores, mass merchants, mail order catalogues & off-price.*
Corp. Office *1824 Byberry Road, Bensalem, Pa. 19020 tel: 215-639-9300*
Web Site *www.feathersgirl.com*
RN Number *RN50110*
Rev. in mil. *11-50*
Contact *Presidents: Bruce Feinberg/Robert Feinberg*

ROYAL APPAREL, INC.

65 Commerce Drive
Hauppauge, NY 11788
sales@royalapparel.net
631 213 8299 Fax : 631 922 8438 866-Royal-1-S

Labels *Royal Apparel*
Products *Basic & fashion forward blanks in a large selection of colors & knit fabrications.*
Price Points *Moderate to better.*
Production *U.S.A.*
Showrooms *New York & Allentown, Pa.*
Sell To *Mass merchants, branded labels, screen printers & department stores.*
Private Label *Yes*
Web Site *www.royalapparel.net*
Contact *President: Morey Mayeri, Owners: Morey Mayeri/Abraham Mayeri*

SISTERS/DIVISION OF FREDINI INC

945 E. 12th Street, Suite A
Los Angeles, CA 90021 customerservice@sistersknit.com
213 955 8000 Fax : 213 955 8005

Labels *Sisters*
Products *Women's private label contemporary apparel, blouses, shirts, knitwear & sweaters.*
Price Points *Better to bridge*
Production *U.S.A. & Import*
Showrooms *New York, Atlanta, Chicago*
Sell To *Department stores, specialty stores & mail order catalogues.*
Private Label *Yes*
Web Site *www.sistersknit.com*
RN Number *RN84332*
Rev. in mil. *2-10*
Contact *President & Owner: Fred Eslamboly, Sales: Fred Eslamboly, Design: Nancy Eslamboly*

STYLE SOURCE INC.

913 Orange Street
Wilmington, NC 28401 geoff@style-source.com
910 399 2288 Fax : 910 399 2289

Labels *Henry Lehr, Mainland Co., Crazy Shirts Hawaii, Motherwear, Garnet Hill*
Products *Product development specialists of cotton knit tops and sportswear and all fabric types.*
Price Points *Moderate to better.*
Production *U.S.A.*
Sell To *Specialty stores, boutiques, mail order catalogues, screenprinters and embroiderers.*
Web Site *www.style-source.com*
RN Number *RN82034*
Contact *President: Geoffrey Krasnov*

STYLEX TEXTILE DBA FABKA FABRICS LLC

2833 Leonis Avenue, Suite 104
Vernon, CA 90058 sharona@fabkafabrics.com
323 588 3000 Fax : 323 588 3636

Products *Basic & fashion forward tee shirts made according to customers designs. Full package.*
Price Points *Budget to better.*
Production *U.S.A.*
Sell To *Specialty stores, boutiques, department stores, mass merchants*
Web Site *www.fabkafabrics.com*
Contact *Sharona Kahen (Cell: 310-991-0366)*

VALENTINE USA

135 West 36th Street, 14th Floor
New York, NY 10018 mng@valentine-usa.com
212 719 3160 Fax : 212 840 8841

Labels *Valentine*
Products *Large size womens apparel for all aspects of life.*
Price Points *Moderate*
Production *U.S.A. & import.*
Showrooms *New York*
Sell To *Department stores, specialty stores, mail order catalogues & mass merchants.*

Private Label *Yes*
RN Number *RN75182, RN64604, RN86643*
Contact *President: Mona Ng*

VICTOR ROSSI

11016 Nacirema Lane
Stevenson, MD 21153
410 337 2714
vr@victorrossi.com

Products *Prival label in bridal, special occasion, eveningwear, cotton garments, sportswear, bags.*
Price Points *Moderate to Designer*
Production *Domestic & Import*
Sell To *Department stores, specialty stores, mail order catalogs, designers & wholesalers.*
Corp. Office *Above*
Private Label *Yes*
Web Site *www.victorrossi.com*
RN Number *102005*
Contact *Manish Singh*

VISHAL ENTERPRISES

226 West 37th Street, 7th Floor
New York, NY 10018
212 629 0880 Fax : 212 629 0882
vishal@vishalent.com

Products *Athleticwear, sportswear, dresses, blouses, skirts, suits, knitwear, tee shirts and denimwear.*
Price Points *Better*
Production *Import*
Sell To *Department stores, boutiques, mail order catalogues*
Private Label *Yes*
Rev. in mil. *2-10*
Contact *Owner: Mahesh Moorjani, Sales: Vishal Moorjani*

BEDHEAD PAJAMAS

3641 10th Avenue
Los Angeles, CA 90018
323 634 0333 Fax : 323 634 0433
joanne@bedheadpjs.com

Labels *Bedhead*
Products *100% original prints on fine cotton sleepwear & intimate apparel. Missy & plus sizes.*
Price Points *Better*
Production *U.S.A.*
Sell To *Department stores, specialty stores, boutiques, mail order catalogues, e-com retailers.*
Corp. Office *Above*
Private Label *Yes*
Web Site *www.bedheadpajamas.com*
Contact *President: Renee Claire, VP Sales: JoAnne Grazzini*

CAPELLI NEW YORK

1 East 33rd Street, 9th Floor
New York, NY 10016
212 684 3344 Fax : 212 686 4895
info@capellinewyork.com

Labels *Capelli New York*
Products *Sleepwear, robes and slippers for women.*
Production *Import*
Showrooms *New York, Canada, Europe and Asia*
Sell To *Department stores, specialty stores, national chain stores*
Private Label *Yes*
Web Site *www.capellinewyork.com*

CHRISTINE VANCOUVER

821 Powell Street
Vancouver, B. C., Canada V6A 1H7
604 253 0350 Fax : 604 253 0351 888 922 0355
kim@christinevancouver.com

Labels *Christine Vancouver*
Products *Loungewear, sleepwear, daywear, trousseau & robes in silk, cotton, lace & linen.*
Price Points *Designer*
Production *Canada*
Showrooms *Dallas/Rita Harris, Tel: 214 905 2006, Toronto/Dee Dee Crosland 416-849-7943*
Sell To *Department stores, specialty stores, boutiques & mail order catlogues.*
Private Label *Yes*
Web Site *www.christinevancouver.com*
Rev. in mil. *2-10*
Contact *President: Christine Morton, Sales: Erin Williams, Design: Christine Morton*

EDWARD CROMARTY ART DESIGN STUDIO *(Rep.)

228 East Route 59, #281
Nanuet, NY 10954
914 288 5171 877 447 2741
edwardcromarty@gmail.com

Labels *Edward Cromarty*
Products *Women's sleepwear, bridal sleepwear & accessories.*
Price Points *High end, designer, reasonable designer pricing.*
Production *U.S.A.*
Showrooms *Please call for an appointment*
Sell To *Department stores, boutiques & specialty stores.*

Private Label *Yes*
Web Site *www.edwardcromarty.com*
RN Number *RN101294*
Rev. in mil. *0-2*
Contact *President & Owner: Edward Cromarty*

GAIAM

833 W South Boulder Road, PO Box 3095
Boulder, CO 80307 customerservice@gaiam.com
303 222 3600 Fax : 303 222 3700 877 989 6321

Labels *Gaiam*
Products *Enviromentally responsible nightwear, loungewear & robes in organic cotton.*
Price Points *Moderate to better.*
Production *U.S.A.*
Sell To *Specialty stores, boutiques & mail order catalogues.*
Web Site *www.gaiam.com*
Contact *President: Lynn Powers*

MANSFIELD INTERNATIONAL *(Rep.)

55 Louvain West, Suite 498
Montreal, Quebec, Canada H4N1A4 p.salhany@kayanna.com
514 274 2407 Fax : 514 274 5697

Labels *KayAnna, Kayanna Spa, Mansfield Hotel and Spa.*
Products *Ladies robes, SPA bathrobes, sleepwear, loungewear.*
Price Points *Moderate to better*
Production *Asia*
Showrooms *Rep: Dallas, Texas: David Willingham 214-577-5116*
Sell To *Department stores, specialty stores, catalogs*
Private Label *Yes*
Web Site *www.kayanna.com*
Rev. in mil. *2-10*
Contact *Sales: Paul Salhany (cell: 514-583-5242).*

PHOOL FASHIONS

241 West 37th Street, Suite 518
New York, NY 10018 phoolfash@aol.com
212 944 0910 Fax : 212 944 0286

Labels *Phool*
Products *Missy, junior & women's updated loungewear.*
Price Points *Moderate*
Production *Import*
Showrooms *New York*
Sell To *Specialty stores, boutiques, mail order catalogues & chain stores.*
Private Label *Yes*
Web Site *www.phoolfashionusa.com*
RN Number *RN80911*
Rev. in mil. *2-10*
Contact *Owner/Sales: Reena Paintal*

RICHARD LEEDS INTERNATIONAL

135 Madison Avenue, 10th Floor
New York, NY 10016 lisa@richardleeds.com
212 532 4546 Fax : 212 683 8571

Labels *French Jenny*
Products *Missy & junior contemporary sleepwear, loungewear & intimate apparel in novelty cottons.*
Price Points *Moderate*
Production *U.S.A. & import.*
Sell To *Department & specialty stores, boutiques & mail order catalogues.*
Private Label *Yes*
Web Site *www.richardleeds.com*
Contact *NY Sales: Lisa Lauricella, Licensing: Rick (rick@richardleeds.com)*

SUSAN DUNN INC.

PO Box 1086
Rancho Santa Fe, CA 92067 susan@susandunn.com
858 832 1086 Fax : 858 832 1087

Labels *Susan Dunn®, Spa Slippurrs™, Spa Sox, Spa Wear*
Products *100% cotton robes, loungewear, spa slippers and socks. Specialize in embroideries.*
Price Points *Designer*
Production *U.S.A.*
Sell To *Specialty stores, boutiques, mail order catalogues, hotels, resorts & spas.*
Private Label *Yes*
Web Site *www.susandunn.com*
RN Number *RN90990*
Rev. in mil. *2-10*
Contact *CEO & President: Susan Dunn*

VENUS FASHION

11711 Marco Beach Drive
Jacksonville, FL 32224 email@venus.com
904 997 4000 Fax : 904 641 0977 888 782 2224

Labels *Winter Silk*
Products *Sleep shirts, pajama sets, long Johns & loungewear.*
Price Points *Moderate to better.*
Production *U.S.A.*
Showrooms *Jacksonville, FL/above.*
Sell To *Specialty stores & boutiques.*
Private Label *No*
Web Site *www.venus.com*
Contact *President and CEO: Jim Brewster*

Notes

ATOPAPPAREL CORP

214 West 39th Street, Suite 604A
New York, NY 10018 info@atopapparel.com
212 221 7685 Fax : 212 221 7587

Labels *Emil Rutenberg, People Like Frank*
Products *Ladies dresses & tops in junior, missy and plus sizes.*
Price Points *Below wholesale prices*
Production *Import*
Showrooms *Same as Above*
Sell To *Department stores, specialty stores, boutiques*
Corp. Office *Same as Above*
Private Label *Yes*
Web Site *www.emilrutenberg.com*
Contact *Customer Service: Amy (347-688-8781)*

B.C.T.C.

3322 South Garfield Avenue
Commerce, CA 90040 edward.hu@bctcapparel.com
323 888 9388

Labels *BCTC*
Products *Women's active sportswear tops & bottoms.*
Price Points *Budget, moderate & better.*
Production *U.S.A. & import*
Showrooms *Los Angeles*
Sell To *Department stores, mass merchants.*
Private Label *Yes*
RN Number *RN69587*
Contact *President and Owner: Even Chew*

BOULEVARD APPAREL

2707 South Alameda Street
Los Angeles, CA 90058 sales@blvapparel.com
213 614 1800 Fax : 213 614 1815 866-967-5919

Products *Denim, jeans, tops, bottoms, activewear plus intimates*
Price Points *Budget to designer*
Production *U.S.A & import*
Sell To *Department stores, specialty stores, boutiques, mass merchants, mail order catalogues.*
Private Label *Yes*
Web Site *www.blvapparel.com*
RN Number *111159*
Rev. in mil. *2-10*
Contact *President & Owner: Eugene Kaplan*

CHRISTINE VANCOUVER

821 Powell Street
Vancouver, B. C., Canada V6A 1H7 kim@christinevancouver.com
604 253 0350 Fax : 604 253 0351 888 922 0355

Labels *Christine Vancouver*
Products *Lingerie, loungewear, sleepwear, daywear, trousseau & robes in luxurious fabrics.*
Price Points *Designer*
Production *Canada*

Showrooms *Dallas/Rita Harris, Tel: 214 905 2006, Toronto/Dee Dee Crosland 416-849-7943*
Sell To *Department stores, specialty stores, boutiques & mail order catlogues.*
Private Label *Yes*
Web Site *www.christinevancouver.com*
Rev. in mil. *2-10*
Contact *President: Christine Morton, Sales: Erin Williams, Design: Christine Morton*

CHRISTOPHER & BANKS CORPORATION

2400 Xenium Lane North
Plymouth, MN 55441 info@christopherandbanks.com
763 551 5000 Fax : 763 551 5198 800 890 9601

Labels *C.J. Banks*
Products *Tops, blouses, pants & skirts for work and leisure in womens sizes 14 and up.*
Price Points *Moderate*
Production *Import*
Sell To *Department stores, specialty stores*
Private Label *Yes*
Web Site *www.christopherandbanks.com*

DANA EMILIA PRESENTS *(Rep.)

264 West 40th, Suite 503
New York, NY 10018 fashion@danaemilia.com
212 391 4104 Fax : 212 391 4153

Labels *Christopher Calvin, Redwood Court, Peacock Ways, Swish, Vanite Couture, Banaris*
Products *Casual to dressy separates in novelty fabrics. Soft separates with versatility.*
Price Points *Better*
Production *U.S.A. & import.*
Showrooms *New York.*
Sell To *Specialty stores, boutiques, chain stores & mail order catalogues.*
Private Label *Yes*
Web Site *www.danaemiliapresents.com*
Contact *President: Dana Harrison*

DEPECHE MODE

230 West 38th Street, 12th Floor
New York, NY 10018 leer@depecheco.com
212 643 6633 Fax : 212 643 1184

Labels *Depeche Mode, Studio*
Products *Day, lunch & dinner dresses & suits.*
Price Points *Better to bridge, plus off-price.*
Production *U.S.A. & import*
Showrooms *New York.*
Sell To *Department & specialty stores, boutiques, mass merchants, catalogues, chains & off-price.*
Private Label *Yes*
Web Site *www.depecheco.com*
RN Number *RN61812*
Contact *President: Lee Rosenthal, Sales: Joy Villa (joyv@depecheco.com)*

ESSEX MANUFACTURING INC.

350 Fifth Avenue, Suite 2400
New York, NY 10118
bbaum@baum-essex.com
212 239 0080 Fax : 212 714 2958 800 648 6010

Labels *Misty Harbor®, CLC*
Products *Large & tall rainwear, specialize in PVC slickers, raincoats & nylon packaway jackets.*
Production *Import*
Showrooms *Chicago, Boston, Cleveland, Philadelphia, San Francisco & New York.*
Sell To *Department stores, specialty stores, mass merchants & mail order catalogues.*
Private Label *Yes*
Web Site *www.baum-essex.com*
Contact *Rainwear & Outerwear: Bill Baum, Umbrellas: Lance Lovett - llovett@baum-essex.com*

J RICHARDS INTERNATIONAL

437 Mamaroneck Avenue
Mamaroneck, NY 10543
richard@jrichardsintl.com
212 819 0444 Fax : 212 819 0587

Labels *J Richards*
Products *Coats, jackets, rainwear in cashmere, lambswool, coated & novelty fabrics. Fur & leather tri*
Price Points *Better, bridge & off-price.*
Production *U.S.A.*
Sell To *Specialty stores, boutiques, department stores.*
Private Label *Yes*
Web Site *www.jrichardsintl.com*
Contact *Designer: Jheri Richards*

JONDEN MANUFACTURING CO., INC.

1410 Broadway, Suite 1103
New York, NY 10018
tsmith@jonden.com
212 730 1741 Fax : 212 730 1742

Labels *Jonden*
Products *Plus size knit tops & related separates.*
Price Points *Moderate*
Production *U.S.A.*
Showrooms *New York/above*
Sell To *Department stores, specialty stores, mass merchants, mail order catalogues & off-price.*
Private Label *Yes*
Web Site *www.jonden.com*
RN Number *RN85224*

LE MIEUX/TARA INTERNATIONAL, INC.

242 Gemini Avenue
Brea, CA 92821
sweta.lmstudio@gmail.com
562 694 6860 Fax : 562 694 6875 877 962 9525

Labels *Le Mieux*
Products *Casual skirts, tops, dresses, 2-piece sets, pants & tees. Large & tall sizes.*
Price Points *Moderate*
Production *U.S.A. & import*
Showrooms *Los Angeles & Texas.*
Sell To *Department, specialty & off-price stores, boutiques, mass merchants & mail order.*
Private Label *Yes*

Web Site *www.lemieux.com*
Contact *President and Owner: Shekhar Agrawal*

LONGITUDE/LONGEVITY BRANDS LLC

250 West 39th Street, 4th Floor
New York, NY 10018 service@longitudeswim.com
212 231 7877 866 315 6555

Labels *Longitude*
Products *Swimwear & cover-ups in large & tall sizes.*
Price Points *Moderate*
Production *U.S.A. & import.*
Sell To *Department stores, specialty stores, mass merchants & mail order catalogues.*
Private Label *Yes*
Web Site *www.longitudeswim.com*
RN Number *WPL08910*
Contact *Sales: Marty Mann (mmann50@verizon.net)*
VP of Merchandising: Brian Epstein (bepstein@swimusa.com)

PENDLETON WOOLEN MILLS, INC.

220 Northwest Broadway
Portland, OR 97209 pendletoncatalog@penwool.com
503 226 4801 Fax : 503 535 5599 800 522 9665

Labels *Pendleton*
Products *Missy and plus size sportswear, outerwear, jackets, westernwear & accessories.*
Price Points *Better*
Production *U.S.A. & import*
Sell To *Specialty stores & mail order catalogues.*
Private Label *No*
Web Site *www.pendleton-usa.com*
RN Number *RN29685, WPL04378*
Rev. in mil. *+500*

PERSONAL TOUCH INC.

23 Commercial Waye
Hanson, MA 02341 info@personaltouchinc.com
781 447 0467 Fax : 781 447 5172 1 888 447 0496

Labels *Personal Touch*
Products *Casual sportswear & career wear for missy & large sizes.*
Price Points *Moderate*
Production *U.S.A.*
Showrooms *New York/above*
Sell To *Department stores, speciality stores & mail order catalogues.*
Private Label *Yes*
Web Site *www.apersonaltouchinc.com*
RN Number *RN60666*
Contact *President: Richard May*

RAGO FOUNDATIONS LLC

18-15 27th Avenue
Long Island City, NY 11102 justin@ragoshapewear.com
718 728 8436 Fax : 718 728 8465 800 982 1113

Labels *Rago, Shapette, Lacette, Special Attention*
Products *Shapewear garments for todays woman in regular & special sizes*
Price Points *Moderate, better*
Production *U.S.A.*
Showrooms *New York/183 Madison Ave., New York, N.Y. 10001 plus reps in LA, Dallas, Atlanta, France, Germany & Japan.*
Sell To *Department stores, specialty stores, boutiques, mail order catalogues*
Private Label *Yes*
Web Site *www.ragoshapewear.com*
Rev. in mil. *11-50*
Contact *President: Justin Chernoff, Marketing: Steve Chernoff*

ROBBIE BEE

1412 Broadway, 8th Floor
New York, NY 10018 rlong@robbiebee.com
212 944 0255 Fax : 212 719 0009

Labels *Robbie Bee*
Products *Casual & dressy dresses in missy and plus sizes.*
Price Points *Moderate.*
Production *U.S.A., Hong Kong, China.*
Showrooms *New York*
Sell To *Department stores, specialty stores, mail order catalogues & off-price.*
Private Label *Yes*
RN Number *RN98582*
Contact *Owner: Maia Chiat*

ROYAL APPAREL, INC.

65 Commerce Drive
Hauppauge, NY 11788 sales@royalapparel.net
631 213 8299 Fax : 631 922 8438 866-Royal-1-S

Labels *Royal Apparel*
Products *Basic & fashion forward blanks, active/athleticwear in a large selection of colors & knit fabr.*
Price Points *Moderate to better.*
Production *U.S.A.*
Showrooms *New York & Allentown, Pa.*
Sell To *Mass merchants, branded labels, screen printers & department stores.*
Private Label *Yes*
Web Site *www.royalapparel.net*
Contact *President: Morey Mayeri, Owners: Morey Mayeri/Abraham Mayeri*

SOPHIE FINZI LTD DBA PASHOOT

255 West 36th Street, Suite 201
New York, NY 10018 sophiefinziltd@aol.com
212 967 4349 Fax : 212 967 5361

Labels *Pashoot, Sophie*
Products *Better sportswear with a European look. Regular & large sizes.*
Price Points *Better*

Showrooms *Chicago/Julie Kipta 219-762-1442, California/Peggy Finnegan 707-778-1592*
Sell To *Specialty stores & boutiques.*
Private Label *No*
Web Site *www.sophiefinzi.com*
Contact *President and Designer: Sophie Finzi*

STANFIELD'S

1 Logan Street, PO Box 190
Truro, Nova Scotia, Canada B2N 5C2 inquiries@stanfields.com
902 895 5406 Fax : 902 893 8187 855-895-5406

Products *Intimate apparel, underwear, bodywear in sizes up to 20-22.*
Price Points *Moderate*
Production *Canada*
Showrooms *Sales Office: 40 University Avenue, Toronto, Ontario Canada M5J 1T1 (416) 598-8086.*
Sell To *Department stores, specialty stores, boutiques & mail order catalogues.*
Private Label *No*
Web Site *www.stanfields.com*

TERI JON

241 West 37th Street, 2nd Floor
New York, NY 10018 sales@terijon.com
212 398 0480 Fax : 212 302 2726

Labels *Rickie Freeman for Teri Jon*
Products *Evening dresses & suits in plus sizes.*
Price Points *Bridge to designer*
Production *U.S.A.*
Showrooms *New York/above, Dallas/214-637-6962*
Sell To *Department stores, boutiques & specialty stores.*
Private Label *Yes*
Web Site *www.terijon.com*
Contact *President: Rickie Freeman*

TOM AND LINDA PLATT

55 West 39th Street, 17th Floor
New York, NY 10018 info@tomandlindaplatt.com
212 764 1210 Fax : 212 719 1213

Labels *Tom and Linda Platt, Tom and Linda Platt Custom*
Products *Day, cocktail, evening dresses and separates in plus sizes.*
Price Points *Designer*
Production *U.S.A.*
Showrooms *New York*
Sell To *Department stores, specialty stores, and private clients.*
Private Label *Yes*
Web Site *www.tomandlindaplatt.com*
Contact *Owners/Designers: Tom and Linda Platt*

VALENTINE USA

135 West 36th Street, 14th Floor
New York, NY 10018 mng@valentine-usa.com
212 719 3160 Fax : 212 840 8841

Labels *Valentine*

Products *Large size womens apparel for all aspects of life.*
Price Points *Moderate*
Production *U.S.A. & import.*
Showrooms *New York*
Sell To *Department stores, specialty stores, mail order catalogues & mass merchants.*
Private Label *Yes*
RN Number *RN75182, RN64604, RN86643*
Contact *President: Mona Ng*

WE BE BOP, INC

448 25th Street, #B
Oakland, CA 94612
510 452 3267
info@webebopinc.com

Labels *We Be Bop*
Products *Fun, chic and classy styles of tops, bottoms, dresses and jackets in sizes 0X-6X.*
Price Points *Better*
Sell To *Department stores, specialty stores, boutiques*
Private Label *Yes*
Web Site *www.webebopinc.com*
Contact *Wholesale orders: Carlos Martinez (carloswebebop@aol.com)*

A PEA IN THE POD

232 Strawbridge Drive
Moorestown, NJ 08057 vendorrelations@destinationmaternity.com
856 291 9700 800 291 7800

Labels *A Pea in the Pod*
Products *Maternity redefined. Sportswear, swim wear, intimate apparel, denim, dresses & knit pieces.*
Price Points *Better*
Sell To *Department stores, boutiques, on-line*
Web Site *www.apeainthepod.com*
Contact *Gail Flesher*

BELLA MATERNA INC.

2000 Westlake Avenue N, Suite 100
Seattle, WA 98109 sales@bellamaterna.com
206 286 8108 Fax : 206 286 2267 888-700-8438

Labels *Bella Materna*
Products *Maternity and nursing bras, camisoles, sleepwear, transition, workout and loungewear.*
Price Points *Contemporary*
Production *U.S.A. and import*
Showrooms *West Coast Maternity (LA Mart), Mama Sooze (Chicago Mart), Hip Mama Sales (Canada).*
Sell To *Department stores, specialty stores, boutiques.*
Web Site *www.bellamaterna.com*
Contact *Sales: Anne Dimond*

JONDEN MANUFACTURING CO., INC.

1410 Broadway, Suite 1103
New York, NY 10018 tsmith@jonden.com
212 730 1741 Fax : 212 730 1742

Labels *Jonden*
Products *Knit tops & related separates.*
Price Points *Moderate*
Production *U.S.A.*
Showrooms *New York/above*
Sell To *Department stores, specialty stores, mass merchants, mail order catalogues & off-price.*
Private Label *Yes*
Web Site *www.jonden.com*
RN Number *RN85224*

ANN TAYLOR

4079 Executive Parkway
Westerville, OH 43081 clientservices@anntaylor.com
800 342 5266 Fax : 866 232 9266 800 342 5266

Labels *Ann Taylor*
Products *Multi-faceted career, casual & dressy collection.*
Price Points *Better*
Production *Import worldwide*
Sell To *Company owned retail stores only.*
Corp. Office *7 Times Square, New York, NY 10036*
Web Site *www.anntaylor.com*

B.C.T.C.

3322 South Garfield Avenue
Commerce, CA 90040 edward.hu@bctcapparel.com
323 888 9388

Labels *BCTC*
Products *Women's active sportswear tops & bottoms.*
Price Points *Budget, moderate & better.*
Production *U.S.A. & import*
Showrooms *Los Angeles*
Sell To *Department stores, mass merchants.*
Private Label *Yes*
RN Number *RN69587*
Contact *President and Owner: Even Chew*

BLUESUITS

200 West 70th Street, Suite 14G
New York, NY 10023 jamak@off7th.com
212 787 0278

Labels *Bluesuits*
Products *Women's business attire including suits, jackets, pants, skirts & dresses in sizes petite 0 to 22.*
Price Points *Designer*
Production *U.S.A.*
Sell To *Department stores & boutiques*
Private Label *Yes*
Web Site *www.bluesuitsonline.com*
Contact *Designer: Jamak Khazra*

CALVIN KLEIN, INC.

205 West 39th Street, 12th Floor
New York, NY 10018 calvinkleincustomerservice@pvh.com
212 719 2600 Fax : 212 292 9131 866-513-0513

Labels *Calvin Klein Petite*
Products *Tops, bottoms, jeans & dresses in petite sizes.*
Price Points *Moderate to better*
Showrooms *New York*
Sell To *Department stores & specialty stores.*
Web Site *www.calvinklein.com*
RN Number *RN54718*

CHRISTINE VANCOUVER

821 Powell Street
Vancouver, B. C., Canada V6A 1H7 kim@christinevancouver.com
604 253 0350 Fax : 604 253 0351 888 922 0355

Labels *Christine Vancouver*
Products *Lingerie, loungewear, sleepwear, daywear, trousseau & robes in luxurious fabrics.*
Price Points *Designer*
Production *Canada*
Showrooms *Dallas/Rita Harris, Tel: 214 905 2006, Toronto/Dee Dee Crosland 416-849-7943*
Sell To *Department stores, specialty stores, boutiques & mail order catlogues*
Private Label *Yes*
Web Site *www.christinevancouver.com*
Rev. in mil. *2-10*
Contact *President: Christine Morton, Sales: Erin Williams, Design: Christine Morton*

DEPECHE MODE

230 West 38th Street, 12th Floor
New York, NY 10018 leer@depecheco.com
212 643 6633 Fax : 212 643 1184

Labels *Depeche Mode, Studio*
Products *Day, lunch & dinner dresses & suits.*
Price Points *Better to bridge, plus off-price.*
Production *U.S.A. & import*
Showrooms *New York.*
Sell To *Department & specialty stores, boutiques, mass merchants, catalogues, chains & off-price.*
Private Label *Yes*
Web Site *www.depecheco.com*
RN Number *RN61812*
Contact *President: Lee Rosenthal, Sales: Joy Villa (joyv@depecheco.com)l*

ESSEX MANUFACTURING INC.

350 Fifth Avenue, Suite 2400
New York, NY 10118 bbaum@baum-essex.com
212 239 0080 Fax : 212 714 2958 800 648 6010

Labels *Misty Harbor®, CLC*
Products *Petite rainwear, specialize in PVC slickers, raincoats & nylon packaway jackets.*
Production *Import*
Showrooms *Chicago, Boston, Cleveland, Philadelphia, San Francisco & New York.*
Sell To *Department stores, specialty stores, mass merchants & mail order catalogues.*
Private Label *Yes*
Web Site *www.baum-essex.com*
Contact *Rainwear & Outerwear: Bill Baum, Umbrellas: Lance Lovett - llovett@baum-essex.com*

JONDEN MANUFACTURING CO., INC.

1410 Broadway, Suite 1103
New York, NY 10018 tsmith@jonden.com
212 730 1741 Fax : 212 730 1742

Labels *Jonden*
Products *Petite size knit tops & related separates.*
Price Points *Moderate*
Production *U.S.A.*

Showrooms *New York/above*
Sell To *Department stores, specialty stores, mass merchants, mail order catalogues & off-price.*
Private Label *Yes*
Web Site *www.jonden.com*
RN Number *RN85224*

LE MIEUX/TARA INTERNATIONAL, INC.

242 Gemini Avenue
Brea, CA 92821
562 694 6860 Fax : 562 694 6875 877 962 9525
sweta.lmstudio@gmail.com

Labels *Le Mieux*
Products *Casual skirts, tops, dresses, 2-piece sets, pants & tees. Petite sizes.*
Price Points *Moderate*
Production *U.S.A. & import*
Showrooms *Los Angeles & Texas.*
Sell To *Department, specialty & off-price stores, boutiques, mass merchants & mail order.*
Private Label *Yes*
Web Site *www.lemieux.com*
Contact *President and Owner: Shekhar Agrawal*

525 AMERICA

525 Seventh Avenue, 10th Floor
New York, NY 10018 mbock@525america.com
212 921 5688 Fax : 212 921 5069 877-246-8609

Labels *525 Womens*
Products *Contemporary knitwear. Luxury yarns including chenilles, boucles & wools.*
Price Points *Better*
Production *U.S.A.*
Showrooms *New York & reps throughout the U.S.*
Sell To *Department stores, specialty stores & mail order catalogues.*
Private Label *Yes*
Web Site *www.525america.com*
Contact *President: Robert Bock, Design: Robert Bock, VP Sales: Marianne Bock*

AIMAI CASHMERE

PO Box 395
Aspen, CO 81612 brian@aimaicashmere.com
970 618 3178 Fax : 970 925 1002

Products *Custom knitted garments plus cashmere garments.*
Price Points *All price points*
Production *Nepal*
Sell To *Department Stores*
Private Label *Yes*
Web Site *www.aimaicashmere.com*
Contact *Sales: Brian Harris*

ANDARI FASHION, INC.

9626 Telstar Avenue
El Monte, CA 91731 info@andari.com
626 575 2759 Fax : 626 575 3629

Products *Private label sweater manufacturer.*
Price Points *Moderate to designer.*
Production *U.S.A. & import*
Sell To *Department stores, specialty stores, boutiques.*
Private Label *Yes*
Web Site *www.andari.com*
Rev. in mil. *2-10*
Contact *Owner: Lillian Wang*

AUGUST SILK, INC.

499 Seventh Avenue, 5th Floor South
New York, NY 10018 francineshane@augustsilk.com
212 643 2400 Fax : 212 244 2155

Labels *August Silk*
Products *Cashmere sweater sets in silk/rayon/nylon, rayon/spandex, silk/bamboo, cotton/nylon.*
Price Points *Moderate*
Production *Import*
Showrooms *New York.*
Sell To *Department stores, specialty stores & boutiques.*
Private Label *Yes*
Contact *Sales: Francine Shane - 212-584-0466*

AUTUMN CASHMERE INC.

231 West 39th Street, Suite#1111
New York, NY 10018 info@autumncashmere.com
888 6 AUTUMN Fax : 212 398 2255 1 888 6 AUTUMN

Labels *Autumn Cashmere*
Products *Fashion & novelty 100% cashmere. 2 to 20 gauge knits.*
Price Points *Better to designer*
Production *China & Hong Kong*
Showrooms *New York/Aci NY, 212-398-2244, CA/Sales: 213-893-6995.*
Sell To *Department & specialty stores, boutiques & mail order catalogues.*
Private Label *Yes*
Web Site *www.autumncashmere.com*
Rev. in mil. *11-50*

B & B SWEATERS

1411 Broadway, Suite 2678
New York, NY 10018 bbsweater@aol.com
212 944 1335 Fax : 212 869 8489

Labels *Jenny, Maddi*
Products *Novelty sweaters & knit tops in missy & large sizes.*
Price Points *Moderate*
Production *Throughout Asia*
Showrooms *New York.*
Sell To *Department stores, specialty stores, boutiques & mass merchants.*
Private Label *Yes*
Contact *Sales: Ari Biderman*

BELLDINI

1428 South Maple Avenue
Los Angeles, CA 90015 info@belldini.com
213 748 4442 Fax : 213 748 3243

Labels *Belldini*
Products *Ladies sweaters & embellished knitwear.*
Price Points *Better*
Production *USA & import from China.*
Showrooms *552 7th Avenue, New York, NY 10018 - 212-302-2140*
Sell To *Department stores, specialty stores, boutiques.*
Corp. Office *Above*
Private Label *Yes*
Web Site *www.belldini.com*

BEREK

270 West 38 Street, 6th Floor
New York, NY 10018 gary@bereksweaters.com
212 575 8255 Fax : 212 354 7634 800-417-0040

Labels *Berek*
Products *"Art you can wear" ladies sweaters& jackets.*
Showrooms *Above*
Sell To *Department stores & specialty stores.*
Private Label *Yes*

Web Site *www.buyberek.com*
Contact *Head Designer: Jill Rogers, Wholesale Sales: Jack Zyman (jackzyman@gmail.com)*

BIBELOT

315 West 39th Street, Suite 1003
New York, NY 10018
212 563 0685 Fax : 212 563 0685
bibelotco@verizon.net

Labels *Bibelot*
Products *A collection of unique and fresh sweaters with a mixture of classicism & whimsey.*
Price Points *Better*
Showrooms *Susan Greenstadt: 215 West 40th Street, New York, NY 10018 tel: 212-302-0600, KLA/Karen Anderson: 127 East 9th Street, Los Angeles, Ca. 90015 tel: 213-622-7447.*
Sell To *Department stores, boutiques, specialty stores throughout the US.*
Web Site *www.bibelotnyc.com*

BLUE PLATE INC.

525 Seventh Avenue, Suite 309
New York, NY 10018
212 382 0069 Fax : 212 997 2413
bpshowroom@aol.com

Labels *Blue Plate*
Products *Sweaters and coordinates in junior and missy sizes.*
Price Points *Moderate*
Production *India*
Showrooms *New York*
Sell To *Department stores, specialty stores, boutiques and mass merchants.*
Private Label *Yes*
Web Site *www.blueplatefashion.com*
Contact *President & Owner: Shashi Anand, Incharge: Seema Anand*

CANADIAN SWEATER CO., LTD.

#39 8528-123rd Street
Surrey, BC, Canada V3W 3V6
604 594 8050 Fax : 604 594 8264
info@canadiansweater.com

Labels *Cowichan, Islander*
Products *Woolen sweaters & winter accessories.*
Price Points *Bridge*
Production *Canada*
Sell To *High end department stores, boutiques.*
Corp. Office *Above*
Private Label *Yes*
Web Site *www.canadiansweater.com*
Contact *President: Kaljit Tmana*

CASHMERE HOUSE

3001 South Croddy Way
Santa Ana, CA 92704
714 957 4000 Fax : 714 957 4004 800 522 2276
info@tse-us.com

Labels *TSE*
Products *Cashmere contemporary collection of separates & accessories*
Price Points *Better*
Showrooms *New York/120 Wooster Street, 2nd Floor, New York, N.Y. 10012, Tel: 800-522-2279.*

Sell To *Specialty stores*
Private Label *Yes*
Web Site *www.tsecashmere.com*
RN Number *RN68088*

COTTON EMPORIUM, INC.

40 83 Street
Glendale, NY 11385 cottonemporium@aol.com
718 894 3365 Fax : 718 894 3374

Labels *Cotton Emporium, C & E*
Products *Missy and junior sweaters, knit tops and knit dresses.*
Price Points *Moderate*
Production *U.S.A.*
Showrooms *530 7th Avenue, Suite 609, New York, NY 10018 212 391 4427*
Private Label *Yes*
RN Number *RN93290*
Contact *President and Owner: Joseph Mosheshvili*

CYRUS

525 Seventh Avenue, Suite 801
New York, NY 10018 sophia@cyrusknits.com
212 764 2555 Fax : 212 819 1920

Labels *Cyrus*
Products *Knitwear & sweaters.*
Price Points *Better*
Production *China*
Showrooms *525 7th Avenue, Suite 1601, New York, N.Y. 10018*
Sell To *Department stores, specialty stores & boutiques.*
Private Label *Yes*
Web Site *www.cyrusknits.com*
Contact *Owner: Stephen Hakakian, Sales: Sophia Bagienski Mangual*

DANA EMILIA PRESENTS *(Rep.)

264 West 40th, Suite 503
New York, NY 10018 fashion@danaemilia.com
212 391 4104 Fax : 212 391 4153

Labels *Christopher Calvin, Redwood Court, Peacock Ways, Swish, Vanite Couture, Banaris*
Products *Sophisticated knit separates in luxury yarns including baby alpaca, linen & cotton/silk blends*
Price Points *Better*
Production *U.S.A. & import.*
Showrooms *New York.*
Sell To *Specialty stores, boutiques, chain stores & mail order catalogues.*
Private Label *Yes*
Web Site *www.danaemiliapresents.com*
Contact *President: Dana Harrison*

DOLORES PISCOTTA

8865 Sixteenth Avenue
Brooklyn, NY 11214 piscotta@msn.com
718 232 1167 Fax : 718 232 1167

Labels *Dolores Piscotta, Piscotta New York*

Products *Cashmere sweater collection, Cotton sweater collection*
Price Points *Better to designer*
Production *U.S.A., Italy, China, Nepal*
Showrooms *Brooklyn, New York - By appointment only*
Additional website: dolorespiscottawholesale.com
Sell To *Department stores, specialty stores, boutiques & catalogues.*
Private Label *Yes*
Web Site *www.dolorespiscotta.com*
RN Number *RN97327*
Contact *Owner and Designer: Dolores Piscotta*

ELE.PAVONI NEW YORK LTD *(Rep.)

159 West 53rd Street, Suite 29D
New York, NY 10019 elepavoni@mac.com
212 397 0108 Fax : 212 397 0366

Labels *Mela Rosa, Flora Fedi*
Products *Merino wool, silk, cashmere, linen, cotton, knits & separates. Printed and painted pieces.*
Price Points *Bridge to designer*
Production *Italy*
Showrooms *New York*
Sell To *Specialty stores & boutiques.*
Private Label *Yes*
Web Site *www.elepavoni.com*
Rev. in mil. *0-2*
Contact *Sales: Eleonora Pavoni*

ELIZABETH GILLETT LTD.

260 West 36th Street, Suite 802
New York, NY 10018 sales@elizabethgillett.com
212 629 7993 Fax : 212 629 7454 1 888 237 4773

Labels *Elizabeth Gillett*
Products *Knit, crochet & embellished sweaters, shrugs & jackets.*
Price Points *Better to designer.*
Production *India*
Showrooms *Dallas (Brad Hughes & Associates), Atlanta (Pepper's Collections),*
Los Angeles (Representing Showroom), New York (Elizabeth Gillett).
Sell To *Private label, specialty stores, boutiques & catalogues.*
Corp. Office *Above*
Private Label *Yes*
Web Site *www.elizabethgillett.com*
Rev. in mil. *2-10*
Contact *President/Owner/Designer: Elizabeth Gillett*

EURO JOY SPORTSWEAR CORP.

108 West 39th Street, Suite 1120
New York, NY 10018 jasoneurojoy@aol.com
212 575 4650 Fax : 212 575 4651

Labels *Euro Joy Sportswear*
Products *Missy sweater line.*
Price Points *Upper moderate*
Production *Overseas*

Showrooms *New York/above*
Sell To *Department stores, specialty stores & catalogues.*
Private Label *Yes*
RN Number *RN57032*
Rev. in mil. *2-10*
Contact *President: Jason Wu*

FORI SHOWROOM *(Rep.)

130 West 25th Street, Suite 10B
New York, NY 10001
646 724 2728
jacopo@jacopofoti.com

Labels *Peserico,Katia Serafini, Argonne, Walter Voulaz, Moorer, Rossopuro*
Products *Sophisticated knitwear & apparel using precious yarns & fabrics.*
Price Points *Bridge*
Production *Italy*
Showrooms *Collection is presented twice a year: Fall and Spring/Summer & sold through specialized agents with showrooms. The best of Made in Italy products.*
Sell To *Specialty stores*
Private Label *Yes*
Web Site *www.forifashion.com*
Rev. in mil. *0-2*

GOLF APPAREL BRANDS

13621 South Main Street
Los Angeles, CA 90061
310 715 1772 Fax : 310 715 1776 800 678 5246
sales@lamode.com

Labels *La Mode, Clark & Gregory*
Products *Women's golf sweaters and vests.*
Price Points *Moderate to better*
Production *Domestic and import from Korea, China, Hong Kong, Malaysia*
Sell To *Specialty stores, off-price and golf shops.*
Private Label *Yes*
Web Site *www.lamode.com*
Contact *President/Owner: Eddie Kahn*

H.M.S. PRODUCTIONS

250 West 39th Street, 18th Floor
New York, NY 10018
212 719 9190 Fax : 212 730 7581
nubby@nubby.com

Labels *Cable & Gage*
Products *Updated sweaters*
Price Points *Better*
Production *U.S.A. & import.*
Showrooms *New York.*
Sell To *Department stores, specialty stores & catalogues*
Private Label *Yes*
Web Site *www.cableandgauge.com*
RN Number *RN98108*
Contact *President and Owner: Spenser Alpern,*
Production: Spenser Alpern, Design: Michelle Antonelli

HOT KNOTS

820 N Street
Arcata, CA 95521
707 822 7562 Fax : 707 822 7512
hotknots@reninet.com

Labels *Tara Handknits*
Products *Handknits. Hats, scarves and sweaters.*
Price Points *Better*
Production *U.S.A. and import.*
Sell To *Specialty stores, boutiques and mail order catalogues.*
Private Label *Yes*
Web Site *www.hotknotsandtara.com*
Contact *Sales: Gayle Shackleton*

KOUROSH NEW YORK

18-42 College Point Blvd.
College Point, NY 11356
718 358 3332 Fax : 718 886 3883
kourosh@kouroshnewyork.com

Labels *Kurosh*
Products *Custom made women's knit suits in sizes zero to forty. 80% wool & 20% viscose.*
Price Points *Better to bridge*
Production *U.S.A.*
Sell To *Department stores, specialty stores*
Private Label *Yes*
Web Site *www.kouroshnewyork.com*
Contact *Kurosh Tehrani (sales@kouroshnewyork.com)*

NEW ORLEANS KNITWEAR

2917 Magazine Street, Suite 105
New Orleans, LA 70115
504 891 4502 Fax : 504 891 3875 800 338 4864
info@neworleansknitwear.com

Labels *New Orleans Knitwear*
Products *Knitwear & sweaters.*
Price Points *Bridge to designer.*
Production *U.S.A.*
Showrooms *New York*
Sell To *Department stores & specialty stores.*
Private Label *Yes*
Web Site *www.neworleansknitwear.com*

NIC + ZOE

323 Speen Street
Natick, MA 01760
508 651 0000 Fax : 508 651 0066 800 822 2939
info@nicandzoe.com

Labels *Nic + Zoe*
Products *Sweaters and knitwear in missy and petite.*
Price Points *Better*
Production *U.S.A. and import.*
Showrooms *New York/561 7th Avenue, Suite 1002 New York, NY 212-768-8500 and have road reps throughout the U.S.*
Sell To *Department stores, specialty stores, mail order catalogues.*
Private Label *Yes*

Web Site *www.nicandzoe.com*
RN Number *RN59351*
Contact *Sales: Julie Jordan Browne*

ODETT ENTERPRISES

109 West 37th Street, Street Level
New York, NY 10018 info@odettfashion.com
212 921 9690 Fax : 212 768 4760

Labels *Odett*
Products *Knitwear for women.*
Price Points *Budget to bridge.*
Production *U.S.A. & Italy*
Showrooms *New York*
Sell To *Specialty stores, boutiques.*
Private Label *Yes*
Web Site *www.odettfashion.com*
Contact *President: Amir Darouvar, Sales: Farah Darouvar*

RAFFI LINEA UOMO

250 West 39th Street, Suite 601
New York, NY 10018 info@raffilineauomo.com
212 307 1416 Fax : 212 957 9735

Labels *Raffi*
Products *Full line of sweaters in cashmere, merino wool and cotton.*
Price Points *Better*
Sell To *Department stores and specialty stores*
Web Site *www.raffionline.com*
Contact *National Sales Manager: Jenny Au, tel: 212-307-1416*

SCOTTEX GLOBAL SOURCING, LLC

1672 Jarrettown Road
Dresher, PA 19025 bradley@scottexglobal.com
215 540 1244 Fax : 215 793 0994 866 333 7630

Products *Factory direct sweater manufacturer specializing in private label product dev & production.*
Price Points *Better & designer.*
Production *U.S.A. & import*
Showrooms *New York: Victoria Watson Showroom - Please call for an appointment 215 540 1244*
Sell To *Department stores, specialty stores & mail order catalogues.*
Private Label *Yes*
Web Site *www.scottexglobal.com*
RN Number *RN104958*
Rev. in mil. *2-10*
Contact *President & Owner: Brad Flickstein*

SISTERS/DIVISION OF FREDINI INC

945 E. 12th Street, Suite A
Los Angeles, CA 90021 customerservice@sistersknit.com
213 955 8000 Fax : 213 955 8005

Labels *Sisters*
Products *Contemporary knitwear, sweaters & outerwear.*
Price Points *Better to bridge*

Production *U.S.A. & import*
Showrooms *New York, Atlanta, Chicago*
Sell To *Department stores, specialty stores & mail order catalogues*
Private Label *Yes*
Web Site *www.sistersknit.com*
RN Number *RN84332*
Rev. in mil. *2-10*
Contact *President & Owner: Fred Eslamboly, Sales: Fred Eslamboly, Design: Nancy Eslamboly*

SOPHIE FINZI LTD DBA PASHOOT

255 West 36th Street, Suite 201
New York, NY 10018 sophiefinziltd@aol.com
212 967 4349 Fax : 212 967 5361

Labels *Pashoot, Sophie*
Products *Missy sweaters.*
Price Points *Better*
Showrooms *Chicago/Julie Kipta 219-762-1442, California/Peggy Finnegan 707-778-1592*
Sell To *Specialty stores & boutiques.*
Private Label *No*
Web Site *www.sophiefinzi.com*
Contact *President and Designer: Sophie Finzi*

SUSAN GREENSTADT & ASSOC. *(Rep.)

215 West 40th Street, 9th Floor
New York, NY 10018 susangreenstadt@aol.com
212 302 0600 Fax : 212 302 0680

Labels *Bibelot*
Products *Bridge & contemporary knit ready-to-wear & sweaters & knit tops.*
Price Points *Better, contemporary & bridge.*
Production *U.S.A. & import.*
Showrooms *New York.*
Sell To *Department stores, better specialty stores, chain stores, mail order catalogues & private label.*
Private Label *Yes*
Contact *President: Susan Greenstadt*

SWEATER BRAND INC. *(Rep.)

86 South 1st Street, Suite BA
Brooklyn, NY 11249 info@sweaterbrand.com
718 797 0505 Fax : 718 875 8028

Labels *Sweater Brand, Knit Avenue, Domani Fashions, Suspicious Lines, Brittany Black*
Products *Private label sweater programs.*
Price Points *Moderate to better.*
Production *U.S.A. & import*
Showrooms *1400 Broadway, Room 808, NYC.*
Sell To *Department stores, specialty stores, mass merchants & manufacturers.*
Private Label *Yes*
RN Number *RN70204*
Rev. in mil. *11-50*
Contact *President & Sales: Moshie Rosenberg, Production: Ben Schlesinger*

TRENDSET ORIGINALS

1407 Broadway, Room 503
New York, NY 10018
212 736 9520 Fax : 212 997 9284
jj@skiva.com

Labels *Trendset*
Products *Missy sweaters & knits.*
Price Points *Budget to moderate.*
Production *Import*
Showrooms *New York*
Sell To *Department stores, specialty stores, mass merchants & off-price retailers.*
Private Label *Yes*
RN Number *RN48829*
Rev. in mil. *51-100*

VIVIANA UCHITEL *(Rep.)

12115 San Vicente Boulevard, Suite 410
Los Angeles , CA 90049
310 472 4955 Fax : 310 472 6054
pamcarone@gmail.com

Labels *Viviana Uchitel*
Products *Knitwear*
Price Points *Moderate to better*
Production *Import*
Showrooms *Los Angeles*
Sell To *Specialty stores & boutiques.*
Web Site *vivianauchitel.com*
Rev. in mil. *0-2*
Contact *Sales: Pamela Carone (cell: 310-994-8483), Design: Vivianna Uchitel*

WOODEN SHIPS

231 West 39th Street
New York, NY 10018
888 717 6700 Fax : 212 221 2329
sales@wooden-ships.com

Labels *Wooden Ships*
Products *Wool blend & cotton sweaters, wraps and ponchos*
Price Points *Better*
Production *Import*
Sell To *Department stores, specialty stores, boutiques & mail order catalogues.*
Private Label *No*
Web Site *www.wooden-ships.com*
Contact *Sales: Randi Weinstein*

A & H SPORTSWEAR CO. INC.

110 Commerce Way
Stockertown, PA 18083
610 759 9550 Fax : 610 746 2379
bruce@swimusa.com

Labels *Miraclesuit®, Penbrooke®, Mainstream® Swimsuits, Eco Swim®, Reebok, Magicsuit®*
Products *Women's fashionable swimsuits*
Price Points *Moderate to Couture*
Production *Domestic and import*
Showrooms *1441 Broadway, Suite 802, New York, NY 10018*
Sell To *Department stores, specialty stores, boutiques, on-line*
Contact *Director of Manufacturing: Bruce Waldman (Cell: 610 390 0977)*

A. CHE

19401 Business Center Drive
Northridge, CA 91324
818773 5000 Fax : 818 773 5100 888 642 4600
sales@acheswimwear.com

Labels *A. Che*
Products *Swimwear with fine Italian fabrics, European flare designed for sophisticated women.*
Price Points *Better*
Production *U.S.A. and import.*
Sell To *Department and specialty stores.*
Private Label *Yes*
Web Site *www.acheswimwear.com*
RN Number *RN84980*
Contact *Design: Amanda Che*

BEACH RAYS/DIV OF J.Y. RAYS, INC.

2023 Chico Avenue
South El Monte, CA 91733
626 941 0388 Fax : 626 941 0386
sales@beachrays.com

Labels *Surfer, Vast, Wet*
Products *Womens & junior swimwear & beachwear.*
Price Points *Moderate to better*
Production *Offshore*
Sell To *Department stores, specialty stores, theme/water parks*
Corp. Office
Private Label *Yes*
Web Site *www.beachrays.com*
Contact *National Sales Manager: Natalie Wierzba*

BREAKING WAVES INTERNATIONAL

1441 Broadway , Rm 2920
New York, NY 10018
646 569 6001
sales@breakingwaves.com

Labels *It Figures!, Leilani, Raisins, Raisins Girls*
Products *Figure enhancing swimwear by body type.*
Price Points *Moderate to better.*
Showrooms *New York*
Sell To *Department & specialty stores, boutiques, mass merchants & mail order catalogues.*
Private Label *Yes*
Web Site *www.breakingwaves.com*

RN Number *RN91106*
Rev. in mil. *11-50*

CARIBBEAN WRAPS INTERNATIONAL

619 N. Birdneck Road
Virginia Beach, VA 26451 sales@allyouneedtowear.com
757 495 8003 Fax : 757 474 4773 800 495 9105

Labels *Caribbean Wraps International*
Products *Beach sarongs, pareos & cover-ups.*
Price Points *Budget to designer*
Production *U.S.A. & import from India, Bali & China*
Sell To *Specialty stores, boutiques & mail order catalogues.*
Private Label *No*
Web Site *www.allyouneedtowear.com*
RN Number *RN107432*
Rev. in mil. *0-2*
Contact *Owner: Victoria & Bruce Begault, Design: Victoria Begault*

CATFISH CALHOUN AKA CALHOUN SPORTSWEAR *(Rep.)

250 Bunting Road
St. Catharines, Ontario, Canada L2M 3Y1 mikev@calhounsportswear.com
905 688 6100 Fax : 905 688 1167 800 263 5729

Labels *Corona, Sons of Anarchy, The Walking Dead, Coors, Molson, Canadian, DC Comics*
Products *Women's licensed apparel, swimwear & jams. Can do custom printing.*
Price Points *Moderate*
Production *Canada & overseas*
Showrooms *Call for reps.*
Sell To *Department stores, specialty stores, boutiques, mass merchants & mail order catalogues.*
Private Label *No*
Web Site *www.calhounsportswear.com*
Contact *Key Accounts Manager: Jodie Bartlett*

CEJON ACCESSORIES INC.

390 Fifth Avenue, Suite 602
New York, NY 10018 rmummert@cejon.com
212 967 4663 Fax : 212 967 4766

Labels *Soaked by Cejon*
Products *Women's swim cover-ups and resort wear.*
Price Points *Moderate*
Production *U.S.A. & import*
Sell To *Department stores, specialty stores, mail order catalogues & off-price retailers.*
Private Label *Yes*
Web Site *www.cejon.com*
Contact *President: David Seeherman, Sales: Robin Mummert*

CORAL HEAD INC./HAWAIIAN ISLAND CREATIONS

1988 West 169th Street
Gardena, CA 90247 baltazar1971@yahoo.com
310 366 7712 Fax : 310 366 6819

Labels *Hawaiian Island Creations*
Products *Surfwear & beachwear.*

Price Points *Moderate*
Production *U.S.A. & import*
Sell To *Specialty stores.*
Private Label *No*
Web Site *www.hicworldwide.com*
RN Number *RN83342*
Rev. in mil. *2-10*
Contact *President: Craig Hara, Marketing: Baltazar Magdirila*

COSABELLA

12186 SW 128th Street
Miami, FL 33186 miami@cosabella.com
305 253 9904 Fax : 305 253 1286 800 451 5393

Labels *Cosabella*
Products *Women's swimwear.*
Price Points *Designer*
Production *Italy*
Showrooms *Los Angeles, New York & Miami. New Jersey rep: Steven Tamarof 973-495-6398.*
Sell To *Department stores, specialty stores & boutiques.*
Private Label *No*
Web Site *www.cosabella.com*
RN Number *RN77351*
Contact *President: Valeria Campello, Design: Ugo Campello*

EVEDEN INC.

65 Sprague Street, Hyde Park
Boston, MA 02136 usaorders@wacoaleurope.com
617 361 7559 Fax : 617 361 7527 800 467 1269

Labels *Fantasie of England, Freya*
Products *Bra-sized swimwear for the full busted woman.*
Price Points *Better to designer.*
Production *Import*
Sell To *Specialty stores & boutiques.*
Private Label *No*
Web Site *www.eveden.com*
Rev. in mil. *2-10*

FREE COUNTRY LTD.

1071 6th Avenue, 9th Floor
New York, NY 10018 rondac@freecountry.com
212 719 4596 Fax : 212 719 2051

Labels *Free Country*
Products *A full line of women's swimwear*
Price Points *Better*
Production *U.S.A. & import*
Showrooms *New York*
Sell To *Department stores, specialty stores & boutiques.*
Private Label *Yes*
Web Site *www.freecountry.com*
RN Number *RN82608*
Rev. in mil. *11-50*

Contact *Design: Ira Schwartz*

G-III APPAREL GROUP

512 Seventh Avenue, 40th Floor
New York, NY 10018 info@g-iii.com
212 403 0500

Labels *Vilebrequin*
Products *Swimwear, accessories and resort wear.*
Price Points *Better*
Production *Import*
Showrooms *Same as Above*
Sell To *Department stores, specialty stores, boutiques*
Corp. Office *Same as Above*
Private Label *Yes*
Web Site *www.g-iii.com*
Contact *Designer: Kisha Beaugris (646 825 9297)*

JANTZEN

424 NE 18th Avenue
Portland, OR 97232 sales@jantzen.com
503 238 5000 Fax : 800 821 6943 1-800-626-0215

Labels *Jantzen, Perry Ellis Swimwear*
Products *Swimwear, resortwear, beachwear, accessories and footwear.*
Price Points *Moderate to better.*
Production *U.S.A. and import worldwide.*
Showrooms *New York: Perry Ellis/1411 Broadway, 24th Floor, NY, NY 10018 646 443 3300*
Jantzen Customer Service: 3000 NW 107th Avenue, Miami, Florida 33172
Sell To *Department stores, specialty stores, mass merchants and mail order catalogues.*
Private Label *Yes*
Web Site *www.jantzen.com*
RN Number *RN37966*
Rev. in mil. *101-500*

LONGITUDE/LONGEVITY BRANDS LLC

250 West 39th Street, 4th Floor
New York, NY 10018 service@longitudeswim.com
212 231 7877 866 315 6555

Labels *Longitude*
Products *Swimwear & cover-ups. Missy, large & tall sizes.*
Price Points *Moderate*
Production *U.S.A. & import.*
Sell To *Department stores, specialty stores, mass merchants & mail order catalogues.*
Private Label *Yes*
Web Site *www.longitudeswim.com*
RN Number *WPL08910*
Contact *Sales: Marty Mann (mmann50@verizon.net)*
VP of Merchandising: Brian Epstein (bepstein@swimusa.com)

LULI FAMA

8785 NW 13th Terrace
Doral, FL 33172
305 234 5656 Fax : 305 234 2968
star@lulifama.com

Labels *Luli Fama, Lulita by Luli Fama*
Products *Designer swimwear separates, cover-ups & resort wear.*
Price Points *Better to designer*
Production *U.S.A.*
Showrooms *Same as above*
Sell To *Swimwear specialty chains, boutiques, luxury resorts worldwide.*
Private Label *Yes*
Web Site *www.lulifama.com*
RN Number *RN97850*
Contact *Sales: Lourdes Hanimian*

MAR CHIQUITA SWIMWEAR INC.

1 N. Atlantic Avenue
Cocoa Beach, FL 32931
321 868 0868 Fax : 321 784 2626
marchiquita@cfl.rr.com

Products *Specialty print and solid swimwear in a variety of fits for juniors.*
Price Points *Moderate and better.*
Production *Domestic*
Showrooms *Above*
Sell To *Department stores, specialty stores and boutiques.*
Corp. Office *Above*
Private Label *Yes*
Contact *President: Rebecca J. Guy*

SWEENIE MANUFACTURING CORPORATION

60 East 9th Street, Suite 315
New York, NY 10003
646 825 5027 Fax : 646 825 5027
diane@sweeniemanufacturing.com

Labels *Shadowplay, Pawa, Bikini Thief, Body Rock Sport, Daniela Corte*
Products *Women, junior, contemporary & maternity swimwear & coverups, graphic tees plus tween sur*
Price Points *Budget to designer*
Production *U.S.A. & import from China, East Asia, Europe & South/Central America*
Sell To *Department stores, specialty stores, boutiques, mass merchants*
Private Label *Yes*
Web Site *www.sweeniemanufacturing.com*
Rev. in mil. *0-2*
Contact *Design & Production: Diane Walker (cell: 914-471-1069), Sales & Marketing: Stacey Demar (cell: 646-772-6113)*

VENUS FASHION

11711 Marco Beach Drive
Jacksonville, FL 32224
904 997 4000 Fax : 904 641 0977 888 782 2224
email@venus.com

Labels *Venus Swimwear*
Products *Women's & junior swimwear company specializing in brights. Swim wraps & beach accessorie*
Price Points *Moderate to better.*
Production *U.S.A.*

Showrooms *Jacksonville, FL/above.*
Sell To *Specialty stores & boutiques.*
Private Label *No*
Web Site *www.venus.com*
Contact *President and CEO: Jim Brewster*

ACTIVE APPAREL, INC.

11076 Venture Drive
Mira Loma, CA 91752
951 361 0060 Fax : 951 361 3120
kashis@activeapparel.net

Products *Women's & juniors printed & embroidered baby rib tees. Plus solid tee shirts & v-necks.*
Price Points *Moderate.*
Production *U.S.A. & import.*
Sell To *Specialty stores, mass merchants & off-price retailers.*
Private Label *Yes*
Web Site *www.activeapparel.net*
RN Number *RN99928*
Rev. in mil. *2-10*
Contact *President: Wasif Siddique, Wholesale Orders: Kashis Hussain*

ALSTYLE

1501 East Cerritos Avenue
Anaheim, CA 92805
714 765 0400 Fax : 714 765 0450 800 225 1364
info@alstyle.com

Labels *AAA™*
Products *All kinds of tees. Organic, short & long sleeve.*
Price Points *Moderate to better*
Showrooms *Sales Reps throughout the USA.*
Sell To *Department stores, mass merchants, mail order catalogs.*
Private Label *Yes*
Web Site *www.alstyle.com*

ANVIL KNITWEAR, INC.

146 West Country Club Road
Hamer, SC 29547
843 774 8211 Fax : 843 841 4963
info@gildan.com

Labels *Anvil®, Cotton Deluxe®, Cotton Deluxe Casuals*
Products *Imprintable & embroiderable sportswear & tee shirts.*
Price Points *Moderate*
Sell To *Wholesalers, department stores, specialty stores & mass merchants.*
Corp. Office *Division of Gildan Activewear SRL (www.gildan.com) - 877 445 3265*
Private Label *Yes*
Web Site *www.anvilknitwear.com*
RN Number *RN38619*
Contact *Arlin Turner Manager*

B & B SWEATERS

1411 Broadway, Suite 2678
New York, NY 10018
212 944 1335 Fax : 212 869 8489
bbsweater@aol.com

Labels *Jenny, Maddi*
Products *Novelty tee shirts in missy & large sizes.*
Price Points *Moderate*
Production *Throughout Asia*
Showrooms *New York.*
Sell To *Department stores, specialty stores, boutiques & mass merchants.*
Private Label *Yes*

Contact *Sales: Ari Biderman*

BRAVADO MERCHANDISING

1755 Broadway, 2nd Floor
New York, NY 10019 tom.bennett@bravado.com
212 445 3400 Fax : 212 445 3499

Labels *Bravado*
Products *Concert & movie tee-shirts. Specialize in rock-n-roll, film & novelty designs.*
Price Points *Moderate*
Production *U.S.A.*
Showrooms *New York, London, Los Angeles, Stockholm*
Sell To *Department stores, specialty stores, mass merchants & mail order catalogues, tour events.*
Private Label *Yes*
Web Site *www.bravadousa.com*
RN Number *RN91889*
Contact *Sales: Tom Bennett*

BUCK WEAR INC.

2900 Cowan Avenue
Baltimore, MD 21223 cjohnson@buckwear.com
410 646 6400 Fax : 410 646 7700 800-813-7708

Products *Printed adult & youth t-shirts. Quality sportswear for those who love the outdoors.*
Sell To *Specialty stores.*
Corp. Office *Above*
Web Site *www.buckwear.com*
Contact *President: David Trapp*

CATFISH CALHOUN AKA CALHOUN SPORTSWEAR *(Rep.)

250 Bunting Road
St. Catharines, Ontario, Canada L2M 3Y1 mikev@calhounsportswear.com
905 688 6100 Fax : 905 688 1167 800 263 5729

Labels *Calhoun*
Products *Women's licensed apparel, unisex tee-shirts, sweatshirts, boxer shorts & jams. Can do custom p*
Price Points *Moderate*
Production *Canada & overseas*
Showrooms *Call for reps.*
Sell To *Department stores, specialty stores, boutiques, mass merchants & mail order catalogues.*
Private Label *No*
Web Site *www.calhounsportswear.com*
Contact *Key Accounts Manager: Jodie Bartlett*

ENVIROTEXTILES LLC.

3214 S. Grand Avenue
Glenwood Springs, CO 81601 info@envirotextile.com
970 945 5986 Fax : 970 945 4456

Products *Hemp T-shirts & promotional apparel.*
Price Points *Moderate*
Production *U.S.A., China & Mexico*
Showrooms *Above*
Sell To *Garment & accessory manufacturers*
Private Label *Yes*

Web Site *www.envirotextile.com*
Rev. in mil. *2-10*
Contact *President: Barbara Filippone*

FAIR HEMP INC.

1717 Troutman Street, #302
Ridgewood, NY 11385 info@fairhemp.com
646 485 0939 Fax : 212 656 1714

Labels *Fair Hemp*
Products *Hemp and organic cotton women's tees and hooded tops.*
Price Points *Better*
Production *Import*
Sell To *Sell blanks to printers and produce private label and custom productions.*
Private Label *Yes*
Web Site *www.fairhemp.com*
RN Number *122157*

GOODWEAR USA

239 Western Avenue, Room 2D
Essex, MA 01929 steve@goodwear.com
978 768 7746 Fax : 800 787 4951 800 338 8895

Labels *Goodwear*
Products *Women's upscale dyeable tee-shirts done in sustainable fabrics: organic cotton & bamboo.*
Price Points *Bridge*
Production *U.S.A.*
Showrooms *Tokyo, Osaka, NYC & Essex*
Sell To *Distributors*
Private Label *Yes*
Web Site *www.goodwear.com*
RN Number *75346*
Contact *President: Martha Liquori, Owner: Stephen & Martha Liquori, Sales: Stephen Liquori*

GRAPHICS GROUP LTD./DBA LATITUDES

2425 NE Riverside Way
Portland, OR 97210 info@latitudespdx.com
503 248 2060 Fax : 503 248 2134 800 700 1073

Labels *Latitudes*
Products *Screenprinted t-shirts & sweatshirts. Boutique-look, sports, multi-media & tie-dye designs.*
Price Points *Moderate to better*
Production *U.S.A.*
Showrooms *Portland, OR*
Sell To *Department stores, specialty stores, boutiques & mail order catalogues.*
Private Label *Yes*
Web Site *www.latitudespdx.com*
Contact *President: L. Thomas, Owner: L. Thomas, Production: Jamie McCrae*

JOE BLOW T'S

8213-B Cloverleaf Drive Rear
Millersville, MD 21108 vanessa@joeblow.com
443 274 2744 Fax : 410 766 9516

Labels *Joe Blow T's Inc.*

Products *T-shirts of all kinds. Made in the USA.*
Price Points *Moderate*
Production *U.S.A.*
Sell To *Department stores, specialty stores & boutiques.*
Private Label *Yes*
Web Site *www.joeblow.com*
Contact *Owner: Stewart Cohen, Sales: Vanessa Harris (cell: 443-962-0278).*

KAMTEX FASHION

2916 NW 28th Street
Lauderdale Lakes, FL 33311 sales@kamtexfashion.com
954 733 1042 Fax : 954 733 1044 1-877-KAMTEX3

Labels *Nina Fresa*
Products *Wholesale distributor of women's tee shirts, hoodies and blanks.*
Price Points *Moderate*
Production *Import*
Web Site *www.kamtexfashion.com*

PILLAGED VILLAGE, THE

31Eagle Court, Suite E
Carlisle, OH 45005 pvsales@pillagedvillage.com
937 743 0685 Fax : 937 743 0697 1-877-793-1066

Labels *The Pillaged Village*
Products *Medieval designed t-shirts.*
Price Points *Moderate*
Showrooms *Same as Above*
Sell To *Boutiques, specialty stores, on-line catalog*
Web Site *www.pillagedvillage.com*
Contact *Owner: Wendy Kimmel*

RICH HONEY

919 E. Slauson Ave
Los Angeles, CA 90011 info@richhoney.us
213 905 3205 Fax : 213 746 9602

Labels *Rich Honey*
Products *Better quality T-shirts using100% combed and ring spun and poly viscose fabrics.*
Price Points *Better*
Production *U.S.A.*
Sell To *Department stores, specialty stores, boutiques*
Private Label *Yes*
Web Site *www.richhoney.us*
Contact *CEO: Luddivina Bowes*

ROYAL APPAREL, INC.

65 Commerce Drive
Hauppauge, NY 11788 sales@royalapparel.net
631 213 8299 Fax : 631 922 8438 866-Royal-1-S

Labels *Royal Apparel*
Products *Basic & fashion forward blanks in a large selection of colors & knit fabrications.*
Price Points *Moderate to better.*
Production *U.S.A.*

Showrooms *New York & Allentown, Pa.*
Sell To *Mass merchants, branded labels, screen printers & department stores.*
Private Label *Yes*
Web Site *www.royalapparel.net*
Contact *President: Morey Mayeri, Owners: Morey Mayeri/Abraham Mayeri*

SLICK DESIGNS

3710 East 10 Court
Hialeah, FL 33013 sales@slickart.com
305 836 7950 Fax : 305 836 7905 1-877-55Slick

Labels *Slick Art*
Products *Wholesaler for novelty & licensed t-shirts & apparel. Specialize in different printing techniqu*
Price Points *Moderate*
Production *U.S.A.*
Sell To *Boutiques, specialty stores*
Web Site *www.slickart.com*
Contact *Vice President: Samuel Ben Yaeesh*

SUGAR AND BRUNO

7260 Georgetown Road
Indianapolis, IN 46268 challen@sugarandbruno.com
317 293 5888 Fax : 317 293 5886 800 875 8559

Labels *Sugar and Bruno*
Products *Fun tees, tanks and hoodies*
Price Points *Moderate*
Production *U.S.A. & China*
Sell To *Specialty stores, boutiques*
Web Site *www.sugarandbruno.com*
RN Number *127789*
Rev. in mil. *2-10*
Contact *President: Challen Powers*

Notes

ALDAN

242 East 137th Street
Bronx, NY 10451
718 665 8699 Fax : 212 473 7003 800 536 8699
lew@aldan.com

Labels *Aldan*
Products *Custom designs for salons, spas, medical, restaurants & leisure resorts.*
Price Points *Better*
Production *U.S.A.*
Web Site *www.aldan.com*
Contact *President: Lew Widoff*

BADGER SPORTSWEAR

111 Badger Lane
Statesville, NC 28625
704 871 0990 Fax : 704 871 0521 888-871-0990
tom@badgersportswear.com

Labels *Badger Sport*
Products *Special order custom team uniforms & warm-ups.*
Price Points *Better*
Production *U.S.A.*
Sell To *Sporting good stores.*
Corp. Office
Private Label *Yes*
Web Site *www.badgersportswear.com*
RN Number *RN55346*
Rev. in mil. *11-50*

BEVERLY HILLS UNIFORMS

565 Barry Street
Bronx, NY 10474
718 378 1188 Fax : 718 378 2889 800 891 7255
sales@bhuniforms.com

Products *Medical uniforms, nursing uniforms, lab coats, print and solid scrubs in sizes XS to 5XL*
Price Points *Moderate*
Sell To *Department stores, specialty stores*
Web Site *www.bhuniforms.com*

BEXAR MANUFACTURING CO.

6623 S. Zarzamora
San Antonio, TX 78211
210 977 9585 Fax : 210 977 8998 877 977 9585
smockers@smockers.com

Labels *Smockers*
Products *Uniforms & fashion smocks for salon, cosmetic & retail.*
Price Points *Moderate*
Production *U.S.A.*
Sell To *Department stores, specialty stores & boutiques.*
Private Label *Yes*
Web Site *www.smockers.com*
RN Number *RN92441*
Contact *President and Owner: Veronica A. DeNeve, CEO: Brian A. Rice*

IN STYLE USA, INC. *(Rep.)

307 West 36th Street, 2nd Floor
New York, NY 10018 pauline.lock@instyleusa.net
212 631 0278 Fax : 212 631 0279

Products *Athleticwear, sportswear, dresses, jeans, uniforms and more.*
Price Points *Better to designer.*
Production *U.S.A. & China*
Showrooms *Above*
Sell To *Department stores, specialty stores & boutiques.*
Corp. Office *Above*
Private Label *Yes*
Web Site *www.instyleusa.net*
Rev. in mil. *2-10*
Contact *President: James Mallon*

K & P WEAVER, LLC

527 Carriage Drive
Orange, CT 06477 kpweaver@aol.com
203 795 9024 Fax : 203 795 4294

Labels *K & P Weaver LLC*
Products *Official licensee of the All-American Girls Professional Baseball League & replica uniforms.*
Production *U.S.A.*
Sell To *Specialty & sport stores, historical institutes, mail order catalogues, gift shops & museum stores*
Private Label *Yes*
Web Site *www.baseballamericaspastime.com*
Rev. in mil. *0-2*
Contact *Owner: Paula Weaver, Production: Kenneth Weaver*

LANDAU

8410 W. Sandidge Road
Olive Branch, MS 38654 darryl.williams@landau.com
800 238 7513 Fax : 662 890 1401

Labels *Landau, Urbane Scrubs, Scrub Zone, Smitten, Lynx*
Products *Trendy, fashionable uniforms & footwear for the healthcare & corporate professional.*
Price Points *Moderate*
Sell To *Department stores, specialty stores, catalogs, internet*
Private Label *No*
Web Site *www.landau.com*
RN Number *33489*
Contact *President: Bruce Landau, Executive VP: Gregg Landau,*
VP Sales, Marketing and Design: Darryl Williams

LIANA UNIFORM

110 West 40th Street, Room 606
New York, NY 10018 customerservice@lianauniforms.com
212 575 0875 Fax : 212 575 0876

Products *Basic scrubs as well as fashionable. New styles & prints every season in sizes XS up to 5X.*
Price Points *Moderate to better*
Sell To *Medical, veterinarian practices, dental, home attendants*
Web Site *www.lianauniforms.com*

MASCOT WORKWEAR U.S./REPCON NW INC

15009 NE Airport Way, Suite 100
Portland, OR 97230
503 252 9760 Fax : 503 252 9651 1-800-325-8707
sales@repconnw.com

Labels *Mascot*
Products *Women's workwear, contractors clothing & accessories.*
Price Points *Moderate*
Production *Import*
Showrooms *Same as Above - Walk In Trade*
Sell To *Department stores, work clothing stores, online retailers, safety/industrial/construction suppli*
Private Label *Yes*
Web Site *www.repconnw.com*
Contact *Sales: Bryan Freeman*

PRIORITY MANUFACTURING

571 N. W. 29th Street
Miami , FL 33127
305 576 3000 Fax : 305 576 2672 800 835 5528
richard@customuniforms.com

Labels *Priority Manufacturing, All American Career Apparel*
Products *Career, casual, formal and industrial uniforms*
Production *U.S.A.*
Sell To *Specialty stores*
Private Label *Yes*
Web Site *www.customuniforms.com*
Rev. in mil. *0-2*
Contact *President: Richard Levy*

VESTS DIRECT

141 Lanza Avenue, Building 10
Garfield, NJ 07026
800 365 9879 Fax : 973 546 8813
info@vestsdirect.com

Products *Custom created corporate wear: vests, bustiers, skirts, shorts for hospitality/casino.*
Price Points *Moderate to High*
Sell To *Corporations*
Web Site *www.vestsdirect.com*
Contact *Joanne Caruselle or Mark Gelles*

WILLIAMSON-DICKIE MFG CO.

509 West Vickery Boulevard
Fort Worth, TX 76104
817 336 7201 Fax : 817 810 4342 866 411 1501
customerservice@dickies.com

Labels *Williamson-Dickie*
Products *Quality & style tops & bottons for workwear & playwear.*
Price Points *Moderate*
Production *U.S.A.*
Showrooms *Dallas, New York*
Sell To *Department stores, specialty stores, uniform outlets.*
Private Label *Yes*
Web Site *www.dickies.com*
Rev. in mil. *+500*
Contact *President: Philip Williamson*

ADIDAS AMERICA, INC.

5055 North Greeley Avenue
Portland, OR 97217
971 234 2300 Fax : 971 234 2450 888 234 3270

Labels *Adidas*
Products *Activewear and athletic apparel.*
Price Points *Moderate to better.*
Production *U.S.A. and import worldwide.*
Sell To *Department stores, mail order catalogues, mass merchants and sporting good stores.*
Private Label *No*
Web Site *www.adidas.com*
Rev. in mil. *+500*

AERO TECH DESIGNS

2345 Preble Avenue
Pittsburgh, PA 15233 cyclewear@aerotechdesigns.com
412 262 3255 Fax : 412 203 1785 800 783 8326

Labels *Aero Tech Designs*
Products *Top quality bicycle apparel.*
Price Points *Better*
Production *U.S.A.*
Sell To *On-line, mail order catalogs*
Web Site *www.aerotechdesigns.com*
Contact *President: Cathy Schnaubelt Rogers*

AKADEMIKS

31 West 34th Street, Suite 401
New York, NY 10001 dclesmere@akademiks.com
212 563 4999 866 425 3657

Labels *Akademiks*
Products *Sweatpants, sweatshirts & tee-shirts.*
Price Points *Better*
Production *Asia*
Showrooms *New York*
Sell To *Department stores, better specialty stores & boutiques.*
Corp. Office *Division of Oved Apparel Group (www.theovedgroup.com)*
Private Label *No*
Web Site *www.akademiks.com*
Rev. in mil. *2-10*
Contact *David Clesmere*

BADGER SPORTSWEAR

111 Badger Lane
Statesville, NC 28625 tom@badgersportswear.com
704 871 0990 Fax : 704 871 0521 888-871-0990

Labels *Badger Sport*
Products *Special order custom team uniforms & warm-ups.*
Price Points *Better*
Production *U.S.A.*
Sell To *Sporting good stores.*
Private Label *Yes*

Web Site *www.badgersportswear.com*
RN Number *RN55346*
Rev. in mil. *11-50*

BALTIERRA SURFBOARDS & BALTI GIRL

788 W 16th Street, Unit B
Costa Mesa, CA 92627 rogerbaltierra@sbcglobal.net
949 645 7873

Labels *Baltierra Surfing*
Products *Mens board shorts, tee-shirts, tank tops & hats.*
Price Points *Moderate*
Production *U.S.A.*
Showrooms *Costa Mesa*
Sell To *Specialty stores.*
Private Label *Yes*
RN Number *SREAA24-776411*
Contact *President & Owner: Roger Baltierra*

BROOKS SPORTS, INC.

3400 Stone Way North, Suite 500
Seattle, WA 98103 Stephen.Cheung@brooksrunning.com
800 227 6657 Fax : 425 489 1975

Labels *Brooks®*
Products *High performance running shoes, apparel and accessories.*
Price Points *Moderate*
Sell To *Department stores*
Web Site *www.brooksrunning.com*
Contact *Global Marketing: Heather Snavely, US Marketing: Stephen Cheung*

CAMBER SPORTSWEAR, INC.

2 DeKalb Pike
Norristown, PA 19401 camberusa@aol.com
610 239 9910 Fax : 610 239 9912 800 345 7518

Labels *Camber*
Products *Athletic wear, workwear, thermals, sweats & sweatshirts.*
Price Points *Moderate to better.*
Production *U.S.A.*
Showrooms *Norristown*
Sell To *Specialty stores, printers & embroiderers.*
Private Label *Yes*
Web Site *www.camberusa.com*
RN Number *RN91210*
Rev. in mil. *2-10*
Contact *President: Barry Schwartz*

CHAMPION ATHLETICWEAR, INC.

1000 East Hanes Mill Road
Winston Salem, NC 27105 linda.barabasova@hanesbrands.com
336 519 6500 Fax : 336 519 7909 800 999 2249

Labels *Champion*
Products *Men's & unisex tee shirts, jogging suits, sport uniforms & all types of active & athletic wear.*

Price Points *Moderate*
Production *U.S.A. & import from the Orient.*
Sell To *Department stores, mass merchants, mail order catalogues & sporting goods retailers.*
Private Label *Yes*
Web Site *www.championusa.com*
RN Number *RN26094*
Contact *Licensing: Linda Barabasova*

DONOUGHE SPORT

721 Donoughe Street
Gallitzin, PA 16641 rmapparel@aol.com
814 886 9272 Fax : 814 886 4228 1-866-366-6844

Labels *Donoughe Sport™*
Products *Designers & manufacturers of quality sports apparel & related products*
Price Points *Moderate*
Production *U.S.A.*
Sell To *Specialty Stores*
Corp. Office *Division of R&M Apparel, Inc.*
Web Site *www.donoughesport.com*

FILA U.S.A. INC.

930 Ridgebrook Road, Suite 200
Sparks, MD 21152 ecommusa@fila.com
410 773 3000 Fax : 410 773 4984 800 845 3452

Labels *Fila*
Products *Active sportswear.*
Price Points *Moderate to better.*
Production *U.S.A., Hong Kong, Thailand, Taiwan & Indonesia.*
Sell To *Department stores, catalogues, mass merchants & sporting goods stores.*
Web Site *www.fila.com*

FREE COUNTRY LTD.

1071 6th Avenue, 9th Floor
New York, NY 10018 rondac@freecountry.com
212 719 4596 Fax : 212 719 2051

Labels *Free Country*
Products *Knit activewear.*
Price Points *Better*
Production *U.S.A. & import*
Showrooms *New York*
Sell To *Department stores, specialty stores & boutiques.*
Private Label *Yes*
Web Site *www.freecountry.com*
RN Number *RN82608*
Rev. in mil. *11-50*
Contact *Design: Ira Schwartz*

FRUIT OF THE LOOM

PO Box 90015
Bowling Green, KY 42102
855 253 4534   Fax : 888 259 6557
fotlcustserv@fruit.com

Labels *Fruit of the Loom, Russell Athletic, Vanity Fair, Russell Outdoors*
Products *All types of underwear and activewear.*
Price Points *Moderate*
Production *U.S.A.*
Sell To *On-line, department stores, specialty stores.*
Private Label *Yes*
Web Site *www.fruit.com*

HOLLOWAY SPORTSWEAR, INC.

2633 Campbell Road
Sidney, OH 45365
937 497 7575   Fax : 937 497 7337   800 852 8798
customercare@hollowayusa.com

Labels *Holloway*
Products *Men's sportswear, running suits & wool jackets.*
Price Points *Moderate*
Production *U.S.A. & import*
Sell To *Dept., specialty & sporting goods stores, catalogues, mass merchants & ASI distributors.*
Private Label *Yes*
Web Site *www.hollowayusa.com*
Rev. in mil. *51-100*

HYBRID APPAREL

10711 Walker Street
Cypress, CA 90630
714 952 3866   Fax : 714 952 3874
mlee@hybridapparel.com

Products *Men's knit tops & licensed tee-shirts.*
Price Points *Moderate*
Showrooms *Los Angeles/ 910 South Los Angeles St, Suite 408, Lost Angeles, Ca 90015, New York/530 7th Avenue, NYC 10018 212-997-4688.*
Sell To *Department stores & mass merchants.*
Web Site *www.hybridapparel.com*
Contact *Wholesale: M. Lee*

NIKE, INC.

1 Bowerman Drive
Beaverton, OR 97005
503 671 6453   Fax : 503 671 6300   800-806-6453

Labels *Nike*
Products *Active & athletic sportswear collection & accessories.*
Price Points *Moderate to Better.*
Production *U.S.A, & worlwide importer.*
Showrooms *Showrooms throughout the U.S.*
Sell To *Department stores, specialty stores, catalogues, mass merchants & Nike retail stores.*
Private Label *Yes*
Web Site *www.nike.com*
Rev. in mil. *+500*
Contact *President: Thomas Clark*

ROYAL APPAREL, INC.

65 Commerce Drive
Hauppauge, NY 11788 sales@royalapparel.net
631 213 8299 Fax : 631 922 8438 866-Royal-1-S

Labels *Royal Apparel*
Products *Basic & fashion forward blanks, active/athleticwear in a large selection of colors & knit fabr.*
Price Points *Moderate to better.*
Production *U.S.A.*
Showrooms *New York & Allentown, Pa.*
Sell To *Mass merchants, branded labels, screen printers & department stores.*
Private Label *Yes*
Web Site *www.royalapparel.net*
Contact *President: Morey Mayeri, Owners: Morey Mayeri/Abraham Mayeri*

SPORTHILL, INC.

725 McKinley Street
Eugene, OR 97402 info@sporthill.com
541 345 9623 Fax : 541 343 7261 888 645 3627

Labels *Sporthill*
Products *Athletic & activewear, gymwear, skiwear & outdoor active sportswear.*
Price Points *Moderate to better.*
Production *U.S.A. & import*
Sell To *Department & specialty stores, catalogues, mass merchants, national & regional chains.*
Private Label *No*
Web Site *www.sporthill.com*
Rev. in mil. *2-10*
Contact *President: James Hill, Production: Taunya Martin*

TOPSON DOWNS

3840 Watseka Avenue
Culver City, CA 90232 info@topsondowns.com
310 558 0300 Fax : 310 774 3666

Labels *Elwood Clothing*
Products *Pants, tees, shorts, tops in ring-spun denim and uniquely dyed wovens.*
Price Points *Better*
Production *Import*
Showrooms *NY Showroom: 530 7th Avenue, Suite 1502, New York, NY 10018 (212) 730 7860.*
Sell To *Department stores, Specialty Stores*
Private Label *Yes*
Web Site *www.topsondowns.com*

WAITEX INTERNATIONAL

135 West 36th Street, 3rd Floor
New York, NY 10018 frankriech@waitex.com
212 967 8100 Fax : 212 967 8266

Labels *Russell Athletic*
Products *Men's activewear, casualwear & athletic uniforms*
Price Points *Moderate*
Production
Sell To *Department stores, specialty stores*

Private Label *Yes*
Web Site *www.waitex.com*
Contact *Frank Reich*

WASATCH CO.

3287 Marjan Drive
Atlanta, GA 30340 info@wasatcht.com
404 634 3000 Fax : 404 634 1338 800 544 9096

Labels *Gildan, Fruit of the Loom, Jerzees Bella+Canvas, KiddyKats, Paradis Point, Q-Tees of Cali*
Products *Sweatpants, sweatshirts & tee-shirts.*
Sell To *Embroiders, screen printers, wholesalers and retail stores.*
Private Label *Yes*
Web Site *www.wasatcht.com*
Contact *Abdul Samad*

WHITE SIERRA

305 Soquel Way
Sunnyvale, CA 94085 wholesale@whitesierra.com
408 980 6688 Fax : 408 980 6670 1 800 980 8688

Labels *White Sierra*
Products *Sport outerwear, hiking apparel & fleece sweatshirt collection.*
Price Points *Moderate*
Production *U.S.A. & Asia*
Sell To *Department stores, specialty stores, mass merchants & sporting good shops.*
Private Label *Yes*
Web Site *www.whitesierra.com*
RN Number *RN58486*
Rev. in mil. *11-50*

Notes

CAMBER SPORTSWEAR, INC.

2 DeKalb Pike
Norristown, PA 19401
camberusa@aol.com
610 239 9910 Fax : 610 239 9912 800 345 7518

Labels *Camber, Camber II*
Products *Sweatshirts & baseball jackets.*
Price Points *Moderate to better.*
Production *U.S.A.*
Showrooms *Norristown*
Sell To *Specialty stores, printers & embroiderers.*
Private Label *Yes*
Web Site *www.camberusa.com*
RN Number *RN91210*
Rev. in mil. *2-10*
Contact *President: Barry Schwartz*

CPT USA, LLC DBA COCKPIT USA

15 West 39th Street, 12th Floor
New York, NY 10018
jacky@cockpitusa.com
212 575 1616 Fax : 212 575 1636 800 228 4739

Labels *Cockpit USA, Blue Eagle by Cockpit USA, Civilian Pilot Training*
Products *Classic American leather jackets & contemporary sportswear inspired by heros & legends.*
Price Points *Better*
Production *U.S.A. & import.*
Showrooms *New York.*
Sell To *Department stores, specialty stores, mail order catalogues, specialty chains & internationally.*
Private Label *Yes on a limited basis.*
Web Site *www.cockpitusa.com*
RN Number *RN114345*
Contact *President: Jeff Clyman, Marketing: Jacky Clyman*

D'ACCORD SHIRTS & GUAYABERAS

7320 NW 12th Street, Unit 115
Miami, FL 33126
rafael@daccordshirts.com
305 576 0926 Fax : 305 576 0196

Labels *DS&G, Paladin*
Products *Big size guayaberas & wedding, retro & casual shirts, safari sets, banded bottom shirts & spo*
Price Points *Moderate to better & off-price.*
Production *U.S.A. & Mexico*
Showrooms *Miami*
Sell To *Department stores, specialty stores, mail order catalogues, restaurants, hotels.*
Corp. Office *DBA: DS&G*
Private Label *Yes*
Web Site *www.daccordshirts.com*
RN Number *RN58706*
Rev. in mil. *11-50*
Contact *President: Rafael Contreras*

DREAM WORLD INTERNATIONAL, INC.

10073 Sandmeyer Lane
Philadelphia, PA 19116
rveltri@dreamworldintl.com
215 320 0200 Fax : 215 320 0201 800 789 7792

Labels *Zacchi, Pacelli, Dreams, XXIOTTI*
Products *Big & tall designer-look styling in mens fashion suits, dress pants & sportswear.*
Price Points *Moderate to bridge*
Production *Import*
Sell To *Specialty stores*
Private Label *Yes*
RN Number *RN99612*
Contact *President: Ross Veltri*

ESSEX MANUFACTURING INC.

350 Fifth Avenue, Suite 2400
New York, NY 10118
bbaum@baum-essex.com
212 239 0080 Fax : 212 714 2958 800 648 6010

Labels *Misty Harbor®, CLC*
Products *Big & tall rainwear, nylon packaway jackets & cold weather accessories.*
Production *Import*
Showrooms *Chicago, Boston, Cleveland, Philadelphia, San Francisco & New York.*
Sell To *Department stores, specialty stores, mass merchants & mail order catalogues.*
Private Label *Yes*
Web Site *www.baum-essex.com*
Contact *Rainwear & Outerwear: Bill Baum, Umbrellas: Lance Lovett - llovett@baum-essex.com*

ROYAL APPAREL, INC.

65 Commerce Drive
Hauppauge, NY 11788
sales@royalapparel.net
631 213 8299 Fax : 631 922 8438 866-Royal-1-S

Labels *Royal Apparel*
Products *Basic & fashion forward blanks in a large selection of colors & knit fabrications.*
Price Points *Moderate to better.*
Production *U.S.A.*
Showrooms *New York & Allentown, Pa.*
Sell To *Mass merchants, branded labels, screen printers & department stores.*
Private Label *Yes*
Web Site *www.royalapparel.net*
Contact *President: Morey Mayeri, Owners: Morey Mayeri/Abraham Mayeri*

WAITEX INTERNATIONAL

135 West 36th Street, 3rd Floor
New York, NY 10018
frankriech@waitex.com
212 967 8100 Fax : 212 967 8266

Labels *Russell Athletic Big and Tall*
Products *Men's activewear, casualwear & athletic uniforms in sizes ranging from boys to big & tall.*
Price Points *Moderate*
Production
Sell To *Department stores, specialty stores*
Private Label *Yes*
Web Site *www.waitex.com*

5TH & OCEAN CLOTHING LLC/NEW ERA CAP CO.

590 West 83 Street
Hialeah, FL 33014 laura.garden@neweracap.com
305 822 4606 Fax : 305 822 4665

Labels *Major League Baseball, NHL, NBA, NFL, Collegiate teams, New Era Men's Line*
Products *Mens sportswear.*
Price Points *Low to moderate.*
Production *Honduras*
Corp. Office *Above*
Private Label *Yes*
Web Site *www.neweracap.com*
RN Number *94989*
Rev. in mil. *11-50*
Contact *Designer: Laura Garden ext. 220*

7 FOR ALL MANKIND

25 West 39th Street, 13th Floor
New York, NY 10018 customerservice@shop.7forallmankind.com
646 839 5400 Fax : 646 839 5435 866 427 1114

Labels *7 for all mankind*
Products *Full collection of casual sportswear, tops and bottoms.*
Price Points *Better to Bridge*
Showrooms *Above, Los Angeles/CA, Dallas/TX*
Sell To *Department stores, boutiques & specialty stores.*
Corp. Office *4440 East 26th Street, Vernon, Ca 90023 tel: 323-406-5300*
Private Label *No*
Web Site *www.7forallmankind.com*

BLUE HAWAII SALES

801 South King Street, Suite 3707
Honolulu, HI 96813 hiblue@hawaii.rr.com
808 277 0368

Labels *Blue Hawaii, Moana*
Products *Casual sportswear collection.*
Price Points *Moderate*
Production *U.S.A.*
Showrooms *Honolulu*
Sell To *Department stores & mass merchants.*
Private Label *Yes*
RN Number *RN85143*
Contact *President and Owner: Joni Albao*

D'ACCORD SHIRTS & GUAYABERAS

7320 NW 12th Street, Unit 115
Miami, FL 33126 rafael@daccordshirts.com
305 576 0926 Fax : 305 576 0196

Labels *DS&G-Rafael Contreras*
Products *Casual sportswear, contemporary western & banded bottoms, linen & European fabrications.*
Price Points *Moderate to better & off-price.*
Production *U.S.A. & Mexico*
Showrooms *Miami*

Sell To *Department stores, specialty stores, mail order catalogues, restaurants, hotels.*
Corp. Office *DBA: DS&G*
Private Label *Yes*
Web Site *www.daccordshirts.com*
RN Number *RN58706*
Rev. in mil. *11-50*
Contact *President: Rafael Contreras*

GRANITE KNITWEAR/CAL CRU CO., INC.

805 S Salisbury Avenue, PO Box 498
Granite Quarry, NC 28072 calcru@mindspring.com
704 279 5526 X254 Fax : 704 279 8205 800 476 9944

Labels *Cal Cru*
Products *Casual sportswear.*
Price Points *Moderate*
Production *U.S.A.*
Showrooms *Granite Quarry, NC/above*
Sell To *Screen printers, embroiderers, gift & souvenir retailers.*
Corp. Office *Same/above*
Private Label *Yes*
Web Site *www.calcru.com*
RN Number *RN41253*
Rev. in mil. *0-2*
Contact *President: Mike Jones, Marketing: Marsha Hartzoge*

HAGGAR CLOTHING CO., INC.

11511 Luna Rd
Dallas, TX 75234 torri.teel@haggar.com
214 352 8481 Fax : 214 956 4644 877 841 2219

Labels *Haggar Casuals*
Products *Men's & young men's casual sportswear coordinates.*
Price Points *Moderate to better.*
Production *U.S.A. & import*
Showrooms *Dallas*
Sell To *Department stores, specialty stores, catalogues, mass merchants & off-price retailers.*
Private Label *No*
Web Site *www.haggar.com*
Rev. in mil. *+500*
Contact *CEO: Paul Buxbaum*

HASELSON INT'L TRADING INC.

32 West 39th Street, 3rd Floor
New York, NY 10118 sales@ringosport.com
212 465 0605 Fax : 212 629 3506 800 217 4478

Labels *Ringo Sport, Triple Play, Swiss Cros, Sahara Club, Roadblock, Aqua, Silver Label*
Products *Men's & boy's knit & woven casual sportswear collections.*
Price Points *Moderate*
Production *Import*
Showrooms *New York, Miami & Houston*
Sell To *Department stores, specialty stores & mass merchants.*
Private Label *Yes*

Web Site *www.haselson.com*

HILO HATTIE

670 Auahi Street, Suite 1-03
Honolulu, HI 96813 sales@hilohattie.com
808 535 6500 Fax : 808 356 1510 1 800 233 8912

Labels *Hilo Hattie*
Products *Hawaiian, casual & resort wear for men.*
Production *Domestic*
Sell To *Retail stores and mass merchants.*
Private Label *Yes*
Web Site *www.hilohattie.com*

J. CREW

770 Broadway, 11th Floor
New York, NY 10003 contactus@jcrew.com
212 209 2500 Fax : 434 385 5750

Labels *J. Crew*
Products *Casual sportswear and lifestyle collection.*
Price Points *Moderate*
Production *Import worldwide*
Sell To *Company owned stores and catalogue only.*
Web Site *www.jcrew.com*

KATE SPADE AND COMPANY

2 Park Avenue
New York, NY 10016 customerservice@jackspade.com
877 917 5225

Labels *Jack Spade*
Products *Updated men's apparel & accessories for all aspects of life.*
Price Points *Moderate to bridge*
Production *U.S.A. & import*
Showrooms *New York/above*
Sell To *Department stores, specialty stores*
Private Label *No*
Web Site *www.jackspade.com*
Contact *CEO: Craig Leavitt*

MODODOC/GENEXUS INTERNATIONAL

1214 W. Jon Street
Torrance, CA 90502 sales@mododoc.com
310 532 7300 Fax : 310 532 7311 888 680 8910

Labels *Mododoc*
Products *Casual sportswear and knits*
Price Points *Better.*
Production *Import*
Showrooms *Los Angeles/127 E. 9th St., #601, L.A., CA 90015, 213-236-0983*
Sell To *Specialty stores, boutiques and mail order catalogues.*
Private Label *Yes*
Web Site *www.mododoc.com*

MOOSE CREEK

20801 Currier Road
City of Industry, CA 91789 richard@moosecreekinc.com
909 869 5859 Fax : 909 869 5873 800 332 2513

Labels *Moose Creek*
Products *Men's active & casual sportswear.*
Price Points *Moderate*
Showrooms *New York/212-967-0999*
Sell To *Department stores & sportsing goods stores.*
Private Label *Yes*
Web Site *www.moosecreekinc.com*
RN Number *RN53623*
Contact *Sales: Richard Bernstein*

PROJECT NO. 8

38 Orchard Street
New York, NY 10002 info@projectno8.com
212 925 5599 Fax : 212 925 5589

Labels *Aspesi, Roberto Collina, Dries Van Noten, Isaac Reina, Maison Martin Margiela, Marni*
Products *Quality shorts, shirts, jeans, pants and jackets.*
Price Points *Designer*
Web Site *www.projectno8.com*

UNIONBAY/SEATTLE PACIFIC INDUSTRIES

1633 Westlake Avenue North, Suite 300
Seattle, WA 98109 cathie.underwood@unionbay.com
253 872 8822 Fax : 253 395 1345

Labels *Unionbay, Reunion*
Products *Casual sportswear, shorts, cargo pants, tank tops & more.*
Price Points *Moderate to better*
Production *Import*
Showrooms *New York/70 West 36th Street, NYC 212-947-1888, plus Los Angeles, Atlanta & Seattle.*
Sell To *Department stores, specialty stores, mail order catalogues, mass merchants & off-price.*
Private Label *Yes*
Web Site *www.unionbay.com*
Rev. in mil. *+500*

WAITEX INTERNATIONAL

135 West 36th Street, 3rd Floor
New York, NY 10018 frankriech@waitex.com
212 967 8100 Fax : 212 967 8266

Labels *Russell Athletic*
Products *Men's activewear, casualwear & athletic uniforms in sizes ranging from boys to big & tall.*
Price Points *Moderate*
Production
Sell To *Department stores, specialty stores*
Private Label *Yes*
Web Site *www.waitex.com*

BILLS KHAKIS

170 Pinesbridge Road
Beacon FallS, CT 06403 jeoff@billskhakis.com
800 435 4254 800 435 4254

Labels *Bills Khakis*
Products *High End men's sportswear.*
Price Points *Designer*
Production *U.S.A.*
Sell To *Specialty stores*
Private Label *No*
Web Site *www.billskhakis.com*

BURMA BIBAS

597 Fifth Avenue, 10th Floor
New York, NY 10017 sales@burmabibas.com
212 750 2500 Fax : 212 750 2834

Labels *Burma Bibas, Campia*
Products *Men's contemporary main-floor sportswear in silk & cottons.*
Price Points *Moderate, better & designer.*
Production *Hong Kong, Korea*
Showrooms *New York*
Sell To *Department & specialty stores, boutiques, catalogues.*
Private Label *Yes*
Web Site *www.burmabibas.com*
RN Number *WPL13185*
Rev. in mil. *11-50*

CPT USA, LLC DBA COCKPIT USA

15 West 39th Street, 12th Floor
New York, NY 10018 jacky@cockpitusa.com
212 575 1616 Fax : 212 575 1636 800 228 4739

Labels *Cockpit USA, Blue Eagle by Cockpit USA, Civilian Pilot Training*
Products *Contemporary Americana themed sportswear, bottoms, denims, wovens, knits & leather.*
Price Points *Better*
Production *U.S.A. & import.*
Showrooms *New York.*
Sell To *Department stores, specialty stores, mail order catalogues, specialty chains & internationally.*
Private Label *Yes on a limited basis.*
Web Site *www.cockpitusa.com*
RN Number *RN114345*
Contact *President: Jeff Clyman, Marketing: Jacky Clyman*

DREAM WORLD INTERNATIONAL, INC.

10073 Sandmeyer Lane
Philadelphia, PA 19116 rveltri@dreamworldintl.com
215 320 0200 Fax : 215 320 0201 800 789 7792

Labels *Zacchi, Pacelli, Dreams, XXIOTTI*
Products *Affordable designer-look styling in mens contemporary suits, pants & sportswear.*
Price Points *Moderate to bridge*
Production *Import*
Sell To *Specialty stores*

Private Label *Yes*
RN Number *RN99612*
Contact *President: Ross Veltri*

FRENCH CONNECTION

512 Seventh Avenue, 25th Floor
New York, NY 10018 frenchconnection@frenchconnection-usa.com
212 221 3157 Fax : 212 302 6839 866-932-3285

Labels *French Connection*
Products *Contemporary sportswear collection, European fabrics.*
Price Points *Better*
Production *Global*
Showrooms *Atlanta, Chicago, Los Angeles & New York.*
Sell To *Department stores, specialty stores, boutiques, mail order catalogues & off-price retailers.*
Corp. Office *184-10 Jamaica Avenue, Hollis, New York 11423*
Private Label *Yes*
Web Site *usa.frenchconnection.com*
RN Number *RN53372*
Rev. in mil. *101-500*
Contact *President: Andrea Hyde*

GUESS, INC.

1444 S. Alameda Street
Los Angeles, CA 90021 vendors@guess.com
213 765 3100 Fax : 213 765 5902 877-44-GUESS

Labels *Guess*
Products *Contemporary sportswear separates & outerwear.*
Price Points *Moderate to better*
Showrooms *New York/119 West 40th St, Suite 420, New York, N.Y. 10018, Tel: 212 730 7200*
Sell To *Department stores & specialty stores.*
Corp. Office *Above*
Web Site *www.guess.com*
Contact *CEO: Paul Marciano*

INSERCH BY MERC USA, INC.

41 Newman Street
Hackensack, NJ 07601 mercusainc@yahoo.com
201 489 3527 Fax : 201 489 7636 800 777 9599

Labels *Inserch*
Products *Contemporary sportswear collection.*
Price Points *Designer*
Production *U.S.A. & imported*
Showrooms *Hackensack, NJ*
Sell To *Specialty stores, boutiques & off-price retailers.*
Private Label *No*
Web Site *www.inserch.com*
RN Number *RN101976*
Rev. in mil. *2-10*
Contact *President: Jahan Astaneha, Sales: Max Astaneha*

MT SHOWROOM *(Rep.)

627 West 27th Street
New York, NY 10001 info@parajumpers.it
212 354 5678 Fax : 212 354 8654

Labels *Parajumpers*
Products *A timeless collection for the modern man based on proven military design.*
Price Points *Better*
Sell To *Department stores, specialty stores, boutiques & own website.*
Private Label *No*
Web Site *www.parajumpers.it*
Rev. in mil. *0-2*

OXFORD GOLF

555 S. Victory Drive
Lyons, GA 30436 info@oxfordgolf.com
866 727 4693 Fax : 212 586 8825

Labels *Oxford Golf*
Products *Golf shirts, pants, shorts, sweaters and jackets.*
Price Points *Better*
Sell To *Golf pro shops, resorts, specialty stores.*
Private Label *Yes*
Web Site *www.oxfordgolf.com*
Rev. in mil. *2-10*
Contact *Beverly Day (bday@oxfordgolf.com), Vicki Robins (vrobins@oxfordgolf.com), Pam Blount (pblount@oxfordgolf.com).*

PROJECT NO. 8

38 Orchard Street
New York, NY 10002 info@projectno8.com
212 925 5599 Fax : 212 925 5589

Labels *Aspesi, Roberto Collina, Dries Van Noten, Isaac Reina, Maison Martin Margiela, Marni*
Products *Quality sweaters, shirts, jackets and pants.*
Price Points *Designer*
Web Site *www.projectno8.com*

TAILOR VINTAGE

12 South Main Street, Unit 403
Norwalk, CT 06854 info@tailorvintage.com
212 840 1871 Fax : 203 286 1055

Labels *Tailor Vintage*
Products *Better contemporary sportswear, shorts, swim, shirts & pants. Preppy Cool.*
Price Points *Better*
Sell To *Department stores, specialty stores & boutiques.*
Private Label *Yes*
Web Site *www.tailorvintage.com*
Contact *Owner & Design: Richard Rosenthal*

ZANETTI INC.

4521 Sherman Oaks Avenue, Suite 401
Sherman Oaks, CA 91403 zanetti@zanetti.com
310 478 8660 Fax : 310 478 6935

Labels *Zanetti*
Products *Men's contemporary sportswear in luxurious fabrics.*
Price Points *Better*
Production *Italy*
Showrooms *New York/147 West 35th Street, Suite 603, New York, NY 10001 212-217-0889..*
Sell To *Deptartment & specialty stores, mass merchants, mail order, boutiques & off-price.*
Corp. Office
Private Label *Yes*
Web Site *www.zanetti.com*
Contact *Owner: Bruce Banafsheha*

BURBERRY

444 Madison Avenue, 14th Floor
New York, NY 10022 us.customerservice@burberry.com
800 284 8480 Fax : 212 977 5521 877-217-4085

Labels *Burberry*
Products *Classic, traditional & casual sportswear, outerwear & rainwear. Cashmere & silk scarves.*
Price Points *Better to designer*
Production *U.S.A. & import*
Sell To *Department stores & specialty stores.*
Private Label *No*
Web Site *www.burberry.com*

HUGO BOSS U.S.A., INC.

55 Water Street, 8th Floor
New York, NY 10041 customerservice@hugoboss-store.com
212 940 0600 Fax : 212 940 0619 800-484-6267

Labels *Hugo Boss, Boss Hugo Boss, Boss Black, Boss Green, Boss Orange*
Products *Suits & traditional sportswear.*
Price Points *Better*
Production *U.S.A. & import*
Sell To *Department stores, specialty stores, mail order catalogues & mass merchants.*
Private Label *No*
Web Site *www.hugoboss.com*
Rev. in mil. *+500*

INSERCH BY MERC USA, INC.

41 Newman Street
Hackensack, NJ 07601 mercusainc@yahoo.com
201 489 3527 Fax : 201 489 7636 800 777 9599

Labels *Inserch*
Products *Contemporary sportswear collection.*
Price Points *Designer*
Production *U.S.A. & imported*
Showrooms *Hackensack, NJ*
Sell To *Specialty stores, boutiques & off-price retailers.*
Private Label *No*
Web Site *www.inserch.com*
RN Number *RN101976*
Contact *President: Jahan Astaneha, Sales: Max Astaneha*

RALPH LAUREN, INC.

650 Madison Avenue
New York, NY 10022 customerassistance@ralphlauren.com
888 475 7674

Labels *Polo Ralph Lauren, Black Label, RRL, Purple Label,*
Products *Complete sportswear collection, plus, shirts, polos, pants, jackets, shorts, swimwear, etc.*
Price Points *Better to designer.*
Production *U.S.A. & import worldwide*
Showrooms *New York/above*
Sell To *Department stores, specialty stores, catalogues, off price & company owned retail shops.*
Web Site *www.ralphlauren.com*

Rev. in mil. *+500*

WEDDING TROPICS

8608 Utica Avenue
Rancho Cucamonga, CA 91730
844 921 0466
kevin@weddingtropics.com

Labels	*Friday Shirts! Wedding Tropics*
Products	*Linen beach wedding attire such as linen pants, linen shirts and linen suits.*
Price Points	*Bridge*
Sell To	*Department stores, specialty stores, boutiques and mass merchants.*
Corp. Office	*Above*
Private Label	*Yes*
Web Site	*www.weddingtropics*
RN Number	*117573*
Rev. in mil.	*0-2*
Contact	*President/Owner: Kevin Baldwin*

ACTIVE EDGE, THE/OLD CITY T-SHIRTS

233 Church Street
Philadelphia, PA 19106 actvej@aol.com
215 925 7860 Fax : 215 925 1597 800 343 1497

Labels *Active Edge*
Products *Organic mens ring-spun cotton tees.*
Price Points *Moderate*
Production *U.S.A.*
Showrooms *Philadelphia.*
Sell To *Specialty stores & boutiques.*
Private Label *Yes*
Web Site *www.theactiveedge.com*
Contact *President: Evan Sharps*

GOODWEAR USA

239 Western Avenue, Room 2D
Essex, MA 01929 steve@goodwear.com
978 768 7746 Fax : 800 787 4951 800 338 8895

Labels *Goodwear*
Products *Men's upscale dyeable tee-shirts done in sustainable fabrics: organic cotton & bamboo.*
Price Points *Bridge*
Production *U.S.A.*
Showrooms *Tokyo, Osaka, NYC & Essex*
Sell To *Distributors*
Private Label *Yes*
Web Site *www.goodwear.com*
RN Number *75346*
Contact *President: Martha Liquori, Owner: Stephen & Martha Liquori, Sales: Stephen Liquori*

INDIGENOUS

6780 Depot Street, Suite 210
Sebastopol, CA 95472 matt@indigenous.com
707 861 9719 Fax : 707 861 9214

Labels *Indigenous*
Products *Contemporary hand made fashion made with organic fibers by artisans worldwide.*
Price Points *Better*
Sell To *Specialty stores*
Private Label *Yes*
Web Site *www.indigenous.com*
Contact *Wholesale Inquiries: Matt Reynolds*

ROYAL APPAREL, INC.

65 Commerce Drive
Hauppauge, NY 11788 sales@royalapparel.net
631 213 8299 Fax : 631 922 8438 866-Royal-1-S

Labels *Royal Apparel*
Products *100% organic apparel for men available in various colors and styles.*
Price Points *Moderate to better.*
Production *U.S.A.*
Showrooms *New York & Allentown, Pa.*
Sell To *Mass merchants, branded labels, screen printers & department stores.*

Private Label	*Yes*
Web Site	*www.royalapparel.net*
Contact	*President: Morey Mayeri, Owners: Morey Mayeri/Abraham Mayeri*

7 DIAMONDS

15778 Gateway Circle
Tustin, CA 92780 sales@7diamonds.com
714 241 7190 Fax : 714 241 7199 877 577 1963

Labels *Seven Diamonds*
Products *Men's jeans & denimwear.*
Price Points *Better*
Showrooms *1071 Avenue of the Americas Room 200 NY NY 10018*
212 997 1777 7diamonds@7diamonds.com
Sell To *Department stores, specialty stores & boutiques.*
Corp. Office *Above*
Private Label *Yes*
Web Site *www.7diamonds.com*
Contact *President: Sami Khalil*

---

7 FOR ALL MANKIND

25 West 39th Street, 13th Floor
New York, NY 10018 customerservice@shop.7forallmankind.com
646 839 5400 Fax : 646 839 5435 866 427 1114

Labels *7 for all mankind*
Products *Men's jeans & denimwear.*
Price Points *Better to Bridge*
Showrooms *Above, Los Angeles/CA, Dallas/TX*
Sell To *Department stores, boutiques & specialty stores.*
Corp. Office *4440 East 26th Street, Vernon, Ca 90023 tel: 323-406-5300*
Private Label *No*
Web Site *www.7forallmankind.com*

ADRIANO GOLDSCHMIED

860 South Los Angeles Street, Suite 316
Los Angeles, CA 90014 david@namasteshowroom.com
213 689 4867 Fax : 213 683 0035

Labels *AG Jeans*
Products *Contemporary detailed jeans.*
Price Points *Better*
Production *U.S.A.*
Showrooms *New York/646-279-8690, Dallas/214-634-3304*
Sell To *Department stores, specialty stores*
Corp. Office *2741 Seminole Avenue, South Gate, CA 90280, tel#: 323-357-1111*
Web Site *www.agjeans.com*
Contact *West Coast Sales: David Coury*

AKADEMIKS

31 West 34th Street, Suite 401
New York, NY 10001 dclesmere@akademiks.com
212 563 4999 866 425 3657

Labels *Akademiks*
Products *Jeans, denim goods & contemporary urbanwear.*
Price Points *Better*
Production *Asia*
Showrooms *New York*

Sell To *Department stores, better specialty stores & boutiques.*
Corp. Office *Division of Oved Apparel Group (www.theovedgroup.com)*
Private Label *No*
Web Site *www.akademiks.com*
Rev. in mil. *2-10*
Contact *David Clesmere*

BERMO ENTERPRISES INC.

12033 U.S. Highway, PO Box 426
Schoolcraft, MI 49087 info@bermoenterprises.com
269 679 2580 Fax : 269 679 2611

Products *Lots of styles & finishes of denimwear*
Showrooms *350 W 34th St, Suite B2501, New York, NY 10001 Ph: 212 239 7483*
Sell To *Off-price clothing wholesaler*
Web Site *www.bermoenterprises.com*

CALVIN KLEIN, INC.

205 West 39th Street, 12th Floor
New York, NY 10018 calvinkleincustomerservice@pvh.com
212 719 2600 Fax : 212 292 9131 866-513-0513

Labels *CK One*
Products *Jean collection*
Price Points *Moderate to better*
Showrooms *New York*
Sell To *Department stores & specialty stores.*
Web Site *www.calvinklein.com*
RN Number *RN54718*

DIESEL PLANET

220 West 19th Street
New York, NY 10011 customerservice@shop.diesel.com
212 755 9200 Fax : 212 255 6641 877.344.8342

Labels *Diesel*
Products *Sportswear & outerwear.*
Price Points *Moderate to better*
Showrooms *New York & Los Angeles/Tel: 310 652 2322*
Sell To *Department stores, mass merchants & boutiques.*
Corp. Office *Above*
Web Site *www.diesel.com*
Contact *Owner: Renzo*

FRENCH CONNECTION

512 Seventh Avenue
New York, NY 10018 frenchconnection@frenchconnection-usa.com
212 221 3157 Fax : 212 302 6839 866-932-3285

Labels *French Connection*
Products *Contemporary sportswear & jean wear collection*
Price Points *Better*
Production *Global*
Showrooms *Atlanta, Chicago, Los Angeles & New York.*
Sell To *Department stores, specialty stores, boutiques, catalogues & off-price retailers.*

Corp. Office *184-10 Jamaica Avenue, Hollis, New York 11423*
Private Label *Yes*
Web Site *usa.frenchconnection.com*
RN Number *RN53372*
Contact *President: Andrea Hyde*

HASELSON INT'L TRADING INC.

32 West 39th Street, 3rd Floor
New York, NY 10118 sales@ringosport.com
212 465 0605 Fax : 212 629 3506 800 217 4478

Labels *Ringo Sport, Triple Play, Swiss Cros, Sahara Club, Roadblock, Aqua, Silver Label*
Products *Men's & boy's knit & woven casual sportswear & jeans collection.*
Price Points *Moderate*
Production *Import*
Showrooms *New York, Miami & Houston*
Sell To *Department stores, specialty stores & mass merchants.*
Private Label *Yes*
Web Site *www.haselson.com*

LEVI STRAUSS & CO.

1155 Battery Street
San Francisco, CA 94111 questions@levistrauss.com
415 501 6000 Fax : 415 501 3939

Labels *Levi's®, Dockers®, Signature by Levi Strauss & Co.™, Denizen*
Products *Casual sportswear, jeans & westernwear.*
Price Points *Moderate*
Showrooms *New York/1411 Broadway, 11th Floor, New York 10018, Tel: 212-704-3200*
Atlanta, Dallas & Chicago
Sell To *Department stores*
Web Site *www.levistrauss.com*
RN Number *RN36665, WPL00423*
Contact *CEO: Chip Bergh*

PARASUCO JEANS INC.

128 Deslauriers Street
St. Laurent, QC, Canada H4N 1V8 customerservice@parasuco.com
514 334 0888 Fax : 514 334 9833 877 PARASUCO

Labels *Parasuco Denim Legend*
Products *Denimwear, sportswear & jeans.*
Price Points *Better*
Production *Canada*
Sell To *Department stores, specialty stores, boutiques & mail order catalogues.*
Corp. Office *Above*
Private Label *Yes*
Web Site *www.parasuco.com*

PIMLICO PERFORMANCE APPAREL LTD.

118 West Hastings Street
Vancouver, BC, Canada V6B 1G8 adriana@pimlicoperformance.com
604 323 0441 Fax : 604 323 0449

Labels *Du'er*

Products *Contemporary men's jeans and denimwear with performance attributes.*
Price Points *Moderate to better*
Sell To *Specialty stores & boutiques.*
Private Label *Yes*
Web Site *www.dishandduer.com*

ROCKSTAR

5901 S. Eastern Avenue
Commerce, CA 90040
323 278 3874 Fax : 323 278 3877
customerservice@rockstaroriginal.com

Labels *Rockstar*
Products *Men's jeans and denimwear.*
Showrooms *New York & Los Angeles*
Sell To *Departmnent stores, boutiques & specialty stores.*
Corp. Office *Above*
Private Label *No*
Web Site *www.rockstarsushi.com*

ANDREW MARC

512 Seventh Avenue
New York, NY 10018 sales@andrewmarc.com
212 840 1800 Fax : 212 575 4717 888 424 6272

Labels *Andrew Marc, Marc New York*
Products *Shearling, leather, suede outerwear & sportswear.*
Price Points *Better*
Production *Asia & Europe*
Showrooms *New York/above*
Sell To *Department stores, specialty stores, boutiques & mail order catalogues.*
Private Label *Yes*
Web Site *www.andrewmarc.com*
Rev. in mil. *11-50*

CPT USA, LLC DBA COCKPIT USA

15 West 39th Street, 12th Floor
New York, NY 10018 jacky@cockpitusa.com
212 575 1616 Fax : 212 575 1636 800 228 4739

Labels *Cockpit USA, Blue Eagle by Cockpit USA, Civilian Pilot Training*
Products *Classic American leather jackets & sportswear inspired by heros, legends & aviation.*
Price Points *Better*
Production *U.S.A. & import.*
Showrooms *New York.*
Sell To *Department stores, specialty stores, mail order catalogues, specialty chains & internationally.*
Private Label *Yes on a limited basis.*
Web Site *www.cockpitusa.com*
RN Number *RN114345*
Contact *President: Jeff Clyman, Marketing: Jacky Clyman*

MONTANACO CLOTHING COMPANY

321 W. Galena Street
Butte, MT 59701 info@montanacoclothing.com
406 723 2332 Fax : 406 723 5267 1-888-265-4128

Labels *Montanaco, Deni, Razer*
Products *Men's leather jackets and vests.*
Price Points *Better*
Production *Domestic*
Corp. Office *Above*
Private Label *No*
Web Site *www.montanacoclothing.com*

SCULLY

Scully Corporate Plaza
Oxnard, CA 93003 brianscully@scullyleather.com
805 483 6339 Fax : 805 483 6439

Labels *Scully*
Products *Leather outerwear, Western apparel and accessories.*
Showrooms *California*
Web Site *www.scullyleather.com*
Contact *Division Director: Brian Scully*

Notes

ASPEN LICENSING INTERNATIONAL, INC.

6615 W. Boynton Beach Boulevard, #349
Boynton Beach, FL 33437
bob@aspenlicensing.com
561 509 8888 Fax : 561 740 0637 1 888 642 7736

Labels *Aspen, Aspen Extreme*
Products *Active & outdoor inspired outerwear, underwear, footwear & accessories.*
Price Points *Moderate*
Production *U.S.A. & Orient.*
Showrooms *Call for licensee's showrooms or if your company would benefit by licensing the Aspen name.*
Sell To *Department stores & mass merchants.*
Web Site *www.aspenbrand.com*
RN Number *RN86959*
Contact *Chairman: Robert Maltz*

CHAMPION ATHLETICWEAR, INC.

1000 East Hanes Mill Road
Winston Salem, NC 27105
linda.barabasova@hanesbrands.com
336 519 6500 Fax : 336 519 7909 800 999 2249

Labels *Champion*
Products *Tee-shirts, jogging suits & all types of active & athletic wear.*
Price Points *Moderate*
Production *U.S.A. & import from the Orient.*
Sell To *Department stores, mass merchants, mail order catalogues & sporting goods retailers.*
Private Label *Yes*
Web Site *www.championusa.com*
RN Number *RN26094*
Contact *Licensing: Nancy Gendimenico - 212 576-8481*

ESSEX MANUFACTURING INC.

350 Fifth Avenue, Suite 2400
New York, NY 10118
bbaum@baum-essex.com
212 239 0080 Fax : 212 714 2958 800 648 6010

Labels *Nautica, Jones New York, Misty Harbor®, CLC*
Products *Licensed rainwear, nylon packaway jackets & cold weather accessories.*
Production *Import*
Showrooms *Chicago, Boston, Cleveland, Philadelphia, San Francisco & New York.*
Sell To *Department stores, specialty stores, mass merchants & mail order catalogues.*
Private Label *Yes*
Web Site *www.baum-essex.com*
Contact *Rainwear & Outerwear: Bill Baum, Umbrellas: Lance Lovett - llovett@baum-essex.com*

GLOBAL BRANDS GROUP

350 Fifth Avenue, 7th Floor
New York, NY 10118
business@globalbrandsgroup.com
646 839 7000

Labels *Calvin Klein, Michael Kors, Frye*
Products *Mens apparel and leather collection.*
Price Points *Moderate & better*
Production *Import*
Showrooms *New York*
Sell To *Department stores, specialty stores, mid-tier, mass merchants & catalogues.*

Private Label *Yes*
Web Site *www.globalbrandsgroup.com*
RN Number *RN82457*
Rev. in mil. *11-50*

HASELSON INT'L TRADING INC.

32 West 39th Street, 3rd Floor
New York, NY 10118 sales@ringosport.com
212 465 0605 Fax : 212 629 3506 800 217 4478

Labels *Marvel, Karl Kani, Pink Panther, Popeye*
Products *Men's & boy's sportswear, outerwear, dress & sport shirts.*
Price Points *Moderate*
Production *Import*
Showrooms *New York, Miami & Houston*
Sell To *Department stores, specialty stores & mass merchants.*
Private Label *Yes*
Web Site *www.haselson.com*

HYBRID APPAREL

10711 Walker Street
Cypress, CA 90630 mlee@hybridapparel.com
714 952 3866 Fax : 714 952 3874

Products *Men's licensed tee-shirts.*
Price Points *Moderate*
Showrooms *Los Angeles/ 910 South Los Angeles St, Suite 408, Lost Angeles, Ca 90015, New York/530 7th Avenue, NYC 10018 212-997-4688.*
Sell To *Department stores & mass merchants.*
Web Site *www.hybridapparel.com*
Contact *Wholesale: M. Lee*

7 DIAMONDS

15778 Gateway Circle
Tustin, CA 92780 sales@7diamonds.com
714 241 7190 Fax : 714 241 7199 877 577 1963

Labels *Seven Diamonds*
Products *Men's outerwear and jackets in cloth and leather.*
Price Points *Better*
Showrooms *1071 Avenue of the Americas Room 200 NY NY 10018*
212 997 1777 7diamonds@7diamonds.com
Sell To *Department stores, specialty stores & boutiques.*
Corp. Office *Above*
Private Label *Yes*
Web Site *www.7diamonds.com*
Contact *President: Sami Khalil*

ALPHA INDUSTRIES, INC.

14200 Park Meadow Drive, Suite 110 South
Chantilly, VA 20151 wholesale@alphaindustries.com
703 378 1420 Fax : 703 378 4910 866 631 0719

Labels *Alpha U.S.A., Knox Armory*
Products *Fashion, military inspired, Americana & cold weather outerwear & apparel.*
Price Points *Moderate to better*
Production *U.S.A., Far East & Middle East*
Showrooms *Washington DC, NYC, Los Angeles, London, Frankfurt, Paris, Seoul, Tokyo, Florence & Shanghai.*
Sell To *Department stores, specialty stores, boutiques & mail order catalogues.*
Private Label *Yes*
Web Site *www.alphaindustries.com*
RN Number *RN35569*

ANDREW MARC

512 Seventh Avenue
New York, NY 10018 sales@andrewmarc.com
212 840 1800 Fax : 212 575 4717 888 424 6272

Labels *Andrew Marc, Marc New York*
Products *Leather, suede, shearling, cashmere/wool & all types of cloth outerwear.*
Price Points *Better*
Production *Asia & Europe*
Showrooms *New York/above*
Sell To *Department stores, specialty stores, boutiques & mail order catalogues.*
Private Label *Yes*
Web Site *www.andrewmarc.com*
Rev. in mil. *11-50*

BLUE DUCK TRADING CO.

463 Seventh Avenue, Suite 1106
New York, NY 10018 barry@blueduckshearling.com
212 268 3122 Fax : 212 268 3125 800 377 9001

Labels *Blue Duck*
Products *Fine luxury outerwear specializing in Spanish Merino Shearlings & fur lined coats & jackets*
Price Points *Better to bridge.*

Production *U.S.A.*
Showrooms *New York*
Sell To *Department stores, specialty stores, boutiques & mail order catalogues.*
Private Label *Yes*
Web Site *www.blueduckshearling.com*
Contact *Founder and CEO Barry Novick*

BURBERRY

444 Madison Avenue, 14th Floor
New York, NY 10022 us.customerservice@burberry.com
800 284 8480 Fax : 212 977 5521 877-217-4085

Labels *Burberry*
Products *Classic, traditional & casual outerwear & rainwear.*
Price Points *Better to designer*
Production *U.S.A. & import*
Sell To *Department stores & specialty stores.*
Private Label *No*
Web Site *www.burberry.com*

COLUMBIA SPORTSWEAR CO., INC.

14375 N.W. Science Park Drive
Portland, OR 97229 sales_info@columbia.com
503 985 4000 Fax : 503 985 5800 800 MA BOYLE

Labels *Columbia Sportswear Co.*
Products *Active outerwear, skiiing, sportswear, footwear & accessories.*
Price Points *Moderate*
Production *U.S.A. & Overseas*
Sell To *Department stores, specialty stores, mass merchants.*
Private Label *No*
Web Site *www.columbia.com*
RN Number *RN69724*
Rev. in mil. *+500*
Contact *Chairman: Gertrude Boyle, CEO: Tim Boyle, VIP Sales: Joseph R. Craig*

CPT USA, LLC DBA COCKPIT USA

15 West 39th Street, 12th Floor
New York, NY 10018 jacky@cockpitusa.com
212 575 1616 Fax : 212 575 1636 800 228 4739

Labels *Cockpit USA, Blue Eagle by Cockpit USA, Civilian Pilot Training*
Products *Classic American leather jackets inspired by heros, legends & aviation.*
Price Points *Better*
Production *U.S.A. & import.*
Showrooms *New York.*
Sell To *Department stores, specialty stores, mail order catalogues, specialty chains & internationally.*
Private Label *Yes on a limited basis.*
Web Site *www.cockpitusa.com*
RN Number *RN114345*
Contact *President: Jeff Clyman, Marketing: Jacky Clyman*

ESSEX MANUFACTURING INC.

350 Fifth Avenue, Suite 2400
New York, NY 10118 bbaum@baum-essex.com
212 239 0080 Fax : 212 714 2958 800 648 6010

Labels *Misty Harbor®, CLC*
Products *Rainwear, specialize in PVC & vinyl slickers, raincoats & nylon pack-away jackets.*
Production *Import*
Showrooms *Chicago, Boston, Cleveland, Philadelphia, San Francisco & New York.*
Sell To *Department stores, specialty stores, mass merchants & mail order catalogues.*
Private Label *Yes*
Web Site *www.baum-essex.com*
Contact *Rainwear & Outerwear: Bill Baum, Umbrellas: Lance Lovett - llovett@baum-essex.com*

FREE COUNTRY LTD.

1071 6th Avenue, 9th Floor
New York, NY 10018 rondac@freecountry.com
212 719 4596 Fax : 212 719 2051 1-888-232-4020

Labels *Free Country*
Products *Outerwear*
Price Points *Better*
Production *U.S.A. & import*
Showrooms *New York*
Sell To *Department stores, specialty stores & boutiques.*
Private Label *Yes*
Web Site *www.freecountry.com*
RN Number *RN82608*
Rev. in mil. *11-50*
Contact *Design: Ira Schwartz*

G-III APPAREL GROUP

512 Seventh Avenue, 40th Floor
New York, NY 10018 info@g-iii.com
212 403 0500

Labels *Calvin Klein, Levi's, Dockers, 100 US Colleges, 4 Major Pro Sports Leagues*
Products *Outerwear and sportswear*
Price Points *Better*
Production *Import*
Showrooms *Same as Above*
Sell To *Department stores, specialty stores, boutiques*
Corp. Office *Same as Above*
Private Label *Yes*
Web Site *www.g-iii.com*
Contact *Designer: Kisha Beaugris (646 825 9297)*

GOLF APPAREL BRANDS

13621 South Main Street
Los Angeles, CA 90061 sales@lamode.com
310 715 1772 Fax : 310 715 1776 800 678 5246

Labels *La Mode, Clark & Gregory, Sahara, Naturetech*
Products *Men's golf rain jackets and rain pants.*
Price Points *Moderate to better*

Production *Domestic and import from Korea, China, Hong Kong, Malaysia*
Sell To *Specialty stores, off-price and golf shops.*
Private Label *Yes*
Web Site *www.lamode.com*
Contact *President/Owner: Eddie Kahn*

HARBOUR INTERNATIONAL LLC

1407 Broadway, Suite 1515
New York, NY 10018 tlewis@harbourintl.net
212 868 9128 Fax : 212 868 9129

Labels *Boston Harbour, Proshield, Habour/One, Emanuel Ungaro*
Products *Outdoor wear in leather and cloth for every occasion*
Price Points *Better*
Production *Import*
Sell To *On-line store*
Private Label *Yes*
Web Site *www.bostonharbour.net*
Contact *CO: Tom Lewis*

HASELSON INT'L TRADING INC.

32 West 39th Street, 3rd Floor
New York, NY 10118 sales@ringosport.com
212 465 0605 Fax : 212 629 3506 800 217 4478

Labels *Ringo Sport, Triple Play, Swiss Cros, Sahara Club, Roadblock, Aqua, Silver Label*
Products *Men's & boy's outerwear collections.*
Price Points *Moderate*
Production *Import*
Showrooms *New York, Miami & Houston*
Sell To *Department stores, specialty stores & mass merchants.*
Private Label *Yes*
Web Site *www.haselson.com*

MARMOT MOUNTAIN LLC.

5789 State Farm Drive, Suite 100
Rohnert Park, CA 94928 ghouser@marmot.com
707 544 4590 Fax : 707 544 1344 1-888-357-3262

Labels *Marmot*
Products *Men's performance outerwear.*
Price Points *Better*
Sell To *Specialty stores and department stores.*
Private Label *No*
Web Site *www.marmot.com*
Contact *Greg Houser*

MARTIN DINGMAN COUNTRYWEAR

14966 Industrial Park Drive
Leadhill, AR 72644 info@martindingman.com
870 422 7151 Fax : 870 422 7379 800 955 BELT

Labels *Martin Dingman*
Products *Men's countrywear collection. Sportcoats, jackets and outerwear.*
Price Points *Better to designer*

Production *U.S.A.*
Showrooms *Show collection in New York during Collective.*
Sell To *Specialty stores, department stores*
Private Label *No*
Web Site *www.martindingman.com*
Contact *President: Gay Dingman, Designer: Martin Dingman, Marketing: Grayson Dingman*

PENDLETON WOOLEN MILLS, INC.

220 Northwest Broadway
Portland, OR 97209 pendletoncatalog@penwool.com
503 226 4801 Fax : 503 535 5599 800 522 9665

Labels *Pendleton*
Products *Outerwear, jackets, vests & westernwear.*
Price Points *Better*
Production *U.S.A. & import*
Sell To *Specialty stores & mail order catalogues.*
Private Label *No*
Web Site *www.pendleton-usa.com*
RN Number *RN29685, WPL04378*
Rev. in mil. *+500*

WASATCH CO.

3287 Marjan Drive
Atlanta, GA 30340 info@wasatcht.com
404 634 3000 Fax : 404 634 1338 800 544 9096

Labels *Gildan, Fruit of the Loom, Jerzees Bella+Canvas, KiddyKats, Paradis Point, Q-Tees of Cali*
Products *Microfiber, lined coach's & satin jackets.*
Sell To *Embroiders, screen printers, wholesalers and retail stores.*
Private Label *Yes*
Web Site *www.wasatcht.com*
Contact *Abdul Samad*

WHITE SIERRA

305 Soquel Way
Sunnyvale, CA 94085 wholesale@whitesierra.com
408 980 6688 Fax : 408 980 6670 1 800 980 8688

Labels *White Sierra*
Products *Sport outerwear.*
Price Points *Moderate*
Production *U.S.A. & Asia*
Sell To *Department stores, specialty stores, mass merchants & sporting good shops.*
Private Label *Yes*
Web Site *www.whitesierra.com*
RN Number *RN58486*
Rev. in mil. *11-50*

Notes

ANDARI FASHION, INC.

9626 Telstar Avenue
El Monte, CA 91731
626 575 2759 Fax : 626 575 3629
info@andari.com

Products *Private label sweater manufacturer.*
Price Points *Moderate to designer.*
Production *U.S.A. & import*
Sell To *Department stores, specialty stores, boutiques.*
Private Label *Yes*
Web Site *www.andari.com*
Rev. in mil. *2-10*
Contact *Owner: Lillian Wang*

AUTUMN CASHMERE INC.

231 West 39th Street, Suite#1111
New York, NY 10018
888 6 AUTUMN Fax : 212 398 2255 1 888 6 AUTUMN
info@autumncashmere.com

Labels *Autumn Cashmere*
Products *Fashion & novelty cashmere & cashmere blend sweaters. 2 to 5 gauge knits.*
Price Points *Better to designer.*
Production *China & Hong Kong*
Showrooms *New York/Aci NY, 212-398-2244, CA/Sales: 213-893-6995.*
Sell To *Department & specialty stores, boutiques & mail order catalogues.*
Private Label *Yes*
Web Site *www.autumncashmere.com*
Rev. in mil. *11-50*

CHATHAM KNITTING MILLS, INC.

119 S. Main Street, PO Box 152
Chatham, VA 24531
434 432 4701 Fax : 434 432 3742
mattharris2006@gmail.com

Products *Windbreaker jackets, work coats, jumpsuits, elastic waist pants, prison clothing*
Price Points *Off-price*
Production *U.S.A.*
Sell To *Off-price & institutional.*
Private Label *Yes*
RN Number *WPL10668*
Contact *President: Matt Harris*

COTTON HERITAGE

6393 E. Washington Blvd.
Commerce, CA 90040
323 722 5592 Fax : 323 724 0045
mickey@cottonheritage.com

Labels *Cotton Heritage*
Products *Men's blank t-shirts, polo's, fleece, outerwear, active and denim wear & jogging sets.*
Price Points *Competitive*
Production *Import*
Showrooms *City of Commerce, CA., Clifton, New Jersey 973-249-5081, Miami, FL. 305-623-1947.*
Sell To *Screenprinters, Embroiders, Resort & Promotional & licensed companies, retailers & discount*
Private Label *Yes*
Web Site *www.cottonheritage.com*

RN Number *75813*
Contact *Vice President: Mickey Sachdeva*

GRUVEN INTERNATIONAL INC.

19 Newgale Gate
Ontario, Canada M1X 5B6 sales@gruven.com
416 292 7331 Fax : 416 754 8675

Products *Active, sportswear & outerwear in knit & woven styles.*
Price Points *Moderate to better.*
Production *Canada & Shanghai, China*
Showrooms *Toronto*
Sell To *Specialty stores & boutiques.*
Private Label *Yes*
Web Site *www.gruven.com*

HART SCHAFFNER MARX

1680 E Touhy Avenue
Des Plaines, IL 60018 info@wdiamondgroup.com
800 327 4466

Labels *HSM*
Products *Men's private label & branded tailored clothing & slacks.*
Price Points *Better*
Production *U.S.A. & import*
Showrooms *New York/above plus reps throughout the U.S.*
Sell To *Department stores, specialty stores, mail order catalogues & off-price retailers.*
Corp. Office *Division of Wdiamondgroup (www.wdiamondgroup.com)*
Private Label *Yes*
Web Site *www.hartschaffnermarx.com*
RN Number *WPL06986*

IN STYLE USA, INC. *(Rep.)

307 West 36th Street, 2nd Floor
New York, NY 10018 pauline.lock@instyleusa.net
212 631 0278 Fax : 212 631 0279

Products *Athleticwear, sportswear, jeans & shirts.*
Price Points *Better to designer.*
Production *U.S.A. & China*
Showrooms *Above*
Sell To *Department stores, specialty stores & boutiques.*
Corp. Office *Above*
Private Label *Yes*
Web Site *www.instyleusa.net*
Rev. in mil. *2-10*
Contact *President: James Mallon*

IN.STYLE EXCHANGE™

1844 W. Division Street, Suite 201
Arlington, TX 76012 info@instyleexchange.com
817 886 9222 Fax : 928 447 3168

Products *Ready-to-wear trendy designs for private label orders.*
Price Points *Competitive to moderate*

Production *U.S.A.*
Sell To *Department stores, specialty stores, boutiques, screenprinters, embroiderers.*
Corp. Office *Arlington, Texas*
Private Label *Yes*
Web Site *www.instyleexchange.com*
Contact *Sales: Jenny Siede*

LEAWOOD APPAREL LLC.

PO Box 55
Flourtown, PA 19031
215 233 1973
leawoodapparel@hotmail.com

Products *Men's private label sweaters and knitwear.*
Price Points *Moderate to better.*
Production *Domestic & Caribbean Basin*
Corp. Office *8900 Carlisle Road, Wyndmoor, PA 19038-7412.*
Private Label *Yes*
Web Site *www.leawoodapparel.vpweb.com*
Contact
President/Owner: Allan Flickstein

MIAMI STYLE INC.

7480 NW 52nd Street
Miami, FL 33166
305 805 1168 Fax : 305 805 0075
customercare@miamistyle.com

Labels *Miami Style*
Products *Manufacturer of active/athletic wear, tee shirts, pants, swimwear & beachwear.*
Price Points *Moderate*
Production *Bangladesh and China*
Sell To *Department stores, specialty stores, boutiques, mass merchants*
Private Label *Yes*
Web Site *www.miamistylebsd.com*
Contact *Owner: Amnon Bensimon, General Manager: Sofia Rincon*

ROYAL APPAREL, INC.

65 Commerce Drive
Hauppauge, NY 11788
631 213 8299 Fax : 631 922 8438 866-Royal-1-S
sales@royalapparel.net

Labels *Royal Apparel*
Products *Basic & fashion forward blanks in a large selection of colors & knit fabrications.*
Price Points *Moderate to better.*
Production *U.S.A.*
Showrooms *New York & Allentown, Pa.*
Sell To *Mass merchants, branded labels, screen printers & department stores.*
Private Label *Yes*
Web Site *www.royalapparel.net*
Contact *President: Morey Mayeri, Owners: Morey Mayeri/Abraham Mayeri*

STYLE SOURCE INC.

913 Orange Street
Wilmington, NC 28401 geoff@style-source.com
910 399 2288 Fax : 910 399 2289

Labels *Henry Lehr, Mainland Co., Crazy Shirts Hawaii, Prince*
Products *Private label and product development specialists of cotton knit shirts and sportswear.*
Price Points *Moderate to better.*
Production *U.S.A.*
Sell To *Specialty stores, boutiques, mail order catalogues, screenprinters and embroiderers.*
Web Site *www.style-source.com*
RN Number *RN82034*
Contact *President: Geoffrey Krasnov*

STYLEX TEXTILE DBA FABKA FABRICS LLC

2833 Leonis Avenue, Suite 104
Vernon, CA 90058 sharona@fabkafabrics.com
323 588 3000 Fax : 323 588 3636

Products *Basic & fashion forward tee shirts made according to customers designs. Full package.*
Price Points *Budget to better.*
Production *U.S.A.*
Sell To *Specialty stores, boutiques, department stores, mass merchants*
Web Site *www.fabkafabrics.com*
Contact *Sharona Kahen (Cell: 310-991-0366)*

VICTOR ROSSI

11016 Nacirema Lane
Stevenson, MD 21153 vr@victorrossi.com
410 337 2714

Products *Prival label in eveningwear, cotton garments, sportswear, bags & footwear.*
Price Points *Moderate to Designer*
Production *Domestic & Import*
Sell To *Department stores, specialty stores, mail order catalogs, designers & wholesalers.*
Corp. Office *Above*
Private Label *Yes*
Web Site *www.victorrossi.com*
RN Number *102005*
Contact *Manish Singh*

VISHAL ENTERPRISES

226 West 37th Street, 7th Floor
New York, NY 10018 vishal@vishalent.com
212 629 0880 Fax : 212 629 0882

Products *Casual sportswear, dress & sport shirts, jeans & denimwear.*
Price Points *Better*
Production *Import*
Sell To *Department stores, boutiques, mail order catalogues*
Private Label *Yes*
Rev. in mil. *2-10*
Contact *Owner: Mahesh Moorjani, Sales: Vishal Moorjani*

7 DIAMONDS

15778 Gateway Circle
Tustin, CA 92780 sales@7diamonds.com
714 241 7190 Fax : 714 241 7199 877 577 1963

Labels *Seven Diamonds*
Products *Men's sport shirts, knits and polos.*
Price Points *Better*
Showrooms *1071 Avenue of the Americas Room 200 NY NY 10018*
212 997 1777 7diamonds@7diamonds.com
Sell To *Department stores, specialty stores & boutiques.*
Corp. Office *Above*
Private Label *Yes*
Web Site *www.7diamonds.com*
Contact *President: Sami Khalil*

ANNE NAMBA DESIGNS

324 Kamani Street
Honolulu, HI 96813 anne@annenamba.com
808 589 1135 Fax : 808 589 1792 877-578-0001

Labels *Anne Namba Designs*
Products *Asian inspired one of a kind shirts.*
Price Points *Designer*
Production *U.S.A.*
Showrooms *Salt & Pepper Sales/Los Angeles*
Sell To *Department stores, specialty stores, boutiques & mail order catalogues.*
Private Label *No*
Web Site *www.annenamba.com*
Rev. in mil. *2-10*
Contact *President & Designer: Anne Namba*

BURMA BIBAS

597 Fifth Avenue, 10th Floor
New York, NY 10017 sales@burmabibas.com
212 750 2500 Fax : 212 750 2834

Labels *Pierre Cardin, Campia, Burma Bibas.*
Products *Men's dress, woven & knit shirts.*
Price Points *Moderate, better & designer.*
Production *Hong Kong, Korea & Europe.*
Showrooms *New York*
Sell To *Department & specialty stores, boutiques, catalogues & off-price retailers.*
Private Label *Yes*
Web Site *www.burmabibas.com*
RN Number *WPL13185*
Rev. in mil. *11-50*

CLASSIX

39360 3rd Street East, #307
Palmdale, CA 93550 vkhachooni@hotmail.com
661 726 9041 Fax : 661 726 9246 800 934-3290

Labels *Classix*
Products *Men's formalwear shirt collection. All our top quality shirts and accessories are always in stoc*

Price Points *Better*
Sell To *Department stores, specialty stores, formalwear shops.*
Web Site *www.classixshirts.com*

D'ACCORD SHIRTS & GUAYABERAS

7320 NW 12th Street, Unit 115
Miami, FL 33126 rafael@daccordshirts.com
305 576 0926 Fax : 305 576 0196

Labels *DS&G-Rafael Contreras*
Products *Guayaberas, casual & dressy shirts with style since 1980. Linen & European fabrications.*
Price Points *Moderate & better.*
Production *U.S.A. & Mexico*
Showrooms *Miami*
Sell To *Department stores, specialty stores, mail order catalogues, restaurants, hotels.*
Corp. Office *DBA: DS&G*
Private Label *Yes*
Web Site *www.daccordshirts.com*
RN Number *RN58706*
Rev. in mil. *11-50*
Contact *President: Rafael Contreras*

DAVID CAREY INC.

2250 Paragon Drive , Suite A
San Jose, CA 95131 sales@davidcareyinc.com
408 453 7843 Fax : 408 453 7848 800 858 TIES

Products *Cotton & cotton/rayon, rayon & silk casual shirts. Licensed t-shirts and camp shirts.*
Price Points *Moderate to better*
Production *U.S.A., Thailand, Korea and China.*
Showrooms *San Jose*
Sell To *Specialty stores, department stores, boutiques & mail order catalogues.*
Private Label *Yes*
Web Site *www.davidcareyinc.com*
RN Number *RN93194*
Rev. in mil. *0-2*
Contact *President: Marc Begun, Design & Production: Mike Murphy*

GOLF APPAREL BRANDS

13621 South Main Street
Los Angeles, CA 90061 sales@lamode.com
310 715 1772 Fax : 310 715 1776 800 678 5246

Labels *La Mode, NatureTech, Clark & Gregory, Sahara*
Products *Men's golf shirts, rain jackets and rain pants.*
Price Points *Moderate to better*
Production *Domestic and import from Korea, China, Hong Kong, Malaysia*
Sell To *Specialty stores, off-price and golf shops.*
Private Label *Yes*
Web Site *www.lamode.com*
Contact *President/Owner: Eddie Kahn*

HASELSON INT'L TRADING INC.

32 West 39th Street, 3rd Floor
New York, NY 10118
212 465 0605 Fax : 212 629 3506 800 217 4478
sales@ringosport.com

Labels *Ringo Sport, Triple Play, Swiss Cros, Sahara Club, Roadblock, Aqua, Silver Label*
Products *Men's & boy's sport & dress shirts.*
Price Points *Moderate*
Production *Import*
Showrooms *New York, Miami & Houston*
Sell To *Department stores, specialty stores & mass merchants.*
Private Label *Yes*
Web Site *www.haselson.com*

HTT HEADWEAR LTD.

41185 Raintree Court
Murrieta, CA 92562
951 304 0400 Fax : 951 304 0410 800 846 8468
sales@httapparel.com

Labels *Head To Toe*
Products *Woven and knit shirts, tees, polos, tanks & sport jerseys.*
Price Points *Better*
Production *U.S.A., China & Pakistan*
Showrooms *Murrieta, CA*
Sell To *Manufacturers*
Private Label *Yes*
Web Site *www.httapparel.com*
Contact *President: Howard Seegar, Owner: Howard Seegar, Customer Service: Luke Fafara*

JUST WHITE SHIRTS

1991 Leslie Street
Toronto, Ontario, Canada M3B 2M3
416 447 2907 Fax : 416 447 8059
alam@justwhiteshirts.com

Labels *JustWhiteShirts, The Shirt Store, Redford*
Products *High quality 100% cotton dress shirts, sport shirts, ties & casual accessories.*
Price Points *Better*
Production *Own manufacturing plant for own brands as well as private label.*
Showrooms *New York Store: 51 East 44th Street, NYC 10017 212-557-8040 or 1-800-289-2744.*
Sell To *Department stores, specialty stores, on-line, catalogues*
Private Label *Yes*
Web Site *www.justwhiteshirts.com*
Contact *President: Alam Najiullah (Cell: 416-837-7448)*

QUEENSBORO SHIRT COMPANY

1400 Marstellar Street
Wilmington, NC 28401
800 847 4478 Fax : 910 251 7771
fredm@queensboro.com

Labels *Queensboro*
Products *Shirts, polo shirts & sweatshirts. Specialize in embroidered, digitally or screenprinted apparel*
Production *USA*
Showrooms *Above*
Private Label *No*
Web Site *www.queensboro.com*

Contact *President: Fred Meyers, Vice President/Operations: Fred Duran*

RUM REGGAE

PO Box 861
Summerland, CA 93067 rumreggae@sbcglobal.net
805 649 4820 Fax : 805 649 5576

Labels *Rum Reggae*
Products *Resort and Hawaiian shirts. Wearable art in hand-crafted Batik. Custom work available.*
Price Points *Moderate*
Sell To *Specialty stores*
Private Label *Yes*
Web Site *www.rumreggae.net*
Contact *President: Karen Proffitt*

SWIFT ORIGINALS

1 W Flatiron Crossing, Ste 2156
Broomfield, CO 80021 swiftoriginals@gmail.com
303 442 9013 Fax : 303 499 6045 866-704-4024

Labels *Swift Originals*
Products *Men's casual cotton shirts.*
Price Points *Moderate*
Production *Import*
Sell To *Specialty stores & boutiques.*
Private Label *Yes*
Web Site *www.facebook.com/swiftoriginals*
Contact *President: Andy McPherson*

ZANETTI INC.

4521 Sherman Oaks Avenue, Suite 401
Sherman Oaks, CA 91403 zanetti@zanetti.com
310 478 8660 Fax : 310 478 6935

Labels *Zanetti*
Products *Men's shirts in luxurious fabrics.*
Price Points *Better*
Production *Italy*
Showrooms *New York/147 West 35th Street, Suite 603, New York, NY 10001 212-217-0889.*
Sell To *Deptartment & specialty stores, mass merchants, mail order, boutiques & off-price.*
Private Label *Yes*
Web Site *www.zanetti.com*
Contact *Owner: Bruce Banafsheha*

2 X IST

1411 Broadway, 8th Floor
New York, NY 10018 ralph@2xist.com
212 741 7731 Fax : 212 741 7932

Labels *2 X ist*
Products *Designer underwear. Briefs, sport brief, thong, trunk and v-neck muscle shirt.*
Price Points *Better to designer*
Production *Import*
Showrooms *New York*
Customer Service: 285 Ridge Road, Suite#3, Dayton, NJ 08810, 1-877-597-5827
Sell To *Department stores, specialty stores & mail order catalogues.*
Private Label *Yes*
Web Site *www.2xist.com*
RN Number *RN97404*
Contact *Vice President Sales: Ralph Beyda*

BEDHEAD PAJAMAS

3641 10th Avenue
Los Angeles, CA 90018 joanne@bedheadpjs.com
323 634 0333 Fax : 323 634 0433

Labels *Bedhead*
Products *Cotton pjs, robes, boxers, shorts and tees.*
Price Points *Better*
Production *U.S.A.*
Sell To *Department stores, specialty stores, boutiques, mail order catalogues, e-com retailers.*
Corp. Office *Above*
Private Label *Yes*
Web Site *www.bedheadpajamas.com*
Contact *President: Renee Claire, VP Sales: JoAnne Grazzini*

CAPELLI NEW YORK

1 East 33rd Street, 9th Floor
New York, NY 10016 info@capellinewyork.com
212 684 3344 Fax : 212 686 4895

Labels *Capelli New York*
Products *Sleepwear, robes and slippers for men.*
Production *Import*
Showrooms *New York, Canada, Europe and Asia*
Sell To *Department stores, specialty stores, national chain stores*
Private Label *Yes*
Web Site *www.capellinewyork.com*

COMME CI COMME CA LTD.

400 Oser Avenue, Suite 900
Hauppauge, NY 11788 liz@malepower.com
631 300 1035 Fax : 631 300 1039 1 800 447 4720

Labels *Male Power*
Products *Men's underwear.*
Price Points *Moderate*
Production *U.S.A.*
Sell To *Retail stores, lingerie stores & mail order catalogues.*

Private Label *Yes*
Web Site *www.malepower.com*
Contact *President: Jeff Baker, Sales: Elizabeth*

EZRASONS, INC.

37 West 37th Street, 10th Floor
New York, NY 10018 ezrajack@ezrasons.com
212 768 8330 Fax : 212 768 8327

Labels *Bottoms Out, Embassy, Ed Hardy, New Balance*
Products *Pajamas, underwear and performance essentials.*
Production *Import*
Web Site *www.ezrasons.com*
Contact *Sales (Bottoms Out and Embassy) Doug Wagner, Sales (New Balance and Ed Hardy) Judah Cattan.*

GOODWEAR USA

239 Western Avenue, Room 2D
Essex, MA 01929 steve@goodwear.com
978 768 7746 Fax : 800 787 4951 800 338 8895

Labels *Goodwear*
Products *Men's 100% cotton upscale dyeable garments, casual sportswear, tee-shirts & underwear.*
Price Points *Bridge*
Production *U.S.A.*
Showrooms *Tokyo, Osaka, NYC & Essex*
Sell To *Distributors*
Private Label *Yes*
Web Site *www.goodwear.com*
RN Number *75346*
Contact *President: Martha Liquori, Owner: Stephen & Martha Liquori, Sales: Stephen Liquori*

INNERWEAR BRANDS INTERNATIONAL

45 West 36th Street, 4th Floor
New York, NY 10018 sales@innerwearbrands.com
212 239 4222 Fax : 212 239 4277

Labels *Andrew Scott*
Products *Mens and boys underwear and loungewear.*
Price Points *Better*
Production *Import*
Sell To *Department stores, off-price, close out outlets*
Private Label *Yes*
Web Site *www.innerwearbrands.com*

ISACO INTERNATIONAL/PAPI INC.

5980 Miami Lakes Drive
Miami Lakes, FL 33014 info@papiinc.com
305 594 4455 Fax : 305 594 4496

Labels *Accents by Isaco, PAPI*
Products *Men's underwear, tanks & tees & hosiery.*
Price Points *Moderate, better & designer.*
Production *U.S.A. & import*
Showrooms *New York/366 Fifth Avenue, #901 New York, N. Y. tel#212 629-0111.*

Sell To *Specialty stores, chain & department stores.*
Corp. Office *5980 Miami Lakes Drive, Miami, FL 33014*
Private Label *Yes*
Web Site *www.papiinc.com*
RN Number *RN59495*
Contact *CEO: Isaac Zelcer, President: Alan Zelcer*

JOCKEY INTERNATIONAL, INC.

2300 60th Street
Kenosha, WI 53140 andy.vacca@jockey.com
262 658 8111 Fax : 262 658 1812 800 Jockey1

Labels *Jockey Classic, Jockey Sport, Next to Nothing, Jockey Pouch®, Elance®*
Products *Sleepwear, underwear and tee-shirts.*
Price Points *Moderate to better*
Production *U.S.A. & import worldwide.*
Showrooms *New York/1411 Broadway Suite 1010 (tel:212 840-4900)*
Sell To *Department stores, specialty stores, catalogues, off-price retailers & mass merchants.*
Private Label *Yes*
Web Site *www.jockey.com*
RN Number *RN61683*
Contact *President: Edward Emma*

SUSAN DUNN INC.

PO Box 1086
Rancho Santa Fe, CA 92067 susan@susandunn.com
858 832 1086 Fax : 858 832 1087

Labels *Susan Dunn®, Spa Slippurrs™, His Spawear*
Products *100% cotton robes, shower wraps & spa slippers.*
Price Points *Designer*
Production *U.S.A.*
Sell To *Specialty stores, boutiques, mail order catalogues, hotels, resorts & spas.*
Private Label *Yes*
Web Site *www.susandunn.com*
RN Number *RN90990*
Rev. in mil. *2-10*
Contact *CEO & President: Susan Dunn*

ALPHA INDUSTRIES, INC.

14200 Park Meadow Drive, Suite 110 South
Chantilly, VA 20151 wholesale@alphaindustries.com
703 378 1420 Fax : 703 378 4910 866 631 0719

Labels *Alpha Industries, Knox Armory*
Products *Fashion, military inspired, Americana & cold weather outerwear & apparel.*
Price Points *Moderate to better*
Production *U.S.A., Far East & Middle East*
Showrooms *Washington DC, NY, Los Angeles, London, Frankfurt, Paris, Seoul, Tokyo, Florence & Shanghai.*
Sell To *Department stores, specialty stores, boutiques & mail order catalogues.*
Private Label *Yes*
Web Site *www.alphaindustries.com*
RN Number *RN35569*

COLUMBIA SPORTSWEAR CO., INC.

14375 N.W. Science Park Drive
Portland, OR 97229 sales_info@columbia.com
503 985 4000 Fax : 503 985 5800 800 MA BOYLE

Labels *Columbia Sportswear Co.*
Products *Hunting, fishing, sportswear, footwear & active outerwear.*
Price Points *Moderate*
Production *U.S.A.*
Sell To *Department stores, specialty stores, mass merchants.*
Private Label *No*
Web Site *www.columbia.com*
RN Number *RN69724*
Rev. in mil. *+500*
Contact *Chairman: Gertrude Boyle, CEO: Tim Boyle, VIP Sales: Joseph R. Craig*

SCENT-LOK/DIV. OF A.L.S. ENTERPRISES

1731 Wierengo Drive
Muskegon, MI 49442 info@scentlok.com
231 777 7565 Fax : 231 767 2824 844 257 9505

Labels *Scent-Lok, A.L.S. Enterprises, Inc.*
Products *Hunting, outdoor & camouflage apparel, with patented odor-absorbing qualities.*
Price Points *Moderate & better.*
Production *U.S.A. & import*
Showrooms *Call for national reps, plus Muskegon, MI.*
Sell To *Specialty stores, mail order catalogues & mass merchants.*
Private Label *Yes*
Web Site *www.scentlok.com*
Contact *President: Greg Sesselmann, Co-Owner: Greg Sesselmann, Co-Owner: George Schrink Production: Mark Sesselmann*

TAYLOR MADE

5545 Fermi Court
Carlsbad, CA 92008 corporate@tmag.com
760 918 6000 800 864 7231

Labels *Ashworth*
Products *Golf inspired lifestyle sportswear. Part of Adidas Group (971-234-2300)*

Price Points *Better*
Sell To *Golf pro shops, resorts, department stores, specialty stores*
Private Label *No*
Web Site *www.taylormadegolf.com*

DREAM WORLD INTERNATIONAL, INC.

10073 Sandmeyer Lane
Philadelphia, PA 19116
215 320 0200 Fax : 215 320 0201 800 789 7792
rveltri@dreamworldintl.com

Labels *Zacchi, Pacelli, Dreams, XXIOTTI, "AT" Collection*
Products *Affordable designer-look suits, dress pants & sportswear. Regular & big & tall sizes.*
Price Points *Moderate to bridge*
Production *Import*
Sell To *Specialty stores*
Private Label *Yes*
RN Number *RN99612*
Contact *President: Ross Veltri*

HAGGAR CLOTHING CO., INC.

11511 Luna Rd
Dallas, TX 75234
214 352 8481 Fax : 214 956 4644 877 841 2219
torri.teel@haggar.com

Labels *Haggar, Haggar Heritage*
Products *Suits, sportcoats, slacks & sportswear.*
Price Points *Moderate to better.*
Production *U.S.A. & import*
Showrooms *Dallas*
Sell To *Department stores, specialty stores, catalogues, mass merchants & off-price retailers.*
Private Label *No*
Web Site *www.haggar.com*
Rev. in mil. *+500*
Contact *CEO: Paul Buxbaum*

HART SCHAFFNER MARX

1680 E Touhy Avenue
Des Plaines, IL 60018
800 327 4466
info@wdiamondgroup.com

Labels *HSM*
Products *Men's private label & branded tailored clothing.*
Price Points *Better*
Production *U.S.A. & import*
Showrooms *New York/above plus reps throughout the U.S.*
Sell To *Department stores, specialty stores, mail order catalogues & off-price retailers.*
Corp. Office *Division of Wdiamondgroup (www.wdiamondgroup.com)*
Private Label *Yes*
Web Site *www.hartschaffnermarx.com*
RN Number *WPL06986*

HUGO BOSS U.S.A., INC.

55 Water Street, 8th Floor
New York, NY 10041
212 940 0600 Fax : 212 940 0619 800-484-6267
customerservice@hugoboss-store.com

Labels *Hugo Boss, Boss Hugo Boss, Boss Black, Boss Green, Boss Orange*
Products *Suits, sportcoats & traditional sportswear*
Price Points *Better*
Production *U.S.A. & import*

Sell To *Department stores, specialty stores, mail order catalogues & mass merchants.*
Private Label *No*
Web Site *www.hugoboss.com*
Rev. in mil. *+500*

PEERLESS CLOTHING INTERNATIONAL

641 Lexington Avenue, 12th Floor
New York, NY 10022
sales@peerless-clothing.com
212 541 8720 Fax : 212 245 1142 800 336 9363

Labels *Lauren Ralph Lauren, Calvin Klein, Tallia, Michael Kors, DKNY, Sean John, John Varvato*
Products *Fine tailored suits, sport coats and trousers.*
Production *Canada*
Showrooms *Distribution Center: 200 Industrial Park Road, St. Albans, VT 05478, Tel: 802-527-1222.*
Corp. Office *Above & Vetements Peerless Clothing, Montreal, Quebec Canada 514-593-9300.*
Private Label *Yes*
Web Site *www.peerless-clothing.com*
Contact *Chairman/CEO: Alvin Segal*

ZANETTI INC.

4521 Sherman Oaks Avenue, Suite 401
Sherman Oaks, CA 91403
zanetti@zanetti.com
310 478 8660 Fax : 310 478 6935

Labels *Zanetti*
Products *Men's suits, tuxedos, jackets & pants in luxurious fabrics.*
Price Points *Better*
Production *Italy*
Showrooms *New York/147 West 35th Street, Suite 603, New York, NY 10001 212-217-0889..*
Sell To *Deptartment & specialty stores, mass merchants, mail order, boutiques & off-price.*
Private Label *Yes*
Web Site *www.zanetti.com*
Contact *Owner: Bruce Banafsheha*

ANDARI FASHION, INC.

9626 Telstar Avenue
El Monte, CA 91731 info@andari.com
626 575 2759 Fax : 626 575 3629

Products *Private label sweater manufacturer.*
Price Points *Moderate to designer.*
Production *U.S.A. & import*
Sell To *Department stores, specialty stores, boutiques.*
Private Label *Yes*
Web Site *www.andari.com*
Rev. in mil. *2-10*
Contact *Owner: Lillian Wang*

AUTUMN CASHMERE INC.

231 West 39th Street, Suite#1111
New York, NY 10018 info@autumncashmere.com
888 6 AUTUMN Fax : 212 398 2255 1 888 6 AUTUMN

Labels *Autumn Cashmere*
Products *Fashion & novelty 100% cashmere & cashmere blend sweaters. 2 to 5 gauge knits.*
Price Points *Better to designer.*
Production *China & Hong Kong*
Showrooms *New York/Aci NY, 212-398-2244, CA/Sales: 213-893-6995.*

Sell To *Department & specialty stores. boutiques & mail order catalogues.*
Private Label *Yes*
Web Site *www.autumncashmere.com*
Rev. in mil. *11-50*

CANADIAN SWEATER CO., LTD.

#39 8528-123rd Street
Surrey, BC, Canada V3W 3V6 info@canadiansweater.com
604 594 8050 Fax : 604 594 8264

Labels *Cowichan, Islander*
Products *Woolen sweaters & winter accessories.*
Price Points *Bridge*
Production *Canada*
Sell To *High end department stores, boutiques.*
Corp. Office *Above*
Private Label *Yes*
Web Site *www.canadiansweater.com*
Contact *President: Kaljit Tmana*

GOLF APPAREL BRANDS

13621 South Main Street
Los Angeles, CA 90061 sales@lamode.com
310 715 1772 Fax : 310 715 1776 800 678 5246

Labels *La Mode, Clark & Gregory*
Products *Men's golf sweaters and vests.*
Price Points *Moderate to better*
Production *Domestic and import from Korea, China, Hong Kong, Malaysia*
Sell To *Specialty stores, off-price and golf shops.*

Private Label *Yes*
Web Site *www.lamode.com*
Contact *President/Owner: Eddie Kahn*

HASELSON INT'L TRADING INC.

32 West 39th Street, 3rd Floor
New York, NY 10118 sales@ringosport.com
212 465 0605 Fax : 212 629 3506 800 217 4478

Labels *Ringo Sport, Triple Play, Swiss Cros, Sahara Club, Roadblock, Aqua, Silver Label*
Products *Men's & boy's dress & casual sweaters.*
Price Points *Moderate*
Production *Import*
Showrooms *New York, Miami & Houston*
Sell To *Department stores, specialty stores & mass merchants.*
Private Label *Yes*
Web Site *www.haselson.com*

RAFFI LINEA UOMO

250 West 39th Street, Suite 601
New York, NY 10018 info@raffilineauomo.com
212 307 1416 Fax : 212 957 9735

Labels *Raffi*
Products *Full line of sweaters in cashmere, merino wool and cotton.*
Price Points *Better*
Sell To *Department stores and specialty stores*
Web Site *www.raffionline.com*
Contact *National Sales Manager: Jenny Au, tel: 212-307-1416*

ZANETTI INC.

4521 Sherman Oaks Avenue, Suite 401
Sherman Oaks, CA 91403 zanetti@zanetti.com
310 478 8660 Fax : 310 478 6935

Labels *Zanetti*
Products *Men's sweaters in luxurious fabrics.*
Price Points *Better*
Production *Italy*
Showrooms *New York/147 West 35th Street, Suite 603, New York, NY 10001 212-217-0889.*
Sell To *Deptartment & specialty stores, mass merchants, mail order, boutiques & off-price.*
Private Label *Yes*
Web Site *www.zanetti.com*
Contact *Owner: Bruce Banafsheha*

BASIX OF AMERICA

2778 NW 31st Avenue
Ft. Lauderdale, FL 33311 info@basixofamerica.com
800 236 8150 Fax : 954 486 6580

Products *Mens swimwear small thru XXL*
Showrooms *Rep: Jessica Corbett - 954-486-6580 - jessicacorbett@basixofamerica.com*
Sell To *Department stores, specialty stores*
Web Site *www.basixofamerica.com*

BEACH RAYS/DIV OF J.Y. RAYS, INC.

2023 Chico Avenue
South El Monte, CA 91733 sales@beachrays.com
626 941 0388 Fax : 626 941 0386

Labels *Surfer, Vast, Wet*
Products *Men's swimwear & beachwear.*
Price Points *Moderate to better*
Production *Offshore*
Sell To *Department stores, specialty stores, theme/water parks*
Corp. Office
Private Label *Yes*
Web Site *www.beachrays.com*
Contact *National Sales Manager: Natalie Wierzba*

CATFISH CALHOUN AKA CALHOUN SPORTSWEAR *(Rep.)

250 Bunting Road
St. Catharines, Ontario, Canada L2M 3Y1 mikev@calhounsportswear.com
905 688 6100 Fax : 905 688 1167 800 263 5729

Labels *Corona, Sons of Anarchy, The Walking Dead, Coors, Molson, Canadian, DC Comics*
Products *Men's licensed apparel, swimwear & jams. Can do custom printing.*
Price Points *Moderate*
Production *Canada & overseas*
Showrooms *Call for reps.*
Sell To *Department stores, specialty stores, boutiques, mass merchants & mail order catalogues.*
Private Label *No*
Web Site *www.calhounsportswear.com*
Contact *Key Accounts Manager: Jodie Bartlett*

COMME CI COMME CA LTD.

400 Oser Avenue, Suite 900
Hauppauge, NY 11788 liz@malepower.com
631 300 1035 Fax : 631 300 1039 1 800 447 4720

Labels *Male Power*
Products *Men's swim & active wear.*
Price Points *Moderate*
Production *U.S.A.*
Sell To *Retail stores, lingerie stores, menswear stores & mail order catalogues.*
Private Label *Yes*
Web Site *www.malepower.com*
Contact *President: Jeff Baker, Sales: Elizabeth*

CORAL HEAD INC./HAWAIIAN ISLAND CREATIONS

1988 West 169th Street
Gardena, CA 90247
baltazar1971@yahoo.com
310 366 7712 Fax : 310 366 6819

Labels *Hawaiian Island Creations*
Products *Surfwear & beachwear.*
Price Points *Moderate*
Production *U.S.A. & import*
Sell To *Specialty stores.*
Private Label *No*
Web Site *www.hicworldwide.com*
RN Number *RN83342*
Rev. in mil. *2-10*
Contact *President: Craig Hara, Marketing: Baltazar Magdirila*

FREE COUNTRY LTD.

1071 6th Avenue, 9th Floor
New York, NY 10018
rondac@freecountry.com
212 719 4596 Fax : 212 719 2051

Labels *Free Country*
Products *A full line of mens swimwear*
Price Points *Better*
Production *U.S.A. & import*
Showrooms *New York*
Sell To *Department stores, specialty stores & boutiques.*
Private Label *Yes*
Web Site *www.freecountry.com*
RN Number *RN82608*
Rev. in mil. *11-50*
Contact *Design: Ira Schwartz*

SWEENIE MANUFACTURING CORPORATION

60 East 9th Street, Suite 315
New York, NY 10003
diane@sweeniemanufacturing.com
646 825 5027 Fax : 646 825 5027

Labels *Torvu, Bilt*
Products *Men's contemporary swimwear & coverups, graphic tees & accessories.*
Price Points *Budget to designer*
Production *U.S.A. & import from China, East Asia, Europe & South/Central America*
Sell To *Department stores, specialty stores, boutiques, mass merchants*
Private Label *Yes*
Web Site *www.sweeniemanufacturing.com*
Rev. in mil. *0-2*
Contact *Design & Production: Diane Walker (cell: 914-471-1069),*
Sales & Marketing: Stacey Demar (cell: 646-772-6113)

2 X IST

1411 Broadway, 8th Floor
New York, NY 10018
212 741 7731 Fax : 212 741 7932
ralph@2xist.com

Labels *2 X ist, Pima, Neon, Modal Collection, SLIQ*
Products *Designer tee-shirts, v-neck muscle tee shirts & blanks*
Price Points *Better to designer*
Production *Import*
Showrooms *New York*
Customer Service: 285 Ridge Road, Suite#3, Dayton, NJ 08810, 1-877-597-5827
Sell To *Department stores, speciality stores & mail order catalogues.*
Private Label *Yes*
Web Site *www.2xist.com*
RN Number *RN97404*
Contact *National Sales Manager: Ralph Beyda*

ACTIVE APPAREL, INC.

11076 Venture Drive
Mira Loma, CA 91752
951 361 0060 Fax : 951 361 3120
kashis@activeapparel.net

Products *Men's solid tee shirts, sweatshirts & v-necks*
Price Points *Moderate.*
Production *U.S.A. & import.*
Sell To *Specialty stores, mass merchants & off-price retailers.*
Private Label *Yes*
Web Site *www.activeapparel.net*
RN Number *RN99928*
Rev. in mil. *2-10*
Contact *President: Wasif Siddique, Wholesale Orders: Kashis Hussain*

ALSTYLE

1501 East Cerritos Avenue
Anaheim, CA 92805
714 765 0400 Fax : 714 765 0450 800 225 1364
info@alstyle.com

Labels *AAA™*
Products *All kinds of tees. Organic, short & long sleeve.*
Price Points *Moderate to better*
Showrooms *Sales Reps throughout the USA.*
Sell To *Department stores, mass merchants, mail order catalogs.*
Private Label *Yes*
Web Site *www.alstyle.com*

ANVIL KNITWEAR, INC.

146 West Country Club Road
Hamer, SC 29547
843 774 8211 Fax : 843 841 4963
info@gildan.com

Labels *Anvil®*
Products *Imprintable & embroiderable knit sportswear blanks.*
Price Points *Moderate*
Sell To *Wholesalers, department stores, specialty stores & mass merchants.*
Corp. Office *Division of Gildan Activewear SRL (www.gildan.com) - 877 445 3265*

Private Label *Yes*
Web Site *www.anvilknitwear.com*
RN Number *RN38619*
Contact *Arlin Turner Manager*

BRAVADO MERCHANDISING

1755 Broadway, 2nd Floor
New York, NY 10019 tom.bennett@bravado.com
212 445 3400 Fax : 212 445 3499

Labels *Bravado*
Products *Concert & movie tee-shirts. Specialize in rock-n-roll, film & novelty designs.*
Price Points *Moderate*
Production *U.S.A.*
Showrooms *New York, London, Los Angeles, Stockholm*
Sell To *Department stores, specialty stores, mass merchants & mail order catalogues, tour events.*
Private Label *Yes*
Web Site *www.bravadousa.com*
RN Number *RN91889*
Contact *Sales: Tom Bennett*

BUCK WEAR INC.

2900 Cowan Avenue
Baltimore, MD 21223 cjohnson@buckwear.com
410 646 6400 Fax : 410 646 7700 800-813-7708

Products *Printed adult & youth t-shirts. Quality sportswear for the Outdoorsman.*
Sell To *Specialty stores.*
Corp. Office *Above*
Web Site *www.buckwear.com*
Contact *President: David Trapp*

CALIFORNIA RAIN CO.

1213 E. 14th Street
Los Angeles, CA 90021 info@californiarainla.com
213 623 6061 Fax : 213 627 5703

Products *Private label manufacturing experts. Men's t-shirts, blanks & polo shirts.*
Price Points *Better*
Production *U.S.A.*
Sell To *Department stores*
Corp. Office *Above*
Private Label *Yes*
Web Site *www.californiarainla.com*
RN Number *75443*
Rev. in mil. *11-50*
Contact *President: Jack Chang*

CAMBER SPORTSWEAR, INC.

2 DeKalb Pike
Norristown, PA 19401 camberusa@aol.com
610 239 9910 Fax : 610 239 9912 800 345 7518

Labels *Camber*
Products *Printable thermals, sweats, sweatshirts & baseball shirts.*

Price Points *Moderate to better.*
Production *U.S.A.*
Showrooms *Norristown*
Sell To *Specialty stores, printers & embroiderers.*
Private Label *Yes*
Web Site *www.camberusa.com*
RN Number *RN91210*
Rev. in mil. *2-10*
Contact *President: Barry Schwartz*

CATFISH CALHOUN AKA CALHOUN SPORTSWEAR *(Rep.)

250 Bunting Road
St. Catharines, Ontario, Canada L2M 3Y1 mikev@calhounsportswear.com
905 688 6100 Fax : 905 688 1167 800 263 5729

Labels *Calhoun*
Products *Men's licensed apparel, unisex tee-shirts, sweatshirts, boxer shorts & jams. Can do custom proa*
Price Points *Moderate*
Production *Canada & overseas*
Showrooms *Call for reps.*
Sell To *Department stores, specialty stores, boutiques, mass merchants & mail order catalogues.*
Private Label *No*
Web Site *www.calhounsportswear.com*

ENVIROTEXTILES LLC.

3214 S. Grand Avenue
Glenwood Springs, CO 81601 info@envirotextile.com
970 945 5986 Fax : 970 945 4456

Products *Hemp T-shirts & promotional apparel.*
Price Points *Moderate*
Production *U.S.A., China & Mexico*
Showrooms *Above*
Sell To *Garment & accessory manufacturers*
Private Label *Yes*
Web Site *www.envirotextile.com*
Rev. in mil. *2-10*
Contact *President: Barbara Filippone*

FAIR HEMP INC.

1717 Troutman Street, #302
Ridgewood, NY 11385 info@fairhemp.com
646 485 0939 Fax : 212 656 1714

Labels *Fair Hemp*
Products *Hemp and organic cotton mens long and short sleeve tees.*
Price Points *Better*
Production *Import*
Sell To *Sell blanks to printers and produce private label and custom productions.*
Private Label *Yes*
Web Site *www.fairhemp.com*
RN Number *122157*

GOODWEAR USA

239 Western Avenue, Room 2D
Essex, MA 01929 steve@goodwear.com
978 768 7746 Fax : 800 787 4951 800 338 8895

Labels *Goodwear*
Products *Men's upscale dyeable tee-shirts done in sustainable fabrics: organic cotton & bamboo.*
Price Points *Bridge*
Production *U.S.A.*
Showrooms *Tokyo, Osaka, NYC & Essex*
Sell To *Distributors*
Private Label *Yes*
Web Site *www.goodwear.com*
RN Number *75346*
Contact *President: Martha Liquori, Owner: Stephen & Martha Liquori, Sales: Stephen Liquori*

GRAPHICS GROUP LTD./DBA LATITUDES

2425 NE Riverside Way
Portland, OR 97210 info@latitudespdx.com
503 248 2060 Fax : 503 248 2134 800 700 1073

Labels *Latitudes*
Products *Screenprinted t-shirts & sweatshirts. "Boutique-look", sports, multi-media & tie-dye designs.*
Price Points *Moderate to better*
Production *U.S.A.*
Showrooms *Portland, OR*
Sell To *Department stores, specialty stores, boutiques & mail order catalogues.*
Private Label *Yes*
Web Site *www.latitudespdx.com*
Contact *President: L. Thomas, Owner: L. Thomas, Production: Jamie McCrae*

JOE BLOW T'S

8213-B Cloverleaf Drive Rear
Millersville, MD 21108 vanessa@joeblow.com
443 274 2744 Fax : 410 766 9516

Labels *Joe Blow T's Inc.*
Products *T-shirts of all kinds. Made in the USA.*
Price Points *Moderate*
Production *U.S.A.*
Sell To *Department stores, specialty stores & boutiques.*
Private Label *Yes*
Web Site *www.joeblow.com*
Contact *Owner: Stewart Cohen, Sales: Vanessa Harris (cell: 443-962-0278).*

KAMTEX FASHION

2916 NW 28th Street
Lauderdale Lakes, FL 33311 sales@kamtexfashion.com
954 733 1042 Fax : 954 733 1044 1-877-KAMTEX3

Labels *Kamtex*
Products *Wholesale distributor of mens tee shirts, hoodies and blanks.*
Price Points *Moderate*
Production *Import*
Web Site *www.kamtexfashion.com*

PILLAGED VILLAGE, THE

31Eagle Court, Suite E
Carlisle, OH 45005
937 743 0685 Fax : 937 743 0697 1-877-793-1066
pvsales@pillagedvillage.com

Labels *The Pillaged Village*
Products *Medieval designed t-shirts.*
Price Points *Moderate*
Showrooms *Same as Above*
Sell To *Boutiques, specialty stores, on-line catalog*
Web Site *www.pillagedvillage.com*
Contact *Owner: Wendy Kimmel*

RICH HONEY

919 E. Slauson Ave
Los Angeles, CA 90011
213 905 3205 Fax : 213 746 9602
info@richhoney.us

Labels *Rich Honey*
Products *Better quality T-shirts using100% combed and ring spun and poly viscose fabrics.*
Price Points *Better*
Production *U.S.A.*
Sell To *Department stores, specialty stores, boutiques*
Private Label *Yes*
Web Site *www.richhoney.us*
Contact *CEO: Luddivina Bowes*

ROYAL APPAREL, INC.

65 Commerce Drive
Hauppauge, NY 11788
631 213 8299 Fax : 631 922 8438 866-Royal-1-S
sales@royalapparel.net

Labels *Royal Apparel*
Products *Basic & fashion forward blanks in a large selection of colors & knit fabrications.*
Price Points *Moderate to better.*
Production *U.S.A.*
Showrooms *New York & Allentown, Pa.*
Sell To *Mass merchants, branded labels, screen printers & department stores.*
Private Label *Yes*
Web Site *www.royalapparel.net*
Contact *President: Morey Mayeri, Owners: Morey Mayeri/Abraham Mayeri*

SLICK DESIGNS

3710 East 10 Court
Hialeah, FL 33013
305 836 7950 Fax : 305 836 7905 1-877-55Slick
sales@slickart.com

Labels *Slick Art*
Products *Wholesaler for novelty & licensed t-shirts & apparel. Specialize in different printing techniqu*
Price Points *Moderate*
Production *U.S.A.*
Sell To *Boutiques, specialty stores*
Web Site *www.slickart.com*
Contact *Vice President: Samuel Ben Yaeesh*

SUGAR AND BRUNO

7260 Georgetown Road
Indianapolis, IN 46268
317 293 5888 Fax : 317 293 5886 800 875 8559
challen@sugarandbruno.com

Labels *Sugar and Bruno*
Products *Fun tees, tanks and hoodies*
Price Points *Moderate*
Production *U.S.A. & China*
Sell To *Specialty stores, boutiques*
Web Site *www.sugarandbruno.com*
RN Number *127789*
Rev. in mil. *2-10*
Contact *President: Challen Powers*

BILLS KHAKIS

170 Pinesbridge Road
Beacon FallS, CT 06403 jeoff@billskhakis.com
800 435 4254 800 435 4254

Labels *Bills Khakis*
Products *Authentic American khakis.*
Price Points *Designer*
Production *U.S.A.*
Sell To *Specialty stores*
Private Label *No*
Web Site *www.billskhakis.com*

HART SCHAFFNER MARX

1680 E Touhy Avenue
Des Plaines, IL 60018 info@wdiamondgroup.com
800 327 4466

Labels *HSM*
Products *Men's private label & branded slacks.*
Price Points *Better*
Production *U.S.A. & import*
Showrooms *New York/above plus reps throughout the U.S.*
Sell To *Department stores, specialty stores, mail order catalogues & off-price retailers.*
Corp. Office *Division of Wdiamondgroup (www.wdiamondgroup.com)*
Private Label *Yes*
Web Site *www.hartschaffnermarx.com*
RN Number *WPL06986*

PEERLESS CLOTHING INTERNATIONAL

641 Lexington Avenue, 12th Floor
New York, NY 10022 sales@peerless-clothing.com
212 541 8720 Fax : 212 245 1142 800 336 9363

Labels *Lauren Ralph Lauren, Calvin Klein, Tallia, Michael Kors, DKNY, Sean John, John Varvato*
Products *Fine tailored suits, sport coats and trousers.*
Production *Canada*
Showrooms *Distribution Center: 200 Industrial Park Road, St. Albans, VT 05478, Tel: 802-527-1222.*
Corp. Office *Above & Vetements Peerless Clothing, Montreal, Quebec Canada 514-593-9300.*
Private Label *Yes*
Web Site *www.peerless-clothing.com*
Contact *Chairman/CEO: Alvin Segal*

Notes

ALDAN

242 East 137th Street
Bronx, NY 10451 lew@aldan.com
718 665 8699 Fax : 212 473 7003 800 536 8699

Labels *Aldan*
Products *Custom designs for salons, spas, medical, restaurants & leisure resorts.*
Price Points *Better*
Production *U.S.A.*
Web Site *www.aldan.com*
Contact *President: Lew Widoff*

BEVERLY HILLS UNIFORMS

565 Barry Street
Bronx, NY 10474 sales@bhuniforms.com
718 378 1188 Fax : 718 378 2889 800 891 7255

Products *Medical uniforms, nursing uniforms, lab coats, print and solid scrubs in sizes XS to 5XL*
Price Points *Moderate*
Sell To *Department stores, specialty stores*
Web Site *www.bhuniforms.com*

BEXAR MANUFACTURING CO.

6623 S. Zarzamora
San Antonio, TX 78211 smockers@smockers.com
210 977 9585 Fax : 210 977 8998 877 977 9585

Labels *Smockers*
Products *Uniforms & fashion smocks for salon, cosmetic & retail.*
Price Points *Moderate*
Production *U.S.A.*
Sell To *Department stores, specialty stores & boutiques.*
Private Label *Yes*
Web Site *www.smockers.com*
RN Number *RN92441*
Contact *President and Owner: Veronica A. DeNeve, CEO: Brian A. Rice*

BLUE HAWAII SALES

801 South King Street, Suite 3707
Honolulu, HI 96813 hiblue@hawaii.rr.com
808 277 0368

Labels *Blue Hawaii*
Products *Custom created corporate wear for your representatives as gifts or simply as uniforms.*
Price Points *Moderate*
Production *U.S.A.*
Showrooms *Honolulu*
Sell To *Department stores & mass merchants.*
Private Label *Yes*
RN Number *RN85143*
Contact *President and Owner: Joni Albao*

HASELSON INT'L TRADING INC.

32 West 39th Street, 3rd Floor
New York, NY 10118 sales@ringosport.com
212 465 0605 Fax : 212 629 3506 800 217 4478

Labels *Preferred School Uniform*
Products *Men's & boy's school uniforms, plus all types of work wear in canvas & twill. Open stock.*
Price Points *Moderate*
Production *Import*
Showrooms *New York, Miami & Houston*
Sell To *Department stores, specialty stores & mass merchants.*
Private Label *Yes*
Web Site *www.haselson.com*

K & P WEAVER, LLC

527 Carriage Drive
Orange, CT 06477 kpweaver@aol.com
203 795 9024 Fax : 203 795 4294

Labels *K & P Weaver LLC*
Products *Manufacturers of vintage baseball uniforms, equipment and more.*
Production *U.S.A.*
Sell To *Specialty & sport stores, historical institutes, mail order catalogs, gift shops & museum stores.*
Private Label *Yes*
Web Site *www.baseballamericaspastime.com*
Rev. in mil. *0-2*
Contact *Owner: Paula Weaver, Production: Kenneth Weaver*

LANDAU

8410 W. Sandidge Road
Olive Branch, MS 38654 darryl.williams@landau.com
800 238 7513 Fax : 662 890 1401

Labels *Landau, Urbane Scrubs, Scrub Zone*
Products *Trendy, fashionable uniforms & footwear for the healthcare & corporate professional.*
Price Points *Moderate*
Sell To *Department stores, specialty stores, catalogs, internet*
Private Label *No*
Web Site *www.landau.com*
RN Number *33489*
Contact *President: Bruce Landau, Executive VP: Gregg Landau,*
VP Sales, Marketing and Design: Darryl Williams

LIANA UNIFORM

110 West 40th Street, Room 606
New York, NY 10018 customerservice@lianauniforms.com
212 575 0875 Fax : 212 575 0876

Products *Basic scrubs as well as fashionable. New styles & prints every season in sizes XS up to 5X.*
Price Points *Moderate to better*
Sell To *Medical, veterinarian practices, dental, home attendants*
Web Site *www.lianauniforms.com*

MASCOT WORKWEAR U.S./REPCON NW INC

15009 NE Airport Way, Suite 100
Portland, OR 97230
503 252 9760 Fax : 503 252 9651 1-800-325-8707
sales@repconnw.com

Labels *Mascot*
Products *Mens workwear, contractors clothing & accessories.*
Price Points *Moderate*
Production *Import*
Showrooms *Same as Above - Walk In Trade*
Sell To *Department stores, work clothing stores, online retailers, safety/industrial/construction suppli*
Private Label *Yes*
Web Site *www.repconnw.com*
Contact *Sales: Bryan Freeman*

PRIORITY MANUFACTURING

571 N. W. 29th Street
Miami , FL 33127
305 576 3000 Fax : 305 576 2672 800 835 5528
richard@customuniforms.com

Labels *Priority Manufacturing, All American Career Apparel*
Products *Career, casual, formal and industrial uniforms*
Production *U.S.A.*
Sell To *Specialty stores*
Private Label *Yes*
Web Site *www.customuniforms.com*
Rev. in mil. *0-2*
Contact *President: Richard Levy*

REPCON NW DBA THE MODERN WORKER

15009 NE Airport Way, Suite 100
Portland, OR 97230
503 252 9760 Fax : 503 252 9651 1-800-325-8707
sales@repconnw.com

Labels *Mascot*
Products *Mens workwear, contractors clothing & accessories.*
Price Points *Moderate*
Production *Import*
By appointment only
Sell To *Department stores, specialty stores, online retailers, safety/industrial/construction suppliers.*
Private Label *No*
Web Site *www.repconnw.com*
Contact *Sales: Bryan Freeman*

WILLIAMSON-DICKIE MFG CO.

509 West Vickery Boulevard
Fort Worth, TX 76104
817 336 7201 Fax : 817 810 4342 866 411 1501
customerservice@dickies.com

Labels *Williamson-Dickie*
Products *Quality workwear*
Price Points *Moderate*
Production *U.S.A.*
Showrooms *Dallas, New York*
Sell To *Department stores, specialty stores, uniform outlets.*

Private Label	*Yes*
Web Site	*www.dickies.com*
Rev. in mil.	*+500*
Contact	*President: Philip Williamson*

LEVI STRAUSS & CO.

1155 Battery Street
San Francisco, CA 94111 questions@levistrauss.com
415 501 6000 Fax : 415 501 3939

Labels *Levi's®, Dockers®, Signature by Levi Strauss & Co.™, Denizen*
Products *Casual sportswear, jeans & westernwear.*
Price Points *Moderate*
Showrooms *New York/1411 Broadway, 11th Floor, New York 10018, Tel: 212-704-3200*
Atlanta, Dallas & Chicago
Sell To *Department stores*
Web Site *www.levistrauss.com*
RN Number *RN36665, WPL00423*
Contact *CEO: Chip Bergh*

PENDLETON WOOLEN MILLS, INC.

220 Northwest Broadway
Portland, OR 97209 pendletoncatalog@penwool.com
503 226 4801 Fax : 503 535 5599 800 522 9665

Labels *Pendleton*
Products *Big & Tall & regular sized sportswear, outerwear, jackets, westernwear & accessories.*
Price Points *Better*
Production *U.S.A. & import*
Sell To *Specialty stores & mail order catalogues.*
Private Label *No*
Web Site *www.pendleton-usa.com*
RN Number *RN29685, WPL04378*
Rev. in mil. *+500*

TONY LAMA COMPANY, INC.

610 West Daggett Street
Fort Worth, TX 76104 vicki.chapman@justinbrands.com
866 240 8854 Fax : 817 390 2566 800-548-1021

Labels *Tony Lama*
Products *Western handcrafted boots for work, play and everything in between.*
Price Points *Better to designer.*
Production *U.S.A.*
Sell To *Department stores, specialty stores & mail order catalogues.*
Private Label *No*
Web Site *www.tonylama.com*
Rev. in mil. *51-100*
Contact *Customer Service: Vicki Chapman*

5TH & OCEAN CLOTHING LLC/NEW ERA CAP CO.

590 West 83 Street
Hialeah, FL 33014
305 822 4606 Fax : 305 822 4665
laura.garden@neweracap.com

Labels *Major League Baseball, NHL, NBA, NFL, Collegiate teams*
Products *Kids/Youth 4/5 through 14 Sportswear.*
Price Points *Low to moderate.*
Production *Honduras*
Corp. Office *Above*
Private Label *Yes*
Web Site *www.neweracap.com*
RN Number *94989*
Rev. in mil. *11-50*
Contact *Designer: Laura Garden ext. 220*

ACTIVE EDGE, THE/OLD CITY T-SHIRTS

233 Church Street
Philadelphia, PA 19106
215 925 7860 Fax : 215 925 1597 800 343 1497
actvej@aol.com

Labels *Active Edge*
Products *Novelty cotton active pieces, garment & tie-dyed garments. Infant, toddler & youth sizes.*
Price Points *Moderate*
Production *U.S.A.*
Showrooms *Philadelphia.*
Sell To *Specialty stores & boutiques.*
Private Label *Yes*
Web Site *www.theactiveedge.com*
Contact *President: Evan Sharps*

AERO TECH DESIGNS

2345 Preble Avenue
Pittsburgh, PA 15233
412 262 3255 Fax : 412 203 1785 800 783 8326
cyclewear@aerotechdesigns.com

Labels *Aero Tech Designs*
Products *Top quality bicycle apparel.*
Price Points *Better*
Production *U.S.A.*
Sell To *On-line, mail order catalogs*
Web Site *www.aerotechdesigns.com*
Contact *President: Cathy Schnaubelt Rogers*

ANVIL KNITWEAR, INC.

146 West Country Club Road
Hamer, SC 29547
843 774 8211 Fax : 843 841 4963
info@gildan.com

Labels *Anvil®*
Products *Imprintable & embroiderable sportswear.*
Price Points *Moderate*
Sell To *Wholesalers, department stores, specialty stores & mass merchants.*
Corp. Office *Division of Gildan Activewear SRL (www.gildan.com) - 877 445 3265*
Private Label *Yes*

Web Site *www.anvilknitwear.com*
RN Number *RN38619*
Contact *Arlin Turner Manager*

BODY WRAPPERS

65 West 36th Street, 5th Floor
New York, NY 10018 info@bodywrappers.com
212 279 3492 Fax : 212 564 3426 800 323 0786

Labels *Body Wrappers®, Princess Aurora™, totalSTRETCH™ Tights, danceBtween™*
Products *Dance, active & team dance apparel, dance tights, dance shoes, liturgical.*
Price Points *Moderate*
Production *U.S.A.*
Showrooms *New York, Denver, Toronto plus reps throughout the U.S, Canada, Europe & Japan.*
Sell To *Dance specialty stores, boutiques, Nordstrom's, mail order catalogues, website.*
Corp. Office *107 Trumbull Street, Elizabeth, NJ 07206*
Private Label *Yes*
Web Site *www.bodywrappers.com*
RN Number *RN60206*
Rev. in mil. *11-50*
Contact *Sales: Michael Lee, tel: 908 354 7218 ext. 231*

CALIFORNIA RAIN CO.

1213 E. 14th Street
Los Angeles, CA 90021 info@californiarainla.com
213 623 6061 Fax : 213 627 5703

Products *Private label manufacturing experts. Sweatshirts, shirts, t-shirts & shorts sizes toddler to yout*
Price Points *Better*
Production *U.S.A.*
Sell To *Department stores*
Corp. Office *Above*
Private Label *Yes*
Web Site *www.californiarainla.com*
RN Number *75443*
Rev. in mil. *11-50*
Contact *President: Jack Chang*

COLUMBIA SPORTSWEAR CO., INC.

14375 N.W. Science Park Drive
Portland, OR 97229 sales_info@columbia.com
503 985 4000 Fax : 503 985 5800 800 MA BOYLE

Labels *Columbia Sportswear Co*
Products *Fishing, sportswear, footwear, active outerwear & active sportswear.*
Price Points *Moderate*
Production *U.S.A.*
Sell To *Department stores, specialty stores, mass merchants.*
Private Label *No*
Web Site *www.columbia.com*
RN Number *RN69724*
Rev. in mil. *+500*
Contact *Chairman: Gertrude Boyle, CEO: Tim Boyle, VIP Sales: Joseph R. Craig*

DONOUGHE SPORT

721 Donoughe Street
Gallitzin, PA 16641 rmapparel@aol.com
814 886 9272 Fax : 814 886 4228 1-866-366-6844

Labels *Donoughe Sport™*
Products *Designers & manufacturers of quality sports apparel & related products*
Price Points *Moderate*
Production *U.S.A.*
Sell To *Specialty Stores*
Corp. Office *Division of R&M Apparel, Inc.*
Web Site *www.donoughesport.com*

FILA U.S.A. INC.

930 Ridgebrook Road, Suite 200
Sparks, MD 21152 ecommusa@fila.com
410 773 3000 Fax : 410 773 4984 800 845 3452

Labels *Fila*
Products *Active sportswear.*
Price Points *Moderate to better.*
Production *U.S.A., Hong Kong, Thailand, Taiwan & Indonesia.*
Sell To *Department stores, catalogues, mass merchants & sporting goods stores.*
Web Site *www.fila.com*

FRENCH TOAST

100 West 33rd Street, Suite 1012
New York, NY 10001 retail@frenchtoast.com
212 594 4740 Fax : 212 268 5160 800 262 KIDS

Labels *French Toast*
Products *Complete line of fashion boy's & girl's ativewear & athletic wear. Sizes 4 to 20.*
Price Points *Budget to moderate.*
Production *U.S.A. & import.*
Sell To *Specialty stores, mass merchants, mail order catalogues & off-price retailers.*
Private Label *Yes*
Web Site *www.frenchtoast.com*
RN Number *RN13706*
Rev. in mil. *101-500*
Contact *Exec Vice President: Richard Sutton, Exec Vice President, Sales: Joseph Sutton*

GRAPHICS GROUP LTD./DBA LATITUDES

2425 NE Riverside Way
Portland, OR 97210 info@latitudespdx.com
503 248 2060 Fax : 503 248 2134 800 700 1073

Labels *Latitudes*
Products *Screenprinted t-shirts & sweatshirts. "Boutique-look", sports, multi-media & tie-dye designs.*
Price Points *Moderate to better*
Production *U.S.A.*
Showrooms *Portland, OR*
Sell To *Department stores, specialty stores, boutiques & mail order catalogues.*
Private Label *Yes*
Web Site *www.latitudespdx.com*
Contact *President: L. Thomas, Owner: L. Thomas, Production: Jamie McCrae*

HOLLOWAY SPORTSWEAR, INC.

2633 Campbell Road
Sidney, OH 45365
customercare@hollowayusa.com
937 497 7575 Fax : 937 497 7337 800 852 8798

Labels *Holloway*
Products *Children's sportswear, running suits & wool jackets.*
Price Points *Moderate*
Production *U.S.A. & import*
Sell To *Dept., specialty & sporting goods stores, catalogues, mass merchants & ASI distributors.*
Private Label *Yes*
Web Site *www.hollowayusa.com*
Rev. in mil. *51-100*

MOTIONWEAR, LLC

1315 Sunday Drive
Indianapolis, IN 46217
bwilson@motionwear.com
317 780 0609 Fax : 317 780 4188 800 869 0609

Labels *Motionwear, Motionwar Gymnastics, Cheer Kids*
Products *Dance, gymnastics & cheerleading apparel for women and girls.*
Price Points *Better*
Production *U.S.A. & import*
Sell To *Specialty stores, boutiques, direct internet*
Web Site *www.motionwear.com*
Contact *President: Bob Wilson*

ROYAL APPAREL, INC.

65 Commerce Drive
Hauppauge, NY 11788
sales@royalapparel.net
631 213 8299 Fax : 631 922 8438 866-Royal-1-S

Labels *Royal Apparel*
Products *Basic & fashion forward blanks, active/athleticwear in a large selection of colors & knit fabr.*
Price Points *Moderate to better.*
Production *U.S.A.*
Showrooms *New York & Allentown, Pa.*
Sell To *Mass merchants, branded labels, screen printers & department stores.*
Private Label *Yes*
Web Site *www.royalapparel.net*
Contact *President: Morey Mayeri, Owners: Morey Mayeri/Abraham Mayeri*

AKADEMIKS

31 West 34th Street, Suite 401
New York, NY 10001 dclesmere@akademiks.com
212 563 4999 866 425 3657

Labels *Akademiks*
Products *Tee-shirts, shirts, shorts and jackets for boys of all sizes.*
Price Points *Better*
Production *Asia*
Showrooms *New York*
Sell To *Department stores, better specialty stores & boutiques.*
Corp. Office *Division of Oved Apparel Group (www.theovedgroup.com)*
Private Label *No*
Web Site *www.akademiks.com*
Rev. in mil. *2-10*
Contact *David Clesmere*

CALVIN CLOTHING COMPANY

108A New South Road
Hicksville, NY 11801 ben@calvinclothes.com
516 937 0400 Fax : 516 937 1342

Labels *Calvin, Europa, Mezzanotte, Dimples by Europa*
Products *Boy's tailored suits, sport coats, dress pants, shirts & ties.*
Price Points *Moderate to better*
Production *Import*
Showrooms *New York*
Sell To *Department stores, speciality stores, boutiques & mail order catalogues.*
Private Label *Yes*
RN Number *RN95393*
Rev. in mil. *11-50*
Contact *President: Gary Calmenson*

EVY OF CALIFORNIA, INC./DBA JALATE

530 Fashion Avenue, Suite 804
New York, NY 10018 suzannem@evy.com
212 594 3670 Fax : 212 971 9131

Labels *Super Charged*
Products *Young men and boys fashion tee line.*
Price Points *Moderate*
Production *U.S.A., Mexico, Dubai, China, Central America, Cambodia, India, Vietnam, Philippines*

Sell To *Department stores, specialty stores, boutiques, mass merchants & mail order catalogues.*
Corp. Office *810A S. Flower St, Los Angeles, Ca. 90017 Tel: 213 763 6100, Fax: 213 748 7475.*
Private Label *Yes*
Web Site *www.evy.com*
RN Number *RN17657, RN106895*
Rev. in mil. *51-100*
Contact *CEO: Kurt Kreiser, Office Manager: Nadine (NY Showroom)*

FRENCH TOAST

100 West 33rd Street, Suite 1012
New York, NY 10001 retail@frenchtoast.com
212 594 4740 Fax : 212 268 5160 800 262 KIDS

Labels *French Toast*
Products *Fashion children's wear. Sizes infant to 20.*
Price Points *Budget to moderate.*
Production *U.S.A. & import.*
Sell To *Specialty stores, mass merchants, mail order catalogues & off-price retailers.*
Private Label *Yes*
Web Site *www.frenchtoast.com*
RN Number *RN13706*
Rev. in mil. *101-500*
Contact *Exec Vice President: Richard Sutton, Exec Vice President, Sales: Joseph Sutton*

GUESS, INC.

1444 S. Alameda Street
Los Angeles, CA 90021 vendors@guess.com
213 765 3100 Fax : 213 765 5902 877-44-GUESS

Labels *Guess Kids*
Products *Boy's contemporary sportswear separates & outerwear, sizes 4 to 7 & 8 to 20.*
Price Points *Moderate to better*
Showrooms *New York/119 West 40th St, Suite 420, New York, N.Y. 10018, Tel: 212 730 7200*
Sell To *Department stores & specialty stores.*
Corp. Office *Above*
Web Site *www.guess.com*
Contact *CEO: Paul Marciano*

LEMUR GROUP, INC.

275 Rue Stinson, Suite 201
Montreal, Quebec, Canada H4N 2E1 info@lemurgroup.com
514 748 6234 Fax : 514 748 6235

Labels *Petit Lem, P.L. Junior*
Products *Playwear for boys 3 mos to 24 mos.*
Price Points *Better*
Production *China*
Sell To *Department stores, specialty stores*
Private Label *Yes*
Web Site *www.petitlem.com*
Contact *President: Gabriel Di Mieele*

LONG STREET

20 West 33rd Street, 12th Floor
New York, NY 10001 elliot@longstreet.com
212 947 4090 Fax : 212 967 2420

Labels *US Polo Association, Genuine School Uniform, 360 Sports, American Hawk,Eddie Bauer*
Products *Boy's sportswear, sleepwear & school uniforms sizes newborn to size 20.*
Price Points *Moderate to better.*
Production *U.S.A. & import*
Showrooms *New York/above*
Sell To *Department stores, speciality stores, boutiques, mass merchants & off-price retailers.*

Private Label *No*
Web Site *www.longstreet.com*
Contact *Vice President: Elliot Tawil*

OSHKOSH B'GOSH/CARTER'S

3438 Peachtree Road
Atlanta, GA 30326
678 791 1000
1-800-692-4674
consumerbgosh@carters.com

Labels *OshKosh B'gosh, Genuine Kids, Carter's*
Products *Overalls, playwear, denimwear & coordinates.*
Price Points *Moderate*
Production *U.S.A. & import worldwide.*
Showrooms *New York*
Sell To *Departments stores, specialty stores, mass markets, catalogues & off-price retailers.*
Private Label *Yes*
Web Site *www.oshkoshbgosh.com*
RN Number *RN96367, RN40103, RN37904*
Rev. in mil. *101-500*

Notes

AKADEMIKS

31 West 34th Street, Suite 401
New York, NY 10001 dclesmere@akademiks.com
212 563 4999 866 425 3657

Labels *Akademiks*
Products *All types of tees, bottoms, jeans and jackets for girls of all ages.*
Price Points *Better*
Production *Asia*
Showrooms *New York*
Sell To *Department stores, better specialty stores & boutiques.*
Corp. Office *Division of Oved Apparel Group (www.theovedgroup.com)*
Private Label *No*
Web Site *www.akademiks.com*
Rev. in mil. *2-10*
Contact *David Clesmere*

EVY OF CALIFORNIA, INC./DBA JALATE

530 Fashion Avenue, Suite 804
New York, NY 10018 suzannem@evy.com
212 594 3670 Fax : 212 971 9131

Labels *Evy, Kidture*
Products *Girl's coordinated separates, all sizes.*
Price Points *Moderate*
Production *U.S.A., Mexico, Dubai, China, Central America, Cambodia, India, Vietnam, Philippines*
Sell To *Department stores, specialty stores, boutiques, mass merchants & mail order catalogues.*
Corp. Office *810A S. Flower St, Los Angeles, Ca. 90017 Tel: 213 763 6100, Fax: 213 748 7475.*
Private Label *Yes*
Web Site *www.evy.com*
RN Number *RN17657, RN106895*
Rev. in mil. *51-100*
Contact *CEO: Kurt Kreiser, Office Manager: Nadine (NY Showroom)*

FRENCH TOAST

100 West 33rd Street, Suite 1012
New York, NY 10001 retail@frenchtoast.com
212 594 4740 Fax : 212 268 5160 800 262 KIDS

Labels *French Toast*
Products *Fashion children's wear. Sizes infant to 18.*
Price Points *Budget to moderate.*
Production *U.S.A. & import.*
Sell To *Specialty stores, mass merchants, mail order catalogues & off-price retailers.*
Private Label *Yes*
Web Site *www.frenchtoast.com*
RN Number *RN13706*
Rev. in mil. *101-500*
Contact *Exec Vice President: Richard Sutton, Exec Vice President, Sales: Joseph Sutton*

GUESS, INC.

1444 S. Alameda Street
Los Angeles, CA 90021 vendors@guess.com
213 765 3100 Fax : 213 765 5902 877-44-GUESS

Labels *Guess Kids*
Products *Girl's contemporary sportswear separates & outerwear sizes 4 -6x & 7 -16.*
Price Points *Moderate to better*
Showrooms *New York/119 West 40th St, Suite 420, New York, N.Y. 10018, Tel: 212 730 7200*
Sell To *Department stores & specialty stores.*
Corp. Office *Above*
Web Site *www.guess.com*
Contact *CEO: Paul Marciano*

KAHN LUCAS

112 West 34th Street, 6th Floor
New York, NY 10120 ebreslow@kahnlucas.com
212 244 4500 Fax : 212 643 1345

Labels *Youngland®, Sweet Heart Rose®, Emily West®, Dollie & Me®, Kahn Lucas*
Products *Girl's sets, activewear & licensed products, size newborn through 16.*
Price Points *Moderate to better*
Production *U.S.A. & import*
Showrooms *New York*
Sell To *Department stores, specialty stores, mass merchants & mail order catalogues.*
Corp. Office *Licensing Inquiries: license@kahnlucas.com*
Private Label *Yes*
Web Site *www.kahnlucas.com*
RN Number *RN16518*
Rev. in mil. *51-100*
Contact *President: Howard Kahn, Sales: Eric Breslow*

KIDCUTETURE

5 Rosalind Road
Lawrenceville, NJ 08648 olga.pantelyat@kidcuteture.com
609 216 7490 Fax : 347 823 1016

Labels *Kashka*
Products *Girly playsuits, coordinates, hats, blankets & one-of-a-kind dresses sizes 3 months to 4T.*
Price Points *Better*
Production *Peru*
Showrooms *Dallas: Annette's 214-637-4446, Atlanta: Janet Hunter Hawkins 404-524-8897, NE: David & Co 781-407-0001, Mid-West: Elite Kids 312-397-0399.*
Sell To *Specialty stores, boutiques, on-line*
Web Site *www.kidcuteture.com*
Contact *Owners: Natasha and Olga Pantelyat*

LEMUR GROUP, INC.

275 Rue Stinson, Suite 201
Montreal, Quebec, Canada H4N 2E1 info@lemurgroup.com
514 748 6234 Fax : 514 748 6235

Labels *Petit Lem, P.L. Junior*
Products *Playwear for girls 3 mos to 24 mos.*
Price Points *Better*

Production *China*
Sell To *Department stores, specialty stores*
Private Label *Yes*
Web Site *www.petitlem.com*
Contact *President: Gabriel Di Mieele*

LIPSTIK GIRLS

3001 East 11th Street
Los Angeles, CA 90023 customerservice@lipstikclothing.com
714 957 1114 Fax : 714 957 1212

Labels *Lipstik Girls, Cach Cach, Elisa B,*
Products *Girl's coordinated separates size 2T thru 14*
Price Points *Better*
Production *U.S.A,*
Showrooms *New York/The Rose Garden 212 564 5100,*
Sell To *Better specialty & department stores.*
Private Label *No*
Web Site *www.lipstikgirlsclothing.com*
RN Number *RN65687*

LONG STREET

20 West 33rd Street, 12th Floor
New York, NY 10001 elliot@longstreet.com
212 947 4090 Fax : 212 967 2420

Labels *US Polo Association, Sweet Vintage, Pinkhouse, Kidzone, Sophie Fae, Genuine School Unifor*
Products *Girl's sportswear, sleepwear & school uniforms.*
Price Points *Moderate to better.*
Production *U.S.A. & import*
Showrooms *New York/above*
Sell To *Department stores, speciality stores, boutiques, mass merchants & off-price retailers.*
Private Label *No*
Web Site *www.longstreet.com*
Contact *Vice President: Elliot Tawil*

NEW ICM, LP

220 Sam Bishkin Road
El Campo, TX 77437 zalmand@newicm.com
979 578 0543 Fax : 979 578 0503 800 987 9008

Labels *Laura Dare, Little Zazzy*
Products *Girl's playwear & coordinated sportswear.*
Price Points *Moderate to better*
Production *U.S.A.*
Sell To *Department stores & specialty stores.*
Private Label *Yes*
Web Site *www.newicm.com*
RN Number *18443*
Contact *President: Daniel Zalman, VP Marketing: Priscilla Hunt*

OSHKOSH B'GOSH/CARTER'S

3438 Peachtree Road
Atlanta, GA 30326
678 791 1000 1-800-692-4674
consumerbgosh@carters.com

Labels *OshKosh B'gosh, Genuine Kids, Carter's*
Products *Overalls, playwear, denimwear & coordinates.*
Price Points *Moderate*
Production *U.S.A. & import worldwide.*
Showrooms *New York*
Sell To *Departments stores, specialty stores, mass markets, catalogues & off-price retailers.*
Corp. Office *Carter's Phipps Tower Suite 1800 Atlanta Ga 678-791-1000*
Private Label *Yes*
Web Site *www.oshkoshbgosh.com*
RN Number *RN96367, RN40103, RN37904*

TRENDSET ORIGINALS

1407 Broadway, Room 503
New York, NY 10018
212 736 9520 Fax : 212 997 9284
jj@skiva.com

Labels *Trendset*
Products *Girl's coordinated sportswear & separates, toddler thru size 14.*
Price Points *Budget to moderate.*
Production *Import*
Showrooms *New York*
Sell To *Department stores, specialty stores, mass merchants & off-price retailers.*
Private Label *Yes*
RN Number *RN48829*
Rev. in mil. *51-100*

EVY OF CALIFORNIA, INC./DBA JALATE

530 Fashion Avenue, Suite 804
New York, NY 10018 suzannem@evy.com
212 594 3670 Fax : 212 971 9131

Labels *Evy, Kidture*
Products *Girl's dresses, jumpers & special occasion, all sizes including Juniors.*
Price Points *Moderate*
Production *U.S.A., Mexico, Dubai, China, Central America, Cambodia, India, Vietnam, Philippines*
Sell To *Department stores, specialty stores, boutiques, mass merchants & mail order catalogues.*
Corp. Office *810A S. Flower St, Los Angeles, Ca. 90017 Tel: 213 763 6100, Fax: 213 748 7475.*
Private Label *Yes*
Web Site *www.evy.com*
RN Number *RN17657, RN106895*
Rev. in mil. *51-100*
Contact *CEO: Kurt Kreiser, Office Manager: Nadine (NY Showroom)*

FOUGER FOR KIDS, INC.

1152 S. Wall Street, #102
Los Angeles, CA 90015 fougerforkids@aol.com
213 748 0648 Fax : 213 748 7430

Labels *Fouger for Kids*
Products *Special occasion dresses & gowns for infant, toddler and girl sizes.*
Price Points *Better*
Sell To *Specialty stores*
Private Label *Yes*
Web Site *www.fouger4kids.com*
Contact *President: Ben Pourebrahim*

HAVENGIRL

2233 Faraday Avenue, Suite H and I
Carlsbad, CA 92008 annmarie@havengirl.com
760 385 6999 Fax : 760 268 1112 800 987 8792

Labels *Havengirl*
Products *Fun designs loaded with an eclectic variety of style and comfort. Sizes 12 months throught 14.*
Production *U.S.A.*
Showrooms *LA/Sylvia Gill Showroom 213-622-8271, San Francisco/Sylvia Gill Showroom 415-255-989 Dallas/Martha Foster Showroom 800-723-3250, New York/Curly Girls 888-35-curly.*
Sell To *Boutiques*
Web Site *www.havengirl.com*

KAHN LUCAS

112 West 34th Street, 6th Floor
New York, NY 10120 ebreslow@kahnlucas.com
212 244 4500 Fax : 212 643 1345

Labels *Youngland®, Sweet Heart Rose®, Emily West®, Dollie & Me®, Kahn Lucas*
Products *Girl's dresses sizes newborn thru size 16.*
Price Points *Moderate to better*
Production *U.S.A. & import*
Showrooms *New York*
Sell To *Department stores, specialty stores, mass merchants & mail order catalogues.*
Corp. Office *Licensing Inquiries: license@kahnlucas.com*

Private Label *Yes*
Web Site *www.kahnlucas.com*
RN Number *RN16518*
Rev. in mil. *51-100*
Contact *President: Howard Kahn, Sales: Eric Breslow*

KIDCUTETURE

5 Rosalind Road
Lawrenceville, NJ 08648 olga.pantelyat@kidcuteture.com
609 216 7490 Fax : 347 823 1016

Labels *KidCuteTure*
Products *Creative & unique clothes for girls sizes newborn to 14. Dresses, rompers, tunics & accessories.*
Price Points *Better*
Production *Peru*
Showrooms *Dallas: Annette's 214-637-4446, Atlanta: Janet Hunter Hawkins 404-524-8897, NE: David & Co 781-407-0001, Mid-West: Elite Kids 312-397-0399.*
Sell To *Specialty stores, boutiques, on-line*
Web Site *www.kidcuteture.com*
Contact *Owners: Natasha and Olga Pantelyat*

NEW ICM, LP

220 Sam Bishkin Road
El Campo, TX 77437 zalmand@newicm.com
979 578 0543 Fax : 979 578 0503 800 987 9008

Labels *Bryan*
Products *Girls and juniors holiday dresses.*
Price Points *Moderate to better*
Production *U.S.A.*
Sell To *Department stores & specialty stores.*
Private Label *Yes*
Web Site *www.newicm.com*
RN Number *18443*
Contact *President: Daniel Zalman, VP Marketing: Priscilla Hunt*

PERSNICKETY

174 S. 1100 E.
American Fork, UT 84003 sales@persnicketyclothing.com
801 658 0400 Fax : 801 877 4328

Labels *Persnickety*
Products *Girls fancy frocks*
Price Points *Better*
Showrooms *Reps throughout the US*
Sell To *Wholesale only*
Web Site *www.persnicketyclothing.com*

PINK CHICKEN

307 Seventh Avenue, Suite 703
New York, NY 10001 customerservice@pinkchicken.com
212 255 9090 Fax : 212 255 9095

Labels *Pink Chicken*
Products *Colorful, fun dresses with great quality*

Price Points *Better*
Showrooms *West Coast/Nicky 213-688-9590, New England/Ellen 617-620-0546*
New York/34 West 33rd Street, New York 212-695-0762
Sell To *Department stores, specialty stores, boutiques*
Private Label *No*
Web Site *www.pinkchicken.com*
Contact *Owner: Stacey Fraser*

THEA HAUTE COUTURE

38 Verandah Place
Brooklyn, NY 11201
718 237 8555 Fax : 718 237 8555
sales@theahautecouture.com

Labels *Thea*
Products *Fine, beautifully crafted white cotton girl's dresses.*
Price Points *Better*
Production *Philippines*
Showrooms *Sales Reps: Atlanta/Lou Pizi 800 524 1462, Dallas/David Willingham 214 631 6493,*
Vermont/CarolAnn Hawkins 518 929 3090.
Sell To *Lingerie stores, department stores, specialty stores, boutiques & mail order catalogues.*
Private Label *Yes*
Web Site *www.theahautecouture.com*
Rev. in mil. *101-500*
Contact *Sales: Derma Gerety, Designer: Marie de la Soudiere*

Notes

ACTIVE EDGE, THE/OLD CITY T-SHIRTS

233 Church Street
Philadelphia, PA 19106 actvej@aol.com
215 925 7860 Fax : 215 925 1597 800 343 1497

Products *Eco-friendly youth ring-spun cotton tees.*
Price Points *Moderate*
Production *U.S.A.*
Showrooms *Philadelphia.*
Sell To *Specialty stores & boutiques.*
Private Label *Yes*
Web Site *www.theactiveedge.com*
Contact *President: Evan Sharps*

CASTLEWARE BABY

1610 K Street
Eureka, CA 95501 info@castleware.com
707 499 9762

Labels *CastleWare*
Products *Organic cotton clothing & bedding. Cozie sacks, footies, pants, dresses, jackets, pj's, blankets.*
Production *U.S.A.*
Sell To *Department stores, specialty stores, boutiques*
Web Site *www.castleware.com*
Contact *Owner: Maureen Smithey*

GARDEN KIDS

3855 East Mira Loma Avenue
Anaheim, CA 92806 paulah@gardenkids.com
714 996 1100

Labels *Garden Kids*
Products *Organic clothes for kids sizes newborn to boys & girls size 12 & size 16 in some organic pj style*
Price Points *Better*
Production *U.S.A.*
Sell To *Department stores, specialty stores, boutiques*
Web Site *www.gardenkids.com*
Contact *Owner: Paula Haddad*

GOODWEAR USA

239 Western Avenue, Room 2D
Essex, MA 01929 steve@goodwear.com
978 768 7746 Fax : 800 787 4951 800 338 8895

Labels *Goodwear*
Products *Children's upscale dyeable tee-shirts done in sustainable fabrics: organic cotton & bamboo.*
Price Points *Bridge*
Production *U.S.A.*
Showrooms *Tokyo, Osaka, NYC & Essex*
Sell To *Distributors*
Private Label *Yes*
Web Site *www.goodwear.com*
RN Number *75346*
Contact *President: Martha Liquori, Owner: Stephen & Martha Liquori, Sales: Stephen Liquori*

ROYAL APPAREL, INC.

65 Commerce Drive
Hauppauge, NY 11788 sales@royalapparel.net
631 213 8299 Fax : 631 922 8438 866-Royal-1-S

Labels *Royal Apparel*
Products *100% organic apparel for youth, infant & toddler available in various colors and styles.*
Price Points *Moderate to better.*
Production *U.S.A.*
Showrooms *New York & Allentown, Pa.*
Sell To *Mass merchants, branded labels, screen printers & department stores.*
Private Label *Yes*
Web Site *www.royalapparel.net*
Contact *President: Morey Mayeri, Owners: Morey Mayeri/Abraham Mayeri*

DIESEL PLANET

220 West 19th Street
New York, NY 10011 customerservice@shop.diesel.com
212 755 9200 Fax : 212 255 6641 877.344.8342

Labels *Diesel Kid*
Products *Sportswear & outerwear.*
Price Points *Moderate to better*
Showrooms *New York & Los Angeles/Tel: 310 652 2322*
Sell To *Department stores, mass merchants & boutiques.*
Corp. Office *Above*
Web Site *www.diesel.com*
Contact *Owner: Renzo*

FRENCH TOAST

100 West 33rd Street, Suite 1012
New York, NY 10001 retail@frenchtoast.com
212 594 4740 Fax : 212 268 5160 800 262 KIDS

Labels *French Toast*
Products *Complete line of fashion boy's & girl's denimwear. Jackets, jeans, shorts, shirts, etc.*
Price Points *Budget to moderate.*
Production *U.S.A. & import.*
Sell To *Specialty stores, mass merchants, mail order catalogues & off-price retailers.*
Private Label *Yes*
Web Site *www.frenchtoast.com*
RN Number *RN13706*
Rev. in mil. *101-500*
Contact *Exec Vice President: Richard Sutton, Exec Vice President, Sales: Joseph Sutton*

LIPSTIK GIRLS

3001 East 11th Street
Los Angeles, CA 90023 customerservice@lipstikclothing.com
714 957 1114 Fax : 714 957 1212

Labels *Lipstik Girls, Cach Cach, Elisa B,*
Products *Denim coordinated separates size 2T thru 7 & 2T thru 14*
Price Points *Better*
Production *U.S.A.*
Showrooms *New York/The Rose Garden 212 564 5100,*
Sell To *Better department & specialty stores.*
Private Label *No*
Web Site *www.lipstikgirlsclothing.com*
RN Number *RN65687*

OSHKOSH B'GOSH/CARTER'S

3438 Peachtree Road
Atlanta, GA 30326 consumerbgosh@carters.com
678 791 1000 1-800-692-4674

Labels *OshKosh B'gosh, Baby B'Gosh, Carter's*
Products *Jeans, overalls, & denim coordinates.*
Price Points *Moderate*
Production *U.S.A. & import worldwide.*
Showrooms *New York*

Sell To *Departments stores, specialty stores, mass markets, catalogues & off-price retailers.*
Corp. Office *Carter's Phipps Tower Suite 1800 Atlanta Ga 678-791-1000*
Private Label *Yes*
Web Site *www.oshkoshbgosh.com*
RN Number *RN96367, RN40103, RN37904*

ASPEN LICENSING INTERNATIONAL, INC.

6615 W. Boynton Beach Boulevard, #349
Boynton Beach, FL 33437 bob@aspenlicensing.com
561 509 8888 Fax : 561 740 0637 1 888 642 7736

Labels *Aspen, Aspen Extreme*
Products *Active & outdoor inspired outerwear, underwear, footwear & accessories.*
Price Points *Moderate*
Production *U.S.A. & Orient.*
Showrooms *Call for licensee's showrooms or if your company would benefit by licensing the Aspen name.*
Sell To *Department stores & mass merchants.*
Web Site *www.aspenbrand.com*
RN Number *RN86959*
Contact *Chairman: Robert Maltz*

FRENCH TOAST

100 West 33rd Street, Suite 1012
New York, NY 10001 retail@frenchtoast.com
212 594 4740 Fax : 212 268 5160 800 262 KIDS

Labels *Cubavera & Havanera, Megaman, Strawberry Shortcake, Cape Bears, Lee Tops*
Products *Boy's & girl's fashion licensed outerwear.*
Price Points *Moderate.*
Production *U.S.A. & import.*
Sell To *Specialty stores, mass merchants, mail order catalogues & off-price retailers.*
Private Label *Yes*
Web Site *www.frenchtoast.com*
RN Number *RN13706*
Rev. in mil. *101-500*
Contact *Exec Vice President: Richard Sutton, Exec Vice President, Sales: Joseph Sutton*

HYBRID APPAREL

10711 Walker Street
Cypress, CA 90630 mlee@hybridapparel.com
714 952 3866 Fax : 714 952 3874

Products *Boys' licensed tee-shirts.*
Price Points *Moderate*
Showrooms *Los Angeles/ 910 South Los Angeles St, Suite 408, Lost Angeles, Ca 90015, New York/530 7th Avenue, NYC 10018 212-997-4688.*
Sell To *Department stores & mass merchants.*
Web Site *www.hybridapparel.com*
Contact *Wholesale: M. Lee*

KAHN LUCAS

112 West 34th Street, 6th Floor
New York, NY 10120 ebreslow@kahnlucas.com
212 244 4500 Fax : 212 643 1345

Labels *Youngland®, Sweet Heart Rose®, Emily West®, Dollie & Me®, Kahn Lucas*
Products *Girl's dresses, jumpers & sweaters sizes newborn through 16.*
Price Points *Moderate to better*
Production *U.S.A. & import*
Showrooms *New York*
Sell To *Department stores, specialty stores, mass merchants & mail order catalogues.*

Corp. Office	*Licensing Inquiries: license@kahnlucas.com*
Private Label	*Yes*
Web Site	*www.kahnlucas.com*
RN Number	*RN16518*
Rev. in mil.	*51-100*
Contact	*President: Howard Kahn, Sales: Eric Breslow*

ACTIVE EDGE, THE/OLD CITY T-SHIRTS

233 Church Street
Philadelphia, PA 19106 actvej@aol.com
215 925 7860 Fax : 215 925 1597 800 343 1497

Labels *Active Edge*
Products *Novelty cotton garments, garment & tie-dyed. Infant & toddler sizes.*
Price Points *Moderate*
Production *U.S.A.*
Showrooms *Philadelphia.*
Sell To *Specialty stores & boutiques.*
Private Label *Yes*
Web Site *www.theactiveedge.com*
Contact *President: Evan Sharps*

BABY JAY INC./GROWING FEET INC.

207 Second Street
Lakewood, NJ 08701 info@babyjay.com
732 905 4980 Fax : 732 363 9195 800 282 3338

Labels *Baby Jay*
Products *Extensive line of 100% European combed cotton infant layette items.*
Price Points *Moderate*
Production *U.K.*
Showrooms *Lakewood, NJ*
Sell To *Specialty stores, boutiques, mail order catalogues, better depart. stores & manufacturers.*
Private Label *Yes*
Web Site *www.babyjay.com*
RN Number *RN89576*
Contact *President: Jacob Phillip*

EVY OF CALIFORNIA, INC./DBA JALATE

530 Fashion Avenue, Suite 804
New York, NY 10018 suzannem@evy.com
212 594 3670 Fax : 212 971 9131

Labels *Evy, Kidture*
Products *Newborn & infant apparel, plus sizes through 16.*
Price Points *Moderate*
Production *U.S.A., Mexico, Dubai, China, Central America, Cambodia, India, Vietnam, Philippines*
Sell To *Department stores, specialty stores, boutiques, mass merchants & mail order catalogues.*
Corp. Office *810A S. Flower St, Los Angeles, Ca. 90017 Tel: 213 763 6100, Fax: 213 748 7475.*
Private Label *Yes*
Web Site *www.evy.com*
RN Number *RN17657, RN106895*
Rev. in mil. *51-100*
Contact *CEO: Kurt Kreiser, Office Manager: Nadine (NY Showroom)*

FOUGER FOR KIDS, INC.

1152 S. Wall Street, #102
Los Angeles, CA 90015 fougerforkids@aol.com
213 748 0648 Fax : 213 748 7430

Labels *Fouger for Kids*
Products *Special occasion Christening clothing.*

Price Points *Better*
Sell To *Specialty stores*
Private Label *Yes*
Web Site *www.fouger4kids.com*
Contact *President: Ben Pourebrahim*

KAHN LUCAS

112 West 34th Street, 6th Floor
New York, NY 10120 ebreslow@kahnlucas.com
212 244 4500 Fax : 212 643 1345

Labels *Sesame Work Shop, Disney, Nickelodeon*
Products *Girl's sets & licensed products, size newborn through 6X.*
Price Points *Moderate to better*
Production *U.S.A. & import*
Showrooms *New York*
Sell To *Department stores, specialty stores, mass merchants & mail order catalogues.*
Corp. Office *Licensing Inquiries: license@kahnlucas.com*
Private Label *Yes*
Web Site *www.kahnlucas.com*
RN Number *RN16518*
Rev. in mil. *51-100*
Contact *President: Howard Kahn, Sales: Eric Breslow*

LIPSTIK GIRLS

3001 East 11th Street
Los Angeles, CA 90023 customerservice@lipstikclothing.com
714 957 1114 Fax : 714 957 1212

Labels *Lipstik Girls, Cach Cach, Elisa B,*
Products *Layette, newborn, infant wear & gift items.*
Price Points *Better*
Production *U.S.A.*
Showrooms *New York/The Rose Garden 212 564 5100*
Sell To *Better department & specialty stores.*
Private Label *No*
Web Site *www.lipstikgirlsclothing.com*
RN Number *RN65687*

MILKBARN, LLC

4208 Old Hillsboro Road
Leiper's Fork, TN 37064 info@milkbarnkids.com
800 269 3512 Fax : 707 657 0324

Labels *Milkbarn*
Products *Eco-friendly modern & vintage designs. One piece, pants, tees, bum covers & bibs.*
Price Points *Better*
Production *U.S.A.*
Sell To *Specialty stores, boutiques, on-line*
Web Site *www.milkbarnkids.com*
Contact *Owner: Stacy Phillips*

NEW ICM, LP

220 Sam Bishkin Road
El Campo, TX 77437 zalmand@newicm.com
979 578 0543 Fax : 979 578 0503 800 987 9008

Labels *Bryan*
Products *Christening, dressy, casual dresses for newborn, infant, 2/4, 4/6X and 7/10.*
Price Points *Moderate to better*
Production *U.S.A.*
Sell To *Department stores & specialty stores.*
Private Label *Yes*
Web Site *www.newicm.com*
RN Number *18443*
Contact *President: Daniel Zalman, VP Marketing: Priscilla Hunt*

OSHKOSH B'GOSH/CARTER'S

3438 Peachtree Road
Atlanta, GA 30326 consumerbgosh@carters.com
678 791 1000 1-800-692-4674

Labels *Baby B'gosh, Carter's*
Products *Infant playwear, denimwear & coordinates.*
Price Points *Moderate*
Production *U.S.A. & import worldwide.*
Showrooms *New York*
Sell To *Departments stores, specialty stores, mass markets, catalogues & off-price retailers.*
Corp. Office *Carter's Phipps Tower Suite 1800 Atlanta Ga 678-791-1000*
Private Label *Yes*
Web Site *www.oshkoshbgosh.com*
RN Number *RN96367, RN40103, RN37904*

PINK CHICKEN

307 Seventh Avenue, Suite 703
New York, NY 10001 customerservice@pinkchicken.com
212 255 9090 Fax : 212 255 9095

Labels *Pink Chicken*
Products *Colorful, fun infant wear with great quality*
Price Points *Better*
Showrooms *West Coast/Nicky 213-688-9590, New England/Ellen 617-620-0546*
New York/34 West 33rd Street, New York 212-695-0762
Sell To *Department stores, specialty stores, boutiques*
Private Label *No*
Web Site *www.pinkchicken.com*
Contact *Owner: Stacey Fraser*

RASHTI & RASHTI/H.J. RASHTI & CO., INC.

875 Avenue of the Americas, 5th Floor
New York, NY 10001 contactus@rashtiandrashti.com
212 594 2939 Fax : 212 594 9102 800 4 RASHTI

Labels *Rashti & Rashti, Carter's, Baby Starters, Taggies, Snuggle Buddy, Boppy, Candlesticks*
Products *Newborn, infant, toddler clothing, accessories, blankets, sleepwear, gift sets, layette, plush.*
Price Points *Budget, moderate & better.*
Production *Import*

Showrooms *New York*
Sell To *Department stores, specialty stores, boutiques, mass merchants & off-price retailers.*
Private Label *Yes*
Web Site *www.rashtiandrashti.com*
RN Number *RN27829*
Rev. in mil. *51-100*
Contact *Sales: Andrew Freed, Merchandising: Sandra Finkelstein, Marketing: Danielle Signorelli*

SUSAN PILLAY

P.O. Box 700
New York, NY 10009
suepillay@aol.com
212 533 9053 Fax : 212 533 9053

Labels *Susan Pillay*
Products *Hand-painted infant wearable art. Natural cottons & non-toxic, washable dyes.*
Price Points *Designer*
Production *U.S.A.*
Sell To *Department stores, specialty stores, boutiques & mail order catalogues.*
Private Label *No*
Web Site *www.susanpillay.com*
Contact *President: Susan Pillay*

THEA HAUTE COUTURE

38 Verandah Place
Brooklyn, NY 11201
sales@theahautecouture.com
718 237 8555 Fax : 718 237 8555

Labels *Thea*
Products *Fine, beautifully crafted white cotton baby clothes & christening gowns.*
Price Points *Better*
Production *Philippines*
Showrooms *Sales Reps: Atlanta/Lou Pizi 800 524 1462, Dallas/David Willingham 214 631 6493, Vermont/CarolAnn Hawkins 518 929 3090.*
Sell To *Lingerie stores, department stores, specialty stores, boutiques & mail order catalogues.*
Private Label *Yes*
Web Site *www.theahautecouture.com*
Rev. in mil. *101-500*
Contact *Sales: Derma Gerety, Designer: Marie de la Soudiere*

WASATCH CO.

3287 Marjan Drive
Atlanta, GA 30340
info@wasatcht.com
404 634 3000 Fax : 404 634 1338 800 544 9096

Labels *Gildan, Fruit of the Loom, Jerzees Bella+Canvas, KiddyKats, Paradis Point, Q-Tees of Cali*
Products *Infant & toddler tees, bibs, underwear & rompers.*
Sell To *Embroiders, screen printers, wholesalers and retail stores.*
Private Label *Yes*
Web Site *www.wasatcht.com*
Contact *Abdul Samad*

ALPHA INDUSTRIES, INC.

14200 Park Meadow Drive, Suite 110 South
Chantilly, VA 20151 wholesale@alphaindustries.com
703 378 1420 Fax : 703 378 4910 866 631 0719

Labels *Alpha Industries, Knox Armory*
Products *Boys fashion, military inspired, Americana & cold weather outerwear & apparel.*
Price Points *Moderate to better*
Production *U.S.A., Far East & Middle East*
Showrooms *Washington DC, NYC, Los Angeles, London, Frankfurt, Paris, Seoul, Tokyo, Florence & Shanghai.*
Sell To *Department stores, specialty stores, boutiques & mail order catalogues.*
Private Label *Yes*
Web Site *www.alphaindustries.com*
RN Number *RN35569*

CEJON ACCESSORIES INC.

390 Fifth Avenue, Suite 602
New York, NY 10018 rmummert@cejon.com
212 967 4663 Fax : 212 967 4766

Labels *Peace of Cake*
Products *Fun fashion for girls. Hats, scarves, vests & outerwear.*
Price Points *Moderate*
Production *U.S.A. & import*
Sell To *Department stores, specialty stores, mail order catalogues & off-price retailers.*
Private Label *Yes*
Web Site *www.cejon.com*
Contact *President: David Seeherman, Sales: Robin Mummert*

COLUMBIA SPORTSWEAR CO., INC.

14375 N.W. Science Park Drive
Portland, OR 97229 sales_info@columbia.com
503 985 4000 Fax : 503 985 5800 800 MA BOYLE

Labels *Columbia Sportswear Co.*
Products *Active outerwear, skiing, sportswear, footwear & accessories.*
Price Points *Moderate*
Production *U.S.A. & Overseas*
Sell To *Department stores, specialty stores, mass merchants.*
Private Label *No*
Web Site *www.columbia.com*
RN Number *RN69724*
Rev. in mil. *+500*
Contact *Chairman: Gertrude Boyle, CEO: Tim Boyle, VIP Sales: Joseph R. Craig*

ESSEX MANUFACTURING INC.

350 Fifth Avenue, Suite 2400
New York, NY 10118 bbaum@baum-essex.com
212 239 0080 Fax : 212 714 2958 800 648 6010

Labels *Misty Harbor®, CLC*
Products *Rainwear, specialize in PVC & vinyl slickers, raincoats & nylon pack-away jackets.*
Production *Import*
Showrooms *Chicago, Boston, Cleveland, Philadelphia, San Francisco & New York.*

Sell To *Department stores, specialty stores, mass merchants & mail order catalogues.*
Private Label *Yes*
Web Site *www.baum-essex.com*
Contact *Rainwear & Outerwear: Bill Baum, Umbrellas: Lance Lovett - llovett@baum-essex.com*

FREE COUNTRY LTD.

1071 6th Avenue, 9th Floor
New York, NY 10018 rondac@freecountry.com
212 719 4596 Fax : 212 719 2051

Labels *Free Country*
Products *Outerwear in sizes 2 through 20.*
Price Points *Better*
Production *U.S.A. & import*
Showrooms *New York*
Sell To *Department stores, specialty stores & boutiques.*
Private Label *Yes*
Web Site *www.freecountry.com*
RN Number *RN82608*
Rev. in mil. *11-50*
Contact *Design: Ira Schwartz*

FRENCH TOAST

100 West 33rd Street, Suite 1012
New York, NY 10001 retail@frenchtoast.com
212 594 4740 Fax : 212 268 5160 800 262 KIDS

Labels *French Toast*
Products *Fashion boy's & girl's outerwear, snowsuits, windsuits & sweaters. All sizes.*
Price Points *Budget to moderate.*
Production *U.S.A. & import.*
Sell To *Specialty stores, mass merchants, mail order catalogues & off-price retailers.*
Private Label *Yes*
Web Site *www.frenchtoast.com*
RN Number *RN13706*
Rev. in mil. *101-500*
Contact *Exec Vice President: Richard Sutton, Exec Vice President, Sales: Joseph Sutton*

IAPPAREL LLC

1407 Broadway, Suite 1721
New York, NY 10018 barry@iapparelny.com
212 695 6343 Fax : 212 764-6475

Labels *Wippette, Big Chill, iXtreme, Pink Platinum*
Products *Fashion forward rainwear & outerwear.*
Price Points *Moderate & better.*
Production *Import*
Showrooms *New York*
Sell To *Moderate to better retailers, mail order catalogues & internet.*
Private Label *Yes*
Web Site *www.wippette.com*
RN Number *RN72348, RN65470*
Rev. in mil. *11-50*
Contact *Owner: Sammy Catton, VP Sales: Barry Newman*

LONG STREET

20 West 33rd Street, 12th Floor
New York, NY 10001
212 947 4090 Fax : 212 967 2420
elliot@longstreet.com

Labels *US Polo Association, Eddie Bauer, American Hawk, Genuine School Uniform*
Products *Boy's & girl's outerwear in sizes newborn to size 20.*
Price Points *Moderate to better.*
Production *U.S.A. & import*
Showrooms *New York/above*
Sell To *Department stores, speciality stores, boutiques, mass merchants & off-price retailers.*
Private Label *No*
Web Site *www.longstreet.com*
Contact *Vice President: Elliot Tawil*

MARMOT MOUNTAIN LLC.

5789 State Farm Drive, Suite 100
Rohnert Park, CA 94928
707 544 4590 Fax : 707 544 1344 1-888-357-3262
ghouser@marmot.com

Labels *Marmot*
Products *Children's performance outerwear.*
Price Points *Better*
Sell To *Specialty stores and department stores.*
Private Label *No*
Web Site *www.marmot.com*
Contact *Greg Houser*

OUTERSTUFF LTD.

1412 Broadway, 18th Floor
New York, NY 10018
212 594 9700 Fax : 212 239 4268
customerservice@outerstuff.com

Labels *Outerstuff, NFL, NHL, NBA, MLB, NCAA, MLS, Adidas, Reebok*
Products *Fashion outerwear, plus professional & college outerwear & windsuits.*
Price Points *Moderate*
Production *Import*
Showrooms *Outerstuff Canada - 905-812-0036*
Sell To *Department stores & specialty stores.*
Private Label *Yes*
Web Site *www.outerstuff.com*
Contact *Sales: Bob Saunders*

TRENDSET ORIGINALS

1407 Broadway, Room 503
New York, NY 10018
212 736 9520 Fax : 212 997 9284
jj@skiva.com

Labels *Trendset*
Products *Girl's jackets toddler thru size 18.*
Price Points *Budget to moderate.*
Production *Import*
Showrooms *New York*
Sell To *Department stores, specialty stores, mass merchants & off-price retailers.*
Private Label *Yes*

RN Number *RN48829*
Rev. in mil. *51-100*

WHITE SIERRA

305 Soquel Way
Sunnyvale, CA 94085
408 980 6688 Fax : 408 980 6670 1 800 980 8688
wholesale@whitesierra.com

Labels *White Sierra*
Products *Boy's & girl's sport outerwear, sizes 8 to 20.*
Price Points *Moderate*
Production *U.S.A. & Asia*
Sell To *Department stores, specialty stores, mass merchants & sporting good shops.*
Private Label *Yes*
Web Site *www.whitesierra.com*
RN Number *RN58486*
Rev. in mil. *11-50*

BABYFAIR, INC.

34 West 33rd Street, Suite 818
New York, NY 10001
212 736 7989 Fax : 212 563 7531
contactus@penelopemack.com

Labels *Penelopemack, mickmack*
Products *Boys & girls coordinated separates sizes toddler thru 20 plus infant & newborn apparel.*
Price Points *Moderate to better.*
Production *Hong Kong, Phillipines, Dominican Republic & China.*
Showrooms *New York*
Sell To *Department stores, specialty stores, boutiques & mass merchants.*
Private Label *Yes*
Web Site *www.penelopemack.com*
RN Number *RN15517*
Contact *President: Ralph Shamah, Sales: Ralph Shamah*

COTTON HERITAGE

6393 E. Washington Blvd.
Commerce, CA 90040
323 722 5592 Fax : 323 724 0045
mickey@cottonheritage.com

Labels *Cotton Heritage*
Products *Blank t-shirts, polo's, fleece, outerwear, active and denim wear. Jogging sets, infant one zees.*
Price Points *Competitive*
Production *Import*
Showrooms *City of Commerce, CA., Clifton, New Jersey 973-249-5081, Miami, FL. 305-623-1947.*
Sell To *Screenprinters, Embroiders, Resort & Promotional & licensed companies, retailers & discount*
Private Label *Yes*
Web Site *www.cottonheritage.com*
RN Number *75813*
Contact *Vice President: Mickey Sachdeva*

FRENCH TOAST

100 West 33rd Street, Suite 1012
New York, NY 10001
212 594 4740 Fax : 212 268 5160 800 262 KIDS
retail@frenchtoast.com

Products *Fashion boys & girls private label sportswear, outerwear, sweaters & beachwear. All sizes.*
Price Points *Budget to moderate.*
Production *U.S.A. & import.*
Sell To *Specialty stores, mass merchants, mail order catalogues & off-price retailers.*
Private Label *Yes*
Web Site *www.frenchtoast.com*
RN Number *RN13706*
Rev. in mil. *101-500*
Contact *Exec Vice President: Richard Sutton, Exec Vice President, Sales: Joseph Sutton*

IN STYLE USA, INC. *(Rep.)

307 West 36th Street, 2nd Floor
New York, NY 10018
212 631 0278 Fax : 212 631 0279
pauline.lock@instyleusa.net

Products *Boy's & girl's coordinated separates.*
Price Points *Better to designer.*
Production *U.S.A. & China*

Showrooms *Above*
Sell To *Department stores, specialty stores & boutiques.*
Corp. Office *Above*
Private Label *Yes*
Web Site *www.instyleusa.net*
Rev. in mil. *2-10*
Contact *President: James Mallon*

IN.STYLE EXCHANGE™

1844 W. Division Street, Suite 201
Arlington, TX 76012
817 886 9222 Fax : 928 447 3168
info@instyleexchange.com

Products *Ready-to-wear trendy designs for private label orders.*
Price Points *Competitive to moderate*
Production *U.S.A.*
Sell To *Department stores, specialty stores, boutiques, screenprinters, embroiderers.*
Corp. Office *Arlington, Texas*
Private Label *Yes*
Web Site *www.instyleexchange.com*
Contact *Sales: Jenny Siede*

LEAWOOD APPAREL LLC.

PO Box 55
Flourtown, PA 19031
215 233 1973
leawoodapparel@hotmail.com

Products *Children's private label sweaters and knitwear.*
Price Points *Moderate to better.*
Production *Domestic & Caribbean Basin*
Corp. Office *8900 Carlisle Road, Wyndmoor, PA 19038-7412.*
Private Label *Yes*
Web Site *www.leawoodapparel.vpweb.com*
Contact
President/Owner: Allan Flickstein

MIAMI STYLE INC.

7480 NW 52nd Street
Miami, FL 33166
305 805 1168 Fax : 305 805 0075
customercare@miamistyle.com

Labels *Miami Style*
Products *Manufacturer of active/athletic wear, tee shirts, sportswear, swimwear & beachwear.*
Price Points *Moderate*
Production *Bangladesh and China*
Sell To *Department stores, specialty stores, boutiques, mass merchants*
Private Label *Yes*
Web Site *www.miamistylebsd.com*
Contact *Owner: Amnon Bensimon, General Manager: Sofia Rincon*

ROYAL APPAREL, INC.

65 Commerce Drive
Hauppauge, NY 11788
631 213 8299 Fax : 631 922 8438 866-Royal-1-S
sales@royalapparel.net

Labels *Royal Apparel*
Products *Basic & fashion forward blanks in a large selection of colors & knit fabrications.*
Price Points *Moderate to better.*
Production *U.S.A.*
Showrooms *New York & Allentown, Pa.*
Sell To *Mass merchants, branded labels, screen printers & department stores.*
Private Label *Yes*
Web Site *www.royalapparel.net*
Contact *President: Morey Mayeri, Owners: Morey Mayeri/Abraham Mayeri*

STYLE SOURCE INC.

913 Orange Street
Wilmington, NC 28401
910 399 2288 Fax : 910 399 2289
geoff@style-source.com

Products *Private label and product development specialists.*
Price Points *Moderate to better.*
Production *U.S.A.*
Sell To *Specialty stores, boutiques, mail order catalogues, screenprint ers and embroiderers.*
Private Label *Yes*
Web Site *www.style-source.com*
RN Number *RN82034*
Contact *President: Geoffrey Krasnov*

VICTOR ROSSI

11016 Nacirema Lane
Stevenson, MD 21153
410 337 2714
vr@victorrossi.com

Products *Prival label in special occasion, cotton garments, sportswear, bags & footwear.*
Price Points *Moderate to Designer*
Production *Domestic & Import*
Sell To *Department stores, specialty stores, mail order catalogs, designers & wholesalers.*
Corp. Office *Above*
Private Label *Yes*
Web Site *www.victorrossi.com*
RN Number *102005*
Contact *Manish Singh*

VISHAL ENTERPRISES

226 West 37th Street, 7th Floor
New York, NY 10018
212 629 0880 Fax : 212 629 0882
vishal@vishalent.com

Products *Specialize in dresses/jumpers*
Price Points *Better*
Production *Import*
Sell To *Department stores, boutiques, mail order catalogues*
Private Label *Yes*
Rev. in mil. *2-10*

Contact *Owner: Mahesh Moorjani, Sales: Vishal Moorjani*

BLUE HAWAII SALES

801 South King Street, Suite 3707
Honolulu, HI 96813
808 277 0368
hiblue@hawaii.rr.com

Labels *Blue Hawaii*
Products *Casual shirts.*
Price Points *Moderate*
Production *U.S.A.*
Showrooms *Honolulu*
Sell To *Department stores & mass merchants.*
Private Label *Yes*
RN Number *RN85143*
Contact *President and Owner: Joni Albao*

CALVIN CLOTHING COMPANY

108A New South Road
Hicksville, NY 11801
516 937 0400 Fax : 516 937 1342
ben@calvinclothes.com

Labels *Calvin, Europa, Mezzanotte, Dimples by Europa*
Products *Boy's woven shirts & ties.*
Price Points *Moderate to better*
Production *Import*
Showrooms *New York*
Sell To *Department stores, speciality stores, boutiques & mail order catalogues.*
Private Label *Yes*
RN Number *RN95393*
Rev. in mil. *11-50*
Contact *President: Joseph Gioia*

CLASSIX

39360 3rd Street East, #307
Palmdale, CA 93550
661 726 9041 Fax : 661 726 9246 800 934-3290
vkhachooni@hotmail.com

Labels *Classix*
Products *Boy's formalwear shirt collection in nine styles.*
Price Points *Better*
Sell To *Department stores, specialty stores, formalwear shops.*
Web Site *www.classixshirts.com*

GOLF APPAREL BRANDS

13621 South Main Street
Los Angeles, CA 90061
310 715 1772 Fax : 310 715 1776 800 678 5246
sales@lamode.com

Labels *La Mode*
Products *Boys cotton pique polos and hoodys*
Price Points *Moderate to better*
Production *Domestic and import from Korea, China, Hong Kong, Malaysia*
Sell To *Specialty stores, off-price and golf shops.*
Private Label *Yes*
Web Site *www.lamode.com*
Contact *President/Owner: Eddie Kahn*

WEDDING TROPICS

8608 Utica Avenue
Rancho Cucamonga, CA 91730
844 921 0466
kevin@weddingtropics.com

Labels *Friday Shirts!, Martinez Montiel!*
Products *Custom & off the rack Guayabera and Hawaiian style children's shirts.*
Price Points *Bridge.*
Sell To *Department stores, specialty stores, boutiques and mass merchants.*
Corp. Office *Above*
Private Label *Yes*
Web Site *www.weddingtropics*
RN Number *117573*
Rev. in mil. *0-2*
Contact *President/Owner: Kevin Baldwin*

CAPELLI NEW YORK

1 East 33rd Street, 9th Floor
New York, NY 10016 info@capellinewyork.com
212 684 3344 Fax : 212 686 4895

Labels *Capelli New York*
Products *Sleepwear, robes and slippers for juniors and children.*
Production *Import*
Showrooms *New York, Canada, Europe and Asia*
Sell To *Department stores, specialty stores, national chain stores*
Private Label *Yes*
Web Site *www.capellinewyork.com*

HYP HATS LTD.

20 West 37th Street
New York, NY 10018 davidf@hyphats.com
212 684 7717 Fax : 212 684 7589 800 331 1181

Labels *Hyp, Disney, Happy Bunny, Baby Phat, Pink Cookie, Mudd, InEssence*
Products *Sleepwear, intimate apparel, socks, slippers and tee shirts.*
Price Points *All*
Production *Taiwan, China*
Showrooms *New York*
Sell To *Department stores, specialty stores, boutiques, mass merchants & mail order catalogues.*
Private Label *Yes*
Web Site *www.hyphats.com*
Rev. in mil. *2-10*
Contact *President: Howard Levy, Sales: David Fisher, Merchandising: David Fisher*
Production: Mike Pascal, Marketing: Howard Levy

LEMUR GROUP, INC.

275 Rue Stinson, Suite 201
Montreal, Quebec, Canada H4N 2E1 info@lemurgroup.com
514 748 6234 Fax : 514 748 6235

Labels *Petit Lem, P.L. Junior*
Products *Coordinated sleepwear for sizes newborn to girls and boys 12 years.*
Price Points *Better*
Production *China*
Sell To *Department stores, specialty stores*
Private Label *Yes*
Web Site *www.petitlem.com*
Contact *President: Gabriel Di Mieele*

NEW ICM, LP

220 Sam Bishkin Road
El Campo, TX 77437 zalmand@newicm.com
979 578 0543 Fax : 979 578 0503 800 987 9008

Labels *Laura Dare, Tom & Jerry, I-C Collections, Zazzy*
Products *Children's sleepwear, slips & underwear.*
Price Points *Moderate to better*
Production *U.S.A.*
Sell To *Department stores & specialty stores.*
Private Label *Yes*

Web Site *www.newicm.com*
RN Number *18443*
Contact *President: Daniel Zalman, VP Marketing: Priscilla Hunt*

CALVIN CLOTHING COMPANY

108A New South Road
Hicksville, NY 11801
516 937 0400 Fax : 516 937 1342
ben@calvinclothes.com

Labels *Calvin, Europa, Mezzanotte, Dimples by Europa*
Products *Boy's tailored suits, sport coats, dress pants, shirts & ties.*
Price Points *Moderate to better*
Production *Import*
Showrooms *New York*
Sell To *Department stores, speciality stores, boutiques & mail order catalogues.*
Private Label *Yes*
RN Number *RN95393*
Rev. in mil. *11-50*
Contact *President: Joseph Gioia*

FOUGER FOR KIDS, INC.

1152 S. Wall Street, #102
Los Angeles, CA 90015
213 748 0648 Fax : 213 748 7430
fougerforkids@aol.com

Labels *Fouger for Kids*
Products *Boy special occasion suits, tuxedos & short sets for infant, toddler & children sizes.*
Price Points *Better*
Sell To *Specialty stores*
Private Label *Yes*
Web Site *www.fouger4kids.com*
Contact *President: Ben Pourebrahim*

SILVER SUIT, INC.

401 E. Washington
Los Angeles, CA 90015
213 748 4535 Fax : 213 748 3039 800-873-6217
silversuitusa@gmail.com

Labels *Silver Suit, Vangoh, Platinum, Silver Line*
Products *Formal boys wear, shirts, pants, suits, vest sets, tuxedos & sportswear, sizes 3 months thru 20.*
Price Points *Moderate*
Production *Import from China, India, Vietnam*
Showrooms *New York: Contact Buzz, tel: 212-965-5151*
Sell To *Department stores, speciality stores, boutiques & mass merchants.*
Private Label *Yes*
Web Site *www.silversuitinc.com*
RN Number *RN85030*
Rev. in mil. *2-10*
Contact *President: Jack/Shan Aghassy*

AUTUMN CASHMERE INC.

231 West 39th Street, Suite#1111
New York, NY 10018 info@autumncashmere.com
888 6 AUTUMN Fax : 212 398 2255 1 888 6 AUTUMN

Labels *Autumn Cashmere*
Products *Fashion & novelty 100% cashmere & cashmere blend sweaters. 2 to 5 gauge knits.*
Price Points *Better to designer.*
Production *China & Hong Kong*
Showrooms *New York/Aci NY, 212-398-2244, CA/Sales: 213-893-6995.*

Sell To *Department & specialty stores. boutiques & mail order catalogues.*
Private Label *Yes*
Web Site *www.autumncashmere.com*
Rev. in mil. *11-50*

CANADIAN SWEATER CO., LTD.

#39 8528-123rd Street
Surrey, BC, Canada V3W 3V6 info@canadiansweater.com
604 594 8050 Fax : 604 594 8264

Labels *Cowichan, Islander*
Products *Woolen sweaters & winter accessories.*
Price Points *Bridge*
Production *Canada*
Sell To *High end department stores, boutiques.*
Corp. Office *Above*
Private Label *Yes*
Web Site *www.canadiansweater.com*
Contact *President: Kaljit Tmana*

Notes

BEACH RAYS/DIV OF J.Y. RAYS, INC.

2023 Chico Avenue
South El Monte, CA 91733 sales@beachrays.com
626 941 0388 Fax : 626 941 0386

Labels *Surfer, Vast, Wet*
Products *Boys and girls swimwear & beachwear.*
Price Points *Moderate to better*
Production *Offshore*
Sell To *Department stores, specialty stores, theme/water parks*
Corp. Office
Private Label *Yes*
Web Site *www.beachrays.com*
Contact *National Sales Manager: Natalie Wierzba*

FRENCH TOAST

100 West 33rd Street, Suite 1012
New York, NY 10001 retail@frenchtoast.com
212 594 4740 Fax : 212 268 5160 800 262 KIDS

Labels *French Toast*
Products *Fashion boy's & girl's beachwear & bathing suits. Sizes 4 to 20.*
Price Points *Budget to moderate.*
Production *U.S.A. & import.*
Sell To *Specialty stores, mass merchants, mail order catalogues & off-price retailers.*
Private Label *Yes*
Web Site *www.frenchtoast.com*
RN Number *RN13706*
Rev. in mil. *101-500*
Contact *Exec Vice President: Richard Sutton, Exec Vice President, Sales: Joseph Sutton*

MAR CHIQUITA SWIMWEAR INC.

1 N. Atlantic Avenue
Cocoa Beach, FL 32931 marchiquita@cfl.rr.com
321 868 0868 Fax : 321 784 2626

Products *Specialty print and solid swimwear in a variety of fits for children.*
Price Points *Moderate and better.*
Production *Domestic*
Showrooms *Above*
Sell To *Department stores, specialty stores and boutiques.*
Corp. Office *Above*
Private Label *Yes*
Contact *President: Rebecca J. Guy*

PINK CHICKEN

307 Seventh Avenue, Suite 703
New York, NY 10001 customerservice@pinkchicken.com
212 255 9090 Fax : 212 255 9095

Labels *Pink Chicken*
Products *Colorful, fun swim wear with great quality*
Price Points *Better*
Showrooms *West Coast/Nicky 213-688-9590, New England/Ellen 617-620-0546*
New York/34 West 33rd Street, New York 212-695-0762

Sell To *Department stores, specialty stores, boutiques*
Private Label *No*
Web Site *www.pinkchicken.com*
Contact *Owner: Stacey Fraser*

SWEENIE MANUFACTURING CORPORATION

60 East 9th Street, Suite 315
New York, NY 10003
646 825 5027 Fax : 646 825 5027
diane@sweeniemanufacturing.com

Labels *Sweenie, Bikini Thief, Body Rock Sport*
Products *Junior & kids contemporary swimwear & coverups, graphic tees & accessories.*
Price Points *Budget to designer*
Production *U.S.A. & import from China, East Asia, Europe & South/Central America*
Sell To *Department stores, specialty stores, boutiques, mass merchants*
Private Label *Yes*
Web Site *www.sweeniemanufacturing.com*
Rev. in mil. *0-2*
Contact *Design & Production: Diane Walker (cell: 914-471-1069), Sales & Marketing: Stacey Demar (cell: 646-772-6113)*

ALSTYLE

1501 East Cerritos Avenue
Anaheim, CA 92805 info@alstyle.com
714 765 0400 Fax : 714 765 0450 800 225 1364

Labels *AAA™*
Products *All kinds of tees. Organic, short & long sleeve.*
Price Points *Moderate to better*
Showrooms *Sales Reps throughout the USA.*
Sell To *Department stores, mass merchants, mail order catalogs.*
Private Label *Yes*
Web Site *www.alstyle.com*

BABY JAY INC./GROWING FEET INC.

207 Second Street
Lakewood, NJ 08701 info@babyjay.com
732 905 4980 Fax : 732 363 9195 800 282 3338

Labels *Baby Jay*
Products *Extensive line of 100% cotton infant & childrens blanks.*
Price Points *Moderate*
Production *U.K.*
Showrooms *Lakewood/NJ*
Sell To *Specialty stores, boutiques, mail order catalogues, better depart. stores & manufacturers.*
Private Label *Yes*
Web Site *www.babyjay.com*
RN Number *RN89576*
Contact *President: Jacob Phillip*

GOODWEAR USA

239 Western Avenue, Room 2D
Essex, MA 01929 steve@goodwear.com
978 768 7746 Fax : 800 787 4951 800 338 8895

Labels *Goodwear*
Products *Children's upscale dyeable tee-shirts done in sustainable fabrics: organic cotton & bamboo.*
Price Points *Bridge*
Production *U.S.A.*
Showrooms *Tokyo, Osaka, NYC & Essex*
Sell To *Distributors*
Private Label *Yes*
Web Site *www.goodwear.com*
RN Number *75346*
Contact *President: Martha Liquori, Owner: Stephen & Martha Liquori, Sales: Stephen Liquori*

HILO HATTIE

670 Auahi Street, Suite 1-03
Honolulu, HI 96813 sales@hilohattie.com
808 535 6500 Fax : 808 356 1510 1 800 233 8912

Labels *Hilo Hattie*
Products *Casual tee shirts for children.*
Production *Domestic*
Sell To *Retail stores and mass merchants.*
Private Label *Yes*

Web Site *www.hilohattie.com*

JOE BLOW T'S

8213-B Cloverleaf Drive Rear
Millersville, MD 21108 vanessa@joeblow.com
443 274 2744 Fax : 410 766 9516

Labels *Joe Blow T's Inc.*
Products *Youth T-shirts of all kinds. Made in the USA.*
Price Points *Moderate*
Production *U.S.A.*
Sell To *Department stores, specialty stores & boutiques.*
Private Label *Yes*
Web Site *www.joeblow.com*
Contact *Owner: Stewart Cohen, Sales: Vanessa Harris (cell: 443-962-0278).*

ROWDY SPROUT

3404 Cloudcroft Drive
Malibu, CA 90265 sales@rowdysprout.com
310 487 7666

Labels *Rowdy Sprout*
Products *Classic rocker tees in hip & funky designs. Sizes 3 months to 8 years*
Price Points *Better*
Production *U.S.A.*
Sell To *Boutiques*
Web Site *www.rowdysprout.com*
Contact *Owner: Laura Angotti*

ROYAL APPAREL, INC.

65 Commerce Drive
Hauppauge, NY 11788 sales@royalapparel.net
631 213 8299 Fax : 631 922 8438 866-Royal-1-S

Labels *Royal Apparel*
Products *Basic & fashion forward blanks in a large selection of colors & knit fabrications.*
Price Points *Moderate to better.*
Production *U.S.A.*
Showrooms *New York & Allentown, Pa.*
Sell To *Mass merchants, branded labels, screen printers & department stores.*
Private Label *Yes*
Web Site *www.royalapparel.net*
Contact *President: Morey Mayeri, Owners: Morey Mayeri/Abraham Mayeri*

SUGAR AND BRUNO

7260 Georgetown Road
Indianapolis, IN 46268 challen@sugarandbruno.com
317 293 5888 Fax : 317 293 5886 800 875 8559

Labels *Sugar and Bruno*
Products *Fun tees, tanks and hoodies*
Price Points *Moderate*
Production *U.S.A. & China*
Sell To *Specialty stores, boutiques*
Web Site *www.sugarandbruno.com*

RN Number *127789*
Rev. in mil. *2-10*
Contact *President: Challen Powers*

Notes

FRENCH TOAST

100 West 33rd Street, Suite 1012
New York, NY 10001 retail@frenchtoast.com
212 594 4740 Fax : 212 268 5160 800 262 KIDS

Labels *French Toast Official School Wear, Lee School Uniforms*
Products *Boy's & girl's school uniforms. Sizes 4 to 20.*
Price Points *Budget to moderate.*
Production *U.S.A. & import.*
Sell To *Specialty stores, mass merchants, mail order catalogues & off-price retailers.*
Private Label *Yes*
Web Site *www.frenchtoast.com*
RN Number *RN13706*
Rev. in mil. *101-500*
Contact *Exec Vice President: Richard Sutton, Exec Vice President, Sales: Joseph Sutton*

LONG STREET

20 West 33rd Street, 12th Floor
New York, NY 10001 elliot@longstreet.com
212 947 4090 Fax : 212 967 2420

Labels *US Polo Association, Genuine School Uniform*
Products *Boy's & Girl's sportswear, sleepwear & school uniforms sizes newborn to size 20.*
Price Points *Moderate to better.*
Production *U.S.A. & import*
Showrooms *New York/above*
Sell To *Department stores, speciality stores, boutiques, mass merchants & off-price retailers.*
Private Label *No*
Web Site *www.longstreet.com*
Contact *Vice President: Elliot Tawil*

RIFLE/KAYNEE *(Rep.)

14-25 Plaza Road, Suite S-2-5
Fair Lawn, NJ 07410 ccomins@kaynee.com
201 796 8101

Labels *Kaynee*
Products *Youth uniform wear including knits, woven shirts and fleece.*
Price Points *Moderate*
Sell To *Select retailers and school uniform suppliers*
Private Label *Yes*
Web Site *www.riflekaynee.com*
Contact *Charlie Comins*

WILLIAMSON-DICKIE MFG CO.

509 West Vickery Boulevard
Fort Worth, TX 76104 customerservice@dickies.com
817 336 7201 Fax : 817 810 4342 866 411 1501

Labels *Williamson-Dickie*
Products *Complete line of school uniforms & playwear for boys, girls and juniors.*
Price Points *Moderate*
Production *U.S.A.*
Showrooms *Dallas, New York*
Sell To *Department stores, specialty stores, uniform outlets.*

Private Label	*Yes*
Web Site	*www.dickies.com*
Rev. in mil.	*+500*
Contact	*President: Philip Williamson*

AQUARIUS LTD.

3200 South Kingshighway
St. Louis, MO 63139 sales@aquariusltd.com
314 664 4498 Fax : 314 664 4482 800-325-2680

Labels *Acquarius*
Products *Men's & young men's fashion belts.*
Price Points *Budget, moderate & better.*
Production *U.S.A. & Asia.*
Showrooms *New York: 1412 Broadway, Suite 1414, New York, N. Y. 10018 212-695-6816.*
Los Angeles: 5901 S. Eastern Ave, Commerce, CA 90040 323 800 2363
Sell To *Department & specialty stores, mass merchants, mail order catalogues & off-price.*
Private Label *Yes*
Web Site *www.aquariusltd.com*
RN Number *RN71327*

BARRONS-HUNTER, INC.

P.O. Box B
Charlottesville, VA 22905 sales@barrons-hunter.com
434 971 7626 Fax : 434 971 9278 800 338 4193

Labels *Barrons-Hunter*
Products *Men's & women's belts including D-Ring ribbon belts, braces & corporate logo accessories.*
Price Points *Moderate to better.*
Production *U.S.A.*
Showrooms *Virginia & New York*
Sell To *Specialty stores & boutiques.*
Private Label *Yes*
Web Site *www.barrons-hunter.com*

BAUXO INC.

9917 110 Street, Unit A
Edmonton, AB, Canada T5K 2N4 info@bauxo.com
780 452 1100 Fax : 780 452 4521 1 888 552 2896

Products *Belts & small leather goods.*
Price Points *Moderate*
Showrooms *Above*
Sell To *Specialty stores, boutiques*
Web Site *www.bauxo.com*
Contact *Owner: Diana DeLuca, Designer: Hariyono*

BELGO LUX INC.

5605 De Gaspe Street, #901
Montreal, Quebec, Canada H2T 2A4 egaranito@belgolux.com
514 279 6328 Fax : 514 271 4429 1-800-363-6328

Labels *Belgo Lux, Bruges, Cobalt, Vermillion*
Products *Fashion belts.*
Price Points *Moderate*
Production *USA & import from China & India.*
Showrooms *10 W. 33rd Street, New York/NY, 212-213-1165*
Sell To *Department stores, specialty stores & boutiques.*
Corp. Office *Above*
Private Label *Yes*

Web Site *www.belgolux.com*
Rev. in mil. *11-50*
Contact *President: Stephen Majnemer, Owner: Stephen & Allen Majnemer, Sales Manager: Andrea Majnemer*

BIG BUDDHA

19 West 34th Street
New York, NY 10001 kirsten@ebigbuddha.com
212 857 9580 Fax : 212 643 7524

Labels *Big Buddha*
Products *Fashionable ladies belts.*
Sell To *Boutiques, specialty stores, department stores.*
Corp. Office *Above*
Private Label *Yes*
Web Site *www.ebigbuddha.com*
Contact *Owner: Jeremy Bassan, Sales Manager: Kirsten Grindeland*

BRAVE LEATHER LTD.

83-87 Colville Road
Toronto, Ontario, Canada M6M 2Y6 info@braveleather.com
416 782 0243 Fax : 416 781 5816 888-655-6905

Products *Leather belts & fashion accessories.*
Price Points *Better*
Production *Canada*
Showrooms *Toronto, Montreal, Vancouver, New York & Los Angeles.*
Sell To *Specialty stores.*
Corp. Office
Private Label *Yes*
Web Site *www.braveleather.com*
Rev. in mil. *2-10*
Contact *CEO: Scott Irvine*

FRENCH CONNECTION

512 Seventh Avenue, 25th Floor
New York, NY 10018 frenchconnection@frenchconnection-usa.com
212 221 3157 Fax : 212 302 6839 866-932-3285

Labels *French Connection*
Products *Contemporary belts.*
Price Points *Better*
Production *Global*
Showrooms *Atlanta, Chicago, Los Angeles & New York.*
Sell To *Department stores, specialty stores, boutiques, catalogues & off-price retailers.*
Corp. Office *184-10 Jamaica Avenue, Hollis, New York 11423*
Private Label *Yes*
Web Site *usa.frenchconnection.com*
RN Number *RN53372*
Rev. in mil. *101-500*
Contact *President: Andrea Hyde*

GEM DANDY INC.

200 West Academy
Madison, NC 27025
336 548 9624 Fax : 336 427 7105 800 334 5101
customerservice@gem-dandy.com

Labels *Collegiate, PGA, G Bar D, John Deere®, Roper®, Real Tree®.*
Products *Leather belts, suspenders & small leather goods. Dress, casual, traditional & western styles.*
Price Points *Better to designer.*
Production *U.S.A., Asia & South America.*
Showrooms *Dallas/Men's Mart, Tokyo & 30 nationwide reps.*
Sell To *Department & specialty stores, mass merchants, mail order & off-price.*
Private Label *Yes*
Web Site *www.gem-dandy.com*
RN Number *WPL06141*
Rev. in mil. *11-50*
Contact *President: Brad Penn*

GILTON COMPANY

1106 West Gardena Boulevard
Gardena, CA 90247
626 241 1958 Fax : 310 327 5020 800 479 1075
sales@giltonco.com

Products *Men's suspenders & wonder buttons.*
Price Points *Moderate*
Production *U.S.A & import.*
Showrooms *Call for catalog*
Sell To *Department stores, specialty stores, mail order catalogues & off-price retailers.*
Private Label *No*
Web Site *giltonco.com*
RN Number *RN64854*
Rev. in mil. *0-2*
Contact *President & Owner: Philip Shar*

HOLD-UP SUSPENDER CO.

21421 Hilltop Street, Suite 16
Southfield, MI 48033
248 386 0252 Fax : 248 352 1185 800 700 4515
sal@suspenders.com

Labels *Hold Up*
Products *Men's & ladies suspenders with the patented "No Slip Clip" for work, dress & sport.*
Price Points *Better*
Production *U.S.A.*
Sell To *Department, chain & specialty stores, mail order catalogues & manufacturers.*
Private Label *Yes*
Web Site *www.suspenders.com*
Contact *Sales: Sal Herman*

KIPPYS *(Rep.)

2096 Newton Avenue
San Diego, CA 92113
619 435 6218 Fax : 619 238 0670
bob@kippys.com

Labels *Kippys*
Products *Embellished leather & suede belts, bags, boots & accessories*
Price Points *Better to designer.*

Showrooms *Regional shows in Dallas, Los Angeles, New York, Denver, Chicago, Las Vegas. International: Milan and Paris.*
Sell To *Specialty stores & mail-order catalagues.*
Private Label *Yes*
Web Site *www.kippys.com*
Rev. in mil. *2-10*
Contact *Designers: Bob Kipperman & Tarin Brouillette*

LA MATERA

204 W 10th Street, Suite 503
New York, NY 11201 sales@lamaterashop.com
917 336 0509

Labels *LaMatera*
Products *Fashionable Belts*
Price Points *Better*
Production *U.S.A.*
Sell To *Boutiques*
Web Site *www.lamaterashop.com*
Contact *Owner: Brook Stroud cell:610 620 3126 brook@lamaterashop.com*

LEATHEROCK INT. INC.

5285 Lovelock Street
San Diego, CA 92110 leatherock@leatherock.com
619 299 7625 Fax : 619 299 7730 800 466 6667

Labels *Leatherock*
Products *Women's designer leather belts.*
Price Points *Moderate to better.*
Production *U.S.A.*
Showrooms *NY/Susan Bonomo, 260 W 39th St., #701, NY, NY, tel: 212 302 4702-bonomo214@aol.com, LA/Engel Showroom, 127 E 9th St., #509, L.A., CA 90015, 213 623 4481-loft809@aol.com*
Sell To *Department stores, specialty stores, boutiques, mass merchants & mail order catalogues.*
Private Label *Yes*
Web Site *www.leatherockwholesale.com*
Rev. in mil. *2-10*
Contact *President & Owner: Laurence Bloch*

MARTIN DINGMAN COUNTRYWEAR

14966 Industrial Park Drive
Leadhill, AR 72644 info@martindingman.com
870 422 7151 Fax : 870 422 7379 800 955 BELT

Labels *Martin Dingman*
Products *Men's leathergoods, belts, gloves, bags, accessories & footwear.*
Price Points *Better to designer*
Production *U.S.A.*
Showrooms *Show collection in New York during Collective.*
Sell To *Specialty stores, department stores*
Private Label *No*
Web Site *www.martindingman.com*
Contact *President: Gay Dingman, Designer: Martin Dingman, Marketing: Grayson Dingman*

MEGA BELTS, INC.

1625 Chabanel West, Suite 484
Montreal, Canada H4N2S7
514 385 4175 Fax : 514 385 3130
josephmingione@qc.aibn.com

Labels *Rebel, Emanuel*
Products *Leather belts & fashion & novelty belts.*
Price Points *Moderate to bridge*
Production *Canada, Taiwan & China*
Showrooms *Montreal, Toronto/Maureen Rankin*
Sell To *Department stores, specialty stores & boutiques.*
Private Label *Yes*
Rev. in mil. *2-10*
Contact *President: Joseph Mingione, Sales: Joseph Mingione*

MIL-IDEE, INC.

9855 Meilleur
Montreal, Quebec, Canada H3L 3J6
514 382 0190 Fax : 514 382 0392
info@mil-idee.com

Labels *Mil-Idee, Pajar®, Lucky 7™, Projek Raw, Report Collection, Point Zero*
Products *Fashionable belts for men and women*
Price Points *Budget to Couture*
Production *Canada and import from China*
Showrooms *Same as Above*
Sell To *Department stores, Specialty Stores, Boutiques, Mass Merchants, Catalogues*
Corp. Office *Same as Above*
Private Label *Yes*
Web Site *mil-idee.com*
Contact *President: Meyer Elkeslassy, Marketing Director: Daniel Elkeslassy*

NOTANONYMOUS *(Rep.)

54 West 39th Street, 10th Floor
New York, NY 10018
212 997 3512 Fax : 212 768 3748
michele@notanonymous.com

Labels *Streets Ahead*
Products *Belts*
Price Points *Better, bridge & designer.*
Production *U.S.A,, Canada, Europe, Asia & South America*
Showrooms *New York*
Sell To *Deptartment stores, specialty stores, boutiques & mail order catalogues.*
Private Label *Yes*
Web Site *www.notanonymous.com*
Contact *President: Maxine Coppersmith, Sales: Michele Beck*

STREETS AHEAD

5510 Soto Street
Vernon, CA 90058
323 277 0860 Fax : 323 277 5565
info@streetsaheadinc.com

Labels *Streets Ahead.*
Products *Leather, suede & embellished denim belts.*
Price Points *Budget, moderate & better.*
Production *U.S.A.*

Showrooms	*Los Angeles: 213-689-9620, New York: 212-997-3512*
Sell To	*Department & specialty stores, boutiques, mass merchants, catalogs & off-price.*
Private Label	*Yes*
Web Site	*www.streetsaheadinc.com*
Contact	*Sales: Kari Woodruff*

WILL LEATHER GOODS

100 Cap Court
Eugene, OR 97402
willservice@willleathergoods.com
541 434 6659 Fax : 541 683 3416 1 877 467 0436

Labels	*Bill Adler Design, Will Leather Goods*
Products	*Belts, bags & wallets.*
Production	*U.S.A.*
Showrooms	*Above*
Private Label	*Yes*
Web Site	*www.willleathergoods.com*
Contact	*President: Bill Adler*

EDWARD CROMARTY ART DESIGN STUDIO *(Rep.)

228 East Route 59, #281
Nanuet, NY 10954 edwardcromarty@gmail.com
914 288 5171 877 447 2741

Labels *Edward Cromarty*
Products *Bridal veils, wraps & shawls.*
Price Points *High end, designer, reasonable designer pricing.*
Production *U.S.A.*
Showrooms *Please call for an appointment*
Sell To *Department stores, boutiques & specialty stores.*
Private Label *Yes*
Web Site *www.edwardcromarty.com*
RN Number *RN101294*
Rev. in mil. *0-2*
Contact *President & Owner: Edward Cromarty*

HAROLD TEPPER STRIBBONS INC.

57-12 260th Street
Little Neck, NY 11362 htepper@stribbons.com
718 423 4598 Fax : 718 423 1494

Products *Drawstring pouches, sachets, cosmetic bags, jewelry bags, tassels, bows & ribbons.*
Price Points *Moderate*
Production *U.S.A. & the Orient*
Showrooms *New York, California, Florida & Chicago*
Sell To *Mass merchants.*
Private Label *Yes*
Web Site *www.stribbons.com*
Rev. in mil. *11-50*
Contact *President Bag & Specialty Division: Harold Tepper (Cell: 917-545-1255).*

LILLIAN ROSE, INC.

475 McKenzie Road, P.O. Box 182
Mukwonago, WI 53149 info@lillianrose.com
262 363 5286 Fax : 800 595 7673 800 521 8760

Labels *Lillian Rose*
Products *Wedding unity candles, guestbooks, glasses, caketops, pillows, garters, favors & baby gifts.*
Price Points *Moderate to better*
Production *U.S.A. & import*
Sell To *Department stores, specialty stores, boutiques & mail order catalogues.*
Private Label *Yes*
Web Site *www.lillianrose.com*
Rev. in mil. *2-10*
Contact *President: Susan D'Amour*

LUSCIOUS LACES LINGERIE

2818 Wabash N.E.
Grand Rapids, MI 49525 lusciouslaces@hotmail.com
616 363 3097 Fax : 616 363 3097 1-800-456-1790

Labels *Luscious Laces Lingerie*
Products *Women's bridal garters, accessories & prom garters.*
Price Points *Moderate to better.*

Production *U.S.A.*
Sell To *Department stores, specialty stores & bridal boutiques.*
Private Label *No*
Web Site *www.lusciouslaces.com*
Contact *Owner: Judith Rice*

MOTHER PLUCKER FEATHER COMPANY INC.

2511 West 3rd Street
Los Angeles, CA 90057 motherplucker@earthlink.net
213 637 0411 Fax : 213 637 0417

Labels *Mother Plucker*
Products *Feather raw goods, wings, boas, and we specialize in custom work.*
Sell To *Wholesaler*
Private Label *Yes*
Web Site *www.motherplucker.com*
Contact *Owner: William Zelowitz, Manager of Production and Design: Lelan Berner*

NOTANONYMOUS *(Rep.)

54 West 39th Street, 10th Floor
New York, NY 10018 michele@notanonymous.com
212 997 3512 Fax : 212 768 3748

Labels *Deborah Grivas, Mystique, Streets Ahead.*
Products *Bridal & evening, leather & beaded handbags, jewelry & scarves.*
Price Points *Better, bridge & designer*
Production *U.S.A,, Canada, Europe, Asia & South America*
Showrooms *New York*
Sell To *Department stores, specialty stores, boutiques & mail order catalogues.*
Private Label *Yes*
Web Site *www.notanonymous.com*
Contact *President: Maxine Coppersmith, Sales: Michele Beck*

SUSAN DUNN INC.

PO Box 1086
Rancho Santa Fe, CA 92067 susan@susandunn.com
858 832 1086 Fax : 858 832 1087

Labels *Spa Slippurrs™, Susan Dunn®, Spa Sox, Spa Wear, Solace per Aqua®*
Products *100% cotton spa slippers, socks, spa wraps, hair wraps & totes.*
Price Points *Designer*
Production *U.S.A.*
Sell To *Specialty stores, boutiques, mail order catalogues, hotels, resorts & spas.*
Private Label *Yes*
Web Site *www.susandunn.com*
RN Number *RN90990*
Rev. in mil. *2-10*
Contact *CEO & President: Susan Dunn*

BABY JAY INC./GROWING FEET INC.

207 Second Street
Lakewood, NJ 08701 info@babyjay.com
732 905 4980 Fax : 732 363 9195 800 282 3338

Labels *Baby Jay*
Products *Extensive line of fine children's socks, baby hats, blankets & bibs.*
Price Points *Moderate*
Production *U.K.*
Showrooms *Lakewood/NJ*
Sell To *Specialty stores, boutiques, hosiery stores, mail order catalogues, manufacturers & designers.*
Private Label *Yes*
Web Site *www.babyjay.com*
RN Number *RN89576*
Contact *President: Jacob Phillip*

BODY WRAPPERS

65 West 36th Street, 5th Floor
New York, NY 10018 info@bodywrappers.com
212 279 3492 Fax : 212 564 3426 800 323 0786

Labels *Body Wrappers®, Princess Aurora™*
Products *Fitness & dance apparel, tights, legwarmers & tutus.*
Price Points *Moderate*
Production *U.S.A., (some accessories imported)*
Showrooms *New York, Denver, Toronto plus reps throughout the U.S, Canada, Europe & Japan.*
Sell To *Dance specialty stores, boutiques, Nordstrom's, mail order catalogues, website.*
Corp. Office *107 Trumbull Street, Elizabeth, NJ 07206 Ph: 908 354 7218*
Private Label *Yes*
Web Site *www.bodywrappers.com*
RN Number *RN60206*
Rev. in mil. *11-50*
Contact *Sales: Michael Lee, tel: 908 354 7218 ext. 231*

FRENCH TOAST

100 West 33rd Street, Suite 1012
New York, NY 10001 retail@frenchtoast.com
212 594 4740 Fax : 212 268 5160 800 262 KIDS

Labels *French Toast*
Products *Fashion children's footwear, leggings, socks & hair accessories.*
Price Points *Budget to moderate.*
Production *U.S.A. & import.*
Sell To *Specialty stores, mass merchants, mail order catalogues & off-price retailers.*
Private Label *Yes*
Web Site *www.frenchtoast.com*
RN Number *RN13706*
Rev. in mil. *101-500*
Contact *Exec Vice President: Richard Sutton, Exec Vice President, Sales: Joseph Sutton*

HYP HATS LTD.

20 West 37th Street
New York, NY 10018
212 684 7717 Fax : 212 684 7589 800 331 1181
davidf@hyphats.com

Labels *Hyp, Disney, Happy Bunny, Baby Phat, Pink Cookie, Mudd, InEssence*
Products *Branded & custom caps, headwear, cold weather accessories, hair accessories & hosiery.*
Price Points *All*
Production *Taiwan, China*
Showrooms *New York*
Sell To *Department stores, specialty stores, boutiques, mass merchants & mail order catalogues.*
Private Label *Yes*
Web Site *www.hyphats.com*
Rev. in mil. *2-10*
Contact *President: Howard Levy, Sales: David Fisher, Merchandising: David Fisher Production: Mike Pascal, Marketing: Howard Levy*

LIN MANUFACTURING & DESIGN

2929 North Main Street, PO Box 6127
North Logan, UT 84341
435 787 8888 Fax : 435 755 9637 888 430 9888
roger@linmfg.com

Labels *Lin Performance, Lin Wellness, Lin Custom, Recycle Lin*
Products *Novelty socks, hosiery & legwear for boys, girls & infants. Made with renewable resources.*
Production *U.S.A., Taiwan & China*
Sell To *Department & specialty stores, boutiques, mass merchants, catalogues & off-price.*
Private Label *Yes*
Web Site *www.linmfg.com*
RN Number *RN84364*
Contact *President: Hillary Lin Ong, Sales: Roger Round, Customer Service: Cole Richards (cs1@linmfg.com)*

SUSAN DUNN INC.

PO Box 1086
Rancho Santa Fe, CA 92067
858 832 1086 Fax : 858 832 1087
susan@susandunn.com

Labels *Susan Dunn®, Spa Slippurrs™, Kids Spa Wear*
Products *100% cotton bibs, hooded towels & slippers.*
Price Points *Designer*
Production *U.S.A.*
Sell To *Specialty stores, boutiques, mail order catalogues, hotels, resorts & spas.*
Private Label *Yes*
Web Site *www.susandunn.com*
RN Number *RN90990*
Rev. in mil. *2-10*
Contact *CEO & President: Susan Dunn*

TIC TAC TOE/BABY LEGS

51 Sullivan Drive
Jericho, NY 11753
516 931 6510 Fax : 516 942 5311 Cell: 516 658 5654
amyhoffmankids@gmail.com

Labels *Tic Tac Toe*
Products *Tights & socks. Specialize in computer prints and seamless toe socks.*

Price Points	*Better*
Production	*U.S.A. & import.*
Showrooms	*34 West 33rd Street, Suite 314, New York, NY 10001 (212-391-4143)*
Sell To	*Department, specialty & high end stores, boutiques, on-line merchants, mail order catalogues.*
Corp. Office	*Baby United LLC, 6333 1st Ave South #8, Seattle, Wa 98108 tel: 206-734-4000.*
Private Label	*Yes*
Web Site	*www.amyhoffmankids.com*
Contact	*Sales Rep: Amy Hoffman*

BELGO LUX INC.

5605 De Gaspe Street, #901
Montreal, Quebec, Canada H2T 2A4 egaranito@belgolux.com
514 279 6328 Fax : 514 271 4429 1-800-363-6328

Labels *Belgo Lux, Vermillion, Bruges*
Products *Fashion Sunglasses*
Price Points *Moderate*
Production *USA & import from China & India.*
Showrooms *10 W. 33rd Street, New York/NY, 212-213-1165*
Sell To *Department stores, specialty stores & boutiques.*
Corp. Office *Above*
Private Label *Yes*
Web Site *www.belgolux.com*
Rev. in mil. *11-50*
Contact *President: Stephen Majnemer, Owner: Stephen & Allen Majnemer, Sales Manager: Andrea Majnemer*

BLUEGEM SUNGLASSES INC.

6381-B Rose Lane
Carpinteria, CA 93013 eye@bluegem.com
800 543 9802 Fax : 805 684 1544

Labels *Blue Gem, DLR, Blue Planet*
Products *All types of sunglasses & eyewear.*
Production *Import*
Sell To *Specialty stores, boutiques, upscale merchandisers & mail order catalogues.*
Private Label *Yes*
Web Site *www.bluegem.com*
Contact *President: David Weinstein, VP Sales: Carolyn Espindola*

DIESEL PLANET

220 West 19th Street
New York, NY 10011 customerservice@shop.diesel.com
212 755 9200 Fax : 212 255 6641 877.344.8342

Labels *Diesel*
Products *Men's & women's fashion eyewear and sun glasses.*
Price Points *Moderate to better*
Showrooms *New York & Los Angeles/Tel: 310 652 2322*
Sell To *Department stores, mass merchants & boutiques.*
Corp. Office *Above*
Web Site *www.diesel.com*
Contact *Owner: Renzo*

FGX INTERNATIONAL/DIV OF ESSILOR

500 George Washington Highway
Smithfield, RI 02917 glazaro@fgxi.com
401 231 3800 Fax : 401 232 7235

Labels *Foster Grant, Magnivision, Gargoyles, Ironman, Dockers, Nine West, Panama Jack*
Products *Designer & marketer of non-prescription reading glasses & value priced sunglasses.*
Price Points *Budget to moderate & designer.*
Production *Europe & Far East.*
Sell To *Department, specialty & optical stores, mass merchants & off-price.*

Private Label *Yes*
Web Site *www.fgxi.com*
Contact *VP Marketing: Gina Lazaro, Director of Marketing: Sal Siano (ssiano@fgxi.com)*
Manager Customer Service: Regina Casey (rcasey@fgxi.com)

FORMART CORPORATION

312 Fifth Avenue , 6th Floor
New York, NY 10001
212 819 1819 Fax : 212 921 1992
bellini_formart@hotmail.com

Labels *Bellini Collections*
Products *Sunglasses. Private label & contracting work only.*
Price Points *Moderate to better.*
Production *U.S.A.*
Showrooms *New York*
Sell To *Department stores, specialty stores, boutiques & mass merchants.*
Private Label *Yes*
Web Site *www.formartcorp.com*
Rev. in mil. *0-2*
Contact *President: Sheung Mei Liu*

HUGO BOSS U.S.A., INC.

55 Water Street, 8th Floor
New York, NY 10041
212 940 0600 Fax : 212 940 0619 800-484-6267
customerservice@hugoboss-store.com

Labels *Hugo Boss, Boss Hugo Boss, Boss Black, Boss Green, Boss Orange*
Products *Men's and women's eyewear.*
Price Points *Better*
Production *U.S.A. & import*
Sell To *Department stores, specialty stores, mail order catalogues & mass merchants.*
Private Label *No*
Web Site *www.hugoboss.com*
Rev. in mil. *+500*

SAFILO U.S.A.

801 Jefferson Road
Parsippany, NJ 07054
973 952 2800 Fax : 212 967 9282
pladines@gmail.com

Labels *Safilo, Kate Spade, Dior, Max Mara, Carerra, Jimmy Choo, Marc Jacobs, Polaroid & many*
Products *Sunglasses, eyeglasses & glasses for sports.*
Price Points *Designer to couture.*
Production *Import*
Showrooms *665 Fifth Avenue, New York, NY , tel: 212 736 5090*
Sell To *Department & specialty stores, boutiques, mail order, mass merchants, off-price.*
Private Label *Yes*
Web Site *www.safilo.com/en*
Contact *Sales: Pedro*

ARMBRUST INTERNATIONAL

735 Allens Avenue
Providence, RI 02905 sales@armbrustintl.com
401 781 3300 Fax : 401 781 2590 866 276 2468

Products *Fashion, chain & fine jewelry.*
Price Points *Moderate to high*
Production *U.S.A.*
Showrooms *Providence, RI & New York, NY*
Sell To *Mass merchants, retailers, designers, private label*
Private Label *Yes*
Web Site *www.armbrustintl.com*
Contact *Sales: Tinah Hall, Kerilyn Rodi, Scott Roberts*

BAUXO INC.

9917 110 Street, Unit A
Edmonton, AB, Canada T5K 2N4 info@bauxo.com
780 452 1100 Fax : 780 452 4521 1 888 552 2896

Products *Fashion jewelry. Earrings, necklaces, bracelets & rings.*
Price Points *Moderate*
Showrooms *Above*
Sell To *Specialty stores, boutiques*
Web Site *www.bauxo.com*
Contact *Owner: Diana DeLuca, Designer: Hariyono*

BY BOE LTD.

253 36th Street, #308
Brooklyn, NY 11232 shop@byboe.com
718 488 0400 Fax : 718 488 0410

Labels *By Boe, INEZ*
Products *Jewelry*
Production *U.S.A.*
Showrooms *Atlanta: AmericaSmart - please call the New York Showroom to make an appointment.*
Sell To *Department stores, specialty stores, boutiques, on-line.*
Web Site *www.byboe.com*
Contact *Designer: Annika Inez*

CHIPITA ACCESSORIES

110 East 7th Street
Walsenburg, CO 81089 chipita@earthlink.net
719 738 3202 Fax : 719 738 2130

Labels *Chipita*
Products *Designer & fashion jewelry. Earrings, necklaces, bracelets, brooches, rings & cufflinks.*
Price Points *Bridge to designer.*
Production *U.S.A.*
Sell To *Department stores, specialty stores & boutiques.*
Private Label *Yes*
Contact *President/Owner: Joan Eagle*

CYNTHIA GALE

8 East 36th Street, 3rd floor
New York, NY 10016
212 481 1845 Fax : 212 481 5296 888 436 2781
info@cynthiagale.com

Labels *Cynthia Gale*
Products *Mens & womens sterling silver jewelry, sterling/genuine stone & sterling/18k & 14k gold ove*
Price Points *Better to designer*
Production *Import*
Showrooms *Atlanta/Tim Philbin Accessories, Mid-Atlantic/Jo D Bond*
Sell To *Department stores, specialty stores, museums, galleries, catalogues & websites.*
Private Label *Yes*
Web Site *www.cynthiagale.com*
Rev. in mil. *2-10*
Contact *Owners: Cynthia & GlennGale, Production: Glenn Gale, Design, Sales & Marketing: Cynthia Gale*

DANECRAFT INC.

One Baker Street
Providence, RI 02905
401 941 7700 Fax : 401 461 8715
bob.soltys@danecraft.com

Labels *Danecraft, Primavera*
Products *Costume jewelry.*
Price Points *Bridge & opening price points.*
Production *U.S.A. & import.*
Showrooms *9 East 38th Street, New York, NY*
Sell To *Department stores, specialty stores*
Private Label *Yes*
Web Site *www.danecraft.com*
Rev. in mil. *11-50*
Contact *President: Robert Soltys*

DIESEL PLANET

220 West 19th Street
New York, NY 10011
212 755 9200 Fax : 212 255 6641 877.344.8342
customerservice@shop.diesel.com

Labels *Diesel*
Products *Men's & women's fashion jewelry and watches.*
Price Points *Moderate to better*
Showrooms *New York & Los Angeles/Tel: 310 652 2322*
Sell To *Department stores, mass merchants & boutiques.*
Corp. Office *Above*
Web Site *www.diesel.com*
Contact *Owner: Renzo*

ERICA LYONS JEWELRY/CRIMZON ROSE

1600 Division Road
West Warwick, RI 02893
401 231 0266 800 619 6588
info@crimzonrose.com

Labels *Erica Lyons, Crimzon rose*
Products *Women's costume jewelry.*

Price Points *Moderate to better*
Production *U.S.A. & import*
Showrooms *385 Fifth Avenue, Suite 1002 , New York NY 10016*
Sell To *Department stores*
Private Label *Yes*
Web Site *www.ericalyons.com*
Contact *www.crimzonrose.com - 401-461-5900*

FORMART CORPORATION

312 Fifth Avenue , 6th Floor
New York, NY 10001 bellini_formart@hotmail.com
212 819 1819 Fax : 212 921 1992

Labels *Bellini Collections*
Products *Fashion jewelry & watches. Private label & contracting work only.*
Price Points *Moderate to better.*
Production *U.S.A.*
Showrooms *New York*
Sell To *Department stores, specialty stores, boutiques & mass merchants.*
Private Label *Yes*
Web Site *www.formartcorp.com*
Rev. in mil. *0-2*
Contact *President: Sheung Mei Liu*

FOUR SEASONS DESIGN GROUP

2400 Merrick Road
Bellmore, NY 11710 info@fourseasonsdesigngroup.com
800 295 6784 Fax : 516 781 8635

Labels *Table Art*
Products *Nature & sea inspired line of jewelry.*
Price Points *Better & designer*
Production *U.S.A.*
Showrooms *Above*
Sell To *Museums, department stores, specialty stores, boutiques & mail order catalogues.*
Private Label *Yes*
Web Site *www.fourseasonsdesigngroup.com*
Contact *President: Steven Lazar*

GILTON COMPANY

1106 West Gardena Boulevard
Gardena, CA 90247 sales@giltonco.com
626 241 1958 Fax : 310 327 5020 800 479 1075

Products *Men's handkerchiefs, wonder buttons, tie racks, travel kits, shave kits & suspenders.*
Price Points *Moderate*
Production *U.S.A & import.*
Showrooms *Call for catalog*
Sell To *Department stores, specialty stores, mail order catalogues & off-price retailers.*
Private Label *No*
Web Site *giltonco.com*
RN Number *RN64854*
Rev. in mil. *0-2*
Contact *President & Owner: Philip Shar*

JOLI JEWELRY

117 Sterling Place, Suite 15
Brooklyn, NY 11217
718 399 9150 Fax : 718 638 4638
sales@jolijewelry.com

Labels *Joli Jewelry*
Products *Limited edition pins, earrings, necklaces, bracelets, barettes made from vintage materials.*
Price Points *Moderate*
Production *U.S.A.*
Showrooms *Brooklyn, NY/above.*
Sell To *Specialty stores, boutiques, museum shops & mail order catalogues.*
Private Label *No*
Web Site *www.jolijewelry.com*
Contact *President: Jody Lyons*

JOY ACCESSORIES

1 Hartford Sq, #E
New Britain, CT 06052
860 612 0439 Fax : 860 612 0510 880-365-4569
joy@joyaccessories.com

Labels *Joy Susan*
Products *Import up-to-date and trendy jewelry of all types.*
Price Points *Moderate*
Production *U.S.A., India, Phillipines, China, Vietnam*
Showrooms *Connecticut and Atlanta*
Sell To *Department stores, specialty stores, boutiques, catalogues*
Private Label *Yes*
Web Site *www.joyaccessories.com*
RN Number *100542*
Rev. in mil. *0-2*
Contact *Sales: Gary Tierney*

L&J ACCESSORIES/CELLINI LLC

140 Candace Drive
Maitland, FL 32751
407 671 0111 Fax : 407 671 4472 800 393 1459
info&landjaccessories.com

Labels *Cellini*
Products *Sterling silver and fashion jewelry*
Price Points *Better*
Production *U.S.A.*
Showrooms *366 5th Avenue Suite 609 Ney York NY 10001*
Sell To *Deaprtment stores, catalogs, on-line*
Web Site *landjaccessories.com*

LORREN BELL, INC.

2050 N. Stemmons Freeway, Unit 158
Dallas , TX 75207
214 651 0110 Fax : 214 651 0550
lorren@lorrenbell.com

Labels *Deluxe by Lorren Bell*
Products *Day and evening ladies jewelry. Specialize in faux tortoise & Austrian crytal looks.*
Price Points *Better*
Production *U.S.A., France & Italy.*
Sell To *Department stores, specialty stores, boutiques & mail order catalogues.*

Private Label *Yes*
Web Site *www.lorrenbell.com*
Rev. in mil. *0-2*
Contact *President & Designer: Lorren Bell*

NOTANONYMOUS *(Rep.)

54 West 39th Street, 10th Floor
New York, NY 10018 michele@notanonymous.com
212 997 3512 Fax : 212 768 3748

Labels *Sonyarenee, Marlyn Schiff, Deborah Grivas*
Products *Sterling, semi-precious & fashion jewelry*
Price Points *Better, bridge & designer*
Production *U.S.A,, Canada, Europe, Asia & South America*
Showrooms *New York*
Sell To *Deptartment stores, specialty stores, boutiques & mail order catalogues.*
Private Label *Yes*
Web Site *www.notanonymous.com*
Contact *President: Maxine Coppersmith, Sales: Michele Beck*

PILLAGED VILLAGE, THE

31Eagle Court, Suite E
Carlisle, OH 45005 pvsales@pillagedvillage.com
937 743 0685 Fax : 937 743 0697 1-877-793-1066

Labels *The Pillaged Village*
Products *Medieval designed jewelry, brooches, anklets, bracelets, dance belts & necklaces.*
Price Points *Moderate*
Showrooms *Same as Above*
Sell To *Boutiques, specialty stores, on-line catalog*
Web Site *www.pillagedvillage.com*
Contact *Owner: Wendy Kimmel*

RHINESTONE JEWELRY CORPORATION

2028 McDonald Avenue
Brooklyn, NY 11223 orders@rhinestone.com
718 336 6788 Fax : 718 645 0355 1 800 458 6625

Products *Rhinestone jewelry and accessories for the bride, evening wear, special occasion or daily wear.*
Price Points *Moderate to designer.*
Production *U.S.A. & import.*
Sell To *Department stores, specialty stores, boutiques.*
Private Label *Yes*
Web Site *www.rhinestonejewelry.com*
Rev. in mil. *2-10*
Contact *President & owner: Jeffrey Levy*

SHAUNE BAZNER ACCESSORIES, INC.

5117 MacArthur Boulevard NW
Washington , DC 20016 service@shaunebazner.com
202 537 2980 Fax : 202 537 2981 800 MEI FA 4U

Labels *Shaune Bazner*
Products *Handmade necklaces, bracelets, earrings & beaded costume jewelry.*
Price Points *Moderate*

Production *U.S.A.*
Showrooms *Reps throughout the US.*
Sell To *Department stores, specialty stores boutiques & mail order catalogues.*
Private Label *No*
Web Site *www.shaunebazner.com*
Rev. in mil. *2-10*
Contact *President/Owner: Shaune Bazner Miller*

SHOWROOM SEVEN/ERICKSON BEAMON *(Rep.)

263 Eleventh Avenue
New York, NY 10001 jean-marc@showroomseven.com
212 643 4810 Fax : 646 763 8940

Labels *Erickson Beamon*
Products *Designer fashion jewelry.*
Price Points *Contemporary, designer & couture*
Production *International*
Showrooms *New York, Los Angeles, Paris*
Sell To *Department stores, specialty stores & boutiques. International and domestic.*
Private Label *Yes*
Web Site *www.showroomseven.com*
Rev. in mil. *11-50*

TOKYO BAY INC.

745 Bryant Street
San Francisco, CA 94107 sales@tokyobayinc.com
415 808 4880 Fax : 415 777 4887 800 653 1771

Labels *Tokyo Bay*
Products *Contemporary, fashion forward watches & accessories for men & women.*
Price Points *Moderate to better.*
Production *Import*
Showrooms *San Francisco, Los Angeles, Atlanta, Seattle, Chicago and Las Vegas*
Sell To *Specialty stores, boutiques & mail order catalogues.*
Private Label *Yes*
Web Site *www.tokyobayinc.com*
Contact *President: Dory Isaacs, Sales Manager: Victoria Son*
Wholesale site: https://nuorder.com/tokyobay

VIESTE-ROSA

21 Mill Street
Johnston, RI 02919 viesterosa@aol.com
401 946 4330 Fax : 401 946 5960

Labels *Vieste Rosa*
Products *Fashion stone jewelry.*
Price Points *Moderate*
Production *U.S.A.*
Showrooms *New York/385 Fifth Avenue, Suite 1410, NY, NY 10016. Tel: 212-686-9287.*
Sell To *Department stores, specialty stores, boutiques & mass merchants.*
Private Label *Yes*
Web Site *www.viesterosa.com*
Contact *President: Anthony Giarrusso, Vice-President: Frank Giarrusso*

YOCHI DESIGNS

11 West 36th Street, 10th Floor
New York, NY 10018
212 947 7826 Fax : 212 947 7859
yochidesignny@yahoo.com

Labels *Yochi*
Products *Necklaces, earrings, belts, pins, brooches & more inset with crystals.*
Price Points *Moderate*
Production *U.S.A.*
Showrooms *New York*
Sell To *Specialty stores & boutiques.*
Web Site *www.yochiny.com*
Contact *Sales: Galetor Yochi*

Notes

525 AMERICA

525 Seventh Avenue, 10th Floor
New York, NY 10018
mbock@525america.com
212 921 5688 Fax : 212 921 5069 877-246-8609

Labels *525 Homewear*
Products *Blankets made of luxury yarns including cotton, chenilles & angora knot throws in solid & tie*
Price Points *Better*
Production *U.S.A.*
Showrooms *New York & reps throughout the U.S.*
Sell To *Department stores, specialty stores & mail order catalogues.*
Private Label *Yes*
Web Site *www.525america.com*
Contact *President: Robert Bock, Design: Robert Bock, VP Sales: Marianne Bock*

ACORN PRODUCTS

9655 International Boulevard
Cincinnati, OH 45246
christian.hilton@totes.com
800 872 2676 Fax : 800 280 4127 1 800 872 2676

Labels *Acorn*
Products *Polartec, sheepskin & leather slippers, comfort footwear, socks & cold weather accessories.*
Price Points *Moderate to better.*
Production *Import*
Showrooms *Call for showrooms.*
Sell To *Specialty stores & mail order catalogues.*
Private Label *Yes*
Web Site *www.acorn.com*

COLORADO SILVER STAR CORP.

975 East 58th Avenue, Suite J
Denver, CO 80216
info@coloradosilverstar.com
303 295 1353 Fax : 303 295 0256 1 800 878 2772

Labels *Colorado Silver Star, Copper Collection*
Products *Handmade German silver & centrifugal casted belt buckles, pins, bolos, antique replicas.*
Price Points *Budget, moderate & better.*
Production *U.S.A.*
Showrooms *Display at Western English Sales Association and Denver Gift & Jewelry Shows*
Sell To *Department & specialty stores, mass merchants, catalogues, western shops & gift stores.*
Private Label *Yes*
Web Site *www.coloradosilverstar.com*
Rev. in mil. *0-2*
Contact *President & Owner: Hilda P. Sanchez, Design & Merchandising: Serafin Sanchez*

CYNTHIA GALE

8 East 36th Street, 3rd floor
New York, NY 10016
info@cynthiagale.com
212 481 1845 Fax : 212 481 5296 888 436 2781

Labels *Cynthia Gale*
Products *Sterling silver gifts.*
Price Points *Better to designer*
Production *Import*
Showrooms *Atlanta/Tim Philbin Accessories, Mid-Atlantic/Jo D Bond*

Sell To *Department stores, specialty stores, museums, galleries, catalogues & websites.*
Private Label *Yes*
Web Site *www.cynthiagale.com*
Rev. in mil. *2-10*
Contact *Owners: Cynthia & GlennGale, Production: Glenn Gale, Design, Sales & Marketing: Cynthia Gale*

DAVID SMITH & ASSOCIATES

One Courageous Court
Salem, MA 01970 smithco200@aol.com
800 776 6100 Fax : 339 440 4873

Labels *David Smith, Gopaks by David Smith*
Products *Custom blankets, pillows & packable jackets.*
Price Points *Moderate to better, plus off-price.*
Production *U.S.A., Hong Kong & Bangladesh.*
Sell To *Specialty stores, college bookstores, country clubs, corporations*
Private Label *Yes*
RN Number *RN#4-3420353*
Rev. in mil. *0-2*
Contact *President: Robert Smith, Vice-President: Linda Smith*

DOLORES PISCOTTA

8865 Sixteenth Avenue
Brooklyn, NY 11214 piscotta@msn.com
718 232 1167 Fax : 718 232 1167

Labels *Dolores Piscotta, Piscotta New York*
Products *A collection of matching cashmere sweaters & accessories for women and dogs.*
Price Points *Better to designer*
Production *U.S.A., Italy, China, Nepal*
Showrooms *Brooklyn, New York - By appointment only*
Additional website: dolorespiscottawholesale.com
Sell To *Department stores, specialty stores, boutiques & catalogues.*
Private Label *Yes*
Web Site *www.dolorespiscotta.com*
RN Number *RN97327*
Contact *Owner and Designer: Dolores Piscotta*

DREAMBAGS, INC.

1225 Shilloh Boulevard, #261
Zion, IL 60099 contact@magmilebrand.com
224 636 8622

Products *Decorative fabric pillows, bolsters, futon covers, pet beds, table runners & bed throws.*
Price Points *Moderate to designer*
Production *U.S.A.*
Sell To *Department stores, specialty stores, boutiques, on-line.*
Private Label *Yes*
Web Site *www.magmilebrand.com*
Rev. in mil. *2-10*
Contact *Owner: Olga Chtiguel*

FORMART CORPORATION

312 Fifth Avenue , 6th Floor
New York, NY 10001
212 819 1819 Fax : 212 921 1992
bellini_formart@hotmail.com

Labels *Bellini Collections*
Products *Pill boxes, picture frames, candle holders, etc. Private label & contracting work only.*
Price Points *Moderate to better.*
Production *U.S.A.*
Showrooms *New York*
Sell To *Department stores, specialty stores, boutiques & mass merchants.*
Private Label *Yes*
Web Site *www.formartcorp.com*
Rev. in mil. *0-2*
Contact *President: Sheung Mei Liu*

FOUR SEASONS DESIGN GROUP

2400 Merrick Road
Bellmore, NY 11710
800 295 6784 Fax : 516 781 8635
info@fourseasonsdesigngroup.com

Labels *Table Art*
Products *Nature & sea inspired line of tabletop & gift items, napkin rings, serving pieces, vases, & pictu*
Price Points *Better & designer*
Production *U.S.A.*
Showrooms *Above*
Sell To *Museums, department stores, specialty stores, boutiques & mail order catalogues.*
Private Label *Yes*
Web Site *www.fourseasonsdesigngroup.com*
Contact *President: Steven Lazar*

GILTON COMPANY

1106 West Gardena Boulevard
Gardena, CA 90247
626 241 1958 Fax : 310 327 5020 800 479 1075
sales@giltonco.com

Products *Men's manicure sets, handkerchiefs, lint lifters, suspenders, travel kits & more.*
Price Points *Moderate*
Production *U.S.A & import.*
Showrooms *Call for catalog*
Sell To *Department stores, specialty stores, mail order catalogues & off-price retailers.*
Private Label *No*
Web Site *giltonco.com*
RN Number *RN64854*
Rev. in mil. *0-2*
Contact *President & Owner: Philip Shar*

JOAN BLACKSHEAR DESIGN COMPANY

P. O. Box 2705
Kailua-Kona, HI 96745
808 324 0766
info@joanblackshear.com

Labels *Joan Blackshear*
Products *Hand painted table top collection, silk wall hangings with bamboo hangers, hat & hair access*
Price Points *Bridge*

Production *U.S.A.*
Sell To *Department stores, specialty stores, boutiques & mail order catalogues*
Private Label *No*
Web Site *www.joanblackshear.com*
RN Number *RN82071*
Contact *Owner: Joan Blackshear*

JOLI JEWELRY

117 Sterling Place, Suite 15
Brooklyn, NY 11217
718 399 9150 Fax : 718 638 4638
sales@jolijewelry.com

Labels *Joli Jewelry*
Products *Decorative home accessories made from vintage & semi-precious materials.*
Price Points *Moderate*
Production *U.S.A.*
Showrooms *Brooklyn, NY/above.*
Sell To *Specialty stores, boutiques & mail order catalogues.*
Private Label *No*
Web Site *www.jolijewelry.com*
Contact *President: Jody Lyons*

NICOLE & CO.

9200 Parc Avenue, Suite 407
Montreal, Canada, H2N1Z4
514 383 5599 Fax : 514 383 5674
hats@nicole-co.com

Labels *Nicole & Co, Procadif*
Products *Fashion shoe clips, bows & accessories. Specialize in all kinds of fashion hats.*
Price Points *Designer to couture*
Production *Canada*
Showrooms *Montreal/9200 Parc Avenue, #407, Montreal*
Sell To *Department stores, specialty stores & boutiques.*
Private Label *Yes*
Web Site *www.nicole-co.com*
Contact *President: Nicole Amram, Production: Yoram Amram, Design: Yoram Amram*

ROYALE LINENS INC.

325 Duffy Avenue
Hicksville, NY 11801
201 997 3700 Fax : 201 997 5008
fsnow@royalelinens.com

Labels *Royale*
Products *Manufacturer of home fashions - sheets, sheet sets, comforters, windows and accessories.*
Price Points *Moderate to better*
Production *Import from Pakistan*
Showrooms *295 Fifth Avenue, New York, N. Y.*
Sell To *Major, regional and independent retailers*
Corp. Office *Subsidiary of Yunus Textile Mills, Ltd.*
Private Label *Open line and private label*
Web Site *www.royalelinens.com*
RN Number *69173*
Rev. in mil. *101-500*
Contact *Merchandising: Frank Snow*

BECKER GLOVE INTERNATIONAL, LLC

4240 Rider Trail
St. Louis, MO 63045 customerinfo@beckerglove.com
314 298 9810 Fax : 314 298 9809 800 875 1244

Labels *Grand Sierra®, Rawlings®Brand, Impulse™Brand, Procure™Brand, Tailgator™Glove*
Products *Large selection of gloves and cold weather accessories for the entire family.*
Sell To *Department stores, specialty stores*
Web Site *www.beckerglove.com*

BETMAR HATS INC.

411 Fifth Avenue
New York, NY 10016 betmarhats@aol.com
212 684 8080 Fax : 212 545 0663 800 678 7676

Labels *Betmar, Plaza Suite*
Products *Hats & millinery. Also, gloves, capes, scarves and handbags.*
Price Points *Moderate to better.*
Production *U.S.A. & import.*
Showrooms *Chicago, Dallas, Atlanta, Boston, New York, New England, West Coast*
Sell To *Department stores, specialty stores, boutiques & mail order catalogues.*
Private Label *Yes*
Web Site *www.betmarhats.com*
Rev. in mil. *11-50*
Contact *President: Bernard Grossman*

CANADIAN SWEATER CO., LTD.

#39 8528-123rd Street
Surrey, BC, Canada V3W 3V6 info@canadiansweater.com
604 594 8050 Fax : 604 594 8264

Labels *Cowichan, Islander*
Products *Winter hats, scarves & gloves for men, women & children.*
Price Points *Bridge*
Production *Canada*
Sell To *High end department stores, boutiques.*
Corp. Office *Above*
Private Label *Yes*
Web Site *www.canadiansweater.com*
Contact *President: Kaljit Tmana*

GILTON COMPANY

1106 West Gardena Boulevard
Gardena, CA 90247 sales@giltonco.com
626 241 1958 Fax : 310 327 5020 800 479 1075

Products *Men's leather gloves and women's white nylon gloves.*
Price Points *Moderate*
Production *U.S.A & import.*
Showrooms *Call for catalog*
Sell To *Department stores, specialty stores, mail order catalogues & off-price retailers.*
Private Label *No*
Web Site *giltonco.com*
RN Number *RN64854*
Rev. in mil. *0-2*

Contact *President & Owner: Philip Shar*

MADEMOISELLE, INC.

4200 W. Schubert Avenue
Chicago, IL 60639 scot210@aol.com
773 394 4555 Fax : 773 394 9495 800 992 5580

Labels *Mademoiselle*
Products *Missy & today's executive women's handbags, gloves & more.*
Price Points *Moderate to better*
Production *U.S.A. & overseas.*
Showrooms *Atlanta, Dallas, Denver plus 15 sales reps nationwide.*
Sell To *Department stores, specialty stores, boutiques, gift shops & online.*
Private Label *Yes*
Web Site *www.mademoiselleinc.com*
Contact *President: Scott Goldstein*

MARMOT MOUNTAIN LLC.

5789 State Farm Drive, Suite 100
Rohnert Park, CA 94928 ghouser@marmot.com
707 544 4590 Fax : 707 544 1344 1-888-357-3262

Labels *Marmot*
Products *Performance gloves for men and women.*
Price Points *Better*
Sell To *Specialty stores and department stores.*
Private Label *No*
Web Site *www.marmot.com*
Contact *Greg Houser*

MARTIN DINGMAN COUNTRYWEAR

14966 Industrial Park Drive
Leadhill, AR 72644 info@martindingman.com
870 422 7151 Fax : 870 422 7379 800 955 BELT

Labels *Martin Dingman*
Products *Men's leather goods, gloves, belts, accessories & footwear.*
Price Points *Better to designer.*
Production *U.S.A.*
Showrooms *Show collection in New York during Collective.*
Sell To *Specialty stores, department stores*
Private Label *No*
Web Site *www.martindingman.com*
Contact *President: Gay Dingman, Designer: Martin Dingman, Marketing: Grayson Dingman*

WOODEN SHIPS

231 West 39th Street
New York, NY 10018 sales@wooden-ships.com
888 717 6700 Fax : 212 221 2329

Labels *Wooden Ships*
Products *Updated scarfs, wraps, ponchos, mittens, gloves & hats*
Price Points *Better*
Production *Import*
Sell To *Department stores, specialty stores, boutiques & mail order catalogues.*

Private Label *No*
Web Site *www.wooden-ships.com*
Contact *Sales: Randi Weinstein*

FORMART CORPORATION

312 Fifth Avenue , 6th Floor
New York, NY 10001
212 819 1819 Fax : 212 921 1992
bellini_formart@hotmail.com

Labels *Bellini Collections*
Products *Fashion hair ornaments. Private label & contracting work only.*
Price Points *Moderate to better.*
Production *U.S.A.*
Showrooms *New York*
Sell To *Department stores, specialty stores, boutiques & mass merchants.*
Private Label *Yes*
Web Site *www.formartcorp.com*
Rev. in mil. *0-2*
Contact *President: Sheung Mei Liu*

JOLI JEWELRY

117 Sterling Place, Suite 15
Brooklyn, NY 11217
718 399 9150 Fax : 718 638 4638
sales@jolijewelry.com

Labels *Joli Jewelry*
Products *Limited edition barettes made from vintage materials.*
Price Points *Moderate*
Production *U.S.A.*
Showrooms *Brooklyn, NY/above.*
Sell To *Specialty stores, boutiques & mail order catalogues.*
Private Label *No*
Web Site *www.jolijewelry.com*
Contact *President: Jody Lyons*

LITTLE MISS JULIA

85 Franklin Road, 1A Hamilton Business Park
Dover, NJ 07801
973 886 8293 Fax : 973 989 1711
info@littlemissjulia.com

Labels *Little Miss Julia*
Products *Hair accessories for girls. Embellished barrettes, alligator clips, headbands, pony tail holders.*
Price Points *Better*
Production *Handmade in the U.S.A.*
Sell To *Specialty stores, boutiques, online retailers.*
Private Label *No*
Web Site *www.littlemissjulia.com*
Rev. in mil. *0-2*
Contact *Owner: Joanne Schlesinger*

LORREN BELL, INC.

2050 N. Stemmons Freeway, Unit 158
Dallas , TX 75207
214 651 0110 Fax : 214 651 0550
lorren@lorrenbell.com

Labels *Deluxe by Lorren Bell*
Products *Hair accessories in faux tortoise and fabrics.*
Price Points *Better*
Production *U.S.A., France & Italy.*

Sell To *Department stores, specialty stores, boutiques & mail order catalogues.*
Private Label *Yes*
Web Site *www.lorrenbell.com*
Rev. in mil. *0-2*
Contact *President & Designer: Lorren Bell*

NICOLE & CO.

9200 Parc Avenue, Suite 407
Montreal, Canada, H2N1Z4
514 383 5599 Fax : 514 383 5674
hats@nicole-co.com

Labels *Nicole & Co.*
Products *Fashion hats, hair clips, scrunchies, combs & bobbie pins.*
Price Points *Designer to couture*
Production *Canada*
Showrooms *Montreal/9200 Parc Avenue, #407, Montreal*
Sell To *Department stores, specialty stores & boutiques.*
Private Label *Yes*
Web Site *www.nicole-co.com*
Contact *President: Nicole Amram, Production: Yoram Amram, Design: Yoram Amram*

RHINESTONE JEWELRY CORPORATION

2028 McDonald Avenue
Brooklyn, NY 11223
718 336 6788 Fax : 718 645 0355 1 800 458 6625
orders@rhinestone.com

Products *Rhinestone hair ornaments, tiaras and jewelry.*
Price Points *Moderate to designer.*
Production *U.S.A. & import.*
Sell To *Department stores, specialty stores, boutiques.*
Private Label *Yes*
Web Site *www.rhinestonejewelry.com*
Rev. in mil. *2-10*
Contact *President & owner: Jeffrey Levy*

SHAUNE BAZNER ACCESSORIES, INC.

5117 MacArthur Boulevard NW
Washington , DC 20016
202 537 2980 Fax : 202 537 2981 800 MEI FA 4U
service@shaunebazner.com

Labels *Shaune Bazner Accessories, Convertibles, Mei Fa*
Products *Hair sticks & other wearable accessories.*
Price Points *Moderate*
Production *U.S.A.*
Showrooms *Reps throughout the US.*
Sell To *Department stores, specialty stores boutiques & mail order catalogues.*
Private Label *No*
Web Site *www.shaunebazner.com*
Rev. in mil. *2-10*
Contact *President/Owner: Shaune Bazner Miller*

VIESTE-ROSA

21 Mill Street
Johnston, RI 02919 viesterosa@aol.com
401 946 4330 Fax : 401 946 5960

Labels	*Vieste Rosa*
Products	*Fashion stone & studded combs, tierras, barrettes & barbie pins.*
Price Points	*Moderate*
Production	*U.S.A.*
Showrooms	*New York/385 Fifth Avenue, Suite 1410, NY, NY 10016. Tel: 212-686-9287.*
Sell To	*Department stores, specialty stores, boutiques & mass merchants.*
Private Label	*Yes*
Web Site	*www.viesterosa.com*
Contact	*President: Anthony Giarrusso, Vice-President: Frank Giarrusso*

APL®

P.O. Box 965
Hallettsville, TX 77964
361 798 5000
apl@aplhandbags.com

Labels *APL®*
Products *Fine leather handbags created by hand. City bags, totes & clutches in natural leather or exoti*
Price Points *Better*
Production *U.S.A.*
Showrooms *Studio: 907 N. Glendale, Hallettsville, Tx 77964 tel: 361-798-2327*
Web Site *www.aplhandbags.com*
Contact *Owner & Designer: Audrey L. Peterson*

AR NEW YORK

121 West 30th Street
New York, NY 10001
212 564 5368 Fax : 212 624 9336
info@arnewyork.us

Products *A large variety of handbags in style and color. Also carry wallets and fashion backpacks.*
Price Points *Budget to moderate*
Showrooms *140 Morgan Avenue, Brooklyn, New York 718-821-8861*
Sell To *Department stores, specialty stores, wholesalers and importers*
Web Site *www.arnewyorkhandbags.com*

AUDISH ACCESSORIES, LLC

2800 E Broadway C-351
Pearland , TX 77581
281 300 3202
bettyaudish@hotmail.com

Labels *Betty Audish Couture®*
Products *Handbags handcrafted in the finest luxury exotic leathers. Python, crocodile, lizard, stingray*
Price Points *Bridge*
Production *U.S.A.*
Showrooms *California: Robert Aruj (robert.aruj@robertaruj.com)*
Sell To *Department stores, specialty stores, boutiques*
Web Site *www.bettyaudish.com*
Contact *Designer: Betty Audish*

BAMBOO 54

11309 Iris Lane
El Monte, CA 91731
626 443 1863 Fax : 626 443 1856
jerry@bamboo54.com

Labels *Bamboo 54*
Products *Handbags, fashion jewelry, hair ornaments with a bamboo look.*
Price Points *Moderate*
Production *China, Vietnam, Indonesia*
Showrooms *Los Angeles, Dallas, Florida, Hawaii and Chicago*
Sell To *Department stores, specialty stores, boutiques, mass merchants & mail order catalogues.*
Corp. Office *Above*
Private Label *Yes*
Web Site *www.bamboo54.com*
Rev. in mil. *2-10*
Contact *President: Jerry Chan, Owners: Jerry & Rick Chan, Sales: Rick Chan*

BCBG MAX AZRIA GROUP

1450 Broadway, 17th Floor
New York, NY 10018 judy.scarpulla@bcbg.com
212 382 1880 Fax : 212 764 6912 866 518 2224

Labels *BCBG Max Azria*
Products *Contemporary leather satchel, tote and clutch handbags.*
Price Points *Better*
Production *U.S.A.*
Showrooms *New York: 1450 Broadway-212-704-4725, Los Angele: 110E 9th St, A571-323-277-5440, Atlanta: 250 Spring St.#11E112-A/B-404-223-2224, Dallas:Ross Ave.-214-744-2226*
Sell To *Department stores & specialty stores.*
Corp. Office *2761 Fruitland Avenue, Vernon, Ca. 90058 - 323-589-2224*
Private Label *Yes*
Web Site *www.bcbg.com*
Contact *President and Owner: Max Azria, President Licensing & International: Sophie Rietdyk, Sales Executive: Judy Scarpulla 212 704-4736*

BEACH HANDBAGS

7402 Mountjoy Drive, Suite B
Huntington Beach, CA 92648 info@beachhandbags.com
714 901 2000 Fax : 714 901 2011

Labels *Beach by CLC*
Products *Handbags, wallets and backpacks in fun and colorful designs.*
Sell To *Specialty stores & boutiques.*
Corp. Office *Above*
Private Label *Yes*
Web Site *www.beachhandbags.com*
Contact *Head of Sales: Amber Ozinga, Creative Director: Karl Ozinga*

BEL ESPRIT SHOWROOM/SHOWROOM INTERNATIONAL *(Rep.)

P.O. Box 30273
Philadelphia, PA 19103 belesprit@ureach.com
215 963 9394 Fax : 419 793 8064

Labels *Bel Esprit, Showroom International*
Products *Handbags.*
Price Points *Casual to designer*
Production *U.S.A. & import*
Showrooms *Bel Esprit Showroom - The International Showroom for Ethical Fashion. Showroom Internat. The International Showroom for Independent Fashion. Moda 360: A Complete Fashion Revo.*
Sell To *Department stores & specialty stores.*
Corp. Office *Additional websites: www.showroominternational.com, www.moda360intl.com*
Private Label *No*
Web Site *www.belesprit.net*
Contact *CEO: Debora Pokallus*

BIG BUDDHA

19 West 34th Street
New York, NY 10001 kirsten@ebigbuddha.com
212 857 9580 Fax : 212 643 7524

Labels *Big Buddha*
Products *Fashion-forward designed handbags with the practicality of everyday use.*

Showrooms *See website.*
Sell To *Boutiques, specialty stores, department stores.*
Corp. Office *Above*
Private Label *Yes*
Web Site *www.ebigbuddha.com*
Contact *Owner: Jeremy Bassan, Sales Manager: Kirsten Grindeland*

BOULEVARD

1340 S. Manhattan Avenue
Fullerton, CA 92831 sales@iloveblvd.com
866 477 5051 Fax : 800 776 8321

Labels *Boulevard*
Products *Handbags & small leather goods.*
Production *Korea, China*
Showrooms *Above*
Sell To *Boutiques & specialty stres.*
Corp. Office *Above*
Web Site *www.iloveblvd.com*
Contact *Sales Executive: Christina Oh*

DREAMBAGS, INC.

1225 Shilloh Boulevard, #261
Zion, IL 60099 contact@magmilebrand.com
224 636 8622

Labels *Mag Mile, Dreambags, Bon Vivant, Bolts, Duke*
Products *Leather, fabric, tapestry & vinyl handbags, evening purses, backpacks, totes, pet carriers, belts.*
Price Points *Moderate to designer*
Production *U.S.A.*
Sell To *Department stores, specialty stores, boutiques, on-line.*
Private Label *Yes*
Web Site *www.magmilebrand.com*
Rev. in mil. *2-10*
Contact *Owner: Olga Chtiguel*

DYNAMIC ASIA INTERNATIONAL, INC.

1372 Wilson Street
Los Angeles, CA 90021 support@dynamicasia.com
213 623 9169 Fax : 213 622 0486

Products *Straw handbags.*
Price Points *Moderate*
Production *China*
Showrooms *Los Angeles*
Sell To *Department & specialty stores, mass merchants, catalogues & off-price.*
Private Label *Yes*
Web Site *www.fashionbyda.com*

ERIC JAVITS, INC.

20 West 22nd Street, 16th Floor
New York, NY 10010 nyshowroom@ericjavits.com
212 213 4949 Fax : 212 213 5281 1 800 374 4287

Labels *Eric Javits*

Products *Designer bags, totes, hats & shoes.*
Price Points *Designer*
Production *U.S.A. & import*
Showrooms *Los Angeles/Ramiro Centeno 213-623-4481, Dallas/Lori Veith 214-630-0541, Atlanta/Lori Veith 404-688-3300.*
Sell To *Department stores, specialty stores, boutiques & mail order catalogues.*
Corp. Office *New York/above*
Private Label *No*
Web Site *www.ericjavits.com*
Rev. in mil. *11-50*
Contact *President: Eric M. Javits, Jr.*

FORMART CORPORATION

312 Fifth Avenue , 6th Floor
New York, NY 10001 bellini_formart@hotmail.com
212 819 1819 Fax : 212 921 1992

Labels *Bellini Collections*
Products *Fashion evening & glitz handbags. Private label & contracting work only.*
Price Points *Moderate to better.*
Production *U.S.A.*
Showrooms *New York*
Sell To *Department stores, specialty stores, boutiques & mass merchants.*
Private Label *Yes*
Web Site *www.formartcorp.com*
Rev. in mil. *0-2*
Contact *President: Sheung Mei Liu*

INGE CHRISTOPHER

141 West 36th Street, Suite 1803
New York, NY 10018 nyshowroom@ingechristopher.com
212 564 1151 Fax : 212 594 2427 800 772 0418

Labels *Inge Christopher, Whiting & Davis*
Products *Evening bags and metal mesh bags.*
Price Points *Moderate to better.*
Production *Import*
Showrooms *West Coast: Raina Paquillo 415-450-8310.*
Sell To *Department stores, specialty stores, boutiques & mail order catalogues.*
Corp. Office *1281 Andersen Drive, #C, San Rafael, CA 94901. Tel:415-457-2595, Fax:415-457-2702.*
Private Label *Yes*
Web Site *www.ingechristopher.com, www.whitinganddavisbags.com*
Rev. in mil. *2-10*
Contact *President: Inge Hendromartono, Director: Christopher Senn*

J.P. OURSE CIE/JOHN COLE COLLECTION

2145 Pulaski Highway
Havre de Grace, MD 21078 kelly@jpourse.com
410 273 0922 Fax : 410 272 8949 800 232 7748

Labels *J.P. Ourse, John Cole Collections*
Products *Fine leather handbags, totes, backpacks & private label manufacturer.*
Price Points *Moderate to better*
Production *Bolivia*

Showrooms *Maryland*
Sell To *Department stores, specialty stores, boutiques & mail order catalogues.*
Private Label *Yes*
Web Site *www.jpourse.com*
Contact *General Manager: Eduardo Velarde, Sales: Kelly Bays.*

JOY ACCESSORIES

1 Hartford Sq, #E
New Britain, CT 06052 joy@joyaccessories.com
860 612 0439 Fax : 860 612 0510 880-365-4569

Labels *Joy Susan*
Products *Import up-to-date and trendy handbags*
Price Points *Moderate*
Production *U.S.A., India, Phillipines, China, Vietnam*
Showrooms *Connecticut and Atlanta*
Sell To *Department stores, specialty stores, boutiques, catalogues*
Private Label *Yes*
Web Site *www.joyaccessories.com*
RN Number *100542*
Rev. in mil. *0-2*
Contact *Sales: Gary Tierney*

LATICO LEATHERS

321 Palmer Road, Suite A
Denville, NJ 07834 info@laticoleathers.com
973 442 9622 Fax : 973 442 3073 800 969 8426

Labels *Latico*
Products *Handcrafted leather weekenders, handbags, wallets, totes, backpacks, briefcases & duffels.*
Price Points *Moderate*
Production *Import*
Showrooms *New York/320 Fifth Ave., Suite 804, NY, NY. By appointment only.*
Sell To *Department stores, specialty stores, luggage stores, boutiques & mail order catalogues.*
Private Label *Yes*
Web Site *www.laticoleathers.com*
Contact *President & Owner: Paul Schreiber, Sales: Lainie Schreiber*

LEATHEROCK INT. INC.

5285 Lovelock Street
San Diego, CA 92110 leatherock@leatherock.com
619 299 7625 Fax : 619 299 7730 800 466 6667

Labels *Leatherock*
Products *Designer leather handbags.*
Price Points *Moderate to better.*
Production *U.S.A.*
Showrooms *NY/Susan Bonomo, 260 W 39th St., #701, NY, NY, tel: 212 302 4702-bonomo214@aol.com, LA/Engel Showroom, 127 E 9th St., #509, L.A., CA 90015, 213 623 4481-loft809@aol.com.*
Sell To *Department stores, specialty stores, boutiques, mass merchants & mail order catalogues.*
Private Label *Yes*
Web Site *www.leatherockwholesale.com*
Rev. in mil. *2-10*
Contact *President & Owner: Laurence Bloch*

LORREN BELL, INC.

2050 N. Stemmons Freeway, Unit 158
Dallas , TX 75207
214 651 0110 Fax : 214 651 0550
lorren@lorrenbell.com

Labels *Deluxe by Lorren Bell*
Products *Handbags designed in fabric with flowers & beaded handles.*
Price Points *Better*
Production *U.S.A., France & Italy.*
Sell To *Department stores, specialty stores. boutiques & catalogues.*
Private Label *Yes*
Web Site *www.lorrenbell.com*
Rev. in mil. *0-2*
Contact *President & Designer: Lorren Bell*

MADEMOISELLE, INC.

4200 W. Schubert Avenue
Chicago, IL 60639
773 394 4555 Fax : 773 394 9495 800 992 5580
scot210@aol.com

Labels *Mademoiselle*
Products *Missy & today's executive women's handbags, gloves & more.*
Price Points *Moderate to better*
Production *U.S.A. & overseas.*
Showrooms *Atlanta, Dallas, Denver plus 15 sales reps nationwide.*
Sell To *Department stores, specialty stores, boutiques, gift shops & online.*
Private Label *Yes*
Web Site *www.mademoiselleinc.com*
Contact *President: Scott Goldstein*

NOTANONYMOUS *(Rep.)

54 West 39th Street, 10th Floor
New York, NY 10018
212 997 3512 Fax : 212 768 3748
michele@notanonymous.com

Labels *Christian Livingston, Streets Ahead*
Products *Leather, non-leather, beaded & novelty handbags.*
Price Points *Better, bridge & designer.*
Production *U.S.A,, Canada, Europe, Asia & South America*
Showrooms *New York*
Sell To *Deptartment stores, specialty stores, boutiques & mail order catalogues.*
Private Label *Yes*
Web Site *www.notanonymous.com*
Contact *President: Maxine Coppersmith, Sales: Michele Beck*

SHOWROOM SEVEN/ERICKSON BEAMON *(Rep.)

263 Eleventh Avenue
New York, NY 10001
212 643 4810 Fax : 646 763 8940
jean-marc@showroomseven.com

Labels *Blumera, Kooba, Maliparmi, Save My Bag, Punchcase by Leslie Hsu*
Products *Women's & men's contemporary handbags, belts, briefcases, laptop carryall.*
Price Points *Contemporary, designer & couture*
Production *International*
Showrooms *New York, Los Angeles, Paris*

Sell To *Department stores, specialty stores & boutiques. International and domestic.*
Private Label *Yes*
Web Site *www.showroomseven.com*
Rev. in mil. *11-50*

STREETS AHEAD

5510 Soto Street
Vernon, CA 90058
323 277 0860 Fax : 323 277 5565
info@streetsaheadinc.com

Labels *Streets Ahead.*
Products *Leather, suede & embellished denim handbags.*
Price Points *Budget, moderate & better.*
Production *U.S.A.*
Showrooms *Los Angeles: 213-689-9620, New York: 212-997-3512*
Sell To *Department & specialty stores, boutiques, mass merchants, catalogs & off-price.*
Private Label *Yes*
Web Site *www.streetsaheadinc.com*
Contact *Sales: Kari Woodruff*

SUSAN DUNN INC.

PO Box 1086
Rancho Santa Fe, CA 92067
858 832 1086 Fax : 858 832 1087
susan@susandunn.com

Labels *Spa Tote*
Products *Totes in nubuck leather, suede, pony fur & satin.*
Price Points *Designer*
Production *U.S.A.*
Sell To *Specialty stores, boutiques, mail order catalogues, hotels, resorts & spas.*
Private Label *Yes*
Web Site *www.susandunn.com*
RN Number *RN90990*
Rev. in mil. *2-10*
Contact *CEO & President: Susan Dunn*

TAKEATOTE LLC

D1950 City Line Road
Auburndale, WI 54412
715 383 4661
info@takeatote.com

Labels *Yvonne Totes*
Products *Custom made line of handbags and totes in tapestry and faux leather.*
Price Points *Better*
Production *U.S.A.*
Sell To *Department stores, specialty stores, boutiques*
Private Label *Yes*
Web Site *www.takeatote.com*
Contact *Owner: Stacey Carolfi*

TUSK LTD.

242 West 26th Street, 1st Floor
New York, NY 10001
212 242 8485 Fax : 212 242 3935 888 GET TUSK
info@tusk.com

Labels *Tusk Ltd.*
Products *Women's upscale leather handbags & wallets.*
Price Points *Better*
Production *U.S.A. & import.*
Sell To *Department stores, specialty stores, boutiques & mail order catalogues.*
Private Label *Yes*
Web Site *www.tusk.com*
Contact *President: Hiten Manseta, Owner: Hiten Manseta*

WAI-CHING

115 Prefontaine Place South, Suite 605
Seattle, WA 98104
206 229 1111
sales@wai-ching.com

Labels *Wai-Ching*
Products *Handbags & belts.*
Price Points *Bridge*
Production *U.S.A.*
Showrooms *Above*
Sell To *Specialty stores & boutiques.*
Corp. Office *Above*
Web Site *www.wai-ching.com*
Contact *Designer: Christine W Ching Leung*

AMERICAN HAT FACTORY, THE

2251 Fraley Street, Building A
Philadelphia, PA 19137 amhat2251@gmail.com
267 345 1141 Fax : 267 345 1144

Labels *Bellini, Seasons, Tim Crawford, Rosebud, Sandra*
Products *Fancy & dressy Sunday-style hats. Fascinators.*
Price Points *Better, bridge & designer*
Production *U.S.A.*
Sell To *Department stores, specialty stores, boutiques & mail order catalogues.*
Private Label *Yes*
Web Site *www.amerahat.com*

ANVIL KNITWEAR, INC.

146 West Country Club Road
Hamer, SC 29547 info@gildan.com
843 774 8211 Fax : 843 841 4963

Labels *Anvil®*
Products *Solid brussed twill caps.*
Price Points *Moderate*
Sell To *Wholesalers, department stores, specialty stores & mass merchants.*
Corp. Office *Division of Gildan Activewear SRL (www.gildan.com) - 877 445 3265*
Private Label *Yes*
Web Site *www.anvilknitwear.com*
RN Number *RN38619*
Contact *Arlin Turner Manager*

BAILEY HATS

411 Fifth Avenue, 2nd Floor
New York, NY 10016 cdistasio@bollmanhats.com
212 981 9900 Fax : 212 981 9901 1-800-859-4653

Labels *Bailey of Hollywood, Bailey Western*
Products *Leather, cloth, felt, fashion & western hats.*
Price Points *Moderate to better*
Sell To *Department stores, specialty stores & boutiques.*
Corp. Office *110 East Main Street, Adamstown, Pa. 19501*
Private Label *Yes*
Web Site *www.baileyhats.com*
Contact *Sales Rep: Jay Rubin 203-919-2276, Marketing Manager: Christine Distasio*

BETMAR HATS INC.

411 Fifth Avenue
New York, NY 10016 betmarhats@aol.com
212 684 8080 Fax : 212 545 0663 800 678 7676

Labels *Betmar, Plaza Suite*
Products *Hats & millinery. Also, gloves, capes, scarves and handbags.*
Price Points *Moderate to better.*
Production *U.S.A. & import.*
Showrooms *Chicago, Dallas, Atlanta, Boston, New York, New England, West Coast*
Sell To *Department stores, specialty stores, boutiques & mail order catalogues.*
Private Label *Yes*
Web Site *www.betmarhats.com*

Rev. in mil. 11-50
Contact *President: Bernard Grossman*

BRAVADO MERCHANDISING

1755 Broadway, 2nd Floor
New York, NY 10019 tom.bennett@bravado.com
212 445 3400 Fax : 212 445 3499

Labels *Bravado*
Products *Concert & movie caps. Specialize in rock-n-roll, film & novelty designs.*
Price Points *Moderate*
Production *U.S.A.*
Showrooms *New York, London, Los Angeles*
Sell To *Department stores, specialty stores, mass merchants & mail order catalogues, tour events.*
Private Label *Yes*
Web Site *www.bravadousa.com*
RN Number *RN91889*
Contact *Sales: Tom Bennett*

BUCK WEAR INC.

2900 Cowan Avenue
Baltimore, MD 21223 cjohnson@buckwear.com
410 646 6400 Fax : 410 646 7700

Products *Printed adult & youth hat & caps. Quality products for the Outdoorsman.*
Sell To *Specialty stores.*
Corp. Office *Above*
Web Site *www.buckwear.com*
Contact *President: David Trapp*

CANADIAN SWEATER CO., LTD.

#39 8528-123rd Street
Surrey, BC, Canada V3W 3V6 info@canadiansweater.com
604 594 8050 Fax : 604 594 8264

Labels *Cowichan, Islander*
Products *Winter hats, scarves & gloves for men, women & children.*
Price Points *Bridge*
Production *Canada*
Sell To *High end department stores, boutiques.*
Corp. Office *Above*
Private Label *Yes*
Web Site *www.canadiansweater.com*
Contact *President: Kaljit Tmana*

CASSIN

922 Riverview Drive
Totowa, NJ 07512 info@cassincollections.com
973 826 1190

Labels *Cassin, sherry cassin new york*
Products *A full range of hats, vests & scarves with a major focus on fur, faux fur & other natural mate*
Price Points *Moderate to designer*
Production *U.S.A. & import.*
Sell To *Department stores, fine specialty stores*

Web Site *www.cassincollections.com*
Contact *Designer: Sherry Cassin*

CONCEPT ONE ACCESSORIES

119 West 40th Street
New York, NY 10018 sgleit@concept1.com
212 868 2590 Fax : 212 868 2595

Labels *IZOD, Levis®, Blue Marlin, Disney, Zoo York, Nickelodeon, VanHeusen, Wrangler*
Products *All types of fashion accessories*
Price Points *Better*
Sell To *Department stores, better specialty stores & boutiques.*
Private Label *Resource for licensed fashion, sports, and entertainment accessories.*
Web Site *www.concept1.com*

COUNTRY GENTLEMAN HEADWEAR, INC.

411 5th Avenue, 2nd Floor
New York, NY 10016 smccabe@bollmanhats.com
212 981 9866 Fax : 888 428 7329 800 792 0896

Labels *Country Gentleman*
Products *Men's felt & straw hats, caps & cut-n-sew headwear.*
Price Points *Moderate to better.*
Production *U.S.A.*
Showrooms *New York*
Sell To *Department stores & specialty stores.*
Private Label *Yes*
Web Site *www.countrygentleman.com*
Contact *Sean McCabe*

DYNAMIC ASIA INTERNATIONAL, INC.

1372 Wilson Street
Los Angeles, CA 90021 support@dynamicasia.com
213 623 9169 Fax : 213 622 0486

Products *Straw hats, winter hats and scarves.*
Price Points *Moderate*
Production *China*
Showrooms *Los Angeles*
Sell To *Department & specialty stores, mass merchants, catalogues & off-price.*
Private Label *Yes*
Web Site *www.fashionbyda.com*

ERIC JAVITS, INC.

20 West 22nd Street, 16th Floor
New York, NY 10010 nyshowroom@ericjavits.com
212 213 4949 Fax : 212 213 5281 1 800 374 HATS

Labels *Eric Javits*
Products *Designer hats, bags & shoes.*
Price Points *Designer*
Production *U.S.A. & import*
Showrooms *Los Angeles/Ramiro Centeno 213-623-4481, Dallas/Lori Veith 214-630-0541, Atlanta/Lori Veith 404-688-3300.*
Sell To *Department stores, specialty stores, boutiques & mail order catalogues.*

Corp. Office *New York/above*
Private Label *No*
Web Site *www.ericjavits.com*
Rev. in mil. *11-50*
Contact *President: Eric M. Javits, Jr.*

F & M HAT CO., INC.

103 Walnut Street
Denver, PA 17517 info@fmhat.com
717 336 5505 Fax : 717 336 0501 800 953 HATS

Labels *F & M Hat, Harley Davidson, Jack Daniels, Silverado, Giovannio, Black Creek*
Products *Fashion & western hats in wool & felt.*
Price Points *Moderate to better.*
Production *U.S.A.*
Sell To *Department stores, specialty stores & mail order catalogues.*
Private Label *Yes*
Web Site *www.fmhat.com*
RN Number *WPL04384*
Rev. in mil. *11-50*
Contact *President/Sales: Ashley Fichthorn*

FAIR HEMP INC.

1717 Troutman Street, #302
Ridgewood, NY 11385 info@fairhemp.com
646 485 0939 Fax : 212 656 1714

Labels *Fair Hemp*
Products *Hemp, recycled plastic and organic cotton caps & bags.*
Price Points *Better*
Production *Import*
Sell To *Sell blanks to printers and produce private label and custom productions.*
Private Label *Yes*
Web Site *www.fairhemp.com*
RN Number *122157*

GOLF APPAREL BRANDS

13621 South Main Street
Los Angeles, CA 90061 sales@lamode.com
310 715 1772 Fax : 310 715 1776 800 678 5246

Labels *La Mode, Clark & Gregory, Sahara*
Products *Men's and women's golf caps, golf visors, golf bucket hats and clip-on visors..*
Price Points *Moderate to better*
Production *Domestic and import from Korea, China, Hong Kong, Malaysia*
Sell To *Specialty stores, off-price and golf shops.*
Private Label *Yes*
Web Site *www.lamode.com*
Contact *President/Owner: Eddie Kahn*

HATCO, INC./ RESISTOL HATS

601 Marion Drive
Garland, TX 75042 rcieslak@hat-co.com
972 494 0511 Fax : 972 494 2369 800 288 6579

Labels *Stetson, Dobb's, Resistol, Charlie One Horse Hats*
Products *Men's cowboy hats, straw hats, felt hats & caps.*
Price Points *Moderate to better.*
Production *U.S.A.*
Showrooms *Denver Apparel Mart*
Sell To *Departments stores, specialty stores, mass merchants, off-price & licensees.*
Private Label *Yes*
Web Site *www.resistolhat.com*
Contact *National Sales Manager Stetson and Dobb's: Gerry Miller (gmiller@hat-co.com)*

HEADWEAR CREATIONS, INC.

200 Wright Street
Newark, NJ 07114 headwrcreations@aol.com
973 622 1144 Fax : 973 622 4309

Labels *Headwear Creations*
Products *High-quality, innovative styles, fashionable hats and caps.*
Price Points *Moderate*
Production *U.S.A.*
Sell To *Department stores, specialty stores, boutiques*
Private Label *Yes*
Web Site *www.headwearcreations.com*
Contact *President: Ruben Spitz*

HENSCHEL HAT CO.

1706 Olive Street
St. Louis, MO 63103 sales@henschelhats.com
314 421 0009 Fax : 314 421 1317 800 872 4287

Labels *Henschel Hat, Breezer, Geoffrey Beene*
Products *Men's high fashion leather, breathable & floatable hats & caps.*
Price Points *Moderate*
Production *U.S.A.*
Showrooms *St. Louis*
Sell To *Department & specialty stores, boutiques, mass merchants & mail order catalogues.*
Private Label *Yes*
Web Site *www.henschelhats.com*
Contact *President: Tarek Deiab, Owner: Ed Henschel*

HTT HEADWEAR LTD.

41185 Raintree Court
Murrieta, CA 92562 sales@httapparel.com
951 304 0400 Fax : 951 304 0410 800 846 8468

Labels *Head To Toe*
Products *Organic, basic & fashion caps & headwear of all types for men, women & children.*
Price Points *Better*
Production *U.S.A., China & Pakistan*
Showrooms *Murrieta, CA*
Sell To *Manufacturers*

Private Label *Yes*
Web Site *www.httapparel.com*
Contact *President: Howard Seegar, Owner: Howard Seegar, Customer Service: Luke Fafara*

HYP HATS LTD.

20 West 37th Street
New York, NY 10018 davidf@hyphats.com
212 684 7717 Fax : 212 684 7589 800 331 1181

Labels *Hyp, Disney, Happy Bunny, Baby Phat, Pink Cookie, Mudd, InEssence*
Products *Branded & custom caps, headwear, cold weather accessories, hair accessories & hosiery.*
Price Points *All*
Production *Taiwan, China*
Showrooms *New York*
Sell To *Department stores, specialty stores, boutiques, mass merchants & mail order catalogues.*
Private Label *Yes*
Web Site *www.hyphats.com*
Contact *President: Howard Levy, Sales: David Fisher, Merchandising: David Fisher Production: Mike Pascal, Marketing: Howard Levy*

IMPERIAL HEADWEAR

One Paramount Drive
Bourbon, MO 65441 eortwein@paifashion.com
800 950 1916 Fax : 800 755 5121

Labels *Imperial*
Products *Golf, tennis, high tech, promotional, green headwear for men, women and children.*
Price Points *Better*
Sell To *Specialty stores*
Private Label *Yes*
Web Site *www.imperialsports.com*
Contact *Wholesale Account: Evelyn Ortwein*

JILL HENNING FINERIES

6058 West Sylvania Avenue
Toledo, OH 43623 jhendesign@aol.com
419 841 9106 Fax : 419 841 9106

Labels *Jill Henning*
Products *Women's couture millinery. Kentucky Derby, Royal Ascot & special occasion hats.*
Price Points *Designer to couture*
Production *U.S.A., England*
Showrooms *Ohio/above*
Sell To *Department stores, boutiques, website retailers.*
Corp. Office *Above*
Private Label *Yes*
Web Site *www.jillhenninghats.com*
Contact *Owner: Jill Henning*

MADEMOISELLE, INC.

4200 W. Schubert Avenue
Chicago, IL 60639 scot210@aol.com
773 394 4555 Fax : 773 394 9495 800 992 5580

Labels *Mademoiselle*

Products *Missy & today's executive women's scarves, hats, dickies, dressing hoods & more.*
Price Points *Moderate to better*
Production *U.S.A. & overseas.*
Showrooms *Atlanta, Dallas, Denver plus 15 sales reps nationwide.*
Sell To *Department stores, specialty stores, boutiques, gift shops & online.*
Private Label *Yes*
Web Site *www.mademoiselleinc.com*
Contact *President: Scott Goldstein*

NICOLE & CO.

9200 Parc Avenue, Suite 407
Montreal, Canada, H2N1Z4 hats@nicole-co.com
514 383 5599 Fax : 514 383 5674

Labels *Nicole & Co.*
Products *Fashion hats.*
Price Points *Designer to couture*
Production *Canada*
Showrooms *Montreal/9200 Parc Avenue, #407, Montreal*
Sell To *Department stores, specialty stores & boutiques.*
Private Label *Yes*
Web Site *www.nicole-co.com*
Contact *President: Nicole Amram, Production: Yoram Amram, Design: Yoram Amram*

PACIFIC SPORTSWEAR & EMBLEM COMPANY

6160 Fairmount Avenue, Suite F
San Diego, CA 92120 quotes@pacificemblem.com
619 281 6688 Fax : 619 281 6687

Labels *UFC, Honda, World Poker Tour, Lasercut, Magicap, Utensil Buddy*
Products *Custom & private label manufacturer of headwear, caps, beanies & all kinds of patches & er*
Price Points *Ppular*
Production *U.S.A. & China*
Sell To *Specialty stores*
Private Label *Yes*
Web Site *www.pacificemblem.com*
Rev. in mil. *0-2*
Contact *Rich "Dr. Patch" Soergel (rich@pacificemblem.com)*

SCREAMER HATS

2401 Utah Ave. South, # 270
Seattle, WA 98178 kimp@screamer.com
206 667 9000 Fax : 206 624 7567 800 437 8430

Labels *Screamer*
Products *Fun, traditional & technical hats for adults and children.*
Production *U.S.A.*
Sell To *Department stores, specialty stores*
Web Site *www.screamer.com*

SHEEPSKIN BY SUSAN BRADFORD

8800 Green Valley Road
Sebastopol, CA 95472
802 371 8236
susanbradforddesigns@charter.net

Labels *Sheepskin by Susan Bradford*
Products *Original, hand-sewn shearling skin hats and caps.*
Price Points *Designer*
Production *U.S.A.*
Sell To *Specialty stores and boutiques.*
Private Label *No*
Web Site *www.sheepskin-by-susan.com*
Contact *Owner: Susan Bradford*

SQUASHT BOUTIQUE

2556 West Chicago Avenue
Chicago, IL 60622
773 292 4123
lesley@squashtboutique.com

Labels *Squasht Boutique*
Products *Retro-styled reversible handcrafted hats, apparel and accessories for women.*
Price Points *Better*
Production *U.S.A.*
Sell To *Boutiques*
Web Site *www.squashtboutique.com*
Contact *Designer & Owner: Lesley Timpe*

TRACYWATTS INC.

119 8th Street, Studio 201
Brooklyn, NY 11215
718 499 7090 Fax : 718 499 7092
info@tracywatts.com

Labels *Tracywatts*
Products *Hats, caps & millinery for women & men.*
Price Points *Designer*
Production *USA*
Showrooms *Above*
Sell To *Department stores, specialty stores, boutiques & mail order catalogues.*
Private Label *Yes*
Web Site *www.tracywatts.com*
Rev. in mil. *0-2*
Contact *President/Owner: Tracy Watts*

WHITTALL & SHON

1201 Broadway, Suite 902
New York, NY 10001
212 594 2626 Fax : 212 268 2862
beauws@aol.com

Labels *Whittall & Shon*
Products *Womens hats & milinery for church, western, fascinators and special events.*
Price Points *Bridge to better*
Production *U.S.A. & Hong Kong.*
Sell To *Department stores, specialty stores, boutiques & mail order catalogues.*
Private Label *Yes*
Web Site *www.whittallandshon.com*

Contact *President: Eliot Whittall, Vice-President: Richard Shon, Design: Richard Shon*

WOODEN SHIPS

231 West 39th Street
New York, NY 10018
888 717 6700 Fax : 212 221 2329
sales@wooden-ships.com

Labels *Wooden Ships*
Products *Updated knit & crochet hats & caps, mittens, gloves, scarfs, wraps & ponchos*
Price Points *Better*
Production *Import*
Sell To *Department stores, specialty stores, boutiques & mail order catalogues.*
Private Label *No*
Web Site *www.wooden-ships.com*
Contact *Sales: Randi Weinstein*

Notes

2 X IST

1411 Broadway, 8th Floor
New York, NY 10018 ralph@2xist.com
212 741 7731 Fax : 212 741 7932

Labels *Socks by 2 X ist*
Products *Mens sport socks in no show, quarter top and crew lengths.*
Price Points *Better to designer*
Production *Import*
Showrooms *New York*
Customer Service: 285 Ridge Road, Suite#3, Dayton, NJ 08810, 1-877-597-5827
Sell To *Department stores, specialty stores & mail order catalogues.*
Private Label *Yes*
Web Site *www.2xist.com*
RN Number *RN97404*
Contact *Vice President Sales: Ralph Beyda*

ABC HOSIERY

640 Park Avenue, PO BOX 218
Youngsville, NC 27596 abc_hosiery@yahoo.com
919 556 5630 Fax : 919 556 0580

Labels *Gildan, Red Rose Hosiery*
Products *All types of hosiery, pantyhose and sport socks for men, women and children.*
Price Points *Moderate*
Sell To *Department stores, outlets*
Web Site *www.myabchosiery.com*
Contact *Sales: Tony or Crystal*

ACORN PRODUCTS

9655 International Boulevard
Cincinnati, OH 45246 christian.hilton@totes.com
800 872 2676 Fax : 800 280 4127 1 800 872 2676

Labels *Acorn*
Products *Polartec & sheepskin slippers, comfort footwear, socks & cold weather accessories.*
Price Points *Moderate to better.*
Production *Import*
Showrooms *Call for showrooms.*
Sell To *Specialty stores & mail order catalogues.*
Private Label *Yes*
Web Site *www.acorn.com*

BABYLEGS® DIV OF UNITED LEGWEAR CO.

48 West 38th Street, 3rd Floor
New York, NY 10018 info@babylegs.com
212 391 4143 800 818 1427

Labels *BabyLegs*
Products *Legwarmers, socks and tights for children.*
Price Points *Moderate*
Sell To *Department stores, specialty stores, boutiques.*
Web Site *www.babylegs.com*

BETSEY JOHNSON

52-16 Barnett Avenue
Long Island City, NY 11104 info@betseyjohnson.com
866-222-4243

Labels *Betsey Johnson*
Products *Women's contemporary lingerie, hosiery, shoe & jewelry collection.*
Price Points *Better*
Sell To *Department stores & specialty stores.*
Web Site *www.betseyjohnson.com*
RN Number *RN77751*

BODY WRAPPERS

65 West 36th Street, 5th Floor
New York, NY 10018 info@bodywrappers.com
212 279 3492 Fax : 212 564 3426 800 323 0786

Labels *totalSTRETCH™*
Products *Activewear & dance tights, legwarmers & accessories.*
Price Points *Moderate*
Production *U.S.A.*
Showrooms *New York, Denver, Toronto plus reps throughout the U.S, Canada, Europe & Japan.*
Sell To *Dance specialty stores, boutiques, Nordstrom's, mail order catalogues, website.*
Corp. Office *107 Trumbull Street, Elizabeth, NJ 07206*
Private Label *Yes*
Web Site *www.bodywrappers.com*
RN Number *RN60206*
Rev. in mil. *11-50*
Contact *Sales: Michael Lee, tel: 908 354 7218 ext. 231*

BOSSONG HOSIERY

840 West Salisbury Street
Ashebo, NC 27204 mowens4bossong@aol.com
845 352 4630 Fax : 336 626 6607

Labels *Ergee, Coco, Town & Country*
Products *Men's, women's & girl's hosiery. Fashion and medical grade hosiery.*
Price Points *Budget to better & off-price.*
Production *U.S.A. - FDA approved factory*
Showrooms *New York.*
Sell To *Department stores, specialty stores, mass merchants & mail order catalogues.*
Private Label *Yes*
Rev. in mil. *11-50*
Contact *Vice President: Matthew Owens (845-352-4630),*
Director of Sales: Diane Serralta 516-931-0927, dserralta@aol.com

CAPELLI NEW YORK

1 East 33rd Street, 9th Floor
New York, NY 10016 info@capellinewyork.com
212 684 3344 Fax : 212 686 4895

Labels *Capelli New York*
Products *Fashion novelty socks, slippersocks, legwear & legwarmers for men, women & children.*
Production *Import*
Showrooms *New York, Canada, Europe and Asia*

Sell To *Department stores, specialty stores, national chain stores*
Private Label *Yes*
Web Site *www.capellinewyork.com*

CRESCENT SOCK COMPANY

527 East Willson Street, PO Box 669
Niota, TN 37826 heather@crescent-inc.com
423 568 2101 Fax : 423 568 2104

Labels *Head®, Dri-Sox®, World's Softest Sock®, FITS, Jack's Socks®, Pajama Socks®*
Products *Men's & women's casual, athletic & sports specific hosiery.*
Price Points *Moderate to better.*
Production *U.S.A.*
Sell To *Department & specialty stores, warehouse clubs, mail order catalogues & off-price retailers.*
Private Label *Yes, plus Licensed Products*
Web Site *www.crescent-inc.com*
Rev. in mil. *11-50*
Contact *CEO: Cathy Allen, Director of Sales: Heather Lingerfelt*

FBF ORIGINALS

1201 South Ohio Street
Martinsville, IN 46151 fbf@fbforiginals.com
765 349 7474 Fax : 765 349 7470

Labels *FBF Originals, NFL, NBA, NHL, College/Universities, MLB, WNBA, MLS, NASCAR*
Products *Socks, footwear, flip flops, wrist bands, headbands & hair accessories.*
Price Points *Budget to better*
Sell To *Department store & specialty stores.*
Private Label *Yes*
Web Site *www.fbforiginals.com*
Contact *President: Kelly Baugh*

FRENCH CONNECTION

512 Seventh Avenue, 25th Floor
New York, NY 10018 frenchconnection@frenchconnection-usa.com
212 221 3157 Fax : 212 302 6839 866-932-3285

Labels *French Connection*
Products *Contemporary socks & tights.*
Price Points *Better*
Production *Global*
Showrooms *Atlanta, Chicago, Los Angeles & New York.*
Sell To *Department stores, specialty stores, boutiques, catalogues & off-price retailers.*
Corp. Office *184-10 Jamaica Avenue, Hollis, New York 11423*
Private Label *Yes*
Web Site *usa.frenchconnection.com*
RN Number *RN53372*
Rev. in mil. *101-500*
Contact *President: Andrea Hyde*

GENE EWING BIS

PCH Fashion District, PO Box 326
Malibu, CA 90265 geneewing@geneewingbis.com
323 839 9647 Fax : 323 839 9647

Labels *Gene Ewing Leglifters®™*
Products *Leg lifters for missy and plus sizes.*
Price Points *Better*
Showrooms *Los Angeles*
Sell To *Specialty stores.*
Corp. Office *Above*
Web Site *www.geneewingbis.com*
Contact *President: Gene Ewing*

GERTEX HOSIERY INC.

9 Densley Avenue
Toronto, Ontario, Canada M6M 2P5 sales@gertex.com
416 241 2345 Fax : 416 241 6904 800-561-2353

Products *Men's, women's, kids fashion, dress & novelty socks, hosiery & panty hose, slippers & headwea*
Price Points *Budget to better*
Production *U.S.A., China, Korea, Turkey, Mexico*
Sell To *Department stores, specialty stores, boutiques, mass merchants, off-price.*
Corp. Office *Above*
Private Label *Yes*
Web Site *www.gertex.ca*
Rev. in mil. *11-50*
Contact *Sales: Aaron Mandelbaum*

KEEPERS INTERNATIONAL

9420 Eton Avenue
Chatsworth, CA 91311 jadamson@keepers.com
800 79 SOCKS Fax : 818 700 1152

Labels *Stacy Adams, Florsheim*
Products *Men's & boy's socks & hosiery*
Price Points *Moderate to better*
Production *U.S.A. & import*
Showrooms *Above*
Sell To *Department stores, specialty stores, mass merchants, mail order catalogues & off-price.*
Corp. Office *Same as Above*
Private Label *Yes*
Web Site *www.keepers.com*
Contact *Customer Service: J Adamson*

LEG RESOURCE INC

350 Fifth Avenue, Suite 6048
New York, NY 10118 wayne@legresource.com
212 736 4574 Fax : 212 736 0245 877 347 6257

Labels *Betsy Johnson, Nicole Miller, Anne Klein, AK by Anne Klein*
Products *Quality branded hosiery, pantyhose, socks, fashion legwear for women & girls.*
Price Points *Better*
Production *U.S.A.*
Sell To *Department stores, specialty stores, boutiques & catalogues.*

Private Label *Yes*
Web Site *www.legresource.com*
Contact *Account Manager: Nancy Felgueiras nancy@legresource.com*

LIN MANUFACTURING & DESIGN

2929 North Main Street, PO Box 6127
North Logan, UT 84341 roger@linmfg.com
435 787 8888 Fax : 435 755 9637 888 430 9888

Labels *Lin Performance, Lin Wellness, Lin Custom, Recycle Lin*
Products *Novelty socks, hosiery, legwear for men, women, kids & infants. Made with renewable resour*
Production *U.S.A., Taiwan & China*
Sell To *Department & specialty stores, boutiques, mass merchants, catalogues & off-price.*
Private Label *Yes*
Web Site *www.linmfg.com*
RN Number *RN84364*
Contact *President: Hillary Lin Ong, Sales: Roger Round, Customer Service: Cole Richards (cs1@linmfg.com)*

OZONE DESIGN INC.

307 Seventh Avenue, Room 1603
New York, NY 10001 contact@ozonesocks.com
212 563 2990 Fax : 212 563 3775

Labels *Ozone*
Products *Men's & women's fashion socks.*
Price Points *Better*
Production *Japan, France & Columbia*
Showrooms *Illinois, Washington, California, Texas, New England & New York.*
Sell To *Department stores, specialty, boutiques, museum shops, shoe stores & mail order catalogues.*
Private Label *Yes*
Web Site *www.ozonesocks.com*
Contact *President/Owner: Laurie Mallet*

SOXLAND INTERNATIONAL, INC.

485 Bloy Street
Hillside, NJ 07205 sreese@soxland.com
908 624 9370 Fax : 908 624 0218 877-289-7699

Labels *Davco, Soxland*
Products *Women's, men's & children's design driven socks & hosiery.*
Price Points *Moderate & better*
Production *U.S.A. & import*
Showrooms *7 West 36th Street, New York, N. Y. 10018 tel: 212-679-4588, fax: 212-679-0263*
Sell To *Department stores, specialty stores, chain stores & mass merchants.*
Private Label *Yes*
Web Site *www.soxland.com*
RN Number *RN74547*
Rev. in mil. *2-10*
Contact *Sales: Susan Reese*

SUGAR AND BRUNO

7260 Georgetown Road
Indianapolis, IN 46268 challen@sugarandbruno.com
317 293 5888 Fax : 317 293 5886 800 875 8559

Labels *Sugar and Bruno*
Products *Fun socks, arm/leg warmers*
Price Points *Moderate*
Production *U.S.A. & China*
Sell To *Specialty stores, boutiques*
Web Site *www.sugarandbruno.com*
RN Number *127789*
Rev. in mil. *2-10*
Contact *President: Challen Powers*

TOTAL FOOT COMFORT

429 27th Street NW
Hickory , NC 28601 admin@totalfootcomfort.com
828 322 2600 Fax : 828 328 1700 866-787-2235

Labels *Phiten®, 10-Seconds® Shoe Laces*
Products *Manufacturer of men's & women's sport socks & shoe laces.*
Production *U.S.A.*
Web Site *www.totalfootcomfort.com*
Contact *President: Robert Bell*

AAA INNOVATIONS

10 Maple Street
Norwood, NJ 07648 diane@aaainnovations.com
201 784 3244 Fax : 201 784 3242 800 426 7446

Labels *Satchels™*
Products *Canvas & leather bags, totes & duffels.*
Price Points *Moderate*
Production *U.S.A. & import*
Sell To *Department stores, specialty stores, mass merchants & mail order catalogues.*
Private Label *Yes*
Web Site *www.aaainnovations.com*
Contact *President: Jeffrey Nanus, Sales: Diane Daly*

BURBERRY

444 Madison Avenue, 14th Floor
New York, NY 10022 us.customerservice@burberry.com
800 284 8480 Fax : 212 977 5521 877-217-4085

Labels *Burberry*
Products *Classic, traditional & casual bags, luggage & personal leather goods.*
Price Points *Better to designer*
Production *U.S.A. & import*
Sell To *Department stores & specialty stores.*
Private Label *No*
Web Site *www.burberry.com*

DREAMBAGS, INC.

1225 Shilloh Boulevard, #261
Zion, IL 60099 contact@magmilebrand.com
224 636 8622

Labels *Mag Mile, Dreambags, Bon Vivant, Bolts, Duke*
Products *Leather & fabric handbags, totes, backpacks, luggage, cosmetic cases, computer cases & small l*
Price Points *Moderate to designer*
Production *U.S.A.*
Sell To *Department stores, specialty stores, boutiques, on-line.*
Private Label *Yes*
Web Site *www.magmilebrand.com*
Rev. in mil. *2-10*
Contact *Owner: Olga Chtiguel*

GILTON COMPANY

1106 West Gardena Boulevard
Gardena, CA 90247 sales@giltonco.com
626 241 1958 Fax : 310 327 5020 800 479 1075

Products *Men's wallets, travel kits, shave kits & manicure sets.*
Price Points *Moderate*
Production *U.S.A & import.*
Showrooms *Call for catalog*
Sell To *Department stores, specialty stores, mail order catalogues & off-price retailers.*
Private Label *No*
Web Site *giltonco.com*
RN Number *RN64854*

Rev. in mil. *0-2*
Contact *President & Owner: Philip Shar*

HAROLD TEPPER STRIBBONS INC.

57-12 260th Street
Little Neck, NY 11362 htepper@stribbons.com
718 423 4598 Fax : 718 423 1494

Products *Drawstring pouches, soft totes, cosmetic bags, jewelry bags & sachets.*
Price Points *Moderate*
Production *U.S.A. & the Orient*
Showrooms *New York, California, Florida & Chicago.*
Sell To *Mass merchants.*
Private Label *Yes*
Web Site *www.stribbons.com*
Contact *President Bag & Specialty Division: Harold Tepper (Cell: 917-545-1255).*

J.P. OURSE CIE/JOHN COLE COLLECTION

2145 Pulaski Highway
Havre de Grace, MD 21078 kelly@jpourse.com
410 273 0922 Fax : 410 272 8949 800 232 7748

Labels *J.P. Ourse, John Cole Collections*
Products *Fine leather wallets, checkbooks, agendas, executive, travel, personal accessories & gifts.*
Price Points *Moderate to better.*
Production *Bolivia*
Showrooms *Maryland*
Sell To *Department stores, specialty stores, boutiques & mail order catalogues.*
Private Label *Yes*
Web Site *www.jpourse.com*
Contact *General Manager: Eduardo Velarde, Sales: Kelly Bays.*

KATE SPADE AND COMPANY

2 Park Avenue
New York, NY 10016 media_relations@katespade.com
212 739 6550

Labels *Kate Spade*
Products *Accessories for all aspects of life: handbags, belts, jewelry, socks, gloves, wallets and more.*
Price Points *Moderate to bridge*
Production *U.S.A. & import*
Showrooms *New York/above*
Sell To *Department stores, specialty stores*
Private Label *No*
Web Site *www.katespadeandcompany.com*
Contact *CEO: Craig Leavitt*

LATICO LEATHERS

321 Palmer Road, Suite A
Denville, NJ 07834 info@laticoleathers.com
973 442 9622 Fax : 973 442 3073 800 969 8426

Labels *Latico*
Products *Handcrafted leather weekenders, handbags, wallets, totes, backpacks, briefcases & duffels.*
Price Points *Moderate*

Production *Import*
Showrooms *New York/320 Fifth Ave., Suite 804, NY, NY. By appointment only.*
Sell To *Department stores, specialty stores, luggage stores, boutiques & mail order catalogues.*
Private Label *Yes*
Web Site *www.laticoleathers.com*
Contact *President & Owner: Paul Schreiber, Sales: Lainie Schreiber*

MARTIN DINGMAN COUNTRYWEAR

14966 Industrial Park Drive
Leadhill, AR 72644 info@martindingman.com
870 422 7151 Fax : 870 422 7379 800 955 BELT

Labels *Martin Dingman*
Products *Men's leathergoods, wallets, belts, gloves, accessories & footwear.*
Price Points *Better to designer.*
Production *U.S.A.*
Showrooms *Show collection in New York during Collective.*
Sell To *Specialty stores, department stores*
Private Label *No*
Web Site *www.martindingman.com*
Contact *President: Gay Dingman, Designer: Martin Dingman, Marketing: Grayson Dingman*

SCULLY

Scully Corporate Plaza
Oxnard, CA 93003 brianscully@scullyleather.com
805 483 6339 Fax : 805 483 6439

Labels *Scully*
Products *Leather bags, luggage, wallets and more.*
Showrooms *California*
Web Site *www.scullyleather.com*
Contact *Division Director: Brian Scully*

TUSK LTD.

242 West 26th Street, 1st Floor
New York, NY 10001 info@tusk.com
212 242 8485 Fax : 212 242 3935 888 GET TUSK

Labels *Tusk Ltd.*
Products *Upscale men's & women's small leather goods.*
Price Points *Better*
Production *U.S.A. & import.*
Sell To *Department stores, specialty stores, boutiques & mail order catalogues.*
Private Label *Yes*
Web Site *www.tusk.com*
Contact *President: Hiten Manseta, Owner: Hiten Manseta*

BEAU TIES LTD. OF VERMONT

69 Industrial Avenue
Middlebury, VT 05753 btl@beautiesltd.com
802 388 0108 Fax : 802 388 7808 800 488 8437

Labels *Beau Ties Ltd.*
Products *Handcrafted bow ties and necktie styles.*
Price Points *Better*
Production *U.S.A.*
Showrooms *Middlebury, VT & direct mail*
Sell To *Specialty stores & mail order catalogues.*
Web Site *www.beautiesltd.com*
Contact *President: Bill Kenerson, Owners: Deb Venman & Bill Kenerson*

BURMA BIBAS

597 Fifth Avenue, 10th Floor
New York, NY 10017 sales@burmabibas.com
212 750 2500 Fax : 212 750 2834

Labels *Pierre Cardin, Campia, Burma Bibas*
Products *Men's woven silk neckwear.*
Price Points *Moderate, better & designer.*
Production *U.S.A.*
Showrooms *New York*
Sell To *Department & specialty stores, boutiques & catalogues.*
Private Label *Yes*
Web Site *www.burmabibas.com*
RN Number *WPL13185*
Rev. in mil. *11-50*

DAVID CAREY INC.

2250 Paragon Drive , Suite A
San Jose, CA 95131 sales@davidcareyinc.com
408 453 7843 Fax : 408 453 7848 800 858 TIES

Products *Conversational & custom silk, cotton & polyester neckwear. Licensed and stock.*
Price Points *Moderate to better*
Production *U.S.A., Thailand, Korea and China.*
Showrooms *San Jose*
Sell To *Department stores, specialty stores, boutiques & mail order catalogues.*
Private Label *Yes*
Web Site *www.davidcareyinc.com*
RN Number *RN93194*
Rev. in mil. *0-2*
Contact *President: Marc Begun, Design & Production: Mike Murphy*

GILTON COMPANY

1106 West Gardena Boulevard
Gardena, CA 90247 sales@giltonco.com
626 241 1958 Fax : 310 327 5020 800 479 1075

Products *Bow ties and ties.*
Price Points *Moderate*
Production *U.S.A & import.*
Showrooms *Call for catalog*

Sell To *Department stores, specialty stores, mail order catalogues & off-price retailers.*
Private Label *No*
Web Site *giltonco.com*
RN Number *RN64854*
Rev. in mil. *0-2*
Contact *President & Owner: Philip Shar*

JUST WHITE SHIRTS

1991 Leslie Street
Toronto, Ontario, Canada M3B 2M3 alam@justwhiteshirts.com
416 447 2907 Fax : 416 447 8059

Labels *JustWhiteShirts, The Shirt Store, Redford*
Products *Printed, solid, stripe & patterned silk ties & casual accessories.*
Price Points *Better*
Production *Own manufacturing plant for own brands as well as private label.*
Showrooms *New York Store: 51 East 44th Street, NYC 10017 212-557-8040 or 1-800-289-2744.*
Sell To *Department stores, specialty stores, on-line, catalogues*
Private Label *Yes*
Web Site *www.justwhiteshirts.com*
Contact *President: Alam Najiullah (Cell: 416-837-7448)*

LARR BRIO ACCESSORIES

141 Lanza Avenue, Building 10
Garfield, NJ 07026 larrbrio@puresilkfabrics.com
800 701 6005 Fax : 973 546 8813

Products *Men's formal wear accessories for weddings, proms including vests, ties, cummerbunds.*
Price Points *Moderate to High*
Sell To *Formal Wear/Bridal Stores, Men's Stores*
Web Site *www.larrbrio.com*
Contact *Owner: Mark Lederman, Sales Manager: Thomas DeYoung*

MMG DIV OF GREAT CHINA EMPIRE

2122 Kratky Road, Suite 150
St. Louis, MO 63114 kronert@mmg-ltd.com
314 421 2182

Labels *Haggar, Steve Harvey, Tango, Rooster, Zanetti, Blake and Hudson, James Campbell*
Products *Men's ties & neckwear.*
Price Points *Budget to designer*
Production *Hong Kong*
Showrooms *1385 Broadway, New York, NY 10018, tel: 212-704-4800, fax: 212-967-4936.*
Sell To *Department stores, specialty stores, mass merchants & mail order catalogues.*
Private Label *Yes*
Contact *Tom Kroner*

RON CORNELL

4570 Van Nuys Boulevard, Suite 411
Sherman Oaks, CA 91403 rc4ties@aol.com
310 441 9601 Fax : 888 502 1829

Labels *J. Blades, Portofino, Nob Hill, Monterey Bay, Enrico Guccini*
Products *Ties, bowties, vests, cumberbunds, ascots, silk pocket squares, suspenders.*
Price Points *Moderate to better.*

Production	*U.S.A., China, Italy*
Showrooms	*Bel Air, California*
Sell To	*Department stores, speciality stores, mass merchants & mail order catalogues.*
Private Label	*Yes*
Web Site	*www.roncornell.com*
RN Number	*RN148175*
Rev. in mil.	*2-10*
Contact	*Owner/President: Ronald Cornell*

Notes

ADRIENNE LANDAU

519 Eighth Avenue, 21st Floor
New York, NY 10018
212 695 8362 Fax : 212 563 2014
sales@adriennelandau.com

Labels *Adrienne Landau*
Products *High end capes, evening wraps plus real & faux fur accessories.*
Price Points *Designer*
Production *U.S.A. & import*
Showrooms *New York*
Sell To *Department stores & specialty stores.*
Private Label *No*
Web Site *www.adriennelandau.com*
Contact *Owner: Adrienne Landau, , Design: Adrienne Landau*

BARRAZA ASSOCIATES LTD

225 West 35th Street, Suite 1502
New York, NY 10001
212 564 6583
barrazany@aol.com

Labels *BarrazaStyle*
Products *Unique collection of scarves, shawls & hats.*
Price Points *Moderate to better.*
Production *U.S.A. & import.*
Sell To *Department stores, specialty stores, boutiques, mail order catalogues.*
Private Label *Yes*
Web Site *www.barrazastyle.com*
Rev. in mil. *2-10*
Contact *President: Maria Barraza, Sales & Marketing: Rafael Romero*

BEL ESPRIT SHOWROOM/SHOWROOM INTERNATIONAL *(Rep.)

P.O. Box 30273
Philadelphia, PA 19103
215 963 9394 Fax : 419 793 8064
belesprit@ureach.com

Labels *Bel Esprit, Showroom International*
Products *Women's scarves, shawls & accessories.*
Price Points *Better to designer*
Production *U.S.A. & import*
Showrooms *Bel Esprit Showroom - The International Showroom for Ethical Fashion. Showroom Internat. The International Showroom for Independent Fashion. Moda 360: A Complete Fashion Revo.*
Sell To *Department stores & specialty stores.*
Corp. Office *Additional websites: www.showroominternational.com, www.moda360intl.com*
Private Label *No*
Web Site *www.belesprit.net*
Contact *CEO: Debora Pokallus*

BETMAR HATS INC.

411 Fifth Avenue
New York, NY 10016
212 684 8080 Fax : 212 545 0663 800 678 7676
betmarhats@aol.com

Labels *Betmar, Plaza Suite*
Products *Hats & millinery. Also, gloves, capes, scarves and handbags.*
Price Points *Moderate to better.*

Production *U.S.A. & import.*
Showrooms *Chicago, Dallas, Atlanta, Boston, New York, New England, West Coast*
Sell To *Department stores, specialty stores, boutiques & mail order catalogues.*
Private Label *Yes*
Web Site *www.betmarhats.com*
Rev. in mil. *11-50*
Contact *President: Bernard Grossman*

BLUE STAR INT'L

15333 Culver Drive, Suite 340-101
Irvine, CA 92606
949 552 1181 Fax : 949 552 1188
bluestarintl@aol.com

Products *Hand embroidered scarves.*
Web Site *www.blue-star-intl.com*
Contact *Marketing Director: Suhaila Reshad*

CASSIN

922 Riverview Drive
Totowa, NJ 07512
973 826 1190
info@cassincollections.com

Labels *Cassin, sherry cassin new york*
Products *A full range of hats, vests & scarves with a major focus on fur, faux fur & other natural mater*
Price Points *Moderate to designer*
Production *U.S.A. & import.*
Sell To *Department stores, fine specialty stores*
Web Site *www.cassincollections.com*
Contact *Designer: Sherry Cassin*

CEJON ACCESSORIES INC.

390 Fifth Avenue, Suite 602
New York, NY 10018
212 967 4663 Fax : 212 967 4766
rmummert@cejon.com

Labels *Cejon*
Products *Ladies & men's scarves.*
Price Points *Moderate*
Production *U.S.A. & import*
Sell To *Department stores, specialty stores, mail order catalogues & off-price retailers.*
Private Label *Yes*
Web Site *www.cejon.com*
Contact *President: David Seeherman, Sales: Robin Mummert*

COLORATURA, INC.

P.O. Box 157
Annville, PA 17003
717 867 1144 Fax : 717 867 1152 800 825 8288
coloratura9@aol.com

Labels *Coloratura*
Products *Decorative capes & scarves in patchwork & applique combining tones, textures & fabrics.*
Price Points *Designer*
Production *U.S.A.*
Showrooms *Denver/Frank Levy, & Annville, P.A.*
Sell To *Specialty stores, boutiques & mail order catalogues.*

Private Label *No*
Web Site *www.coloratura.com*
Contact *President: Alan J. Resnick*

ELIZABETH GILLETT LTD.

260 West 36th Street, Suite 802
New York, NY 10018 sales@elizabethgillett.com
212 629 7993 Fax : 212 629 7454 1 888 237 4773

Labels *Elizabeth Gillett*
Products *Feminine, unique scarves & wraps made from the softest modal, silk, wool and cashmere.*
Price Points *Better to designer.*
Production *India*
Showrooms *Dallas (Brad Hughes & Associates), Atlanta (Pepper's Collections), Los Angeles (Representing Showroom), New York (Elizabeth Gillett).*
Sell To *Private label, specialty stores, boutiques & catalogues.*
Corp. Office *Above*
Private Label *Yes*
Web Site *www.elizabethgillett.com*
Rev. in mil. *2-10*
Contact *President/Owner/Designer: Elizabeth Gillett*

FITZSIMMONS FABRICS, LTD

115 East 87th Street, Suite 22B
New York, NY 10128 info@fitzfabltd.com
212 876 2868 Fax : 212 410 1485

Products *Silk woven & cashmere/silk knit scarfs.*
Price Points *Couture*
Production *France*
Showrooms *Rep Soieries Brochiers in Lyons France. Elegant 100% silk scarves in hundreds of patterns. Also rep Bianchini-Ferier. Their 35% silk/65% cashmere is ideal for throws, scarves or yard*
Sell To *Department stores, boutiques, specialty stores*
Private Label *Yes*
Contact *Owner: Beverly Fitzsimmons*

JOY ACCESSORIES

1 Hartford Sq, #E
New Britain, CT 06052 joy@joyaccessories.com
860 612 0439 Fax : 860 612 0510 880-365-4569

Labels *Joy Susan*
Products *Domestic & imported up-to-date and trendy scarves & shawls of all types.*
Price Points *Moderate*
Production *U.S.A., India, Phillipines, China, Vietnam*
Showrooms *Connecticut and Atlanta*
Sell To *Department stores, specialty stores, boutiques, catalogues*
Private Label *Yes*
Web Site *www.joyaccessories.com*
RN Number *100542*
Rev. in mil. *0-2*
Contact *Sales: Gary Tierney*

LINDA RICHARDS

209 West 38th Street, Suite 505
New York, NY 10018 info@lindarichards.com
212 382 2257 Fax : 212 382 1793

Labels *Linda Richards*
Products *Cashmere & fur scarves, wraps, vests & jackets.*
Price Points *Better*
Production *U.S.A.*
Sell To *Department stores, specialty stores & boutiques.*
Corp. Office *Above*
Private Label *Yes*
Web Site *www.lindarichards.com*
RN Number *RN28278*
Contact *Sales: Merrisa Alfano (malfano@lindarichards.com*

MADEMOISELLE, INC.

4200 W. Schubert Avenue
Chicago, IL 60639 scot210@aol.com
773 394 4555 Fax : 773 394 9495 800 992 5580

Labels *Mademoiselle*
Products *Missy & executive women's scarves, hats, dickies, dressing hoods & more.*
Price Points *Moderate to better*
Production *U.S.A. & overseas.*
Showrooms *Atlanta, Dallas, Denver plus 15 sales reps nationwide.*
Sell To *Department stores, specialty stores, boutiques, gift shops & online.*
Private Label *Yes*
Web Site *www.mademoiselleinc.com*
Contact *President: Scott Goldstein*

MANN & BROS INC/IMPERIAL HANDKERCHIEFS

48 West 37th Street, Suite 700
New York, NY 10018 susan@mannbro.com
212 868 3535 Fax : 212 643 1406 1 800 275 1230

Labels *Van Heusen, Geoffrey Beene*
Products *Men's handkerchiefs & scarves.*
Price Points *Moderate, better & designer, plus off-price.*
Production *Import*
Showrooms *New York/above.*
Sell To *Department & specialty stores, mass merchants, mail order catalogues & off-price.*
Private Label *Yes*
RN Number *RN18731*
Contact *Sales: Susan Agosto*

NICOLE & CO.

9200 Parc Avenue, Suite 407
Montreal, Canada, H2N1Z4 hats@nicole-co.com
514 383 5599 Fax : 514 383 5674

Labels *Nicole & Co.*
Products *Fashion scarves & hats.*
Price Points *Designer to couture*
Production *Canada*

Showrooms *Montreal/9200 Parc Avenue, #407, Montreal*
Sell To *Department stores, specialty stores & boutiques.*
Private Label *Yes*
Web Site *www.nicole-co.com*
Contact *President: Nicole Amram, Production: Yoram Amram, Design: Yoram Amram*

ODETT ENTERPRISES

109 West 37th Street, Street Level
New York, NY 10018
212 921 9690 Fax : 212 768 4760
info@odettfashion.com

Labels *Odett*
Products *Shawls & capes in cashmere, wool & fur trim (mink & rabbit).*
Price Points *Budget to bridge.*
Production *U.S.A. & Italy*
Showrooms *New York*
Sell To *Specialty stores, boutiques.*
Private Label *Yes*
Web Site *www.odettfashion.com*
Contact *President: Amir Darouvar, Sales: Farah Darouvar*

PILLAGED VILLAGE, THE

31Eagle Court, Suite E
Carlisle, OH 45005
937 743 0685 Fax : 937 743 0697 1-877-793-1066
pvsales@pillagedvillage.com

Labels *The Pillaged Village*
Products *Medieval designed scarves, veils, capes & cloaks.*
Price Points *Moderate*
Showrooms *Same as Above*
Sell To *Boutiques, specialty stores, on-line catalog*
Web Site *www.pillagedvillage.com*
Contact *Owner: Wendy Kimmel*

PUR CASHMERE

74-804 Joni Drive, Suite 5A
Palm Desert, CA 92260
800 225 9157 Fax : 240 536 0094
info@purcashmere.com

Labels *Pur Cashmere*
Products *Modern, classic heirloom cashmere scarf & shawl designs.*
Price Points *Better*
Sell To *Specialty stores, on-line*
Private Label *Yes*
Web Site *www.purcashmere.com*
Contact *CEO: Leslie Deane Roth*

RAJ IMPORTS

850 S. Broadway , #1101
Los Angeles, CA 90014
213 629 5375 Fax : 213 629 5376
rajimports@hotmail.com

Labels *Raj Imports*
Products *Scarves in unique modern bohemian designs with Indian aesthetics.*
Price Points *Better*

Production *Import*
Sell To *Department stores, boutiques, specialty stores*
Web Site *www.rajimports.net*

REDWOOD COURT BY SILK BOX

PO Box 3019
Princeton Jct, NJ 08543 info@lotusa.com
609 275 4403 Fax : 609 897 1118

Labels *Silk Box*
Products *Specialty handbags & shawls in silk novelty fabrications.*
Price Points *Better*
Production *Import*
Showrooms *None*
Sell To *Department stores & boutiques.*
Private Label *Yes*
Web Site *www.redwoodcourt.com*
Rev. in mil. *0-2*
Contact *Sales: Shirley Fang 609-275-0350 (shirleymfang@gmail.com)*

ROBIN ASCHER

PO Box 5
Piermont, NH 03779 roba24@aol.com
603 989 9829

Labels *Ascher*
Products *High quality cashmere and silk screen printed scarves.*
Price Points *Better*
Production *Italy*
Sell To *Department stores, specialty stores, boutiques.*
Web Site *www.aschersquares.com*
Contact *Sales: Robin Ascher*

SHOWROOM SEVEN/ERICKSON BEAMON *(Rep.)

263 Eleventh Avenue
New York, NY 10001 jean-marc@showroomseven.com
212 643 4810 Fax : 646 763 8940

Labels *Pashma Cashmere*
Products *Women's scarves*
Price Points *Contemporary, designer & couture*
Production *International*
Showrooms *New York, Los Angeles, Paris*
Sell To *Department stores, specialty stores & boutiques. International and domestic.*
Private Label *Yes*
Web Site *www.showroomseven.com*
Rev. in mil. *11-50*

SMARTWORKS INC.

37 Pike Road West
Sheffield, MA 01257 smartworks.design@gmail.com
413 229 2130 Fax : 413 229 0014

Labels *Smartworks Inc.*
Products *Contemporary knitted scarves & wraps.*

Price Points *Bridge*
Production *U.S.A.*
Sell To *Department stores, specialty stores, boutiques & mail order catalogues.*
Private Label *No*
Web Site *www.smARTwks.com*
Rev. in mil. *0-2*
Contact *Owner: Sonya Mackintosh, Design: Sonya Mackintosh*

VISMAYA

112 West 9th Street, Suite 1000
Los Angeles, CA 90015 shivani@vismayacollection.com
213 623 8567 Fax : 310 919 0400

Labels *Vismaya, Shivani*
Products *Shawls, scarves, wraps and ponchos in stylish trends & sophisticated classics in colorful designs.*
Price Points *Moderate*
Production *India*
Sell To *Department stores, specialty stores, boutiques*
Corp. Office *Los Angeles and Delhi, India*
Private Label *Yes*
Web Site *www.vismayacollection.com*
RN Number *127802*
Rev. in mil. *0-2*
Contact *Shivani Mehrotra/Yatin Narula*

WOODEN SHIPS

231 West 39th Street
New York, NY 10018 sales@wooden-ships.com
888 717 6700 Fax : 212 221 2329

Labels *Wooden Ships*
Products *Updated scarfs, wraps, ponchos, mittens, gloves & hats*
Price Points *Better*
Production *Import*
Sell To *Department stores, specialty stores, boutiques & mail order catalogues.*
Private Label *No*
Web Site *www.wooden-ships.com*
Contact *Sales: Randi Weinstein*

AAA INNOVATIONS

10 Maple Street
Norwood, NJ 07648 diane@aaainnovations.com
201 784 3244 Fax : 201 784 3242 800 426 7446

Labels *AAA Umbrella*
Products *Fashion umbrellas, golf umbrellas and folding umbrellas.*
Price Points *Moderate*
Production *U.S.A. & import*
Sell To *Department stores, specialty stores, mass merchants & mail order catalogues.*
Private Label *Yes*
Web Site *www.aaainnovations.com*
Contact *President: Jeffrey Nanus, Sales: Diane Daly*

BURBERRY

444 Madison Avenue, 14th Floor
New York, NY 10022 us.customerservice@burberry.com
800 284 8480 Fax : 212 977 5521 877-217-4085

Labels *Burberry*
Products *Classic, traditional umbrellas.*
Price Points *Better to designer*
Production *U.S.A. & import.*
Sell To *Department stores & specialty stores.*
Private Label *No*
Web Site *www.burberry.com*
Rev. in mil. *11-50*

ESSEX MANUFACTURING INC.

350 Fifth Avenue, Suite 2400
New York, NY 10118 bbaum@baum-essex.com
212 239 0080 Fax : 212 714 2958 800 648 6010

Labels *Nautica, Jones New York, Misty Harbor®, Nicole Miller, Ellen Tracy*
Products *Men's & women's umbrellas.*
Production *Import*
Showrooms *Chicago, Boston, Cleveland, Philadelphia, San Francisco & New York.*
Sell To *Department stores, specialty stores, mass merchants & mail order catalogues.*
Private Label *Yes*
Web Site *www.baum-essex.com*
Contact *Rainwear & Outerwear: Bill Baum, Umbrellas: Lance Lovett - llovett@baum-essex.com*

GILTON COMPANY

1106 West Gardena Boulevard
Gardena, CA 90247 sales@giltonco.com
626 241 1958 Fax : 310 327 5020 800 479 1075

Labels *Jones New York*
Products *Men's umbrellas.*
Price Points *Moderate*
Production *U.S.A & import.*
Showrooms *Call for catalog*
Sell To *Department stores, specialty stores, mail order catalogues & off-price retailers.*
Private Label *No*
Web Site *giltonco.com*

RN Number *RN64854*
Rev. in mil. *0-2*
Contact *President & Owner: Philip Shar*

SHEDRAIN CORP.

366 Fifth Avenue, Suite 1001
New York, NY 10001 iraw@shedrain.com
212 685 5555 Fax : 212 447 0888 800 722 7246

Labels *ShedRain, Shedrays, Gellas, Windpro, WalkSafe, Rain Essentials, Windjammer*
Products *Umbrellas, rainhats & fashion rainwear.*
Price Points *Budget, moderate & better.*
Production *U.S.A. & Asia*
Showrooms *New York & Portland, Oregon*
Sell To *Department & specialty stores, boutiques, mass merchants, catalogues & corporate sales.*
Corp. Office *8303 N.E. Killingsworth, Portland, OR 97220, Tel:503-255-2200*
Private Label *Yes*
Web Site *www.shedrain.com*
Contact *President: Jeffrey Blauer*

AIMAI CASHMERE

PO Box 395
Aspen, CO 81612
970 618 3178 Fax : 970 925 1002
brian@aimaicashmere.com

Products *Hand-woven cashmere & silk pashmina scarves, shawls, mufflers plus cashmere garments.*
Price Points *All price points*
Production *Nepal*
Sell To *Department Stores*
Private Label *Yes*
Web Site *www.aimaicashmere.com*
Contact *Sales: Brian Harris*

Company	Category		Page
2 X IST	HOSIERY/SOCKS/LEGWEAR	A	335
	SLEEPWEAR & UNDERWEAR	M	207
	TEE SHIRTS & BLANKS	M	219
525 AMERICA	CONTEMPORARY SPORTSWEAR	W	29
	GIFT ITEMS	A	305
	SWEATERS & KNITWEAR	W	135
5TH & OCEAN CLOTHING LLC/NEW ERA	ACTIVE/ATHLETICWEAR	C	233
	CASUAL SPORTSWEAR	W	23
	CASUAL SPORTSWEAR	M	172
	JUNIOR SPORTSWEAR	W	81
7 DIAMONDS	JEANS & DENIMWEAR	M	185
	OUTERWEAR/COATS & JACKETS	M	193
	SHIRTS: DRESS & SPORT	M	203
7 FOR ALL MANKIND	CASUAL SPORTSWEAR	W	23
	CASUAL SPORTSWEAR	M	172
	JEANS & DENIMWEAR	W	77
	JEANS & DENIMWEAR	M	185
A & H SPORTSWEAR CO. INC.	SWIMWEAR & BEACHWEAR	W	145
A PEA IN THE POD	SPECIAL SIZES/MATERNITY	W	129
A'NUE LIGNE	BLOUSES/SHIRTS/TOPS	W	10
A. CHE	SWIMWEAR & BEACHWEAR	W	145
AAA INNOVATIONS	LUGGAGE/BAGS/LEATHER GOODS	A	341
	UMBRELLAS	A	357
ABC HOSIERY	HOSIERY/SOCKS/LEGWEAR	A	335
ABS BY ALLEN SCHWARTZ	DESIGNER COLLECTIONS	W	47
	DRESSES/SEPARATES/SUITS	W	55
ACORN PRODUCTS	GIFT ITEMS	A	305
	HOSIERY/SOCKS/LEGWEAR	A	335
ACTIVE APPAREL, INC.	TEE SHIRTS & BLANKS	W	151
	TEE SHIRTS & BLANKS	M	219
ACTIVE EDGE, THE/OLD CITY T-SHIRTS	ACTIVE/ATHLETICWEAR	C	233
	ECOLOGICAL & ORGANIC	W	65
	ECOLOGICAL & ORGANIC	M	183
	ECOLOGICAL & ORGANIC	C	249
	NEWBORN/LAYETTE/INFANT	C	255
ADEA	INTIMATE APPAREL & LINGERIE	W	69
ADIDAS AMERICA, INC.	ACTIVE/ATHLETICWEAR	W	1
	ACTIVE/ATHLETICWEAR	M	162
ADK FASHIONS	BRIDAL & EVENINGWEAR	W	15
	DESIGNER COLLECTIONS	W	47
ADRIANNA PAPELL LLC.	DESIGNER COLLECTIONS	W	47

Company	Category		Page
ADRIANO GOLDSCHMIED	JEANS & DENIMWEAR	W	77
	JEANS & DENIMWEAR	M	185
ADRIENNE LANDAU	OUTERWEAR/COATS & JACKETS	W	101
	SCARVES & SHAWLS	A	349
ADVANCE APPARELS INC.	DRESSES/SEPARATES/SUITS	W	55
AERO TECH DESIGNS	ACTIVE/ATHLETICWEAR	W	1
	ACTIVE/ATHLETICWEAR	M	162
	ACTIVE/ATHLETICWEAR	C	233
AIDAN MATTOX	BRIDAL & EVENINGWEAR	W	15
	DESIGNER COLLECTIONS	W	48
AIMAI CASHMERE	SCARVES & SHAWLS		359
	SWEATERS & KNITWEAR	W	135
AKADEMIKS	ACTIVE/ATHLETICWEAR	M	162
	COORDINATED SPORTSWEAR-BOYS	C	237
	COORDINATED SPORTSWEAR-GIRLS	C	241
	JEANS & DENIMWEAR	M	186
ALDAN	UNIFORMS	W	157
	UNIFORMS	M	227
ALICE AND OLIVIA	CONTEMPORARY SPORTSWEAR	W	29
	DRESSES/SEPARATES/SUITS	W	55
ALPHA INDUSTRIES, INC.	OUTERWEAR/COATS & JACKETS	W	101
	OUTERWEAR/COATS & JACKETS	M	193
	OUTERWEAR/COATS & JACKETS	C	259
	SPORTSMEN'S APPAREL	M	211
ALSTYLE	TEE SHIRTS & BLANKS	W	151
	TEE SHIRTS & BLANKS	M	219
	TEE SHIRTS & BLANKS	C	277
AMERICAN HAT FACTORY, THE	HATS/CAPS/MILLINERY	A	325
ANDARI FASHION, INC.	PRIVATE LABEL	W	111
	PRIVATE LABEL	M	199
	SWEATERS & KNITWEAR	W	135
	SWEATERS	M	215
ANDERSEN-BECKER INC.	DECORATED/EMBELLISHED APPAREL	W	43
ANDREW MARC	LEATHER & SUEDE	W	87
	LEATHER & SUEDE	M	189
	OUTERWEAR/COATS & JACKETS	W	101
	OUTERWEAR/COATS & JACKETS	M	193
ANN TAYLOR	DRESSES/SEPARATES/SUITS	W	55
	LIFESTYLE COLLECTIONS	W	91
	SPECIAL SIZES/PETITE	W	131
ANNA SUI	DESIGNER COLLECTIONS	W	48

Company	Category		Page
ANNE KLEIN	LIFESTYLE COLLECTIONS	W	91
	MISSY/UPDATED SPORTSWEAR	W	95
ANNE NAMBA DESIGNS	DECORATED/EMBELLISHED APPAREL	W	43
	DRESSES/SEPARATES/SUITS	W	56
	SHIRTS: DRESS & SPORT	M	203
ANVIL KNITWEAR, INC.	ACTIVE/ATHLETICWEAR	C	234
	HATS/CAPS/MILLINERY	A	325
	TEE SHIRTS & BLANKS	W	151
	TEE SHIRTS & BLANKS	M	220
APL®	HANDBAGS	A	317
AQUARIUS LTD.	BELTS	A	283
AR NEW YORK	HANDBAGS	A	317
ARABESQUE DESIGN/PATRICIA	INTIMATE APPAREL & LINGERIE	W	69
ARAKS	LIFESTYLE COLLECTIONS	W	91
AREA CODE 212 INC.	CASUAL SPORTSWEAR	W	23
ARMBRUST INTERNATIONAL	FASHION JEWELRY & WATCHES	A	297
ASPEN LICENSING INTERNATIONAL, INC.	LICENSED APPAREL	W	89
	LICENSED APPAREL	M	191
	LICENSED APPAREL	C	253
ATOPAPPAREL CORP	BLOUSES/SHIRTS/TOPS	W	10
	SPECIAL SIZES/LARGE	W	121
AUDISH ACCESSORIES, LLC	HANDBAGS	A	317
AUGUST SILK, INC.	CASUAL SPORTSWEAR	W	23
	SWEATERS & KNITWEAR	W	135
AUTUMN CASHMERE INC.	PRIVATE LABEL	W	111
	PRIVATE LABEL	M	199
	SWEATERS & KNITWEAR	W	136
	SWEATERS	M	215
	SWEATERS	C	273
AVALIN LIMITED	CONTEMPORARY SPORTSWEAR	W	29
AZIBI LTD.	CONTEMPORARY SPORTSWEAR	W	30
	DRESSES/SEPARATES/SUITS	W	56
B & B DESIGNS COLLECTION INC.	BLOUSES/SHIRTS/TOPS	W	10
	CONTEMPORARY SPORTSWEAR	W	30
B & B SWEATERS	SWEATERS & KNITWEAR	W	136
	TEE SHIRTS & BLANKS	W	152
B. BRONSON	CASUAL SPORTSWEAR	W	24
B.C.T.C.	ACTIVE/ATHLETICWEAR	W	1
	SPECIAL SIZES/LARGE	W	121
	SPECIAL SIZES/PETITE	W	131
BABETTE	CONTEMPORARY SPORTSWEAR	W	30

Company	Category	Section	Page
	OUTERWEAR/COATS & JACKETS	W	102
BABY JAY INC./GROWING FEET INC.	CHILDREN	A	291
	NEWBORN/LAYETTE/INFANT	C	255
	TEE SHIRTS & BLANKS	C	277
BABYFAIR, INC.	PRIVATE LABEL	C	263
BABYLEGS® DIV OF UNITED LEGWEAR	HOSIERY/SOCKS/LEGWEAR	A	335
BADGER SPORTSWEAR	ACTIVE/ATHLETICWEAR	W	2
	ACTIVE/ATHLETICWEAR	M	163
	UNIFORMS	W	157
BAILEY HATS	HATS/CAPS/MILLINERY	A	325
BALTIERRA SURFBOARDS & BALTI GIRL	ACTIVE/ATHLETICWEAR	W	2
	ACTIVE/ATHLETICWEAR	M	163
BAMBOO 54	HANDBAGS	A	317
BARAMI/FASHION CONCEPTS/PATRIZIA	CONTEMPORARY SPORTSWEAR	W	30
	DRESSES/SEPARATES/SUITS	W	56
BARRAZA ASSOCIATES LTD	ACTIVE/ATHLETICWEAR	W	2
	BRIDAL & EVENINGWEAR	W	15
	CONTEMPORARY SPORTSWEAR	W	31
	ECOLOGICAL & ORGANIC	W	65
	OUTERWEAR/COATS & JACKETS	W	102
	PRIVATE LABEL	W	111
	SCARVES & SHAWLS	A	349
BARRONS-HUNTER, INC.	BELTS	A	283
BASIX OF AMERICA	CONTEMPORARY SPORTSWEAR	W	31
	SWIMWEAR & BEACHWEAR	M	217
BAUXO INC.	BELTS	A	283
	FASHION JEWELRY & WATCHES	A	297
BCBG MAX AZRIA GROUP	BRIDAL & EVENINGWEAR	W	16
	CONTEMPORARY SPORTSWEAR	W	31
	HANDBAGS	A	318
BEACH HANDBAGS	HANDBAGS	A	318
BEACH RAYS/DIV OF J.Y. RAYS, INC.	JUNIOR SPORTSWEAR	W	81
	SWIMWEAR & BEACHWEAR	W	145
	SWIMWEAR & BEACHWEAR	M	217
	SWIMWEAR & BEACHWEAR	C	275
BEAU TIES LTD. OF VERMONT	MEN'S TIES & NECKWEAR	A	345
BECKER GLOVE INTERNATIONAL, LLC	GLOVES	A	310
BEDHEAD PAJAMAS	SLEEPWEAR & UNDERWEAR	M	207
	SLEEPWEAR & LOUNGEWEAR	W	117
BEL ESPRIT SHOWROOM/SHOWROOM	CONTEMPORARY SPORTSWEAR	W	32
	HANDBAGS	A	318

Company	Category	Section	Page
	SCARVES & SHAWLS	A	349
BELASSE COLLECTION LLC	DRESSES/SEPARATES/SUITS	W	57
BELGO LUX INC.	BELTS	A	284
	EYEWEAR	A	295
BELLA MATERNA INC.	SPECIAL SIZES/MATERNITY	W	129
BELLDINI	SWEATERS & KNITWEAR	W	136
BEREK	SWEATERS & KNITWEAR	W	137
BERGER & STEVENS	BRIDAL & EVENINGWEAR	W	16
	CONTEMPORARY SPORTSWEAR	W	32
BERMO ENTERPRISES INC.	JEANS & DENIMWEAR	W	77
	JEANS & DENIMWEAR	M	186
BETMAR HATS INC.	GLOVES	A	310
	HATS/CAPS/MILLINERY	A	326
	SCARVES & SHAWLS	A	350
BETSEY JOHNSON	CONTEMPORARY SPORTSWEAR	W	32
	DESIGNER COLLECTIONS	W	48
	HOSIERY/SOCKS/LEGWEAR	A	336
BEVERLY HILLS UNIFORMS	UNIFORMS	W	157
	UNIFORMS	M	227
BEXAR MANUFACTURING CO.	UNIFORMS	W	157
	UNIFORMS	M	227
BIANCA NERO	DRESSES/SEPARATES/SUITS	W	57
BIBELOT	SWEATERS & KNITWEAR	W	137
BIG BUDDHA	BELTS	A	284
	HANDBAGS	A	319
BILL BLASS FASHIONS LLC	BRIDAL & EVENINGWEAR	W	16
	DESIGNER COLLECTIONS	W	48
BILLS KHAKIS	CONTEMPORARY SPORTSWEAR	M	177
	TROUSERS & SLACKS	M	225
BLUE DUCK TRADING CO.	OUTERWEAR/COATS & JACKETS	W	102
	OUTERWEAR/COATS & JACKETS	M	194
BLUE HAWAII SALES	CASUAL SPORTSWEAR	W	24
	CASUAL SPORTSWEAR	M	172
	SHIRTS: DRESS & SPORT	C	267
	UNIFORMS	M	227
BLUE PLATE INC.	BLOUSES/SHIRTS/TOPS	W	11
	JUNIOR SPORTSWEAR	W	81
	SWEATERS & KNITWEAR	W	137
BLUE STAR INT'L	SCARVES & SHAWLS	A	350
BLUEGEM SUNGLASSES INC.	EYEWEAR	A	295
BLUESUITS	DESIGNER COLLECTIONS	W	49

Company	Category	Code	Page
	DRESSES/SEPARATES/SUITS	W	57
	MISSY/UPDATED SPORTSWEAR	W	95
	SPECIAL SIZES/PETITE	W	131
BODY WRAPPERS	ACTIVE/ATHLETICWEAR	W	2
	ACTIVE/ATHLETICWEAR	C	234
	CHILDREN	A	291
	HOSIERY/SOCKS/LEGWEAR	A	336
BOSSONG HOSIERY	HOSIERY/SOCKS/LEGWEAR	A	336
BOULEVARD	HANDBAGS	A	319
BOULEVARD APPAREL	JEANS & DENIMWEAR	W	77
	SPECIAL SIZES/LARGE	W	121
BRAVADO MERCHANDISING	HATS/CAPS/MILLINERY	A	326
	TEE SHIRTS & BLANKS	W	152
	TEE SHIRTS & BLANKS	M	220
BRAVE LEATHER LTD.	BELTS	A	284
BRAZILROXX INC.	JEANS & DENIMWEAR	W	78
BREAKING WAVES INTERNATIONAL	SWIMWEAR & BEACHWEAR	W	146
BROOKS SPORTS, INC.	ACTIVE/ATHLETICWEAR	W	3
	ACTIVE/ATHLETICWEAR	M	163
BUCK WEAR INC.	HATS/CAPS/MILLINERY	A	326
	TEE SHIRTS & BLANKS	W	152
	TEE SHIRTS & BLANKS	M	220
BURBERRY	DESIGNER COLLECTIONS	M	181
	LIFESTYLE COLLECTIONS	W	91
	LUGGAGE/BAGS/LEATHER GOODS	A	341
	OUTERWEAR/COATS & JACKETS	W	102
	OUTERWEAR/COATS & JACKETS	M	194
	UMBRELLAS	A	357
BURMA BIBAS	CONTEMPORARY SPORTSWEAR	M	177
	MEN'S TIES & NECKWEAR	A	345
	SHIRTS: DRESS & SPORT	M	203
BY BOE LTD.	FASHION JEWELRY & WATCHES	A	297
C.T.C. INC.	CONTEMPORARY SPORTSWEAR	W	32
	DRESSES/SEPARATES/SUITS	W	57
CALIFORNIA RAIN CO.	ACTIVE/ATHLETICWEAR	W	3
	ACTIVE/ATHLETICWEAR	C	234
	PRIVATE LABEL	W	112
	TEE SHIRTS & BLANKS	M	220
CALVIN CLOTHING COMPANY	COORDINATED SPORTSWEAR-BOYS	C	237
	SHIRTS: DRESS & SPORT	C	267
	SUITS/SPECIAL OCCASION	C	271

Company	Category		Page
CALVIN KLEIN, INC.	INTIMATE APPAREL & LINGERIE	W	69
	JEANS & DENIMWEAR	W	78
	JEANS & DENIMWEAR	M	186
	SPECIAL SIZES/PETITE	W	131
CAMBER SPORTSWEAR, INC.	ACTIVE/ATHLETICWEAR	M	163
	BIG & TALL	M	169
	TEE SHIRTS & BLANKS	M	221
CANADIAN SWEATER CO., LTD.	GLOVES	A	310
	HATS/CAPS/MILLINERY	A	326
	SWEATERS & KNITWEAR	W	137
	SWEATERS	M	215
	SWEATERS	C	273
CAPELLI NEW YORK	HOSIERY/SOCKS/LEGWEAR	A	337
	SLEEPWEAR & UNDERWEAR	M	207
	SLEEPWEAR & UNDERWEAR	C	269
	SLEEPWEAR & LOUNGEWEAR	W	117
CARIBBEAN WRAPS INTERNATIONAL	SWIMWEAR & BEACHWEAR	W	146
CARMEN MARC VALVO	BRIDAL & EVENINGWEAR	W	17
CAROL PERETZ	BRIDAL & EVENINGWEAR	W	17
	CONTEMPORARY SPORTSWEAR	W	33
	DESIGNER COLLECTIONS	W	49
CARRIEAMBER INTIMATES	INTIMATE APPAREL & LINGERIE	W	69
	PRIVATE LABEL	W	112
CARTISE INTERNATIONAL	CASUAL SPORTSWEAR	W	24
	DRESSES/SEPARATES/SUITS	W	58
CASHMERE HOUSE	SWEATERS & KNITWEAR	W	138
CASSIN	HATS/CAPS/MILLINERY	A	327
	OUTERWEAR/COATS & JACKETS	W	103
	SCARVES & SHAWLS	A	350
CASTLEWARE BABY	ECOLOGICAL & ORGANIC	C	249
CATFISH CALHOUN AKA CALHOUN	SWIMWEAR & BEACHWEAR	W	146
	SWIMWEAR & BEACHWEAR	M	217
	TEE SHIRTS & BLANKS	W	152
	TEE SHIRTS & BLANKS	M	221
CEJON ACCESSORIES INC.	OUTERWEAR/COATS & JACKETS	W	103
	OUTERWEAR/COATS & JACKETS	C	259
	SCARVES & SHAWLS	A	350
	SWIMWEAR & BEACHWEAR	W	146
CHAMPION ATHLETICWEAR, INC.	ACTIVE/ATHLETICWEAR	W	3
	ACTIVE/ATHLETICWEAR	M	164
	LICENSED APPAREL	W	89

Company	Category		Page
	LICENSED APPAREL	M	191
CHANTELLE LINGERIE INC.	INTIMATE APPAREL & LINGERIE	W	70
CHARLEY MORGAN, INC.	INTIMATE APPAREL & LINGERIE	W	70
CHATHAM KNITTING MILLS, INC.	PRIVATE LABEL	W	112
	PRIVATE LABEL	M	199
CHIPITA ACCESSORIES	FASHION JEWELRY & WATCHES	A	297
CHRISTINE VANCOUVER	INTIMATE APPAREL & LINGERIE	W	70
	SLEEPWEAR & LOUNGEWEAR	W	117
	SPECIAL SIZES/LARGE	W	122
	SPECIAL SIZES/PETITE	W	132
CHRISTOPHER & BANKS CORPORATION	CONTEMPORARY SPORTSWEAR	W	33
	SPECIAL SIZES/LARGE	W	122
CLASSIX	BLOUSES/SHIRTS/TOPS	W	11
	SHIRTS: DRESS & SPORT	M	204
	SHIRTS: DRESS & SPORT	C	267
COLLECTION ARIANNE	BLOUSES/SHIRTS/TOPS	W	11
	INTIMATE APPAREL & LINGERIE	W	71
COLORADO SILVER STAR CORP.	GIFT ITEMS	A	305
COLORATURA, INC.	DECORATED/EMBELLISHED APPAREL	W	43
	OUTERWEAR/COATS & JACKETS	W	103
	SCARVES & SHAWLS	A	351
COLUMBIA SPORTSWEAR CO., INC.	ACTIVE/ATHLETICWEAR	W	4
	ACTIVE/ATHLETICWEAR	C	234
	OUTERWEAR/COATS & JACKETS	W	104
	OUTERWEAR/COATS & JACKETS	M	194
	OUTERWEAR/COATS & JACKETS	C	259
	SPORTSMEN'S APPAREL	M	211
COMME CI COMME CA LTD.	INTIMATE APPAREL & LINGERIE	W	71
	SLEEPWEAR & UNDERWEAR	M	208
	SWIMWEAR & BEACHWEAR	M	217
CONCEPT ONE ACCESSORIES	HATS/CAPS/MILLINERY	A	327
COOBIE INTIMATES	INTIMATE APPAREL & LINGERIE	W	71
CORAL HEAD INC./HAWAIIAN ISLAND	SWIMWEAR & BEACHWEAR	W	147
	SWIMWEAR & BEACHWEAR	M	218
COSABELLA	INTIMATE APPAREL & LINGERIE	W	71
	SWIMWEAR & BEACHWEAR	W	147
COTTON EMPORIUM, INC.	JUNIOR SPORTSWEAR	W	82
	SWEATERS & KNITWEAR	W	138
COTTON HERITAGE	PRIVATE LABEL	W	112
	PRIVATE LABEL	M	200
	PRIVATE LABEL	C	263

Company	Category		Page
COUNTRY GENTLEMAN HEADWEAR, INC.	HATS/CAPS/MILLINERY	A	327
CPT USA, LLC DBA COCKPIT USA	BIG & TALL	M	169
	CONTEMPORARY SPORTSWEAR	W	33
	CONTEMPORARY SPORTSWEAR	M	177
	LEATHER & SUEDE	M	189
	OUTERWEAR/COATS & JACKETS	M	194
CRESCENT SOCK COMPANY	HOSIERY/SOCKS/LEGWEAR	A	337
CYNTHIA GALE	FASHION JEWELRY & WATCHES	A	298
	GIFT ITEMS	A	306
CYNTHIA ROWLEY	CONTEMPORARY SPORTSWEAR	W	33
	DESIGNER COLLECTIONS	W	49
CYNTHIA STEFFE	CONTEMPORARY SPORTSWEAR	W	34
	DESIGNER COLLECTIONS	W	50
CYRUS	SWEATERS & KNITWEAR	W	138
D'ACCORD SHIRTS & GUAYABERAS	BIG & TALL	M	169
	CASUAL SPORTSWEAR	M	173
	SHIRTS: DRESS & SPORT	M	204
DAILY WEAR SPORTSWEAR/FOREVER	MISSY/UPDATED SPORTSWEAR	W	95
DAMIANOU	BRIDAL & EVENINGWEAR	W	17
DANA EMILIA PRESENTS	BLOUSES/SHIRTS/TOPS	W	11
	CONTEMPORARY SPORTSWEAR	W	34
	DECORATED/EMBELLISHED APPAREL	W	44
	MISSY/UPDATED SPORTSWEAR	W	96
	SPECIAL SIZES/LARGE	W	122
	SWEATERS & KNITWEAR	W	138
DANECRAFT INC.	FASHION JEWELRY & WATCHES	A	298
DARIAN GROUP INC.	BRIDAL & EVENINGWEAR	W	17
	DRESSES/SEPARATES/SUITS	W	58
DAVID CAREY INC.	MEN'S TIES & NECKWEAR	A	345
	SHIRTS: DRESS & SPORT	M	204
DAVID SMITH & ASSOCIATES	GIFT ITEMS	A	306
DAYLEEN INTIMATES INC.	INTIMATE APPAREL & LINGERIE	W	71
DEBORA RACHELLE INC.	BRIDAL & EVENINGWEAR	W	18
DEPECHE MODE	BRIDAL & EVENINGWEAR	W	18
	CONTEMPORARY SPORTSWEAR	W	34
	DRESSES/SEPARATES/SUITS	W	58
	SPECIAL SIZES/LARGE	W	122
	SPECIAL SIZES/PETITE	W	132
DESSY CREATIONS & AFTER SIX	BRIDAL & EVENINGWEAR	W	18
DIANE VON FURSTENBERG STUDIO, L.P.	DESIGNER COLLECTIONS	W	50
DIESEL PLANET	EYEWEAR	A	295

Company	Category	Section	Page
	FASHION JEWELRY & WATCHES	A	298
	JEANS & DENIMWEAR	W	78
	JEANS & DENIMWEAR	M	186
	JEANS & DENIMWEAR	C	251
DIVINA DANCEWEAR	ACTIVE/ATHLETICWEAR	W	4
DKNY	CONTEMPORARY SPORTSWEAR	W	35
DOLLHOUSE	JUNIOR SPORTSWEAR	W	82
DOLORES PISCOTTA	ECOLOGICAL & ORGANIC	W	65
	GIFT ITEMS	A	306
	OUTERWEAR/COATS & JACKETS	W	104
	SWEATERS & KNITWEAR	W	139
DONNA KARAN COLLECTIONS	DESIGNER COLLECTIONS	W	50
DONOUGHE SPORT	ACTIVE/ATHLETICWEAR	W	4
	ACTIVE/ATHLETICWEAR	M	164
	ACTIVE/ATHLETICWEAR	C	235
DORMAN FASHION INC.	BLOUSES/SHIRTS/TOPS	W	12
DREAM WORLD INTERNATIONAL, INC.	BIG & TALL	M	170
	CONTEMPORARY SPORTSWEAR	M	178
	SUITS & SPORTCOATS	M	213
DREAMBAGS, INC.	GIFT ITEMS	A	306
	HANDBAGS	A	319
	LUGGAGE/BAGS/LEATHER GOODS	A	341
DREW PHILIPS CORP.	CONTEMPORARY SPORTSWEAR	W	35
	DRESSES/SEPARATES/SUITS	W	58
DUE PER DUE/209WST	CONTEMPORARY SPORTSWEAR	W	35
DYNAMIC ASIA INTERNATIONAL, INC.	HANDBAGS	A	319
	HATS/CAPS/MILLINERY	A	327
EASTWEST CLOTHING	CASUAL SPORTSWEAR	W	24
EDWARD CROMARTY ART DESIGN	BRIDAL/SPECIAL/INTIMATE	A	289
	BRIDAL & EVENINGWEAR	W	19
	SLEEPWEAR & LOUNGEWEAR	W	118
EILEEN FISHER INC.	MISSY/UPDATED SPORTSWEAR	W	96
ELAN INTERNATIONAL	CONTEMPORARY SPORTSWEAR	W	35
ELE.PAVONI NEW YORK LTD	BLOUSES/SHIRTS/TOPS	W	12
	DESIGNER COLLECTIONS	W	50
	SWEATERS & KNITWEAR	W	139
ELIE TAHARI LTD.	DESIGNER COLLECTIONS	W	51
	MISSY/UPDATED SPORTSWEAR	W	96
ELIZABETH GILLETT LTD.	SCARVES & SHAWLS	A	351
	SWEATERS & KNITWEAR	W	139
EMA SAVAHL DESIGN	BRIDAL & EVENINGWEAR	W	19

Company	Category	Section	Page
	DECORATED/EMBELLISHED APPAREL	W	44
EMIL RUTENBERG	CONTEMPORARY SPORTSWEAR	W	36
ENVIROTEXTILES LLC.	TEE SHIRTS & BLANKS	W	153
	TEE SHIRTS & BLANKS	M	221
ERIC JAVITS, INC.	HANDBAGS	A	320
	HATS/CAPS/MILLINERY	A	328
ERICA LYONS JEWELRY/CRIMZON ROSE	FASHION JEWELRY & WATCHES	A	299
ESCADA USA	DESIGNER COLLECTIONS	W	51
ESSEX MANUFACTURING INC.	BIG & TALL	M	170
	LICENSED APPAREL	M	191
	OUTERWEAR/COATS & JACKETS	W	104
	OUTERWEAR/COATS & JACKETS	M	195
	OUTERWEAR/COATS & JACKETS	C	260
	SPECIAL SIZES/LARGE	W	123
	SPECIAL SIZES/PETITE	W	132
	UMBRELLAS	A	357
EURO JOY SPORTSWEAR CORP.	CASUAL SPORTSWEAR	W	25
	MISSY/UPDATED SPORTSWEAR	W	96
	OUTERWEAR/COATS & JACKETS	W	104
	SWEATERS & KNITWEAR	W	140
EVANESE, INC.	DRESSES/SEPARATES/SUITS	W	59
EVEDEN INC.	INTIMATE APPAREL & LINGERIE	W	72
	SWIMWEAR & BEACHWEAR	W	147
EVY OF CALIFORNIA, INC./DBA JALATE	COORDINATED SPORTSWEAR-BOYS	C	237
	COORDINATED SPORTSWEAR-GIRLS	C	241
	DRESSES	C	245
	JUNIOR SPORTSWEAR	W	82
	NEWBORN/LAYETTE/INFANT	C	255
EZRASONS, INC.	SLEEPWEAR & UNDERWEAR	M	208
F & M HAT CO., INC.	HATS/CAPS/MILLINERY	A	328
FAIR HEMP INC.	HATS/CAPS/MILLINERY	A	328
	TEE SHIRTS & BLANKS	W	153
	TEE SHIRTS & BLANKS	M	221
FBF ORIGINALS	HOSIERY/SOCKS/LEGWEAR	A	337
FGX INTERNATIONAL/DIV OF ESSILOR	EYEWEAR	A	296
FILA U.S.A. INC.	ACTIVE/ATHLETICWEAR	W	4
	ACTIVE/ATHLETICWEAR	M	164
	ACTIVE/ATHLETICWEAR	C	235
FITZSIMMONS FABRICS, LTD	SCARVES & SHAWLS	A	351
FLATIRON WORKSHOP	BLOUSES/SHIRTS/TOPS	W	12
FLEUR'T, INC./MONTELLE	INTIMATE APPAREL & LINGERIE	W	72

Company	Category		Page
FLORA NIKROOZ/DIVISION OF AGE	INTIMATE APPAREL & LINGERIE	W	72
FORI SHOWROOM	OUTERWEAR/COATS & JACKETS	W	105
	SWEATERS & KNITWEAR	W	140
FORMART CORPORATION	EYEWEAR	A	296
	FASHION JEWELRY & WATCHES	A	299
	GIFT ITEMS	A	307
	HAIR ORNAMENTS	A	313
	HANDBAGS	A	320
FORT KNOX LINGERIE	INTIMATE APPAREL & LINGERIE	W	73
FOUGER FOR KIDS, INC.	DRESSES	C	245
	NEWBORN/LAYETTE/INFANT	C	256
	SUITS/SPECIAL OCCASION	C	271
FOUR SEASONS DESIGN GROUP	FASHION JEWELRY & WATCHES	A	299
	GIFT ITEMS	A	307
FREE COUNTRY LTD.	ACTIVE/ATHLETICWEAR	M	164
	OUTERWEAR/COATS & JACKETS	W	105
	OUTERWEAR/COATS & JACKETS	M	195
	OUTERWEAR/COATS & JACKETS	C	260
	SWIMWEAR & BEACHWEAR	W	148
	SWIMWEAR & BEACHWEAR	M	218
FRENCH CONNECTION	BELTS	A	284
	CONTEMPORARY SPORTSWEAR	W	36
	CONTEMPORARY SPORTSWEAR	M	178
	HOSIERY/SOCKS/LEGWEAR	A	337
	JEANS & DENIMWEAR	W	78
	JEANS & DENIMWEAR	M	187
	OUTERWEAR/COATS & JACKETS	W	105
FRENCH TOAST	ACTIVE/ATHLETICWEAR	C	235
	CHILDREN	A	291
	COORDINATED SPORTSWEAR-BOYS	C	238
	COORDINATED SPORTSWEAR-GIRLS	C	241
	JEANS & DENIMWEAR	C	251
	LICENSED APPAREL	C	253
	OUTERWEAR/COATS & JACKETS	C	260
	PRIVATE LABEL	C	263
	SWIMWEAR & BEACHWEAR	C	275
	UNIFORMS	C	281
FRUIT OF THE LOOM	ACTIVE/ATHLETICWEAR	W	4
	ACTIVE/ATHLETICWEAR	M	165
G-III APPAREL GROUP	LIFESTYLE COLLECTIONS	W	92
	OUTERWEAR/COATS & JACKETS	M	195

Company	Category		Page
	SWIMWEAR & BEACHWEAR	W	148
GAIAM	CONTEMPORARY SPORTSWEAR	W	36
	ECOLOGICAL & ORGANIC	W	66
	SLEEPWEAR & LOUNGEWEAR	W	118
GARDEN KIDS	ECOLOGICAL & ORGANIC	C	249
GELMART INDUSTRIES INC.	INTIMATE APPAREL & LINGERIE	W	73
GEM DANDY INC.	BELTS	A	285
GENE EWING BIS	HOSIERY/SOCKS/LEGWEAR	A	338
	MISSY/UPDATED SPORTSWEAR	W	97
GERTEX HOSIERY INC.	HOSIERY/SOCKS/LEGWEAR	A	338
GILTON COMPANY	BELTS	A	285
	FASHION JEWELRY & WATCHES	A	299
	GIFT ITEMS	A	307
	GLOVES	A	311
	LUGGAGE/BAGS/LEATHER GOODS	A	342
	MEN'S TIES & NECKWEAR	A	346
	UMBRELLAS	A	358
GLOBAL BRANDS GROUP	LICENSED APPAREL	W	89
	LICENSED APPAREL	M	192
GOLF APPAREL BRANDS	BLOUSES/SHIRTS/TOPS	W	13
	HATS/CAPS/MILLINERY	A	328
	OUTERWEAR/COATS & JACKETS	W	106
	OUTERWEAR/COATS & JACKETS	M	196
	SHIRTS: DRESS & SPORT	M	204
	SHIRTS: DRESS & SPORT	C	267
	SWEATERS & KNITWEAR	W	140
	SWEATERS	M	216
GOODWEAR USA	ECOLOGICAL & ORGANIC	W	66
	ECOLOGICAL & ORGANIC	M	183
	ECOLOGICAL & ORGANIC	C	249
	SLEEPWEAR & UNDERWEAR	M	208
	TEE SHIRTS & BLANKS	W	153
	TEE SHIRTS & BLANKS	M	222
	TEE SHIRTS & BLANKS	C	277
GRANITE KNITWEAR/CAL CRU CO., INC.	CASUAL SPORTSWEAR	W	25
	CASUAL SPORTSWEAR	M	173
GRAPHICS GROUP LTD./DBA LATITUDES	ACTIVE/ATHLETICWEAR	C	235
	TEE SHIRTS & BLANKS	W	153
	TEE SHIRTS & BLANKS	M	222
GREEN DRAGON	ECOLOGICAL & ORGANIC	W	66
GRUVEN INTERNATIONAL INC.	PRIVATE LABEL	W	113

Company	Category	Section	Page
	PRIVATE LABEL	M	200
GUESS, INC.	CONTEMPORARY SPORTSWEAR	M	178
	COORDINATED SPORTSWEAR-BOYS	C	238
	COORDINATED SPORTSWEAR-GIRLS	C	242
	JUNIOR SPORTSWEAR	W	82
H.M.S. PRODUCTIONS	CONTEMPORARY SPORTSWEAR	W	37
	DRESSES/SEPARATES/SUITS	W	59
	SWEATERS & KNITWEAR	W	140
HAGGAR CLOTHING CO., INC.	CASUAL SPORTSWEAR	M	173
	SUITS & SPORTCOATS	M	213
HARBOUR INTERNATIONAL LLC	OUTERWEAR/COATS & JACKETS	W	106
	OUTERWEAR/COATS & JACKETS	M	196
HAROLD TEPPER STRIBBONS INC.	BRIDAL/SPECIAL/INTIMATE	A	289
	LUGGAGE/BAGS/LEATHER GOODS	A	342
HART SCHAFFNER MARX	PRIVATE LABEL	M	200
	SUITS & SPORTCOATS	M	213
	TROUSERS & SLACKS	M	225
HASELSON INT'L TRADING INC.	CASUAL SPORTSWEAR	M	174
	JEANS & DENIMWEAR	M	187
	LICENSED APPAREL	M	192
	OUTERWEAR/COATS & JACKETS	M	196
	SHIRTS: DRESS & SPORT	M	205
	SWEATERS	M	216
	UNIFORMS	M	228
HATCO, INC./ RESISTOL HATS	HATS/CAPS/MILLINERY	A	329
HAVENGIRL	DRESSES	C	245
HEADWEAR CREATIONS, INC.	HATS/CAPS/MILLINERY	A	329
HEISEL	CONTEMPORARY SPORTSWEAR	W	37
HENRY AND BELLE	JEANS & DENIMWEAR	W	79
HENSCHEL HAT CO.	HATS/CAPS/MILLINERY	A	329
HILO HATTIE	CASUAL SPORTSWEAR	W	25
	CASUAL SPORTSWEAR	M	174
	TEE SHIRTS & BLANKS	C	278
HOLD-UP SUSPENDER CO.	BELTS	A	285
HOLLOWAY SPORTSWEAR, INC.	ACTIVE/ATHLETICWEAR	W	5
	ACTIVE/ATHLETICWEAR	M	165
	ACTIVE/ATHLETICWEAR	C	236
HOT KNOTS	SWEATERS & KNITWEAR	W	141
HTT HEADWEAR LTD.	BLOUSES/SHIRTS/TOPS	W	13
	HATS/CAPS/MILLINERY	A	330
	SHIRTS: DRESS & SPORT	M	205

Company	Category	Section	Page
HUGO BOSS U.S.A., INC.	DESIGNER COLLECTIONS	W	51
	DESIGNER COLLECTIONS	M	181
	EYEWEAR	A	296
	SUITS & SPORTCOATS	M	214
HYBRID APPAREL	ACTIVE/ATHLETICWEAR	M	165
	LICENSED APPAREL	W	90
	LICENSED APPAREL	M	192
	LICENSED APPAREL	C	253
HYP HATS LTD.	CHILDREN	A	292
	HATS/CAPS/MILLINERY	A	330
	SLEEPWEAR & UNDERWEAR	C	269
HYPERCLASH	ECOLOGICAL & ORGANIC	W	66
	JUNIOR SPORTSWEAR	W	83
IAPPAREL LLC	OUTERWEAR/COATS & JACKETS	C	260
IMPERIAL HEADWEAR	HATS/CAPS/MILLINERY	A	330
IN STYLE USA, INC.	PRIVATE LABEL	W	113
	PRIVATE LABEL	M	200
	PRIVATE LABEL	C	264
	UNIFORMS	W	158
IN.STYLE EXCHANGE™	PRIVATE LABEL	W	113
	PRIVATE LABEL	M	201
	PRIVATE LABEL	C	264
INDIGENOUS	ECOLOGICAL & ORGANIC	W	67
	ECOLOGICAL & ORGANIC	M	183
INGE CHRISTOPHER	HANDBAGS	A	320
INNERWEAR BRANDS INTERNATIONAL	SLEEPWEAR & UNDERWEAR	M	208
INSERCH BY MERC USA, INC.	CONTEMPORARY SPORTSWEAR	M	178
	DESIGNER COLLECTIONS	M	181
ISACO INTERNATIONAL/PAPI INC.	SLEEPWEAR & UNDERWEAR	M	209
J RICHARDS INTERNATIONAL	OUTERWEAR/COATS & JACKETS	W	106
	SPECIAL SIZES/LARGE	W	123
J. CREW	CASUAL SPORTSWEAR	M	174
	LIFESTYLE COLLECTIONS	W	92
J.D. FINE	CONTEMPORARY SPORTSWEAR	W	37
	DRESSES/SEPARATES/SUITS	W	59
J.P. OURSE CIE/JOHN COLE COLLECTION	HANDBAGS	A	321
	LUGGAGE/BAGS/LEATHER GOODS	A	342
JANTZEN	SWIMWEAR & BEACHWEAR	W	148
JBD NEW YORK	LIFESTYLE COLLECTIONS	W	92
JILL HENNING FINERIES	HATS/CAPS/MILLINERY	A	330
JLM COUTURE	BRIDAL & EVENINGWEAR	W	19

Company	Category	Section	Page
JOAN BLACKSHEAR DESIGN COMPANY	GIFT ITEMS	A	308
JOCKEY INTERNATIONAL, INC.	INTIMATE APPAREL & LINGERIE	W	73
	SLEEPWEAR & UNDERWEAR	M	209
JOE BLOW T'S	TEE SHIRTS & BLANKS	W	154
	TEE SHIRTS & BLANKS	M	222
	TEE SHIRTS & BLANKS	C	278
JOLI JEWELRY	FASHION JEWELRY & WATCHES	A	300
	GIFT ITEMS	A	308
	HAIR ORNAMENTS	A	313
JONDEN MANUFACTURING CO., INC.	JUNIOR SPORTSWEAR	W	83
	MISSY/UPDATED SPORTSWEAR	W	97
	SPECIAL SIZES/LARGE	W	123
	SPECIAL SIZES/MATERNITY	W	129
	SPECIAL SIZES/PETITE	W	133
JONES APPAREL GROUP USA, INC	MISSY/UPDATED SPORTSWEAR	W	97
JOU JOU DESIGNS	JEANS & DENIMWEAR	W	79
	JUNIOR SPORTSWEAR	W	83
	OUTERWEAR/COATS & JACKETS	W	106
JOY ACCESSORIES	FASHION JEWELRY & WATCHES	A	300
	HANDBAGS	A	321
	SCARVES & SHAWLS	A	351
JOYOUS AND FREE	LIFESTYLE COLLECTIONS	W	93
JULIE HUTTON INC.	PRIVATE LABEL	W	113
JUSSARA LEE	BRIDAL & EVENINGWEAR	W	19
	CONTEMPORARY SPORTSWEAR	W	37
JUST WHITE SHIRTS	MEN'S TIES & NECKWEAR	A	346
	SHIRTS: DRESS & SPORT	M	205
K & P WEAVER, LLC	ACTIVE/ATHLETICWEAR	W	5
	UNIFORMS	W	158
	UNIFORMS	M	228
KAHN LUCAS	COORDINATED SPORTSWEAR-GIRLS	C	242
	DRESSES	C	246
	LICENSED APPAREL	C	254
	NEWBORN/LAYETTE/INFANT	C	256
KAMTEX FASHION	TEE SHIRTS & BLANKS	W	154
	TEE SHIRTS & BLANKS	M	222
KATE SPADE AND COMPANY	CASUAL SPORTSWEAR	M	174
	LIFESTYLE COLLECTIONS	W	93
	LUGGAGE/BAGS/LEATHER GOODS	A	342
	MISSY/UPDATED SPORTSWEAR	W	98
KEEPERS INTERNATIONAL	HOSIERY/SOCKS/LEGWEAR	A	338

Company	Category		Page
KELLWOOD COMPANY	BRIDAL & EVENINGWEAR	W	20
	CONTEMPORARY SPORTSWEAR	W	38
	JUNIOR SPORTSWEAR	W	83
KEMBALI LTD.	MISSY/UPDATED SPORTSWEAR	W	98
KIDCUTETURE	COORDINATED SPORTSWEAR-GIRLS	C	242
	DRESSES	C	246
KIPPYS	BELTS	A	286
	DECORATED/EMBELLISHED APPAREL	W	44
	LEATHER & SUEDE	W	87
KOUROSH NEW YORK	SWEATERS & KNITWEAR	W	141
L&J ACCESSORIES/CELLINI LLC	FASHION JEWELRY & WATCHES	A	300
LA MATERA	BELTS	A	286
LANDAU	UNIFORMS	W	158
	UNIFORMS	M	228
LARR BRIO ACCESSORIES	MEN'S TIES & NECKWEAR	A	346
LATICO LEATHERS	HANDBAGS	A	321
	LUGGAGE/BAGS/LEATHER GOODS	A	343
LE MIEUX/TARA INTERNATIONAL, INC.	MISSY/UPDATED SPORTSWEAR	W	98
	SPECIAL SIZES/LARGE	W	124
	SPECIAL SIZES/PETITE	W	133
LEATHEROCK INT. INC.	BELTS	A	286
	HANDBAGS	A	321
LEAWOOD APPAREL LLC.	PRIVATE LABEL	W	114
	PRIVATE LABEL	M	201
	PRIVATE LABEL	C	264
LEG RESOURCE INC	HOSIERY/SOCKS/LEGWEAR	A	339
LEMUR GROUP, INC.	COORDINATED SPORTSWEAR-BOYS	C	238
	COORDINATED SPORTSWEAR-GIRLS	C	243
	SLEEPWEAR & UNDERWEAR	C	269
LEVI STRAUSS & CO.	JEANS & DENIMWEAR	W	79
	JEANS & DENIMWEAR	M	187
	WESTERNWEAR	M	231
LIANA UNIFORM	UNIFORMS	W	158
	UNIFORMS	M	228
LIANCARLO	BRIDAL & EVENINGWEAR	W	20
LIFE & STYLE FASHIONS INC.	CASUAL SPORTSWEAR	W	26
LILLIAN ROSE, INC.	BRIDAL/SPECIAL/INTIMATE	A	289
LIN MANUFACTURING & DESIGN	CHILDREN	A	292
	HOSIERY/SOCKS/LEGWEAR	A	339
LINDA RICHARDS	OUTERWEAR/COATS & JACKETS	W	107
	SCARVES & SHAWLS	A	352

Company	Category		Page
LIPSTIK GIRLS	COORDINATED SPORTSWEAR-GIRLS	C	243
	JEANS & DENIMWEAR	C	251
	NEWBORN/LAYETTE/INFANT	C	256
LITTLE MISS JULIA	HAIR ORNAMENTS	A	313
LONG STREET	COORDINATED SPORTSWEAR-BOYS	C	239
	COORDINATED SPORTSWEAR-GIRLS	C	243
	OUTERWEAR/COATS & JACKETS	C	261
	UNIFORMS	C	281
LONGITUDE/LONGEVITY BRANDS LLC	SPECIAL SIZES/LARGE	W	124
	SWIMWEAR & BEACHWEAR	W	148
LORREN BELL, INC.	FASHION JEWELRY & WATCHES	A	301
	HAIR ORNAMENTS	A	314
	HANDBAGS	A	322
LULI FAMA	SWIMWEAR & BEACHWEAR	W	149
LUSCIOUS LACES LINGERIE	BRIDAL/SPECIAL/INTIMATE	A	290
MADEMOISELLE, INC.	GLOVES	A	311
	HANDBAGS	A	322
	HATS/CAPS/MILLINERY	A	331
	SCARVES & SHAWLS	A	352
MANN & BROS INC/IMPERIAL	SCARVES & SHAWLS	A	352
MANSFIELD INTERNATIONAL	SLEEPWEAR & LOUNGEWEAR	W	118
MAR CHIQUITA SWIMWEAR INC.	SWIMWEAR & BEACHWEAR	W	149
	SWIMWEAR & BEACHWEAR	C	275
MARC BOUWER	BRIDAL & EVENINGWEAR	W	20
	DRESSES/SEPARATES/SUITS	W	60
MARMOT MOUNTAIN LLC.	GLOVES	A	311
	OUTERWEAR/COATS & JACKETS	W	107
	OUTERWEAR/COATS & JACKETS	M	196
	OUTERWEAR/COATS & JACKETS	C	261
MARTIN DINGMAN COUNTRYWEAR	BELTS	A	286
	GLOVES	A	311
	LUGGAGE/BAGS/LEATHER GOODS	A	343
	OUTERWEAR/COATS & JACKETS	M	197
MASCOT WORKWEAR U.S./REPCON NW	UNIFORMS	W	159
	UNIFORMS	M	229
MEGA BELTS, INC.	BELTS	A	287
MEHERA SHAW TEXTILES PVT. LTD.	ECOLOGICAL & ORGANIC	W	67
MELANIE HARRIS	DESIGNER COLLECTIONS	W	51
MIAMI STYLE INC.	PRIVATE LABEL	W	114
	PRIVATE LABEL	M	201
	PRIVATE LABEL	C	264

Company	Category		Page
MICHAEL KORS	DESIGNER COLLECTIONS	W	52
MIL-IDEE, INC.	BELTS	A	287
MILKBARN, LLC	NEWBORN/LAYETTE/INFANT	C	256
MISOOK	DRESSES/SEPARATES/SUITS	W	60
MISTER NOAH	ACTIVE/ATHLETICWEAR	W	5
	JUNIOR SPORTSWEAR	W	84
	PRIVATE LABEL	W	114
MMG DIV OF GREAT CHINA EMPIRE	MEN'S TIES & NECKWEAR	A	346
MODODOC/GENEXUS INTERNATIONAL	CASUAL SPORTSWEAR	W	26
	CASUAL SPORTSWEAR	M	174
MONTANACO CLOTHING COMPANY	LEATHER & SUEDE	W	87
	LEATHER & SUEDE	M	189
MOOSE CREEK	CASUAL SPORTSWEAR	W	26
	CASUAL SPORTSWEAR	M	175
MOTHER PLUCKER FEATHER COMPANY	BRIDAL/SPECIAL/INTIMATE	A	290
MOTIONWEAR, LLC	ACTIVE/ATHLETICWEAR	W	6
	ACTIVE/ATHLETICWEAR	C	236
MT SHOWROOM	CONTEMPORARY SPORTSWEAR	M	179
	LIFESTYLE COLLECTIONS	W	93
	OUTERWEAR/COATS & JACKETS	W	107
NATORI CO.	INTIMATE APPAREL & LINGERIE	W	73
NEW ICM, LP	COORDINATED SPORTSWEAR-GIRLS	C	243
	DRESSES	C	246
	NEWBORN/LAYETTE/INFANT	C	257
	SLEEPWEAR & UNDERWEAR	C	270
NEW ORLEANS KNITWEAR	CASUAL SPORTSWEAR	W	26
	SWEATERS & KNITWEAR	W	141
NIC + ZOE	LIFESTYLE COLLECTIONS	W	93
	SWEATERS & KNITWEAR	W	142
NICOLE & CO.	GIFT ITEMS	A	308
	HAIR ORNAMENTS	A	314
	HATS/CAPS/MILLINERY	A	331
	SCARVES & SHAWLS	A	353
NIKE, INC.	ACTIVE/ATHLETICWEAR	W	6
	ACTIVE/ATHLETICWEAR	M	165
NORMA KAMALI	DESIGNER COLLECTIONS	W	52
NOTANONYMOUS	BELTS	A	287
	BRIDAL/SPECIAL/INTIMATE	A	290
	FASHION JEWELRY & WATCHES	A	301
	HANDBAGS	A	322
NUTHATCH	CONTEMPORARY SPORTSWEAR	W	38

Company	Category		Page
ODETT ENTERPRISES	DRESSES/SEPARATES/SUITS	W	60
	MISSY/UPDATED SPORTSWEAR	W	98
	OUTERWEAR/COATS & JACKETS	W	108
	SCARVES & SHAWLS	A	353
	SWEATERS & KNITWEAR	W	142
ONLY HEARTS	BLOUSES/SHIRTS/TOPS	W	13
	DRESSES/SEPARATES/SUITS	W	61
	INTIMATE APPAREL & LINGERIE	W	74
OSHKOSH B'GOSH/CARTER'S	COORDINATED SPORTSWEAR-BOYS	C	239
	COORDINATED SPORTSWEAR-GIRLS	C	244
	JEANS & DENIMWEAR	C	252
	NEWBORN/LAYETTE/INFANT	C	257
OUTERSTUFF LTD.	OUTERWEAR/COATS & JACKETS	C	261
OXFORD GOLF	CONTEMPORARY SPORTSWEAR	W	38
	CONTEMPORARY SPORTSWEAR	M	179
OZONE DESIGN INC.	HOSIERY/SOCKS/LEGWEAR	A	339
PACIFIC SPORTSWEAR & EMBLEM	HATS/CAPS/MILLINERY	A	331
PARASUCO JEANS INC.	CONTEMPORARY SPORTSWEAR	W	38
	JEANS & DENIMWEAR	W	80
	JEANS & DENIMWEAR	M	187
PARISA	INTIMATE APPAREL & LINGERIE	W	74
PEERLESS CLOTHING INTERNATIONAL	SUITS & SPORTCOATS	M	214
	TROUSERS & SLACKS	M	225
PENDLETON WOOLEN MILLS, INC.	OUTERWEAR/COATS & JACKETS	W	108
	OUTERWEAR/COATS & JACKETS	M	197
	SPECIAL SIZES/LARGE	W	124
	WESTERNWEAR	M	231
PERSNICKETY	DRESSES	C	246
PERSONAL TOUCH INC.	CASUAL SPORTSWEAR	W	27
	SPECIAL SIZES/LARGE	W	124
PHOOL FASHIONS	CONTEMPORARY SPORTSWEAR	W	39
	DRESSES/SEPARATES/SUITS	W	61
	SLEEPWEAR & LOUNGEWEAR	W	118
PILLAGED VILLAGE, THE	FASHION JEWELRY & WATCHES	A	301
	SCARVES & SHAWLS	A	353
	TEE SHIRTS & BLANKS	W	154
	TEE SHIRTS & BLANKS	M	223
PIMLICO PERFORMANCE APPAREL LTD.	JEANS & DENIMWEAR	W	80
	JEANS & DENIMWEAR	M	188
	LIFESTYLE COLLECTIONS	W	94
PINK CHICKEN	DRESSES	C	247

Company	Category		Page
	NEWBORN/LAYETTE/INFANT	C	257
	SWIMWEAR & BEACHWEAR	C	276
PRIORITY MANUFACTURING	UNIFORMS	W	159
	UNIFORMS	M	229
PROJECT NO. 8	CASUAL SPORTSWEAR	M	175
	CONTEMPORARY SPORTSWEAR	M	179
PUR CASHMERE	SCARVES & SHAWLS	A	353
PVH CORPORATION	LIFESTYLE COLLECTIONS	W	94
QUEENSBORO SHIRT COMPANY	SHIRTS: DRESS & SPORT	M	206
RAFFI LINEA UOMO	SWEATERS & KNITWEAR	W	142
	SWEATERS	M	216
RAGO FOUNDATIONS LLC	INTIMATE APPAREL & LINGERIE	W	74
	SPECIAL SIZES/LARGE	W	125
RAJ IMPORTS	SCARVES & SHAWLS	A	354
RALPH LAUREN, INC.	DESIGNER COLLECTIONS	W	52
	DESIGNER COLLECTIONS	M	182
RASHTI & RASHTI/H.J. RASHTI & CO., INC.	NEWBORN/LAYETTE/INFANT	C	258
REBECCA TAYLOR	DRESSES/SEPARATES/SUITS	W	61
REDWOOD COURT BY SILK BOX	BLOUSES/SHIRTS/TOPS	W	13
	DRESSES/SEPARATES/SUITS	W	61
	SCARVES & SHAWLS	A	354
REPCON NW DBA THE MODERN WORKER	UNIFORMS	M	229
RHINESTONE JEWELRY CORPORATION	FASHION JEWELRY & WATCHES	A	301
	HAIR ORNAMENTS	A	314
RICH HONEY	TEE SHIRTS & BLANKS	W	154
	TEE SHIRTS & BLANKS	M	223
RICHARD LEEDS INTERNATIONAL	SLEEPWEAR & LOUNGEWEAR	W	119
RIFLE/KAYNEE	UNIFORMS	C	281
ROBBIE BEE	DRESSES/SEPARATES/SUITS	W	62
	SPECIAL SIZES/LARGE	W	125
ROBIN ASCHER	SCARVES & SHAWLS	A	354
ROCKSTAR	JEANS & DENIMWEAR	W	80
	JEANS & DENIMWEAR	M	188
RODEL U.S.A. INC.	DESIGNER COLLECTIONS	W	53
	OUTERWEAR/COATS & JACKETS	W	108
RON CORNELL	MEN'S TIES & NECKWEAR	A	347
ROSE TAFT	BRIDAL & EVENINGWEAR	W	20
	DESIGNER COLLECTIONS	W	53
ROWDY SPROUT	TEE SHIRTS & BLANKS	C	278
ROYAL APPAREL, INC.	ACTIVE/ATHLETICWEAR	W	6
	ACTIVE/ATHLETICWEAR	M	166

Company	Category		Page
	ACTIVE/ATHLETICWEAR	C	236
	BIG & TALL	M	170
	ECOLOGICAL & ORGANIC	W	67
	ECOLOGICAL & ORGANIC	M	184
	ECOLOGICAL & ORGANIC	C	250
	JUNIOR SPORTSWEAR	W	84
	PRIVATE LABEL	W	114
	PRIVATE LABEL	M	201
	PRIVATE LABEL	C	265
	SPECIAL SIZES/LARGE	W	125
	TEE SHIRTS & BLANKS	W	155
	TEE SHIRTS & BLANKS	M	223
	TEE SHIRTS & BLANKS	C	278
ROYALE LINENS INC.	GIFT ITEMS	A	308
RUM REGGAE	SHIRTS: DRESS & SPORT	M	206
SAFILO U.S.A.	EYEWEAR	A	296
SARA MIQUE	BRIDAL & EVENINGWEAR	W	21
SCENT-LOK/DIV. OF A.L.S. ENTERPRISES	SPORTSMEN'S APPAREL	M	211
SCOTTEX GLOBAL SOURCING, LLC	SWEATERS & KNITWEAR	W	142
SCREAMER HATS	HATS/CAPS/MILLINERY	A	331
SCULLY	CONTEMPORARY SPORTSWEAR	W	39
	LEATHER & SUEDE	W	87
	LEATHER & SUEDE	M	189
	LUGGAGE/BAGS/LEATHER GOODS	A	343
SENTIMENTAL INC.	BRIDAL & EVENINGWEAR	W	21
	CONTEMPORARY SPORTSWEAR	W	39
	DRESSES/SEPARATES/SUITS	W	62
SHAUNE BAZNER ACCESSORIES, INC.	FASHION JEWELRY & WATCHES	A	302
	HAIR ORNAMENTS	A	314
SHEDRAIN CORP.	OUTERWEAR/COATS & JACKETS	W	108
	UMBRELLAS	A	358
SHEEPSKIN BY SUSAN BRADFORD	HATS/CAPS/MILLINERY	A	332
	OUTERWEAR/COATS & JACKETS	W	109
SHOWROOM SEVEN/ERICKSON BEAMON	CONTEMPORARY SPORTSWEAR	W	40
	DESIGNER COLLECTIONS	W	53
	FASHION JEWELRY & WATCHES	A	302
	HANDBAGS	A	323
	SCARVES & SHAWLS	A	354
SILVER SUIT, INC.	SUITS/SPECIAL OCCASION	C	271
SIMON SHOWROOM	CONTEMPORARY SPORTSWEAR	W	40
	JUNIOR SPORTSWEAR	W	84

Company	Category		Page
SISTERS/DIVISION OF FREDINI INC	PRIVATE LABEL	W	115
	SWEATERS & KNITWEAR	W	143
SLICK DESIGNS	TEE SHIRTS & BLANKS	W	155
	TEE SHIRTS & BLANKS	M	223
SMARTWORKS INC.	SCARVES & SHAWLS	A	355
SOPHIE FINZI LTD DBA PASHOOT	CONTEMPORARY SPORTSWEAR	W	40
	SPECIAL SIZES/LARGE	W	126
	SWEATERS & KNITWEAR	W	143
SOSSY BAGHDOIAN	BRIDAL & EVENINGWEAR	W	21
SOXLAND INTERNATIONAL, INC.	HOSIERY/SOCKS/LEGWEAR	A	339
SPORTHILL, INC.	ACTIVE/ATHLETICWEAR	W	6
	ACTIVE/ATHLETICWEAR	M	166
SQUASHT BOUTIQUE	HATS/CAPS/MILLINERY	A	332
SQUASHT BY LES	BLOUSES/SHIRTS/TOPS	W	14
ST. JOHN	DESIGNER COLLECTIONS	W	53
	JEANS & DENIMWEAR	W	80
STANFIELD'S	ACTIVE/ATHLETICWEAR	W	7
	INTIMATE APPAREL & LINGERIE	W	74
	SPECIAL SIZES/LARGE	W	126
STEEL PONY	DECORATED/EMBELLISHED APPAREL	W	44
STREETS AHEAD	BELTS	A	288
	HANDBAGS	A	323
STYLE SOURCE INC.	ECOLOGICAL & ORGANIC	W	67
	PRIVATE LABEL	W	115
	PRIVATE LABEL	M	202
	PRIVATE LABEL	C	265
STYLEX TEXTILE DBA FABKA FABRICS	PRIVATE LABEL	W	115
	PRIVATE LABEL	M	202
SUGAR AND BRUNO	HOSIERY/SOCKS/LEGWEAR	A	340
	TEE SHIRTS & BLANKS	W	155
	TEE SHIRTS & BLANKS	M	224
	TEE SHIRTS & BLANKS	C	279
SURVIVAL INC.	JUNIOR SPORTSWEAR	W	85
SUSAN DUNN INC.	BRIDAL/SPECIAL/INTIMATE	A	290
	CHILDREN	A	292
	HANDBAGS	A	323
	SLEEPWEAR & UNDERWEAR	M	209
	SLEEPWEAR & LOUNGEWEAR	W	119
SUSAN ELIAS	BRIDAL & EVENINGWEAR	W	21
	CONTEMPORARY SPORTSWEAR	W	40
	DESIGNER COLLECTIONS	W	54

Company	Category	Section	Page
	DRESSES/SEPARATES/SUITS	W	62
SUSAN GREENSTADT & ASSOC.	MISSY/UPDATED SPORTSWEAR	W	99
	SWEATERS & KNITWEAR	W	143
SUSAN PILLAY	NEWBORN/LAYETTE/INFANT	C	258
SWEATER BRAND INC.	SWEATERS & KNITWEAR	W	143
SWEENIE MANUFACTURING	ACTIVE/ATHLETICWEAR	W	7
	SWIMWEAR & BEACHWEAR	W	149
	SWIMWEAR & BEACHWEAR	M	218
	SWIMWEAR & BEACHWEAR	C	276
SWIFT ORIGINALS	DRESSES/SEPARATES/SUITS	W	62
	SHIRTS: DRESS & SPORT	M	206
TAILOR VINTAGE	CONTEMPORARY SPORTSWEAR	W	41
	CONTEMPORARY SPORTSWEAR	M	179
TAKEATOTE LLC	HANDBAGS	A	323
TASHA POLIZZI	BLOUSES/SHIRTS/TOPS	W	14
	CONTEMPORARY SPORTSWEAR	W	41
	LEATHER & SUEDE	W	88
	OUTERWEAR/COATS & JACKETS	W	109
TAYLOR MADE	SPORTSMEN'S APPAREL	M	212
TERI JON	BRIDAL & EVENINGWEAR	W	22
	DESIGNER COLLECTIONS	W	54
	SPECIAL SIZES/LARGE	W	126
THEA HAUTE COUTURE	DRESSES	C	247
	INTIMATE APPAREL & LINGERIE	W	75
	NEWBORN/LAYETTE/INFANT	C	258
TIC TAC TOE/BABY LEGS	CHILDREN	A	293
TOKYO BAY INC.	FASHION JEWELRY & WATCHES	A	302
TOM AND LINDA PLATT	DESIGNER COLLECTIONS	W	54
	DRESSES/SEPARATES/SUITS	W	63
	SPECIAL SIZES/LARGE	W	126
TONY LAMA COMPANY, INC.	WESTERNWEAR	M	231
TOPSON DOWNS	ACTIVE/ATHLETICWEAR	M	166
	CONTEMPORARY SPORTSWEAR	W	41
	JUNIOR SPORTSWEAR	W	85
TOTAL FOOT COMFORT	HOSIERY/SOCKS/LEGWEAR	A	340
TRACYWATTS INC.	HATS/CAPS/MILLINERY	A	332
TRAMP	CONTEMPORARY SPORTSWEAR	W	41
TRENDSET ORIGINALS	COORDINATED SPORTSWEAR-GIRLS	C	244
	JUNIOR SPORTSWEAR	W	85
	OUTERWEAR/COATS & JACKETS	W	109
	OUTERWEAR/COATS & JACKETS	C	262

Company	Category		Page
	SWEATERS & KNITWEAR	W	144
TRIPP NYC	JUNIOR SPORTSWEAR	W	85
TUSK LTD.	HANDBAGS	A	324
	LUGGAGE/BAGS/LEATHER GOODS	A	343
UNIONBAY/SEATTLE PACIFIC	CASUAL SPORTSWEAR	M	175
	JUNIOR SPORTSWEAR	W	86
VALENTINE USA	PRIVATE LABEL	W	116
	SPECIAL SIZES/LARGE	W	127
VENUS FASHION	CASUAL SPORTSWEAR	W	27
	DRESSES/SEPARATES/SUITS	W	63
	SLEEPWEAR & LOUNGEWEAR	W	119
	SWIMWEAR & BEACHWEAR	W	150
VESTS DIRECT	UNIFORMS	W	159
VICTOR ROSSI	PRIVATE LABEL	W	116
	PRIVATE LABEL	M	202
	PRIVATE LABEL	C	265
VIESTE-ROSA	FASHION JEWELRY & WATCHES	A	302
	HAIR ORNAMENTS	A	315
VISHAL ENTERPRISES	PRIVATE LABEL	W	116
	PRIVATE LABEL	M	202
	PRIVATE LABEL	C	266
VISMAYA	SCARVES & SHAWLS	A	355
VIVIANA UCHITEL	DRESSES/SEPARATES/SUITS	W	63
	SWEATERS & KNITWEAR	W	144
WAI-CHING	DECORATED/EMBELLISHED APPAREL	W	45
	HANDBAGS	A	324
WAITEX INTERNATIONAL	ACTIVE/ATHLETICWEAR	M	167
	BIG & TALL	M	170
	CASUAL SPORTSWEAR	M	175
WASATCH CO.	ACTIVE/ATHLETICWEAR	W	7
	ACTIVE/ATHLETICWEAR	M	167
	NEWBORN/LAYETTE/INFANT	C	258
	OUTERWEAR/COATS & JACKETS	M	197
WE BE BOP, INC	SPECIAL SIZES/LARGE	W	127
WEARABLE INTEGRITY/BARBARA LESSER	CASUAL SPORTSWEAR	W	27
	MISSY/UPDATED SPORTSWEAR	W	99
WEDDING TROPICS	BRIDAL & EVENINGWEAR	W	22
	DESIGNER COLLECTIONS	M	182
	SHIRTS: DRESS & SPORT	C	268
WHITE SIERRA	ACTIVE/ATHLETICWEAR	W	7
	ACTIVE/ATHLETICWEAR	M	167

Company	Category	Code	Page
	OUTERWEAR/COATS & JACKETS	W	109
	OUTERWEAR/COATS & JACKETS	M	197
	OUTERWEAR/COATS & JACKETS	C	262
WHITTALL & SHON	HATS/CAPS/MILLINERY	A	333
WILL LEATHER GOODS	BELTS	A	288
WILLIAMSON-DICKIE MFG CO.	CASUAL SPORTSWEAR	W	28
	UNIFORMS	W	159
	UNIFORMS	M	230
	UNIFORMS	C	282
WOODEN SHIPS	GLOVES	A	312
	HATS/CAPS/MILLINERY	A	333
	SCARVES & SHAWLS	A	355
	SWEATERS & KNITWEAR	W	144
XOXO	CONTEMPORARY SPORTSWEAR	W	42
YOCHI DESIGNS	FASHION JEWELRY & WATCHES	A	303
YON DESIGN, INC.	CONTEMPORARY SPORTSWEAR	W	42
ZANETTI INC.	CONTEMPORARY SPORTSWEAR	M	180
	SHIRTS: DRESS & SPORT	M	206
	SUITS & SPORTCOATS	M	214
	SWEATERS	M	216
ZELDA	DRESSES/SEPARATES/SUITS	W	64
	MISSY/UPDATED SPORTSWEAR	W	99

JOY ACCESSORIES	100 542
VICTOR ROSSI	102 005
BOULEVARD APPAREL	111 159
WEDDING TROPICS	117 573
FAIR HEMP INC.	122 157
SENTIMENTAL INC.	124 825
SUGAR AND BRUNO	127 789
VISMAYA	127 802
JULIE HUTTON INC.	134 008432
NEW ICM, LP	184 43
BELASSE COLLECTION LLC	240 8904
LANDAU	334 89
ROYALE LINENS INC.	691 73
GOODWEAR USA	753 46
CALIFORNIA RAIN CO.	754 43
COTTON HERITAGE	758 13
5TH & OCEAN CLOTHING LLC/NEW ERA CAP CO.	949 89
J.D. FINE	978 84
DAVID SMITH & ASSOCIATES	RN #4-3420353
FRENCH TOAST	RN 13706
BABYFAIR, INC.	RN 15517
KAHN LUCAS	RN 16518
EVY OF CALIFORNIA, INC./DBA JALATE	RN 17657
MANN & BROS INC/IMPERIAL HANDKERCHIEFS	RN 18731
CHAMPION ATHLETICWEAR, INC.	RN 26094
RASHTI & RASHTI/H.J. RASHTI & CO., INC.	RN 27829
LINDA RICHARDS	RN 28278
PENDLETON WOOLEN MILLS, INC.	RN 29685
ALPHA INDUSTRIES, INC.	RN 35569
LEVI STRAUSS & CO.	RN 36665
OSHKOSH B'GOSH/CARTER'S	RN 37904
JANTZEN	RN 37966
BILL BLASS FASHIONS LLC	RN 38344
ANVIL KNITWEAR, INC.	RN 38619
OSHKOSH B'GOSH/CARTER'S	RN 40103
GRANITE KNITWEAR/CAL CRU CO., INC.	RN 41253
NORMA KAMALI	RN 47494
TRENDSET ORIGINALS	RN 48829
MISTER NOAH	RN 50110
FRENCH CONNECTION	RN 53372
MOOSE CREEK	RN 53623

CALVIN KLEIN, INC.	RN 54718
BADGER SPORTSWEAR	RN 55346
EURO JOY SPORTSWEAR CORP.	RN 57032
WHITE SIERRA	RN 58486
D'ACCORD SHIRTS & GUAYABERAS	RN 58706
BILL BLASS FASHIONS LLC	RN 59126
NIC + ZOE	RN 59351
ISACO INTERNATIONAL/PAPI INC.	RN 59495
ADRIANNA PAPELL LLC.	RN 59782
AIDAN MATTOX	RN 59782
BODY WRAPPERS	RN 60206
PERSONAL TOUCH INC.	RN 60666
JOCKEY INTERNATIONAL, INC.	RN 61683
DEPECHE MODE	RN 61812
VALENTINE USA	RN 64604
GILTON COMPANY	RN 64854
IAPPAREL LLC	RN 65470
LIPSTIK GIRLS	RN 65687
CASHMERE HOUSE	RN 68088
B.C.T.C.	RN 69587
COLUMBIA SPORTSWEAR CO., INC.	RN 69724
SWEATER BRAND INC.	RN 70204
AQUARIUS LTD.	RN 71327
IAPPAREL LLC	RN 72348
SOXLAND INTERNATIONAL, INC.	RN 74547
CYNTHIA ROWLEY	RN 75150
VALENTINE USA	RN 75182
COSABELLA	RN 77351
CYNTHIA STEFFE	RN 77456
LIFE & STYLE FASHIONS INC.	RN 77511
BETSEY JOHNSON	RN 77751
TRIPP NYC	RN 78061
EILEEN FISHER INC.	RN 78121
JBD NEW YORK	RN 80911
PHOOL FASHIONS	RN 80911
STYLE SOURCE INC.	RN 82034
ANNE KLEIN	RN 82060
JOAN BLACKSHEAR DESIGN COMPANY	RN 82071
GLOBAL BRANDS GROUP	RN 82457
FREE COUNTRY LTD.	RN 82608
CORAL HEAD INC./HAWAIIAN ISLAND CREATIONS	RN 83342

SISTERS/DIVISION OF FREDINI INC	RN 84332
LIN MANUFACTURING & DESIGN	RN 84364
A. CHE	RN 84980
PARISA	RN 84980
SILVER SUIT, INC.	RN 85030
BLUE HAWAII SALES	RN 85143
JONDEN MANUFACTURING CO., INC.	RN 85224
VALENTINE USA	RN 86643
ASPEN LICENSING INTERNATIONAL, INC.	RN 86959
B & B DESIGNS COLLECTION INC.	RN 87230
BARAMI/FASHION CONCEPTS/PATRIZIA LUCA	RN 87729
JUSSARA LEE	RN 89094
AVALIN LIMITED	RN 89128
BABY JAY INC./GROWING FEET INC.	RN 89576
DARIAN GROUP INC.	RN 89700
SUSAN DUNN INC.	RN 90990
BREAKING WAVES INTERNATIONAL	RN 91106
CAMBER SPORTSWEAR, INC.	RN 91210
BRAVADO MERCHANDISING	RN 91889
DESSY CREATIONS & AFTER SIX	RN 91947
BEXAR MANUFACTURING CO.	RN 92441
DAVID CAREY INC.	RN 93194
COTTON EMPORIUM, INC.	RN 93290
DAILY WEAR SPORTSWEAR/FOREVER YOUNG	RN 93450
DAMIANOU	RN 93780
EASTWEST CLOTHING	RN 94062
BARAMI/FASHION CONCEPTS/PATRIZIA LUCA	RN 94992
CALVIN CLOTHING COMPANY	RN 95393
AZIBI LTD.	RN 96314
OSHKOSH B'GOSH/CARTER'S	RN 96367
DOLORES PISCOTTA	RN 97327
2 X IST	RN 97404
LULI FAMA	RN 97850
H.M.S. PRODUCTIONS	RN 98108
ROBBIE BEE	RN 98582
TRAMP	RN 99610
DREAM WORLD INTERNATIONAL, INC.	RN 99612
ACTIVE APPAREL, INC.	RN 99928
EDWARD CROMARTY ART DESIGN STUDIO	RN 101294
INSERCH BY MERC USA, INC.	RN 101976
SCOTTEX GLOBAL SOURCING, LLC	RN 104958

EVY OF CALIFORNIA, INC./DBA JALATE	RN 106895
CARIBBEAN WRAPS INTERNATIONAL	RN 107432
CPT USA, LLC DBA COCKPIT USA	RN 114345
RON CORNELL	RN 148175
BALTIERRA SURFBOARDS & BALTI GIRL	SRE AA24-776411
LEVI STRAUSS & CO.	WPL 00423
PENDLETON WOOLEN MILLS, INC.	WPL 04378
F & M HAT CO., INC.	WPL 04384
GEM DANDY INC.	WPL 06141
HART SCHAFFNER MARX	WPL 06986
LONGITUDE/LONGEVITY BRANDS LLC	WPL 08910
CHATHAM KNITTING MILLS, INC.	WPL 10668
BURMA BIBAS	WPL 13185

"AT" Collection M-SUITS — DREAM WORLD INTERNATIONAL, page 213
10-Seconds® Shoe Laces A-HOSIERY/SOCKS/LEGWEAR — TOTAL FOOT COMFORT page 340
100 US Colleges M-OUTERWEAR/COATS & JACKETS — G-III APPAREL GROUP page 195
2 X ist M-SLEEPWEAR — 2 X IST page 207
2 X ist M-TEE — 2 X IST page 219
2nd Day W-CONTEMPORARY SPORTSWEAR — SHOWROOM SEVEN/ERICKSON page 40
360 Sports C-COORDINATED SPORTSWEAR-BOYS — LONG STREET page 239
4 Major Pro Sports Leagues M-OUTERWEAR/COATS & JACKETS — G-III APPAREL GROUP page 195
525 Homewear A-GIFT — 525 AMERICA page 305
525 Womens W-CONTEMPORARY SPORTSWEAR — 525 AMERICA page 29
525 Womens W-SWEATERS & KNITWEAR — 525 AMERICA page 135
7 for all mankind W-CASUAL — 7 FOR ALL MANKIND page 23
7 for all mankind W-JEANS — 7 FOR ALL MANKIND page 77
7 for all mankind M-CASUAL — 7 FOR ALL MANKIND page 172
7 for all mankind M-JEANS — 7 FOR ALL MANKIND page 185
A Pea in the Pod W-SPECIAL — A PEA IN THE POD page 129
A'nue Ligne W-BLOUSES/SHIRTS/TOPS — A'NUE LIGNE page 10
A. Che W-SWIMWEAR & BEACHWEAR — A. CHE page 145
A.L.S. Enterprises M-SPORTSMEN'S — SCENT-LOK/DIV. OF A.L.S. page 211
AAA Umbrella A-UMBRELLAS — AAA INNOVATIONS page 357
AAA™ W-TEE — ALSTYLE page 151
AAA™ M-TEE — ALSTYLE page 219
AAA™ C-TEE — ALSTYLE page 277
ABS by Allen Schwartz W-DESIGNER — ABS BY ALLEN SCHWARTZ page 47
ABS by Allen Schwartz W-DRESSES/SEPARATES/SUITS — ABS BY ALLEN SCHWARTZ page 55
ABS Collection W-DESIGNER — ABS BY ALLEN SCHWARTZ page 47
ABS Collection W-DRESSES/SEPARATES/SUITS — ABS BY ALLEN SCHWARTZ page 55
Accents by Isaco M-SLEEPWEAR — ISACO INTERNATIONAL/PAPI INC. page 209
Acorn A-GIFT — ACORN PRODUCTS page 305
Acorn A-HOSIERY/SOCKS/LEGWEAR — ACORN PRODUCTS page 335
Acquarius A-BELTS — AQUARIUS LTD. page 283
Active Edge W-ECOLOGICAL & ORGANIC — ACTIVE EDGE, THE/OLD CITY page 65
Active Edge M-ECOLOGICAL & ORGANIC — ACTIVE EDGE, THE/OLD CITY page 183
Active Edge C-ACTIVE/ATHLETICWEAR — ACTIVE EDGE, THE/OLD CITY page 233
Active Edge C-NEWBORN/LAYETTE/INFANT — ACTIVE EDGE, THE/OLD CITY page 255
Adagio W-INTIMATE APPAREL & LINGERIE — ARABESQUE DESIGN/PATRICIA page 69
Adea W-INTIMATE APPAREL & LINGERIE — ADEA page 69
Adidas W-ACTIVE/ATHLETICWEAR — ADIDAS AMERICA, INC. page 1
Adidas M-ACTIVE/ATHLETICWEAR — ADIDAS AMERICA, INC. page 162
Adidas C-OUTERWEAR/COATS & JACKETS — OUTERSTUFF LTD. page 261
Adrianna Papell W-DESIGNER — ADRIANNA PAPELL LLC. page 47
Adrienne Landau W-OUTERWEAR/COATS & JACKETS — ADRIENNE LANDAU page 101
Adrienne Landau A-SCARVES — ADRIENNE LANDAU page 349
Aero Tech Designs W-ACTIVE/ATHLETICWEAR — AERO TECH DESIGNS page 1
Aero Tech Designs M-ACTIVE/ATHLETICWEAR — AERO TECH DESIGNS page 162
Aero Tech Designs C-ACTIVE/ATHLETICWEAR — AERO TECH DESIGNS page 233
AG Jeans W-JEANS — ADRIANO GOLDSCHMIED page 77
AG Jeans M-JEANS — ADRIANO GOLDSCHMIED page 185
Aidan W-BRIDAL & EVENINGWEAR — AIDAN MATTOX page 15
Aidan W-DESIGNER — AIDAN MATTOX page 48
Aidan Mattox W-BRIDAL & EVENINGWEAR — AIDAN MATTOX page 15
Aidan Mattox W-DESIGNER — AIDAN MATTOX page 48
AK W-LIFESTYLE COLLECTIONS — ANNE KLEIN page 91
AK W-MISSY/UPDATED SPORTSWEAR — ANNE KLEIN page 95
AK by Anne Klein A-HOSIERY/SOCKS/LEGWEAR — LEG RESOURCE INC page 339
Akademiks M-ACTIVE/ATHLETICWEAR — AKADEMIKS page 162
Akademiks M-JEANS — AKADEMIKS page 186
Akademiks C-COORDINATED SPORTSWEAR-BOYS — AKADEMIKS page 237
Akademiks C-COORDINATED SPORTSWEAR-GIRLS — AKADEMIKS page 241
Aldan W-UNIFORMS — ALDAN page 157

Label Index

Aldan M-UNIFORMS — ALDAN page 227

Alfred Sung W-BRIDAL & EVENINGWEAR — DESSY CREATIONS & AFTER SIX page 18

Alice and Olivia W-CONTEMPORARY SPORTSWEAR — ALICE AND OLIVIA page 29

Alice and Olivia W-DRESSES/SEPARATES/SUITS — ALICE AND OLIVIA page 55

All American Career Apparel W-UNIFORMS — PRIORITY MANUFACTURING page 159

All American Career Apparel M-UNIFORMS — PRIORITY MANUFACTURING page 229

Allen B. by Allen Schwartz W-DESIGNER — ABS BY ALLEN SCHWARTZ page 47

Allen B. by Allen Schwartz W-DRESSES/SEPARATES/SUITS — ABS BY ALLEN SCHWARTZ page 55

Alpha Industries W-OUTERWEAR/COATS & JACKETS — ALPHA INDUSTRIES, INC. page 101

Alpha Industries M-SPORTSMEN'S — ALPHA INDUSTRIES, INC. page 211

Alpha Industries C-OUTERWEAR/COATS & JACKETS — ALPHA INDUSTRIES, INC. page 259

Alpha U.S.A. W-OUTERWEAR/COATS & JACKETS — ALPHA INDUSTRIES, INC. page 101

Alpha U.S.A. M-OUTERWEAR/COATS & JACKETS — ALPHA INDUSTRIES, INC. page 193

Alvina Valenta W-BRIDAL & EVENINGWEAR — JLM COUTURE page 19

Amanda W-BLOUSES/SHIRTS/TOPS — B & B DESIGNS COLLECTION INC. page 10

Amanda W-CONTEMPORARY SPORTSWEAR — B & B DESIGNS COLLECTION INC. page 30

American Hawk C-COORDINATED SPORTSWEAR-BOYS — LONG STREET page 239

American Hawk C-OUTERWEAR/COATS & JACKETS — LONG STREET page 261

AMO W-CONTEMPORARY SPORTSWEAR — SIMON SHOWROOM page 40

AMO W-JUNIOR SPORTSWEAR — SIMON SHOWROOM page 84

Anamaria Couture W-DESIGNER — SHOWROOM SEVEN/ERICKSON page 53

Andrew Marc W-LEATHER — ANDREW MARC page 87

Andrew Marc W-OUTERWEAR/COATS & JACKETS — ANDREW MARC page 101

Andrew Marc M-LEATHER — ANDREW MARC page 189

Andrew Marc M-OUTERWEAR/COATS & JACKETS — ANDREW MARC page 193

Andrew Scott M-SLEEPWEAR — INNERWEAR BRANDS page 208

Angelo Luzio® Shoes W-ACTIVE/ATHLETICWEAR — BODY WRAPPERS page 2

Ann Taylor W-DRESSES/SEPARATES/SUITS — ANN TAYLOR page 55

Ann Taylor W-LIFESTYLE COLLECTIONS — ANN TAYLOR page 91

Ann Taylor W-SPECIAL — ANN TAYLOR page 131

Anna Sui W-DESIGNER — ANNA SUI page 48

Anne Klein W-LIFESTYLE COLLECTIONS — ANNE KLEIN page 91

Anne Klein W-MISSY/UPDATED SPORTSWEAR — ANNE KLEIN page 95

Anne Klein A-HOSIERY/SOCKS/LEGWEAR — LEG RESOURCE INC page 339

Anne Namba Designs W-DECORATED/EMBELLISHED APPAREL — ANNE NAMBA DESIGNS page 43

Anne Namba Designs W-DRESSES/SEPARATES/SUITS — ANNE NAMBA DESIGNS page 56

Anne Namba Designs M-SHIRTS: — ANNE NAMBA DESIGNS page 203

Antik Batik W-CONTEMPORARY SPORTSWEAR — SIMON SHOWROOM page 40

Antik Batik W-JUNIOR SPORTSWEAR — SIMON SHOWROOM page 84

Anvil® W-TEE — ANVIL KNITWEAR, INC. page 151

Anvil® M-TEE — ANVIL KNITWEAR, INC. page 220

Anvil® C-ACTIVE/ATHLETICWEAR — ANVIL KNITWEAR, INC. page 234

Anvil® A-HATS/CAPS/MILLINERY — ANVIL KNITWEAR, INC. page 325

APL® A-HANDBAGS — APL® page 317

Aqua M-CASUAL — HASELSON INT'L TRADING INC. page 174

Aqua M-JEANS — HASELSON INT'L TRADING INC. page 187

Aqua M-OUTERWEAR/COATS & JACKETS — HASELSON INT'L TRADING INC. page 196

Aqua M-SHIRTS: — HASELSON INT'L TRADING INC. page 205

Aqua M-SWEATERS — HASELSON INT'L TRADING INC. page 216

Araks W-LIFESTYLE COLLECTIONS — ARAKS page 91

Area Code 212 W-CASUAL — AREA CODE 212 INC. page 23

Argonne W-OUTERWEAR/COATS & JACKETS — FORI SHOWROOM page 105

Argonne W-SWEATERS & KNITWEAR — FORI SHOWROOM page 140

Arianne W-BLOUSES/SHIRTS/TOPS — COLLECTION ARIANNE page 11

Arianne W-INTIMATE APPAREL & LINGERIE — COLLECTION ARIANNE page 71

Ascher A-SCARVES — ROBIN ASCHER page 354

Ashton Bradley W-PRIVATE LABEL — JULIE HUTTON INC. page 113

Ashworth M-SPORTSMEN'S — TAYLOR MADE page 212

Aspen W-LICENSED — ASPEN LICENSING INTERNATIONAL, page 89

Aspen M-LICENSED — ASPEN LICENSING INTERNATIONAL, page 191

Label	Category	Company	Page
Aspen	C-LICENSED	ASPEN LICENSING INTERNATIONAL,	page 253
Aspen Extreme	W-LICENSED	ASPEN LICENSING INTERNATIONAL,	page 89
Aspen Extreme	M-LICENSED	ASPEN LICENSING INTERNATIONAL,	page 191
Aspen Extreme	C-LICENSED	ASPEN LICENSING INTERNATIONAL,	page 253
Aspesi	M-CASUAL	PROJECT NO. 8	page 175
Aspesi	M-CONTEMPORARY SPORTSWEAR	PROJECT NO. 8	page 179
August Silk	W-CASUAL	AUGUST SILK, INC.	page 23
August Silk	W-SWEATERS & KNITWEAR	AUGUST SILK, INC.	page 135
Autumn Cashmere	W-PRIVATE LABEL	AUTUMN CASHMERE INC.	page 111
Autumn Cashmere	W-SWEATERS & KNITWEAR	AUTUMN CASHMERE INC.	page 136
Autumn Cashmere	M-PRIVATE LABEL	AUTUMN CASHMERE INC.	page 199
Autumn Cashmere	M-SWEATERS	AUTUMN CASHMERE INC.	page 215
Autumn Cashmere	C-SWEATERS	AUTUMN CASHMERE INC.	page 273
Avalin	W-CONTEMPORARY SPORTSWEAR	AVALIN LIMITED	page 29
Azibi	W-CONTEMPORARY SPORTSWEAR	AZIBI LTD.	page 30
Azibi	W-DRESSES/SEPARATES/SUITS	AZIBI LTD.	page 56
Babette	W-CONTEMPORARY SPORTSWEAR	BABETTE	page 30
Babette	W-OUTERWEAR/COATS & JACKETS	BABETTE	page 102
Baby B'Gosh	C-JEANS	OSHKOSH B'GOSH/CARTER'S	page 252
Baby B'gosh	C-NEWBORN/LAYETTE/INFANT	OSHKOSH B'GOSH/CARTER'S	page 257
Baby Jay	C-NEWBORN/LAYETTE/INFANT	BABY JAY INC./GROWING FEET INC.	page 255
Baby Jay	C-TEE	BABY JAY INC./GROWING FEET INC.	page 277
Baby Jay	A-CHILDREN	BABY JAY INC./GROWING FEET INC.	page 291
Baby Phat	C-SLEEPWEAR	HYP HATS LTD.	page 269
Baby Phat	A-CHILDREN	HYP HATS LTD.	page 292
Baby Phat	A-HATS/CAPS/MILLINERY	HYP HATS LTD.	page 330
Baby Starters	C-NEWBORN/LAYETTE/INFANT	RASHTI & RASHTI/H.J. RASHTI & CO.,	page 258
BabyLegs	A-HOSIERY/SOCKS/LEGWEAR	BABYLEGS® DIV OF UNITED	page 335
Badger Sport	W-ACTIVE/ATHLETICWEAR	BADGER SPORTSWEAR	page 2
Badger Sport	W-UNIFORMS	BADGER SPORTSWEAR	page 157
Badger Sport	M-ACTIVE/ATHLETICWEAR	BADGER SPORTSWEAR	page 163
Bailey of Hollywood	A-HATS/CAPS/MILLINERY	BAILEY HATS	page 325
Bailey Western	A-HATS/CAPS/MILLINERY	BAILEY HATS	page 325
Balti Girl	W-ACTIVE/ATHLETICWEAR	BALTIERRA SURFBOARDS & BALTI	page 2
Baltierra Surfing	M-ACTIVE/ATHLETICWEAR	BALTIERRA SURFBOARDS & BALTI	page 163
Bamboo 54	A-HANDBAGS	BAMBOO 54	page 317
Banaris	W-BLOUSES/SHIRTS/TOPS	DANA EMILIA PRESENTS	page 11
Banaris	W-CONTEMPORARY SPORTSWEAR	DANA EMILIA PRESENTS	page 34
Banaris	W-DECORATED/EMBELLISHED APPAREL	DANA EMILIA PRESENTS	page 44
Banaris	W-MISSY/UPDATED SPORTSWEAR	DANA EMILIA PRESENTS	page 96
Banaris	W-SPECIAL	DANA EMILIA PRESENTS	page 122
Banaris	W-SWEATERS & KNITWEAR	DANA EMILIA PRESENTS	page 138
Barami	W-CONTEMPORARY SPORTSWEAR	BARAMI/FASHION	page 30
Barami	W-DRESSES/SEPARATES/SUITS	BARAMI/FASHION	page 56
Barbara Lesser	W-CASUAL	WEARABLE INTEGRITY/BARBARA	page 27
Barbara Lesser	W-MISSY/UPDATED SPORTSWEAR	WEARABLE INTEGRITY/BARBARA	page 99
BarrazaStyle	W-BRIDAL & EVENINGWEAR	BARRAZA ASSOCIATES LTD	page 15
BarrazaStyle	W-CONTEMPORARY SPORTSWEAR	BARRAZA ASSOCIATES LTD	page 31
BarrazaStyle	W-OUTERWEAR/COATS & JACKETS	BARRAZA ASSOCIATES LTD	page 102
BarrazaStyle	A-SCARVES	BARRAZA ASSOCIATES LTD	page 349
Barrons-Hunter	A-BELTS	BARRONS-HUNTER, INC.	page 283
Basil & Maude	W-LIFESTYLE COLLECTIONS	JOYOUS AND FREE	page 93
bbs	W-ACTIVE/ATHLETICWEAR	SWEENIE MANUFACTURING	page 7
BCBG Max Azria	W-BRIDAL & EVENINGWEAR	BCBG MAX AZRIA GROUP	page 16
BCBG Max Azria	W-CONTEMPORARY SPORTSWEAR	BCBG MAX AZRIA GROUP	page 31
BCBG Max Azria	A-HANDBAGS	BCBG MAX AZRIA GROUP	page 318
BCTC	W-ACTIVE/ATHLETICWEAR	B.C.T.C.	page 1
BCTC	W-SPECIAL	B.C.T.C.	page 121
BCTC	W-SPECIAL	B.C.T.C.	page 131
Beach by CLC	A-HANDBAGS	BEACH HANDBAGS	page 318

Label Index

Beau Ties Ltd. — A-MEN'S — BEAU TIES LTD. OF VERMONT — page 345

Bedhead — W-SLEEPWEAR & LOUNGEWEAR — BEDHEAD PAJAMAS — page 117

Bedhead — M-SLEEPWEAR — BEDHEAD PAJAMAS — page 207

Bel Esprit — W-CONTEMPORARY SPORTSWEAR — BEL ESPRIT — page 32

Bel Esprit — A-HANDBAGS — BEL ESPRIT — page 318

Bel Esprit — A-SCARVES — BEL ESPRIT — page 349

Belasse — W-DRESSES/SEPARATES/SUITS — BELASSE COLLECTION LLC — page 57

Belgo Lux — A-BELTS — BELGO LUX INC. — page 284

Belgo Lux — A-EYEWEAR — BELGO LUX INC. — page 295

Bella Materna — W-SPECIAL — BELLA MATERNA INC. — page 129

Belldini — W-SWEATERS & KNITWEAR — BELLDINI — page 136

Bellini — A-HATS/CAPS/MILLINERY — AMERICAN HAT FACTORY, THE — page 325

Bellini Collections — A-EYEWEAR — FORMART CORPORATION — page 296

Bellini Collections — A-FASHION — FORMART CORPORATION — page 299

Bellini Collections — A-GIFT — FORMART CORPORATION — page 307

Bellini Collections — A-HAIR — FORMART CORPORATION — page 313

Bellini Collections — A-HANDBAGS — FORMART CORPORATION — page 320

Berek — W-SWEATERS & KNITWEAR — BEREK — page 137

Bergdorf Goodman Collection exclusi — W-INTIMATE APPAREL & LINGERIE — ARABESQUE DESIGN/PATRICIA — page 69

Betmar — A-GLOVES — BETMAR HATS INC. — page 310

Betmar — A-HATS/CAPS/MILLINERY — BETMAR HATS INC. — page 326

Betmar — A-SCARVES — BETMAR HATS INC. — page 350

Betsey Johnson — W-CONTEMPORARY SPORTSWEAR — BETSEY JOHNSON — page 32

Betsey Johnson — W-DESIGNER — BETSEY JOHNSON — page 48

Betsey Johnson — A-HOSIERY/SOCKS/LEGWEAR — BETSEY JOHNSON — page 336

Betsy Johnson — A-HOSIERY/SOCKS/LEGWEAR — LEG RESOURCE INC — page 339

Betty Audish Couture® — A-HANDBAGS — AUDISH ACCESSORIES, LLC — page 317

Bianca Nero — W-DRESSES/SEPARATES/SUITS — BIANCA NERO — page 57

Bibelot — W-SWEATERS & KNITWEAR — BIBELOT — page 137

Bibelot — W-SWEATERS & KNITWEAR — SUSAN GREENSTADT & ASSOC. — page 143

Big Buddha — A-BELTS — BIG BUDDHA — page 284

Big Buddha — A-HANDBAGS — BIG BUDDHA — page 319

Big Chill — C-OUTERWEAR/COATS & JACKETS — IAPPAREL LLC — page 260

Bijou — W-INTIMATE APPAREL & LINGERIE — CHARLEY MORGAN, INC. — page 70

Bikini Thief — W-SWIMWEAR & BEACHWEAR — SWEENIE MANUFACTURING — page 149

Bikini Thief — C-SWIMWEAR & BEACHWEAR — SWEENIE MANUFACTURING — page 276

Bill Adler Design — A-BELTS — WILL LEATHER GOODS — page 288

Bill Blass — W-BRIDAL & EVENINGWEAR — BILL BLASS FASHIONS LLC — page 16

Bill Blass — W-DESIGNER — BILL BLASS FASHIONS LLC — page 48

Bills Khakis — M-CONTEMPORARY SPORTSWEAR — BILLS KHAKIS — page 177

Bills Khakis — M-TROUSERS — BILLS KHAKIS — page 225

Bilt — M-SWIMWEAR & BEACHWEAR — SWEENIE MANUFACTURING — page 218

Bis Woman — W-MISSY/UPDATED SPORTSWEAR — GENE EWING BIS — page 97

Black Creek — A-HATS/CAPS/MILLINERY — F & M HAT CO., INC. — page 328

Black Label — W-DESIGNER — RALPH LAUREN, INC. — page 52

Black Label — M-DESIGNER — RALPH LAUREN, INC. — page 182

Blair Stanley — W-CONTEMPORARY SPORTSWEAR — BERGER & STEVENS — page 32

Blake and Hudson — A-MEN'S — MMG DIV OF GREAT CHINA EMPIRE — page 346

Blue Duck — W-OUTERWEAR/COATS & JACKETS — BLUE DUCK TRADING CO. — page 102

Blue Duck — M-OUTERWEAR/COATS & JACKETS — BLUE DUCK TRADING CO. — page 194

Blue Eagle by Cockpit USA — W-CONTEMPORARY SPORTSWEAR — CPT USA, LLC DBA COCKPIT USA — page 33

Blue Eagle by Cockpit USA — M-BIG — CPT USA, LLC DBA COCKPIT USA — page 169

Blue Eagle by Cockpit USA — M-CONTEMPORARY SPORTSWEAR — CPT USA, LLC DBA COCKPIT USA — page 177

Blue Eagle by Cockpit USA — M-LEATHER — CPT USA, LLC DBA COCKPIT USA — page 189

Blue Eagle by Cockpit USA — M-OUTERWEAR/COATS & JACKETS — CPT USA, LLC DBA COCKPIT USA — page 194

Blue Gem — A-EYEWEAR — BLUEGEM SUNGLASSES INC. — page 295

Blue Hawaii — W-CASUAL — BLUE HAWAII SALES — page 24

Blue Hawaii — M-CASUAL — BLUE HAWAII SALES — page 172

Blue Hawaii — M-UNIFORMS — BLUE HAWAII SALES — page 227

Blue Hawaii — C-SHIRTS: — BLUE HAWAII SALES — page 267

Blue Label RALPH LAUREN, INC.
W-DESIGNER page 52

Blue Marlin CONCEPT ONE ACCESSORIES
A-HATS/CAPS/MILLINERY page 327

Blue Planet BLUEGEM SUNGLASSES INC.
A-EYEWEAR page 295

Blue Plate BLUE PLATE INC.
W-BLOUSES/SHIRTS/TOPS page 11

Blue Plate BLUE PLATE INC.
W-JUNIOR SPORTSWEAR page 81

Blue Plate BLUE PLATE INC.
W-SWEATERS & KNITWEAR page 137

Bluesuits BLUESUITS
W-DESIGNER page 49

Bluesuits BLUESUITS
W-DRESSES/SEPARATES/SUITS page 57

Bluesuits BLUESUITS
W-MISSY/UPDATED SPORTSWEAR page 95

Bluesuits BLUESUITS
W-SPECIAL page 131

Blumera SHOWROOM SEVEN/ERICKSON
A-HANDBAGS page 323

Blush by JLM JLM COUTURE
W-BRIDAL & EVENINGWEAR page 19

Body Rock Sport SWEENIE MANUFACTURING
W-SWIMWEAR & BEACHWEAR page 149

Body Rock Sport SWEENIE MANUFACTURING
C-SWIMWEAR & BEACHWEAR page 276

Body Wrappers® BODY WRAPPERS
W-ACTIVE/ATHLETICWEAR page 2

Body Wrappers® BODY WRAPPERS
C-ACTIVE/ATHLETICWEAR page 234

Body Wrappers® BODY WRAPPERS
A-CHILDREN page 291

Bodynaturals GELMART INDUSTRIES INC.
W-INTIMATE APPAREL & LINGERIE page 73

Bolts DREAMBAGS, INC.
A-HANDBAGS page 319

Bolts DREAMBAGS, INC.
A-LUGGAGE/BAGS/LEATHER page 341

Bon Vivant DREAMBAGS, INC.
A-HANDBAGS page 319

Bon Vivant DREAMBAGS, INC.
A-LUGGAGE/BAGS/LEATHER page 341

Boppy RASHTI & RASHTI/H.J. RASHTI & CO.,
C-NEWBORN/LAYETTE/INFANT page 258

Boss Black HUGO BOSS U.S.A., INC.
W-DESIGNER page 51

Boss Black HUGO BOSS U.S.A., INC.
M-DESIGNER page 181

Boss Black HUGO BOSS U.S.A., INC.
M-SUITS page 214

Boss Black HUGO BOSS U.S.A., INC.
A-EYEWEAR page 296

Boss Green HUGO BOSS U.S.A., INC.
W-DESIGNER page 51

Boss Green HUGO BOSS U.S.A., INC.
M-DESIGNER page 181

Boss Green HUGO BOSS U.S.A., INC.
M-SUITS page 214

Boss Green HUGO BOSS U.S.A., INC.
A-EYEWEAR page 296

Boss Hugo Boss HUGO BOSS U.S.A., INC.
W-DESIGNER page 51

Boss Hugo Boss HUGO BOSS U.S.A., INC.
M-DESIGNER page 181

Boss Hugo Boss HUGO BOSS U.S.A., INC.
M-SUITS page 214

Boss Hugo Boss HUGO BOSS U.S.A., INC.
A-EYEWEAR page 296

Boss Orange HUGO BOSS U.S.A., INC.
W-DESIGNER page 51

Boss Orange HUGO BOSS U.S.A., INC.
M-DESIGNER page 181

Boss Orange HUGO BOSS U.S.A., INC.
M-SUITS page 214

Boss Orange HUGO BOSS U.S.A., INC.
A-EYEWEAR page 296

Boston Harbour HARBOUR INTERNATIONAL LLC
W-OUTERWEAR/COATS & JACKETS page 106

Boston Harbour HARBOUR INTERNATIONAL LLC
M-OUTERWEAR/COATS & JACKETS page 196

Bottoms Out EZRASONS, INC.
M-SLEEPWEAR page 208

Boulevard BOULEVARD
A-HANDBAGS page 319

Bravado BRAVADO MERCHANDISING
W-TEE page 152

Bravado BRAVADO MERCHANDISING
M-TEE page 220

Bravado BRAVADO MERCHANDISING
A-HATS/CAPS/MILLINERY page 326

BrazilRoxx Jeans BRAZILROXX INC.
W-JEANS page 78

Breezer HENSCHEL HAT CO.
A-HATS/CAPS/MILLINERY page 329

Briggs New York KELLWOOD COMPANY
W-CONTEMPORARY SPORTSWEAR page 38

Brittany Black SWEATER BRAND INC.
W-SWEATERS & KNITWEAR page 143

Brooks® BROOKS SPORTS, INC.
W-ACTIVE/ATHLETICWEAR page 3

Brooks® BROOKS SPORTS, INC.
M-ACTIVE/ATHLETICWEAR page 163

Bruges BELGO LUX INC.
A-BELTS page 284

Bruges BELGO LUX INC.
A-EYEWEAR page 295

Bryan NEW ICM, LP
C-DRESSES page 246

Bryan NEW ICM, LP
C-NEWBORN/LAYETTE/INFANT page 257

Burberry BURBERRY
W-LIFESTYLE COLLECTIONS page 91

Burberry BURBERRY
W-OUTERWEAR/COATS & JACKETS page 102

Burberry BURBERRY
M-DESIGNER page 181

Burberry BURBERRY
M-OUTERWEAR/COATS & JACKETS page 194

Label Index

Burberry BURBERRY
A-LUGGAGE/BAGS/LEATHER page 341

Burberry BURBERRY
A-UMBRELLAS page 357

Burma Bibas BURMA BIBAS
M-CONTEMPORARY SPORTSWEAR page 177

Burma Bibas BURMA BIBAS
A-MEN'S page 345

Burma Bibas. BURMA BIBAS
M-SHIRTS: page 203

By Boe BY BOE LTD.
A-FASHION page 297

C & E COTTON EMPORIUM, INC.
W-JUNIOR SPORTSWEAR page 82

C & E COTTON EMPORIUM, INC.
W-SWEATERS & KNITWEAR page 138

C.J. Banks CHRISTOPHER & BANKS
W-SPECIAL page 122

C.T.C. C.T.C. INC.
W-CONTEMPORARY SPORTSWEAR page 32

C.T.C. C.T.C. INC.
W-DRESSES/SEPARATES/SUITS page 57

Cable & Gage H.M.S. PRODUCTIONS
W-SWEATERS & KNITWEAR page 140

Cable & Gauge H.M.S. PRODUCTIONS
W-CONTEMPORARY SPORTSWEAR page 37

Cach Cach LIPSTIK GIRLS
C-COORDINATED SPORTSWEAR-GIRLS page 243

Cach Cach LIPSTIK GIRLS
C-JEANS page 251

Cach Cach LIPSTIK GIRLS
C-NEWBORN/LAYETTE/INFANT page 256

Cal Cru GRANITE KNITWEAR/CAL CRU CO.,
W-CASUAL page 25

Cal Cru GRANITE KNITWEAR/CAL CRU CO.,
M-CASUAL page 173

Calhoun CATFISH CALHOUN AKA CALHOUN
W-TEE page 152

Calhoun CATFISH CALHOUN AKA CALHOUN
M-TEE page 221

Calvin CALVIN CLOTHING COMPANY
C-COORDINATED SPORTSWEAR-BOYS page 237

Calvin CALVIN CLOTHING COMPANY
C-SHIRTS: page 267

Calvin CALVIN CLOTHING COMPANY
C-SUITS/SPECIAL page 271

Calvin Klein GLOBAL BRANDS GROUP
W-LICENSED page 89

Calvin Klein PVH CORPORATION
W-LIFESTYLE COLLECTIONS page 94

Calvin Klein GLOBAL BRANDS GROUP
M-LICENSED page 192

Calvin Klein G-III APPAREL GROUP
M-OUTERWEAR/COATS & JACKETS page 195

Calvin Klein PEERLESS CLOTHING
M-SUITS page 214

Calvin Klein PEERLESS CLOTHING
M-TROUSERS page 225

Calvin Klein Petite CALVIN KLEIN, INC.
W-SPECIAL page 131

Camber CAMBER SPORTSWEAR, INC.
M-ACTIVE/ATHLETICWEAR page 163

Camber CAMBER SPORTSWEAR, INC.
M-BIG page 169

Camber CAMBER SPORTSWEAR, INC.
M-TEE page 221

Camber II CAMBER SPORTSWEAR, INC.
M-BIG page 169

Campia BURMA BIBAS
M-CONTEMPORARY SPORTSWEAR page 177

Campia BURMA BIBAS
M-SHIRTS: page 203

Campia BURMA BIBAS
A-MEN'S page 345

Canadian CATFISH CALHOUN AKA CALHOUN
W-SWIMWEAR & BEACHWEAR page 146

Canadian CATFISH CALHOUN AKA CALHOUN
M-SWIMWEAR & BEACHWEAR page 217

Candlesticks RASHTI & RASHTI/H.J. RASHTI & CO.,
C-NEWBORN/LAYETTE/INFANT page 258

Cape Bears FRENCH TOAST
C-LICENSED page 253

Capelli New York CAPELLI NEW YORK
W-SLEEPWEAR & LOUNGEWEAR page 117

Capelli New York CAPELLI NEW YORK
M-SLEEPWEAR page 207

Capelli New York CAPELLI NEW YORK
C-SLEEPWEAR page 269

Capelli New York CAPELLI NEW YORK
A-HOSIERY/SOCKS/LEGWEAR page 337

Carerra SAFILO U.S.A.
A-EYEWEAR page 296

Caribbean Wraps International CARIBBEAN WRAPS
W-SWIMWEAR & BEACHWEAR page 146

Carisa Rene SIMON SHOWROOM
W-CONTEMPORARY SPORTSWEAR page 40

Carisa Rene SIMON SHOWROOM
W-JUNIOR SPORTSWEAR page 84

Carmen Marc Valvo Collection Black ar CARMEN MARC VALVO
W-BRIDAL & EVENINGWEAR page 17

Carmen Marc Valvo Couture CARMEN MARC VALVO
W-BRIDAL & EVENINGWEAR page 17

Carol Peretz CAROL PERETZ
W-BRIDAL & EVENINGWEAR page 17

Carol Peretz CAROL PERETZ
W-DESIGNER page 49

Carrie Amber CARRIEAMBER INTIMATES
W-INTIMATE APPAREL & LINGERIE page 69

Carrie Amber CARRIEAMBER INTIMATES
W-PRIVATE LABEL page 112

Carter's OSHKOSH B'GOSH/CARTER'S
C-COORDINATED SPORTSWEAR-BOYS page 239

Carter's OSHKOSH B'GOSH/CARTER'S
C-COORDINATED SPORTSWEAR-GIRLS page 244

Carter's OSHKOSH B'GOSH/CARTER'S
C-JEANS page 252

Carter's OSHKOSH B'GOSH/CARTER'S
C-NEWBORN/LAYETTE/INFANT page 257

Carter's RASHTI & RASHTI/H.J. RASHTI & CO.,
C-NEWBORN/LAYETTE/INFANT page 258

Cartise W-CASUAL — CARTISE INTERNATIONAL page 24
Cartise W-DRESSES/SEPARATES/SUITS — CARTISE INTERNATIONAL page 58
Cassin W-OUTERWEAR/COATS & JACKETS — CASSIN page 103
Cassin A-HATS/CAPS/MILLINERY — CASSIN page 327
Cassin A-SCARVES — CASSIN page 350
CastleWare C-ECOLOGICAL & ORGANIC — CASTLEWARE BABY page 249
CeCe by Cynthia Steffe W-CONTEMPORARY SPORTSWEAR — CYNTHIA STEFFE page 34
CeCe by Cynthia Steffe W-DESIGNER — CYNTHIA STEFFE page 50
Cejon W-OUTERWEAR/COATS & JACKETS — CEJON ACCESSORIES INC. page 103
Cejon A-SCARVES — CEJON ACCESSORIES INC. page 350
Cellini A-FASHION — L&J ACCESSORIES/CELLINI LLC page 300
Champion W-ACTIVE/ATHLETICWEAR — CHAMPION ATHLETICWEAR, INC. page 3
Champion W-LICENSED — CHAMPION ATHLETICWEAR, INC. page 89
Champion M-ACTIVE/ATHLETICWEAR — CHAMPION ATHLETICWEAR, INC. page 164
Champion M-LICENSED — CHAMPION ATHLETICWEAR, INC. page 191
Chantelle W-INTIMATE APPAREL & LINGERIE — CHANTELLE LINGERIE INC. page 70
Charlie One Horse Hats A-HATS/CAPS/MILLINERY — HATCO, INC./ RESISTOL HATS page 329
Cheer Kids C-ACTIVE/ATHLETICWEAR — MOTIONWEAR, LLC page 236
Chetta B W-BRIDAL & EVENINGWEAR — DARIAN GROUP INC. page 17
Chetta B W-DRESSES/SEPARATES/SUITS — DARIAN GROUP INC. page 58
Chipita A-FASHION — CHIPITA ACCESSORIES page 297
Christian Livingston A-HANDBAGS — NOTANONYMOUS page 322
Christine Vancouver W-INTIMATE APPAREL & LINGERIE — CHRISTINE VANCOUVER page 70
Christine Vancouver W-SLEEPWEAR & LOUNGEWEAR — CHRISTINE VANCOUVER page 117
Christine Vancouver W-SPECIAL — CHRISTINE VANCOUVER page 122
Christine Vancouver W-SPECIAL — CHRISTINE VANCOUVER page 132
Christopher & Banks W-CONTEMPORARY SPORTSWEAR — CHRISTOPHER & BANKS page 33
Christopher Calvin W-BLOUSES/SHIRTS/TOPS — DANA EMILIA PRESENTS page 11
Christopher Calvin W-CONTEMPORARY SPORTSWEAR — DANA EMILIA PRESENTS page 34
Christopher Calvin W-DECORATED/EMBELLISHED APPAREL — DANA EMILIA PRESENTS page 44
Christopher Calvin W-MISSY/UPDATED SPORTSWEAR — DANA EMILIA PRESENTS page 96
Christopher Calvin W-SPECIAL — DANA EMILIA PRESENTS page 122
Christopher Calvin W-SWEATERS & KNITWEAR — DANA EMILIA PRESENTS page 138
Cinzia Rocca W-DESIGNER — RODEL U.S.A. INC. page 53
Cinzia Rocca W-OUTERWEAR/COATS & JACKETS — RODEL U.S.A. INC. page 108
Civilian Pilot Training W-CONTEMPORARY SPORTSWEAR — CPT USA, LLC DBA COCKPIT USA page 33
Civilian Pilot Training M-BIG — CPT USA, LLC DBA COCKPIT USA page 169
Civilian Pilot Training M-CONTEMPORARY SPORTSWEAR — CPT USA, LLC DBA COCKPIT USA page 177
Civilian Pilot Training M-LEATHER — CPT USA, LLC DBA COCKPIT USA page 189
Civilian Pilot Training M-OUTERWEAR/COATS & JACKETS — CPT USA, LLC DBA COCKPIT USA page 194
CK One W-INTIMATE APPAREL & LINGERIE — CALVIN KLEIN, INC. page 69
CK One W-JEANS — CALVIN KLEIN, INC. page 78
CK One M-JEANS — CALVIN KLEIN, INC. page 186
Clark & Gregory W-BLOUSES/SHIRTS/TOPS — GOLF APPAREL BRANDS page 13
Clark & Gregory W-OUTERWEAR/COATS & JACKETS — GOLF APPAREL BRANDS page 106
Clark & Gregory W-SWEATERS & KNITWEAR — GOLF APPAREL BRANDS page 140
Clark & Gregory M-OUTERWEAR/COATS & JACKETS — GOLF APPAREL BRANDS page 196
Clark & Gregory M-SHIRTS: — GOLF APPAREL BRANDS page 204
Clark & Gregory M-SWEATERS — GOLF APPAREL BRANDS page 216
Clark & Gregory A-HATS/CAPS/MILLINERY — GOLF APPAREL BRANDS page 328
Classix W-BLOUSES/SHIRTS/TOPS — CLASSIX page 11
Classix M-SHIRTS: — CLASSIX page 204
Classix C-SHIRTS: — CLASSIX page 267
CLC W-OUTERWEAR/COATS & JACKETS — ESSEX MANUFACTURING INC. page 104
CLC W-SPECIAL — ESSEX MANUFACTURING INC. page 123
CLC W-SPECIAL — ESSEX MANUFACTURING INC. page 132
CLC M-BIG — ESSEX MANUFACTURING INC. page 170
CLC M-LICENSED — ESSEX MANUFACTURING INC. page 191
CLC M-OUTERWEAR/COATS & JACKETS — ESSEX MANUFACTURING INC. page 195
CLC C-OUTERWEAR/COATS & JACKETS — ESSEX MANUFACTURING INC. page 260

Coach GLOBAL BRANDS GROUP
W-LICENSED page 89

Cobalt BELGO LUX INC.
A-BELTS page 284

Cockpit USA CPT USA, LLC DBA COCKPIT USA
W-CONTEMPORARY SPORTSWEAR page 33

Cockpit USA CPT USA, LLC DBA COCKPIT USA
M-BIG page 169

Cockpit USA CPT USA, LLC DBA COCKPIT USA
M-CONTEMPORARY SPORTSWEAR page 177

Cockpit USA CPT USA, LLC DBA COCKPIT USA
M-LEATHER page 189

Cockpit USA CPT USA, LLC DBA COCKPIT USA
M-OUTERWEAR/COATS & JACKETS page 194

Coco CHARLEY MORGAN, INC.
W-INTIMATE APPAREL & LINGERIE page 70

Coco BOSSONG HOSIERY
A-HOSIERY/SOCKS/LEGWEAR page 336

College/Universities FBF ORIGINALS
A-HOSIERY/SOCKS/LEGWEAR page 337

Collegiate GEM DANDY INC.
A-BELTS page 285

Collegiate teams 5TH & OCEAN CLOTHING LLC/NEW
W-CASUAL page 23

Collegiate teams 5TH & OCEAN CLOTHING LLC/NEW
W-JUNIOR SPORTSWEAR page 81

Collegiate teams 5TH & OCEAN CLOTHING LLC/NEW
M-CASUAL page 172

Collegiate teams 5TH & OCEAN CLOTHING LLC/NEW
C-ACTIVE/ATHLETICWEAR page 233

Colorado Silver Star COLORADO SILVER STAR CORP.
A-GIFT page 305

Coloratura COLORATURA, INC.
W-DECORATED/EMBELLISHED APPAREL page 43

Coloratura COLORATURA, INC.
W-OUTERWEAR/COATS & JACKETS page 103

Coloratura COLORATURA, INC.
A-SCARVES page 351

Columbia Sportswear Co COLUMBIA SPORTSWEAR CO., INC.
C-ACTIVE/ATHLETICWEAR page 234

Columbia Sportswear Co. COLUMBIA SPORTSWEAR CO., INC.
W-ACTIVE/ATHLETICWEAR page 4

Columbia Sportswear Co. COLUMBIA SPORTSWEAR CO., INC.
W-OUTERWEAR/COATS & JACKETS page 104

Columbia Sportswear Co. COLUMBIA SPORTSWEAR CO., INC.
M-OUTERWEAR/COATS & JACKETS page 194

Columbia Sportswear Co. COLUMBIA SPORTSWEAR CO., INC.
M-SPORTSMEN'S page 211

Columbia Sportswear Co. COLUMBIA SPORTSWEAR CO., INC.
C-OUTERWEAR/COATS & JACKETS page 259

Comfies® JOCKEY INTERNATIONAL, INC.
W-INTIMATE APPAREL & LINGERIE page 73

Convertibles SHAUNE BAZNER ACCESSORIES,
A-HAIR page 314

Coobie COOBIE INTIMATES
W-INTIMATE APPAREL & LINGERIE page 71

Coors CATFISH CALHOUN AKA CALHOUN
W-SWIMWEAR & BEACHWEAR page 146

Coors CATFISH CALHOUN AKA CALHOUN
M-SWIMWEAR & BEACHWEAR page 217

Copper Collection COLORADO SILVER STAR CORP.
A-GIFT page 305

Corona CATFISH CALHOUN AKA CALHOUN
W-SWIMWEAR & BEACHWEAR page 146

Corona CATFISH CALHOUN AKA CALHOUN
M-SWIMWEAR & BEACHWEAR page 217

Cosabella COSABELLA
W-INTIMATE APPAREL & LINGERIE page 71

Cosabella COSABELLA
W-SWIMWEAR & BEACHWEAR page 147

Cotton Club FORT KNOX LINGERIE
W-INTIMATE APPAREL & LINGERIE page 73

Cotton Deluxe Casuals ANVIL KNITWEAR, INC.
W-TEE page 151

Cotton Deluxe® ANVIL KNITWEAR, INC.
W-TEE page 151

Cotton Emporium COTTON EMPORIUM, INC.
W-JUNIOR SPORTSWEAR page 82

Cotton Emporium COTTON EMPORIUM, INC.
W-SWEATERS & KNITWEAR page 138

Cotton Heritage COTTON HERITAGE
W-PRIVATE LABEL page 112

Cotton Heritage COTTON HERITAGE
M-PRIVATE LABEL page 200

Cotton Heritage COTTON HERITAGE
C-PRIVATE LABEL page 263

Country Gentleman COUNTRY GENTLEMAN
A-HATS/CAPS/MILLINERY page 327

Cowichan CANADIAN SWEATER CO., LTD.
W-SWEATERS & KNITWEAR page 137

Cowichan CANADIAN SWEATER CO., LTD.
M-SWEATERS page 215

Cowichan CANADIAN SWEATER CO., LTD.
C-SWEATERS page 273

Cowichan CANADIAN SWEATER CO., LTD.
A-GLOVES page 310

Cowichan CANADIAN SWEATER CO., LTD.
A-HATS/CAPS/MILLINERY page 326

Crazy Shirts Hawaii STYLE SOURCE INC.
W-ECOLOGICAL & ORGANIC page 67

Crazy Shirts Hawaii STYLE SOURCE INC.
W-PRIVATE LABEL page 115

Crazy Shirts Hawaii STYLE SOURCE INC.
M-PRIVATE LABEL page 202

Crimzon rose ERICA LYONS JEWELRY/CRIMZON
A-FASHION page 299

Cristina Ruales SHOWROOM SEVEN/ERICKSON
W-DESIGNER page 53

Cubavera & Havanera FRENCH TOAST
C-LICENSED page 253

Cupio H.M.S. PRODUCTIONS
W-CONTEMPORARY SPORTSWEAR page 37

Cynthia Gale CYNTHIA GALE
A-FASHION page 298

Cynthia Gale CYNTHIA GALE
A-GIFT page 306

Cynthia Rowley CYNTHIA ROWLEY
W-CONTEMPORARY SPORTSWEAR page 33

Cynthia Rowley CYNTHIA ROWLEY
W-DESIGNER page 49

Cynthia Steffe W-CONTEMPORARY SPORTSWEAR — CYNTHIA STEFFE page 34
Cynthia Steffe W-DESIGNER — CYNTHIA STEFFE page 50
Cyrus W-SWEATERS & KNITWEAR — CYRUS page 138
Daang Goodman W-JUNIOR SPORTSWEAR — TRIPP NYC page 85
Daily Wear W-MISSY/UPDATED SPORTSWEAR — DAILY WEAR page 95
Damianou W-BRIDAL & EVENINGWEAR — DAMIANOU page 17
danceBtween™ C-ACTIVE/ATHLETICWEAR — BODY WRAPPERS page 234
Danecraft A-FASHION — DANECRAFT INC. page 298
Daniela Corte W-ACTIVE/ATHLETICWEAR — SWEENIE MANUFACTURING page 7
Daniela Corte W-SWIMWEAR & BEACHWEAR — SWEENIE MANUFACTURING page 149
Davco A-HOSIERY/SOCKS/LEGWEAR — SOXLAND INTERNATIONAL, INC. page 339
David Meister - manufactured under W-BRIDAL & EVENINGWEAR — KELLWOOD COMPANY page 20
David Smith A-GIFT — DAVID SMITH & ASSOCIATES page 306
DC Comics W-SWIMWEAR & BEACHWEAR — CATFISH CALHOUN AKA CALHOUN page 146
DC Comics M-SWIMWEAR & BEACHWEAR — CATFISH CALHOUN AKA CALHOUN page 217
DeBora Rachelle W-BRIDAL & EVENINGWEAR — DEBORA RACHELLE INC. page 18
Deborah Grivas A-BRIDAL/SPECIAL/INTIMATE — NOTANONYMOUS page 290
Deborah Grivas A-FASHION — NOTANONYMOUS page 301
Deluxe by Lorren Bell A-FASHION — LORREN BELL, INC. page 301
Deluxe by Lorren Bell A-HAIR — LORREN BELL, INC. page 314
Deluxe by Lorren Bell A-HANDBAGS — LORREN BELL, INC. page 322
Deni W-LEATHER — MONTANACO CLOTHING COMPANY page 87
Deni M-LEATHER — MONTANACO CLOTHING COMPANY page 189
Denizen W-JEANS — LEVI STRAUSS & CO. page 79
Denizen M-JEANS — LEVI STRAUSS & CO. page 187
Denizen M-WESTERNWEAR — LEVI STRAUSS & CO. page 231
Depeche Mode W-BRIDAL & EVENINGWEAR — DEPECHE MODE page 18
Depeche Mode W-CONTEMPORARY SPORTSWEAR — DEPECHE MODE page 34
Depeche Mode W-DRESSES/SEPARATES/SUITS — DEPECHE MODE page 58
Depeche Mode W-SPECIAL — DEPECHE MODE page 122
Depeche Mode W-SPECIAL — DEPECHE MODE page 132
Dessy Creations & After Six W-BRIDAL & EVENINGWEAR — DESSY CREATIONS & AFTER SIX page 18
Diane by Diane Von Furstenberg W-DESIGNER — DIANE VON FURSTENBERG STUDIO, page 50
Diesel W-JEANS — DIESEL PLANET page 78
Diesel M-JEANS — DIESEL PLANET page 186
Diesel A-EYEWEAR — DIESEL PLANET page 295
Diesel A-FASHION — DIESEL PLANET page 298
Diesel Kid C-JEANS — DIESEL PLANET page 251
Dimples by Europa C-COORDINATED SPORTSWEAR-BOYS — CALVIN CLOTHING COMPANY page 237
Dimples by Europa C-SHIRTS: — CALVIN CLOTHING COMPANY page 267
Dimples by Europa C-SUITS/SPECIAL — CALVIN CLOTHING COMPANY page 271
Dior A-EYEWEAR — SAFILO U.S.A. page 296
Dish W-JEANS — PIMLICO PERFORMANCE APPAREL page 80
Dish W-LIFESTYLE COLLECTIONS — PIMLICO PERFORMANCE APPAREL page 94
Disney C-NEWBORN/LAYETTE/INFANT — KAHN LUCAS page 256
Disney C-SLEEPWEAR — HYP HATS LTD. page 269
Disney A-CHILDREN — HYP HATS LTD. page 292
Disney A-HATS/CAPS/MILLINERY — CONCEPT ONE ACCESSORIES page 327
Disney A-HATS/CAPS/MILLINERY — HYP HATS LTD. page 330
Divina Dancewear W-ACTIVE/ATHLETICWEAR — DIVINA DANCEWEAR page 4
DKNY W-CONTEMPORARY SPORTSWEAR — DKNY page 35
DKNY M-SUITS — PEERLESS CLOTHING page 214
DKNY M-TROUSERS — PEERLESS CLOTHING page 225
DLR A-EYEWEAR — BLUEGEM SUNGLASSES INC. page 295
Dobb's A-HATS/CAPS/MILLINERY — HATCO, INC./ RESISTOL HATS page 329
Dockers M-OUTERWEAR/COATS & JACKETS — G-III APPAREL GROUP page 195
Dockers A-EYEWEAR — FGX INTERNATIONAL/DIV OF page 296
Dockers® W-JEANS — LEVI STRAUSS & CO. page 79
Dockers® M-JEANS — LEVI STRAUSS & CO. page 187
Dockers® M-WESTERNWEAR — LEVI STRAUSS & CO. page 231

Label Index

Dollhouse DOLLHOUSE
W-JUNIOR SPORTSWEAR page 82

Dollie & Me® KAHN LUCAS
C-COORDINATED SPORTSWEAR-GIRLS page 242

Dollie & Me® KAHN LUCAS
C-DRESSES page 246

Dollie & Me® KAHN LUCAS
C-LICENSED page 254

Dolores Piscotta DOLORES PISCOTTA
W-ECOLOGICAL & ORGANIC page 65

Dolores Piscotta DOLORES PISCOTTA
W-OUTERWEAR/COATS & JACKETS page 104

Dolores Piscotta DOLORES PISCOTTA
W-SWEATERS & KNITWEAR page 139

Dolores Piscotta DOLORES PISCOTTA
A-GIFT page 306

Domani Fashions SWEATER BRAND INC.
W-SWEATERS & KNITWEAR page 143

Dominique DAYLEEN INTIMATES INC.
W-INTIMATE APPAREL & LINGERIE page 71

Donna Karan DONNA KARAN COLLECTIONS
W-DESIGNER page 50

Donoughe Sport™ DONOUGHE SPORT
W-ACTIVE/ATHLETICWEAR page 4

Donoughe Sport™ DONOUGHE SPORT
M-ACTIVE/ATHLETICWEAR page 164

Donoughe Sport™ DONOUGHE SPORT
C-ACTIVE/ATHLETICWEAR page 235

Dorman Fashion DORMAN FASHION INC.
W-BLOUSES/SHIRTS/TOPS page 12

Dreambags DREAMBAGS, INC.
A-HANDBAGS page 319

Dreambags DREAMBAGS, INC.
A-LUGGAGE/BAGS/LEATHER page 341

Dreams DREAM WORLD INTERNATIONAL,
M-BIG page 170

Dreams DREAM WORLD INTERNATIONAL,
M-CONTEMPORARY SPORTSWEAR page 178

Dreams DREAM WORLD INTERNATIONAL,
M-SUITS page 213

Drew DREW PHILIPS CORP.
W-CONTEMPORARY SPORTSWEAR page 35

Drew DREW PHILIPS CORP.
W-DRESSES/SEPARATES/SUITS page 58

Dri-Sox® CRESCENT SOCK COMPANY
A-HOSIERY/SOCKS/LEGWEAR page 337

Dries Van Noten PROJECT NO. 8
M-CASUAL page 175

Dries Van Noten PROJECT NO. 8
M-CONTEMPORARY SPORTSWEAR page 179

DS&G D'ACCORD SHIRTS & GUAYABERAS
M-BIG page 169

DS&G-Rafael Contreras D'ACCORD SHIRTS & GUAYABERAS
M-CASUAL page 173

DS&G-Rafael Contreras D'ACCORD SHIRTS & GUAYABERAS
M-SHIRTS: page 204

Du'er PIMLICO PERFORMANCE APPAREL
M-JEANS page 188

Due Per Due/209Wst DUE PER DUE/209WST
W-CONTEMPORARY SPORTSWEAR page 35

Duke DREAMBAGS, INC.
A-HANDBAGS page 319

Duke DREAMBAGS, INC.
A-LUGGAGE/BAGS/LEATHER page 341

Eco Swim® A & H SPORTSWEAR CO. INC.
W-SWIMWEAR & BEACHWEAR page 145

Ed Hardy EZRASONS, INC.
M-SLEEPWEAR page 208

Eddie Bauer LONG STREET
C-COORDINATED SPORTSWEAR-BOYS page 239

Eddie Bauer LONG STREET
C-OUTERWEAR/COATS & JACKETS page 261

Edward Cromarty EDWARD CROMARTY ART DESIGN
W-SLEEPWEAR & LOUNGEWEAR page 118

Edward Cromarty EDWARD CROMARTY ART DESIGN
A-BRIDAL/SPECIAL/INTIMATE page 289

Edward Cromarty Art Design Studio EDWARD CROMARTY ART DESIGN
W-BRIDAL & EVENINGWEAR page 19

Edward Cromarty Bridal Design Studi EDWARD CROMARTY ART DESIGN
W-BRIDAL & EVENINGWEAR page 19

Eileen Fisher EILEEN FISHER INC.
W-MISSY/UPDATED SPORTSWEAR page 96

EKAT SHOWROOM SEVEN/ERICKSON
W-CONTEMPORARY SPORTSWEAR page 40

EKAT SHOWROOM SEVEN/ERICKSON
W-DESIGNER page 53

Elance® JOCKEY INTERNATIONAL, INC.
W-INTIMATE APPAREL & LINGERIE page 73

Elance® JOCKEY INTERNATIONAL, INC.
M-SLEEPWEAR page 209

Elan™ ELAN INTERNATIONAL
W-CONTEMPORARY SPORTSWEAR page 35

Elie Tahari ELIE TAHARI LTD.
W-DESIGNER page 51

Elie Tahari ELIE TAHARI LTD.
W-MISSY/UPDATED SPORTSWEAR page 96

Elisa B LIPSTIK GIRLS
C-COORDINATED SPORTSWEAR-GIRLS page 243

Elisa B LIPSTIK GIRLS
C-JEANS page 251

Elisa B LIPSTIK GIRLS
C-NEWBORN/LAYETTE/INFANT page 256

Elizabeth Gillett ELIZABETH GILLETT LTD.
W-SWEATERS & KNITWEAR page 139

Elizabeth Gillett ELIZABETH GILLETT LTD.
A-SCARVES page 351

Ellen Tracy ESSEX MANUFACTURING INC.
A-UMBRELLAS page 357

Elomi EVEDEN INC.
W-INTIMATE APPAREL & LINGERIE page 72

Elwood Clothing TOPSON DOWNS
M-ACTIVE/ATHLETICWEAR page 166

Ema Savahl Couture EMA SAVAHL DESIGN
W-BRIDAL & EVENINGWEAR page 19

Ema Savahl Couture EMA SAVAHL DESIGN
W-DECORATED/EMBELLISHED APPAREL page 44

Emanuel MEGA BELTS, INC.
A-BELTS page 287

Emanuel Ungaro HARBOUR INTERNATIONAL LLC
W-OUTERWEAR/COATS & JACKETS page 106

Emanuel Ungaro HARBOUR INTERNATIONAL LLC
M-OUTERWEAR/COATS & JACKETS page 196

Embassy EZRASONS, INC.
M-SLEEPWEAR page 208

Emerson Fry JULIE HUTTON INC.
W-PRIVATE LABEL page 113

Emil Rutenberg ATOPAPPAREL CORP
W-BLOUSES/SHIRTS/TOPS page 10

Emil Rutenberg EMIL RUTENBERG
W-CONTEMPORARY SPORTSWEAR page 36

Emil Rutenberg ATOPAPPAREL CORP
W-SPECIAL page 121

Emily West® KAHN LUCAS
C-COORDINATED SPORTSWEAR-GIRLS page 242

Emily West® KAHN LUCAS
C-DRESSES page 246

Emily West® KAHN LUCAS
C-LICENSED page 254

Enrico Guccini RON CORNELL
A-MEN'S page 347

Ergee BOSSONG HOSIERY
A-HOSIERY/SOCKS/LEGWEAR page 336

Eric Javits ERIC JAVITS, INC.
A-HANDBAGS page 320

Eric Javits ERIC JAVITS, INC.
A-HATS/CAPS/MILLINERY page 328

Erica Lyons ERICA LYONS JEWELRY/CRIMZON
A-FASHION page 299

Erickson Beamon SHOWROOM SEVEN/ERICKSON
A-FASHION page 302

Escada USA ESCADA USA
W-DESIGNER page 51

Eshel ADK FASHIONS
W-BRIDAL & EVENINGWEAR page 15

Essentiel SIMON SHOWROOM
W-CONTEMPORARY SPORTSWEAR page 40

Essentiel SIMON SHOWROOM
W-JUNIOR SPORTSWEAR page 84

Etienne Marcel SHOWROOM SEVEN/ERICKSON
W-CONTEMPORARY SPORTSWEAR page 40

Eugenio Vazzano ELE.PAVONI NEW YORK LTD
W-DESIGNER page 50

Euro Joy Sportswear EURO JOY SPORTSWEAR CORP.
W-CASUAL page 25

Euro Joy Sportswear EURO JOY SPORTSWEAR CORP.
W-MISSY/UPDATED SPORTSWEAR page 96

Euro Joy Sportswear EURO JOY SPORTSWEAR CORP.
W-OUTERWEAR/COATS & JACKETS page 104

Euro Joy Sportswear EURO JOY SPORTSWEAR CORP.
W-SWEATERS & KNITWEAR page 140

Europa CALVIN CLOTHING COMPANY
C-COORDINATED SPORTSWEAR-BOYS page 237

Europa CALVIN CLOTHING COMPANY
C-SHIRTS: page 267

Europa CALVIN CLOTHING COMPANY
C-SUITS/SPECIAL page 271

Eva and Claudi BERGER & STEVENS
W-CONTEMPORARY SPORTSWEAR page 32

Evanese EVANESE, INC.
W-DRESSES/SEPARATES/SUITS page 59

Evy EVY OF CALIFORNIA, INC./DBA
C-COORDINATED SPORTSWEAR-GIRLS page 241

Evy EVY OF CALIFORNIA, INC./DBA
C-DRESSES page 245

Evy EVY OF CALIFORNIA, INC./DBA
C-NEWBORN/LAYETTE/INFANT page 255

F & M Hat F & M HAT CO., INC.
A-HATS/CAPS/MILLINERY page 328

Fair Hemp FAIR HEMP INC.
W-TEE page 153

Fair Hemp FAIR HEMP INC.
M-TEE page 221

Fair Hemp FAIR HEMP INC.
A-HATS/CAPS/MILLINERY page 328

Faith JOYOUS AND FREE
W-LIFESTYLE COLLECTIONS page 93

Fantasie of England EVEDEN INC.
W-INTIMATE APPAREL & LINGERIE page 72

Fantasie of England EVEDEN INC.
W-SWIMWEAR & BEACHWEAR page 147

Fashion Concept BARAMI/FASHION
W-CONTEMPORARY SPORTSWEAR page 30

Fashion Concept BARAMI/FASHION
W-DRESSES/SEPARATES/SUITS page 56

Fauve EVEDEN INC.
W-INTIMATE APPAREL & LINGERIE page 72

FBF Originals FBF ORIGINALS
A-HOSIERY/SOCKS/LEGWEAR page 337

Feathers MISTER NOAH
W-ACTIVE/ATHLETICWEAR page 5

Feathers MISTER NOAH
W-JUNIOR SPORTSWEAR page 84

Fila FILA U.S.A. INC.
W-ACTIVE/ATHLETICWEAR page 4

Fila FILA U.S.A. INC.
M-ACTIVE/ATHLETICWEAR page 164

Fila FILA U.S.A. INC.
C-ACTIVE/ATHLETICWEAR page 235

Fire TOPSON DOWNS
W-CONTEMPORARY SPORTSWEAR page 41

FITS CRESCENT SOCK COMPANY
A-HOSIERY/SOCKS/LEGWEAR page 337

Flatiron Workshop FLATIRON WORKSHOP
W-BLOUSES/SHIRTS/TOPS page 12

Fleurish EVY OF CALIFORNIA, INC./DBA
W-JUNIOR SPORTSWEAR page 82

Fleurt FLEUR'T, INC./MONTELLE
W-INTIMATE APPAREL & LINGERIE page 72

Flex CARRIEAMBER INTIMATES
W-INTIMATE APPAREL & LINGERIE page 69

Flex CARRIEAMBER INTIMATES
W-PRIVATE LABEL page 112

Flora Fedi ELE.PAVONI NEW YORK LTD
W-SWEATERS & KNITWEAR page 139

Flora Nikrooz Collection FLORA NIKROOZ/DIVISION OF AGE
W-INTIMATE APPAREL & LINGERIE page 72

Flora Nikrooz Gold Label FLORA NIKROOZ/DIVISION OF AGE
W-INTIMATE APPAREL & LINGERIE page 72

Florsheim KEEPERS INTERNATIONAL
A-HOSIERY/SOCKS/LEGWEAR page 338

Forever Young — DAILY WEAR
W-MISSY/UPDATED SPORTSWEAR — page 95

Foster Grant — FGX INTERNATIONAL/DIV OF
A-EYEWEAR — page 296

Fouger for Kids — FOUGER FOR KIDS, INC.
C-DRESSES — page 245

Fouger for Kids — FOUGER FOR KIDS, INC.
C-NEWBORN/LAYETTE/INFANT — page 256

Fouger for Kids — FOUGER FOR KIDS, INC.
C-SUITS/SPECIAL — page 271

Foundrae — SIMON SHOWROOM
W-CONTEMPORARY SPORTSWEAR — page 40

Foundrae — SIMON SHOWROOM
W-JUNIOR SPORTSWEAR — page 84

Free Country — FREE COUNTRY LTD.
W-OUTERWEAR/COATS & JACKETS — page 105

Free Country — FREE COUNTRY LTD.
W-SWIMWEAR & BEACHWEAR — page 148

Free Country — FREE COUNTRY LTD.
M-ACTIVE/ATHLETICWEAR — page 164

Free Country — FREE COUNTRY LTD.
M-OUTERWEAR/COATS & JACKETS — page 195

Free Country — FREE COUNTRY LTD.
M-SWIMWEAR & BEACHWEAR — page 218

Free Country — FREE COUNTRY LTD.
C-OUTERWEAR/COATS & JACKETS — page 260

French Connection — FRENCH CONNECTION
W-CONTEMPORARY SPORTSWEAR — page 36

French Connection — FRENCH CONNECTION
W-JEANS — page 78

French Connection — FRENCH CONNECTION
W-OUTERWEAR/COATS & JACKETS — page 105

French Connection — FRENCH CONNECTION
M-CONTEMPORARY SPORTSWEAR — page 178

French Connection — FRENCH CONNECTION
M-JEANS — page 187

French Connection — FRENCH CONNECTION
A-BELTS — page 284

French Connection — FRENCH CONNECTION
A-HOSIERY/SOCKS/LEGWEAR — page 337

French Jenny — RICHARD LEEDS INTERNATIONAL
W-SLEEPWEAR & LOUNGEWEAR — page 119

French Toast — FRENCH TOAST
C-ACTIVE/ATHLETICWEAR — page 235

French Toast — FRENCH TOAST
C-COORDINATED SPORTSWEAR-BOYS — page 238

French Toast — FRENCH TOAST
C-COORDINATED SPORTSWEAR-GIRLS — page 241

French Toast — FRENCH TOAST
C-JEANS — page 251

French Toast — FRENCH TOAST
C-OUTERWEAR/COATS & JACKETS — page 260

French Toast — FRENCH TOAST
C-SWIMWEAR & BEACHWEAR — page 275

French Toast — FRENCH TOAST
A-CHILDREN — page 291

French Toast Official School Wear — FRENCH TOAST
C-UNIFORMS — page 281

Freya — EVEDEN INC.
W-INTIMATE APPAREL & LINGERIE — page 72

Freya — EVEDEN INC.
W-SWIMWEAR & BEACHWEAR — page 147

Friday Shirts! — WEDDING TROPICS
C-SHIRTS: — page 268

Friday Shirts! Wedding Tropics — WEDDING TROPICS
M-DESIGNER — page 182

Fruit of the Loom — FRUIT OF THE LOOM
W-ACTIVE/ATHLETICWEAR — page 4

Fruit of the Loom — WASATCH CO.
W-ACTIVE/ATHLETICWEAR — page 7

Fruit of the Loom — FRUIT OF THE LOOM
M-ACTIVE/ATHLETICWEAR — page 165

Fruit of the Loom — WASATCH CO.
M-ACTIVE/ATHLETICWEAR — page 167

Fruit of the Loom — WASATCH CO.
M-OUTERWEAR/COATS & JACKETS — page 197

Fruit of the Loom — WASATCH CO.
C-NEWBORN/LAYETTE/INFANT — page 258

Frye — GLOBAL BRANDS GROUP
W-LICENSED — page 89

Frye — GLOBAL BRANDS GROUP
M-LICENSED — page 192

G Bar D — GEM DANDY INC.
A-BELTS — page 285

Gaiam — GAIAM
W-CONTEMPORARY SPORTSWEAR — page 36

Gaiam — GAIAM
W-ECOLOGICAL & ORGANIC — page 66

Gaiam — GAIAM
W-SLEEPWEAR & LOUNGEWEAR — page 118

Garden Kids — GARDEN KIDS
C-ECOLOGICAL & ORGANIC — page 249

Gargoyles — FGX INTERNATIONAL/DIV OF
A-EYEWEAR — page 296

Garnet Hill — STYLE SOURCE INC.
W-ECOLOGICAL & ORGANIC — page 67

Garnet Hill — STYLE SOURCE INC.
W-PRIVATE LABEL — page 115

Gellas — SHEDRAIN CORP.
A-UMBRELLAS — page 358

Gene Ewing Bis — GENE EWING BIS
W-MISSY/UPDATED SPORTSWEAR — page 97

Gene Ewing Leglifters®™ — GENE EWING BIS
A-HOSIERY/SOCKS/LEGWEAR — page 338

Genuine Kids — OSHKOSH B'GOSH/CARTER'S
C-COORDINATED SPORTSWEAR-BOYS — page 239

Genuine Kids — OSHKOSH B'GOSH/CARTER'S
C-COORDINATED SPORTSWEAR-GIRLS — page 244

Genuine School Uniform — LONG STREET
C-COORDINATED SPORTSWEAR-BOYS — page 239

Genuine School Uniform — LONG STREET
C-OUTERWEAR/COATS & JACKETS — page 261

Genuine School Uniform — LONG STREET
C-UNIFORMS — page 281

Genuine School Uniform. — LONG STREET
C-COORDINATED SPORTSWEAR-GIRLS — page 243

Geoffrey Beene — HENSCHEL HAT CO.
A-HATS/CAPS/MILLINERY — page 329

Geoffrey Beene — MANN & BROS INC/IMPERIAL
A-SCARVES — page 352

Georges Chakra "Edition" W-BRIDAL & EVENINGWEAR — ADK FASHIONS page 15
Georges Chakra "Edition" W-DESIGNER — ADK FASHIONS page 47
Gildan W-ACTIVE/ATHLETICWEAR — WASATCH CO. page 7
Gildan M-ACTIVE/ATHLETICWEAR — WASATCH CO. page 167
Gildan M-OUTERWEAR/COATS & JACKETS — WASATCH CO. page 197
Gildan C-NEWBORN/LAYETTE/INFANT — WASATCH CO. page 258
Gildan A-HOSIERY/SOCKS/LEGWEAR — ABC HOSIERY page 335
Giovannio A-HATS/CAPS/MILLINERY — F & M HAT CO., INC. page 328
Goddess W-INTIMATE APPAREL & LINGERIE — EVEDEN INC. page 72
Goodwear W-ECOLOGICAL & ORGANIC — GOODWEAR USA page 66
Goodwear W-TEE — GOODWEAR USA page 153
Goodwear M-ECOLOGICAL & ORGANIC — GOODWEAR USA page 183
Goodwear M-SLEEPWEAR — GOODWEAR USA page 208
Goodwear M-TEE — GOODWEAR USA page 222
Goodwear C-ECOLOGICAL & ORGANIC — GOODWEAR USA page 249
Goodwear C-TEE — GOODWEAR USA page 277
Gopaks by David Smith A-GIFT — DAVID SMITH & ASSOCIATES page 306
Gossip W-BLOUSES/SHIRTS/TOPS — ELE.PAVONI NEW YORK LTD page 12
Grand Sierra® A-GLOVES — BECKER GLOVE INTERNATIONAL, page 310
Green Dragon W-ECOLOGICAL & ORGANIC — GREEN DRAGON page 66
Guess W-JUNIOR SPORTSWEAR — GUESS, INC. page 82
Guess M-CONTEMPORARY SPORTSWEAR — GUESS, INC. page 178
Guess Kids C-COORDINATED SPORTSWEAR-BOYS — GUESS, INC. page 238
Guess Kids C-COORDINATED SPORTSWEAR-GIRLS — GUESS, INC. page 242
Habour/One W-OUTERWEAR/COATS & JACKETS — HARBOUR INTERNATIONAL LLC page 106
Habour/One M-OUTERWEAR/COATS & JACKETS — HARBOUR INTERNATIONAL LLC page 196
Haggar M-SUITS — HAGGAR CLOTHING CO., INC. page 213
Haggar A-MEN'S — MMG DIV OF GREAT CHINA EMPIRE page 346
Haggar Casuals M-CASUAL — HAGGAR CLOTHING CO., INC. page 173
Haggar Heritage M-SUITS — HAGGAR CLOTHING CO., INC. page 213
Happy Bunny C-SLEEPWEAR — HYP HATS LTD. page 269
Happy Bunny A-CHILDREN — HYP HATS LTD. page 292
Happy Bunny A-HATS/CAPS/MILLINERY — HYP HATS LTD. page 330
Harley Davidson A-HATS/CAPS/MILLINERY — F & M HAT CO., INC. page 328
Havengirl C-DRESSES — HAVENGIRL page 245
Hawaiian Island Creations W-SWIMWEAR & BEACHWEAR — CORAL HEAD INC./HAWAIIAN page 147
Hawaiian Island Creations M-SWIMWEAR & BEACHWEAR — CORAL HEAD INC./HAWAIIAN page 218
Hayley Paige W-BRIDAL & EVENINGWEAR — JLM COUTURE page 19
Head® A-HOSIERY/SOCKS/LEGWEAR — CRESCENT SOCK COMPANY page 337
Head To Toe W-BLOUSES/SHIRTS/TOPS — HTT HEADWEAR LTD. page 13
Head To Toe M-SHIRTS: — HTT HEADWEAR LTD. page 205
Head To Toe A-HATS/CAPS/MILLINERY — HTT HEADWEAR LTD. page 330
Headwear Creations A-HATS/CAPS/MILLINERY — HEADWEAR CREATIONS, INC. page 329
Heisel W-CONTEMPORARY SPORTSWEAR — HEISEL page 37
Henry & Belle W-JEANS — HENRY AND BELLE page 79
Henry Lehr W-ECOLOGICAL & ORGANIC — STYLE SOURCE INC. page 67
Henry Lehr W-PRIVATE LABEL — STYLE SOURCE INC. page 115
Henry Lehr M-PRIVATE LABEL — STYLE SOURCE INC. page 202
Henschel Hat A-HATS/CAPS/MILLINERY — HENSCHEL HAT CO. page 329
Heritage Brands W-LIFESTYLE COLLECTIONS — PVH CORPORATION page 94
Herve Leger W-BRIDAL & EVENINGWEAR — BCBG MAX AZRIA GROUP page 16
Hilo Hattie W-CASUAL — HILO HATTIE page 25
Hilo Hattie M-CASUAL — HILO HATTIE page 174
Hilo Hattie C-TEE — HILO HATTIE page 278
His Spawear M-SLEEPWEAR — SUSAN DUNN INC. page 209
Hold Up A-BELTS — HOLD-UP SUSPENDER CO. page 285
Holloway W-ACTIVE/ATHLETICWEAR — HOLLOWAY SPORTSWEAR, INC. page 5
Holloway M-ACTIVE/ATHLETICWEAR — HOLLOWAY SPORTSWEAR, INC. page 165
Holloway C-ACTIVE/ATHLETICWEAR — HOLLOWAY SPORTSWEAR, INC. page 236
Honda A-HATS/CAPS/MILLINERY — PACIFIC SPORTSWEAR & EMBLEM page 331

Hotdrop W-ACTIVE/ATHLETICWEAR — SWEENIE MANUFACTURING page 7
House of King W-PRIVATE LABEL — JULIE HUTTON INC. page 113
HSM M-PRIVATE LABEL — HART SCHAFFNER MARX page 200
HSM M-SUITS — HART SCHAFFNER MARX page 213
HSM M-TROUSERS — HART SCHAFFNER MARX page 225
Hugo Boss W-DESIGNER — HUGO BOSS U.S.A., INC. page 51
Hugo Boss M-DESIGNER — HUGO BOSS U.S.A., INC. page 181
Hugo Boss M-SUITS — HUGO BOSS U.S.A., INC. page 214
Hugo Boss A-EYEWEAR — HUGO BOSS U.S.A., INC. page 296
Hyp C-SLEEPWEAR — HYP HATS LTD. page 269
Hyp A-CHILDREN — HYP HATS LTD. page 292
Hyp A-HATS/CAPS/MILLINERY — HYP HATS LTD. page 330
Hyperclash W-ECOLOGICAL & ORGANIC — HYPERCLASH page 66
Hyperclash W-JUNIOR SPORTSWEAR — HYPERCLASH page 83
I-C Collections C-SLEEPWEAR — NEW ICM, LP page 270
Imperial A-HATS/CAPS/MILLINERY — IMPERIAL HEADWEAR page 330
Impulse™Brand A-GLOVES — BECKER GLOVE INTERNATIONAL, page 310
Inc. W-DRESSES/SEPARATES/SUITS — EVANESE, INC. page 59
Inc. M-SPORTSMEN'S — SCENT-LOK/DIV. OF A.L.S. page 211
Indigenous W-ECOLOGICAL & ORGANIC — INDIGENOUS page 67
Indigenous M-ECOLOGICAL & ORGANIC — INDIGENOUS page 183
InEssence C-SLEEPWEAR — HYP HATS LTD. page 269
InEssence A-CHILDREN — HYP HATS LTD. page 292
InEssence A-HATS/CAPS/MILLINERY — HYP HATS LTD. page 330
INEZ A-FASHION — BY BOE LTD. page 297
Inge Christopher A-HANDBAGS — INGE CHRISTOPHER page 320
Inserch M-CONTEMPORARY SPORTSWEAR — INSERCH BY MERC USA, INC. page 178
Inserch M-DESIGNER — INSERCH BY MERC USA, INC. page 181
Intimate Moments W-INTIMATE APPAREL & LINGERIE — CHARLEY MORGAN, INC. page 70
IRO W-CONTEMPORARY SPORTSWEAR — SIMON SHOWROOM page 40
IRO W-JUNIOR SPORTSWEAR — SIMON SHOWROOM page 84
Ironman A-EYEWEAR — FGX INTERNATIONAL/DIV OF page 296
Isaac Reina M-CASUAL — PROJECT NO. 8 page 175
Isaac Reina M-CONTEMPORARY SPORTSWEAR — PROJECT NO. 8 page 179
Islander W-SWEATERS & KNITWEAR — CANADIAN SWEATER CO., LTD. page 137
Islander M-SWEATERS — CANADIAN SWEATER CO., LTD. page 215
Islander C-SWEATERS — CANADIAN SWEATER CO., LTD. page 273
Islander A-GLOVES — CANADIAN SWEATER CO., LTD. page 310
Islander A-HATS/CAPS/MILLINERY — CANADIAN SWEATER CO., LTD. page 326
It Figures! W-SWIMWEAR & BEACHWEAR — BREAKING WAVES INTERNATIONAL page 146
iXtreme C-OUTERWEAR/COATS & JACKETS — IAPPAREL LLC page 260
IZOD A-HATS/CAPS/MILLINERY — CONCEPT ONE ACCESSORIES page 327
J Richards W-OUTERWEAR/COATS & JACKETS — J RICHARDS INTERNATIONAL page 106
J Richards W-SPECIAL — J RICHARDS INTERNATIONAL page 123
J. Blades A-MEN'S — RON CORNELL page 347
J. Crew W-LIFESTYLE COLLECTIONS — J. CREW page 92
J. Crew M-CASUAL — J. CREW page 174
J.P. Ourse A-HANDBAGS — J.P. OURSE CIE/JOHN COLE page 321
J.P. Ourse A-LUGGAGE/BAGS/LEATHER — J.P. OURSE CIE/JOHN COLE page 342
Jack Daniels A-HATS/CAPS/MILLINERY — F & M HAT CO., INC. page 328
Jack Spade M-CASUAL — KATE SPADE AND COMPANY page 174
Jack's Socks® A-HOSIERY/SOCKS/LEGWEAR — CRESCENT SOCK COMPANY page 337
Jamais Rae W-BRIDAL & EVENINGWEAR — DEBORA RACHELLE INC. page 18
James Campbell A-MEN'S — MMG DIV OF GREAT CHINA EMPIRE page 346
Jantzen W-SWIMWEAR & BEACHWEAR — JANTZEN page 148
JBD New York W-LIFESTYLE COLLECTIONS — JBD NEW YORK page 92
Jenna Leigh W-INTIMATE APPAREL & LINGERIE — GELMART INDUSTRIES INC. page 73
Jenny W-SWEATERS & KNITWEAR — B & B SWEATERS page 136
Jenny W-TEE — B & B SWEATERS page 152
Jerzees Bella+Canvas W-ACTIVE/ATHLETICWEAR — WASATCH CO. page 7

Jerzees Bella+Canvas WASATCH CO.
M-ACTIVE/ATHLETICWEAR page 167

Jerzees Bella+Canvas WASATCH CO.
M-OUTERWEAR/COATS & JACKETS page 197

Jerzees Bella+Canvas WASATCH CO.
C-NEWBORN/LAYETTE/INFANT page 258

Jessica Taylor LIFE & STYLE FASHIONS INC.
W-CASUAL page 26

Jill Henning JILL HENNING FINERIES
A-HATS/CAPS/MILLINERY page 330

Jim Hjelm JLM COUTURE
W-BRIDAL & EVENINGWEAR page 19

Jimmy Choo SAFILO U.S.A.
A-EYEWEAR page 296

jj threads JULIE HUTTON INC.
W-PRIVATE LABEL page 113

Joan Blackshear JOAN BLACKSHEAR DESIGN
A-GIFT page 308

Joan Vass NEW ORLEANS KNITWEAR
W-CASUAL page 26

Jockey Classic JOCKEY INTERNATIONAL, INC.
W-INTIMATE APPAREL & LINGERIE page 73

Jockey Classic JOCKEY INTERNATIONAL, INC.
M-SLEEPWEAR page 209

Jockey Pouch® JOCKEY INTERNATIONAL, INC.
M-SLEEPWEAR page 209

Jockey Silks® JOCKEY INTERNATIONAL, INC.
W-INTIMATE APPAREL & LINGERIE page 73

Jockey Sport JOCKEY INTERNATIONAL, INC.
W-INTIMATE APPAREL & LINGERIE page 73

Jockey Sport JOCKEY INTERNATIONAL, INC.
M-SLEEPWEAR page 209

Joe Blow T's Inc. JOE BLOW T'S
W-TEE page 154

Joe Blow T's Inc. JOE BLOW T'S
M-TEE page 222

Joe Blow T's Inc. JOE BLOW T'S
C-TEE page 278

John Cole Collections J.P. OURSE CIE/JOHN COLE
A-HANDBAGS page 321

John Cole Collections J.P. OURSE CIE/JOHN COLE
A-LUGGAGE/BAGS/LEATHER page 342

John Deere® GEM DANDY INC.
A-BELTS page 285

John Varvatos PEERLESS CLOTHING
M-SUITS page 214

John Varvatos PEERLESS CLOTHING
M-TROUSERS page 225

Joli Jewelry JOLI JEWELRY
A-FASHION page 300

Joli Jewelry JOLI JEWELRY
A-GIFT page 308

Joli Jewelry JOLI JEWELRY
A-HAIR page 313

Jon TERI JON
W-DESIGNER page 54

Jonden JONDEN MANUFACTURING CO.,
W-JUNIOR SPORTSWEAR page 83

Jonden JONDEN MANUFACTURING CO.,
W-MISSY/UPDATED SPORTSWEAR page 97

Jonden JONDEN MANUFACTURING CO.,
W-SPECIAL page 123

Jonden JONDEN MANUFACTURING CO.,
W-SPECIAL page 129

Jonden JONDEN MANUFACTURING CO.,
W-SPECIAL page 133

Jones New York JONES APPAREL GROUP USA, INC
W-MISSY/UPDATED SPORTSWEAR page 97

Jones New York ESSEX MANUFACTURING INC.
M-LICENSED page 191

Jones New York ESSEX MANUFACTURING INC.
A-UMBRELLAS page 357

Jones New York GILTON COMPANY
A-UMBRELLAS page 358

Josie NATORI CO.
W-INTIMATE APPAREL & LINGERIE page 73

JOTA+GE ADK FASHIONS
W-DESIGNER page 47

Jou Jou JOU JOU DESIGNS
W-JEANS page 79

Jou Jou JOU JOU DESIGNS
W-JUNIOR SPORTSWEAR page 83

Jou Jou JOU JOU DESIGNS
W-OUTERWEAR/COATS & JACKETS page 106

Joy Susan JOY ACCESSORIES
A-FASHION page 300

Joy Susan JOY ACCESSORIES
A-HANDBAGS page 321

Joy Susan JOY ACCESSORIES
A-SCARVES page 351

Joyous and Free JOYOUS AND FREE
W-LIFESTYLE COLLECTIONS page 93

Julie Vino ADK FASHIONS
W-BRIDAL & EVENINGWEAR page 15

Jussara Lee JUSSARA LEE
W-BRIDAL & EVENINGWEAR page 19

Jussara Lee JUSSARA LEE
W-CONTEMPORARY SPORTSWEAR page 37

JustWhiteShirts JUST WHITE SHIRTS
M-SHIRTS: page 205

JustWhiteShirts JUST WHITE SHIRTS
A-MEN'S page 346

K & P Weaver LLC K & P WEAVER, LLC
W-ACTIVE/ATHLETICWEAR page 5

K & P Weaver LLC K & P WEAVER, LLC
W-UNIFORMS page 158

K & P Weaver LLC K & P WEAVER, LLC
M-UNIFORMS page 228

Kahn Lucas KAHN LUCAS
C-COORDINATED SPORTSWEAR-GIRLS page 242

Kahn Lucas KAHN LUCAS
C-DRESSES page 246

Kahn Lucas KAHN LUCAS
C-LICENSED page 254

Kamtex KAMTEX FASHION
M-TEE page 222

Karl Kani HASELSON INT'L TRADING INC.
M-LICENSED page 192

Kashka KIDCUTETURE
C-COORDINATED SPORTSWEAR-GIRLS page 242

Kate Spade KATE SPADE AND COMPANY
W-LIFESTYLE COLLECTIONS page 93

Kate Spade KATE SPADE AND COMPANY
W-MISSY/UPDATED SPORTSWEAR page 98

Kate Spade SAFILO U.S.A.
A-EYEWEAR page 296

Kate Spade KATE SPADE AND COMPANY
A-LUGGAGE/BAGS/LEATHER page 342

Katia Serafini FORI SHOWROOM
W-OUTERWEAR/COATS & JACKETS page 105

Katia Serafini FORI SHOWROOM
W-SWEATERS & KNITWEAR page 140

KayAnna MANSFIELD INTERNATIONAL
W-SLEEPWEAR & LOUNGEWEAR page 118

Kayanna Spa MANSFIELD INTERNATIONAL
W-SLEEPWEAR & LOUNGEWEAR page 118

Kaynee RIFLE/KAYNEE
C-UNIFORMS page 281

Kembali KEMBALI LTD.
W-MISSY/UPDATED SPORTSWEAR page 98

Kensie G-III APPAREL GROUP
W-LIFESTYLE COLLECTIONS page 92

KidCuteTure KIDCUTETURE
C-DRESSES page 246

KiddyKats WASATCH CO.
W-ACTIVE/ATHLETICWEAR page 7

KiddyKats WASATCH CO.
M-ACTIVE/ATHLETICWEAR page 167

KiddyKats WASATCH CO.
M-OUTERWEAR/COATS & JACKETS page 197

KiddyKats WASATCH CO.
C-NEWBORN/LAYETTE/INFANT page 258

Kids Spa Wear SUSAN DUNN INC.
A-CHILDREN page 292

Kidture EVY OF CALIFORNIA, INC./DBA
C-COORDINATED SPORTSWEAR-GIRLS page 241

Kidture EVY OF CALIFORNIA, INC./DBA
C-DRESSES page 245

Kidture EVY OF CALIFORNIA, INC./DBA
C-NEWBORN/LAYETTE/INFANT page 255

Kidzone LONG STREET
C-COORDINATED SPORTSWEAR-GIRLS page 243

Kippys KIPPYS
W-DECORATED/EMBELLISHED APPAREL page 44

Kippys KIPPYS
W-LEATHER page 87

Kippys KIPPYS
A-BELTS page 286

Knit Avenue SWEATER BRAND INC.
W-SWEATERS & KNITWEAR page 143

Knox Armory ALPHA INDUSTRIES, INC.
M-OUTERWEAR/COATS & JACKETS page 193

Knox Armory ALPHA INDUSTRIES, INC.
M-SPORTSMEN'S page 211

Knox Armory ALPHA INDUSTRIES, INC.
C-OUTERWEAR/COATS & JACKETS page 259

Kooba SHOWROOM SEVEN/ERICKSON
A-HANDBAGS page 323

Kurosh KOUROSH NEW YORK
W-SWEATERS & KNITWEAR page 141

La Mode GOLF APPAREL BRANDS
W-BLOUSES/SHIRTS/TOPS page 13

La Mode GOLF APPAREL BRANDS
W-OUTERWEAR/COATS & JACKETS page 106

La Mode GOLF APPAREL BRANDS
W-SWEATERS & KNITWEAR page 140

La Mode GOLF APPAREL BRANDS
M-OUTERWEAR/COATS & JACKETS page 196

La Mode GOLF APPAREL BRANDS
M-SHIRTS: page 204

La Mode GOLF APPAREL BRANDS
M-SWEATERS page 216

La Mode GOLF APPAREL BRANDS
C-SHIRTS: page 267

La Mode GOLF APPAREL BRANDS
A-HATS/CAPS/MILLINERY page 328

Lacette RAGO FOUNDATIONS LLC
W-INTIMATE APPAREL & LINGERIE page 74

Lacette RAGO FOUNDATIONS LLC
W-SPECIAL page 125

Lady M GELMART INDUSTRIES INC.
W-INTIMATE APPAREL & LINGERIE page 73

Lalla Bee ADK FASHIONS
W-BRIDAL & EVENINGWEAR page 15

Lalla Bee ADK FASHIONS
W-DESIGNER page 47

LaMatera LA MATERA
A-BELTS page 286

Landau LANDAU
W-UNIFORMS page 158

Landau LANDAU
M-UNIFORMS page 228

Language Los Angeles EASTWEST CLOTHING
W-CASUAL page 24

Lasercut PACIFIC SPORTSWEAR & EMBLEM
A-HATS/CAPS/MILLINERY page 331

Latico LATICO LEATHERS
A-HANDBAGS page 321

Latico LATICO LEATHERS
A-LUGGAGE/BAGS/LEATHER page 343

Latitudes GRAPHICS GROUP LTD./DBA
W-TEE page 153

Latitudes GRAPHICS GROUP LTD./DBA
M-TEE page 222

Latitudes GRAPHICS GROUP LTD./DBA
C-ACTIVE/ATHLETICWEAR page 235

Laura Dare NEW ICM, LP
C-COORDINATED SPORTSWEAR-GIRLS page 243

Laura Dare NEW ICM, LP
C-SLEEPWEAR page 270

Lauren RALPH LAUREN, INC.
W-DESIGNER page 52

Lauren Ralph Lauren PEERLESS CLOTHING
M-SUITS page 214

Lauren Ralph Lauren PEERLESS CLOTHING
M-TROUSERS page 225

Lazaro JLM COUTURE
W-BRIDAL & EVENINGWEAR page 19

Le Mieux LE MIEUX/TARA INTERNATIONAL
W-MISSY/UPDATED SPORTSWEAR page 98

Le Mieux W-SPECIAL — LE MIEUX/TARA INTERNATIONAL, page 124

Le Mieux W-SPECIAL — LE MIEUX/TARA INTERNATIONAL, page 133

Leatherock A-BELTS — LEATHEROCK INT. INC. page 286

Leatherock A-HANDBAGS — LEATHEROCK INT. INC. page 321

Lee Andersen W-DECORATED/EMBELLISHED APPAREL — ANDERSEN-BECKER INC. page 43

Lee School Uniforms C-UNIFORMS — FRENCH TOAST page 281

Lee Tops C-LICENSED — FRENCH TOAST page 253

Leilani W-SWIMWEAR & BEACHWEAR — BREAKING WAVES INTERNATIONAL page 146

Levi's M-OUTERWEAR/COATS & JACKETS — G-III APPAREL GROUP page 195

Levi's® W-JEANS — LEVI STRAUSS & CO. page 79

Levi's® M-JEANS — LEVI STRAUSS & CO. page 187

Levi's® M-WESTERNWEAR — LEVI STRAUSS & CO. page 231

Levis® A-HATS/CAPS/MILLINERY — CONCEPT ONE ACCESSORIES page 327

Liancarlo W-BRIDAL & EVENINGWEAR — LIANCARLO page 20

Lillian Rose A-BRIDAL/SPECIAL/INTIMATE — LILLIAN ROSE, INC. page 289

Lin Custom A-CHILDREN — LIN MANUFACTURING & DESIGN page 292

Lin Custom A-HOSIERY/SOCKS/LEGWEAR — LIN MANUFACTURING & DESIGN page 339

Lin Performance A-CHILDREN — LIN MANUFACTURING & DESIGN page 292

Lin Performance A-HOSIERY/SOCKS/LEGWEAR — LIN MANUFACTURING & DESIGN page 339

Lin Wellness A-CHILDREN — LIN MANUFACTURING & DESIGN page 292

Lin Wellness A-HOSIERY/SOCKS/LEGWEAR — LIN MANUFACTURING & DESIGN page 339

Linda Richards W-OUTERWEAR/COATS & JACKETS — LINDA RICHARDS page 107

Linda Richards A-SCARVES — LINDA RICHARDS page 352

Lipstik Girls C-COORDINATED SPORTSWEAR-GIRLS — LIPSTIK GIRLS page 243

Lipstik Girls C-JEANS — LIPSTIK GIRLS page 251

Lipstik Girls C-NEWBORN/LAYETTE/INFANT — LIPSTIK GIRLS page 256

Little Miss Julia A-HAIR — LITTLE MISS JULIA page 313

Little Zazzy C-COORDINATED SPORTSWEAR-GIRLS — NEW ICM, LP page 243

Lolakimoni W-ECOLOGICAL & ORGANIC — MEHERA SHAW TEXTILES PVT. LTD. page 67

Longitude W-SPECIAL — LONGITUDE/LONGEVITY BRANDS page 124

Longitude W-SWIMWEAR & BEACHWEAR — LONGITUDE/LONGEVITY BRANDS page 148

Lorraine Claire W-PRIVATE LABEL — JULIE HUTTON INC. page 113

Love W-CONTEMPORARY SPORTSWEAR — TOPSON DOWNS page 41

Lucky 7™ A-BELTS — MIL-IDEE, INC. page 287

Luli Fama W-SWIMWEAR & BEACHWEAR — LULI FAMA page 149

Lulita by Luli Fama W-SWIMWEAR & BEACHWEAR — LULI FAMA page 149

Luna Luz W-CONTEMPORARY SPORTSWEAR — AZIBI LTD. page 30

Luna Luz W-DRESSES/SEPARATES/SUITS — AZIBI LTD. page 56

Luscious Laces Lingerie A-BRIDAL/SPECIAL/INTIMATE — LUSCIOUS LACES LINGERIE page 290

Lust W-INTIMATE APPAREL & LINGERIE — COMME CI COMME CA LTD. page 71

Lynx W-UNIFORMS — LANDAU page 158

Maddi W-SWEATERS & KNITWEAR — B & B SWEATERS page 136

Maddi W-TEE — B & B SWEATERS page 152

Made with Love W-INTIMATE APPAREL & LINGERIE — CHARLEY MORGAN, INC. page 70

Mademoiselle A-GLOVES — MADEMOISELLE, INC. page 311

Mademoiselle A-HANDBAGS — MADEMOISELLE, INC. page 322

Mademoiselle A-HATS/CAPS/MILLINERY — MADEMOISELLE, INC. page 331

Mademoiselle A-SCARVES — MADEMOISELLE, INC. page 352

Mag Mile A-HANDBAGS — DREAMBAGS, INC. page 319

Mag Mile A-LUGGAGE/BAGS/LEATHER — DREAMBAGS, INC. page 341

Magicap A-HATS/CAPS/MILLINERY — PACIFIC SPORTSWEAR & EMBLEM page 331

Magicsuit® W-SWIMWEAR & BEACHWEAR — A & H SPORTSWEAR CO. INC. page 145

Magnivision A-EYEWEAR — FGX INTERNATIONAL/DIV OF page 296

Mainland Co. W-ECOLOGICAL & ORGANIC — STYLE SOURCE INC. page 67

Mainland Co. W-PRIVATE LABEL — STYLE SOURCE INC. page 115

Mainland Co. M-PRIVATE LABEL — STYLE SOURCE INC. page 202

Mainstream® Swimsuits W-SWIMWEAR & BEACHWEAR — A & H SPORTSWEAR CO. INC. page 145

Maison Martin Margiela M-CASUAL — PROJECT NO. 8 page 175

Maison Martin Margiela M-CONTEMPORARY SPORTSWEAR — PROJECT NO. 8 page 179

Major League Baseball W-CASUAL — 5TH & OCEAN CLOTHING LLC/NEW page 23

Major League Baseball — 5TH & OCEAN CLOTHING LLC/NEW
W-JUNIOR SPORTSWEAR — page 81

Major League Baseball — 5TH & OCEAN CLOTHING LLC/NEW
M-CASUAL — page 172

Major League Baseball — 5TH & OCEAN CLOTHING LLC/NEW
C-ACTIVE/ATHLETICWEAR — page 233

Male Power — COMME CI COMME CA LTD.
M-SLEEPWEAR — page 208

Male Power — COMME CI COMME CA LTD.
M-SWIMWEAR & BEACHWEAR — page 217

Maliparmi — SHOWROOM SEVEN/ERICKSON
W-CONTEMPORARY SPORTSWEAR — page 40

Maliparmi — SHOWROOM SEVEN/ERICKSON
W-DESIGNER — page 53

Maliparmi — SHOWROOM SEVEN/ERICKSON
A-HANDBAGS — page 323

Manage á Trois — KIPPYS
W-DECORATED/EMBELLISHED APPAREL — page 44

Mansfield Hotel and Spa. — MANSFIELD INTERNATIONAL
W-SLEEPWEAR & LOUNGEWEAR — page 118

Marc Bouwer — MARC BOUWER
W-BRIDAL & EVENINGWEAR — page 20

Marc Bouwer — MARC BOUWER
W-DRESSES/SEPARATES/SUITS — page 60

Marc Jacobs — SAFILO U.S.A.
A-EYEWEAR — page 296

Marc New York — ANDREW MARC
W-LEATHER — page 87

Marc New York — ANDREW MARC
W-OUTERWEAR/COATS & JACKETS — page 101

Marc New York — ANDREW MARC
M-LEATHER — page 189

Marc New York — ANDREW MARC
M-OUTERWEAR/COATS & JACKETS — page 193

Maria Coca — ADK FASHIONS
W-BRIDAL & EVENINGWEAR — page 15

Maria Coca — ADK FASHIONS
W-DESIGNER — page 47

Marisa Baratelli — BERGER & STEVENS
W-BRIDAL & EVENINGWEAR — page 16

Marlyn Schiff — NOTANONYMOUS
A-FASHION — page 301

Marmot — MARMOT MOUNTAIN LLC.
W-OUTERWEAR/COATS & JACKETS — page 107

Marmot — MARMOT MOUNTAIN LLC.
M-OUTERWEAR/COATS & JACKETS — page 196

Marmot — MARMOT MOUNTAIN LLC.
C-OUTERWEAR/COATS & JACKETS — page 261

Marmot — MARMOT MOUNTAIN LLC.
A-GLOVES — page 311

Marni — PROJECT NO. 8
M-CASUAL — page 175

Marni — PROJECT NO. 8
M-CONTEMPORARY SPORTSWEAR — page 179

Martin Dingman — MARTIN DINGMAN COUNTRYWEAR
M-OUTERWEAR/COATS & JACKETS — page 197

Martin Dingman — MARTIN DINGMAN COUNTRYWEAR
A-BELTS — page 286

Martin Dingman — MARTIN DINGMAN COUNTRYWEAR
A-GLOVES — page 311

Martin Dingman — MARTIN DINGMAN COUNTRYWEAR
A-LUGGAGE/BAGS/LEATHER — page 343

Martinez Montiel! — WEDDING TROPICS
C-SHIRTS: — page 268

Marvel — HASELSON INT'L TRADING INC.
M-LICENSED — page 192

Mascot — MASCOT WORKWEAR U.S./REPCON
W-UNIFORMS — page 159

Mascot — MASCOT WORKWEAR U.S./REPCON
M-UNIFORMS — page 229

Mascot — REPCON NW DBA THE MODERN
M-UNIFORMS — page 229

Max Mara — SAFILO U.S.A.
A-EYEWEAR — page 296

Max Volmary and Alora Knits. — BERGER & STEVENS
W-CONTEMPORARY SPORTSWEAR — page 32

Megaman — FRENCH TOAST
C-LICENSED — page 253

Meher & Riddhima — ADK FASHIONS
W-BRIDAL & EVENINGWEAR — page 15

Mehera Shaw — MEHERA SHAW TEXTILES PVT. LTD.
W-ECOLOGICAL & ORGANIC — page 67

Mei Fa — SHAUNE BAZNER ACCESSORIES,
A-HAIR — page 314

Mela Rosa — ELE.PAVONI NEW YORK LTD
W-BLOUSES/SHIRTS/TOPS — page 12

Mela Rosa — ELE.PAVONI NEW YORK LTD
W-DESIGNER — page 50

Mela Rosa — ELE.PAVONI NEW YORK LTD
W-SWEATERS & KNITWEAR — page 139

Melanie Harris — MELANIE HARRIS
W-DESIGNER — page 51

Mezzanotte — CALVIN CLOTHING COMPANY
C-COORDINATED SPORTSWEAR-BOYS — page 237

Mezzanotte — CALVIN CLOTHING COMPANY
C-SHIRTS: — page 267

Mezzanotte — CALVIN CLOTHING COMPANY
C-SUITS/SPECIAL — page 271

Miami Style — MIAMI STYLE INC.
W-PRIVATE LABEL — page 114

Miami Style — MIAMI STYLE INC.
M-PRIVATE LABEL — page 201

Miami Style — MIAMI STYLE INC.
C-PRIVATE LABEL — page 264

Michael by Michael Kors — MICHAEL KORS
W-DESIGNER — page 52

Michael Kor's — MICHAEL KORS
W-DESIGNER — page 52

Michael Kors — GLOBAL BRANDS GROUP
W-LICENSED — page 89

Michael Kors — GLOBAL BRANDS GROUP
M-LICENSED — page 192

Michael Kors — PEERLESS CLOTHING
M-SUITS — page 214

Michael Kors — PEERLESS CLOTHING
M-TROUSERS — page 225

mickmack — BABYFAIR, INC.
C-PRIVATE LABEL — page 263

Mil-Idee — MIL-IDEE, INC.
A-BELTS — page 287

Milkbarn MILKBARN, LLC
C-NEWBORN/LAYETTE/INFANT page 256

Miraclesuit® A & H SPORTSWEAR CO. INC.
W-SWIMWEAR & BEACHWEAR page 145

Misook MISOOK
W-DRESSES/SEPARATES/SUITS page 60

Mister Noah MISTER NOAH
W-ACTIVE/ATHLETICWEAR page 5

Misty Harbor® ESSEX MANUFACTURING INC.
W-OUTERWEAR/COATS & JACKETS page 104

Misty Harbor® ESSEX MANUFACTURING INC.
W-SPECIAL page 123

Misty Harbor® ESSEX MANUFACTURING INC.
W-SPECIAL page 132

Misty Harbor® ESSEX MANUFACTURING INC.
M-BIG page 170

Misty Harbor® ESSEX MANUFACTURING INC.
M-LICENSED page 191

Misty Harbor® ESSEX MANUFACTURING INC.
M-OUTERWEAR/COATS & JACKETS page 195

Misty Harbor® ESSEX MANUFACTURING INC.
C-OUTERWEAR/COATS & JACKETS page 260

Misty Harbor® ESSEX MANUFACTURING INC.
A-UMBRELLAS page 357

MLB OUTERSTUFF LTD.
C-OUTERWEAR/COATS & JACKETS page 261

MLB FBF ORIGINALS
A-HOSIERY/SOCKS/LEGWEAR page 337

MLS OUTERSTUFF LTD.
C-OUTERWEAR/COATS & JACKETS page 261

MLS FBF ORIGINALS
A-HOSIERY/SOCKS/LEGWEAR page 337

Moana BLUE HAWAII SALES
M-CASUAL page 172

Modal Collection 2 X IST
M-TEE page 219

Mododoc MODODOC/GENEXUS
W-CASUAL page 26

Mododoc MODODOC/GENEXUS
M-CASUAL page 174

Molson CATFISH CALHOUN AKA CALHOUN
W-SWIMWEAR & BEACHWEAR page 146

Molson CATFISH CALHOUN AKA CALHOUN
M-SWIMWEAR & BEACHWEAR page 217

Montanaco MONTANACO CLOTHING COMPANY
W-LEATHER page 87

Montanaco MONTANACO CLOTHING COMPANY
M-LEATHER page 189

Monterey Bay RON CORNELL
A-MEN'S page 347

Moorer FORI SHOWROOM
W-OUTERWEAR/COATS & JACKETS page 105

Moorer FORI SHOWROOM
W-SWEATERS & KNITWEAR page 140

Moose Creek MOOSE CREEK
W-CASUAL page 26

Moose Creek MOOSE CREEK
M-CASUAL page 175

Mother Plucker MOTHER PLUCKER FEATHER
A-BRIDAL/SPECIAL/INTIMATE page 290

Motherwear STYLE SOURCE INC.
W-ECOLOGICAL & ORGANIC page 67

Motherwear STYLE SOURCE INC.
W-PRIVATE LABEL page 115

Motionwar Gymnastics MOTIONWEAR, LLC
W-ACTIVE/ATHLETICWEAR page 6

Motionwar Gymnastics MOTIONWEAR, LLC
C-ACTIVE/ATHLETICWEAR page 236

Motionwear MOTIONWEAR, LLC
W-ACTIVE/ATHLETICWEAR page 6

Motionwear MOTIONWEAR, LLC
C-ACTIVE/ATHLETICWEAR page 236

Motionwear Cheer MOTIONWEAR, LLC
W-ACTIVE/ATHLETICWEAR page 6

Mudd HYP HATS LTD.
C-SLEEPWEAR page 269

Mudd HYP HATS LTD.
A-CHILDREN page 292

Mudd HYP HATS LTD.
A-HATS/CAPS/MILLINERY page 330

My Michelle KELLWOOD COMPANY
W-JUNIOR SPORTSWEAR page 83

Mystique NOTANONYMOUS
A-BRIDAL/SPECIAL/INTIMATE page 290

Naked Sportswear SWEENIE MANUFACTURING
W-ACTIVE/ATHLETICWEAR page 7

NASCAR FBF ORIGINALS
A-HOSIERY/SOCKS/LEGWEAR page 337

Natori NATORI CO.
W-INTIMATE APPAREL & LINGERIE page 73

Naturals JOCKEY INTERNATIONAL, INC.
W-INTIMATE APPAREL & LINGERIE page 73

NatureTech GOLF APPAREL BRANDS
W-BLOUSES/SHIRTS/TOPS page 13

Naturetech GOLF APPAREL BRANDS
M-OUTERWEAR/COATS & JACKETS page 196

NatureTech GOLF APPAREL BRANDS
M-SHIRTS: page 204

Nautica ESSEX MANUFACTURING INC.
M-LICENSED page 191

Nautica ESSEX MANUFACTURING INC.
A-UMBRELLAS page 357

NBA 5TH & OCEAN CLOTHING LLC/NEW
W-CASUAL page 23

NBA 5TH & OCEAN CLOTHING LLC/NEW
W-JUNIOR SPORTSWEAR page 81

NBA 5TH & OCEAN CLOTHING LLC/NEW
M-CASUAL page 172

NBA 5TH & OCEAN CLOTHING LLC/NEW
C-ACTIVE/ATHLETICWEAR page 233

NBA OUTERSTUFF LTD.
C-OUTERWEAR/COATS & JACKETS page 261

NBA FBF ORIGINALS
A-HOSIERY/SOCKS/LEGWEAR page 337

NCAA OUTERSTUFF LTD.
C-OUTERWEAR/COATS & JACKETS page 261

Neon 2 X IST
M-TEE page 219

New Balance EZRASONS, INC.
M-SLEEPWEAR page 208

Label Index

New Era Men's Line — M-CASUAL — 5TH & OCEAN CLOTHING LLC/NEW — page 172

New Orleans Knitwear — W-SWEATERS & KNITWEAR — NEW ORLEANS KNITWEAR — page 141

Next to Nothing — M-SLEEPWEAR — JOCKEY INTERNATIONAL, INC. — page 209

NFL — W-CASUAL — 5TH & OCEAN CLOTHING LLC/NEW — page 23

NFL — W-JUNIOR SPORTSWEAR — 5TH & OCEAN CLOTHING LLC/NEW — page 81

NFL — M-CASUAL — 5TH & OCEAN CLOTHING LLC/NEW — page 172

NFL — C-ACTIVE/ATHLETICWEAR — 5TH & OCEAN CLOTHING LLC/NEW — page 233

NFL — C-OUTERWEAR/COATS & JACKETS — OUTERSTUFF LTD. — page 261

NFL — A-HOSIERY/SOCKS/LEGWEAR — FBF ORIGINALS — page 337

NHL — W-CASUAL — 5TH & OCEAN CLOTHING LLC/NEW — page 23

NHL — W-JUNIOR SPORTSWEAR — 5TH & OCEAN CLOTHING LLC/NEW — page 81

NHL — M-CASUAL — 5TH & OCEAN CLOTHING LLC/NEW — page 172

NHL — C-ACTIVE/ATHLETICWEAR — 5TH & OCEAN CLOTHING LLC/NEW — page 233

NHL — C-OUTERWEAR/COATS & JACKETS — OUTERSTUFF LTD. — page 261

NHL — A-HOSIERY/SOCKS/LEGWEAR — FBF ORIGINALS — page 337

Nic + Zoe — W-LIFESTYLE COLLECTIONS — NIC + ZOE — page 93

Nic + Zoe — W-SWEATERS & KNITWEAR — NIC + ZOE — page 142

Nickelodeon — C-NEWBORN/LAYETTE/INFANT — KAHN LUCAS — page 256

Nickelodeon — A-HATS/CAPS/MILLINERY — CONCEPT ONE ACCESSORIES — page 327

Nicole & Co — A-GIFT — NICOLE & CO. — page 308

Nicole & Co. — A-HAIR — NICOLE & CO. — page 314

Nicole & Co. — A-HATS/CAPS/MILLINERY — NICOLE & CO. — page 331

Nicole & Co. — A-SCARVES — NICOLE & CO. — page 353

Nicole Miller — A-HOSIERY/SOCKS/LEGWEAR — LEG RESOURCE INC — page 339

Nicole Miller — A-UMBRELLAS — ESSEX MANUFACTURING INC. — page 357

Nike — W-ACTIVE/ATHLETICWEAR — NIKE, INC. — page 6

Nike — M-ACTIVE/ATHLETICWEAR — NIKE, INC. — page 165

Nina Fresa — W-TEE — KAMTEX FASHION — page 154

Nine West — A-EYEWEAR — FGX INTERNATIONAL/DIV OF — page 296

Nob Hill — A-MEN'S — RON CORNELL — page 347

Norma Kamali — W-DESIGNER — NORMA KAMALI — page 52

Nuthatch — W-CONTEMPORARY SPORTSWEAR — NUTHATCH — page 38

Odett — W-DRESSES/SEPARATES/SUITS — ODETT ENTERPRISES — page 60

Odett — W-MISSY/UPDATED SPORTSWEAR — ODETT ENTERPRISES — page 98

Odett — W-OUTERWEAR/COATS & JACKETS — ODETT ENTERPRISES — page 108

Odett — W-SWEATERS & KNITWEAR — ODETT ENTERPRISES — page 142

Odett — A-SCARVES — ODETT ENTERPRISES — page 353

ON TREND — W-CONTEMPORARY SPORTSWEAR — SENTIMENTAL INC. — page 39

ON TREND — W-DRESSES/SEPARATES/SUITS — SENTIMENTAL INC. — page 62

Only Hearts — W-BLOUSES/SHIRTS/TOPS — ONLY HEARTS — page 13

Only Hearts — W-DRESSES/SEPARATES/SUITS — ONLY HEARTS — page 61

Only Hearts — W-INTIMATE APPAREL & LINGERIE — ONLY HEARTS — page 74

OshKosh B'gosh — C-COORDINATED SPORTSWEAR-BOYS — OSHKOSH B'GOSH/CARTER'S — page 239

OshKosh B'gosh — C-COORDINATED SPORTSWEAR-GIRLS — OSHKOSH B'GOSH/CARTER'S — page 244

OshKosh B'gosh — C-JEANS — OSHKOSH B'GOSH/CARTER'S — page 252

Outerstuff — C-OUTERWEAR/COATS & JACKETS — OUTERSTUFF LTD. — page 261

Oxford Golf — W-CONTEMPORARY SPORTSWEAR — OXFORD GOLF — page 38

Oxford Golf — M-CONTEMPORARY SPORTSWEAR — OXFORD GOLF — page 179

Ozone — A-HOSIERY/SOCKS/LEGWEAR — OZONE DESIGN INC. — page 339

P.L. Junior — C-COORDINATED SPORTSWEAR-BOYS — LEMUR GROUP, INC. — page 238

P.L. Junior — C-COORDINATED SPORTSWEAR-GIRLS — LEMUR GROUP, INC. — page 243

P.L. Junior — C-SLEEPWEAR — LEMUR GROUP, INC. — page 269

Pacelli — M-BIG — DREAM WORLD INTERNATIONAL, — page 170

Pacelli — M-CONTEMPORARY SPORTSWEAR — DREAM WORLD INTERNATIONAL, — page 178

Pacelli — M-SUITS — DREAM WORLD INTERNATIONAL, — page 213

Pajama Socks® — A-HOSIERY/SOCKS/LEGWEAR — CRESCENT SOCK COMPANY — page 337

Pajar® — A-BELTS — MIL-IDEE, INC. — page 287

Paladin — M-BIG — D'ACCORD SHIRTS & GUAYABERAS — page 169

Panama Jack — A-EYEWEAR — FGX INTERNATIONAL/DIV OF — page 296

PAPI — M-SLEEPWEAR — ISACO INTERNATIONAL/PAPI INC. — page 209

Paradis Point W-ACTIVE/ATHLETICWEAR — WASATCH CO. page 7
Paradis Point M-ACTIVE/ATHLETICWEAR — WASATCH CO. page 167
Paradis Point M-OUTERWEAR/COATS & JACKETS — WASATCH CO. page 197
Paradis Point C-NEWBORN/LAYETTE/INFANT — WASATCH CO. page 258
Parajumpers W-LIFESTYLE COLLECTIONS — MT SHOWROOM page 93
Parajumpers W-OUTERWEAR/COATS & JACKETS — MT SHOWROOM page 107
Parajumpers M-CONTEMPORARY SPORTSWEAR — MT SHOWROOM page 179
Parasuco Denim Legend W-CONTEMPORARY SPORTSWEAR — PARASUCO JEANS INC. page 38
Parasuco Denim Legend W-JEANS — PARASUCO JEANS INC. page 80
Parasuco Denim Legend M-JEANS — PARASUCO JEANS INC. page 187
Parisa W-INTIMATE APPAREL & LINGERIE — PARISA page 74
Pashma Cashmere A-SCARVES — SHOWROOM SEVEN/ERICKSON page 354
Pashoot W-CONTEMPORARY SPORTSWEAR — SOPHIE FINZI LTD DBA PASHOOT page 40
Pashoot W-SPECIAL — SOPHIE FINZI LTD DBA PASHOOT page 126
Pashoot W-SWEATERS & KNITWEAR — SOPHIE FINZI LTD DBA PASHOOT page 143
Passionata W-INTIMATE APPAREL & LINGERIE — CHANTELLE LINGERIE INC. page 70
PatBo W-CONTEMPORARY SPORTSWEAR — SHOWROOM SEVEN/ERICKSON page 40
Patricia Bonaldi W-DESIGNER — SHOWROOM SEVEN/ERICKSON page 53
Patricia Fieldwalker W-INTIMATE APPAREL & LINGERIE — ARABESQUE DESIGN/PATRICIA page 69
Patrizia Luca W-CONTEMPORARY SPORTSWEAR — BARAMI/FASHION page 30
Patrizia Luca W-DRESSES/SEPARATES/SUITS — BARAMI/FASHION page 56
Pawa W-SWIMWEAR & BEACHWEAR — SWEENIE MANUFACTURING page 149
Paz W-ACTIVE/ATHLETICWEAR — BARRAZA ASSOCIATES LTD page 2
Paz W-ECOLOGICAL & ORGANIC — BARRAZA ASSOCIATES LTD page 65
Peace of Cake C-OUTERWEAR/COATS & JACKETS — CEJON ACCESSORIES INC. page 259
Peacock Ways W-BLOUSES/SHIRTS/TOPS — DANA EMILIA PRESENTS page 11
Peacock Ways W-CONTEMPORARY SPORTSWEAR — DANA EMILIA PRESENTS page 34
Peacock Ways W-DECORATED/EMBELLISHED APPAREL — DANA EMILIA PRESENTS page 44
Peacock Ways W-MISSY/UPDATED SPORTSWEAR — DANA EMILIA PRESENTS page 96
Peacock Ways W-SPECIAL — DANA EMILIA PRESENTS page 122
Peacock Ways W-SWEATERS & KNITWEAR — DANA EMILIA PRESENTS page 138
Penbrooke® W-SWIMWEAR & BEACHWEAR — A & H SPORTSWEAR CO. INC. page 145
Pendleton W-OUTERWEAR/COATS & JACKETS — PENDLETON WOOLEN MILLS, INC. page 108
Pendleton W-SPECIAL — PENDLETON WOOLEN MILLS, INC. page 124
Pendleton M-OUTERWEAR/COATS & JACKETS — PENDLETON WOOLEN MILLS, INC. page 197
Pendleton M-WESTERNWEAR — PENDLETON WOOLEN MILLS, INC. page 231
Penelopemack C-PRIVATE LABEL — BABYFAIR, INC. page 263
People Like Frank W-BLOUSES/SHIRTS/TOPS — ATOPAPPAREL CORP page 10
People Like Frank W-SPECIAL — ATOPAPPAREL CORP page 121
Pepin W-CONTEMPORARY SPORTSWEAR — SIMON SHOWROOM page 40
Pepin W-JUNIOR SPORTSWEAR — SIMON SHOWROOM page 84
Perry Ellis Swimwear W-SWIMWEAR & BEACHWEAR — JANTZEN page 148
Persnickety C-DRESSES — PERSNICKETY page 246
Personal Touch W-CASUAL — PERSONAL TOUCH INC. page 27
Personal Touch W-SPECIAL — PERSONAL TOUCH INC. page 124
Peserico W-OUTERWEAR/COATS & JACKETS — FORI SHOWROOM page 105
Peserico W-SWEATERS & KNITWEAR — FORI SHOWROOM page 140
Petit Lem C-COORDINATED SPORTSWEAR-BOYS — LEMUR GROUP, INC. page 238
Petit Lem C-COORDINATED SPORTSWEAR-GIRLS — LEMUR GROUP, INC. page 243
Petit Lem C-SLEEPWEAR — LEMUR GROUP, INC. page 269
PGA A-BELTS — GEM DANDY INC. page 285
Phiten® A-HOSIERY/SOCKS/LEGWEAR — TOTAL FOOT COMFORT page 340
Phool W-CONTEMPORARY SPORTSWEAR — PHOOL FASHIONS page 39
Phool W-DRESSES/SEPARATES/SUITS — PHOOL FASHIONS page 61
Phool W-SLEEPWEAR & LOUNGEWEAR — PHOOL FASHIONS page 118
Pier Antonio Gaspari W-DESIGNER — SHOWROOM SEVEN/ERICKSON page 53
Pierre Cardin M-SHIRTS: — BURMA BIBAS page 203
Pierre Cardin A-MEN'S — BURMA BIBAS page 345
Pima M-TEE — 2 X IST page 219
Pink Chicken C-DRESSES — PINK CHICKEN page 247

Label Index

Pink Chicken C-NEWBORN/LAYETTE/INFANT — PINK CHICKEN page 257

Pink Chicken C-SWIMWEAR & BEACHWEAR — PINK CHICKEN page 276

Pink Cookie C-SLEEPWEAR — HYP HATS LTD. page 269

Pink Cookie A-CHILDREN — HYP HATS LTD. page 292

Pink Cookie A-HATS/CAPS/MILLINERY — HYP HATS LTD. page 330

Pink Lotus W-ECOLOGICAL & ORGANIC — GREEN DRAGON page 66

Pink Panther M-LICENSED — HASELSON INT'L TRADING INC. page 192

Pink Platinum C-OUTERWEAR/COATS & JACKETS — IAPPAREL LLC page 260

Pinkhouse C-COORDINATED SPORTSWEAR-GIRLS — LONG STREET page 243

Piscotta New York W-ECOLOGICAL & ORGANIC — DOLORES PISCOTTA page 65

Piscotta New York W-OUTERWEAR/COATS & JACKETS — DOLORES PISCOTTA page 104

Piscotta New York W-SWEATERS & KNITWEAR — DOLORES PISCOTTA page 139

Piscotta New York A-GIFT — DOLORES PISCOTTA page 306

Platinum C-SUITS/SPECIAL — SILVER SUIT, INC. page 271

Plaza Suite A-GLOVES — BETMAR HATS INC. page 310

Plaza Suite A-HATS/CAPS/MILLINERY — BETMAR HATS INC. page 326

Plaza Suite A-SCARVES — BETMAR HATS INC. page 350

Point Zero A-BELTS — MIL-IDEE, INC. page 287

Polaroid & many more. A-EYEWEAR — SAFILO U.S.A. page 296

Polo Ralph Lauren M-DESIGNER — RALPH LAUREN, INC. page 182

Popeye M-LICENSED — HASELSON INT'L TRADING INC. page 192

Portofino A-MEN'S — RON CORNELL page 347

Preferred School Uniform M-UNIFORMS — HASELSON INT'L TRADING INC. page 228

Premiere Collection™ W-ACTIVE/ATHLETICWEAR — BODY WRAPPERS page 2

Primavera A-FASHION — DANECRAFT INC. page 298

Prince M-PRIVATE LABEL — STYLE SOURCE INC. page 202

Princess Aurora™ C-ACTIVE/ATHLETICWEAR — BODY WRAPPERS page 234

Princess Aurora™ A-CHILDREN — BODY WRAPPERS page 291

Priority Manufacturing W-UNIFORMS — PRIORITY MANUFACTURING page 159

Priority Manufacturing M-UNIFORMS — PRIORITY MANUFACTURING page 229

Procadif A-GIFT — NICOLE & CO. page 308

Procure™Brand A-GLOVES — BECKER GLOVE INTERNATIONAL, page 310

Projek Raw A-BELTS — MIL-IDEE, INC. page 287

Proshield W-OUTERWEAR/COATS & JACKETS — HARBOUR INTERNATIONAL LLC page 106

Proshield M-OUTERWEAR/COATS & JACKETS — HARBOUR INTERNATIONAL LLC page 196

Punchcase by Leslie Hsu A-HANDBAGS — SHOWROOM SEVEN/ERICKSON page 323

Pur Cashmere A-SCARVES — PUR CASHMERE page 353

Purple Label M-DESIGNER — RALPH LAUREN, INC. page 182

Q-Tees of California W-ACTIVE/ATHLETICWEAR — WASATCH CO. page 7

Q-Tees of California. M-ACTIVE/ATHLETICWEAR — WASATCH CO. page 167

Q-Tees of California. M-OUTERWEAR/COATS & JACKETS — WASATCH CO. page 197

Q-Tees of California. C-NEWBORN/LAYETTE/INFANT — WASATCH CO. page 258

Queen W-CONTEMPORARY SPORTSWEAR — BERGER & STEVENS page 32

Queensboro M-SHIRTS: — QUEENSBORO SHIRT COMPANY page 206

Raffi W-SWEATERS & KNITWEAR — RAFFI LINEA UOMO page 142

Raffi M-SWEATERS — RAFFI LINEA UOMO page 216

Rago W-INTIMATE APPAREL & LINGERIE — RAGO FOUNDATIONS LLC page 74

Rago W-SPECIAL — RAGO FOUNDATIONS LLC page 125

Rain Essentials A-UMBRELLAS — SHEDRAIN CORP. page 358

Raisins W-SWIMWEAR & BEACHWEAR — BREAKING WAVES INTERNATIONAL page 146

Raisins Girls W-SWIMWEAR & BEACHWEAR — BREAKING WAVES INTERNATIONAL page 146

Raj Imports A-SCARVES — RAJ IMPORTS page 354

Rashti & Rashti C-NEWBORN/LAYETTE/INFANT — RASHTI & RASHTI/H.J. RASHTI & CO., page 258

Rawlings®Brand A-GLOVES — BECKER GLOVE INTERNATIONAL, page 310

Razer W-LEATHER — MONTANACO CLOTHING COMPANY page 87

Razer M-LEATHER — MONTANACO CLOTHING COMPANY page 189

Real Tree®. A-BELTS — GEM DANDY INC. page 285

Rebecca Taylor W-DRESSES/SEPARATES/SUITS — REBECCA TAYLOR page 61

Rebel A-BELTS — MEGA BELTS, INC. page 287

Recycle Lin A-CHILDREN — LIN MANUFACTURING & DESIGN page 292

Recycle Lin A-HOSIERY/SOCKS/LEGWEAR — LIN MANUFACTURING & DESIGN page 339
Red Rose Hosiery A-HOSIERY/SOCKS/LEGWEAR — ABC HOSIERY page 335
Redford M-SHIRTS: — JUST WHITE SHIRTS page 205
Redford A-MEN'S — JUST WHITE SHIRTS page 346
Redwood Court W-BLOUSES/SHIRTS/TOPS — DANA EMILIA PRESENTS page 11
Redwood Court W-BLOUSES/SHIRTS/TOPS — REDWOOD COURT BY SILK BOX page 13
Redwood Court W-CONTEMPORARY SPORTSWEAR — DANA EMILIA PRESENTS page 34
Redwood Court W-DECORATED/EMBELLISHED APPAREL — DANA EMILIA PRESENTS page 44
Redwood Court W-MISSY/UPDATED SPORTSWEAR — DANA EMILIA PRESENTS page 96
Redwood Court W-SPECIAL — DANA EMILIA PRESENTS page 122
Redwood Court W-SWEATERS & KNITWEAR — DANA EMILIA PRESENTS page 138
Reebok W-SWIMWEAR & BEACHWEAR — A & H SPORTSWEAR CO. INC. page 145
Reebok C-OUTERWEAR/COATS & JACKETS — OUTERSTUFF LTD. page 261
Report Collection A-BELTS — MIL-IDEE, INC. page 287
Resistol A-HATS/CAPS/MILLINERY — HATCO, INC / RESISTOL HATS page 329
Reunion W-JUNIOR SPORTSWEAR — UNIONBAY/SEATTLE PACIFIC page 86
Reunion M-CASUAL — UNIONBAY/SEATTLE PACIFIC page 175
Rewind W-JUNIOR SPORTSWEAR — KELLWOOD COMPANY page 83
Rich Honey W-TEE — RICH HONEY page 154
Rich Honey M-TEE — RICH HONEY page 223
Rickie Freeman for Teri Jon W-BRIDAL & EVENINGWEAR — TERI JON page 22
Rickie Freeman for Teri Jon W-DESIGNER — TERI JON page 54
Rickie Freeman for Teri Jon W-SPECIAL — TERI JON page 126
Ringo Sport M-CASUAL — HASELSON INT'L TRADING INC. page 174
Ringo Sport M-JEANS — HASELSON INT'L TRADING INC. page 187
Ringo Sport M-OUTERWEAR/COATS & JACKETS — HASELSON INT'L TRADING INC. page 196
Ringo Sport M-SHIRTS: — HASELSON INT'L TRADING INC. page 205
Ringo Sport M-SWEATERS — HASELSON INT'L TRADING INC. page 216
Rivieras W-CONTEMPORARY SPORTSWEAR — SIMON SHOWROOM page 40
Rivieras W-JUNIOR SPORTSWEAR — SIMON SHOWROOM page 84
RLX W-DESIGNER — RALPH LAUREN, INC. page 52
Roadblock M-CASUAL — HASELSON INT'L TRADING INC. page 174
Roadblock M-JEANS — HASELSON INT'L TRADING INC. page 187
Roadblock M-OUTERWEAR/COATS & JACKETS — HASELSON INT'L TRADING INC. page 196
Roadblock M-SHIRTS: — HASELSON INT'L TRADING INC. page 205
Roadblock M-SWEATERS — HASELSON INT'L TRADING INC. page 216
Robbie Bee W-DRESSES/SEPARATES/SUITS — ROBBIE BEE page 62
Robbie Bee W-SPECIAL — ROBBIE BEE page 125
Roberto Collina M-CASUAL — PROJECT NO. 8 page 175
Roberto Collina M-CONTEMPORARY SPORTSWEAR — PROJECT NO. 8 page 179
Rockalicious W-INTIMATE APPAREL & LINGERIE — CARRIEAMBER INTIMATES page 69
Rockalicious W-PRIVATE LABEL — CARRIEAMBER INTIMATES page 112
Rockstar W-JEANS — ROCKSTAR page 80
Rockstar M-JEANS — ROCKSTAR page 188
Rooster A-MEN'S — MMG DIV OF GREAT CHINA EMPIRE page 346
Roper® A-BELTS — GEM DANDY INC. page 285
Rose Taft Couture W-BRIDAL & EVENINGWEAR — ROSE TAFT page 20
Rose Taft Couture W-DESIGNER — ROSE TAFT page 53
Rosebud A-HATS/CAPS/MILLINERY — AMERICAN HAT FACTORY, THE page 325
Rossopuro W-OUTERWEAR/COATS & JACKETS — FORI SHOWROOM page 105
Rossopuro W-SWEATERS & KNITWEAR — FORI SHOWROOM page 140
Rowdy Sprout C-TEE — ROWDY SPROUT page 278
Royal Apparel W-ACTIVE/ATHLETICWEAR — ROYAL APPAREL, INC. page 6
Royal Apparel W-ECOLOGICAL & ORGANIC — ROYAL APPAREL, INC. page 67
Royal Apparel W-JUNIOR SPORTSWEAR — ROYAL APPAREL, INC. page 84
Royal Apparel W-PRIVATE LABEL — ROYAL APPAREL, INC. page 114
Royal Apparel W-SPECIAL — ROYAL APPAREL, INC. page 125
Royal Apparel W-TEE — ROYAL APPAREL, INC. page 155
Royal Apparel M-ACTIVE/ATHLETICWEAR — ROYAL APPAREL, INC. page 166
Royal Apparel M-BIG — ROYAL APPAREL, INC. page 170

Royal Apparel ROYAL APPAREL, INC.
M-ECOLOGICAL & ORGANIC page 184

Royal Apparel ROYAL APPAREL, INC.
M-PRIVATE LABEL page 201

Royal Apparel ROYAL APPAREL, INC.
M-TEE page 223

Royal Apparel ROYAL APPAREL, INC.
C-ACTIVE/ATHLETICWEAR page 236

Royal Apparel ROYAL APPAREL, INC.
C-ECOLOGICAL & ORGANIC page 250

Royal Apparel ROYAL APPAREL, INC.
C-PRIVATE LABEL page 265

Royal Apparel ROYAL APPAREL, INC.
C-TEE page 278

Royale ROYALE LINENS INC.
A-GIFT page 308

RRL RALPH LAUREN, INC.
W-DESIGNER page 52

RRL RALPH LAUREN, INC.
M-DESIGNER page 182

Rum Reggae RUM REGGAE
M-SHIRTS: page 206

Russell Athletic FRUIT OF THE LOOM
W-ACTIVE/ATHLETICWEAR page 4

Russell Athletic FRUIT OF THE LOOM
M-ACTIVE/ATHLETICWEAR page 165

Russell Athletic WAITEX INTERNATIONAL
M-ACTIVE/ATHLETICWEAR page 167

Russell Athletic WAITEX INTERNATIONAL
M-CASUAL page 175

Russell Athletic Big and Tall WAITEX INTERNATIONAL
M-BIG page 170

Russell Outdoors FRUIT OF THE LOOM
W-ACTIVE/ATHLETICWEAR page 4

Russell Outdoors FRUIT OF THE LOOM
M-ACTIVE/ATHLETICWEAR page 165

Safilo SAFILO U.S.A.
A-EYEWEAR page 296

Sag Harbor® KELLWOOD COMPANY
W-CONTEMPORARY SPORTSWEAR page 38

Sahara GOLF APPAREL BRANDS
W-BLOUSES/SHIRTS/TOPS page 13

Sahara GOLF APPAREL BRANDS
W-OUTERWEAR/COATS & JACKETS page 106

Sahara GOLF APPAREL BRANDS
M-OUTERWEAR/COATS & JACKETS page 196

Sahara GOLF APPAREL BRANDS
M-SHIRTS: page 204

Sahara GOLF APPAREL BRANDS
A-HATS/CAPS/MILLINERY page 328

Sahara Club HASELSON INT'L TRADING INC.
M-CASUAL page 174

Sahara Club HASELSON INT'L TRADING INC.
M-JEANS page 187

Sahara Club HASELSON INT'L TRADING INC.
M-OUTERWEAR/COATS & JACKETS page 196

Sahara Club HASELSON INT'L TRADING INC.
M-SHIRTS: page 205

Sahara Club HASELSON INT'L TRADING INC.
M-SWEATERS page 216

Sandra AMERICAN HAT FACTORY, THE
A-HATS/CAPS/MILLINERY page 325

Sara Mique SARA MIQUE
W-BRIDAL & EVENINGWEAR page 21

Sassy Cyclist JULIE HUTTON INC.
W-PRIVATE LABEL page 113

Satchels™ AAA INNOVATIONS
A-LUGGAGE/BAGS/LEATHER page 341

Save My Bag SHOWROOM SEVEN/ERICKSON
A-HANDBAGS page 323

Scent-Lok SCENT-LOK/DIV. OF A.L.S.
M-SPORTSMEN'S page 211

Screamer SCREAMER HATS
A-HATS/CAPS/MILLINERY page 331

Scrub Zone LANDAU
W-UNIFORMS page 158

Scrub Zone LANDAU
M-UNIFORMS page 228

Scully SCULLY
W-CONTEMPORARY SPORTSWEAR page 39

Scully SCULLY
W-LEATHER page 87

Scully SCULLY
M-LEATHER page 189

Scully SCULLY
A-LUGGAGE/BAGS/LEATHER page 343

Sean John PEERLESS CLOTHING
M-SUITS page 214

Sean John PEERLESS CLOTHING
M-TROUSERS page 225

Seasons AMERICAN HAT FACTORY, THE
A-HATS/CAPS/MILLINERY page 325

Selmark FORT KNOX LINGERIE
W-INTIMATE APPAREL & LINGERIE page 73

Sentimental NY SENTIMENTAL INC.
W-BRIDAL & EVENINGWEAR page 21

Sentimental NY SENTIMENTAL INC.
W-CONTEMPORARY SPORTSWEAR page 39

Sesame Work Shop KAHN LUCAS
C-NEWBORN/LAYETTE/INFANT page 256

Seven 'til Midnight CARRIEAMBER INTIMATES
W-INTIMATE APPAREL & LINGERIE page 69

Seven 'til Midnight CARRIEAMBER INTIMATES
W-PRIVATE LABEL page 112

Seven Diamonds 7 DIAMONDS
M-JEANS page 185

Seven Diamonds 7 DIAMONDS
M-OUTERWEAR/COATS & JACKETS page 193

Seven Diamonds 7 DIAMONDS
M-SHIRTS: page 203

Shadowplay SWEENIE MANUFACTURING
W-SWIMWEAR & BEACHWEAR page 149

Shapette RAGO FOUNDATIONS LLC
W-INTIMATE APPAREL & LINGERIE page 74

Shapette RAGO FOUNDATIONS LLC
W-SPECIAL page 125

Shaune Bazner SHAUNE BAZNER ACCESSORIES,
A-FASHION page 302

Shaune Bazner Accessories SHAUNE BAZNER ACCESSORIES,
A-HAIR page 314

ShedRain W-OUTERWEAR/COATS & JACKETS — SHEDRAIN CORP. page 108
ShedRain A-UMBRELLAS — SHEDRAIN CORP. page 358
Shedrays A-UMBRELLAS — SHEDRAIN CORP. page 358
Sheepskin W-OUTERWEAR/COATS & JACKETS — SHEEPSKIN BY SUSAN BRADFORD page 109
Sheepskin by Susan Bradford A-HATS/CAPS/MILLINERY — SHEEPSKIN BY SUSAN BRADFORD page 332
sherry cassin new york W-OUTERWEAR/COATS & JACKETS — CASSIN page 103
sherry cassin new york A-HATS/CAPS/MILLINERY — CASSIN page 327
sherry cassin new york A-SCARVES — CASSIN page 350
Shivani A-SCARVES — VISMAYA page 355
Showroom International W-CONTEMPORARY SPORTSWEAR — BEL ESPRIT page 32
Showroom International A-HANDBAGS — BEL ESPRIT page 318
Showroom International A-SCARVES — BEL ESPRIT page 349
Signature by Levi Strauss & Co.™ W-JEANS — LEVI STRAUSS & CO. page 79
Signature by Levi Strauss & Co.™ M-JEANS — LEVI STRAUSS & CO. page 187
Signature by Levi Strauss & Co.™ M-WESTERNWEAR — LEVI STRAUSS & CO. page 231
Silk Box W-DRESSES/SEPARATES/SUITS — REDWOOD COURT BY SILK BOX page 61
Silk Box A-SCARVES — REDWOOD COURT BY SILK BOX page 354
Silver Label M-CASUAL — HASELSON INT'L TRADING INC. page 174
Silver Label M-JEANS — HASELSON INT'L TRADING INC. page 187
Silver Label M-OUTERWEAR/COATS & JACKETS — HASELSON INT'L TRADING INC. page 196
Silver Label M-SHIRTS — HASELSON INT'L TRADING INC. page 205
Silver Label M-SWEATERS — HASELSON INT'L TRADING INC. page 216
Silver Line C-SUITS/SPECIAL — SILVER SUIT, INC. page 271
Silver Suit C-SUITS/SPECIAL — SILVER SUIT, INC. page 271
Silverado A-HATS/CAPS/MILLINERY — F & M HAT CO., INC. page 328
Sisters W-PRIVATE LABEL — SISTERS/DIVISION OF FREDINI INC page 115
Sisters W-SWEATERS & KNITWEAR — SISTERS/DIVISION OF FREDINI INC page 143
Slick Art W-TEE — SLICK DESIGNS page 155
Slick Art M-TEE — SLICK DESIGNS page 223
SLIQ M-TEE — 2 X IST page 219
Smartworks Inc. A-SCARVES — SMARTWORKS INC. page 355
Smitten W-UNIFORMS — LANDAU page 158
Smockers W-UNIFORMS — BEXAR MANUFACTURING CO. page 157
Smockers M-UNIFORMS — BEXAR MANUFACTURING CO. page 227
Snuggle Buddy C-NEWBORN/LAYETTE/INFANT — RASHTI & RASHTI/H.J. RASHTI & CO., page 258
Soaked by Cejon W-SWIMWEAR & BEACHWEAR — CEJON ACCESSORIES INC. page 146
Socks by 2 X ist A-HOSIERY/SOCKS/LEGWEAR — 2 X IST page 335
Solace per Aqua® A-BRIDAL/SPECIAL/INTIMATE — SUSAN DUNN INC. page 290
Sons of Anarchy W-SWIMWEAR & BEACHWEAR — CATFISH CALHOUN AKA CALHOUN page 146
Sons of Anarchy M-SWIMWEAR & BEACHWEAR — CATFISH CALHOUN AKA CALHOUN page 217
Sonyarenee A-FASHION — NOTANONYMOUS page 301
Sophie W-CONTEMPORARY SPORTSWEAR — SOPHIE FINZI LTD DBA PASHOOT page 40
Sophie W-SPECIAL — SOPHIE FINZI LTD DBA PASHOOT page 126
Sophie W-SWEATERS & KNITWEAR — SOPHIE FINZI LTD DBA PASHOOT page 143
Sophie Fae C-COORDINATED SPORTSWEAR-GIRLS — LONG STREET page 243
Sossy Baghdoian W-BRIDAL & EVENINGWEAR — SOSSY BAGHDOIAN page 21
Soxland A-HOSIERY/SOCKS/LEGWEAR — SOXLAND INTERNATIONAL, INC. page 339
Spa Slippurrs™ W-SLEEPWEAR & LOUNGEWEAR — SUSAN DUNN INC. page 119
Spa Slippurrs™ M-SLEEPWEAR — SUSAN DUNN INC. page 209
Spa Slippurrs™ A-BRIDAL/SPECIAL/INTIMATE — SUSAN DUNN INC. page 290
Spa Slippurrs™ A-CHILDREN — SUSAN DUNN INC. page 292
Spa Sox W-SLEEPWEAR & LOUNGEWEAR — SUSAN DUNN INC. page 119
Spa Sox A-BRIDAL/SPECIAL/INTIMATE — SUSAN DUNN INC. page 290
Spa Tote A-HANDBAGS — SUSAN DUNN INC. page 323
Spa Wear W-SLEEPWEAR & LOUNGEWEAR — SUSAN DUNN INC. page 119
Spa Wear A-BRIDAL/SPECIAL/INTIMATE — SUSAN DUNN INC. page 290
Special Attention W-INTIMATE APPAREL & LINGERIE — RAGO FOUNDATIONS LLC page 74
Special Attention W-SPECIAL — RAGO FOUNDATIONS LLC page 125
SPENSE W-DRESSES/SEPARATES/SUITS — H.M.S. PRODUCTIONS page 59
Spense Blouse W-CONTEMPORARY SPORTSWEAR — H.M.S. PRODUCTIONS page 37

Label Index

Spense Dress H.M.S. PRODUCTIONS
W-CONTEMPORARY SPORTSWEAR page 37

Spense Knits H.M.S. PRODUCTIONS
W-CONTEMPORARY SPORTSWEAR page 37

Sporthill SPORTHILL, INC.
W-ACTIVE/ATHLETICWEAR page 6

Sporthill SPORTHILL, INC.
M-ACTIVE/ATHLETICWEAR page 166

Spreegirl CARRIEAMBER INTIMATES
W-INTIMATE APPAREL & LINGERIE page 69

Spreegirl CARRIEAMBER INTIMATES
W-PRIVATE LABEL page 112

Squasht Boutique SQUASHT BOUTIQUE
A-HATS/CAPS/MILLINERY page 332

Squasht by Les SQUASHT BY LES
W-BLOUSES/SHIRTS/TOPS page 14

St. John ST. JOHN
W-DESIGNER page 53

St. John ST. JOHN
W-JEANS page 80

Stacy Adams KEEPERS INTERNATIONAL
A-HOSIERY/SOCKS/LEGWEAR page 338

Steel Pony STEEL PONY
W-DECORATED/EMBELLISHED APPAREL page 44

Stetson HATCO, INC./ RESISTOL HATS
A-HATS/CAPS/MILLINERY page 329

Steve Harvey MMG DIV OF GREAT CHINA EMPIRE
A-MEN'S page 346

Strawberry Shortcake FRENCH TOAST
C-LICENSED page 253

Streets Ahead NOTANONYMOUS
A-BELTS page 287

Streets Ahead NOTANONYMOUS
A-HANDBAGS page 322

Streets Ahead. STREETS AHEAD
A-BELTS page 288

Streets Ahead. NOTANONYMOUS
A-BRIDAL/SPECIAL/INTIMATE page 290

Streets Ahead. STREETS AHEAD
A-HANDBAGS page 323

Studio DEPECHE MODE
W-BRIDAL & EVENINGWEAR page 18

Studio DEPECHE MODE
W-CONTEMPORARY SPORTSWEAR page 34

Studio DEPECHE MODE
W-DRESSES/SEPARATES/SUITS page 58

Studio DEPECHE MODE
W-SPECIAL page 122

Studio DEPECHE MODE
W-SPECIAL page 132

Sugar and Bruno SUGAR AND BRUNO
W-TEE page 155

Sugar and Bruno SUGAR AND BRUNO
M-TEE page 224

Sugar and Bruno SUGAR AND BRUNO
C-TEE page 279

Sugar and Bruno SUGAR AND BRUNO
A-HOSIERY/SOCKS/LEGWEAR page 340

Sundry SIMON SHOWROOM
W-CONTEMPORARY SPORTSWEAR page 40

Sundry SIMON SHOWROOM
W-JUNIOR SPORTSWEAR page 84

Super Charged EVY OF CALIFORNIA, INC./DBA
C-COORDINATED SPORTSWEAR-BOYS page 237

SUPmerge SWEENIE MANUFACTURING
W-ACTIVE/ATHLETICWEAR page 7

Surfer BEACH RAYS/DIV OF J.Y. RAYS, INC.
W-JUNIOR SPORTSWEAR page 81

Surfer BEACH RAYS/DIV OF J.Y. RAYS, INC.
W-SWIMWEAR & BEACHWEAR page 145

Surfer BEACH RAYS/DIV OF J.Y. RAYS, INC.
M-SWIMWEAR & BEACHWEAR page 217

Surfer BEACH RAYS/DIV OF J.Y. RAYS, INC.
C-SWIMWEAR & BEACHWEAR page 275

Survival SURVIVAL INC.
W-JUNIOR SPORTSWEAR page 85

Susan Dunn® SUSAN DUNN INC.
W-SLEEPWEAR & LOUNGEWEAR page 119

Susan Dunn® SUSAN DUNN INC.
M-SLEEPWEAR page 209

Susan Dunn® SUSAN DUNN INC.
A-BRIDAL/SPECIAL/INTIMATE page 290

Susan Dunn® SUSAN DUNN INC.
A-CHILDREN page 292

Susan Elias SUSAN ELIAS
W-BRIDAL & EVENINGWEAR page 21

Susan Elias SUSAN ELIAS
W-CONTEMPORARY SPORTSWEAR page 40

Susan Elias SUSAN ELIAS
W-DESIGNER page 54

Susan Elias SUSAN ELIAS
W-DRESSES/SEPARATES/SUITS page 62

Susan Pillay SUSAN PILLAY
C-NEWBORN/LAYETTE/INFANT page 258

Suspicious Lines SWEATER BRAND INC.
W-SWEATERS & KNITWEAR page 143

Sweater Brand SWEATER BRAND INC.
W-SWEATERS & KNITWEAR page 143

Sweenie SWEENIE MANUFACTURING
C-SWIMWEAR & BEACHWEAR page 276

Sweet Blossom MEHERA SHAW TEXTILES PVT. LTD.
W-ECOLOGICAL & ORGANIC page 67

Sweet Heart Rose® KAHN LUCAS
C-COORDINATED SPORTSWEAR-GIRLS page 242

Sweet Heart Rose® KAHN LUCAS
C-DRESSES page 246

Sweet Heart Rose® KAHN LUCAS
C-LICENSED page 254

Sweet Vintage LONG STREET
C-COORDINATED SPORTSWEAR-GIRLS page 243

Swift Originals SWIFT ORIGINALS
W-DRESSES/SEPARATES/SUITS page 62

Swift Originals SWIFT ORIGINALS
M-SHIRTS: page 206

Swish DANA EMILIA PRESENTS
W-BLOUSES/SHIRTS/TOPS page 11

Swish DANA EMILIA PRESENTS
W-CONTEMPORARY SPORTSWEAR page 34

Swish DANA EMILIA PRESENTS
W-DECORATED/EMBELLISHED APPAREL page 44

Swish W-MISSY/UPDATED SPORTSWEAR — DANA EMILIA PRESENTS page 96
Swish W-SPECIAL — DANA EMILIA PRESENTS page 122
Swish W-SWEATERS & KNITWEAR — DANA EMILIA PRESENTS page 138
Swiss Cros M-CASUAL — HASELSON INT'L TRADING INC. page 174
Swiss Cros M-JEANS — HASELSON INT'L TRADING INC. page 187
Swiss Cros M-OUTERWEAR/COATS & JACKETS — HASELSON INT'L TRADING INC. page 196
Swiss Cros M-SHIRTS: — HASELSON INT'L TRADING INC. page 205
Swiss Cros M-SWEATERS — HASELSON INT'L TRADING INC. page 216
Table Art A-FASHION — FOUR SEASONS DESIGN GROUP page 299
Table Art A-GIFT — FOUR SEASONS DESIGN GROUP page 307
Taggies C-NEWBORN/LAYETTE/INFANT — RASHTI & RASHTI/H.J. RASHTI & CO., page 258
Tailgator™Glove A-GLOVES — BECKER GLOVE INTERNATIONAL, page 310
Tailor Vintage W-CONTEMPORARY SPORTSWEAR — TAILOR VINTAGE page 41
Tailor Vintage M-CONTEMPORARY SPORTSWEAR — TAILOR VINTAGE page 179
Tallia M-SUITS — PEERLESS CLOTHING page 214
Tallia M-TROUSERS — PEERLESS CLOTHING page 225
Tango A-MEN'S — MMG DIV OF GREAT CHINA EMPIRE page 346
Tara Handknits W-SWEATERS & KNITWEAR — HOT KNOTS page 141
Tara Keely W-BRIDAL & EVENINGWEAR — JLM COUTURE page 19
Tart Collections W-CONTEMPORARY SPORTSWEAR — J.D. FINE page 37
Tart Collections W-DRESSES/SEPARATES/SUITS — J.D. FINE page 59
Tasha Polizzi W-BLOUSES/SHIRTS/TOPS — TASHA POLIZZI page 14
Tasha Polizzi W-CONTEMPORARY SPORTSWEAR — TASHA POLIZZI page 41
Tasha Polizzi W-LEATHER — TASHA POLIZZI page 88
Tasha Polizzi W-OUTERWEAR/COATS & JACKETS — TASHA POLIZZI page 109
Tatras W-CONTEMPORARY SPORTSWEAR — SIMON SHOWROOM page 40
Tatras W-JUNIOR SPORTSWEAR — SIMON SHOWROOM page 84
Teri Jon W-DESIGNER — TERI JON page 54
The Essence W-PRIVATE LABEL — JULIE HUTTON INC. page 113
The Pillaged Village W-TEE — PILLAGED VILLAGE, THE page 154
The Pillaged Village M-TEE — PILLAGED VILLAGE, THE page 223
The Pillaged Village A-FASHION — PILLAGED VILLAGE, THE page 301
The Pillaged Village A-SCARVES — PILLAGED VILLAGE, THE page 353
The Shirt Store M-SHIRTS: — JUST WHITE SHIRTS page 205
The Shirt Store A-MEN'S — JUST WHITE SHIRTS page 346
The Walking Dead W-SWIMWEAR & BEACHWEAR — CATFISH CALHOUN AKA CALHOUN page 146
The Walking Dead M-SWIMWEAR & BEACHWEAR — CATFISH CALHOUN AKA CALHOUN page 217
Thea W-INTIMATE APPAREL & LINGERIE — THEA HAUTE COUTURE page 75
Thea C-DRESSES — THEA HAUTE COUTURE page 247
Thea C-NEWBORN/LAYETTE/INFANT — THEA HAUTE COUTURE page 258
Tic Tac Toe A-CHILDREN — TIC TAC TOE/BABY LEGS page 293
Tim Crawford A-HATS/CAPS/MILLINERY — AMERICAN HAT FACTORY, THE page 325
Tinseltown W-JUNIOR SPORTSWEAR — TOPSON DOWNS page 85
Tokyo Bay A-FASHION — TOKYO BAY INC. page 302
Tom & Jerry C-SLEEPWEAR — NEW ICM, LP page 270
Tom and Linda Platt W-DESIGNER — TOM AND LINDA PLATT page 54
Tom and Linda Platt W-DRESSES/SEPARATES/SUITS — TOM AND LINDA PLATT page 63
Tom and Linda Platt W-SPECIAL — TOM AND LINDA PLATT page 126
Tom and Linda Platt Custom W-DESIGNER — TOM AND LINDA PLATT page 54
Tom and Linda Platt Custom W-DRESSES/SEPARATES/SUITS — TOM AND LINDA PLATT page 63
Tom and Linda Platt Custom W-SPECIAL — TOM AND LINDA PLATT page 126
Tommy Hilfiger W-LIFESTYLE COLLECTIONS — PVH CORPORATION page 94
Tony Lama M-WESTERNWEAR — TONY LAMA COMPANY, INC. page 231
Torvu W-ACTIVE/ATHLETICWEAR — SWEENIE MANUFACTURING page 7
Torvu M-SWIMWEAR & BEACHWEAR — SWEENIE MANUFACTURING page 218
totalSTRETCH™ A-HOSIERY/SOCKS/LEGWEAR — BODY WRAPPERS page 336
totalSTRETCH™ Tights W-ACTIVE/ATHLETICWEAR — BODY WRAPPERS page 2
totalSTRETCH™ Tights C-ACTIVE/ATHLETICWEAR — BODY WRAPPERS page 234
Town & Country A-HOSIERY/SOCKS/LEGWEAR — BOSSONG HOSIERY page 336
Tracywatts A-HATS/CAPS/MILLINERY — TRACYWATTS INC. page 332

Label Index

Tramp TRAMP
W-CONTEMPORARY SPORTSWEAR page 41

Trendset TRENDSET ORIGINALS
W-JUNIOR SPORTSWEAR page 85

Trendset TRENDSET ORIGINALS
W-OUTERWEAR/COATS & JACKETS page 109

Trendset TRENDSET ORIGINALS
W-SWEATERS & KNITWEAR page 144

Trendset TRENDSET ORIGINALS
C-COORDINATED SPORTSWEAR-GIRLS page 244

Trendset TRENDSET ORIGINALS
C-OUTERWEAR/COATS & JACKETS page 262

Tricot Chic ELE.PAVONI NEW YORK LTD
W-DESIGNER page 50

Triple Play HASELSON INT'L TRADING INC.
M-CASUAL page 174

Triple Play HASELSON INT'L TRADING INC.
M-JEANS page 187

Triple Play HASELSON INT'L TRADING INC.
M-OUTERWEAR/COATS & JACKETS page 196

Triple Play HASELSON INT'L TRADING INC.
M-SHIRTS: page 205

Triple Play HASELSON INT'L TRADING INC.
M-SWEATERS page 216

Tripp NYC TRIPP NYC
W-JUNIOR SPORTSWEAR page 85

TSE CASHMERE HOUSE
W-SWEATERS & KNITWEAR page 138

Tusk Ltd. TUSK LTD.
A-HANDBAGS page 324

Tusk Ltd. TUSK LTD.
A-LUGGAGE/BAGS/LEATHER page 343

Twisted by Carol Peretz CAROL PERETZ
W-CONTEMPORARY SPORTSWEAR page 33

UFC PACIFIC SPORTSWEAR & EMBLEM
A-HATS/CAPS/MILLINERY page 331

Unionbay UNIONBAY/SEATTLE PACIFIC
W-JUNIOR SPORTSWEAR page 86

Unionbay UNIONBAY/SEATTLE PACIFIC
M-CASUAL page 175

Urbane Scrubs LANDAU
W-UNIFORMS page 158

Urbane Scrubs LANDAU
M-UNIFORMS page 228

US Polo Association LONG STREET
C-COORDINATED SPORTSWEAR-BOYS page 239

US Polo Association LONG STREET
C-COORDINATED SPORTSWEAR-GIRLS page 243

US Polo Association LONG STREET
C-OUTERWEAR/COATS & JACKETS page 261

US Polo Association LONG STREET
C-UNIFORMS page 281

Utensil Buddy PACIFIC SPORTSWEAR & EMBLEM
A-HATS/CAPS/MILLINERY page 331

Valentine VALENTINE USA
W-PRIVATE LABEL page 116

Valentine VALENTINE USA
W-SPECIAL page 127

Van Heusen MANN & BROS INC/IMPERIAL
A-SCARVES page 352

Vangoh SILVER SUIT, INC.
C-SUITS/SPECIAL page 271

VanHeusen CONCEPT ONE ACCESSORIES
A-HATS/CAPS/MILLINERY page 327

Vanite Couture DANA EMILIA PRESENTS
W-BLOUSES/SHIRTS/TOPS page 11

Vanite Couture DANA EMILIA PRESENTS
W-CONTEMPORARY SPORTSWEAR page 34

Vanite Couture DANA EMILIA PRESENTS
W-DECORATED/EMBELLISHED APPAREL page 44

Vanite Couture DANA EMILIA PRESENTS
W-MISSY/UPDATED SPORTSWEAR page 96

Vanite Couture DANA EMILIA PRESENTS
W-SPECIAL page 122

Vanite Couture DANA EMILIA PRESENTS
W-SWEATERS & KNITWEAR page 138

Vanity Fair FRUIT OF THE LOOM
W-ACTIVE/ATHLETICWEAR page 4

Vanity Fair FRUIT OF THE LOOM
M-ACTIVE/ATHLETICWEAR page 165

Vast BEACH RAYS/DIV OF J.Y. RAYS, INC.
W-JUNIOR SPORTSWEAR page 81

Vast BEACH RAYS/DIV OF J.Y. RAYS, INC.
W-SWIMWEAR & BEACHWEAR page 145

Vast BEACH RAYS/DIV OF J.Y. RAYS, INC.
M-SWIMWEAR & BEACHWEAR page 217

Vast BEACH RAYS/DIV OF J.Y. RAYS, INC.
C-SWIMWEAR & BEACHWEAR page 275

Venus Fashion VENUS FASHION
W-CASUAL page 27

Venus Fashion VENUS FASHION
W-DRESSES/SEPARATES/SUITS page 63

Venus Swimwear VENUS FASHION
W-SWIMWEAR & BEACHWEAR page 150

Vermillion BELGO LUX INC.
A-BELTS page 284

Vermillion BELGO LUX INC.
A-EYEWEAR page 295

Vicedomini ADK FASHIONS
W-DESIGNER page 47

Vieste Rosa VIESTE-ROSA
A-FASHION page 302

Vieste Rosa VIESTE-ROSA
A-HAIR page 315

Vilebrequin G-III APPAREL GROUP
W-SWIMWEAR & BEACHWEAR page 148

Vismaya VISMAYA
A-SCARVES page 355

Vitamin BERGER & STEVENS
W-CONTEMPORARY SPORTSWEAR page 32

Viviana Uchitel VIVIANA UCHITEL
W-DRESSES/SEPARATES/SUITS page 63

Viviana Uchitel VIVIANA UCHITEL
W-SWEATERS & KNITWEAR page 144

Wai-Ching WAI-CHING
W-DECORATED/EMBELLISHED APPAREL page 45

Wai-Ching WAI-CHING
A-HANDBAGS page 324

WalkSafe SHEDRAIN CORP.
W-OUTERWEAR/COATS & JACKETS page 108

WalkSafe SHEDRAIN CORP.
A-UMBRELLAS page 358

Walter Voulaz FORI SHOWROOM
W-OUTERWEAR/COATS & JACKETS page 105

Walter Voulaz FORI SHOWROOM
W-SWEATERS & KNITWEAR page 140

We Be Bop WE BE BOP, INC
W-SPECIAL page 127

Wedding Tropics WEDDING TROPICS
W-BRIDAL & EVENINGWEAR page 22

Wet BEACH RAYS/DIV OF J.Y. RAYS, INC.
W-JUNIOR SPORTSWEAR page 81

Wet BEACH RAYS/DIV OF J.Y. RAYS, INC.
W-SWIMWEAR & BEACHWEAR page 145

Wet BEACH RAYS/DIV OF J.Y. RAYS, INC.
M-SWIMWEAR & BEACHWEAR page 217

Wet BEACH RAYS/DIV OF J.Y. RAYS, INC.
C-SWIMWEAR & BEACHWEAR page 275

White Sierra WHITE SIERRA
W-ACTIVE/ATHLETICWEAR page 7

White Sierra WHITE SIERRA
W-OUTERWEAR/COATS & JACKETS page 109

White Sierra WHITE SIERRA
M-ACTIVE/ATHLETICWEAR page 167

White Sierra WHITE SIERRA
M-OUTERWEAR/COATS & JACKETS page 197

White Sierra WHITE SIERRA
C-OUTERWEAR/COATS & JACKETS page 262

Whiting & Davis INGE CHRISTOPHER
A-HANDBAGS page 320

Whittall & Shon WHITTALL & SHON
A-HATS/CAPS/MILLINERY page 333

Will Leather Goods WILL LEATHER GOODS
A-BELTS page 288

Williamson-Dickie WILLIAMSON-DICKIE MFG CO.
W-CASUAL page 28

Williamson-Dickie WILLIAMSON-DICKIE MFG CO.
W-UNIFORMS page 159

Williamson-Dickie WILLIAMSON-DICKIE MFG CO.
M-UNIFORMS page 230

Williamson-Dickie WILLIAMSON-DICKIE MFG CO.
C-UNIFORMS page 282

Windjammer SHEDRAIN CORP.
A-UMBRELLAS page 358

Windpro SHEDRAIN CORP.
A-UMBRELLAS page 358

Winter Silk VENUS FASHION
W-SLEEPWEAR & LOUNGEWEAR page 119

Wippette IAPPAREL LLC
C-OUTERWEAR/COATS & JACKETS page 260

WNBA FBF ORIGINALS
A-HOSIERY/SOCKS/LEGWEAR page 337

Wooden Ships WOODEN SHIPS
W-SWEATERS & KNITWEAR page 144

Wooden Ships WOODEN SHIPS
A-GLOVES page 312

Wooden Ships WOODEN SHIPS
A-HATS/CAPS/MILLINERY page 333

Wooden Ships WOODEN SHIPS
A-SCARVES page 355

World Poker Tour PACIFIC SPORTSWEAR & EMBLEM
A-HATS/CAPS/MILLINERY page 331

World's Softest Sock® CRESCENT SOCK COMPANY
A-HOSIERY/SOCKS/LEGWEAR page 337

Wrangler CONCEPT ONE ACCESSORIES
A-HATS/CAPS/MILLINERY page 327

XOXO KELLWOOD COMPANY
W-CONTEMPORARY SPORTSWEAR page 38

XOXO XOXO
W-CONTEMPORARY SPORTSWEAR page 42

XXIOTTI DREAM WORLD INTERNATIONAL,
M-BIG page 170

XXIOTTI DREAM WORLD INTERNATIONAL,
M-CONTEMPORARY SPORTSWEAR page 178

XXIOTTI DREAM WORLD INTERNATIONAL,
M-SUITS page 213

Yochi YOCHI DESIGNS
A-FASHION page 303

YonDesign YON DESIGN, INC.
W-CONTEMPORARY SPORTSWEAR page 42

Youngland® KAHN LUCAS
C-COORDINATED SPORTSWEAR-GIRLS page 242

Youngland® KAHN LUCAS
C-DRESSES page 246

Youngland® KAHN LUCAS
C-LICENSED page 254

Yvonne Totes TAKEATOTE LLC
A-HANDBAGS page 323

Z by Zelda ZELDA
W-MISSY/UPDATED SPORTSWEAR page 99

Zacchi DREAM WORLD INTERNATIONAL,
M-BIG page 170

Zacchi DREAM WORLD INTERNATIONAL,
M-CONTEMPORARY SPORTSWEAR page 178

Zacchi DREAM WORLD INTERNATIONAL,
M-SUITS page 213

Zanetti ZANETTI INC.
M-CONTEMPORARY SPORTSWEAR page 180

Zanetti ZANETTI INC.
M-SHIRTS: page 206

Zanetti ZANETTI INC.
M-SUITS page 214

Zanetti ZANETTI INC.
M-SWEATERS page 216

Zanetti MMG DIV OF GREAT CHINA EMPIRE
A-MEN'S page 346

Zazzy NEW ICM, LP
C-SLEEPWEAR page 270

Zelda ZELDA
W-DRESSES/SEPARATES/SUITS page 64

Zoo York CONCEPT ONE ACCESSORIES
A-HATS/CAPS/MILLINERY page 327

Sthenos SWEENIE MANUFACTURING
W-ACTIVE/ATHLETICWEAR page 7

2 X IST www.2xist.com ralph@2xist.com 212 741 7731

525 AMERICA www.525america.com mbock@525america.com 212 921 5688

5TH & OCEAN CLOTHING LLC/NEW ERA CAP CO. www.neweracap.com laura.garden@neweracap.com 305 822 4606

7 DIAMONDS www.7diamonds.com sales@7diamonds.com 714 241 7190

7 FOR ALL MANKIND www.7forallmankind.com customerservice@shop.7forallmankind. 646 839 5400

A & H SPORTSWEAR CO. INC. bruce@swimusa.com 610 759 9550

A PEA IN THE POD www.apeainthepod.com vendorrelations@destinationmaternity. 856 291 9700

A'NUE LIGNE www.anueligne.com admin@anueligne.com 305 436 5828

A. CHE www.acheswimwear.com sales@acheswimwear.com 818773 5000

AAA INNOVATIONS www.aaainnovations.com diane@aaainnovations.com 201 784 3244

ABC HOSIERY www.myabchosiery.com abc_hosiery@yahoo.com 919 556 5630

ABS BY ALLEN SCHWARTZ www.absstyle.com kfoster@absstyle.com 213 895 4400

ACORN PRODUCTS www.acorn.com christian.hilton@totes.com 800 872 2676

ACTIVE APPAREL, INC. www.activeapparel.net kashis@activeapparel.net 951 361 0060

ACTIVE EDGE, THE/OLD CITY T-SHIRTS www.theactiveedge.com actvej@aol.com 215 925 7860

ADEA www.myadea.com info@myadea.com 866 798 2332

ADIDAS AMERICA, INC. www.adidas.com 971 234 2300

ADK FASHIONS www.adkfashions.com adk@adkfashions.com 212 714 1177

ADRIANNA PAPELL LLC. www.adriannapapell.com customerservice@adriannapapell.com 212 695 5244

ADRIANO GOLDSCHMIED www.agjeans.com david@namasteshowroom.com 213 689 4867

ADRIENNE LANDAU www.adriennelandau.com sales@adriennelandau.com 212 695 8362

ADVANCE APPARELS INC. www.advanceapparelsny.com sales@advanceapparelsny.com 212 481 7246

AERO TECH DESIGNS www.aerotechdesigns.com cyclewear@aerotechdesigns.com 412 262 3255

AIDAN MATTOX www.aidanmattox.com customerservice@aidanmattox.com 212 764 5870

AIMAI CASHMERE www.aimaicashmere.com brian@aimaicashmere.com 970 618 3178

AKADEMIKS www.akademiks.com dclesmere@akademiks.com 212 563 4999

ALDAN www.aldan.com lew@aldan.com 718 665 8699

ALICE AND OLIVIA www.aliceandolivia.com info@aliceandolivia.com 646 747 1461

ALPHA INDUSTRIES, INC. www.alphaindustries.com wholesale@alphaindustries.com 703 378 1420

ALSTYLE www.alstyle.com info@alstyle.com 714 765 0400

AMERICAN HAT FACTORY, THE www.amerahat.com amhat2251@gmail.com 267 345 1141

ANDARI FASHION, INC. www.andari.com info@andari.com 626 575 2759

ANDERSEN-BECKER INC. www.leeandersen.com info@leeandersen.com 301 725 5555

ANDREW MARC www.andrewmarc.com sales@andrewmarc.com 212 840 1800

ANN TAYLOR www.anntaylor.com clientservices@anntaylor.com 800 342 5266

ANNA SUI www.annasui.com contactus@annasui.com 212 768 1004

ANNE KLEIN www.anneklein.com customer_relations@anneklein.com 888 841 2229

ANNE NAMBA DESIGNS www.annenamba.com anne@annenamba.com 808 589 1135

ANVIL KNITWEAR, INC. www.anvilknitwear.com info@gildan.com 843 774 8211

APL® www.aplhandbags.com apl@aplhandbags.com 361 798 5000

AQUARIUS LTD. www.aquariusltd.com sales@aquariusltd.com 314 664 4498

AR NEW YORK www.arnewyorkhandbags.com info@arnewyork.us 212 564 5368

ARABESQUE DESIGN/PATRICIA FIELDWALKER www.pfieldwalker.com inquiries@arabesquedesign.com 604 689 1210

ARAKS www.araks.com sales@araks.com 212 982 5652

AREA CODE 212 INC. ac@areacode.net www.areacode212.net 212 465 9072

ARMBRUST INTERNATIONAL www.armbrustintl.com sales@armbrustintl.com 401 781 3300

ASPEN LICENSING INTERNATIONAL, INC. www.aspenbrand.com bob@aspenlicensing.com 561 509 8888

ATOPAPPAREL CORP www.emilrutenberg.com info@atopapparel.com 212 221 7685

AUDISH ACCESSORIES, LLC www.bettyaudish.com bettyaudish@hotmail.com 281 300 3202

AUGUST SILK, INC. francineshane@augustsilk.com 212 643 2400

AUTUMN CASHMERE INC. www.autumncashmere.com info@autumncashmere.com 888 6 AUTUMN

AVALIN LIMITED www.avalinknits.com info@avalinknits.com 212 997 0011

AZIBI LTD. www.lunaluz.net goodrep@gmail.com 212 869 6550

B & B DESIGNS COLLECTION INC. www.amandafashion.com info@amandafashion.com 323 261 0000

B & B SWEATERS bbsweater@aol.com 212 944 1335

B. BRONSON www.bbronson.com sales@bbronson.com 213 747 0501

B.C.T.C. edward.hu@bctcapparel.com 323 888 9388

BABETTE www.shopbabette.com mary@babettesf.com 510 625 8500

BABY JAY INC./GROWING FEET INC. www.babyjay.com info@babyjay.com 732 905 4980

BABYFAIR, INC. www.penelopemack.com contactus@penelopemack.com 212 736 7989

BABYLEGS® DIV OF UNITED LEGWEAR CO. www.babylegs.com info@babylegs.com 212 391 4143

BADGER SPORTSWEAR www.badgersportswear.com tom@badgersportswear.com 704 871 0990

BAILEY HATS www.baileyhats.com cdistasio@bollmanhats.com 212 981 9900

BALTIERRA SURFBOARDS & BALTI GIRL rogerbaltierra@sbcglobal.net 949 645 7873

BAMBOO 54 www.bamboo54.com jerry@bamboo54.com 626 443 1863

BARAMI/FASHION CONCEPTS/PATRIZIA LUCA www.barami.com baman@barami.com 212 629 6464

BARRAZA ASSOCIATES LTD www.barrazastyle.com barrazany@aol.com 212 564 6583

BARRONS-HUNTER, INC. www.barrons-hunter.com sales@barrons-hunter.com 434 971 7626

Company	Website	E-mail	Phone
BASIX OF AMERICA	www.basixofamerica.com	info@basixofamerica.com	800 236 8150
BAUXO INC.	www.bauxo.com	info@bauxo.com	780 452 1100
BCBG MAX AZRIA GROUP	www.bcbg.com	judy.scarpulla@bcbg.com	212 382 1880
BEACH HANDBAGS	www.beachhandbags.com	info@beachhandbags.com	714 901 2000
BEACH RAYS/DIV OF J.Y. RAYS, INC.	www.beachrays.com	sales@beachrays.com	626 941 0388
BEAU TIES LTD. OF VERMONT	www.beautiesltd.com	btl@beautiesltd.com	802 388 0108
BECKER GLOVE INTERNATIONAL, LLC	www.beckerglove.com	customerinfo@beckerglove.com	314 298 9810
BEDHEAD PAJAMAS	www.bedheadpajamas.com	joanne@bedheadpjs.com	323 634 0333
BEL ESPRIT SHOWROOM/SHOWROOM INTERNA	www.belesprit.net	belesprit@ureach.com	215 963 9394
BELASSE COLLECTION LLC	www.belassecollection.com	info@belassecollection.com	404 892 5030
BELGO LUX INC.	www.belgolux.com	egaranito@belgolux.com	514 279 6328
BELLA MATERNA INC.	www.bellamaterna.com	sales@bellamaterna.com	206 286 8108
BELLDINI	www.belldini.com	info@belldini.com	213 748 4442
BEREK	www.buyberek.com	gary@bereksweaters.com	212 575 8255
BERGER & STEVENS	www.bergerandstevens.com	aberger@bergerandstevens.com	212 768 0050
BERMO ENTERPRISES INC.	www.bermoenterprises.com	info@bermoenterprises.com	269 679 2580
BETMAR HATS INC.	www.betmarhats.com	betmarhats@aol.com	212 684 8080
BETSEY JOHNSON	www.betseyjohnson.com	info@betseyjohnson.com	866-222-4243
BEVERLY HILLS UNIFORMS	www.bhuniforms.com	sales@bhuniforms.com	718 378 1188
BEXAR MANUFACTURING CO.	www.smockers.com	smockers@smockers.com	210 977 9585
BIANCA NERO	www.biancanero.com	info@biancanero.com	213 236 9282
BIBELOT	www.bibelotnyc.com	bibelotco@verizon.net	212 563 0685
BIG BUDDHA	www.ebigbuddha.com	kirsten@ebigbuddha.com	212 857 9580
BILL BLASS FASHIONS LLC	www.billblass.com	allison@billblass.com	212 689 8957
BILLS KHAKIS	www.billskhakis.com	jeoff@billskhakis.com	800 435 4254
BLUE DUCK TRADING CO.	www.blueduckshearling.com	barry@blueduckshearling.com	212 268 3122
BLUE HAWAII SALES		hiblue@hawaii.rr.com	808 277 0368
BLUE PLATE INC.	www.blueplatefashion.com	bpshowroom@aol.com	212 382 0069
BLUE STAR INT'L	www.blue-star-intl.com	bluestarintl@aol.com	949 552 1181
BLUEGEM SUNGLASSES INC.	www.bluegem.com	eye@bluegem.com	800 543 9802
BLUESUITS	www.bluesuitsonline.com	jamak@off7th.com	212 787 0278
BODY WRAPPERS	www.bodywrappers.com	info@bodywrappers.com	212 279 3492
BOSSONG HOSIERY		mowens4bossong@aol.com	845 352 4630
BOULEVARD	www.iloveblvd.com	sales@iloveblvd.com	866 477 5051
BOULEVARD APPAREL	www.blvapparel.com	sales@blvapparel.com	213 614 1800
BRAVADO MERCHANDISING	www.bravadousa.com	tom.bennett@bravado.com	212 445 3400
BRAVE LEATHER LTD.	www.braveleather.com	info@braveleather.com	416 782 0243
BRAZILROXX INC.	www.brazilroxx.com	eliana@brazilroxx.com	817 886 6710
BREAKING WAVES INTERNATIONAL	www.breakingwaves.com	sales@breakingwaves.com	646 569 6001
BROOKS SPORTS, INC.	www.brooksrunning.com	Stephen.Cheung@brooksrunning.com	800 227 6657
BUCK WEAR INC.	www.buckwear.com	cjohnson@buckwear.com	410 646 6400
BURBERRY	www.burberry.com	us.customerservice@burberry.com	800 284 8480
BURMA BIBAS	www.burmabibas.com	sales@burmabibas.com	212 750 2500
BY BOE LTD.	www.byboe.com	shop@byboe.com	718 488 040
C.T.C. INC.		turnercarol22@aol.com	325 947 210
CALIFORNIA RAIN CO.	www.californiarainla.com	info@californiarainla.com	213 623 6061
CALVIN CLOTHING COMPANY		ben@calvinclothes.com	516 937 040
CALVIN KLEIN, INC.	www.calvinklein.com	calvinkleincustomerservice@pvh.com	212 719 260
CAMBER SPORTSWEAR, INC.	www.camberusa.com	camberusa@aol.com	610 239 991
CANADIAN SWEATER CO., LTD.	www.canadiansweater.com	info@canadiansweater.com	604 594 805
CAPELLI NEW YORK	www.capellinewyork.com	info@capellinewyork.com	212 684 334
CARIBBEAN WRAPS INTERNATIONAL	www.allyouneedtowear.com	sales@allyouneedtowear.com	757 495 800
CARMEN MARC VALVO	www.carmenmarcvalvo.com	customerservice@carmenmarcvalvo.c	212 944 737
CAROL PERETZ	www.carolperetz.com	info@carolperetz.com	516 248 630
CARRIEAMBER INTIMATES	www.carrieamber.com	sales@carrieamber.com	626 371 198
CARTISE INTERNATIONAL	www.cartise.ca	customerservice@cartise.ca	514 383 349
CASHMERE HOUSE	www.tsecashmere.com	info@tse-us.com	714 957 400
CASSIN	www.cassincollections.com	info@cassincollections.com	973 826 119
CASTLEWARE BABY	www.castleware.com	info@castleware.com	707 499 976
CATFISH CALHOUN AKA CALHOUN SPORTSWEAR	www.calhounsportswear.com	ev@calhounsportswear.com	905 688 610
CEJON ACCESSORIES INC.	www.cejon.com	rmummert@cejon.com	212 967 466
CHAMPION ATHLETICWEAR, INC.	www.championusa.com	linda.barabasova@hanesbrands.com	336 519 650
CHANTELLE LINGERIE INC.	www.chantelle.com	lgeerhart@chantelle.com	212 689 473
CHARLEY MORGAN, INC.	www.charleymorganusa.com	info@charleymorganusa.com	213 747 704
CHATHAM KNITTING MILLS, INC.		mattharris2006@gmail.com	434 432 470
CHIPITA ACCESSORIES		chipita@earthlink.ne	719 738 320
CHRISTINE VANCOUVER	www.christinevancouver.com	kim@christinevancouver.com	604 253 035
CHRISTOPHER & BANKS CORPORATION	www.christopherandbanks.com	info@christopherandbanks.com	763 551 500

Company	Web	E-mail	Phone
CLASSIX	www.classixshirts.com	vkhachooni@hotmail.com	661 726 9041
COLLECTION ARIANNE	www.ariannelingerie.com	webmaster@ariannelingerie.com	514 385 9393
COLORADO SILVER STAR CORP.	www.coloradosilverstar.com	info@coloradosilverstar.com	303 295 1353
COLORATURA, INC.	www.coloratura.com	coloratura9@aol.com	717 867 1144
COLUMBIA SPORTSWEAR CO., INC.	www.columbia.com	sales_info@columbia.com	503 985 4000
COMME CI COMME CA LTD.	www.magicsilk.com	liz@malepower.com	631 300 1035
COMME CI COMME CA LTD.	www.malepower.com	liz@malepower.com	631 300 1035
CONCEPT ONE ACCESSORIES	www.concept1.com	sgleit@concept1.com	212 868 2590
COOBIE INTIMATES	www.coobieintimates.com	coobieintimates1@gmail.com	562 906 5200
CORAL HEAD INC./HAWAIIAN ISLAND CREATIO	www.hicworldwide.com	baltazar1971@yahoo.com	310 366 7712
COSABELLA	www.cosabella.com	miami@cosabella.com	305 253 9904
COTTON EMPORIUM, INC.		cottonemporium@aol.com	718 894 3365
COTTON HERITAGE	www.cottonheritage.com	mickey@cottonheritage.com	323 722 5592
COUNTRY GENTLEMAN HEADWEAR, INC.	www.countrygentleman.com	smccabe@bollmanhats.com	212 981 9866
CPT USA, LLC DBA COCKPIT USA	www.cockpitusa.com	jacky@cockpitusa.com	212 575 1616
CRESCENT SOCK COMPANY	www.crescent-inc.com	heather@crescent-inc.com	423 568 2101
CYNTHIA GALE	www.cynthiagale.com	info@cynthiagale.com	212 481 1845
CYNTHIA ROWLEY	www.cynthiarowley.com	kfiorentino@cynthiarowley.com	212 242 0847
CYNTHIA STEFFE	www.cynthiasteffe.com	info@cynthiasteffe.com	212 403 6210
CYRUS	www.cyrusknits.com	sophia@cyrusknits.com	212 764 2555
D'ACCORD SHIRTS & GUAYABERAS	www.daccordshirts.com	rafael@daccordshirts.com	305 576 0926
DAILY WEAR SPORTSWEAR/FOREVER YOUNG		dailywearsports@aol.com	212 278 0038
DAMIANOU	www.damianouny.com	sales@damianouny.com	718 204 5600
DANA EMILIA PRESENTS	www.danaemiliapresents.com	fashion@danaemilia.com	212 391 4104
DANECRAFT INC.	www.danecraft.com	bob.soltys@danecraft.com	401 941 7700
DARIAN GROUP INC.	www.dariangroupinc.com	martin@dariangroupinc.com	212 944 6500
DAVID CAREY INC.	www.davidcareyinc.com	sales@davidcareyinc.com	408 453 7843
DAVID SMITH & ASSOCIATES		smithco200@aol.com	800 776 6100
DAYLEEN INTIMATES INC.	www.dominiqueapparel.com	mchernoff@dayleen.com	914 840 2729
DEBORA RACHELLE INC.	www.deborarachelle.com	info@deborarachelle.com	218 727 8100
DEPECHE MODE	www.depecheco.com	leer@depecheco.com	212 643 6633
DESSY CREATIONS & AFTER SIX	www.dessy.com	alan@dessy.com	646 638 9600
DIANE VON FURSTENBERG STUDIO, L.P.	www.dvf.com	M.Graniela@dvf.com	212 741 6607
DIESEL PLANET	www.diesel.com	customerservice@shop.diesel.com	212 755 9200
DIVINA DANCEWEAR	www.divinadancewear.com	divinadancewearusa@gmail.com	800 360 6008
DKNY	www.donnakaran.com		212 789 1500
DOLLHOUSE	www.dollhouse.com	racampora@joujou.com	212 997 0230
DOLORES PISCOTTA	www.dolorespiscotta.com	piscotta@msn.com	718 232 1167
DONNA KARAN COLLECTIONS	www.donnakaran.com		212 789 1500
DONOUGHE SPORT	www.donoughesport.com	rmapparel@aol.com	814 886 9272
DORMAN FASHION INC.	www.dormanfashion.com	sales@dormanfashion.com	213 623 7188
DREAM WORLD INTERNATIONAL, INC.		rveltri@dreamworldintl.com	215 320 0200
DREAMBAGS, INC.	www.magmilebrand.com	contact@magmilebrand.com	224 636 8622
DREW PHILIPS CORP.	www.drewclothing.com	gigi@drewphilipscorp.com	212 354 0095
DUE PER DUE/209WST	www.dueperdue.com	amyho@dueperdue.com	212 921 7650
DYNAMIC ASIA INTERNATIONAL, INC.	www.fashionbyda.com	support@dynamicasia.com	213 623 9169
EASTWEST CLOTHING	www.languagelosangeles.com	avril@languagelosangeles.com	323 980 1177
EDWARD CROMARTY ART DESIGN STUDIO	www.edwardcromarty.com	edwardcromarty@gmail.com	914 288 5171
EILEEN FISHER INC.	www.eileenfisher.com	customercare@eileenfisher.com	212 420 5900
ELAN INTERNATIONAL	www.elan-usa.com	elan@elan-usa.com	954 962 9166
ELE.PAVONI NEW YORK LTD	www.elepavoni.com	elepavoni@mac.com	212 397 0108
ELIE TAHARI LTD.	www.elietahari.com	questions@elietahari.com	212 763 2000
ELIZABETH GILLETT LTD.	www.elizabethgillett.com	sales@elizabethgillett.com	212 629 7993
EMA SAVAHL DESIGN	www.emasavahl.com	sales@emasavahl.com	305 754 6717
EMIL RUTENBERG	www.emilrutenberg.com	info@emilrutenberg.com	213 489 4374
ENVIROTEXTILES LLC.	www.envirotextile.com	info@envirotextile.com	970 945 5986
ERIC JAVITS, INC.	www.ericjavits.com	nyshowroom@ericjavits.com	212 213 4949
ERICA LYONS JEWELRY/CRIMZON ROSE	www.ericalyons.com	info@crimzonrose.com	401 231 0266
ESCADA USA	www.escada.com	customerservice@escadausa.com	212 852 5300
ESSEX MANUFACTURING INC.	www.baum-essex.com	bbaum@baum-essex.com	212 239 0080
EURO JOY SPORTSWEAR CORP.		jasoneurojoy@aol.com	212 575 4650
EVANESE, INC.	www.evanese.net	info@evanese.net	310 532 7004
EVEDEN INC.	www.eveden.com	usaorders@wacoaleurope.com	617 361 7559
EVY OF CALIFORNIA, INC./DBA JALATE	www.evy.com	suzannem@evy.com	212 594 3670
EZRASONS, INC.	www.ezrasons.com	ezrajack@ezrasons.com	212 768 8330
F & M HAT CO., INC.	www.fmhat.com	info@fmhat.com	717 336 5505
FAIR HEMP INC.	www.fairhemp.com	info@fairhemp.com	646 485 0939
FBF ORIGINALS	www.fbforiginals.com	fbf@fbforiginals.com	765 349 7474

Company	Web	E-Mail	Phone
FGX INTERNATIONAL/DIV OF ESSILOR	www.fgxi.com	glazaro@fgxi.com	401 231 3800
FILA U.S.A. INC.	www.fila.com	ecommusa@fila.com	410 773 3000
FITZSIMMONS FABRICS, LTD		info@fitzfabltd.com	212 876 2868
FLATIRON WORKSHOP	www.flatironworkshop.com	flatironworkshop@gmail.com	212 924 8795
FLEUR'T, INC./MONTELLE	www.fleurtintimates.com	info@fleurtintimates.com	866 278 3739
FLORA NIKROOZ/DIVISION OF AGE GROUP	www.flora-nikrooz.com	info@agegroupltd.com	212 213 9500
FORI SHOWROOM	www.forifashion.com	jacopo@jacopofoti.com	646 724 2728
FORMART CORPORATION	www.formartcorp.com	bellini_formart@hotmail.com	212 819 1819
FORT KNOX LINGERIE	www.cottonclub.it, www.selmark.es	fortknoxlingerie@comcast.net	561 625 9594
FOUGER FOR KIDS, INC.	www.fouger4kids.com	fougerforkids@aol.com	213 748 0648
FOUR SEASONS DESIGN GROUP	www.fourseasonsdesigngroup.com	info@fourseasonsdesigngroup.com	800 295 6784
FREE COUNTRY LTD.	www.freecountry.com	rondac@freecountry.com	212 719 4596
FRENCH CONNECTION	usa.frenchconnection.com	frenchconnection@frenchconnection-u	212 221 3157
FRENCH TOAST	www.frenchtoast.com	retail@frenchtoast.com	212 594 4740
FRUIT OF THE LOOM	www.fruit.com	fotlcustserv@fruit.com	855 253 4534
G-III APPAREL GROUP	www.g-iii.com	info@g-iii.com	212 403 0500
GAIAM	www.gaiam.com	customerservice@gaiam.com	303 222 3600
GARDEN KIDS	www.gardenkids.com	paulah@gardenkids.com	714 996 1100
GELMART INDUSTRIES INC.	www.gelmart.com	ezran@gelmart.com	212 743 6900
GEM DANDY INC.	www.gem-dandy.com	customerservice@gem-dandy.com	336 548 9624
GENE EWING BIS	www.geneewingbis.com	geneewing@geneewingbis.com	323 839 9647
GERTEX HOSIERY INC.	www.gertex.ca	sales@gertex.com	416 241 2345
GILTON COMPANY	giltonco.com	sales@giltonco.com	626 241 1958
GLOBAL BRANDS GROUP	www.globalbrandsgroup.com	business@globalbrandsgroup.com	646 839 7000
GOLF APPAREL BRANDS	www.lamode.com	sales@lamode.com	310 715 1772
GOODWEAR USA	www.goodwear.com	steve@goodwear.com	978 768 7746
GRANITE KNITWEAR/CAL CRU CO., INC.	www.calcru.com	calcru@mindspring.com	704 279 5526 X254
GRAPHICS GROUP LTD./DBA LATITUDES	www.latitudespdx.com	info@latitudespdx.com	503 248 2060
GREEN DRAGON	www.greendragonstyle.com	info@greendragonstyle.com	714 892 7354
GRUVEN INTERNATIONAL INC.	www.gruven.com	sales@gruven.com	416 292 7331
GUESS, INC.	www.guess.com	vendors@guess.com	213 765 3100
H.M.S. PRODUCTIONS	www.cableandgauge.com	nubby@nubby.com	212 719 9190
HAGGAR CLOTHING CO., INC.	www.haggar.com	torri.teel@haggar.com	214 352 8481
HARBOUR INTERNATIONAL LLC	www.bostonharbour.net	tlewis@harbourintl.net	212 868 9128
HAROLD TEPPER STRIBBONS INC.	www.stribbons.com	htepper@stribbons.com	718 423 4598
HART SCHAFFNER MARX	www.hartschaffnermarx.com	info@wdiamondgroup.com	800 327 4466
HASELSON INT'L TRADING INC.	www.haselson.com	sales@ringosport.com	212 465 0605
HATCO, INC./ RESISTOL HATS	www.resistolhat.com	rcieslak@hat-co.com	972 494 0511
HAVENGIRL	www.havengirl.com	annmarie@havengirl.com	760 385 6999
HEADWEAR CREATIONS, INC.	www.headwearcreations.com	headwrcreations@aol.com	973 622 1144
HEISEL	www.heisel.co	contact@heisel.co	212 719 3916
HENRY AND BELLE	www.henryandbelle.com	meganw@henryandbelle.com	312 242 2500
HENSCHEL HAT CO.	www.henschelhats.com	sales@henschelhats.com	314 421 0009
HILO HATTIE	www.hilohattie.com	sales@hilohattie.com	808 535 6500
HOLD-UP SUSPENDER CO.	www.suspenders.com	sal@suspenders.com	248 386 0252
HOLLOWAY SPORTSWEAR, INC.	www.hollowayusa.com	customercare@hollowayusa.com	937 497 7575
HOT KNOTS	www.hotknotsandtara.com	hotknots@reninet.com	707 822 7562
HTT HEADWEAR LTD.	www.httapparel.com	sales@httapparel.com	951 304 0400
HUGO BOSS U.S.A., INC.	www.hugoboss.com	customerservice@hugoboss-store.com	212 940 0600
HYBRID APPAREL	www.hybridapparel.com	mlee@hybridapparel.com	714 952 3866
HYP HATS LTD.	www.hyphats.com	davidf@hyphats.com	212 684 7717
HYPERCLASH	www.hyperclash.com	wholesale@hyperclash.com	505 820 0520
IAPPAREL LLC	www.wippette.com	barry@iapparelny.com	212 695 6343
IMPERIAL HEADWEAR	www.imperialsports.com	eortwein@paifashion.com	800 950 1916
IN STYLE USA, INC.	www.instyleusa.net	pauline.lock@instyleusa.net	212 631 0278
IN.STYLE EXCHANGE™	www.instyleexchange.com	info@instyleexchange.com	817 886 9222
INDIGENOUS	www.indigenous.com	matt@indigenous.com	707 861 9719
INGE CHRISTOPHER	www.ingechristopher.com, www.whitinganddavisbags.com	nyshowroom@ingechristopher.com	212 564 1151
INNERWEAR BRANDS INTERNATIONAL	www.innerwearbrands.com	sales@innerwearbrands.com	212 239 4222
INSERCH BY MERC USA, INC.	www.inserch.com	mercusainc@yahoo.com	201 489 3527
ISACO INTERNATIONAL/PAPI INC.	www.papiinc.com	info@papiinc.com	305 594 4455
J RICHARDS INTERNATIONAL	www.jrichardsintl.com	richard@jrichardsintl.com	212 819 0444
J. CREW	www.jcrew.com	contactus@jcrew.com	212 209 2500
J.D. FINE	www.tartcollections.com	jamief@jdfine.com	925 521 3300
J.P. OURSE CIE/JOHN COLE COLLECTION	www.jpourse.com	kelly@jpourse.com	410 273 0922
JANTZEN	www.jantzen.com	sales@jantzen.com	503 238 5000
JBD NEW YORK	www.jbdnewyork.com	vijay@jbdnewyork.com	212 944 0910
JILL HENNING FINERIES	www.jillhenninghats.com	jhendesign@aol.com	419 841 9106

JLM COUTURE — www.jlmcouture.com — tammy@jlmcinc.com — 800 686 7880

JOAN BLACKSHEAR DESIGN COMPANY — www.joanblackshear.com — info@joanblackshear.com — 808 324 0766

JOCKEY INTERNATIONAL, INC. — www.jockey.com — andy.vacca@jockey.com — 262 658 8111

JOE BLOW T'S — www.joeblow.com — vanessa@joeblow.com — 443 274 2744

JOLI JEWELRY — www.jolijewelry.com — sales@jolijewelry.com — 718 399 9150

JONDEN MANUFACTURING CO., INC. — www.jonden.com — tsmith@jonden.com — 212 730 1741

JONES APPAREL GROUP USA, INC — www.jny.com — 212 642 3860

JOU JOU DESIGNS — www.joujou.com — racampora@joujou.com — 212 997 0230

JOY ACCESSORIES — www.joyaccessories.com — joy@joyaccessories.com — 860 612 0439

JOYOUS AND FREE — www.joyousandfree.com — sales@joyousandfree.com — 760 385 6999

JULIE HUTTON INC. — www.juliehuttoninc.com — julie@juliehuttoninc.com — 212 532 5126

JUSSARA LEE — www.jussaralee.com — mail@jussaralee.com — 212 242 4128

JUST WHITE SHIRTS — www.justwhiteshirts.com — alam@justwhiteshirts.com — 416 447 2907

K & P WEAVER, LLC — www.baseballamericaspastime.com — kpweaver@aol.com — 203 795 9024

KAHN LUCAS — www.kahnlucas.com — ebreslow@kahnlucas.com — 212 244 4500

KAMTEX FASHION — www.kamtexfashion.com — sales@kamtexfashion.com — 954 733 1042

KATE SPADE AND COMPANY — www.jackspade.com — customerservice@jackspade.com — 877 917 5225

KATE SPADE AND COMPANY — www.katespadeandcompany.com — media_relations@katespade.com — 212 739 6550

KEEPERS INTERNATIONAL — www.keepers.com — jadamson@keepers.com — 800 79 SOCKS

KELLWOOD COMPANY — www.kellwood.com — corp_communications@kellwood.com — 314 576 3100

KEMBALI LTD. — kembali@optonline.net — 914 965 2183

KIDCUTETURE — www.kidcuteture.com — olga.pantelyat@kidcuteture.com — 609 216 7490

KIPPYS — www.kippys.com — bob@kippys.com — 619 435 6218

KOUROSH NEW YORK — www.kouroshnewyork.com — kourosh@kouroshnewyork.com — 718 358 3332

L&J ACCESSORIES/CELLINI LLC — landjaccessories.com — info&landjaccessories.com — 407 671 0111

LA MATERA — www.lamaterashop.com — sales@lamaterashop.com — 917 336 0509

LANDAU — www.landau.com — darryl.williams@landau.com — 800 238 7513

LARR BRIO ACCESSORIES — www.larrbrio.com — larrbrio@puresilkfabrics.com — 800 701 6005

LATICO LEATHERS — www.laticoleathers.com — info@laticoleathers.com — 973 442 9622

LE MIEUX/TARA INTERNATIONAL, INC. — www.lemieux.com — sweta.lmstudio@gmail.com — 562 694 6860

LEATHEROCK INT. INC. — www.leatherockwholesale.com — leatherock@leatherock.com — 619 299 7625

LEAWOOD APPAREL LLC. — www.leawoodapparel.vpweb.com — leawoodapparel@hotmail.com — 215 233 1973

LEG RESOURCE INC — www.legresource.com — wayne@legresource.com — 212 736 4574

LEMUR GROUP, INC. — www.petitlem.com — info@lemurgroup.com — 514 748 6234

LEVI STRAUSS & CO. — www.levistrauss.com — questions@levistrauss.com — 415 501 6000

LIANA UNIFORM — www.lianauniforms.com — customerservice@lianauniforms.com — 212 575 0875

LIANCARLO — www.liancarlo.com — info@liancarlo.com — 305 591 7332

LIFE & STYLE FASHIONS INC. — sunnykakar@hotmail.com — 212 629 7314

LILLIAN ROSE, INC. — www.lillianrose.com — info@lillianrose.com — 262 363 5286

LIN MANUFACTURING & DESIGN — www.linmfg.com — roger@linmfg.com — 435 787 8888

LINDA RICHARDS — www.lindarichards.com — info@lindarichards.com — 212 382 2257

LIPSTIK GIRLS — www.lipstikgirlsclothing.com — customerservice@lipstikclothing.com — 714 957 1114

LITTLE MISS JULIA — www.littlemissjulia.com — info@littlemissjulia.com — 973 886 8293

LONG STREET — www.longstreet.com — elliot@longstreet.com — 212 947 4090

LONGITUDE/LONGEVITY BRANDS LLC — www.longitudeswim.com — service@longitudeswim.com — 212 231 7877

LORREN BELL, INC. — www.lorrenbell.com — lorren@lorrenbell.com — 214 651 0110

LULI FAMA — www.lulifama.com — star@lulifama.com — 305 234 5656

LUSCIOUS LACES LINGERIE — www.lusciouslaces.com — lusciouslaces@hotmail.com — 616 363 3097

MADEMOISELLE, INC. — www.mademoiselleinc.com — scot210@aol.com — 773 394 4555

MANN & BROS INC/IMPERIAL HANDKERCHIEFS — susan@mannbro.com — 212 868 3535

MANSFIELD INTERNATIONAL — www.kayanna.com — p.salhany@kayanna.com — 514 274 2407

MAR CHIQUITA SWIMWEAR INC. — marchiquita@cfl.rr.com — 321 868 0868

MARC BOUWER — www.marcbouwer.com — info@marcbouwer.com — 212 242 7510

MARMOT MOUNTAIN LLC. — www.marmot.com — ghouser@marmot.com — 707 544 4590

MARTIN DINGMAN COUNTRYWEAR — www.martindingman.com — info@martindingman.com — 870 422 7151

MASCOT WORKWEAR U.S./REPCON NW INC — www.repconnw.com — sales@repconnw.com — 503 252 9760

MEGA BELTS, INC. — josephmingione@qc.aibn.com — 514 385 4175

MEHERA SHAW TEXTILES PVT. LTD. — www.meherashaw.com — info@meherashaw.com — 919 969 2572

MELANIE HARRIS — www.melanieharrisny.com — melanieharrisdesignspr@gmail.com — 646 504 9608

MIAMI STYLE INC. — www.miamistylebsd.com — customercare@miamistyle.com — 305 805 1168

MICHAEL KORS — www.michaelkors.com — inquiries@michaelkors.com — 212 201 8100

MIL-IDEE, INC. — mil-idee.com — info@mil-idee.com — 514 382 0190

MILKBARN, LLC — www.milkbarnkids.com — info@milkbarnkids.com — 800 269 3512

MISOOK — www.misook.com — customerservice@misook.com — 800 447 3556

MISTER NOAH — www.feathersgirl.com — noah@mrnoah.com — 212 354 1700

MMG DIV OF GREAT CHINA EMPIRE — kronert@mmg-ltd.com — 314 421 2182

MODODOC/GENEXUS INTERNATIONAL — www.mododoc.com — sales@mododoc.com — 310 532 7300

MONTANACO CLOTHING COMPANY — www.montanacoclothing.com — info@montanacoclothing.com — 406 723 2332

MOOSE CREEK
www.moosecreekinc.com
richard@moosecreekinc.com
909 869 5859

MOTHER PLUCKER FEATHER COMPANY INC.
www.motherplucker.com
motherplucker@earthlink.net
213 637 0411

MOTIONWEAR, LLC
www.motionwear.com
bwilson@motionwear.com
317 780 0609

MT SHOWROOM
www.parajumpers.it
info@parajumpers.it
212 354 5678

NATORI CO.
www.natori.com
custserv@natori.com
212 532 7796

NEW ICM, LP
www.newicm.com
zalmand@newicm.com
979 578 0543

NEW ORLEANS KNITWEAR
www.neworleansknitwear.com
info@neworleansknitwear.com
504 891 4502

NIC + ZOE
www.nicandzoe.com
info@nicandzoe.com
508 651 0000

NICOLE & CO.
www.nicole-co.com
hats@nicole-co.com
514 383 5599

NIKE, INC.
www.nike.com
503 671 6453

NORMA KAMALI
www.normakamalicollection.com
sales@normakamalicollection.com
212 957 9797

NOTANONYMOUS
www.notanonymous.com
michele@notanonymous.com
212 997 3512

NUTHATCH
www.shopnuthatch.com
sales@shopnuthatch.com
207 596 0880

ODETT ENTERPRISES
www.odettfashion.com
info@odettfashion.com
212 921 9690

ONLY HEARTS
www.onlyhearts.com
customerservice@onlyhearts.com
212 268 0886

OSHKOSH B'GOSH/CARTER'S
www.oshkoshbgosh.com
consumerbgosh@carters.com
678 791 1000

OUTERSTUFF LTD.
www.outerstuff.com
customerservice@outerstuff.com
212 594 9700

OXFORD GOLF
www.oxfordgolf.com
info@oxfordgolf.com
866 727 4693

OZONE DESIGN INC.
www.ozonesocks.com
contact@ozonesocks.com
212 563 2990

PACIFIC SPORTSWEAR & EMBLEM COMPANY
www.pacificemblem.com
quotes@pacificemblem.com
619 281 6688

PARASUCO JEANS INC.
www.parasuco.com
customerservice@parasuco.com
514 334 0888

PARISA
www.parisausa.com
sales@parisausa.com
818773 5000

PEERLESS CLOTHING INTERNATIONAL
www.peerless-clothing.com
sales@peerless-clothing.com
212 541 8720

PENDLETON WOOLEN MILLS, INC.
www.pendleton-usa.com
pendletoncatalog@penwool.com
503 226 4801

PERSNICKETY
www.persnicketyclothing.com
sales@persnicketyclothing.com
801 658 0400

PERSONAL TOUCH INC.
www.apersonaltouchinc.com
info@personaltouchinc.com
781 447 0467

PHOOL FASHIONS
www.phoolfashionusa.com
phoolfash@aol.com
212 944 0910

PILLAGED VILLAGE, THE
www.pillagedvillage.com
pvsales@pillagedvillage.com
937 743 0685

PIMLICO PERFORMANCE APPAREL LTD.
www.dishandduer.com
adriana@pimlicoperformance.com
604 323 0441

PINK CHICKEN
www.pinkchicken.com
customerservice@pinkchicken.com
212 255 9090

PRIORITY MANUFACTURING
www.customuniforms.com
richard@customuniforms.com
305 576 3000

PROJECT NO. 8
www.projectno8.com
info@projectno8.com
212 925 5599

PUR CASHMERE
www.purcashmere.com
info@purcashmere.com
800 225 9157

PVH CORPORATION
www.pvh.com
contactus@pvh.com
212 287 8000

QUEENSBORO SHIRT COMPANY
www.queensboro.com
fredm@queensboro.com
800 847 4478

RAFFI LINEA UOMO
www.raffionline.com
info@raffilineauomo.com
212 307 1416

RAGO FOUNDATIONS LLC
www.ragoshapewear.com
justin@ragoshapewear.com
718 728 8436

RAJ IMPORTS
www.rajimports.net
rajimports@hotmail.com
213 629 5375

RALPH LAUREN, INC.
www.ralphlauren.com
customerassistance@ralphlauren.com
888 475 7674

RASHTI & RASHTI/H.J. RASHTI & CO., INC.
www.rashtiandrashti.com
contactus@rashtiandrashti.com
212 594 2939

REBECCA TAYLOR
www.rebeccataylor.com
sales@rebeccataylor.com
212 704 0607

REDWOOD COURT BY SILK BOX
www.redwoodcourt.com
info@lotusa.com
609 275 4403

REPCON NW DBA THE MODERN WORKER
www.repconnw.com
sales@repconnw.com
503 252 9760

RHINESTONE JEWELRY CORPORATION
www.rhinestonejewelry.com
orders@rhinestone.com
718 336 6788

RICH HONEY
www.richhoney.us
info@richhoney.us
213 905 3205

RICHARD LEEDS INTERNATIONAL
www.richardleeds.com
lisa@richardleeds.com
212 532 4546

RIFLE/KAYNEE
www.riflekaynee.com
ccomins@kaynee.com
201 796 8101

ROBBIE BEE
rlong@robbiebee.com
212 944 0255

ROBIN ASCHER
www.aschersquares.com
roba24@aol.com
603 989 9829

ROCKSTAR
www.rockstarsushi.com
customerservice@rockstaroriginal.com
323 278 3874

RODEL U.S.A. INC.
www.cinziarocca.com
rodelusa@aol.com
212 997 9767

RON CORNELL
www.roncornell.com
re4ties@aol.com
310 441 9601

ROSE TAFT
www.melanieharrisny.com
mdm@rosetaft.com
212 279 8580

ROWDY SPROUT
www.rowdysprout.com
sales@rowdysprout.com
310 487 7666

ROYAL APPAREL, INC.
www.royalapparel.net
sales@royalapparel.net
631 213 8299

ROYALE LINENS INC.
www.royalelinens.com
fsnow@royalelinens.com
201 997 3700

RUM REGGAE
www.rumreggae.net
rumreggae@sbcglobal.net
805 649 4820

SAFILO U.S.A.
www.safilo.com/en
pladines@gmail.com
973 952 2800

SARA MIQUE
www.saramique.com
info@saramique.com
954 531 6800

SCENT-LOK/DIV. OF A.L.S. ENTERPRISES
www.scentlok.com
info@scentlok.com
231 777 7565

SCOTTEX GLOBAL SOURCING, LLC
www.scottexglobal.com
bradley@scottexglobal.com
215 540 1244

SCREAMER HATS
www.screamer.com
kimp@screamer.com
206 667 9000

SCULLY
www.scullyleather.com
brianscully@scullyleather.com
805 483 6339

SENTIMENTAL INC.
www.sentimentalny.com
sam@sentimentalny.com
212 221 0282

SHAUNE BAZNER ACCESSORIES, INC.
www.shaunebazner.com
service@shaunebazner.com
202 537 2980

SHEDRAIN CORP.
www.shedrain.com
iraw@shedrain.com
212 685 5555

SHEEPSKIN BY SUSAN BRADFORD
www.sheepskin-by-susan.com
susanbradforddesigns@charter.net
802 371 8230

SHOWROOM SEVEN/ERICKSON BEAMON
www.showroomseven.com
jean-marc@showroomseven.com
212 643 4810

SILVER SUIT, INC. silversuitusa@gmail.com
www.silversuitinc.com 213 748 4535

SIMON SHOWROOM info@simonshowroom.com
www.simonshowroom.com 212 242 1565

SISTERS/DIVISION OF FREDINI INC customerservice@sistersknit.com
www.sistersknit.com 213 955 8000

SLICK DESIGNS sales@slickart.com
www.slickart.com 305 836 7950

SMARTWORKS INC. smartworks.design@gmail.com
www.smARTwks.com 413 229 2130

SOPHIE FINZI LTD DBA PASHOOT sophiefinziltd@aol.com
www.sophiefinzi.com 212 967 4349

SOSSY BAGHDOIAN sossy.b@sbcglobal.net
www.sossysbridals.com 818 766 5008

SOXLAND INTERNATIONAL, INC. sreese@soxland.com
www.soxland.com 908 624 9370

SPORTHILL, INC. info@sporthill.com
www.sporthill.com 541 345 9623

SQUASHT BOUTIQUE lesley@squashtboutique.com
www.squashtboutique.com 773 292 4123

SQUASHT BY LES les@squashtbyles.com
www.squashtbyles.com 773 292 4123

ST. JOHN info@sjk.com
www.sjk.com 949 863 1171

STANFIELD'S inquiries@stanfields.com
www.stanfields.com 902 895 5406

STEEL PONY joanne@steelpony.com
www.steelpony.com 215 467 6065

STREETS AHEAD info@streetsaheadinc.com
www.streetsaheadinc.com 323 277 0860

STYLE SOURCE INC. geoff@style-source.com
www.style-source.com 910 399 2288

STYLEX TEXTILE DBA FABKA FABRICS LLC sharona@fabkafabrics.com
www.fabkafabrics.com 323 588 3000

SUGAR AND BRUNO challen@sugarandbruno.com
www.sugarandbruno.com 317 293 5888

SURVIVAL INC. sanjay@survivalrules.com
www.survivalrules.com 631 385 5060

SUSAN DUNN INC. susan@susandunn.com
www.susandunn.com 858 832 1086

SUSAN ELIAS eliascouture@gmail.com
www.eliascouture.com 727 452 6637

SUSAN GREENSTADT & ASSOC. susangreenstadt@aol.com
212 302 0600

SUSAN PILLAY suepillay@aol.com
www.susanpillay.com 212 533 9053

SWEATER BRAND INC. info@sweaterbrand.com
718 797 0505

SWEENIE MANUFACTURING CORPORATION diane@sweeniemanufacturing.com
www.sweeniemanufacturing.com 646 825 5027

SWIFT ORIGINALS swiftoriginals@gmail.com
www.facebook.com/swiftoriginals 303 442 9013

TAILOR VINTAGE info@tailorvintage.com
www.tailorvintage.com 212 840 1871

TAKEATOTE LLC info@takeatote.com
www.takeatote.com 715 383 4661

TASHA POLIZZI jane@tashapolizzi.com
www.tashapolizzi.com 413 528 6500

TAYLOR MADE corporate@tmag.com
www.taylormadegolf.com 760 918 6000

TERI JON sales@terijon.com
www.terijon.com 212 398 0480

THEA HAUTE COUTURE sales@theahautecouture.com
www.theahautecouture.com 718 237 8555

TIC TAC TOE/BABY LEGS amyhoffmankids@gmail.com
www.amyhoffmankids.com 516 931 6510

TOKYO BAY INC. sales@tokyobayinc.com
www.tokyobayinc.com 415 808 4880

TOM AND LINDA PLATT info@tomandlindaplatt.com
www.tomandlindaplatt.com 212 764 1210

TONY LAMA COMPANY, INC. vicki.chapman@justinbrands.com
www.tonylama.com 866 240 8854

TOPSON DOWNS info@topsondowns.com
www.topsondowns.com 310 558 0300

TOTAL FOOT COMFORT admin@totalfootcomfort.com
www.totalfootcomfort.com 828 322 2600

TRACYWATTS INC. info@tracywatts.com
www.tracywatts.com 718 499 7090

TRAMP tramp@trampny.com
212 398 1428

TRENDSET ORIGINALS jj@skiva.com
212 736 9520

TRIPP NYC wholesale@trippnyc.com
www.trippnyc.com 212 979 8238

TUSK LTD. info@tusk.com
www.tusk.com 212 242 8485

UNIONBAY/SEATTLE PACIFIC INDUSTRIES cathie.underwood@unionbay.com
www.unionbay.com 253 872 8822

VALENTINE USA mng@valentine-usa.com
212 719 3160

VENUS FASHION email@venus.com
www.venus.com 904 997 4000

VESTS DIRECT info@vestsdirect.com
www.vestsdirect.com 800 365 9879

VICTOR ROSSI vr@victorrossi.com
www.victorrossi.com 410 337 2714

VIESTE-ROSA viesterosa@aol.com
www.viesterosa.com 401 946 4330

VISHAL ENTERPRISES vishal@vishalent.com
212 629 0880

VISMAYA shivani@vismayacollection.com
www.vismayacollection.com 213 623 8567

VIVIANA UCHITEL pamcarone@gmail.com
vivianauchitel.com 310 472 4955

WAI-CHING sales@wai-ching.com
www.wai-ching.com 206 229 1111

WAITEX INTERNATIONAL frankriech@waitex.com
www.waitex.com 212 967 8100

WASATCH CO. info@wasatcht.com
www.wasatcht.com 404 634 3000

WE BE BOP, INC info@webebopinc.com
www.webebopinc.com 510 452 3267

WEARABLE INTEGRITY/BARBARA LESSER mlesser@barbaralesser.com
www.barbaralesser.com 310 742 7444

WEDDING TROPICS kevin@weddingtropics.com
www.weddingtropics 844 921 0466

WHITE SIERRA wholesale@whitesierra.com
www.whitesierra.com 408 980 6688

WHITTALL & SHON beauws@aol.com
www.whittallandshon.com 212 594 2626

WILL LEATHER GOODS willservice@willleathergoods.com
www.willleathergoods.com 541 434 6659

WILLIAMSON-DICKIE MFG CO. customerservice@dickies.com
www.dickies.com 817 336 7201

WOODEN SHIPS sales@wooden-ships.com
www.wooden-ships.com 888 717 6700

XOXO suzanne.desiderio@kellwood.com
www.kellwood.com 212 575 0273

YOCHI DESIGNS yochidesignny@yahoo.com
www.yochiny.com 212 947 7826

YON DESIGN, INC. yondesigninc@me.com
www.yondesign.com 954 973 7771

ZANETTI INC. zanetti@zanetti.com
www.zanetti.com 310 478 8660

ZELDA info@zelda-intl.com
www.zeldacollection.com 212 764 0020

Sourcing Made Simpler/On-line Access

Sourcing Made Simpler/On-line Access Online access to over 2,000 nationwide suppliers of all types of fabrics, trims, notions, forecast services, swatch design studios, CAD services & much more for the apparel industry. "**one click**" to contact suppliers via email and or website. 1 year subscription.

Listings include:
Company address, phone, fax, and email; Sales manager names; Products they sell or manufacture and/or services they provide; If goods are domestic or imported and where they import from; Minimum quantities for production; Price points; Markets they cater to; and more.

Fabric and trim manufacturers, converters, jobbers, agents, mills and reps listed. Over 65 categories serve all your industry sourcing needs.

Ref: 001 $ 99.00 1 year subscription

order online: www.fashiondex.com/store or by phone 212 647 0051

Sourcing

The Apparel Industry Sourcebook

Comprehensive directory for apparel manufacturers, designers, merchandisers, trim and fabric buyers and production sourcing departments in the men's, women's, children's and accessory markets.

A complete and up-to-date sourcebook listing over 2,000 nationwide suppliers of all fabrics, trims, notions, forecast services, swatch studios, CAD services and more for the apparel industry.

Listings include:
Company address, phone, fax, and email; Sales manager names; Products they sell or manufacture and/or services they provide; If goods are domestic or imported and where they import from; Minimum quantities for production; Price points; Markets they cater to; and more.

Fabric and trim manufacturers, converters, jobbers, agents, mills and reps listed. Over 65 categories serve all your industry sourcing needs.

Reference: 101 $ 135.00

The Small Design Company's Guide to Wholesale Fabrics and Trims

The perfect sourcebook for companies requiring smaller yardage quantities of production fabric.

This concise directory lists over 400 fabric suppliers selling low minimum (500 yards or less) of a fabric, to the fashion trade. Also listed are suppliers and jobbers of no minimum and in-stock goods.

Listings are grouped by fabric category, and each listing includes company address, phone, fax, email and website address. Also listed is the sales manager name, the fabric qualities they sell, price points, minimum yardage quantities for production, and more!

The sourcebook begins with an excellent introduction chapter which instructs the how-tos' when one is shopping the wholesale fabric market!

Specifically created for start-up companies, small design houses, and home sewing businesses.

Reference: 106 On Sale! 65.00

order online: www.fashiondex.com/store or by phone 212 647 0051

The Fashion Designer's Sustainable Sourcebook (A Guide to Eco and Slow Fashion Suppliers)

The first directory of apparel industry suppliers who collectively want to help lessen the impact our industry is making on our environment.

Geared to designers, manufacturers, merchandisers and buyers in the men's, women's, children's, accessory, wearable tech and home fashion markets.

Reference: 100 $ 65.00

The Apparel Production Sourcebook American Edition

Up-to-date directory committed to solving your production sourcing and contracting needs in the Americas. Hundreds of contractors open for production, includes sewing, CMT & finishing contractors, & production services from the U.S. Listings include: contact info; specialty areas; package capabilities; machinery; minimums; and more!

Excellent tool for all production sourcing departments.

Reference: 102 $ 125.00

Directory of Brand Name Apparel Manufacturers and Importers

Up-to-date directory lists brand name and private label manufacturers and importers of women's, men's, and children's wear and accessories. Developed and targeted for retail store and catalogue buyers to shop the apparel and accessory markets easily.

Over 1,800 brand name labels listed, broken down by type of apparel classification. No cross-referencing. Listings include: labels; line types; types of retailers sold; showroom/sales rep locations; whether products are domestic/import; price points; and RN numbers.

Reference: 104 $ 135.00

order online: www.fashiondex.com/store or by phone 212 647 0051

Birnbaum's Global Guide to Agents and Buying Offices

Today, the difference between a first class and a mediocre middleman is the difference between success and bankruptcy.

Reference: 240 $ 45.00

Crisis in the 21st Century Garment Industry

Last man standing may well be an accurate description of the steps that we must take to survive the current downturn. Everything depends on how fast the players understand that the rules of survival have changed.

Reference: 226 $ 45.00

Birnbaum's Global Guide to Material Sourcing

You can no longer depend on how you sourced materials a few years ago, those methods are already antiquated. Is your company on the leading edge, or are you falling behind?

Reference: 220 $ 45.00

Birnbaum's Global Guide to Winning the Great Garment War

The premier book on garment costing and sourcing, and the ultimate book for all garment industry professionals.

Reference: 201 $ 35.00

Sourcing A,B,C'S

We published this 16 page booklet to assist all new designers and entrepreneurs sourcing apparel production for the first time.

You have an idea for a new garment, apparel concept, clothing line or product that doesn't exist at retail... or.... You are a designer planning to start out on your own... or.... Your existing locally-made product line has grown and you need to outsource production...

If any of the these scenarios are the case and you are traveling to a trade show or sourcing event to research how to produce this new idea/garment/ product line, then this booklet is for you.

Reference: 120 $ 9.99

order online: www.fashiondex.com/store or by phone 212 647 0051

Apparel Design and Production Handbook- A Technical Reference

Invaluable reference book for fashion designers, merchandisers, technical designers, production managers, apparel-making factories, patternmakers, and all industry executives working in the men's, women's and children's markets today.

Chapters include:
•How to measure the body for apparel production.
•Standard body measurements for regular and special sizes of men's, women's and children's wear.
•How to measure garments for apparel production.
•Standard garment specifications and flats for basic styles.
•Grading charts for all markets and sizes.
•Blank costing and specification sheets.
•Croquis drawings for design, illustration, tracing and more.

Reference 105 $ 95.00

The Vendor Compliance Handbook with Forms and Data Templates 2nd Edition

This book outlines everything a designer or a garment manufacturer needs to know about producing a compliant garment from start to finish.

This in-depth handbook explains all standards and guidelines of all production phases, so that garments are delivered compliant and disconcerting incidents, such as chargebacks and late deliveries, are avoided.

A must-have for every garment production department!

Reference 228 $ 60.00

How to Start a Fashion Company

Straight forward step-by-step guide for designers and entrepreneurs wanting to start their own line. Book contains all the necessary fashion terms you need to know to start a line; basic information on Making Prototypes, Costing, Marketing, and Production.

Reference 230 $ 45.00

Stitch Sample Kit

A comprehensive guide, providing both technical and creative solutions for garment construction. The Stitch Sample Kit contains over 80 mounted swatches of current stitches and techniques used within the garment industry today. You will find the Stitch Sample Kit both informative and inspirational.

- Stitches are organized by type; thread is color-coded
- Swatches are pre-mounted
- Includes required specs, ISO #'s and approximate US cost, where applicable

Reference: 231 $ 150.00

A Picture Speaks A Thousand Words

This book demonstrates the use of computer–aided design to create clearly detailed technical information for factories through the stages of design, development and manufacture, using graphic illustration wherever possible.

The specification is a critical document to be shared by all involved in the buying, selling, design and manufacture of the product. A style can be amended many times before the start of production, and specifications created by CAD can be quickly amended in minutes and circulated to everyone involved.

The book takes the reader through a variety of specifications step by step and explains the reasoning behind creating each page; a complete detailed specification may have up to 20 pages depending on the style and construction detail. This book is a practical, hands-on approach to the subject written with many years experience in the industry. The message is that good graphics is an international language, which helps to avoid misunderstandings; details that are in text can be lost in translation.

A recent quote from a source in China states that the most common issue between buyers and suppliers is the lack of communication and unclear specifications for products that leads to mistakes and that Quality Control is your most effective tool to getting the correct product when your specifications/expectations are clear.

This book is a definitive approach to specification writing for the clothing and related industries, demonstrating the advantages of using CAD.

This book will help those working in the industry and students starting textile courses to view specifications as an integral part of product development, quality assurance and manufacturing.

Reference: 123 $ 45.00

CPSIA information can be obtained
at www.ICGtesting.com
Printed in the USA
BVOW11s2053240616
453352BV00003B/9/P

9 780971 486751